THE FORT WORTH
PUBLIC LIBRARY

FOUNDATION

1993—2003

In celebration of
The Fort Worth Public
Library Foundation's
10th Anniversary
this book is given in honor of

Lockheed Martin Tactical Aircraft Systems

100 YEARS OF AIR POWER AND AVIATION

Number Five:
Centennial of Flight Series
Roger D. Launius, General Editor

100 YEARS OF AIR POWER & AVIATION

ROBIN HIGHAM

Texas A&M University Press
College Station

The paper used in this book meets the minimum requirements
of the American National Standard for Permanence
of Paper for Printed Library Materials, Z39.48–1984.
Binding materials have been chosen for durability.
♾
Library of Congress Cataloging-in-Publication Data

Higham, Robin D. S.
    100 years of air power and aviation / Robin Higham.—1st ed.
       p. cm. — (Centennial of flight series ; no. 5)
Originally published: Air Power. New York : St. Martin's Press,
1972.
    ISBN 1-58544-241-0 (cloth : alk. paper)
    1. Air power—History. I. Title: One hundred years of air
power and aviation. II. Higham, Robin D. S. Air power. III.
Title. IV. Series.
    UG630 .H573   2004
    359'.009—dc21
                                                    2003003577

Originally published as *Air Power: A Concise History,* 1972,
St. Martin's Press
Copyright © 1972 by Robin Higham
Enlarged second edition, 1984; revised third edition, 1988,
Sunflower University Press
© 1984 and © 1988 by Sunflower University Press
Revised and enlarged under the new title, 2003

CONTENTS

CONTENTS

FIGURES AND TABLES

To those who have made the history of aviation, have made it possible, and have fallen en route

ACKNOWLEDGMENTS

I wish to thank all those companies and others who have supplied me over the years with photographs, information, and assistance. Unless otherwise acknowledged, all photographs are from the author's collection.

Many thanks are due to Carol A. Williams, long-time associate, for editing; to Nedra Sylvis and Marolyn Caldwell for typing; and to the staff of the Texas A&M University Press for their faith in the work.

100 YEARS OF AIR POWER AND AVIATION

INTRODUCTION

The story of aviation and air power in the twentieth century is one of patterns, problems, and promoting peace, using military, corporate, educational, technical, and historic forces.

Aviation was to the twentieth century what electricity, steam, and railways were to the nineteenth. Yet the progress of air power has been paradoxical. On the one hand man has destroyed his own and has polluted the earth with air power, and on the other he has endeavored to compress time and distance to create a pacific unified world in which civil aviation has been the catalyst.

Flight has forever captured the imagination. The boyish Charles A. Lindbergh epitomized this in his 1927 trans-Atlantic journey. The legacy of escapism, symbolized by the white-scarfed aces of the 1914–18 era, continued throughout the twentieth century, in part due to the characterization of the Red Baron in the renowned Charles Schulz Snoopy cartoons.

In World War II, the Battle of Britain's heroes were the young Royal Air Force (RAF) pilots looking skyward, in their light blue uniforms, and immortalized by Prime Minister Winston Churchill's, "Never have so many owed so much to so few." Ever since, those young, romanticized victors have been known as "the few"—in contrast to their black-uniformed *Luftwaffe* op-

ponents. And, later, air shows perpetuated these idealized images.

Hand-in-hand with the romance of the aviators was the evolution of structurally beautiful airplanes. "If it looks right, it will fly right," was enshrined in the public mind along with an image of technical beauty. Thus the Supermarine Spitfire epitomized the sleek and appealing form of the single-seat piston-engined fighter as opposed to the boxy Messerschmitt Me-109, and the elegant Avro Lancaster as opposed to the awkward-looking Heinkel He-177. Later, the 1936 de Havilland Albatross, the 1946 Lockheed Constellation, and the 1954 de Havilland Comet I airliners set the visual standard. Subsequently, however, Mach numbers dictated designs that tended to look alike.

Technology has been central to the progress of civilization, especially since the mid-nineteenth century. In many ways, aviation is the epitome of the nineteenth-century concept of progress and the twentieth-century concept of technological perfection—which at times has been revolutionary. Yet, though innovation and invention have been the product of necessity, they have been stifled by bureaucracy.

Part of the bonding of air power with culture has been the carryover of technology from one segment of society to another, just as bridge-building benefitted from stress-calculations for biplanes and rigid airships. Thus, intractable realities have been overcome, enabling us to go from the Wright brothers to well beyond the sound barrier in three generations. But increasingly, engineers and designers, operators and the public, have to be concerned with the effect of aviation on the environment.

The history of aviation and air power in the last one hundred years is also one of the relationship of dynamic forces and criticism of action or inaction. And it is a tale of management and the search for cost-effective efficiency, of doing more with less, and of consumption and wastage, as well of ever-increasing range and larger payloads.

Two approaches have been taken in this work, one of civilian aviation, one of military aviation. The civilian side of aviation moved along economic paths, toward making a profit, whether in general aviation's light aircraft and flying clubs, in the airline business, or in manufacturing. Weight, speed, range, and costs (capital and operational) always have to be melded and balanced, while at the same time offering sales appeal. Success remains a constant struggle.

Management and efficiency on the military side are somewhat different. While affected by economic and political cycles, the rule of thumb for air forces has been plethora in war, poverty in peace—yet they have always expected to be an instrument of policy. After 1945, especially, much was demanded of air power, often with little realization of the time, doctrine, and sinews needed to make it effective. Production lead times have risen from the six months for conception to operations during the 1914–18 war, to twenty years or more in 2003.

Simplicity and availability are the measure of readiness, and decent production rates can only be achieved by planning. Tied into this is the importance of maintenance and spares—another theme that recurs time and again in the twentieth century.

The use of computer technology, starting from the ENIAC in 1944 to the ubiquitous contemporary laptops, has enabled not only vast calculations to be completed mechanically in milliseconds, but also the miniaturization of these wonder chips into our aircraft, weapons systems, and essentially all phases of modern life. Conversely, however, fascination with the abilities of this technology can sometimes lead to unacceptable conclusions, as was evidenced in the third London airport (Foulness/Maplin) inquiry of 1971. The computerized interpolation of data had resulted in an enormously expensive proposal for this third airport, causing the British government to cancel the project shortly thereafter.

Automation has been a constant in the pressure to lower costs, especially of labor. Thus developed flight simulators, which reduced flying hours and the need to use pilots in the air as instructors and evaluators. By 2003, the trend had swept through to manufacturing, with the whole process speeded up from four years to only months per aircraft ordered.

Aviation, air power, the military, and space have all stimulated the study of innovation and the dynamics of technology and organizations. But, in contrast, little effort has been devoted to determining when programs should be stopped, just as no attention has been paid to the causes for the defeat of air forces.

PERIODIZATION

In order to understand the progress of aviation, it is necessary to have a chronological framework upon which to hang events and developments.

Aviation was and is a product of the Victorian era of imperialism, adventure, and advancement. It is less spiritual than realistic, yet its forward movement has depended upon vision and faith, as well as scientific and mechanical ability. Many of its leading lights up to the 1960s did not have a university degree, but were intuitive, self-taught men. Women in aviation, except for a few daring aviatrix, came to prominence only in the last quarter of the twentieth century.

The pre-1903 history of aviation is largely one filled with ideas that could not be brought to fruition because of deficiencies of knowledge, of suitable materials, and of a lightweight power source. Even simple gliding was handicapped by the inadequate understanding of control.

The Wright brothers inaugurated practical knowledge with their innovations in controls and in the steps to a light usable engine. They introduced this to Europe in 1908, to the air meet at Rheims, France—a virtual takeoff point.

From there to 1927, aviation was able to advance rapidly, due to the World War I ability to experiment, remedy, and develop multiple models. But much of the attitude was Victorian and mechanical; if a plane crashed, it was the pilot's fault, even as engine reliability was refined.

Lindbergh's non-stop flight from New York to Paris in 1927 proved the dependability of engines and airframes. And contemporaneously, the Guggenheim Fund for Aviation was another quiet contributor to progress through sponsorship of innovation and safety.

Soon all sorts of revolutions began to take place, a number of them in the realm of continuity and change. Technological progress was stimulated by the rise of Stalin and Hitler, whose economic and technical management has been overshadowed by their heinous crimes.

Rearmament and the Second World War, from 1935 to 1945, again provided a stimulant to aviation in glider clubs and airlines, and to air power in the clash of armed forces. By 1939 the latter had become mature enough to evolve from ancillary to equal partners with the surface and submarine forces. Concepts and methods of training rapidly changed to match the realities of global war.

Between 1935 and 1945, the piston engine was perfected and brought to its peak, the jet was taken off the workbench and made operational, and aircraft of the future were envisioned. The postwar boom in aviation was launched by the building of

airfields worldwide, and by the free training and accreditation by governments for air and ground crew, as well as for the infrastructure of both military and civil aviation.

The next milestone was reached in 1958 when regular jet travel was inaugurated by the airlines, together with regional turboprop services, and when cargo was accepted as a normal specialty. At the same time, flying ceased to be an upper-class perquisite, with the introduction of tourist/economy class. By the 1960s, over one million people annually were flying across the North Atlantic, and the great ocean liners were being withdrawn.

Also part of this equation was the defeat of France in 1940, and Germany and Japan in 1945, which brought economic aid in the case of the latter two and no defense costs until the 1950s. In the meantime, the two new superpowers, the United States and Russia, had entered the Cold War (1947–91), keeping their countries on a fortress basis. Elsewhere, notably in the Middle East, fear stimulated arms sales, with restraints on the selling of secret technology, while in the Far East, China created its new aviation.

After 1958, there was not only the technical refinement of the jet engine in power and lower fuel consumption—especially after the 1973 Arab oil embargo, but further consolidations of the industry, signified by the 1963 Anglo-French Concorde agreement to build a supersonic transport— the SST—based upon German World War II swept-wing testing. At the same time, costs and competing demands of social programs, as well as the Vietnam War, saw the development and introduction of new military aircraft dragged out or canceled. In addition to the Boeing 747, the most notable civil airliner progress was made in the introduction of the Airbus machines that used "fly-by-wire" technology—computers to control the aircraft electronically; the stretching of basic Boeings, in part because of certification costs; and the development of regional airliners finally able to replace the 1936 Douglas DC-3.

In 1978, commercial aviation was deregulated

in the United States, and with the implementation of the European Community (EC) in 1993, alliances, and privatization, the freedom of European skies was expected in the twenty-first century. Coupled with all of this, from 1960 on, the swamping of air-traffic control had been—and remains—a constant concern as facilities, for reasons of potential economy, cannot be expanded rapidly enough to get ahead of the traffic curve.

Just as the trans-oceanic airlines sank the great liners and forced the steamship companies eventually to develop the air-linked cruise ships, the railways in Japan and Europe similarly countered regional on-time competition with high-speed non-stop trains, placing their stations in airports for seamless service. This was a solution not really possible in the United States due to the automobile culture and lack of public transport.

By 2003, aviation in general would reach a plateau, much as perhaps had the personal computer market. In fact, both may have peaked, as television conferencing and business jets had cut into airline revenues and the military/naval aircraft on hand would be adequate for foreseeable limited wars.

About Air Power

Air power is a perpetual struggle between grand-strategic bombing and strategic and tactical attack forces, but it also includes civil and general aviation, especially the airlines, the aircraft industry and its economic and governmental support bases, and the national will and character. All factor into air power.

Very basic to air power was the development of airfield construction, from five years pre-World War II for a simple grass field with permanent buildings, to nine months in wartime for a station with concrete runways and prefabricated buildings—or three days to lay perforated-steel-plate (PSP) runways and set up tents.

Channeling the progress of air power has been doctrine and planning. Doctrine is a body of principles designed to guide the development and employment of military power in support of national policies or ends. It requires a knowledge of past experience with a vision of future realities, in harmony with the means available. Without doctrine, written or believed, there can be neither strategy nor operational planning, nor use of air power as an instrument of policy.

Of interest in this regard is the Israeli Air Force, which has operated from fixed bases with great flexibility against at least three enemies and often under diplomatic constraints, yet it is still an instrument of policy.

From 1918 the effectiveness of bombing was over-accepted. By 1939, the fear of it remained, but the realities had not been tested. By 1945, not the atomic bomb, but the 4.5-pound incendiary and special deep-penetration weapons had shown what air power could do behind the lines, while tactical air forces, notably of German and Soviet armies and in the Japanese navy—and then in Allied hands—had become highly effective.

This work emphasizes grand strategy, the formulation and execution of national and allied policy. In recent years professionals have become cognizant of this aspect of war and peace, and it is thus included here for the benefit of less militarily educated readers. Grand-strategic air campaigns are treated as such when they were not connected to surface actions.

In any potentially conflicting situation, a good deal depends upon perceived national grand strategies, military strategy, and operational art. Tactics and effects can be determined from minor wars, but high policy may be based more upon one's own actions and needs than upon an assessment of the enemy's.

In 1918, the French air service had 4,500 aircraft in 260 squadrons, the RAF 3,000 in 191. As a result of disarmament, by 1932 they both were reduced to handfuls.

In the days before the Spanish Civil War of 1936–39, many of the discussions of roles, doctrine, equipment, and training were sterile in view of the lack of study of the lessons of the 1914–18 war, of the shortage of funds, and of modern aircraft. The assumptions made by the English engineer F. W. Lanchester (1915) and the Italian Guilio Douhet (1921), that air power and bombing could win all wars, ignored defense—an omission that another Italian, Colonel Amadeo Mecozzi, began to rectify in the 1930s. Others, however, sought to provide the army with support and the air forces with planes, as well as a doctrine that would allow a Douhetian long-range bombing of the enemy heartland. A multi-purpose machine for such strategy, though unsuccessful, came into being in the mid-1930s with the French BCR (bomber-combat-reconnaissance) aircraft, but the goal was not achieved until the de Havilland Mosquito in 1942.

The problems of small air forces were even more acute. The Australians had the same alternating chiefs of staff for nearly twenty years, and no indigenous aircraft industry. The Greeks fell in 1941 for a variety of causes, not the least of which was that their aircraft had all come from French, Polish, and Czech factories overrun from 1939 to 1940 by the enemy Germans. Their new ally, Britain, was too short of machines to resupply them, and the United States was bogged in peacetime paperwork. Only the Hellenes' enemy, the Italians, had the same caliber weapons.

Ironically, when Greece fell, 132 qualified pilots escaped, but anti-colonialism sent them to be trained again in Iraq. Superior countries, as in the case of the United States in Vietnam, do not believe lesser peoples can do what they themselves can.

Airlines—as opposed to general aviation—and air forces can collapse suddenly. Airlines go bankrupt because of debts, low load factors, the consequences of accidents, regulations, and mismanagement. Air forces are defeated in part or in whole when they lack the resilience, airfields, supplies, bases, and command management and organization to permit them to absorb losses and to remain serviceable.

Before World War I, airmen had entertained with their daring flights, while at the same time pioneering technology and techniques. The 1914–18 war was, as wars usually are, a hothouse of progress in aerodynamics, airframes, engines, and the techniques of flight, as well as an impetus to the development of aerial photography, cartography, radios, long-range navigation, and the equipment and adventurous spirit (really a Victorian legacy) for both postwar record-breaking and the pioneer airlines.

The interwar years saw air power used for economical pacification in Iraq and along the Northwest Frontier of India. But during these years, both Britain and France were the victims of Douhetian-style thought and of their own air forces' hatred of army cooperation.

The latter 1930s saw a series of revolutionary developments, which meant that after 1945—indeed after 1941—air power was very different than before 1934, even though it still had the same, albeit a better trained, human element. Foremost in this 1934–45 period was the technical development in airframes, all-metal construction, engines, fuels, electronics, airfield construction, flying control, computers, and the atomic bomb, as well as jet engines. Not only did this progress make aviation costs rise dramatically, while being offset by multiple copies and subsidized developments, but also a program as complex as manufacturing the B-29 Superfortress, for example, had to be managed by a senior officer. All this was a civilian logistical challenge, akin to providing the correct parts and POL (petrol, oil, and lubricants) to forces all over the world for well-trained personnel to use to carry out the High Command's plans.

In World War II three grand-strategic campaigns affected air power. First was the Allied air campaign against Germany, which was designed to cripple the Nazis by destroying their industry and their air force, when it rose to protect the "Fatherland's" vitals. A similar shorter campaign was waged late in the war against Japan, adopting some of the techniques used in Europe. Another grand-strategic campaign was that waged by German and American submarines against enemy supply lines. In the Atlantic theater this was countered by air power, very effectively in the second half of the war. However, this was not the case in the Pacific, for that was a different kind of war.

Grand-strategic bombing, because it affected civilians, became a highly controversial, moral debate. More recently this imponderable surfaced again in Kosovo in 1999, aided by skillful propaganda by Serbia. The more access the enemy has to the media, the more appeals there will be to the opponent's emotions, free speech, and democratic weakness.

Air superiority, then, is important but is not an absolute requirement in major wars. It was achieved over Iraq in 1991 and over Kosovo in 1999, though it did not ensure victory; and it was not everywhere all the time in World War II. Rarely has theoretical air superiority been achieved for long periods over all fronts, Afghanistan in the 2001–02 conflict being an exception. And it can be countered by guerrilla tactics, a point the People's Republic of China's Air Force recognizes.

Aviation and Air Power

The history of aviation and air power is that of a logarithmic development of power, as seen in Efficiency Ratings (ERs). Roughly at 1 in 1918, ERs had risen to 30 by 1939 and to about 100 from 1945 to 1950. But in the next fifty years, they rose to over 8,000, and by 2006 would approach 11,000.

On the military side, lethality had exploded with fire raids on cities, and with the 1945 atomic bomb, but thereafter the growth was restrained by the unusable nature of nuclear weapons. Instead, miniaturization, accuracy, and increased conventional lethality made the military aircraft subject to command, control, communications, computers, and intelligence (C^4I) so much more devastating.

Put another way, the story about to be told is of the increasing range of aircraft and their infrastructural support until, in the twenty-first century, they have global reach in communications and navigation, if not yet commonly in flight.

But more than this, the story of aviation and air power depicts as well the evolution from an escapist dream to a social nuisance, raising noise and environmental concerns—the human factor.

These human factors have been responsible for sound-proofing and comfort control, auto pilots, automatic landing devices, inertial navigation, and center-of-gravity calculations. They have come into being, including duty-time limitations, for safety, efficiency, and to preserve capital assets—whether an aircraft, its crew, or airports. And within this mix are accidents, which have been not only riddles to solve, but the trigger for legal actions and insurance claims, as well as for important correctives.

The final exposition of human factors—the one constant—is the individual in aviation, who though perhaps better educated, yet essentially is the same physical being as Orville and Wilbur Wright. There is, however, one difference. The Wrights had to explore the unknown, while their "descendants" can be tempted to believe implicitly in the machine. And thus, training aims to teach the paradox of both belief and skepticism.

In any field of human affairs, patterns of history are evident, linked by human behavior. Those patterns in aviation parallel those in military affairs, in corporate activity, and in technological innovation and advancement, as well as in society. How clearly they are seen depends upon the perception, vision, understanding, and vicarious education or experience of the viewer/reader.

Aviation and air power have been positive forces in the development of meteorology and diplomacy (such as evolved from the 1944 international conference on civil aviation in Chicago), and have been influential scientifically and technologically in radar, in the development of piston and then jet engines, in the extension of the medical fields of tropical health and of high-altitude travel, and, ideologically, in the attitudes and worship of things aeronautical. Economically, aviation and air power via the aircraft industry, air forces, and airlines, as well as airports, are large employers with a local, regional, national, and international ripple effect.

The Aircraft Industry

The aircraft and airline industries provide the basis for the exercise of air power outside its purely military aspects, and thus the aircraft industry—more than the airline industry, which was born at least a decade later—has been subject to the pattern of war and peace, as well as to the overall growth pattern of air power. In China, the aircraft industry has especially been subject to the vicissitudes of politics.

The aircraft industry has been more often the target of attacks on profit-making than most others. Aircraft manufacturers have indeed made great gains. But it has also been true that although the industry has enjoyed enormous short, sharp, wartime peaks, it has suffered long hand-to-mouth peacetime years as well. And after the Second World War, the industry experienced a drastic rise in costs of materials and components and the compelling need to undertake increasingly expensive research and development.

One facet of the history of air power, which is at present inadequately studied, is the combined influence of economic considerations and political developments on the growth and decline of the aircraft industry in various nations. The simple

assumption that competition is the reason is not of itself sufficient.

In aviation, two economic laws have joined— one, that the simple inevitably becomes more complex and costly, and another, that organizations become increasingly complex and bureaucratic.

It is ironic that the first graduate of the RAF College at Cranwell to become Chief of the Air Staff (CAS) did not do so until 1956, when the British air force had already peaked. It remains to be seen whether or not Parkinson's Law relating to Great Buildings applies to the U.S. Air Force Academy, founded in 1954.

These two developments with the British and the Americans occurred at a time when it appeared that missiles would replace manned aircraft, the arrival of the practical ballistic missile inspiring talk of its being the ultimate weapon, making all others obsolete. Historical analogy, however, suggests that this may not happen. The field gun did not outmode the pistol or rifle. As armies were used more and more merely to guard frontiers, firepower became less important to them, but there was a long period in which the pistol remained useful in minor contests. And so it appears to be with air power. The nuclear ballistic missiles have created their own stalemate, thus making the manned tactical airplane, the transport airplane, or the remotely piloted vehicle (RPV) and the unmanned aerial vehicle (UAV) far more valuable.

Careers

Corresponding to the growth of aviation from infancy to middle age and retirement are the careers of many of the men who have taken part in this development. Sociologically, airmen form a group, drawn largely from the middle and lower middle classes, which has certain recognizable characteristics (though this caste awaits a study such as Janowitz's *The Professional Soldier*). The young airmen of 1914 did not retire as chiefs of staff until the 1950s; and in the aircraft industry, many of those who had pioneered the aeronautical business were actually only leaving it in the 1960s—in the Soviet Union a decade later, in China not until the twenty-first century. Thus the management of the industry, at least in Britain, has tended to reflect the age of the founder of the firm.

A powerful leader rarely produces an equally dynamic heir, for who with ambition wants to play second fiddle to a strong man unwilling to give up the reins in the foreseeable future? This is true for any nation or industry, though in the United States, where competition has been more ruthless than elsewhere, the aviation companies by the end of the Second World War were becoming far more corporate and far less one-man shows. Yet in the U.S. airline business in the 1960s, the founders Juan Trippe, C. R. Smith, W. A. Patterson, Eddie Rickenbacker, and Robert Six were still running systems that were nonetheless highly competitive and dynamic.

SOME PATTERNS OR MODELS OF DEVELOPMENT

History is complex and is affected by diplomatic, military, political, economic, scientific and technological, medical, social, and ideological factors. Models, such as the Wave and Plateau theories, used within this work are approximations, designed to give readers and students comprehension of patterns otherwise hidden by minutiae.

The Cause and Effect Cube suggests many of the influences that must be taken into account in analyzing a single incident or a complex operation.

And the Wave pattern shows the cycle of peace and war affecting the aircraft industry: a peacetime equilibrium, disturbed by rearmamental instability, then settling into the controlled activity

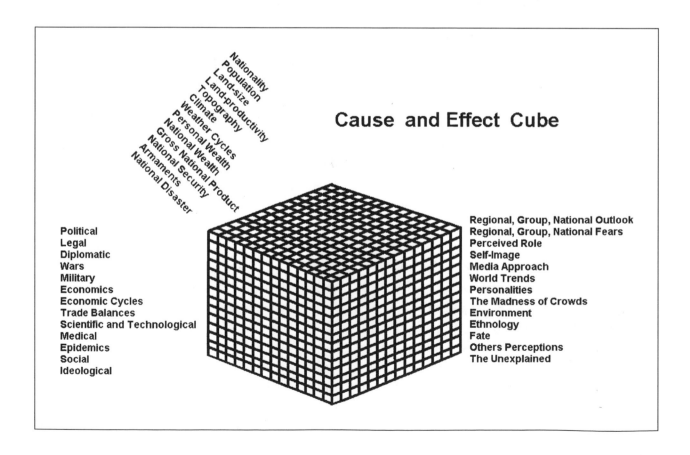

Cause and Effect Cube

Nationality
Population
Land-size
Land-productivity
Topography
Climate
Weather Cycles
Personal Wealth
National Wealth
Gross National Product
National Security
Armaments
National Disaster

Political
Legal
Diplomatic
Wars
Military
Economics
Economic Cycles
Trade Balances
Scientific and Technological
Medical
Epidemics
Social
Ideological

Regional, Group, National Outlook
Regional, Group, National Fears
Perceived Role
Self-Image
Media Approach
World Trends
Personalities
The Madness of Crowds
Environment
Ethnology
Fate
Others Perceptions
The Unexplained

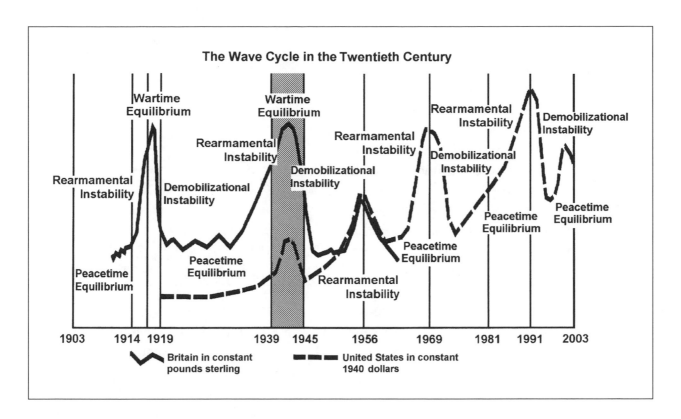

The Wave Cycle in the Twentieth Century

Rearmamental Instability

Wartime Equilibrium

Demobilizational Instability

Peacetime Equilibrium

Rearmamental Instability

Wartime Equilibrium

Demobilizational Instability

Rearmamental Instability

Peacetime Equilibrium

Rearmamental Instability

Demobilizational Instability

Peacetime Equilibrium

Rearmamental Instability

Demobilizational Instability

Peacetime Equilibrium

1903   1914 1919   1939 1945   1956   1969   1981 1991   2003

⌇⌇⌇ Britain in constant pounds sterling   ▬ ▬ ▬ United States in constant 1940 dollars

of wartime equilibrium with full production; and, before the war is over, renewed demobilizational instability, phasing into a new peacetime equilibrium.

This pattern was first developed from a study of the British aircraft industry, in which the process could be measured in terms of either the numbers of aircraft produced or the money appropriated for the air force. In either case, the pattern emphasized that, at least in a technological service, the beginnings and ends of wars do not coincide with the formal dates assigned to these phenomena. Thus, in Britain, accelerated purchasing began in 1913 and 1934, many months before war was declared. (The Korean War, however, caught that government flatfooted, and the instability of rearmament began after the crisis started and continued after it ended.) The level of steady British wartime production was not reached until 1916 or later in the First World War and carried on until shortly after it ended. In the Second World War, it was not reached until mid-1942 (about the same three years after the war began as

before) but the running-down process began in 1944, nearly a year before the conflict terminated.

After 1918, the political situation at home in Britain dictated using war-surplus aircraft for years, in order to save money in a day of orthodox finance. The continuing unsettled state of Europe created the demand for the British Home Defence Air Force of 1923, which resulted in some aircraft purchases, but that program was stretched out over more than ten years, during which technology began to change rapidly.

The wave can be discerned in the overall history of aviation since its beginning. The airplane, the airship, and aeronautics in general were in their infancy before 1914. Only by about 1917 did military aviation begin to mature. Its period as an ancillary weapon in war was very short and came to an effective end with the Armistice of November 1918. Like the boy born about 1900 who had enlisted in 1917, military aviation had scarcely been properly blooded when the fighting stopped.

Untrained for other jobs, but with airy dreams, aviators sought for a significant place in a world where until then they had been nothing more than a Sunday afternoon entertainment. It was a long and painful struggle for military and civil aviation, for manufacturers, ancillary industries, and airlines alike, and it lasted for nearly two decades.

Air power did not reach maturity until well into the Second World War, and only after 1945 did it enter a full hard-working middle age. At least this was true for the United States and the Soviet Union; in other countries, notably Britain, the manned air forces, after a brief resurgence as a result of the Korean War, began a gentle extended decline toward retirement.

The evolution of British aviation provides a framework that is known to be applicable to American and Russian development, but that has not as yet been tested for other aeronautical countries, in particular France, Germany, Japan, and China.

The post-1950 wave is based upon U.S. figures.

Another model, or tool, for the understanding of technology is the Plateau theory, which notes that progress runs about three generations before it levels off, caused not by the inability to continue to develop an item but by political, economic, social, and ideological resistance, or ordering of priorities.

The learning curve combined with the Plateau concept suggests that about twenty-five years after a technology is developed, its design and use becomes established. While further advances will be made whether driven by war or economics, the whole can be calculated and managed relatively routinely.

More advanced versions of a technology, or radical changes, may be made if the money is available or if management is willing to gamble. But no progress can be made until there is a new technological breakthrough.

Another model is the Bamboo Basket, of the Invisible Infrastructure, which can help to understand the complexity of the elements that had to be bound together to allow an aircraft to take off for an operational sortie or scheduled airline service—from wishful order or command to actual

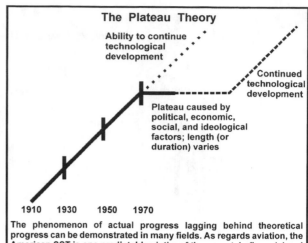

The phenomenon of actual progress lagging behind theoretical progress can be demonstrated in many fields. As regards aviation, the American SST is one predictable victim of the uncertain financial and political climate of the early 1970's.

departure. Everything has to fit together to a timetable. And after takeoff, a whole new set of factors have to be counted in.

Although the Bamboo Basket points to the complexity of the flow of essentials to an airfield as symbolic of air power, this does not make plain the other vital points.

The first is that all action is based upon an invisible infrastructure, especially in a general wide-flung war, and that airlines are in conflict all the time. Direction, management, ordering, and accounting for all the contributory pieces and personnel are needed to make an airline efficient and productive.

The other point affecting airline or miliary operations, especially over distances, is "Pipeline Purdah"—the operational unavailability of supplies and personnel because they are in transit whether marching on foot, in convoys at sea, or being flown in. They just are not operationally available.

EFFICIENCY RATINGS

Interpretation of the growth of air power requires an understanding of the significance of Efficiency Ratings. The changing nature of both aviation and air power in part can be seen in the ER—a technical measure—and in part by

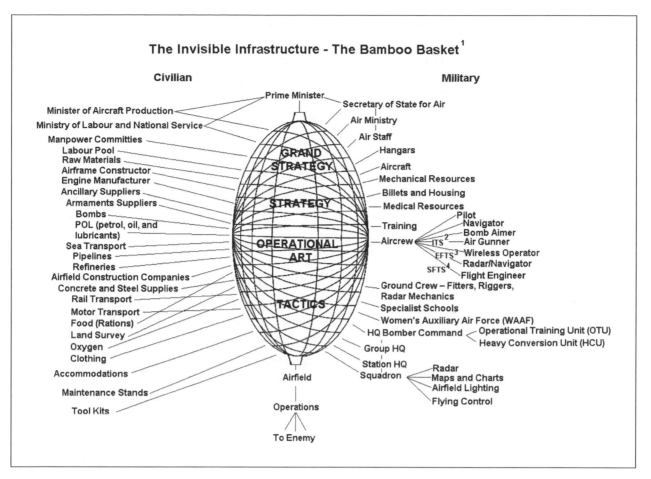

The Invisible Infrastructure - The Bamboo Basket [1]

¹Based on the British model, used in *The Bases of Air Strategy*, by Robin Higham (Shrewsbury, U.K.: Airlife Publications, 2000).
²Initial Training School.
³Elementary Flying Training School.
⁴Service Flying Training School.

the evolving appreciation and understanding of the subject by politicians, the public, and practitioners, and vice versa.

Yet, there is the growth of power and possibilities, of range, lethality, and accuracy, balanced by the dampening effects of deflation of overclaims for effectiveness and efficiency.

Efficiency Ratings are a simple formula designed to allow meaningful comparisons between aircraft at various times. In order to be as consistent as possible, the data herein has been taken from Enzio Angelucci's two-volume *Encyclopedia of Military and Civil Aviation* (Chartwell, 2001), from *The Complete Encylcopedia of World Aircraft,* edited by David Donald (Barnes & Noble, 1997),

and from the Putnam Aeronautical volumes. Dates are more related to an era than a year due to variances as to conception, first flight, or operational use. ERs vary for particular types, depending upon the date, the model, and the configuration, as well as whether or not the range is combat or ferry miles. Manufacturer names are those current at the time being discussed. ERs are given at first mention of an aircraft, and most usually are only repeated in a comparison of machines, or for a particular emphasis. ERs not available are noted as "ER n/a."

Knots quoted have been multiplied by 1.17 to get miles per hour; and where radius of action rather than range was given, the figure was multiplied by 2.5 (distance out and return plus a re-serve). The formula used shifted the decimal place two removals to the left. The 500 divisor was chosen empirically to provide usable figures. The formula, therefore, is:

$$\frac{\text{maximum weight x maximum speed x maximum range}}{500} = ER$$

Thus for the 1940 Martin Maryland we get:

$$\frac{168.00 \times 2.78 \times .18}{500} = 16.8$$

For the 1942 Martin Baltimore II, its successor:

$$\frac{266.00 \times 3.2 \times 9.5}{500} = 16.4$$

These two aircraft are examples of the designers' compromise between weight, speed, and range (and only implicitly ceiling), which show that the earlier, less well-armed but longer-ranged machine actually gets a better ER.

Comparisons can be made to show growth, as in the case of the Supermarine Spitfire, where the Mark I had a 1.9, the Mark IX a 2.63, and the Mark XIV a 3.5, while the ultimate British piston-engine fighter, the Hawker Tempest V, had a 15 and the first RAF jet, the Gloster Meteor III, a 15.3.

In actual fact, the ER depended in practice on how the aircraft was employed and the model whose data are used.

ERs, however, can be misleading. In the 1943 World War II Allied arsenal, the Boeing B-17E Flying Fortress, perhaps the better of the heavies, had an ER of 101, due to ferry range, compared to Consolidated's B-24D Liberator at 103 and, later, to the Boeing's B-29 Superfortress at ER 414. But in operational assessments, though the B-17 lacked bomb load due to defensive armament, it could absorb punishment; in contrast, the B-24 dropped like a brick with more than one engine out. Both on the return journey were lightened by consumption of fuel and ammunition.

On the RAF side, the Short Stirling, with an ER of 72, was dropped out of Bomber Command in part for ground handling accidents, and in part because of lack of ceiling. And the Handley Page Halifax, with an ER of 91, was clearly an inferior machine to the Avro Lancaster, ER 103, which did not have handling problems.

On the other hand, close differences in ERs may not reflect actual appraisals. The Vickers Valiant, ER 652, and the Avro Vulcan, ER 653, were apparently equal, but the Vulcan handled much better at both high and low altitudes.

Between about 1910 and 1975, aviation and air power made quantum leaps. Fighter aircraft rose from an ER of just above 0 to almost 1, and bombers from and ER of 1 to 2 by 1918. The First World War had been a virtual incubator, with the benefits of mass production and rapid evolution of not only airframes and engines, but also of professional expertise. And the interwar years saw the consolidation of knowledge and practice to make for reliability, though the acceptance of accident investigation and more penetrating knowledge of causes only slowly developed from engine failure, followed by pilot error, to a realization that structural failure might exist and have many causes.

Those years also saw the beginnings of the ten technological and technical revolutions of the decade 1934–45 noted earlier. In addition, developments in laboratories, wind tunnels, designers' minds, and—from practical experience—long-distance, high-altitude, and speed record-breaking were applied. The fruits of this were seen in the later 1930s as fighter ERs doubled from 0.18 to 1.9, bombers from 2 to 30, and transports from 2 to 19, with engines rising in horsepower from 300 to 1,000.

The Second World War was another hothouse period when designers and industry, as well as specification writers, surged ahead to meet operational demands. The lag between inquiries and operational products ranged from four to eight years from the beginning of rearmament in 1934. This meant that the 1934–36 designs only became operational during the 1938–42 period, and that the postwar designs were mostly on the drawing boards, if only experimentally, by 1940–43.

But the developmental wonders were in evidence, such as the North American P-51 Mustang (ER 9.63), which progressed from sketch to flight in ninety days, and the de Havilland Goblin jet engine, which was in operation only 248 days after conception.

On the other hand, the Consolidated B-36 Peacemaker, ER 2,042, originated in 1941, but did not reach operational status until 1947. During the same 1935–45 period, airlines went from an ER of 19.14 for the Douglas DC-3, to an ER of 83 for the DC-4.

From 1945 to 1975, the inflammatory wars in Korea and Vietnam and the Cold War of the United States and NATO versus the USSR and the Warsaw Pact also maintained an incubating atmosphere in aviation, with the continuing infusion of funds at a high level. Fighter ERs went from the 15.3 of the jet Meteor III to the 187 of the McDonnell Douglas F-15A Eagle and 157 of the MiG-29. Bombers rose from the 103 of the Consolidated B-24 Liberator of 1943 to the 6,336 of Boeing's B-52 Stratofortress of 1953.

Airliners at this time bifurcated and rose from an ER of 124 for the Lockheed Constellation L-749 to 5,989 for the Boeing 747-100, 183.5 for the de Havilland Comet I of 1952, 106 for the Sud Caravelle of 1959, and 4,262 for the British Aircraft Corporation/Aerospatiale Concorde of 1976. But, thereafter, progress was evolutionary rather than revolutionary. This is to be seen in the development of the 747-100's ER of 5,989 to that of the 747-400 twenty years later, of 8,760.

In the meantime, in nearly sixty years, the jet engine had gone from a puny 2,000 pounds in 1941 to 100,000 pounds by the end of the century, without afterburner (reheat).

That all of this was possible was due to the switch from slide rules before the 1950s to computers from then on, to the developments in metallurgy from aluminum S2024 of the 1930s to titanium—though S2024 was still in use in 2003. Aluminum's limitation was Mach 2, where the skin temperature at speed, in spite of sub-zero degrees at 50,000 feet, began to weaken it.

The miniaturization of electronics and computers in the past half-century has allowed labor-saving in the cockpit and vastly increased productivity per employee. The latter rose from a worker efficiency rating of less than 1 to 125 in British Overseas Airways Corporaation (BOAC) between 1947 and 1974 alone, meaning that on a base of 100 for the year 1947, real fares have hardly increased at all. In part, this has been due to the economies of scale as airline traffic has grown phenomenally, and as non-stop range has risen from 2,000 to 8,000 or more miles.

At the same time, military machines have grown more powerful, but speeds have plateaued at about 1,600 mph for fighters, while heavy bombers have stayed subsonic, as has the Northrop B-2 Spirit, ER 1,460, though some such as the Tupolev Tu-160 Blackjack, ER 6,698, and the North American Rockwell B-1 Lancer, ER 6,279, can do Mach 2.

The usefulness of Efficiency Ratings can be seen by comparing the power of a squadron of bombers in 1918, 1939, 1945, and 1990.

Assuming a squadron of nine aircraft and two reserve machines, in 1918 a squadron of Handley Page 0/400s (ER 1.95) had a total ER of 8.547; in 1939, a similar unit of twelve Vickers Wellingtons (ER 30) and two reserves had a total ER of 420; and in 1945, an Avro Lancaster (ER 67) squadron, of eighteen aircraft, had a total ER of 1,206. However, due to serviceability, only about 60 percent of ER power could actually be used against enemy targets, and even then that impact was vitiated by aircraft that turned back, failed to find the target, could not bomb accurately, were shot down, or ran out of fuel and were lost on the way home.

By 1990, the total ER power of a twelve-machine squadron of two-seat British Aircraft Corporation (BAC) Tornadoes (ER 72) was 864, a figure which, while showing a dramatic increase since 1945, did not reflect the explosive lethality of new munitions and the accuracy of their guidance systems.

Aviation and air power have come a long way technically since 1903, but also humanely. While the capacity to strike deep into enemy territory has carried war to civilians, accuracy has limited casualties to a fraction of those of either World War II or of tribal warfare in Africa in the late twentieth century. And on the peaceful side, not only has airlift aided the victims of national disasters, but the enormous flow of business, family, and tourist passengers and of express and freight have brought the world closer together and have stimulated the economies as population has grown from 1.6 billion in 1903 to an estimated 6 billion—a four-fold worldwide increase in one hundred years.

NOTE TO THE READER

This volume is not solely about aviation and air power in a technical and operational sense, for it also aims to show, especially in the pages on Africa post-1945 and on China post-1949, the many complex factors that surround and influence air power and that are themselves affected by it. In Africa the whole has been complicated by the anarchy and the three Africas—North, Tropical, and South—and in China by the size of the country and its monolithic Communist regime. Thus, the reader needs to juxtapose these areas with their multi-faceted aspects.

In addition, there are two reasons why space flight is not treated in this work. The first is the present length of the manuscript; the second is that as highly technological and computerized as the subject is, it had by 2003 only reached, after some forty-five years, where steamships were in the 1840s, the railways in the 1880s, and aviation by about 1940, if that. But this is not meant to suggest that the field, by 2020, may be approaching the plateau where its progress technically will be limited by political, economic, and social factors.

And finally, it is the inevitable nature of historical narrative that the story must move back and forth chronologically to pick up themes. The photo gallery, however, inasmuch as possible, is chronological, to show the evolution of aircraft and air power.

CHAPTER 1

EARLY ATTITUDES TOWARD AIR POWER

The history of air power has been much confused, both by the glamour surrounding flight and by a lack in the past of historical perspective on the part of its proponents.

To pierce this confusion, we must examine the context in which the airplane first flew. Its arrival coincided with the beginning of widespread industrialization and with the closure of frontiers in the United States, Russia, Australia, South Africa, and South America. Humans were now confined to known geographic boundaries and their frustrations were accentuated by the stalemate of the First World War when airmen—the romantic frontiersmen of the day—appeared to be as free as the birds.

Man had taken to the air in the 1890s, just after the tabloid newspapers of the sensational yellow press were started. This, and the fact that flying grew up with the cinema and shared its young heroes in the 1920s with radio, made glamorization inevitable. Flying somehow fit into each nation's idealized characteristics. In America, the Wright brothers were upper-class theoretical and practical mechanics; elsewhere, pioneer fliers were more often gentry, manufacturers, or engineers as in Britain, France, and Russia, or even nobility as in Germany and Japan. That at least was the popular impression, if not always the fact. Above all else there emerged the picture of the daring

pilot, his white scarf streaming in the wind, as man once again fought against nature. Other members of the aircrew were largely ignored, even in wartime.

Those early publications that raved about the magic of flight also delighted in portraying its accidents. In flying's infancy, these were often spectacular, though not always fatal. The public, enchanted by the misfortunes of those who dared, liked to read about air disasters, though far fewer people were killed in these than in vehicles on the ground.

Somehow, too, the impression was created that the air was a new element with unknown dangers and unknown rules—that nothing learned from the past applied. Everything seemed new; but actually, in order to fly, man had converted the automobile engine and bird-wing propellers and had adopted for his vehicle the shape of a bird. Likewise, his subsequent organization of the developing air forces followed that of ground-bound armies and navies. In fact, the utilization of most new weapons is perforce based on old organizations, because adaptable manuals exist; and military aviation, much as the cavalry or submarine units, was originally manned by those who saw it only as another branch of the their own service.

The history of air power has also been confused by the bragging of its prophets and the derision of its enemies. Too often vision has outrun reality and resulted in disappointment and reaction. As newcomers, forced to plead from a position of weakness, airmen carried arguments to their logical extremes as they talked about what air power was going to be able to do. Their listeners tended to forget that these were prognostications, accepting them instead as imminent realities. Illustrative of this is the fact that not until the post-1945 perfection of air-to-air refueling and the creation of the atomic bomb was it technically possible for the aircraft of a single power to devastate a city anywhere in the world. Yet before that the psychological impact of air power on people, notably civilians, was greater than the physical blow in terms of numbers involved. And in spite of the actual destruction that did take place in war, the impact of air power was discussed more widely by its partisans than by its victims, not all of whom died. The real effect of air power thus in many ways fell far short of the claims of its early supporters.

The history of air power must be considered within the general intellectual and emotional background sketched above, but it must also be approached in other terms and from other angles. First, it must be seen within the general patterns not only of military history but of all human experience. Applicable to an understanding of aviation events and trends is the Cause and Effect Cube, a matrix of intersecting forces that apply to historical as well as current situations. The aerial means and the medium applied to particular situations were novel, but human elements and influences have remained unchanged.

One of the failures of earlier students of air power was to claim for it immunity from the trends of history. But we can now see that the usual patterns of administrative, commercial, and logistical past experience apply, with their changing political and economic pressures, feasts and famines, bureaucratic rigidity, and human foibles. And one pattern that applies especially to air history is the economic imperative to consolidation.

Before 1914, in their wave-cycle state of peace-time equilibrium, air services simply strove to be recognized and survive. Officers were attached on a temporary basis so that their careers would not be ruined, and equipment was flimsy and scarce. Then came the mushroom wartime expansion of 1914 when regulars were promoted rapidly to High Command, or "high heaven," and massive recruitment and constantly changing matériel disrupted the services. Wartime equilibrium in World War I was reached about 1917. At last the machinery ran smoothly, and with the arrival of properly trained pilots and crews, tactics were stabilized and losses became less alarming.

What really affected at least the French, the RAF in 1918, and later the U.S. Air Service, is that they joined in the trench battles in a ground-support role and took very heavy casualties, stemming the German March offensive. They then went over to a tactical offensive again with more heavy casualties. After the Great War, the Germans, who had usually successfully stayed on the defensive, taking fewer casualties, wished to forget that offensive experience—and, in fact, the RAF did.

The General Background to 1914

Before 1914, even really before 1917, air forces hardly existed. In 1914 the major European powers each fielded about fifty aircraft. Each squadron was composed of assorted types—monoplanes or biplanes. None had reliable engines, nor were they equipped to fight. In fact, exactly what they were there for was not very clear. The German general staff took the tactical view that aircraft might provide battlefield information after a movement had started, though the French were more anxious to use them to locate enemy armies and observe their movements in order to prepare for battle. The Germans had the means in the Zeppelins to cruise well behind the enemy front lines, whereas the French did not; and because the Zeppelin was the symbol of German power, the

French favored airplanes. Thus, national *mentalité,* among many other factors, entered into the creation of air forces.

By the 1880s, before the Wright brothers, both the British and the Germans had developed military balloon units run by the engineers. But later—just as the engineers did not always control automobile transport when it appeared—the artillery officers claimed that powered airplanes came under their jurisdiction, arguing that airplanes had to be transportable by road. On land, the transport staff emphasized, aircraft must be towable and easy to erect or disassemble. Although this requirement resulted in a lack of airworthiness, not until a number of accidents had occurred, due to structural weakness, was it changed. Thus, early designers and aviators—and they were sometimes the same people—had to fight vested interests that had laid down rules with no relevance to the nature of flight.

At the same time, reaction to the arrival of the airplane and the airship varied. Some of those who feared or disdained these craft criticized them unreasonably, discounting the Zeppelin, for example, because it could not turn as tightly as the non-rigid airship. Detractors saw to it that aircraft were not given the scope on maneuvers to demonstrate their real abilities.

In contrast, however, those who supported aeronautics sometimes claimed too much for their fragile, temperamental, and unweatherly birds. But the enthusiasts also went ahead with their own experiments in bomb-dropping, mounting machine guns, and aerial photography. None of these developments had reached a useful stage or had been adopted officially when World War I broke out, except in the veteran Italian air forces after 1911. Nor had artillery spotting been accepted, except, again, by the Italians, because until the advent of workable wireless sets, communication between spotter and gunner was better maintained via a telephone line from the new sausage-shaped observation balloons.

Those who were worried about aircraft also sought the development of anti-aircraft guns. Here, again, the conflict between established groups was evident. The artillery advocated the adaptation of field guns, but these could not be traversed fast enough or elevated sufficiently to be effective even against the very slow aircraft of the day. A much better device appeared to be special guns mounted upon automobile chassis and firing shrapnel. But no resolution of this conflict had appeared before the war broke out in 1914.

Another unanswered question at this time concerned the actual size of the air arms. Much like the "missile gap" of the 1960s, in the early 1900s, and indeed again in the 1930s, there was talk of an aircraft or machine gap. Politicians, faced with vociferous and well-intentioned, though not always well-informed, questioners made their usual vague statements. Of course, a vast difference existed between the number of aircraft officially on charge and those actually able to fly, and a vast difference, too, between the latter and machines ready for war. This contradiction and the related matter of the funding for aircraft caused the fall of a French government in 1912.

In Britain the situation reached a ridiculous point when members of Parliament actually went around to verify the number of aircraft on each field. Rumors flew, secret missions were sent abroad, and journalists were encouraged. The new aviation magazines took up the cry, for it was good business to demand more orders for their advertisers. Appeals were made to national pride, and subscriptions were raised to help pay for Zeppelins in Germany, new aircraft for the French army, or "condolences" for a dead Japanese flier. International competitions were sponsored, and prizes and orders given to the winners. However, sometimes this backfired, for on occasion the judges made their award to a product that turned out to be useless. Yet they can hardly be blamed, for nobody had a very clear idea about what was really wanted for aviation.

The Germans and the British were in some ways more concerned with quality than with quantity, whereas in the United States almost no airplanes were on hand until 1916. Nevertheless, the military desire to standardize came early to the fore, and by 1912 the British were seeking the ideal airplane, recognizing that at least three should be built of each type developed. One would be used as the basis for production, another for the development of modifications and for training, and the third as the basis for the aircraft's next generation. The rapidity of progress was largely limited by the development of engines and the survival rate of pilots.

In the United States before 1917 the Wright brothers' patents in the courts, and personalities, accidents, and distrust in the U.S. Army Signal Corps, frustrated the development of Army aviation. The U.S. Navy, in contrast, was far more successful in making progress—as in the case of the Royal Naval Air Service (RNAS)—due to an understanding of new technology, notably the submarine.

Training and Manufacturing

Pilots in the early days of aviation were a commodity both in great potential supply and in acute actual shortage. When volunteers were called for, bored young officers happily stepped forward. But few could be taken, because training facilities were limited by the lack of instructors and aircraft, and the need for perfectly still or windless flying days. The whole training process was hampered by lack of flying knowledge and by the non-existence of a training philosophy. It was not until the development of such simple things as the Gosport intercom tube and dual controls that an instructor could both run through his patter and demonstrate in the air. Moreover, accidents were not investigated with any understanding either of what airmen were trying to do or of likely causes and the complex factors involved. Even such commonplace phenomena as stalls and spins were not understood until well into World War I, though some skillful pilots had discovered how to get out of them before the war started. The result was

that when quick recovery of the aircraft was essential, many pilots were injured or killed in accidents close to the ground. And thus, the monoplane was banned in Britain as inherently unstable.

Structural testing was also somewhat primitive at this time, and dynamic testing did not exist. Moreover, parachutes, though available by 1913 as static models attached to the machine, were not used until late in the war, and then only by the Germans. It was argued that if airmen could bail out, they would abandon costly equipment in the face of the enemy. The attitude prevailed that airmen were not to be trusted, largely due to their boisterous behavior, which perhaps in many cases was really a cover for their fear of flying and of receiving the traditional "white feather" for cowardice. Coupled with this was the managerial failure to consider what high casualty rates could mean to an elite branch such as aviation, which might be relentlessly ground down in continuous combat. Hence, the view evolved that the fear of flying could be handled by sending people up again—by yet more flying—or by dishonorably discharging aircrew, as in shell-shock cases (later called "lack of moral fiber," or LMF).

And thus, training up to and during the First World War remained primitive. At the worst, pilots might be sent into action with as few as seventeen hours of flying time in unstable aircraft. They became easy victims.

In the better organizations, and as training became a more recognized and standardized operation, pilots were given some fifty hours, which included both elementary flying instruction and advanced work on the kind of craft they would use in combat, together with gunnery and navigational practice. By 1939 this had risen to some 150 hours before combat, and by 1945 was likely to have reached 300 or more when aircrew were becoming a surplus commodity on the Allied side. But in countries such as Germany in 1918 and 1945, and Japan by 1945, fuel shortages sharply restricted training in those days before useful simulators existed.

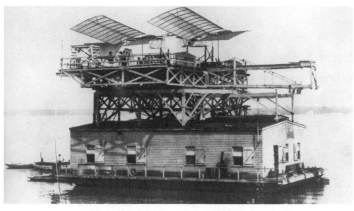

The unsuccessful Samuel Pierpont Langley "aerodrome" is ready to be launched from a houseboat on the Potomac River, Washington, D. C., December 1903.

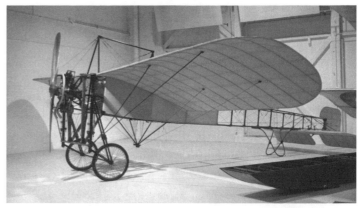

The Frenchman Louis Blériot flew the English Channel in 1909 in one of these aircraft of his own design. This replica of the Blériot XI (ER 0.035) is in the RAF Museum, Hendon, London. (Stuart Howe)

Lts. Benjamin Foulois and Frank Coffyn learning new skills on a Wright Model B Flyer about 1910. Note that the pilots are seated in order to balance the weight of the offset engine. (NASM)

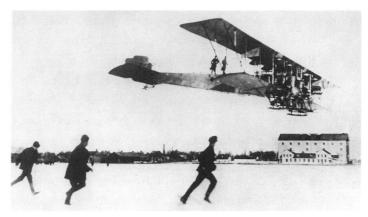

Russian aircraft designer Igor Sikorsky's famous giant aircraft design, the Ilýa Mourometz (ER 0.52), was an improved modification of the 1913 *Russky Vitaz,* the world's first four-engine aircraft. The Ilýa Mourometz was first a civil transport, then subsequently used by the tsarist air arm as a reconnaissance machine and bomber. Its slow speed can be noted by the men running alongside and those standing atop the machine. (Sikorsky Aircraft)

The original Royal Navy rigid airship is seen here after launching from its floating building shed in 1911. But because of Admiralty requirements that it carry an anchor, capstan, and towing hawser, it was too heavy to get airborne. It also suffered from early metal fatigue, and collapsed shortly after being withdrawn from its shed. (Vickers)

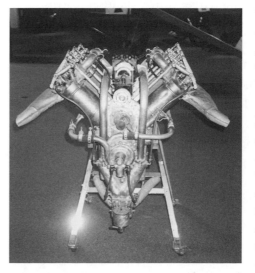

The Liberty 12-A engine was America's best technical contribution to the 1917–18 war. Designed by an automotive team, 20,478 were manufactured by six different companies, and the type continued into the 1930s. (S. Liebler)

One of the enduring problems of air-training organizations was their detachment from operational realities. Before 1914, the small elite stations, mostly catering to officers, did not know what they were really training their pilots for, as the role of aviation in war was largely undecided. Thus the emphasis was simply upon learning to fly; employment on maneuvers was largely limited to primitive tactical reconnaissance. Training staff tended to be non-operational personnel; they adhered to peacetime concepts and rules, and were loath to change unless forced by an influx of men experienced in fighting. Even then, jealousy could make vanquishing the expert more important than training the fighting force. This hostility, however, was less notable at operational training units, which were closer to battle both in terms of men and machines, and which were more heavily staffed with veterans, and thus lacked the often petty outlook of training commands. No doubt there were exceptions, but in general this behavior applies to training in both World Wars.

It was also at this period that flying pay was granted to those who obtained a pilot's brevet—his wings—reinforcing the idea that the airman was something special. And perhaps he was—for few others except air gunners in the services were likely to have such a short life.

If early training was primitive, so was manufacturing. Up to the start of steady orders in 1914, design and manufacture was strictly a small-team, limited, manual operation. Rival establishments loudly touted their own wares, scrambled for orders, and gloated over others' failures. Firms were often started with one wealthy silent partner (who might also take a hand at sales), a designer (who might or might not be an engineer or a pilot, or both), a pilot, and a half-dozen workmen. Each model was hand built, and, after each accident, rebuilt. Most aircraft were a combination of wooden frames, fabric covering, and wire bracing, powered by an unreliable reciprocating gasoline (petrol) engine. Airships used heavier fabric, a metal framework, and sometimes diesel engines, as well as highly inflammable hydrogen for lifting power. Early airplanes were not too expensive for some officers to possess their own, just as they owned cars and horses.

Prewar Air Operations, 1911–12

In 1911, the Italians took an odd assortment of biplanes to the war in Libya. Aircraft had been assigned to the army in 1910, and on maneuvers in August 1911 each of the "contending" armies had been allotted four. It was soon obvious that far more aircraft were needed. In a matter of three days, half of one "air force" was out of action due to forced landings. And other lessons were learned: observers were needed to make notes of ground activity; and more pilots as well as more aircraft had to be available, which in turn required a better servicing organization. In these early exercises, airborne observers, who had been given a crash twenty-day course, undertook strategic reconnaissance of some sixty-five miles each way twice a day, then scouted for the attacker, located the units engaged, and plotted the extent of the front. It was the results of these operations that convinced the Italian armed forces of the value of small airships and led to their dispatch to the Libyan front.

Because of transportation problems and bad weather, active operations in Tripoli with airships, balloons, and airplanes were not begun until October 23, 1911. In November, the magazine *La Stampa Sportiva* of Turin sent out two flights of its own to Derna and Tobruk, under the command of the president of the Italian Aero Club. Naval aviators were established at Benghazi.

These actions in Libya again made plain some of the new requirements as well as the uses to which aircraft could be put. Of primary importance was the need for better maps, and this led to aerial photography. Observation of artillery bombardments was less fruitful, as airmen could not communicate with the gunners to correct their aim or choice of target.

The first bombs dropped from the aircraft were the 4.5-pounders, which the pilot flung over the side after pulling the pin with his teeth. The effect on the press was probably greater than that on the Turks, and immediately the moral-humanitarian issue was raised. The Turks claimed a hospital had been hit, though the bombs used were basically hand grenades lobbed a somewhat abnormal distance. These early bombs were soon followed by a special box, which held ten of the 4.5-pound type; a safety catch on the bomb fuse was released automatically when a bomb fell from the box, and the pilot or observer in an airship could choose to drop one singly or all ten bombs together. Occasionally airmen also engaged in leaflet-dropping and night-flying, for which they soon devised instruments, lighting, and runway illumination.

At the same time, consideration was given to the possible challenge posed if the Turks obtained airplanes, and to the more immediate threat of the increasing accuracy of their anti-aircraft gunfire. Despite all these side developments, the main task of the Italian pilots was observation, and this they performed so well that headquarters came to rely to a great extent upon their confirmation of intelligence gathered from other sources that were not always reliable.

It is interesting that not until August 25, 1912, was the first pilot killed, and that was when he lost control after takeoff and plunged into the sea. On September 10, the first pilot was captured by the enemy, when his engine failed and he landed behind the lines. Other incidents occurred, but on the whole very few considering the nature of the enemy's country, the fact that the aircraft could not reach over 3,000 feet even with only one man aboard, and the remarkable accuracy of the enemy riflemen.

As the Italians demonstrated in Libya in 1911–12, there is nothing like a war, especially a minor one, for pointing up weaknesses and showing the areas in which developments may be profitable. Participation in such a campaign counts far more than maneuvers, for the targets are real and there are no umpires, except the press. Success or failure depends upon training, equipment, tactics, leadership, and empirical response. Yet the lessons learned can be as misleading as those from maneuvers, for the enemy may not be typical or the results may be over-interpreted.

Just as the Russo-Japanese War of 1904–05 provided many lessons for the coming world conflict, the Libyan War did as well, as far as air power was concerned. Too few Europeans troubled to learn these lessons, or even to observe them, but the Italians gained invaluable experience and in a quiet way their air force undertook a number of unusual operations in the First World War. The Libyan campaign had taught the Italians, at least, the usefulness and the rapidity, as well as the reliability, of air reconnaissance of the other side of the hill, the need for accuracy in bombing, the dangers of ground fire, and the limitations of equipment.

In the United States, prewar status had lasted until 1917. Before that date, in 1914 the U.S. Navy had aircraft at Vera Cruz, Mexico, and in 1916 Gen. John J. Pershing had taken aircraft into the field in pursuit of Pancho Villa.

Although up to 1914 air power had been hampered by many problems, it was also learning roles to develop for the future. Peacetime aviation had attracted the bored, the adventurous, and the ambitious, requiring, however, that they be either wealthy enough to pay for flying lessons or technically bright enough to be useful. The military air arm was both an extension of and a potential rival to artillery and engineers; and as international rivalry became more dangerous, and as aircraft began to receive the support of such notables as Prince Henry of Prussia, funds started to flow and growth became assured.

In both peace and war American airmen were quick to seize opportunities for publicity and to combine their efforts with those of popular journalists to impress the general public as well as politicians and senior officers. And they were doing this at a time when the major aeronautical nations were well aware of the growing political power of the man in the street.

Early Attitudes toward Air Power

Yet at this time air power was still frail. Senior officers perhaps recognized that if an elite were created, other units of the services might well be weakened by a siphoning off of the best officers. Certainly before 1914 the air services were regarded largely as another arm of the surface forces and not as separate services. Moreover, their equipment made them capable of no more than tactical action and strategic reconnaissance.

The wars in Tripoli and Mexico showed that although the air service had much scope, its role was essentially auxiliary and not independent. Many years would pass before airmen would have the power and the range to operate independently in an effective manner. But visionaries talked and wrote as though their dreams were already about to become reality.

PATTERNS, POST-1918

In late 1918, demobilizational instability suddenly appeared for the Germans and the Allies, along with its uncertainties, which had started before the end of the conflict with the cutting back of procurement orders. Once the fighting had stopped, the wholesale reduction in force continued along with the disposal or storage of equipment. Those who had hoped to make the air force a career found themselves discharged, unless they belonged to the correct clique, as in the case of the Chief of the Air Staff of the RAF, who hand-picked his regular officers from the Western Front and virtually excluded anyone from the Royal Naval Air Service.

Some former airmen found employment in the new commercial airlines, a few barnstormed, but most could only dream of the good old flying days. Those who did stay in the service found themselves dropped two ranks, bound into an often boring routine, and compelled to wait years for promotion. In addition, equipment remained war surplus until roughly 1924–30. With little room at the top, many younger officers found the flying

career limited and ended up elsewhere. The result was that in World War II, most of the top air posts went to those who had served in 1914–18 and who often thought in terms of that war. Much of the aviation theory and doctrine of 1919–39 was based on First World War combat experience and its apparent lessons or upon colonial conditions of limited validity in conflicts between modern armed forces, and not on the history of war.

But after World War II, civilian airlines were expanding at a rate of 14 percent per annum, into the late 1960s, and their need for manpower and equipment created a demand for pilots, mechanics, management, and air-traffic controllers. The airline expansion kept the postwar surviving aircraft manufacturers in business, as did the new Cold War. At the same time, the private or general aircraft market at last blossomed, twenty years after predictions, providing more jobs in aeronautics. In countries where defense or the airlines became big business, retirement from the military services often meant only a sidestep into a new career in the defense industry or the airlines. However, in the air forces of powers with no belligerent future, notably in Latin America, careers became sour enough for pilots to turn to politics. And in those countries, the future of the air forces still remains a question mark.

The struggle of the airmen for identity during the early growth cycle of air power was not an abnormal phenomenon, but one to be observed in many human groupings. Thus airmen sought a separate service and uniform, in order to fight as equals and brothers with the older services and even, ultimately, in some cases such as in Canada, to wear the same uniform again in one single triphibious service—land, sea, and air—at least for a while.

In Britain, in peacetime, the post of Permanent Under-Secretary for the British Air Ministry was usually filled from civil servants already working inside the Ministry, as opposed to that of British Secretary of State for Air, who was always a politician. But in the Second World War, when the position became more powerful and important, it was taken over by a small coterie of high civil servants associated with the top-level Board of Trade, with the result that the permanent "managing director" was a man who knew the civil service rules rather than aeronautical technology. After the 1956 failed Anglo-French attempt to retake the Suez Canal, and the explanatory 1957 White Paper—*Cmnd. 124,* which presumed the next war would only last three days—the Permanent Secretary at the Air Ministry was again chosen from inside that organization, for the post experienced declining prestige. And after 1964, the Air Department became a division of the Ministry of Defence, without its head in the Cabinet.

In the United States, the Department of the Air Force and an independent U.S. Air Force came into being in September 1947. However, naval aviation remained under U.S. Navy control. The U.S. Secretary of the Air Force and Secretary of the Navy each controlled their air arms.

In the USSR, the naval air force was unimportant, and the Red Air Force and the Defense Forces divided the air assets under ultimate Kremlin control—meaning whoever controlled the Kremlin controlled the air forces.

In China, after 1949, the air force was—as in Russia—under control of several ministries and of the Communist Party leadership.

AIR POWER—SOME CONSIDERATIONS

Air power is the ability to go where—and when—you wish, and to prevent your enemy from doing likewise, coupled with the realization that complete air superiority rarely exists. More importantly, air power has to include both the military and civilian infrastructure and the factors affecting them. This can be assessed in part by using Rear Adm. Alfred Thayer Mahan's criteria and the Higham Cause and Effect Cube.

Mahan noted that physical yardsticks for sea power were extent of territory, territorial con-

formation and natural resources, and number and usefulness of ports. His other three criteria were human—the population number, the nature of the population, and the character of the government. The same criteria can be used for air power as for naval power, with the reminder that since 1935, when aircraft could reach higher altitudes, there have been no natural physical choke points—straits or channels—in the air, similar to those that still remain at sea. Moreover, it appears that air power has to apply many principles of war and is more affected by technology than other services. Furthermore, like naval power, air power is four-dimensional: land, sea, air, and submarine. Airmen and naval aviators, therefore, must be able to think and act in all dimensions.

Put yet another way, air power is the management of force delivered by air, whether offensive or defensive. It is an instrument of policy, and as such has to be an essential element of grand strategy. And grand strategy is the continual projection of national policy by a plan that is ever evolving. This plan should take into account diplomatic, political, military, economic, scientific, technological, medical, social, and ideological factors. The policy may be offensive, defensive, or neutral. Decision-making will rarely be black and white. Moreover grand strategy has to recognize the strengths and weaknesses of both sides or of all parties.

The 1938 RAF over-optimistic assessment of its ally the French Air Force, for example, was plain wishful thinking; the British dreams were shattered in May 1940. The month before, the British had unrealistically attempted to pass two battalions through Trondheim, Norway, with the intention of implementing a plan to prevent the Narvik iron ore from reaching Germany via the Swedish railways and the Baltic ports. But the British were so muffled up in winter clothing that they could not move in the snow.

This helps make the point that those who command any force—including air power—have to understand its assets and liabilities as well as its technical side. Commanders have to recognize that aviation is affected by the historical precedent of all the old rules—military and corporate patterns, optimism or pessimism, and human nature, as well as geography, climate, and weather—for the introduction of aircraft and space machines, in essence, parallels the chronology of that of the steam warship.

Air power requires leadership and dedicated followers. But it is unlike the other services generally, in that a very small elite bears the brunt of combat, unless the anti-aircraft establishment is under the same command.

Moreover, concepts of and approaches to air power are inevitably different in countries with a significant aircraft industry and economic infrastructure than in states dependent upon foreign suppliers. Even so, today the replacement rate of complex systems may make major powers as vulnerable as minor ones due to such variables as accidents, parsimony, resupply concepts, enemy action, computer viruses, and shortages from foreign suppliers.

Airmen, especially in the United States, Russia, and now in China, like to talk about air superiority, in particular with reference to certain fighter types. Like so many phrases, this often has been misinterpreted. Air space, indeed, has almost no boundaries, though in the past distance and ceiling have imposed limitations upon air activity, and today radar forms a kind of barrier. In the First World War, however, when bombers (and more devastatingly shellfire) followed spotter planes, some air commanders saw their responsibility as keeping the skies clear over whole battlefields, a policy wasteful both in wear on patrolling aircraft and crews and in casualties. With forces spread over greater areas in the Second World War, commanders learned, using radar, to attempt to achieve air superiority only over decisive points, either for attack or for defense. In some local wars, of course, air superiority may go to one side by default. But as in Vietnam, the grounded opponent can de-

velop effective anti-aircraft defenses and adapt tactics and camouflage to his lack of air cover.

On the whole, we hear discussions on the use of aviation by theorists in major powers, who live in a different environment than do small air forces. But those theories may be changing, and the major air forces' thinkers, planners, and strategists may find themselves looking much more at the handling methods of their smaller allies and rivals. As the service numbers of the major powers shrink, allocation of forces and resources will become more critical; there will be much more need to adjust ends to means, as well as to protect against rivalry from competing services.

The Cold War made evident for those who were not blinded by political lights that the Soviet Air Force was designed to a very different philosophy than that of the West and commanded in a different manner. The key to the approach was the peasant/worker background and at times dual military and party control. To the mid-1970s, the design bureau had money and a free hand, and production was as much based upon full-employment policies as upon defense and doctrinal necessities. Aircraft were designed to be simple to build and maintain, rugged and easy to repair, and most often able to use grass airfields. Late in the Cold War the sophistication of Soviet equipment surprised Western observers, but not the rigidity of their command.

Essential, but generally overlooked, in these air forces is the management factor. This exists to make grand-strategy possible by providing all the means needed from industrial and food production and delivery, to foreign, medical, and social policy and welfare. Slack, inappropriate, or inefficient management can vitiate power, especially if economics are neglected.

And if grand strategy is a seamless national policy, then strategy is the art of the commander-in-chief to see that forces are available and in place to carry out contemplated operations in the face of potential or real enemies. Operational art links strategy and tactics to provide planning, guidance, and the means to win. And tactics are the conceptions governing the use of force when actively seeking or engaged with the enemy.

Aiding in the quest for air power, scientific research and improved technology saw piston engines make a quantum leap, between 1934 and 1944, due to metallurgical advances, octane ratings, tetraethyl-lead additives to prevent knock, and improved ignition systems, as well as refined airframes. In recent years, armaments and guidance systems, as well as stealth design have produced a new revolution in striking power and lethality as well as in the defenses.

And, finally, essential to air power is the critical element of doctrine—a body of principles designed to guide the development and employment of military power in support of national policies or ends. It requires the knowledge of past experience with a vision of future politics, in harmony with the means available. Without doctrine, written or believed, there can be neither strategy nor operational planning.

THE PRINCIPLES OF WAR AND AIR POWER

Air power is now an integral part of warfare, and any historical or theoretical study of its use must take into account the general principles of war. In most of the world, up to 1920, these principles, though often referred to, had not been spelled out.

However, in the May 1920 issue of the *Journal of the Royal United Service Institution* the leading British pundit of tank warfare, Col. (later Major General) J. F. Fuller, laid down the principles of war as follows:

1. The principle of the objective
2. The principle of the offensive
3. The principle of security
4. The principle of concentration
5. The principle of economy of force
6. The principle of movement
7. The principle of surprise
8. The principle of cooperation

These are affected in war by time, space, ground, weather, numbers, morale, communications and information, supply, armament, obstacles, formations, and observation.

But Fuller's principles neither went far enough, nor were they interpreted broadly enough, nor have they been considered from a purely air basis. To his list I would add:

1. The principle of a unified command of grand strategy
2. The principle of bases
3. The principle of simplicity
4. The principle of training
5. The principle of infrastructure
6. The principle of procurement and production
7. The principle of management of the economy
8. The principle of the allocation of manpower and other raw materials
9. The principle of the control of the population
10. The principle of cooperation
11. The principle of the protection of the lines of communication

To these also may be added British military historian Sir Basil Liddell Hart's aphorisms:

- adjust your ends to your means
- keep your object, once selected, always in mind
- choose a line or a course of action of least expectation
- surprise
- exploit a line of least resistance

- take a line of operations that offers alternative objectives
- ensure that both plan and disposition are flexible and adaptable to the circumstances

and two negatives:

- do not throw your weight into a stroke when your enemy is on guard
- never renew an attack along the same line, or in the same form, after it has once failed

The principles of war can be applied on the grand-strategic, strategic, operational art, and tactical levels. Distinctions must be made. War is the continuation of national policy by other than outwardly pacific means and in the operational art.

The theory of war, in spite of the writings of a number of authors from Machiavelli to Jomini and Clausewitz, was not well studied in the nineteenth century. Too often writing was limited either to compiling manuals or to reporting on campaigns. This has been less true in the twentieth century, but airmen until recently have written relatively little on theory. The only air-power theorists worth mentioning are Douhet, Trenchard, Mitchell, de Seversky, Slessor, Kingston-McCloughry, Richard Williams, Asher Lee, Bernard Brodie, R. A. Mason, and Colonel John Warden. None except Mason has attempted a balanced history of air power, and only a very few books, such as those by Alan Stephens, about development within single countries, have yet been published.

Clausewitz, in an unfinished work in the early years of the nineteenth century, placed the theory of war in its context as the extension of diplomacy, recognizing that in the modern state system it was unlikely that most disputes would lead to more than limited wars for limited objectives. In other words, the objective of war would usually be an early peace, normally to be achieved by seizing and holding small territories with or without the decisive defeat of the enemy's forces in the field. The British application of this theory, if there was any awareness of it at all, was naval and consisted generally in picking up colonies overseas while preventing the opponent from coming to their rescue, a mercantilist approach in the nineteenth century called imperialism.

Toward the end of that century and into the twentieth, Clausewitz's common sense was lost sight of—if indeed most military men had ever read Clausewitz or Jomini. Instead, they fastened upon the Napoleonic *esprit,* or the will to win battles. A logical extension of this was to couple it to the democratic idea that a nation responds to the will of its people, and, therefore, the will of the enemy's people must be broken. To airmen this meant skipping over the battlefields to strike directly at the citizens. And this in its turn became linked with the long-held fascination of generals with capital cities as a strategic objective.

Thus, with the aerial weapon came the temptation to turn wars for limited objectives into unlimited ones on the assumption that a paralyzing stroke at the enemy's capital would destroy his will to fight and thereby quickly assure victory. The fallacies in this argument were that it presupposed accurate destructive capacity, denied any stiffening patriotic feelings or natural human resentment on the part of the population, and failed to realize that occupation of enemy ground (or at least defeat of its surface forces) was a prerequisite to success. Moreover, airmen tend to be unwilling to credit the enemy with totally effective stopping power, assuming that some of the bombers would always get through.

In actuality, however, until the massed raids of 1944 and the advent in 1945 of the atomic bomb, the amount of damage that could be done with air power was strictly limited both by the force of the bombs available and by the accuracy or inaccuracy of the bombing, except in a few firestorm raids. Thus, a paradox developed in the application of the aerial weapon within the total military effort. Powers whose policy was normally defensive tended toward the offensive counterstrike deterrent theory, whereas those with aggressive intentions developed tactical air forces to enable their armies to take and hold ground. Defensive powers assumed that aggressors would think as they did, and thus prepared themselves against the wrong kind of attack. *Blitzkrieg*—a lightning-quick mechanized thrust—for instance, was specifically designed to avoid a war of attrition on the ground or in the air. Aggressive powers intended to wage a limited, inexpensive war, whereas the defenders' strategy was to extend the conflict, gaining time, as was the Anglo-French strategy at the beginning of World War II.

One of the ironies of modern war has been that military casualties have moved from the battlefields, as in World War I, to civilian victims in the cities, or to the population in general in guerrilla warfare.

In the past, an independent air force and its use of air power has at times led to the neglect of the overall war effort, notably in the Second World War. Air strategy, however, must be effectively related to both grand strategy and any particular surface campaigns, either current or contemplated. Whether or not a nation can afford to use air power depends—as Mahan pointed out for sea power—on its territorial position and resources as well as upon its human might and technical skill. Psychological factors also affect the use of air power, and they vary considerably.

Both British and German civilians, for example, proved unexpectedly stoic under bombing in World War II, to the surprise of most British politicians, even to such a military expert as Maj. Gen. J. F. C. Fuller. British leaders perhaps had been unduly influenced by the devastating effect of German bombing raids on London between 1915 and 1918; and perhaps they forgot that German veterans of the First World War, who had gone through worse experiences in Flanders, by the Second World War were among those citizens undergoing attack at home and were providing stiffening for the will to resist. In fact, recent evidence seems to show that a naturally stoic people such as the North Vietnamese in the 1960s responded to bombing much as did others in the Second World War in Europe—the attacks, close to home, increased the peoples' resolution and support for their leaders. The conflict had immediate and personal meaning for them.

Air power has also been used inappropriately or inadequately in maritime warfare. Nations whose lifeblood depends upon the sea should think in terms of protecting their shipping by both air and sea arms. But in World War II, both the Germans and the Americans scored heavily on the convoys of their opponents, for air power had not been applied to safeguarding the lines of maritime communication, one of the most elementary of all principles of war.

It is clear that many aspects of aerial warfare within the context of overall military theory are yet to be adequately understood. Even in limited wars, air power must be used with swift tactical precision, and its effectiveness will be restricted by the many factors determining grand strategy. Particularly in such wars, numbers and readiness may be more important than the most modern equipment or most sophisticated methods. These considerations hold for all warfare, and they can only be applied by a commander who understands his objective. This may well mean, in terms of air power, that a single air force should be commanded by an airman—a force perhaps including contingents from several different air arms, with a commander who is the immediate deputy of the supreme commander of all the armed forces involved. By the end of the Second World War, the Allied Higher Direction understood this. Even so, efficient command depended upon personalities, planning, production, and communications, no matter which service was involved.

War is intended to obtain the political objective as quickly as possible with the least cost to either side. It calls for the most efficient use of all the forces available to bring victory, so that peace may be restored and trade resumed. Marshal Maurice de Saxe in the eighteenth century, and Field Marshal Sir Archibald Wavell in the twentieth, said that a pyramid of skulls or other evidence of butchery are not the signs of great generalship. To this may be added the claim that politicians who go to war without a long-term policy, a plan, or the power to wage the war dynamically are not statesmen.

The efficient conduct of war depends upon the development of doctrines that are flexible enough to be applicable to the situations that emerge. German success with *Blitzkrieg* in the Second World War was due to the development of a doctrine and the appropriate equipment and training in the interwar years, and to their correct application until mid-1941 in limited campaigns. Similarly, the most effective use of aircraft carriers was made by the Japanese and the Americans because they had developed the doctrines necessary for intelligent command (including the rudiments of resupply) and because they saw carriers as weapons in themselves and not just as vessels subordinate to the main fleet.

In assessing the place of air power in war it is useful to go back once more to the thoughts of Mahan. Grand strategy in air warfare, or what might be called grand-strategic bombing independent of surface forces, has to take into account all of Mahan's factors. Success presupposes that the enemy's geographical position can be reached; that the enemy has concentrated vital industries and transportation or military facilities; that the loss of any of these would leave no alternative to support war-like action; that the enemy's population cannot stand losses and has not the will to war; and that the national government is weak and ill-prepared mentally and physically.

A nation with adequate room in which to disperse its vital organizations, with a government prepared to wage war, and with a people experienced in war or strongly policed, will not easily become defeatist. A lack of understanding of this point from misreading the evidence of the First World War left some leaders believing that the Second World War could be won by an air blow. But in that sort of strategy the campaign has to be as much psychological as physical to have immediate effects.

In 1940, the Germans underestimated Mahan's intangibles in the case of Britain. True, the many British fighter airfields were vital and vulnerable, as was the sector-control system, but even more so were the ports and roads, and the railways leading out of them. The Japanese in China and the Germans again in the Soviet Union made the same mistakes. The United States, in the pre-intercontinental days, enjoyed all the assets Mahan required for success. Whether the atomic, hydrogen, or biological weapons, or terrorism, have nullified some of these assets remains to be seen. And of the major air powers, only France defeated herself with her lack of foresight.

INDUSTRIAL AND TECHNOLOGICAL LEGACY

War in the twentieth century has been a legacy of the industrial and technological revolutions. In the Russo-Japanese conflict and the First World War most soldiers and seamen saw the solution to their troubles simply as bigger and better guns, more shells, and a greater wastage of manpower. But in the Second World War, the younger officers who had faced the actual blood-bath caused by the machine gun in 1914–18 knew they could not afford to repeat those tactics; instead, they made greater use of improved mobile and armored warfare. Navies, too, moved beyond the point at which the British, the United States, and the Imperial Japanese navies left off—the only major fleets with an air component—as well as the German navy, which had advanced ideas about using air power. This meant at least a beginning of three-dimensional warfare.

By the 1930s the air forces were split philosophically. The British, the Italian in theory, the American, and possibly the Japanese army forces favored "strategic bombing" but had not the wherewithal to carry it out. When their bluffs were called by their opponents, they were not in a position to do more than engage in a war of attrition on the 1918 scale. The real successes of 1939–42 were won by tactical air forces in cooperation with surface forces. And that includes the Battle of Britain. The ultimate absurdity of the called bluff was reached in Vietnam in 1968, where grand-strategic bombers were used to drop antipersonnel bombs in tactical raids, and tactical aircraft were used in strategic raids on grand-strategic targets. Insult to air power was added to injury by a slow escalation, which vitiated the grand-strategic air force's most important weapon—a devastating surprise blow. The blame for this kind of mismanagement has to be placed on those political leaders whose knowledge of military affairs is too limited to enable them to understand their professional advisers, let alone overrule them when their proposals or doctrine run counter to the possible, credible, or acceptable in both political and military terms.

The air weapon is essentially a technical weapon. Such an instrument of policy in trained professional hands can be a superbly efficient tool for a *coup de main*—a knockout blow—at the beginning of a conflict, whether declared or not. But it must have the power to be used quickly, ruthlessly, and absolutely effectively, not as in Kosovo in 1999 when the air-power strategy took 78 days to bring a minor Balkan power to surrender, and this after the Balkan power's negative publicity battle almost had been won.

Part of the problem with our complex new air age and its weapons is that effectiveness decreases rapidly when the professional military force has to be diluted with "hostilities only" civilians—though ultimately these weapons may well evolve to be better operationally than if in regular hands. The irony, however, is that in the interim, hostilities-only combatants still may do enough damage to stimulate the opponent's fighting spirit. Examples of this, in addition to the American bombing of North Vietnam in the 1960s, are the German use of U-boats, Germany's air attacks on London in the

Table 1. Bomb Loads, 1914–60

Year	Pounds
1914	100
1918	2,000
1939	4,500
1945	22,000
1965	42,000

1914 war, and Britain's attacks on Germany in the 1939–45 war. The Israelis seem to have understood this best—that if you attack civilians, you arouse the enemy nation—for their 1967 preemptive strike against Arab aggression was a perfect example of the proper use of air power: simple, direct, and limited to military objectives. Civilians without martyrs cannot long be venomous; to attack them is to arouse the previously uncommitted.

Success or failure in war is, of course, directly related to the weapons available as well as how they are employed. A notable feature of air power has been the rapid and significant increase in the kinds of weapons that aircraft have been able to bring to bear on an opponent. Armament has been directly related to technological developments in innovation, manufacture, logistics, and maintenance; to operational suitability and command imagination; and last, but by no means least, to the lifting capacity of the aircraft itself. The power of aircraft, as evidenced by bomb loads, has increased immensely. In 1914, aircraft could carry a bomb load of less than one hundred pounds of gunpowder about one hundred miles; fighters could with difficulty lug one machine gun and a few hundred rounds into the air. By the end of the war, bombers were capable of delivering a 2,000-pound weapon several hundred miles, and fighters carried two or more machine guns.

The next advance in weapons came in the late 1930s and during the Second World War with the introduction of multiple machine guns and cannon in fighters, the development of a better range of high explosives, and the mass production of incendiary bombs. The latter particularly emphasized another factor in war: the bigger and better weapon may not be the most effective; the cheap 4.5-pound incendiary proved to be perhaps the most destructive non-battlefield weapon of the 1939 war.

Both at sea and on land, the airborne rocket gave aircraft new hitting power. Another new armament, napalm—a jellied gasoline fire bomb for battlefield use—has itself become a target, both emotional and political. A further ramification of wartime research, in this case into the means to protect or free friendly soldiers from natural hazards, was the development of herbicides. Thus, even the transport, fitted with tanks and spraying apparatus, has become a combat aircraft capable of defoliating the countryside.

The ultimate development, the atomic bomb, evolved under a crash Anglo-American program and enabled just one airman to hold an entire city ransom. The subsequent mating of a nuclear weapon with a ballistic missile raised the question of the future role of manned aircraft.

It can be argued that technology takes about sixty years to reach an acceptable plateau of development, after which for some time the public is unwilling to support further progress. Today, for example, the massive cost of new systems, subsystems, and their antidotes are effectively limiting the number of new developments, even of airframes and engines. And historically, reaction to some of the new weapons, including rapid-fire guns adopted specially for strafing, has focused on the air forces because they have been the most spectacular users.

The absolutist conception of the efficacy of air operations, on the part of air-power advocates, has stimulated—especially since 1935—scientific and technological advances of all sorts. These advances would not have been possible without government support, although this support, especially for what we refer to today as "weapons of mass destruction," often was without an understanding of the significance for the future of mankind. And at the same time, this support often was driven by government fears that "the enemy" would go ahead and development the new weapons anyway. In a vaguely tacit way, these weapons also had citizen support, although radar and the atomic bomb demonstrate that often development has been undertaken in secret, so that knowledge of a weapon's existence may not become public until after it has been used.

One final point to remember about new ideas and technological progress is that acceptance rarely is as immediate as supporters claim. Blind landings, for example, were used in flying-boat operations by 1918, and by the slow German Junkers Ju-52 in the late 1930s, with the Lorenz standard beam approach. In 1944, the British perfected a true system, but not until 1969 would the airlines accept—or perhaps trust—the system. And it was not a lack of mechanical perfection, but human doubt and reluctance that caused the delay.

CHAPTER 2

THE FIRST WORLD WAR

The Great War erupted across Europe in August 1914, following the Austrian declaration of war against Serbia in late July. Russia and Germany went to war at the same time, and Germany attempted early to eliminate France, but crossed into neutral Belgium and thus Britain also declared war. Turkey joined the struggle in late 1914. In 1915 the war spread to the Middle East. Italy joined during 1915. The United States did not enter the conflict until April 1917, and Russia withdrew in March 1918 after its Revolution. The war ended in 1918 as the Central Powers (Germany, Austria, Hungary, and Turkey) collapsed and made peace at Paris in 1919 and 1920. The 1914–18 war was the baptism of what would become an ancillary air service.

Training, Command, and Equipment

During the First World War, airmen continued their struggle for recognition and independent power against a background of romantic journalism and an often hostile military establishment. Neither in 1914 nor at the end of the war were they in a position to deliver decisive military blows independently, although under certain conditions air power could exert considerable psychological pressure. The complaint of soldiers in the trenches, however, was centered on the fact that enemy observation planes were able to bring down artillery fire upon those on the ground. Aircraft made little direct impact, except perhaps in strafing runs along the length of a trench, and that only late in the war. Aircraft were more effective generally in bombing raids over civilian and resource areas, as was demonstrated in German raids on London. The argument for a grand-strategic air force, independent of an army commander, was based on this function.

Bombers during World War I could have been more effective if army commanders had used more imagination in their employment, and if airmen had been more rational in their assessment of the damage they were doing. The Royal Naval Air Service, for instance, found that at night its heavy bombers could range more widely, unmolested by enemy fighters, than in daytime; they could fly lower and bomb more accurately. But while naval commanders were less afraid of night operations than their landlubber brothers, the latter generally regarded night fighting as ungentlemanly, liable to confusion, and downright dangerous to their reputations. The real reason for this prejudice may well have been that in fact night bombing was almost never tried in training exercises, so that none of the hazards were thoroughly examined and a means of overcoming them devised. Apart from a few attempts at night flight made in early 1916 by the Royal Flying Corps (RFC), bombing was limited until the German breakthrough in March 1918.

It is difficult to glamorize a bomber crew unless it undertakes some spectacular daylight operation and a cameraman is along. But the lone fighter pilots appeared to the public as valiant gentlemen of the clouds, like the knights of old, fighting gallant duels in the air. Newspapers were clamoring for popular heroes, yet the land-based massive bloodbaths in the Flanders mud and at Verdun produced few. The realities of aerial fighting were little understood or analyzed. Fighting between aircraft started largely to prevent enemy observers from gaining information, and not until the last year or so of the war were the forces engaged sizable—a point often overlooked.

It should also be noted that although a great deal of glamour was attached to the fighter pilots, many died. A single day's loss of aircraft could be as high as 23 percent in squadrons engaged in low-level work. On August 8, 1918, the RAF lost forty-five aircraft over the front lines and fifty-two wrecked or damaged on landing. My own World War II squadron, No. 48, fighting in the First World War, from March to November 1918, lost 165 killed or died of wounds, 13 injured, and 13 POWs, out of an establishment in March 1918 of 16 officers, flying 18 new Bristol Fighters, and 83 other ranks. No. 48 Squadron's losses amounted to 60 percent of all personnel, a bit higher than for the infantry.

Wastage in fighters in Britain and on the Western Front in World War I totaled 66 percent per month—the same as for horses in the British army in the Boer War of 1899–1902. The French replacement rate for the last two years of the war was 50 percent.

The reasons for these figures are not hard to find. Many of the casualties were officers who scarcely knew how to fly—but the breakfast table was never allowed to have empty places. So insistent was Hugh Trenchard of the RFC to keep on the offensive that in 1917 pilots were being sent into action who had flown less than twenty hours. They could hardly have been masters of their machines, let alone of aerial combat. British casualties in the air were high also because, unlike the Germans, British airmen often took the offensive regardless of the odds; it was considered cowardly not to do so. This holdover from a knightly code and colonial warfare was costly, resulting in a 50 percent pilot loss for the RFC/RAF for 1914–18.

Less well endowed with matériel, the Germans refined aerodynamics to produce better and better aircraft with a limited development of engines. More especially they conserved their pilots by giving them sixty-five hours training, plus OTU (operational training unit) for a week, before sending them to squadrons. They only engaged when victory appeared assured—a professional approach. The results were that the Germans had a three to one kill ratio over the RFC. The Germans were more successful, as they did not attack ground targets until 1918 with the armored Junkers CL-I (ER 0.092).

The *offensive à l'outrance*—the maximum effort—in the air eventually killed almost all the aces. For the French and the Americans, an ace was anyone who had shot down five enemy aircraft; in the German air force, twenty victories were required. The RFC did not recognize the ace concept for some time, and the Russians, Austrians, and Italians never did, thus, perhaps, putting more emphasis on doing the task assigned than on scoring.

Obviously, after a few combat victories, a pilot's experience placed him way ahead of the fledgling. Yet, those who survived were generally those who had entered the game late, like the Canadian Billy Bishop or the American Eddie Rickenbacker. Aces were sometimes killed because their judgment was warped by combat fatigue and a sense of honor, or fear of accusations of loss of nerve, which kept them airborne when they should have been on leave or posted home. Fatalities were unnecessarily high because although parachutes were available before 1914, they were not actually used until toward the end of the conflict, and not in the RAF until 1926. In all, it is said, 55,000 airmen were lost in World War I; the Germans had 16,054 air casualties, the British 16,623, and the French 7,259. The figures for other combatants are not known reliably.

Although the British air force acquired some 35,000 machines during the war, the increase in strength was slow. In August 1914 the British had four squadrons in France, in January 1915 six, and a year later about twenty-four. In early 1917 it had fifty-eight squadrons, and at the beginning of the last year of the war around one hundred.

The reason for Britain's paucity of aircraft in 1914 was that there was no invisible infrastructure—the manufacturing organization. Although the RFC had expected 100 percent wastage, the only aircraft industry was the Royal Aircraft Factory at Farnborough, which could produce but two machines per month. Orders had not been placed for large numbers of aircraft because there was no standard design and no satisfactory British engines—nor was there an experienced staff of officers. Resupply for the British Expeditionary Force (BEF) air wing was bought in France. When war came, the whole peacetime annual budget for aviation was spent in a week!

By comparison, in March 1918 the Germans had about 200 squadrons; and the French ended the war with 260 on the Western Front alone. British aircraft elsewhere overseas were spread far thinner, though there the French often took up the slack. In September 1918, British General Sir Edmund Allenby at Megiddo, in the Near East, had only four RAF, one Australian, and one French squadron, compared to some one hundred under Field Marshal Lord Haig on the Western Front. In the great March 1918 German offensive, the British in two months lost 1,032 of their 1,232 machines on hand when the battle started, and of these 528 were fighters. On the last day of March, when only three combats were fought in the air, the RFC lost ten aircraft in action and thirty-eight

wrecked. The fact that most of the latter were in landing accidents emphasizes the costliness of inadequate training. During the war, the Germans lost 27,637 aircraft (57 percent), the British 35,973 (62 percent), and the French 52,640 (77 percent), even with many aircraft being rebuilt.

At this time, the command of the air forces was still evolving. The history of organizational change shows that a new administrative unit is developed according to past precedent and procedure. The army modeled the new force upon the cavalry, as a reconnaissance arm; in the navy, the organization followed that of cruiser squadrons. But while it was easy to organize an ancillary air service on paper, it was a much greater problem in practice. The army had less awareness than the navy of the heavy demands that complex, and as yet unreliable, machinery makes upon manpower resources. The British air services grew from some 2,000 officers and men in 1914 to about 300,000 in 1918, but the destruction of the elite youth in the flying services was very high, and it can be roughly calculated that one in every four officers who joined the British air services died. Interestingly, the organizational establishment of the RFC was laid down in 1915 and remained the same in the RAF in 2003.

To be fair to those who commanded the air forces, it must be noted that their position was often not enviable. Because of the very youth of air services, those in command were generally low in rank, sometimes no higher than major. They had, then, more tactical skills than experience in commanding large forces. Some—and, later in the war, many—had never been to staff college. Furthermore, some of the air commanders were misfits or gadflies from other units. In general, officer aircrew lived fast and developed rakish traditions of conduct and dress that tended to appall stuffy senior officers. And thus commanding an air unit required a combination of political finesse and fatherly oversight that was often foreign to those in charge. Moreover, anxious to build their own empires while at the same time not letting their side down, airmen made promises they could not carry out, and, when they failed, they blamed lack of equipment rather than poor generalship.

In the higher headquarters the airman's position was also difficult. Although a few admirals—such as Sir John Jellicoe and Sir David Beatty on the British side and Reinhard Scheer among the Germans—had some knowledge of aeronautics and had helped in its development, the bulk of generals were not so trained. And as the importance of aviation was thrust upon them, they sought out a congenial air adviser. Thus, in Britain, Hugh Trenchard found himself suddenly raised from a major in charge of a training base to a major general and chief air adviser to the commander-in-chief of the British Expeditionary Force in France. And no doubt there were those who were jealous. Until more thorough studies are available, it is only possible to suggest that one of the problems in the First World War was that airmen had not been trained for power; and after the war, because they had exercised this command, they had a tendency to feel they knew all about it.

But the conduct of war in the air is not simply a matter of manpower and commanders; it is also a technical battle. The aircraft available in 1914 were underpowered and could often barely climb with two men aboard. Moreover, their speed was so slow—50 mph—that with any headwind they had trouble returning to base. Gradually new craft appeared with higher horsepower, able to climb first to 10,000 and later to 20,000 feet, although slowly. At the start of the war, most units were outfitted with a ragged assortment of aircraft, which could neither fly together effectively nor be easily maintained on the ground. But by 1915, the need for coordinated firepower in the air and for ease of maintenance began to dictate changes. Formation flying in pairs, flights, and squadrons, and finally in wings, groups, or circuses demanded aircraft of a standard type, and the development of these automatically eased the spares and maintenance problem.

One asset the British did have at this time was the ability to locate airfields; and they were literally that—a nice flat piece of grass with limited obstructions around the periphery and room for some canvas-and-wood hangars. Thus, in the great March 1918 retreat, as a result of the successful German advance, RFC airfields could be pulled back overnight to another site fifteen miles behind the front.

A further technical problem at this time, however, was the location and operation of guns. The pusher-type aircraft, with its engine and propeller behind, in pursuit had a clear field of fire forward; but it was generally slower, and for protection to the rear it had to rely on alertness and maneuverability—and sometimes the observer standing on his seat to fire over the top wing! The pusher was not thought of as a weapon itself but as a platform for a movable gun, and thus it had to carry the additional weight of a gunner. In contrast, the single-seat tractor machine—with the engine and propeller up front—carried less weight, but for some time had the insuperable problem of the pilot flying while standing up and trying to fire a machine gun mounted on the top of the upper wing, or aiming one aligned nearly forty-five degrees out of the flight path. Moreover, early airborne machine guns were drum fed, and in the case of the British Lewis gun, the drum originally only held forty-seven rounds and had to be changed while maneuvering. Added to all that, the guns frequently jammed because of wind pressure and had to be cleared with a wooden mallet.

The French were first to invent a system of protecting the propeller blades with metal wedges, allowing a fixed machine gun to be fired through the propeller arc, but this system made the blades of the airscrew (propeller) less efficient. Technologically, it was fortunate that the only French machine so equipped was forced to land behind the German lines and was captured intact before the pilot could destroy it. The Germans promptly turned it over to Fokker, the company owned by Dutch engineer and designer Anthony Fokker. By building on German work in progress, in four days Fokker produced a proper interrupter gear that enabled the pilot to fire fixed guns at random through the propeller arc, aiming his whole machine at his opponent. The Allies, however, did not have the German luck, due in part to the prevailing westerly wind and in part to German defensive tactics, which forced them to do most of their fighting on the German side of the line. It was nearly mid-1916 before they had aircraft equipped with an effective interrupter gear.

One of the truisms of aeronautical development has been that airframes generally have been available before engines. At the beginning of World War I, the Germans were ahead with 200 hp motors while the Allies lagged with most of theirs closer to 80 hp, and production difficulties delayed the output of aircraft. Again, it was not until after 1916 that many of these problems began to be solved.

Because the Germans had few new design engines, they spent a lot of time on smoothing designs. Using the same horsepower, they obtained vastly improved performance from better airfoils, lenticular (streamlined) struts, and monocoque plywood fuselages to reduce drag. ERs went up from the 0.0096 of the Bleriot BE-2C of 1914 to the 0.83 of the Fokker D-VII and the 0.18 of the Royal Aircraft Factory SE-5A of 1917–18.

Designing was simpler than production, because most aircraft manufacturers were amateurs with little or no idea of mass production. Moreover, the military was not in a position to write specifications for new equipment, and often, in the absence of an overall ministry of munitions to allocate industrial resources, the services competed against one another for supplies. This was most true in Britain, where the Royal Naval Air Service was a clear rival to the Royal Flying Corps. Rivalry was less acute in Germany, Russia, and Italy, where the navy was no more than an auxiliary. But in France, there was a triangle consisting of the General Headquarters at the front, the bureaucracy in Paris, and the manufacturers, mostly clustered in the capital's suburbs. The position in the United States was similar to that in Britain, but far more chaotic because of confusing counsel and industrial haste, as America entered late into the war, in 1917.

Some indication of the amount of effort that went into the production of aeronautical matériel for the war can be gauged from the few figures available. Germany turned out 48,000 airframes and 41,000 engines; France, 67,000 airframes (of which 9,500 were for her allies) and 92,000 engines (of which 28,000 were for allies, especially the British); and Britain, 58,000 airframes and engines. The Italian figures give some indication of the growth of manufacturing, for in 1915 only 382 aircraft and 606 engines were produced, whereas in 1918 the figures were 6,488 and 14,840, respectively.

A great deal of the success of aircraft production depended upon flexibility and the availability of topnotch designers. What happened without these is best illustrated by the American case. In April 1917 the Air Service had 350 aircraft on order, but of such obsolete designs that the manufacturers asked to be released from their contracts. An ambitious program was then developed to produce 22,000 aircraft by July 1918, which with spares meant about 40,000 machines. Production lagged badly, sometimes because of such simple errors as the use in drawings of metric measurements, unfamiliar to American craftsmen. In the end, the United States produced only 11,950 planes for the U.S. Army, which also bought 5,198 abroad. Engine development in the United States was another story, because the automobile industry was at that time still closely related technologically to the aircraft engine business. Thus, the Liberty engine was a success, and 15,572 were delivered by the end of November 1918.

Russia had a very small national aircraft industry at this time, in which Igor Sikorsky was outstanding. But his big bombers—Ilýa Mouromets (ER 0.52)—lacked suitable targets and were converted to reconnaissance in the vast Russian spaces where there was little air opposition, especially as

The First World War

A replica 1914 British BE-2C (ER 0.0096) at the Flying Circus Aerodrome, Old Rhinebeck, New York. (Flying Circus)

U.S. Air Service pilots of the 1st Aero Squadron in San Antonio, Texas, 1915. (USAF)

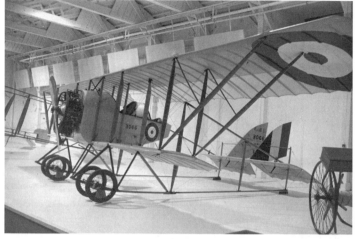

The French Caudron GIII of 1915 (ER 0.013) at the RAF Museum, Hendon, London. (Stuart Howe)

The Cradle of Aviation Museum's Jenny (ER 0.039) at the Nassau Air Museum, Mitchel Field, Garden City, Long Island, New York. (Photo by Fred J. Freketic, courtesy of the curator, CAM)

A mixed bag of officer-pilots "seconded"—on loan—from their British Army regiments to the Royal Flying Corps, some with pilot's brevets and others apparently observers. The aircraft is a Royal Aircraft Factory FE-8 of 1916 (ER 0.3) and is unusual in that observer is manning an early movie camera instead of a gun. (RAF)

The German ace Freiherr Baron Manfred von Richthofen (center) and some of his pilots on the Western Front, ca. 1917. Note the heavy leather flying coats and boots. (Source unknown).

Blimps, inflatable airships, were used for coastal and fleet patrols. They could be temperamental, especially if the engines stopped ceasing the flow of air into the bag to keep it rigid. (Royal Naval Air Service)

The relative speed of the ship and the airplane was so low during this 1917 landing attempt on an "aircraft carrier" that fellow officers could grab hold of the Sopwith Pup (ER 0.934) and haul it down to the deck. Takeoff, with the ship at speed into the wind, was fifteen feet. (Fleet Air Arm Museum)

Italian Gen. Guilio Douhet began writing on the topic of air power about 1909, as did others. His *The Command of the Air* was published in 1921 and translated into English in 1942. (Italian Air Force Historical Office)

Austria-Hungary lacked aviation resources. The uprisings of 1917 essentially finished the Imperial Russian Air Force.

Because manufacturing depended upon the allocation of raw materials and labor, priorities eventually had to be set. The labor force was especially critical. Although women had always been employed in production, during the war their numbers increased dramatically, even in the face of opposition by skilled craftsmen who saw jobs broken down into smaller and smaller pieces so that unskilled labor could handle them. By 1918, in Britain the work force consisted of up to 50 percent women and boys.

FIGHTER OPERATIONS

As soon as the war began, all the participants sent airships, airplanes, and balloons to the front. The four squadrons of the Royal Flying Corps, together with their mixed collection of aircraft, were shipped over to France. The French mobilized the aircraft and talents of the freelance fliers who had been entertaining civilians in the years before the war. The Germans sent their little Gotha LE-3 Taube (Dove) monoplanes (ER 0.006). The Russians trundled out some early Sikorskys and a diverse collection of French Farmans and Voisins (ER 0.007) in various states of repair. At first, most of these machines, with the exception of those of the Russians, bore no national markings, and in many cases they were hard to identify, because no one had been trained in aircraft recognition.

On August 22, 1914, the first engagement in the air took place, and it at once became obvious that markings would be needed. The RFC first adopted the idea of painting a Union Jack on the aircraft, but allowed each pilot to decide on size and arrangement. Yet, identification from the air was not the only problem. Troops who had hardly ever seen an airplane fired at whatever came within range, though fortunately for the fliers very few

units had anything approaching anti-aircraft guns. To counter this, British Field Headquarters ordered Union Jacks to be painted on the underside of the wings, the entire width—full chord. But even this was unsatisfactory because it could be confused with the *Cross Patée* used by the Germans and Austrians on both wing and rudder surfaces. By October 1914, the French found a satisfactory solution—the roundel. The British simply reversed the French color scheme so that red was the central concentric circle. Almost the only change made in this from late 1914 to the present has been that the tail stripe order was reversed for the Second World War. Roundels soon appeared on fuselage sides and on the top of the wing, and with the introduction in 1916 of camouflage, a thin circle of white was used to outline them. In the late 1930s, the markings were made less visible, until the natural aluminum finish was adopted in late World War II, which made the aircraft obvious.

Early aircraft were easily visible. British airplane finishes came out in shades varying from buff to primrose pink, depending upon the varnish used on doped fabric, though most metal was finished in gray or black. German machines were pale cream, but this usually became a dirty white after operations. Then in 1916 came black-dot gray followed shortly afterward by a blotchy effect of green-purple and brown. In 1917 the Germans went farther and introduced an octagonal "lozenge-printed" fabric; the Allies went to khaki green, though the shade varied tremendously. As would happen later in the 1939–45 war, however, not everyone attempted to merge with his background. The Fokker triplanes of German ace Manfred von Richthofen's World War I "circus" were painted bright red, while RNAS flying boats adopted the same dazzle paint applied to ships from 1917 onward.

At the start, relatively little damage was done by pilots and observers firing rifles or pistols at enemy planes, largely because the very few aircraft in the air at any one time had a great deal of trouble even getting near each other. British pilots found that their Royal Aircraft Factory BEs (Bleriot Experimental) aircraft, with a speed of 60 mph and a ceiling of 3,000 feet, simply could not catch other aircraft. A German was shot down by two Britishers on August 26, but though the British pilots landed at once and pursued the enemy with pistols drawn, the German aircrew escaped into a forest and disappeared! It still was not quite an aerial war—though it soon would be.

Even before the war, individual pilots had tried machine guns on their aircraft, but to the German ace Oswald Boelcke must go the credit for developing the first disciplined attack techniques. Aged twenty-three, he had by the end of 1914 made forty-two operational flights without being involved in a fight. Early in 1915 he asked to be transferred to a squadron that was equipped with the new Aviatik C (ER n/a) two-seater, which had been fitted with a machine gun in the after cockpit. On July 6, 1915, after a thirty-minute stalk and twenty minutes of combat at speeds from 35 to 80 mph, he shot down an enemy aircraft. As luck would have it, Fokker soon delivered the first of his new Eindekker E-1s (ER 0.029)—called the Fokker Scourge—to Boelcke's airfield, and Boelcke was given the job of testing the new machine in combat. He soon found that the best scheme was to loiter at his 5,000-foot ceiling and to pounce from cloud or sun on any Allied plane that strayed below him. He then dived down, closed as quickly as possible, aimed his plane, fired, and climbed away.

At about this time Max Immelmann, another pilot in the same squadron, developed the technique of diving below his opponent, pulling up in order to fire into him from the vulnerable position under the tail, then at the top of his climb kicking on hard rudder and dropping back down for a new strike from the opposite direction. This method worked as long as the Fokker was faster than its opponent, but as soon as the Allied planes developed the power to climb after him, the German pilot was vulnerable as he made his stall turn.

The British RFC continued to fly offensive missions and long reconnaissance flights, and Boelcke's tactics, with Immelmann as his wingman or extra pair of eyes, were paying handsome dividends as the enemy constantly came into his territory. Their successes were not unnoticed in the German command, and more pairs of scouts were ordered upon the initiative of Major Stempel, the 6th Army's Aviation Staff Officer. But in the spring of 1916, the Allies began to dominate the little Fokkers with new types—the de Havilland DH-2 (ER 0.064), the Farman FE-2B (Farman Experimental)(ER 0.095), and the French Nieuport 17 (ER 0.037)—and by midsummer 1916 they were using early formation tactics. At first, formation had simply consisted of providing three escorts for each reconnaissance machine, but as the escorts were often nothing more than other two-seaters, the system resulted in a formation, rather than in a proper escort arrangement. To counter escorts, Boelcke had already begun to consider formation flying and was by 1916 organizing his fighters into squadron formations. Hand signals were required, because aircraft were not until many years later fitted with voice radios (R/T, radio telephone). To identify the squadron leader, streamers were tied to his wingtips; these were supplemented by the use of colored paint.

Tactical formations not unnaturally developed from infantry and cavalry maneuvers, practiced at first in pairs and then in fours, and finally in squadron formations of twelve or more aircraft. Each squadron was subdivided into diamonds of four led by a flight commander. The slow evolution of these tactics must be stressed. The aircraft themselves were not easy to fly, the pilots were often inexperienced, and the leaders were anxious to avoid non-battle casualties. Formation flying demanded that 75 percent of a pilot's attention be devoted to watching his leader.

As in the case of escort work, the development of formation flying was considerably retarded by the long lag in equipping squadrons with a single kind of machine so that all pilots would have aircraft of more or less identical performance. The

The First World War

Germans had largely achieved uniformity in late 1915 with the Fokker Eindeckers, but the RFC, the French, and the Italians did not reach this stage until the summer of 1916. By July the Fokker Scourge had been mastered, but as the Germans brought out new aircraft and developed new tactics, aerial supremacy continued to move from one side to the other.

The French continued to work on the tractor aircraft and in the Nieuport 17 produced one that could reach 10,000 feet in nine minutes and fly at 107 mph, in contrast to the single-seat pusher British de Havilland DH-2, which took twenty-four minutes to gain the same altitude and could only do 90 mph. Thereafter, pushers became oddities, until the advent of the jet engine in the 1940s.

In August 1916 the Germans started forming their new elite *Jagdstaffeln* or *Jasta* (Squadron). These were equipped with the Halberstadt D-11 (ER 0.04), with two synchronized machine guns, and the Albatros D-1 (ER 0.03). Though the former did not last long, the latter remained in service with the German air force until almost the end of the war. Boelcke's *Jasta 2* was extremely effective, and by the time of his death on October 28, 1916, in a combat collision, he had shot down thirty-five Allied aircraft.

In the five months from July to November 1916, the RFC in France grew from 421 to 550 serviceable machines, of which 173 were rebuilds. Of the total of 1,179 new or rebuilt aircraft supplied after or on hand on July 1, 782 were struck off squadron charge. In other words, consumption and wastage was high and replacement vital to both take care of losses and allow for growth. The squadrons each needed ten fresh aircraft per month. Similarly, roughly 25 percent per month pilot casualties (killed, wounded, and missing), or 113 per month plus other aircrew (676 all told), needed to be replaced to allow pilot numbers to grow from 426 to 585 as the squadrons rose from 27 to 35.

The winter of 1916–17 saw many changes. The German air units were redistributed into fighter, reconnaissance, and bombing groups. Ever larger formations were developed to counter the arrival in the field of new Allied aircraft such as the Sopwith Pup (ER 0.934), the first British aircraft fitted with a synchronized machine gun. On the British side, the RFC was licking its wounds from the Battle of the Somme, in which airmen had been thrown into action just as ruthlessly and with about as little planning as had troops on the ground. Albert Ball, one of the British aces, was in twenty-three battles in fourteen days before finally being allowed to go home for a rest. Though at the beginning of 1917 the RFC had thirty-five squadrons at the front, most were ill-trained and no match for the elite German *Jastas.* The French also had suffered from the mauling they had taken at Verdun and had sensibly largely withdrawn their squadrons for refitting. But their mastery of the air then led in 1917 to the formation of the Duval Division, a mobile air reserve that could be used to gain superiority at a decisive point.

The Anglo-German contest still favored the Germans in the spring of 1917 because their fighters were superior to the FE-2B and the BE-2C that the British were still using. And, although by then the RFC could deploy some 550 aircraft or more, in April 1917 it lost 140. Manfred von Richthofen was in his prime and shot down five airplanes in one day, while at the same time seriously damaging the faith of the RFC in the Bristol F-2B "Brisfit" (ER 0.24), a new two-seater with a powerful armament of a forward-firing synchronized gun and twin Lewis guns for the observer. In the vital action on April 28, Richthofen attacked a group of six Bristol F-2Bs led by Leefe Robinson, the man who had won a British Victoria Cross for shooting down a Zeppelin. Robinson's crews were not yet accustomed to their powerful machines, and their tactics had not been properly worked out. The result was that four aircraft were lost and Robinson captured. Training improved, however, and by the end of the war the "Brisfit" was the dominant British two-seater.

At this same time, the Germans also began to

face the new SE-5A (ER 0.18), which in the hands of British squadrons proved to be a highly efficient counter to the thirty-five German *Jastas.* In addition, the RFC was beginning to get the de Havilland DH-4 (ER 0.0096), a two-seater day bomber that was at least as fast as many enemy fighters.

Meanwhile Gen. Erich von Ludendorff had decided that the German air arm needed its own separate organization and had placed Gen. Ernst von Hoeppner in command of the forces in October 1916. To counter what appeared to be dangerous developments on the Allied side, including the American declaration of war, Hoeppner organized four *Jastas* into a *Jagdgeschwader,* or wing. Richthofen was placed in command of the new circus, and his duty was to lead his outfit to battle over any part of the front upon which the Germans found themselves threatened. Thus reorganizing their forces, Richthofen and his experienced fighters followed successfully the principles of concentration and economy of force. The circus flaunted brightly colored Albatros aircraft as a psychological threat to all who saw them. But even when equipped with the new Pfalz D-III (ER 0.1) scouts, the circus increasingly came up against tougher opposition as the SE-5s and the new Sopwith Camels (ER 0.96) came into action, as well as the newer French fighters such as the SPAD XIII (ER 0.135) and the Nieuport 28 (ER 0.07). Even when the circus got its Fokker Dr-I (ER 0.03) triplanes, which were extremely maneuverable but slower both in level and climbing flight, it still never regained the supremacy that it had enjoyed in the early summer of 1917.

Although Germans like Werner Voss still occasionally made lone sorties across the lines on stalking expeditions, the British had finally learned to operate in groups, such as the one that jumped Voss on his last flight. Moreover, the Fokker triplane turned out to have a weakness—its canvas-covered upper wing disintegrated in steep dives. By the end of the war, the new Fokker D-VII (ER 0.83) was the mainstay of the German fighter force, and indeed its surrender was required as part of the peace settlement in order to make sure that the Allies maintained their aerial-fighting superiority. Although not as fast as some Allied fighters, the D-VII's biggest asset was its maneuverability at the then high altitude of 10,000 or more feet.

General Hoeppner's plan of June 1917, sometimes called the Amerika Program, was designed to help win the war before trans-Atlantic power could be applied on the Western Front. Helped by the collapse of Russia, the German air force was built up to 155 squadrons and seven heavy bomber groups by the time the great March 1918 offensive was opened. But the leaders were beginning to suffer from chronic battle fatigue brought on by daily dicing with death. Richthofen had become in many respects an old man. He was obsessed with thoughts of fire in the air. On April 21, 1918, just as the German offensive petered out, he entered one more dogfight, as usual picking on a fledgling pilot. The conflict was fought at a low altitude, and whether he was shot down from the air or from the ground has remained a matter of argument. Certain it is, however, that he went the way of most aces who stayed too long in combat.

Richthofen's immediate successor was subsequently killed testing a new craft designed to replace the well-worn Albatros still in use, and command of his circus for the rest of the war devolved upon a lesser ace, Hermann Goering, later to be the leader of the *Luftwaffe,* the German air force in the Second World War. But the Richthofen myth had been so built up in the early German air force, that his death caused a steady deterioration of morale among men pushed hard against increasingly great odds.

Production was by then seriously hampered by the Allied blockade, which was at last having a significant effect, and the airmen were increasingly facing the same losses due to inexperience that had earlier weakened the Royal Flying Corps. Yet in many ways, the Germans failed to learn the lessons of the First World War and in the Second made the same fatal mistakes of standardizing too

The First World War

early and of not estimating the wave pattern of war in order to be able to take advantage of the flow and stem the ebb of supplies.

In the long May–October 1917 British Flanders offensive, for the first time a truly comprehensive modern air campaign appeared—the Germans had integral air defenses and used their new two-seater metal ground-attack strafing machines, flown by specially trained crews, as well as radios in artillery-spotting aircraft.

In 1918 the Germans stealthily moved their squadrons up at night and camouflaged them by day to help achieve surprise in the March 1918 forerunner of *Blitzkrieg.* Transport and logistical targets and air superiority were sought, and campaigns waged against enemy airfields and air forces.

The German March offensive was halted at the end of two weeks in part due to the selfless low-level (wheels hitting the ground) attacks of RFC pilots and the artillery observation and intelligence gathering of the photo-reconnaissance airplanes. Trenchard's well-laid plans had included regular photographic sorties and analysis of the prints, artillery barrages, and low-level attacks upon rear areas and upon the fourteen new airfields discovered. But the German attack on March 21 opened by shelling RFC airfields, among other targets. British counter-battery efforts failed, however, because its artillery, the most effective weapon, was on the move and failed to erect its wireless telegraph (W/T) aerials.

The next most effective action was the RFC strafing of massed men on the move in the rear. The Germans concentrated in helping their own front-line advance and ignored the RFC's rear areas, including forty-five new RFC airfields, which were spared their own defense. And the British squadrons were supported by logistical flying squads carrying fuel, ammunition, and spares so that all squadrons were kept up to strength in spite of abandoning aircraft on shelled fields.

While the Germans engaged in a day-and-night grand-strategic attack on Britain first by Zeppelins and then with Gotha bombers, the High Command concluded that the Allied attacks upon the Fatherland were but pinpricks. The Allies, in fact, lost one bomber for every 154 tons dropped, not at all cost effective, even if bombs had hit the targets. German defenses were by late in the war composed of 37 mm to 88 mm guns and machine guns. In September and October 1918 these 2,558 guns shot down 260 Allied aircraft. In March 1918, the German air force had about 200 squadrons spread between the Western and Italian fronts with six squadrons in Turkey.

By the end of the war, the RAF on the Western Front had been built up to 97 squadrons with 36 more overseas, 55 at home, and 199 in the training system. The French air force contained 260 squadrons on the Western Front alone, of which 135 were reconnaissance, 10 were for strategic observation for army headquarters, 83 were fighter squadrons, and 32 were bomber units. In addition, seventy-two squadrons were on home defense or overseas, including three in Russia and one in Palestine.

In later 1917, Colonel Duval of the French Army Air Service had managed to muster his assets into a formidable resource, controlled from headquarters rather than farmed out in "penny packets" to each infantry division. This had followed the approach at Verdun in 1916 where the objective had been to gain air superiority over the Germans. In the summer of 1918, the American General Billy Mitchell had claimed credit for applying the Duval Division concept to the Meuse-Argonne and St. Michiel offensives, by which time the Germans were in retreat. The Duval Division was the correct application of force and concentration, at the decisive point.

The Italians did not enter the war until late May 1915, and their opponents, the Austrians, were not of the same fighting caliber as the Germans. Moreover, because the Italians suffered the great reverse at Caporetto in 1917, because they became Hitler's ally in the Second World War, and because little has been written in English of their actions, it has long been assumed that the Italian air effort was not worth recording. The truth is the opposite.

Italian exercise of air power was conditioned by geographical location and physical features. Ground fighting quickly became stalemated along the Isonzo River in northern Italy. But the Austrians had to be supplied through the Ljubljana Gap, between Italy and Austria, and the mountainous nature of the terrain meant that they were forced to concentrate in other areas as well. At the same time, their navy operated from the few bases available at the head of the Adriatic, notably Fiume and Pola. Because of the limited enemy supply routes, the Italians were able to develop a number of features of air power, which received less attention elsewhere. Rather than merely fighting for air superiority, Italian airmen undertook long-range photo-reconnaissance flights, which took them as much as 300 miles through enemy territory, along the enemy communication lines. Control of photo-reconnaissance work was at army headquarters, and the information gathered was used for strategic raids to disrupt the Austrian rear. Although the 1917 Austrian breakthrough at Caporetto was a disaster for the Italians, cost them many forward airfields, and compelled a reorganization of the air service on a more independent basis, it did not stop the Italian air offensive, as most raids flew directly across the Adriatic. In view of the claims of the American air-power propagandist Gen. William "Billy" Mitchell, it should be pointed out that the Italians had used massed tactical air units as early as 1916 during ground operations, while at the battle of Vittorio Veneto (October–November 1918) they employed 600 aircraft, 36 balloons, and 7 airships.

Douhet may have been misled in his theory that bombers alone could destroy an opponent by the Austrian situation, one in which a small Italian bomber force might have struck a psychological blow at Vienna with its limited industry. Austria-Hungary was not a major industrial state with multiple resources.

On the Russian front, the situation is much less clear, due to the general absence of historical reports, at least in English, and to the historiographical impact of the 1917 Revolution. It appears that the Russian air force never amounted to more than some 300 effective machines, many of which were castoffs from the Allied air forces in the West. Some craft of foreign design were manufactured under license in Russia, together with a few advanced designs of Russian origin such as the Grigorovich M.24 flying boats (ER n/a), and the Sikorsky Ilýa Mouromets four-engine bombers. But Russian maintenance was pitiful, and much of the equipment was in disrepair even before the Revolution. Thus, because on the whole the Germans did not face great opposition on the Eastern Front, except for occasional raids by the large Russian bombers, they were able to concentrate in the West. Very little is known even of the desultory naval strikes in the Baltic, which produced Alexandre de Seversky, later an apostle of victory through air power.

The U.S. contribution to the 1914–18 air war was at first limited to volunteer pilots in outfits such as the Lafayette Escadrille, named for the French hero of the American Revolution; but gradually an Army Air Service using Allied equipment was built up. The United States also lent its training fields in the Sun Belt to Canadian training units. The Air Service's most notable operation was the use of the Duval-like 1,500-aircraft cover provided during the reduction of the St. Mihiel salient in September 1918. In October, General Mitchell followed Italian practice by using large bomber forces against concentrated targets in the Meuse-Argonne.

On the whole, both sides overlooked the significance of massing additional air power in the lesser theaters where victories, even if of no great strategic import, could be used for propaganda leverage elsewhere. Aircraft in these overseas theaters were particularly valuable for reconnaissance, although they were in short supply. The British also used aircraft occasionally for resupplying forces as at Kut, in Mesopotamia; and the destruction of

The FE-2B Bristol Fighter (ER 0.24) was regarded as the best two-seat aircraft of the 1914–18 war and remained in service until the end of the 1920s. This original, belonging to the Shuttleworth Collection at Old Warden Aerodrome, Biggleswade, Bedfordshire, United Kingdom, is powered by the oldest running Rolls-Royce engine. (Shuttleworth Collection)

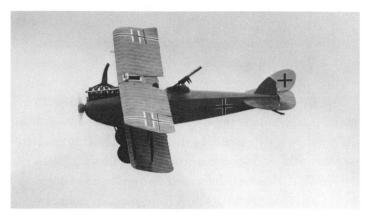

A 1917 Halberstadt C VI (ER 0.22) of the Shuttlesworth Collection, the only original German fighter of that era still flying. (Shuttleworth Collection)

The famous Fokker Triplane Dr-I (ER 0.03) was a Dutch design manufactured in Germany. Painted red, it was flown by von Richthofen and his circus. Total wingspan was nearly sixty feet, but it was so short-coupled (a man can put one hand on the trailing edge of the wing and the other on the leading edge of the tailplane) that it was highly maneuverable.

Late in World War I the Germans introduced the Fokker DVII (ER 0.09), an excellent fighter that used aerodynamic refinements to make up for lack of German engine developments. The Swiss Air Force built the aircraft in 1929, and their pilots went directly from these machines to the P-51D Mustang (ER 9.63) in 1947. (Source unknown)

The famous French ace, Capt. Charles Guynemer, with his Spad XIII (ER 0.134) with an Eclair propeller. (Avions Marcel Dassault)

The American ace Eddie Rickenbacker, who went on to head Eastern Air Lines, seen with his Spad S.XIII (ER 0.135) in 1918. (USAF)

The Royal Aircraft Factory SE-5A of 1918 (ER 0.18) was regarded as the best fighter of the First World War. (H. M. Banner, provenance unknown)

The Germans were adept at converting guns to flak use; this one was truck-mounted for mobility. (Canadian Forces)

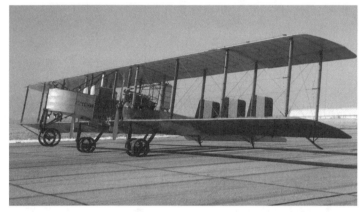

A trimotored Italian Caproni Ca. 46 (ER 1.05) was derived from a 1914 design and remained in service with the *Regia Aeronautica* until 1929. This example is on loan from the Caproni Museum to the USAF Museum at Dayton, Ohio. (Uncopyrighted postcard)

A Handley Page 0/100 (ER 0.52) heavy bomber of 1918 with which the Independent Air Force in France was being equipped in late 1918. This aircraft has been modernized for civilian operations. (Source unknown)

U.S. airmen riggers are here under instruction in a British aircraft repair depot in France in 1918. A very large percentage of combat aircraft were rebuilds. (USAF)

The U.S. Army 7th Corps being reviewed by Gen. John J. Pershing, General Officer Commanding of the American Expeditionary Force, at Treves, France. The size of the airship shed in the background is evident from the scale of the men. Such hangars were a major capital investment.

the German cruiser *Königsberg* in Africa's Rufiji River was accomplished by naval monitors guided by two seaplanes. One notable attempt by the Germans to make use of air transport was the abortive flight of the Zeppelin *L-59* to take ammunition and medical supplies to the elusive German commander in East Africa, Paul Emil von Lettow-Vorbeck. The Zeppelin turned back to its Balkan base after reaching the vicinity of Khartoum in the Sudan, considerably north of the German force.

The Allied campaign in the Turkish Dardanelles might have been successful if a more advanced and less heterogeneous collection of aircraft had been sent out to Gallipoli in 1915. As it was, the aircraft operating from the island base of Tenedos (for only one temporary landing ground was made available on the Gallipoli peninsula) made a number of significant contributions to the development of aerial warfare, including the first successful destruction of a ship with an air-launched torpedo. In particular, more squadrons with better equipment might have panicked Constantinople by psychological bombing as well as by providing competent photographic reconnaissance before the actual Gallipoli landings.

Air Power in Action: The Ideal

The Palestine campaign under General Sir Edmund Allenby during the last months of World War I was for its day as perfect an example of the proper application of air power as the later German *Blitzkriegs* in 1940 or the Israeli campaign of 1967. Although the Turkish army was weakened by malnutrition and lack of supplies, and was therefore a less formidable opponent than some other units, Allenby's Megiddo operation of September 1918 was almost the breakthrough and envelopment that leaders on other fronts had dreamed about throughout the war. He achieved it by a combination of tactical deceptions and feints, cavalry, armored cars, and air power. He made use of five air squadrons, all but one with modern aircraft, to achieve complete domination over the opposing air force, so that by September 1918 the Turks were virtually without either reconnaissance or air cover.

Immediately prior to the attack, British aircraft bombed the central Turkish telephone exchange and Turkish army headquarters, upsetting the enemy's balance in a way the cavalry could not get through to do. A patrol of two SE-5As flew constantly over the main Turkish airfield, dropping bombs from time to time as an additional harassment. While the British advanced on the ground, RAF aircraft provided them with smoke-screens and intelligence. Late on September 19, two Turkish divisions were in retreat, and they were caught in a narrow defile by RAF fighters and bombers and badly mangled.

Quality photo-intelligence had enabled Allenby to predict all routes of Turkish retreat and to intersect them with cavalry and armored cars. The psychological effect of the sudden appearance of these units caused a precipitate withdrawal, which the RAF was able to turn into a rout. Farther out in the desert, along Allenby's right flank, the Arab forces of the mysterious T. E. Lawrence suffered from the attacks of German aircraft, which the three British fighters assigned to him could not beat off until Lawrence managed to arrange a reinforcement of three more fighters.

Much of the success of Allenby's subsequent campaign, which moved some 300 miles in six weeks, was due to the way in which supplies were rushed forward, often by air. Thus the fighters and bombers of the RAF could continue to apply both a physical and a psychological spearhead, while the Turks found themselves without their German air cover. Strangely, the ability to move squadrons forward with great rapidity had to be learned all over again in the Western Desert in World War II.

This use of the RAF and the Australian Flying Corps in Palestine in 1918 was much more imaginative and of a sounder tactical nature than were RAF assignments in Europe. The explanation for it lies both in the mentality of the High Command and in geography. On the Western Front, Allenby had been under leaders of generally conservative vision. But when he became a commander-in-chief, he was free to operate as he saw fit (and the same could be said of Britain's Maude in Iraq). The maps of the Middle East area, in comparison to those of Europe, lacked detail, and aircraft were sent out to undertake long reconnaissance flights, in the Italian manner. It was necessary to consider great distances in moving supplies, over ground not potholed by incessant shellfire but rather so arid that water supply was one of the chief limitations. Thus, it is evident that the lack of supplies and the difficulty of transporting them, together with the small number of airplanes available, meant that resources were used with more skill than in France, where abundance stultified generalship.

Another theater in which air power was used efficiently was Macedonia, where the Hellenic air force had operated in 1913. The British diversionary attack from Salonika in September 1918 was supported by only three squadrons, but by the end of the month the Bulgarians had started to retreat and had been caught in a mountain pass and demoralized. There, as in the Palestine campaign, part of the secret of the air force's success lay in the nature of the country, which was sparse, mountainous, and with very few roads along which any army could move. And, thus, the side with command of the air was likely to be the victor, from the application of both psychological and physical pressure.

AIR POWER AT SEA

Naval air power in the First World War was heavily dominated, as might be expected, by the Royal Navy, which was then the largest fleet in the world. Moreover, though the British navy was moribund in many respects from a century of peace, it did have the advantage of leaders with technical competence, and in the formative years was commanded first by Adm. Sir John "Jacky" Fisher, followed by Winston Churchill, and then the combination of the two.

Fisher launched naval aviation, and Churchill became an enthusiastic supporter. Naval airmen, despite the shipbuilding precedent of the Royal Dockyards, were not tied to an official factory and energetically looked for supplies from other sources. Thus, for much of the war, the RNAS matériel was superior to that of the RFC because the navy was a better organized service and was accustomed to technical change. In addition, its officers apparently better understood the need for training than did those in the other services; and this, coupled with a less reckless offensive policy, even in France, meant that on the whole the RNAS developed more highly qualified squadrons. Although the bulk of naval air activity was connected with the Grand Fleet and the protection of trade, as an offshoot of these responsibilities it operated a bomber and fighter base on the northern French coast. Although most of its flights had a tactical purpose, a few were strategic strikes.

Other naval air forces were less prominent. Apart from Zeppelins, most of the German naval air effort was either connected with the few sorties made by the fleet or were defensive, against the incursions of British ships or aircraft. French and Italian efforts were concentrated mainly in the area of anti-submarine warfare. Russian and Austro-Hungarian operations were negligible. And the embryo U.S. naval air service followed in the wake of the RNAS. Under these circumstances, then, any description of the war at sea must inevitably deal primarily with the British experience.

The RNAS established bases at Dover and Dunkirk when the Germans seized the Belgian coast in 1914. Seaplanes were used to raid the new U-boat bases, but with little effect. When intelligence showed that the Germans were assembling coastal U-boats in the shipyards at Antwerp, a strike against these was laid on, but the three aircraft that succeeded in dropping a total of twelve twenty-pound bombs did little damage. The Admiralty thus decided upon a much wider program, to include better protection of shipping, and its plan led to two important developments: the SS—submarine-searching or scout—airships, and the heavy bombers. The former were very rapidly improvised from non-rigid airship bags and the fuselages of BE-2C aircraft, an arrangement that produced a ship capable of an eight-hour flight with a crew of two, 160 pounds of bombs, and, most importantly, a wireless set. But because throughout the war the anti-submarine craft were not fitted with detection aids, their effectiveness was limited to visual distances.

Although the attacks made by non-rigid airships were not many, their presence was disliked by U-boats because they could alert destroyers. Thus, shipping escorted by a blimp was generally immune to U-boat attack. The truth of this was shown in the Mediterranean where the blimps were slow to arrive and losses to U-boats were high until they appeared. By the end of the war, blimps had been developed that could stay on patrol for nearly two days and could achieve speeds close to 60 mph. But they were always limited by the weather, and attempts to use them with the fleet were unsuccessful when the wind reached 30 mph, for this reduced their surface speed into the wind to that of the cruisers. British attempts to imitate Zeppelins and provide long-range fast airships for fleet scouting and long anti-submarine patrols over the Western Approaches were nullified by the fact that designs were copied from the Germans and were thus usually four years behind.

The other solution, then, to both the U-boat problem and fleet requirements was the development of airplanes. For the anti-submarine-warfare (ASW) role both seaplanes and flying boats were produced. The former had the advantage that they could be carried at sea by ships and launched from smooth water alongside, whereas the latter were generally operated from harbors, though some attempts were made to tow them closer to their patrol areas on lighters—a decked barge—from which they could be slipped for takeoff. The seaplane was more maneuverable, but the flying boat had much greater range and could carry a heavier armament, including a 37 mm recoilless gun. This gun, however, was not always successful, for it did not use a rocket but provided a bag of buckshot to absorb recoil, which was exhausted to the rear, sometimes to the detriment of the upper wing—or the engines! In 1917, landplanes were taken to war, flying off platforms either on gun turrets or forward of the bridge. A cruiser doing 30 knots into the wind allowed an aircraft to take off in fifteen feet.

The Germans were unable, due to American pressure, to start on a full-scale U-boat offensive until February 1917, and by then the Allies had been able to develop much of the equipment, though not yet the convoys, needed to protect commerce. It might, however, be argued that if the Germans had attacked earlier at a time when they had fewer submarines, the advantages would have been placed more firmly in Allied hands, for they would have been forced to undertake convoying and other measures much sooner. As it was, Allied convoys, started in June 1917 to and from the United Kingdom, were soon given air cover, and the same practice was adopted in the Mediterranean with Japanese surface escorts.

Besides protecting trade, the British navy took rapid steps to make use of air power in its strictly military operations. When, on the outbreak of war, the Admiralty had appointed the quiet Sir John Jellicoe to command the Grand Fleet, it sent to sea a man who was familiar with submarines and who was the one flag officer to have flown in a Zeppelin. Jellicoe was alarmed by these two weapons, as the British navy had no counters, and he set to work with the help of Jacky Fisher, who had been recalled to the Admiralty to join Churchill, to remedy the deficiency. Thus, throughout the war the RNAS engaged in a strong program to take air power to sea. Seaplane tenders were developed to enable airplanes to be used either from secluded harbors or with the ships at sea. Platforms were mounted on the turrets of battleships, so that aircraft could be flown off, and were erected over the sterns so that aircraft could land on. And eventually it was recognized that a ship was needed that had its funnels set over to one side, so that planes could land and take off on an unobstructed surface, immune to the deflecting boiler fumes.

All of this took a great deal of time and had not been realized in practice when the war ended. Nevertheless, when the Grand Fleet went to sea in 1918 it carried with it some 150 fighters ready to fly off and do battle with any enemy, and was shortly to include torpedo-bombers for attack on the opposing German High Seas Fleet. At the same time, the submarine menace had been partially countered by towing kite-balloons, which, although they tended to give away the fleet's position, warned U-boats that destroyers were likely to be directed onto them if they approached.

To carry the war home to the Germans in their own waters, S. C. Porte, who commanded the naval air station at Felixstowe and had been at the Hammondsport, New York, Curtiss Aeroplane Company before the war, began building some large flying boats on the American Curtiss lines. These F-2A machines of 1917 (ER 1.189) dwarfed the standard airplanes of the day with their two 345 hp engines, crew of four, up to seven machine guns, two 230-pound bombs, and overall weight of 11,000 pounds (compared to the 1,200-pound Sopwith Pup fighter (ER 0.934). Able to patrol for eight hours, the F-2As were assigned to the so-called spiderwebs in which they searched that part of some 4,000 square miles of the North Sea where the Admiralty suspected a U-boat was lurking. On May 20, 1917, *UC-36* became the first submarine sunk from the air when hit by a bomb from a Porte flying boat. The flying boats also

managed to pick off two Zeppelins (*L-22* and *L-43*) while the latter were flying over their home waters. This sort of insult compelled the Germans to strengthen their naval air service, with the result that offensive seaplane patrols began to be a nuisance to British airmen, and a seesaw battle continued to the end of the war.

An improvement, of necessity, came to the flying boats when because of frequent failing of solid copper fuel lines due to vibration and the dangers of descent onto a glassy sea or through fog, Porte produced a simple blind-landing gear, which saved many boats.

The development of a naval strategic strike force came from the desire of the British fleet to be rid of Zeppelins. On September 22, 1914, the RNAS had staged a pair of raids with two airplanes each against the Zeppelin sheds at Dusseldorf and Cologne. Only one pilot reached the target and only one of his bombs exploded—the one that missed. But on October 6, two more planes set out. One jettisoned its bombs on the Cologne railway station, but the other hit the sheds at Dusseldorf and destroyed the new German army Zeppelin *Z-1X*. On November 21, a strike of three Avros hit the Zeppelin factory at Friedrichshafen, but just failed to do any damage—a penetration of 150 miles into enemy territory was a notable achievement in itself in those days. A further attempt to damage the Zeppelins was made on Christmas Day 1914 by seaplanes ferried to their takeoff point in converted cross-Channel steamers. Although none of the seven planes found the Cuxhaven Zeppelin sheds in Denmark, a thorough reconnaissance of the Wilhelmshafen naval base was accomplished. No new attacks were made until July 19, 1918, when the new aircraft carrier *Furious* was used to launch a strike against the airship sheds at Tondern, northern Germany. This was successful with two aircraft destroying Zeppelins *L-54* and *L-60* by dropping forty-pound bombs from a height of only one hundred feet as they passed over the sheds. Not only was the German

Naval Airship Division left in a state of nerves that lasted to the end of the war, but at Tondern, used as an advanced emergency landing ground, both a strategic and tactical surprise had been achieved and a psychologically strategic effect created.

Meanwhile, in an attempt to deal with the Germans on the Belgian coast, the British Admiralty had asked in 1915 for a true heavy strategic bomber. The response was the Handley Page 0/100 (ER 0.52) through 0/400 (ER 1.95), but the first was not delivered to the Dunkirk base until November 1916 and the third, due to a navigational error, was landed intact behind the German lines two months later. At first they were employed as intended on patrols off the coast, but during the summer they switched over to night bombing, striking at strategic points behind the German lines while refraining from attacks on purely civilian targets. Although one squadron of the four available was loaned to the RFC for grand-strategic bombing, on the whole the Navy was successful in keeping these bombers for its own purposes.

GRAND-STRATEGIC BOMBING CAMPAIGNS

The Italian, British, and German grand-strategic (a better term for some of them is psychological) bombing campaigns started as much from the demands of the navy as from those of army commanders.

Many claims were made before the war that air power would strike at the heart of an opposing power, but this was largely long-term guessing. The Italian Giulio Douhet's claims must be taken with a pinch of Caproni salt.

Strategic bombing divides into two categories: attacks against targets that were legitimate military objectives, such as ammunition dumps, supply routes, and factories out of tactical reach of surface forces; and grand-strategic attacks against enemy cities undertaken for psychological reasons. Into the first class clearly fall many of the early

French and British raids against German rear areas in France and against airship sheds and constructional facilities in Germany, together with Italian raids on Ljubljana, Pola, Trieste, and Fiume. Into the second must be placed the raids starting with the French reaction to the German attacks on Paris in September 1914. Apart from a lone raid in August against a Zeppelin shed near Metz, the French waited until the end of the year, when they began to organize first five- and then twenty-bomber squadrons. Under Captain Happe, they began to penetrate as far as Karlsruhe (June 13, 1915), and one aircraft struck Munich (November 17).

It is not at all clear that a deliberate doctrine of retaliation upon civilian centers had yet evolved, but by 1916 the French consciously began such revenge with an attack on Karlsruhe, in reprisal for German attacks on French towns that had been declared "open"—non-military zones. A combination of the early German Zeppelin attacks and naval bombardment of Britain, coupled with the friction between the politicians in London, Paris, and Rome and their generals in the field in 1917, probably brought on in frustration the development of a grand-strategic bombing force independent of High Commands of the armies on the Western Front. This frustration probably also led to the decision on the part of some leaders that the grand-strategic force should be one of destructive retaliation.

Another element in the decisions to bomb civilian centers stemmed from the still-primitive nature of air warfare. As defenses developed (as inevitably they always do), the planes were forced to drop their bomb loads from higher altitudes or to fly at night. Both courses led to greater inaccuracy. In part, therefore, politically to justify inaccurate bombing, airmen developed the defensive thesis that war workers in their homes were directly connected to the will to make war and could properly be attacked.

A peculiarity of the British system under Churchill in 1915 was that the navy had been put in charge of home defense in general, in addition to its particular responsibility for that of fleet bases. In the early German raids, the Zeppelins had several advantages. Not only were they simply frightening, but they could hover while dropping their bombs, and the defenses were so sparse that neither anti-aircraft fire nor airplanes were for some time very effective against them. In fact, it was not until June 1915 that the first Zeppelin was brought down by an airplane, and not until September 1916 that one was brought down over England.

On the whole, these early Zeppelin raids on Britain were not very effective in physical terms. *LZ-13* dropped the first high-explosive bombs on London on the night of September 8, 1915, killing thirteen and wounding eighty-seven persons, but at that time casualties in Flanders were already running to several thousand per day. As far as the defenses were concerned, the Zeppelins had greater effect; they raised a political storm, which ultimately resulted in air defense being handed back to the War Office, and they stimulated the defenses to prepare for the next challenge, which came in the form of daylight German airplane raids starting on November 28, 1916. Night attacks followed, however, and in pre-radio and pre-radar days, finding an attacking enemy aircraft was difficult. Although by 1917 many aircraft were scrambled to intercept enemy raiders, few were even attacked, let alone shot down. The Germans were able to obtain a great deal of information about the effectiveness of their raids, and they were encouraged to believe that they could quickly bring Britain to her knees.

One spin-off of the German attack in the first Battle of Britain was that Maj. Gen. E. B. Ashmore was called in to mastermind the air defense. With air experience, he devised a reporting and analyzing system that could respond in five minutes. He remained in command until 1929, and thus by the time radar became available in 1939, coupled to sector-control fighter direction, the RAF had an effective system for meeting enemy aircraft on their approach to targets.

The cycle of German raids against Britain was the same for naval Zeppelins and for army Gotha heavy bombers: first came daylight attacks, then night raids, then the raids were finally abandoned because the defenses became too accurate and the losses too great. Even the Gothas flying in daylight could not be escorted by long-range fighters, for not until the 1930s would the Japanese navy develop long-range tanks for operational use. The Gothas usually escaped destruction at the hands of fighters because their defensive armament and formation were sufficient to counter the few defending fighters that reached them. But the Zeppelins were 700-foot long gasbags filled with hydrogen and slower than mid-war fighters. The lessons learned from this were rudely shattered in 1939 when the RAF relied on formation flying and First World War machine guns against cannon-armed fighters, and in 1942 when the U.S. Army Air Forces (USAAF) repeated the mistake.

Although it was not ultimately directly successful, the German bombing of Britain did accomplish several things. The threat of air raids and the sounding of the air-raid alarms caused suspension of production, and the fear of air raids caused the recall of some fighter squadrons from France. This in itself was not really serious, despite the insistence of Field Marshal Haig's headquarters that every aircraft possible should be diverted to his cause. It could well be argued that the rest period in England—being assigned to Home defense—was, in fact, beneficial to men who were being flown too much. More importantly, German raids meant that Allied squadrons were not sent to the Middle East, where even one extra unit made the difference between air superiority and inferiority. Also the raids meant some diversion of resources into attempts to develop long-range machines to conduct retaliatory operations against German targets and eventually against Berlin, though no aircraft were ready for this great adventure until the war was over. But lastly, and most important of all, the raids brought to a peak the complaints about air defenses and production problems, which led to the formation in Britain of the independent Air Ministry and of the Royal Air Force in 1918.

It is true that the newly arrived Field Marshal Jan Christian Smuts of South Africa was the man who wrote the final report to the Cabinet, which called for this late 1917 turn of events, but it was by no means simply the few daylight raids he had witnessed that convinced Smuts. The German attacks acted as a catalyst in a political-industrial quarrel that had been raging from the start of the war. The Royal Naval Air Service had steadily worked to acquire a large chunk of the production of British aircraft and engine manufacturing facilities. Naval officers had also applied their knowledge of technological developments to produce increasingly effective aircraft, while at the same time they had not had to waste their aircrew in constant battle over the Western Front. In contrast, the army had attempted to standardize too early, and it was concurrently undertaking constant offensive action. To this basic dichotomy of outlook has to be added the fact that private manufacturers had a direct interest in putting the Royal Aircraft Factory out of business. And on top of all this, not only was a former private manufacturer calling the government murderers in Parliamentary debates, but his targets were themselves not at all sure that the army's conduct of the war on the Western Front was sound.

Prime Minister Herbert Asquith's Liberal government had attempted to get around the problem by the usual British compromise, the establishment of a joint Air Board, which under Lord Curzon, a distinguished politician of strong character but with no training in technological matters, was supposed to arbitrate without any executive powers. This unsatisfactory position continued until well after Lloyd George became Prime Minister in December 1916. After the German raids in July 1917, Smuts was asked to adjudicate, as someone fresh to the English scene and therefore untainted with political or military prejudices. He was supplied with a lengthy memorandum by Gen. Sir David Henderson, a man "high in the direction"—the administration—of the RFC. Henderson urged that air defense and retaliatory bombing would have to be undertaken by the air service, and Smuts was willing to go along with this, while at the same time turning down the rebuttals supplied from British Headquarters in France. The assumptions upon which he made his decisions, however, were based on the predictions of a surplus of aircraft over the army's needs by mid-1918. In fact, his assumptions were optimistic and were largely vitiated by problems with engine production and by the failure of the American aircraft program.

Still, the Smuts report of September 1917 did not recommend an independent air arm. It was only in October that a War Production Committee was finally established when Churchill pressed for the total rather than piecemeal allocation of resources so that the whole of the war effort was logically planned. This in effect meant that when the new Air Ministry came into being in January 1918 it was really an Air Board with executive powers. The creation of the Royal Air Force as of April 1 was a logical, if debatable, afterthought. Certainly it would cause endless trouble in the years to come.

One other side effect of the German raids should be mentioned. Damage was actually very light—£3,000,000 in four years—for it has been calculated that rats destroyed matériel worth £70,000,000 per year. But the casualties of a chance bomb raid of January 28, 1918, in which one hit Odham's printing plant and caused thirty-eight killed and eighty-five wounded, were used in the following years by statistically unsophisticated air force planners to create a horrible specter of the power of the bomb. Although the vision was largely out of touch with reality, it may be said to have played a part in the coming of the Second World War. A little knowledge truly is a dangerous thing.

The British response to the German psychological bombing was the development of a retaliatory strategy for the new air force, calling for raids against targets in German cities. The British had been persuaded in the summer of 1916, before the Asquith government fell, to add a force to the French strategic-bomber squadrons. The Admiralty had supported this, while Field Marshal Haig protested against dilution of effort. But before all the difficulties could be resolved (and they centered about problems of aircraft procurement), the German daylight raids caused urgent government acceptance of an expansion of the air forces to include forty long-range bomber squadrons. Haig opposed the idea again, but by mid-October 1917 a wing had begun to operate. By May 1918, the British Independent Bombing Force in France had four squadrons, and on June 6 these became officially the Independent Bombing Force. The name change was prompted by three motives: to remove the force from the commander-in-chief in France and from the control of the new Allied Generalissimo Ferdinand Foch of France; to provide a high-sounding post for Sir Hugh Trenchard, recently relieved as Chief of the Air Staff of the new RAF; and to provide the government at home with a retaliatory air force. Because of its small size, the Independent Bombing Force accomplished little during the war, but by misinterpretation of the word "independent," it became far more significant afterward.

Strategic bombing on the Italian front (striking at targets just along the battle line), where Ca 30 (ER n/a) and Ca 42 (ER n/a) trimotored Caproni bombers were available to the Italians by August 1915, began with a raid on Ljubljana on February 18, 1916. This was followed by occasional sorties against targets behind the Austrian lines, including army headquarters, and by a succession of attacks in August and September 1917 against the naval base at Pola; the last of the series, on October 2, involved 148 Caproni bombers and 11 flying boats. A year later, the last major raid of the war was again against Pola when on October 22, 1918, 142 flying boats and 56 Capronis took part. These strikes are correctly called strategic, in that they were aimed at essentially military targets.

After the retreat from Caporetto had been halted at the Piave River, the suggestion was made that a token psychological "raid" be made against Vienna. Work started at once with a trial long-distance flight within the Italian lines on September 4, 1917. The poet Gabriel d'Annunzio, later famous for his postwar capture of Fiume in 1919, took up the cause, and on August 9, 1918, he led five aircraft on a long leaflet-dropping journey, using an evasive route both going and returning. The Italians appreciated the raid at its face value—a psychological rather than grand-strategic effort—and at least semi-official Italian sources do not give Douhet credit for its conception.

On the whole, the psychological lessons learned from bombing in the First World War were that the shock effect was initially great upon civilians long undisturbed by war, especially when the defenses appeared to be unable to stop the attackers, but that both physical and psychological defenses were fairly quickly built up. Churchill was undoubtedly right in the long run when, in a lengthy October 1917 memorandum to the British Cabinet, he pointed out that attacking civilians only in the end stiffened the opponents' will to make war. What would have been the effect upon the German nation of one psychological raid against Berlin, before the end of the war, remains an interesting speculation.

In the last two years of the war, matériel was more plentiful than in 1914 and 1915, but the problem of standardization still plagued all air forces. In feverish attempts to gain air superiority, a plethora of designs were rushed into production, of which only a very small number actually proved useful on operations. Maintenance problems were often accentuated by trying to keep too many kinds of aircraft in the field. The political and military powers did not always recognize that it was necessary to standardize, yet at the same time essential to deal with the constant challenges of the rapidly developing aerial warfare. Flexible measures were required in defense against aerial attack and in the training of crews, as well as in production. As warfare in the air became more complex, more thorough training also became necesary; and, as fighting became more regular, the organization of larger formations was required, as well as planning of mass tactics, and training of personnel in aerial gunnery. At the other end of the spectrum, it was equally important to recall that the war in the air was still a conflict in which the principles of war applied. Concentration, surprise, protection, mobility, and a clear objective were still important. And to these could be added the knowledge that a comparatively small diversion of force to a theater in which existing forces were weak could make a significant contribution psychologically as well as physically.

Aircraft industries in general during 1914–18 had to overcome technical, financial, legal, and bureaucratic barriers. Because of the infancy of aviation in 1914, only design offices and workshops existed with staffs of under one hundred—if even over ten, the whole to design and hand build at the craft level. Profits, if any, were limited, stock offerings meager, and indebtedness slight. Managerial skills could largely be devoted to design and flight. Bureaucratic oversight was mostly benign, technical developments progressed by observation, and plans and modification drawings were not much in use.

War brought not only a technical revolution, but also managerial, organizational, and financial changes: estimates made of future production a year hence, materials and power secured (often by sub-contract), workers organized for serial production, unskilled and even female labor trained, government inspectors hired and certified, and the whole financed against eventual payment upon delivery. Wartime production did not really get into full swing until late 1916, while debts mounted rapidly in preparation, and governments stumbled over costs, prices, loans, grants, and payments as civil servants and politicians failed to perceive the needs or to understand the difficulties facing patriotic manufacturers. Firms suffered roughly five-month delays between types, even if orders were consecutive, though if engines were on schedule, production demands were usually met. But the aircraft constructors left the war exhausted and in debt, and many were bankrupt. On the bright side, all parties learned how to handle the business aspects of the renewed aircraft production from 1934 onward.

CONCLUSIONS

A Mahanian assessment of the power of aeronautical countries in 1914 has only to cover Russia, Germany, Austria, France, Italy, Britain, and the United States.

Russia had the most potential, but lacked the finances, management, and skilled labor to produce an air force. Germany had almost all the assets to be an air power, except engine manufacturing potential and fuel sources. Austria lacked the capacity for successful aviation and the coal needed to keep factories warm; fortunately, physical conditions limited the effectiveness of her opponents. Italy had enough resources plus the imaginative leadership to be an air power, as well as a mountain barrier to the north and surrounding seas. France had the space, the resources, the engineering know-how and the higher direction to be the leading air power as long as her armies could hold on the ground. Like Germany, she had some understanding of economy of force. Britain also enjoyed similar advantages in industrial and financial assets and higher direction, but suffered from a wasteful offensive spirit and a shortage of engines. In all the countries, the effects and legacies of the 1914–18 war would affect their activities to 1940 and beyond.

In the First World War were sown the seeds of future progress and of future disaster. Many heroic traditions were created and many illusions generated. The fighter pilot was glorified and the ace immortalized. Too much credit was given to bombs, which often in the early years were no bigger than portable typewriters. And just as myths emerged, so did mythical personalities. Sir Hugh Trenchard and Gen. Billy Mitchell came out of the war with reputations that history does not substantiate. Trenchard was originally an advocate of a tactical air force, and in the long run he may well have been right in opposing grand-strategic bombing; but he made the mistake in 1921 of adopting it. Mitchell was at his best as a Duvalian tactical man and a propagandist of air power. His postwar notoriety overshadowed his real work during the conflict in forming the American air services. Douhet in later years also achieved a reputation for support of the efficacy of bombing that is today much more open to question than it was in 1933. And on the French side, Duval was the father of the battle for air superiority and for attack aviation.

In the 1920s and 1930s many air forces were torn internally and externally by quarrels over their desire to be able to bomb independently and the surface forces' demand for cooperation—as well as for their own official air arms.

The German air force ended the First World War as it concluded the Second, gallantly fighting despite increasing supply difficulties and rapidly dwindling reserves of men and machines. Its commander, General von Hoeppner, remains a shadowy figure, at least in the English-speaking world, yet he should rank as one of the geniuses of early aviation organization. The Germans should also get credit for conserving their forces and not always taking the bait of battle, knowing they could not afford the losses.

That the airplane had at least reached puberty may be seen from the limited figures which show that at the end of the war France had 4,511 aircraft on hand, Britain 3,300, Germany 2,390, and the United States 740.

Too much of the writing of aviation history has taken place in the Anglo-Saxon world with the result that erroneous impressions have persisted. The RAF managed to perpetuate the belief that at the end of the war it was the world's largest air force; in fact, history shows that it was not—the French service was bigger. An impressive British claim, however, is that of the 55,000 airmen lost, about 30 percent were British. It was a magnificent show, but was it the way a war should be fought?

Of importance for the later interwar years (1919–39) was the fact that during 1914–18 a new design could go from a sketch to operations in six months. By 1936, peacetime lethargy lengthened this, when combined with new technologies and construction materials, to four years for a fighter, six for a medium bomber, and eight for a heavy bomber. Thus, to be out of synchronization with other powers, as the Russians were in Spain during 1936–37, or the French and the Americans were during 1936–40, could mean disaster unless extraordinary measures were taken.

Although the biplane persisted into World War II, it was technically obsolete; but much of the practical knowledge of the ebb and flow of battle, of the difficulties of defense and of production, would carry over through the interwar years to the Second World War. In part this was because the highly placed air commanders of 1939–45 had been pilots in 1914–18, veterans of linked wars.

CHAPTER 3

THE INTERWAR YEARS

The end of the First World War left the victorious powers with a large surplus of matériel and a mixed bag of officers and men, some eager to be demobilized as fast as possible and others still dreaming of glory and anxious to make flying a career. Many were too young to have known any other life work.

The vanquished were left with shattered forces that were soon eliminated, either under armistice or peace-treaty terms, or at the hands of their own men. In the case of Germany, at least, technological advantage lay ultimately in being defeated, for all her matériel was destroyed and she was forbidden to undertake military construction. Thus, she was compelled to concentrate upon the development of new, technically reliable, and efficient civil machines, while at the same time training her personnel outside her borders, operating them in such climatic extremes as Russia and Latin America.

In all countries, demobilization brought a severe constriction in terms of men, matériel, and monies. And because air arms in most nations had to compete against older and better-established services, the members of the newest and youngest branch of war again had to attempt to justify their existence. Doctrine and conceptions once more sometimes outran reality, and airmen's claims sometimes annoyed their fraternal opponents into taking more active parts in the overall military re-

organization. This was particularly true in America, where opposition to the messianic views of Billy Mitchell drove the U.S. Navy along the path to the creation of the carrier task force. Perhaps even more than in wartime, it is essential for a military force in peacetime to have an "enemy," even if it is only a rival service or arm—with victory in terms of money, not territory—for a challenge may lead to coherent planning. Of course, if political power is too oppressive on one side or the other, or if verbal combat is mostly acrimonious, then the effects may be undesirable.

It is of interest that the RAF, belonging to the only postwar superpower and concerned with its own existence, failed to evolve a corps of staff officers and to learn how to plan for all eventualities. Instead, as late as 1936 it would have difficulty getting ten aircraft airborne for an exercise, let alone plan for attacks upon Germany, for which it did not even have maps. Thus, in France and Britain the "air menace" became a fear-inspiring straw man.

NEW MILITARY ROLES AND RELATIONSHIPS

The interwar years saw progress made toward new military roles and relationships. Air forces from 1919 to 1941 were split between those who followed air proponent Giulio Douhet, seeing their focus as grand-strategic bombing—or who like the RAF had come independently to that stance, and those who put the emphasis upon strategic and tactical attacks in cooperation with the surface services. The British (1918), Italians (1921), and the French (1928) created independent Air Ministries and later pursued grand-strategic bombing, neglected fighter and anti-aircraft defenses, and detested "cooperation." But in the 1930s the Italian Col. Amadeo Mecozzi, of the independent *Regia Aeronautica,* called for attack aviation modeled on France's Duval Air Division of 1917–18, and by the late 1930s this had led to the development of a doctrine for light bomber-fighters for dive-bombing, low-level attack aircraft, and level bombers. The role especially of the fighter-bombers was to avoid combat with enemy forces until after they had struck their targets, then to be able to fight their way home. The French air service had begun to adapt this, but aircrew and equipment had only trickled into units by the time of the Battle of France in May–June 1940. The U.S. Army Air Corps was in a similar predicament.

The exponents of tactical air forces were the *Wehrmacht*-controlled *Luftwaffe* and the Soviet air forces, followed after 1941 by the RAF and US-AAF Tactical Air Forces.

In the meantime, from 1936, one-third of the Home RAF was devoted to fighters and was augmented and coordinated with searchlights, guns, and the new radar, just in time to win the Battle of Britain in the summer of 1940.

Although the French air arm was the largest in the world in 1918, it was still part of the French army. And while Colonel Duval had been able to create a central air reserve—the Duval Division—for use in 1917–18, the organization of the air service had not been resolved, though its logistical system was effective. The contrast here is with the Royal Air Force across the Channel in which the air revolution provided mechanical efficiency, with the aim of conserving manpower. As important

as was the vision of modern war of Lt. Col. Frederick Sykes, his establishment in 1915 of the basic organizational structure of the Royal Flying Corps and in 1918 of the RAF was equally essential. Under the economic and political stresses of peacetime parsimony, the Home RAF was consolidated in 1924 under the Air Defence of Great Britain Command (ADGB), which controlled the RAF in the United Kingdom until 1936, when functional commands were created to meet the needs of expansion and war.

The fall of the French air force from victory as the world's largest in 1918 to absolute defeat in 1940 was a complex tale. In the 1920s, the force was the moribund air arm of the army, with whom the airmen quarreled constantly over doctrine: was aviation to be the handmaiden of the ground forces, to be allocated a little at a time, or was it to be a general reserve *à la* the Duval Division, to be used *en masse* by army headquarters? These issues were complicated by the development of a new concept of air power advocated by Guilio Douhet—the devastation of enemy cities and industry by surprise preemptive air strike at the outset of war. As this concept gained adherents, in 1928 an Air Ministry was established. At the beginning of the 1930s, Douhetian doctrine really began to take hold and in 1933, when the Socialist Pierre Cot became Air Minister and General Denain his Chief of the Air Staff, *L'Armée de l'Air* (the French Air Force) was created by decree and legitimized in July 1934.

A new structure had to be formed and the force re-equipped. But due to continuing arguments with the army, an order for over 1,000 planes was compromised by the development of a multi-place, multi-purpose machine, the BCR (bomber-combat-reconnaissance) that was obsolete at birth. Moreover, the aircraft industry was still artisan in nature, accustomed to building only one machine at a time. Not until mid-1938, with nationalization of the factories, restructuring, and rationalization, did the industry become productive. A similar consolidation for efficiency had taken place

Lt. Cmdr. A. C. Read and his crew prepare to depart from Long Island, New York, for their trans-Atlantic hops in May 1919, in a Curtiss NC-4 flying boat (ER 7.49). This aircraft is preserved in the U.S. Naval Aviation Museum at Pensacola, Florida. (USN)

Lt. Commander Read and his crew of the Curtiss NC-4, in May 1919. This was the only flying boat to go all the way across the Atlantic from the United States to Great Britain. (USN)

The Vickers Vimy Commercial (ER 0.95) taking off in June 1919 with the Australian Charles Kingsford-Smith at the start of his ground-breaking journey from England to Australia. Former Royal Flying Corps officers Capt. John Alcock and Lt. Arthur W. Brown had flown a similar biplane aircraft non-stop, in about sixteen hours, from Newfoundland to Ireland also in June of 1919. (Vickers)

Sir Charles Kingsford-Smith in front of his 1928 Fokker F-VII (ER 1.15).

Maj. Gen. Sir Hugh Trenchard, the "father of the RAF," was the Air Officer Commander-in-Chief of the Royal Flying Corps in France from 1915 to 1918, then Chief of the Air Staff of the Royal Air Force in early 1918 and from 1919 to 1930. His long tenure and grasp of the organizational needs of the new air arm made him influential. (Source unknown)

R-34 was a British copy of the German Zeppelin shot down intact over Britain in 1916. In July 1919, this rigid airship flew non-stop from Scotland to Long Island, New York, and after refueling, flew back across the North Atlantic to England. The lighter-than-air ship is seen here on Long Island. (USN)

Maj. Gen. Mason M. Patrick led the U.S. Air Service in its early years, here in 1923 with Brig. Gen. Billy Mitchell, his second in command. Mitchell, however, was determined to have an independent air force, disobeyed orders, was insubordinate, and was court-martialed in 1925 and "exiled." (USAF)

Rear Adm. William F. Moffett, was Chief of the Bureau of Aeronautics, U.S. Navy from 1921 until his death in the *Akron* airship crash in 1933. Moffett had the tact that Mitchell lacked and made naval aviation a creditable response to Billy Mitchell's claims for a single, independent air force. (USN)

World War I spawned airfields, especially in the Sun Belt, such as this one at Brooks Field, Texas, built on a grand scale. One of the hangars in this 1920 view is still preserved. (USAF)

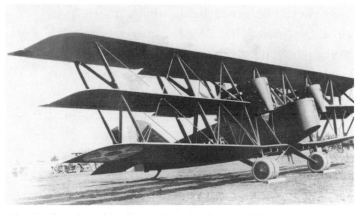

The Barling bomber (ER n/a) was designed by an ex-patriot Englishman, with one prototype built in the United States. The aircraft was so underpowered that it could not get over the mountains between Ohio and Washington, D.C.

Air policing of the British Empire colonies involved not only aircraft, but also RAF armored cars on Rolls-Royce chassis, here seen in Iraq in 1923. (Source unknown)

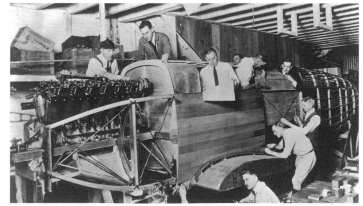

One of the World Cruisers (ER 3.07) of the U.S. Army's 1924 round-the-world flight is here being constructed at Douglas Aircraft Company in Los Angeles. Donald Douglas, Sr., is standing in the cockpit just aft of the engine fitter. (Douglas)

Two Douglas World Cruisers ready to depart from the West Coast in 1924. Automobiles and clothing make it possible to date this photograph. One of the machines is preserved at the U.S. Air Force Museum in Dayton, Ohio, and another at the National Air and Space Museum in Washington, D.C. (McDonnell Douglas)

earlier in Britain. By 1940, the French industry was producing 350 aircraft per month, the British over 600 modern machines. As a result, the FAF entered the war in September 1939 with less than 400 modern fighters, including 130 imported Curtiss P-36 Mohawks (ER 1.6) and only 20 bombers, facing a *Luftwaffe* of nearly 3,000 first-line modern aircraft.

The FAF was not helped in the late 1930s by constant political changes and international crises. In March 1936, the French did nothing when the Germans remilitarized the Rhineland, having revealed their new, modern *Luftwaffe* and a superior rate of aircraft production. France was paralyzed by fear of the air menace when she was defenseless. That nakedness also reached a nadir at Munich in September 1938 when France signed the conciliatory Accords, as did Britain, allowing Hitler to annex a portion of Czechoslovakia in exchange for a hollow promise of peace.

French difficulties were also caused not only by political troubles but by the fact that French technology had been allowed to slip out of synchronization with that of the rest of the aeronautical world. France's 1934 orders, delivered in 1936–37, were for 1928–32 designs. Aircraft equivalent to the German designs of 1935 and their British contemporaries were still being tested in France when war came.

Unfortunately, in 1935, the French Air Force was still seeking an efficient organization, still arguing doctrine with the army, and only on the verge of specifying the new modern aircraft needed. The French situation was exacerbated by the withholding of credits until 1938, which hampered French prototype development. In contrast, the RAF's budget had gone from £16 million pounds sterling in 1932 to over £450 million by the time war came; and one of the payoffs of the cost plus ten percent contracts used by the Air Ministry in London was the Rolls-Royce Merlin engine.

Moreover, because of the slowness and lack of vision of the prototype policy under peacetime financing and leisurely work schedules, France lacked the expertise to jump immediately to modern types. At the same time, the dominance of Douhetism until the late 1930s helped create an incoherent doctrine that, apart from the faultily conceived BCR aircraft, left France without much attack or army cooperation aviation. In addition, the victory of the Popular Front in 1936 saw the nationalization of production and a shift of such facilities southwest away from Paris. Without doubt, the French aircraft industry and the FAF suffered from a political economy that had shortsightedly cut funds in the early 1930s, just when the technological revolutions needed to work through prototypes to producible, viable designs.

It should be noted that at this same time, in 1934, the Soviet's Red Air Force was the world's largest, though its fleet would be outclassed by the Germans in Spain, just as the Japanese seized air superiority over China. The Italians were close behind and the British about equal. The United States had advanced prototypes and in some cases production aircraft, such as the Curtiss 75 Hawks (ER 1.67) the French ordered in 1939.

Due to plenty of time and minimal orders, aircraft companies in the years 1919–34 were simply design offices with a workshop attached. Political demands for competition and low bids meant that the successful design might not be built by the winner but by another company, which did not have to include design costs in its bid. In Russia the design office continued to have a workshop that could build and modify prototypes, whereas production was assigned to separate factories as part of the full-employment policy. Not until after the collapse of the USSR were the design offices forced, in 1997, to amalgamate with the factories as part of the restructuring of the Russian economy on a capitalist/cost basis. And in 2000, all were pushed into a national company.

Even more than words, deeds were essential to make industrialists, politicians, and the public— and thus the legislatures—aware of the importance of air power. Here airmen were gifted with an ideal vehicle for publicity, in an era of individualism, demonstrations, and cameras. Throughout the interwar years, at least until the Great Depression, airmen sought to stir the public mind with record-breaking headlines and aerobatic displays. And not unnaturally, although some of these activities (such as the development of air racing and long-distance machines) had practical applications in the creation of matériel and techniques, inevitably other facets tended to become ends in themselves. Thus, a squadron might spend nine months of the year practicing a set of maneuvers for the annual public display; but the other three months left little time for military training once leave had been taken.

Peacetime brought other problems. Because the air services had hardly existed before World War I, they had no permanent bases, schools, stores, or positions in the defense spectrum. Nor did they have traditions, which may have been a good thing. In each case it was necessary to establish an organization to create a permanent force, which would in itself form the cadre of another wartime air force, if one should be needed. Yet, how was this to be done with the funding available?

The solutions varied according to the situation each nation faced. The Germans created a disguised air force in their gliding clubs and airlines, and through advisers sent to foreign air forces. The French stayed tensely on guard against another German attack. They remained especially fearful when the Anglo-American Guarantee Treaty to protect French borders failed to be ratified after the Treaty of Versailles in 1919 had ended the Anglo-Franco-Italian war against Germany. The French even regarded Britain as a likely enemy in the critical days over the Ruhr in 1923, when British airliners flew currency into the Germans in that area soon occupied by the French.

The Italians followed the British lead and established an Air Ministry. The rehabilitated Gen. Guilio Douhet, in favor with the newly risen dictator Benito Mussolini, found acceptable his ideas of a counterstrike deterrent against the enemy

while the infantry held the Alpine passes. The British, unable to re-divide the RAF as originally planned, took the view that as there would be no major war for ten years, the best thing to do was cut the service back to a cadre force while building anew from the ground up. Sir Hugh Trenchard was unspoken—perhaps fortunately—unlike America's Billy Mitchell; British parliamentary procedure did not allow the public brawling between services that was possible in American congressional committees. The United States, however, had the unique opportunities for an air service, with its vast amount of internal air space and reasonably good weather.

Although strapped for cash and almost without airplanes at home, the RAF carried on the air defense system devised by Gen. E. B. Ashmore in 1917 and essentially commanded by him until 1929. This strategic air defense became the base, with its observer corps and reporting system, that Air Chief Marshal Sir Hugh Dowding would use in the exercises of 1936–39 to pre-test Fighter Command's battle system, in which radar was the vital added ingredient enabling his minimum of fifty-two squadrons to successfully fight the Battle of Britain in 1940.

Both British and American doctrine developed the concept of an air defense against a seaborne invasion, but the controversies resulted in different conclusions. In Britain, the naval air arm was subordinated to and manned by the RAF. In America, the U.S. Navy retained and developed under Rear Adm. William A. Moffett its own air force, to counter General Mitchell's claims that the Army Air Service could defend the country at sea. Ironically, the ex-Royal Naval Air Service professionals followed naval tradition and went out to train the Japanese naval air arm, thus laying the trap for the humiliation of the Royal Navy in 1941–42. The Royal Navy was allowed to start Fleet Air Arm (FAA) training in 1924, but it was not until 1937 that the FAA was brought fully under Admiralty control. It is interesting to speculate about the outcome of the war at sea if the

RNAS had remained a naval air arm after 1918 and had not trained the Japanese. British airmen have claimed the Admiralty did not want them until the RAF took them, but the challenges created by both the Americans and Japanese, whose first aircraft carrier entered service in 1923, coupled with the evidence of air-mindedness in Adm. Sir John Jellicoe's 1919 proposals for a Far Eastern Fleet, suggest that a naval air arm of some kind would have been maintained. And Japanese-American rivalries, no doubt, would have created an oriental carrier fleet anyway.

While the Royal Navy was uncertain about the future of naval aviation and was entangled in fights with the Air Ministry, the U.S. Navy moved rapidly ahead. The USN had a solid, if small, background in aviation from the prewar days, when Glenn Curtiss had trained officer pilots in San Diego and Lt. J. H. Towers had flown out to sea off Guantanamo Bay in 1913 and had spotted "the enemy" approaching. In 1917–18, USN airmen had flown from France and Britain.

Postwar, the USN owed its progress to several things, not the least of which was that the country's leading practical airman-politician was a naval officer. In his day, Rear Adm. Moffett was the Hyman Rickover—from 1950 to 1980 a nuclear leader—and also the Trenchard. Like the RAF leader, Moffett enjoyed an exceptionally long tenure of office, from 1921 until his accidental death in 1933, as head of the Bureau of Aeronautics. It was Moffett who guided the U.S. Navy past Mitchellian rocks and along the channels of the carrier task force. Moffett was careful; he never openly antagonized either his superiors or Congress, but he took full advantage of the power of a bureau chief and of the publicity value of aviation. As a result, the U.S. Navy found itself escaping the odium heaped upon the U.S. Army's Mitchell, whose antics and attacks made Navy brass all the more ready to fight fire with fire.

To prevent the usurpation of the U.S. Navy's traditional coast-defense role by the U.S. Air Service, the Navy developed patrol bombers and carriers. At the same time, Moffett was helped by the fact that by 1922 the great battleship advocate, Adm. William S. Sims, had become converted by games played under his own command at the Naval War College, and Sims's endorsement of carriers influenced other officers. Aviation was included in annual fleet maneuvers starting in 1921, but not until Fleet Problem V in 1925 was a carrier present, the USS *Langley,* and not until 1929 were two modern carriers available, the *Lexington* and the *Saratoga.* From then on, progress was steady. The U.S. Navy was able to order its own aircraft and train its own crews, and a permanent cadre of naval aviators came into being with equipment that they had specified, tried, and modified. It was American naval airmen who worked up—or perfected—the dive-bomber, and it was their new biplane Curtiss SBC Helldiver (ER 10.36) that the German Ernst Udet saw in 1935, bought with state funds, and took back to Germany and "sold" to Hermann Goering and the *Luftwaffe.* Thus, the U.S. Navy was indirectly responsible for the German Ju-87 Stuka (ER 2.22) dive-bomber design, which started operational life in the Spanish Civil War, then spearheaded the 1939–40 *Blitzkrieg,* before being used in the war at sea and over the USSR. The U.S. Navy's grasp of politics was one of the basic reasons for its ultimate success.

The development and evolution of the Royal Navy's and the U.S. Navy's aircraft carrier was a study in national perceptions and attitudes toward the future and new ideas. In Britain, the RN had invented the aircraft carrier and ended the war with three converted battlecruisers—*Furious, Glorious,* and *Courageous.* The USN did not reach that stage until 1929 with the *Saratoga* and the *Lexington.* In both navies the innovation process was tempered by their view of the Imperial Japanese Navy as a potential enemy. On the other hand, conscious that it would have to operate within range of European land-based air power, the new Royal Navy carrier of the 1930s was constructed around an armored box, whereas the USN carrier had a wooden flight deck—a contrast evident in 1945 in the *kamikaze* age.

Perhaps more important than the technical questions were the institutional and organizational differences. While the Admiralty had a Fifth Sea Lord on the Board, the U.S. Navy had Rear Admiral Moffett heading the Bureau of Aeronautics and close liaison with innovative designers, especially at the Douglas and Grumman aircraft companies.

Yet the Royal Navy had started out in 1919 with Admiral Jellicoe's plan for Pacific carrier fleets to oppose the then friendly Imperial Japanese Navy, influenced by popular journalist Hector Bywater's *The Great Pacific War,* a 1922 fictional conflict that was won by Allied carrier task forces. In the end, the Royal Navy became the victim of its own vision of war, which the naval staff failed to scrutinize, in part because of the battles with Trenchard over the Fleet Air Arm in the 1920s. The U.S. Navy, meanwhile, strove to get as many aircraft as possible aboard a carrier. War would show who had the better crystal ball.

Whereas the French helped the Japanese army, it was a British Air Mission, sent out in April 1921 and staying until the end of 1923, that helped with naval developments. Though not regarded as particularly apt pupils by their instructors, the Japanese were aware of what needed to be done. Thus, the *Hosho* was laid down in 1919 as an aircraft carrier and commissioned by early 1923, when active flying trials aboard her began. Although an economy drive in 1923 created some problems, the Japanese were vigorous in their desire to learn about flying and soon acquired British aircraft and equipment, which they often proceeded to copy as the first step toward creating their own home-built aircraft. The British Air Mission suffered from the Air Ministry's reluctance to release the latest information, as it wished to keep its developments at least a year ahead of rivals; but the Japanese in any case soon progressed more rapidly than the Fleet Air Arm, even as early as 1923 en-

gaging in night-flying operations. As an island kingdom, Japan had good reason to develop a naval air arm and was in a political position to do so.

Yet in both the Japanese and the American navies, airmen had trouble developing their tactics, because the navies were dominated by battleship admirals who predicted that the next war would be won at sea in one great big free-for-all clash of the classic example of the Russo-Japanese Battle of Tsushima in 1905. Thus, aircraft carriers were tied to the battle fleet, not always with positive results, as when in the 1929 U.S. Naval War College games the *Lexington* was caught by the "enemy" surface forces while steaming away from her own battle line to launch her planes. In Fleet Problem IX, a carrier task force proved that the Panama Canal could be surprised and that naval aircraft could attack land targets. Later, the USN would successfully attack Pearl Harbor on maneuvers in 1932, while the Royal Navy would do the same at Singapore in 1937. Although in the 1930 American maneuvers a separate striking group was built around the *Saratoga,* the idea seems not to have occurred to the Japanese, who began fleet air maneuvers in 1931. Their vision was blinded by the apparent necessity, similar to that facing the Germans up to 1918, to cut down the size of the U.S. Navy's battle line. The ratio established at the 1922 Washington Naval Conference was that the American and British fleets would be equal and the Japanese only 60 percent of the size of either; and the Japanese placed too great an emphasis at one time upon the possibility of the presence of all the American fleet in the Pacific. In preparing to reduce the American battle line, their carriers were heavily outfitted with dive- and torpedo-bombers, whereas American carriers had a higher proportion of fighters. Only gradually did the Japanese realize that the U.S. carriers were their main problem, and not until about 1940 were these made the principal target.

What influenced the Japanese were the ideas brought back from Britain, by their naval air at-

Sir Alan Cobham and Sir Sefton Brancker. Cobham, former Royal Flying Corps member and de Havilland test pilot, made historic long-distance flights in the 1920s. He had been selected to accompany Brancker, Director of Civil Aviation, to India and Burma to look into the feasibility of airship routes. Brancker came back convinced of the aeroplane's ultimate success.

A Swedish Malmo J-3 high-wing monoplane (ER n/a) being tested for structural strength in 1923. The designer is in the foreground with Lt. Nils Söderberg, test pilot, above him and, highest of all, the commandant of the Fighter Pilot's School. (RSAF)

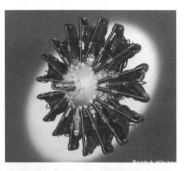

The original Pratt & Whitney Wasp R-1340 engine was refined over the years from 425 hp of 1926 to the 2,000 hp Double Wasp R-2800 of 1942, and the R-4300 3000 hp of 1945. (Pratt & Whitney)

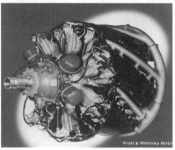

Above: Wasp Major engine, 2,000 hp, 1942. Right: Double Wasp engine, 3,000 hp, 1945.

Charles A. Lindbergh's 1927 solo west-to-east trans-Atlantic flight gave aviation a tremendous boost. Lindy was not simply lucky, but rather a careful planner. He departed from New York and landed in Paris, well-covered by the press, and his shyness made him an endearing hero. More than this, the reliability of his engine, which ran non-stop for thirty-three hours, made a name for radials and boosted the reputation of flying's reliability and its safety. (USAF)

The replica of Lindbergh's Ryan Aeronautical *Spirit of St. Louis* (ER 0.48), flying past the St. Louis Arch. The machine now hangs in the passenger terminal at Lambert Field; the original is in the National Air and Space Museum, Washington, D.C.

In 1927, Clyde Cessna and his staff and workers pose in front of their hangar workshop in Wichita, Kansas. (Cessna)

Walter H. Beech and his test pilot, Art Goebel, with the firm's Travel Air 5000, *Woolaroc* (ER 0.48), in which Goebel won the August 1927 Dole Pacific Race from California to Hawaii. (Beech)

The wooden Fokker F-7 (ER 3.3) was one of the various designs that the famous Dutchman Anthony Fokker made in the United States, and in 1928 was Pan Am's first service plane. An advance in efficiency, the aircraft well suited the trans-continental routes being developed in the country. (Pan American Airways)

The Fokkers were succeeded by the famous Ford Trimotors (ER 3), this one seen in Eastern Air Transport livery, with passengers and agent standing by for boarding. (Eastern Air Lines)

Operations in cold climates such as Alaska, Canada, Russia, and Finland called for extraordinary measures. Here, a Finnish pilot heats the oil before pouring it in a Junkers W-13 (n/a) so that the engine will start. (Finnair)

Dr. Hugo Junkers (1859–1935) was the pioneer German all-metal aircraft constructor. Perhaps his most successful design antedates the Douglas DC-3 (ER 19.14) of the mid-1930s. The Ju-52 (ER 6.7) entered airline service in 1929, and three are still being flown by the Swiss Air Force Museum at Dübendorf, near Zurich.

Finnish mechanics work on a Junkers W-13 (ER n/a). Note the all-metal construction and corrugated skin, which were Junkers trademarks up through the Ju-52 (ER 6.7) of 1929. (Finnair)

The 1929 Dornier Do-X (ER 28.5) was a twelve-engine monster designed for ocean crossings, seen here at New York. Only one was built. (Fairchild-Dornier)

taché, after the British surprise attack on the anchored Italian fleet at Taranto in 1940. Lt. Cdr. Minoru Genda concluded that air superiority was essential, that strikes must be by at least one hundred bombers, and that carriers had to have armored decks. Partly as a result of these observations and of a newsreel of the four U.S. carriers steaming together, the Japanese had by 1941 developed the doctrine that for attacks on land targets their carriers should steam in company; but in order to avoid "mutual kill," as they termed it, in air actions at sea the carriers should be separated. The object of the characteristic Japanese separation of forces was the entrapment of the enemy fleet in a box, which would allow them to strike from four directions at once—the tactic they had in mind at Midway in 1942.

What gave strength to both the Japanese and American naval airmen was the fact that their services were separate from other air forces; their struggles were fought within their own services, which controlled their matériel and expected to fight battles basically in their own environment.

In their search for a postwar role, airmen could justify themselves in part by their wartime actions. But, on the whole, they found themselves really doing no more than making a case for an arm of one of the surface establishments. Naval airmen could not, for instance, show that they had played a significant independent role against enemy navies; even in anti-submarine warfare their role had been ancillary. They sought to claim that they could sink ships with torpedoes and that they could take over the coast-defense role; and they did demonstrate that bombs could harm battleships, although in this they were outshone by Billy Mitchell and the U.S. Army.

In Germany, naval airmen for a while were given a role in coast defense, but this was more an arbitrary administrative division of covert activities than a real function. What naval airmen basically could claim—a fact that the RNAS had demonstrated and that the U.S. and Imperial Japanese navies would prove—was that unless the fleet controlled its own air arm, it would suffer from three fatal defects. First, its aircraft would not be designed for its own needs, but usually would be variations of land-based machines whose operational weaknesses would become more apparent as size increased. (It must be noted here that the poor design of British naval aircraft came from a variety of factors connected both with the history of the Fleet Air Arm and with the nature of the aircraft industry.) Second, the fleet's personnel would not be dedicated naval officers, but would belong to an alien service. And third, most clearly demonstrated in the German case in the Second World War, the fleet's entire air arm could be siphoned off to other tasks more rewarding in the eyes of the air force High Command or of other career officers. Even in Britain, the great example of an independent third service was compromised (as Trenchard had envisaged that it would be when money was available) by the creation first between 1924 and 1937 of the Fleet Air Arm, and then in the midst of the Second World War of an army air arm. And this army air arm would be manned partly by army officers and partly by "hostilities-only" RAF aircrew who had no overriding loyalty to either service. Two other factors must be noted as affecting the issue. Most of the difficulties and rivalries were among the *prima donnas* in the top echelons; individuals at the lower levels got along when they had a common concern. But in the days of strapped budgets, anything that could be passed over to someone else's account scored a point in budgetary gamesmanship. Also to be considered was the adverse publicity that could easily be associated with air crashes and with excessive profits of aircraft firms, singled out in particular by the disarmers whose attacks on private manufacture of arms reached their climax in the American Nye Committee hearings in 1935.

Yet, although naval airman had their problems, in some countries they were able to make progress by quiet work at sea and successful efforts on maneuvers. German and Soviet naval aviators, however, got almost nowhere; and in the British navy, airmen were hampered by their affiliation with the RAF and by the fact that umpires on maneuvers were often conservative gunnery officers who might overlook or nullify the contribution of aviation. Thus, tactics tended to become sterile, and only real warfare would sharpen them to viability in combat.

Land-based airmen had an equally difficult time arguing that they had a separate role and were not an arm of the army. Even in Britain in 1917 it was only intended that the unified air service should exist until wartime production problems were solved; after the Armistice it was assumed that the RNAS and the RFC would be recreated, most likely under the same names. In Italy, the United States, France, and Britain airmen sought a separate identify because of their frustration at operating under the control of older ground-bound officers, who they felt did not understand air power. Progress toward complete separation between air and surface commands, however, was slow and uneven.

In the new Russia—the USSR after 1917—aviation played a small role first in the civil war and then in that against Poland until 1922. Thereafter, the state institutionalized and fostered the training of the second generation of aviators and designers. With few grand-strategic targets in range and the need to perfect aircraft, engines, and techniques, the Red Air Force developed into a tactical air force, the handmaiden of the armies (and to a much lesser extent of the navies). Stalin's brilliant managerial five-year plans, prepared with the military's help from 1924, mobilized industry from 1928. Thus, when Germany invaded in 1941, the Soviets had the makings of a powerful tactical air force in spite of the purges of the leadership in the 1937 trials.

CEMENTING NEW ATTITUDES
AND NEW ROLES

Acceptance of new technologies appears to go through a cycle, starting with battles in which the lines are sharply drawn in public between unabashed admirers and fervently reactionary opponents. If the item is eventually accepted, it is assumed at first to be a cure-all. Once that adulatory phase passes with some disillusionment, it is possible to come to a rational understanding of the real capabilities and limitations of the new technological creation. In the meantime, in the twenty years or so which this process takes, technology itself may have advanced far enough to give some realism to the claims made for the machine in its early days. With air power, the twenty-year period was up in 1939.

Although it was true that airmen discovered that in colonial operations—against tribesmen lacking even anti-aircraft guns—they could apparently act swiftly, economically, and therefore effectively as policemen, colonial activities between the wars produced little more than general-purpose tactical air forces used in a limited strategic sense. Moreover, the very conditions under which these forces operated created a frame of mind that was a liability in a modern, mechanized continental war. British and French airmen suffered, too, from their isolation, in such activities, from the very people with whom they would have to cooperate in wartime.

That the RAF, for instance, did not fare worse in the Second World War was probably in part due to a dominant aspect of the British character—the willingness to team together, in spite of diversity, to get a job done. In the United States, where army airmen had few if any tasks, they were never able to obtain more than corps status (1926) until 1941, when the U.S. Army Air Corps was promoted to the U.S. Army Air Forces. In other countries, such as Japan and the Soviet Union, to whom no grand-strategic targets were open, the air arms remained essentially tactical. And in Germany, where former fighter pilot Hermann Goering made much of his air force as opposed to the needs of the navy, he nevertheless saw a tactical role, in basically the style of the First World War, in support of the army.

In their attempt to achieve a self-confident independent identity—necessary before they could willingly join their strength to that of a larger community—airmen found a niche in which they could make a special claim, though even that could be disputed by anti-aircraft proponents. The apparent lessons of the German air attacks on Britain in the First World War, in British eyes, were that the next war would open with a devastating air attack and that only an independent air force could protect the nation from this third-dimensional blow. A corollary developed was that the best defense was a solid deterrent offensive threat. But the intellectual simplicity of these approaches was made difficult by internal political and economic clouds as well as by diplomatic and geographic obstacles. If the air-power nations of the interwar years are surveyed, it will be noted that each reacted in a different way and suffered a different fate. And at least a part of the result was due to semantic difficulties over the word "strategic," which we have suggested should be redefined as either strategic in the older army sense, designating military contacts beyond the immediate battlefield— or grand strategic in the sense of independent operations, not directly connected with a surface campaign. That this confusion arose and still persists was due to the lack of defense education on the part of politicians and their unwillingness even to listen in an era in which the emphasis was upon disarmament—and due as well to a natural human tendency to assume that both parties in a dialogue are using the same terms in the same way.

The attitude taken by the Soviets and the Japanese was largely governed by the lack of an apparent grand-strategic threat and by a dearth of external targets. But it was also dictated by the absence of a champion within the state. In the Russian case, Igor Sikorsky and Alexandre de Seversky left the country for the United States, where Sikorsky turned to building passenger aircraft and helicopters, as the idea of grand-strategic bombing was given little support in an American isolationist era. Despite the fact that the Germans had been the instigators of grand-strategic bombing,

the German officers who trained the Soviet Air Force were essentially tactically oriented. The 1936–38 Soviet purge of general officers ended any chance that those who had read the work of Italy's Douhet, whose doctrines the Germans did not accept, would have power. By 1939 Soviet heavy bombers were obsolete and converted to transport roles, while the rest of the air force was recuperating from the Spanish Civil War.

By the time the Sino-Japanese incident broke out in July 1937, the Japanese air forces had developed long-range bombers, which were used first for strategic attacks against Chinese airfields and then, when these strikes caught and nearly destroyed the Chinese Air Force (CAF) on the ground, for larger strategic raids against the principal bases outside Chinese cities. In the 1939 Manchurian Nomonhan war against the Soviets, however, the Japanese never were in a position to undertake strategic bombing due to the overwhelming numbers of Soviet fighters. Each side, of course, claimed that the other suffered severe losses, but neither established air superiority.

In Germany, where the air force was suppressed until after the rise of Adolf Hitler, the concentration was on air transport and after 1933 on tactical aircraft, in part because Goering, the head of the *Luftwaffe,* had been a fighter pilot and in part because the only advocate of grand-strategic bombing, Gen. Walther Wever, was killed in an air crash in 1936. Moreover, it is questionable whether grand-strategic attacks would have suited Hitler's policy, which was to avoid arousing other powers while quickly snapping up victims. As for the French, even in the First World War they had been most careful not to arouse the Germans due to the fragile state of their own morale, for they had already lost many of their industrial towns to the German army, and they did not want retaliation. Thus, they had resisted the British establishment of an independent air force outside the control of Allied Generalissimo Foch for these very reasons. If the British wanted to retaliate against the Germans, they concluded, let it be clearly a British action with the consequences upon the heads of their stubborn allies.

But in the case of three air forces (possibly intellectually interlinked), the doctrine of grand "strategic bombing" or of "the counterstrike deterrent" held sway. In Italy and in Britain the airpower enthusiasts were led to advocate a doctrine of offensive bombardment by the willingness of politicians to consider some other way to win the war than through appalling casualties for local ground actions, which brought no apparent result in a war of attrition. After the 1914 war, military men began to appreciate that no nation could fight another war with manpower losses anywhere near what had just been experienced. Instinctively people sought a weapon that would prevent another war from starting, or that would win a war in a very short order without terrible casualties to either side.

In Italy, the chief advocate of this cause was Gen. Guilio Douhet, though the impetus may have come from Count Caproni, a bomber manufacturer. The Italian situation reflected the frustration of the nineteen battles of the Izonso River and the Caporetto disaster in 1917, which Douhet had predicted. Douhet and Caproni could argue from the Italian geographical environment that provided a natural defensive position behind the Alps, from which there was little prospect of sallying. To Italy, air blows that would paralyze her adversaries made good sense as a defensive grand strategy.

But, ironically, the whole Italian approach lacked vitality for two reasons. First, when war came, it was fought not against a Continental power with vulnerable industrial centers, but in 1935 against primitive Ethiopians, and then, from 1940, against colonial British forces in East Africa and in the desolation of the Western Desert of North Africa. (The battle against France in 1940 was essentially over the corpse of the French state.) And second, not only was Italian equipment going out of phase in 1940 and 1941, but the Italian character was not that of the consistently aggres-

sive and successful Julius Caesar and the Roman legionary. Individually daring and superb fliers (who collectively became the Italian Air Force of World War II), with the exception of anti-shipping strikes, were ineffective. And Douhet's bombastic 1921 *The Command of the Air* fails to credit the enemy with any air defenses. Douhet also advocated the use of gas, but was ignorant of the problems of carrying it to the target and making it effective. And Mussolini's need politically to keep the services at odds, and his aggressive foreign policy, did not allow him to adopt what Italy could not afford, a grand-strategic bomber force.

American officers had some contact with Caproni, who tactfully had his doctrine printed in English, and strategic bombing and the concept of an independent air force for them went hand in hand. But they had no enemy and, equally significant, they had in the first crucial years Billy Mitchell as their mouthpiece. Mitchell was intellectually a plagiarizer, in the best military manner, and temperamentally a propagandist.

Mitchell's and Douhet's careers have a number of parallels, but the timing was significantly different. Douhet was court-martialed and imprisoned in 1916, but a turn of the tide of war (Caporetto in 1917) exonerated him, and the rise of Mussolini in 1922 catapulted him into a place of influence in a government determined to glorify Italy. Mitchell was just about three years too late. Isolationism lasted a full decade and a half after his 1925 court-martial. Even more ironically, although Douhet's name appeared in English as early as 1922, and some of his writings became available in the U.S. Army in 1933, his renaissance and fame in the English-speaking world did not come until the publication of the Dino Ferrari English translation of *The Command of the Air* in 1942. And then he was glorified because he was an outside expert who posthumously backed up the ideas of American air-power strategists.

In the meantime, what America really needed was an Air Corps leader like the U.S. Navy's later Hyman Rickover, someone who would be a quiet,

James Doolittle, a pioneer in blind-flying, was a technical genius of the U.S. Army Air Corps, with a Ph.D. from the Massachusetts Institute of Technology. In 1929, he made the first takeoff and landing "under the hood," using Sperry gyro instruments and funded by Guggenheim money. (USAF)

The epitome of a "hot" sport aircraft, the Beech Javelin (ER 0.48) of 1929, with NACA cowling and low-drag, spatted wheels. (Beech)

Well-dressed fighter pilots, circa 1929, in front of a U.S. Air Corps Boeing P-12 (ER 0.59)—the images of heroes in their aerobatic fighters with their white scarves blowing in the wind. (Lt. John Doherty)

Boeing F4B-3 fighters (ER 0.79) with telescopic gunnery sights, Townend ring cowled engines, and early arrester gear between the wheels. (Boeing)

The Boeing Company's first manufacturing plant became the initial wing of the Seattle Museum of Flight. The "Red Barn" opened in 1983 with exhibits focusing on the early days of aviation. The restoration of this historic 1909 structure was accomplished by the Seattle architectural firm of Ibsen Nelsen and Associates. The building is listed on the National Register of Historic Places. (Museum of Flight)

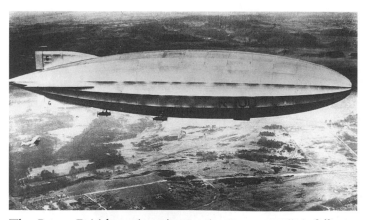

The R-100, British engineering genius Barnes Wallis's fully streamline rigid airship, crossed the Atlantic and back in 1930, only to be crushed by steamrollers in 1931 when the program was canceled. (Vickers)

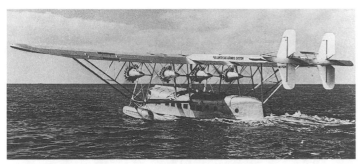

Pan Am's Sikorsky S-40 flying boat (ER n/a) of 1930 used the highly efficient, streamlined boat hull with the wing and tail high out of the spray from takeoffs and landings. (Pan Am)

The Supermarine S-6B (ER 0.496) in 1931 captured the Schneider Trophy for Britain at over 400 mph with a 2,300 hp engine. R. J. Mitchell's design was a decade ahead of fighter top speeds. This racer was remarkable for its fuel in the floats and radiators in the wings and fuselage skin. (Vickers)

The 1932 Martin B-10 (ER 4.19) was one of the aircraft beginning the technological revolution—a monoplane with a retractable undercarriage, fully cowled engines, and stressed-skin construction, and was the winner of the 1932 Collier Trophy for achievement in aviation. The Royal Thai Air Force was still flying these machines in 1946, when the author was an airfield controller with the Royal Air Force in Bangkok. (USAF)

The Ju-52/3m (ER 6.7) entered Lufthansa airline operations in 1932. An armada of these German transports had ferried Loyalist forces under Gen. Francisco Franco from Spanish Morocco to the motherland, the first tactical airlifts in history. The Loyalist "X" markings are seen here on the rudders.

One of the first United Air Lines types (1930s) was the radical new Boeing 247 (ER 3.84), a contemporary of the Martin B-10. It was a ten-passenger machine with a stewardess. (Boeing)

The increasing complexity of cockpits (as in this Boeing 247D) is evident in multi-engine aircraft fitted with autopilots to prevent pilot fatigue. (Boeing)

The monocoque construction of the Boeing 247D fuselage/cabin is well-illustrated here. Planes flew low enough and slow enough that large windows made the trips less boring in an unpressurized cabin. (Boeing)

knowledgeable, and able advocate of air power who could win the genuine support of Congress—or even a man like Gen. Amos Fries, who saved the U.S. Army's Chemical Warfare Service in 1919. As it was, after his court-martial, Billy Mitchell's Air Corps friends took up his legacy in the remote safety of Randolph Field, Texas, and evolved an offensive doctrine of grand-strategic bombing. They believed that the advent of the Boeing B-17A Flying Fortress in 1935 gave them their victory weapon.

The Second World War was to prove how overly optimistic they were and to what extent they, like most airmen, overestimated the power of the 500-pound bomb and underestimated the toughness of populations either inured to hardship as in Spain and China, endowed with a stoic outlook as in Japan, or stiffened with veterans of trench warfare as in Britain and Nazi-dominated Germany. Moreover, by the Second World War, the novelty of air power, and the horror leading to panic with which it had been viewed in 1914–18, had worn off. Women evacuated from London in September 1939 returned that same night, preferring to face bombs in a familiar environment rather than the unknown of a blacked-out countryside. The U.S. Army Air Corps in 1941 had bomber advocates firmly entrenched in its leadership, when in fact it needed armor-oriented tactical airmen. This is not to say that the Air Corps did not develop tactical doctrine and planes; but in terms of the war that had to be fought, the emphasis turned out to be unbalanced and had to be reshaped in the cauldron of battle to include fighters and fighter-bombers.

Yet, for all this, the inevitable must be recognized—that in the search for an independent and respectable identity, the brass of the U.S. Army Air Corps would seek out the one role—grand-strategic bombing—that appeared to free airmen from domination by the older service chiefs. Such action was a form of escapism, often politically necessary within the establishment, but marred by the vitriolic nature of the Mitchell crusade, which made it difficult to reconcile roles and budgets.

What happened in the United States was in many respects parallel to what happened in Britain, but as the British national character was more privacy, privilege, and Parliament conscious than the American, the battle was fought out largely behind closed doors, proving almost equally dangerous. One thing that can be said for the British pattern was that it probably owed absolutely nothing to Douhet, because Britain had produced its own air-power theorists—at least as early as the Italian general—in F. W. Lanchester, P. R. C. Groves, and Sir Frederick Sykes. It is questionable whether or not Trenchard would have adopted these grand-strategic bombing views had he not heard in 1921 that the French Generalissimo J. C. J. Joffre accepted them, had the Royal Navy not pushed the RAF over coastal defense, and had Trenchard, as head of the RAF, not become concerned about the organization's separate survival. Trenchard was a tactical and strategic man only in the limited army sense of those terms—that is, he was closer to a ground-bound Haig than to a grand-strategic Sykes.

In Britain, the RAF discovered that it could have three roles: colonial policing, air defense, and anti-invasion. In the interwar years it managed to keep its active squadrons largely abroad engaged in policing, while it argued at home for roles in air and coastal defense. It was awarded the former in 1922 and 1923 Cabinet decisions, and a Home Defence counterstrike deterrent force—composed two-thirds of bombers—was initiated. The logic of this decision was marred because antiaircraft equipment and troops were never placed under RAF command. Trenchard, in fact, did not want them; not only would they have hurt his budgets, but he did not believe that there really was a defense against bombers—the civilian population would just have to grin and bear it until the morale of the enemy population collapsed in an aerial war of attrition.

The argument that the bomber would always get through was in large measure true only because little work was done on defensive measures by offensively minded air marshals who refused to take into account the lessons of the 1915–18 air battle of London and set up exercises on World War I models. In fact, one of the problems of the postwar RAF was that Trenchard virtually hand-picked the officer corps from RFC veterans of the Western Front. Others, too, overlooked the study of all-around defense until their cities were attacked and political pressures upset rational defensive planning and diluted resources.

Yet it must also be remembered that what was said and what was done were two quite different things, as a study of RAF procurement shows. At the very time when the counterstrike deterrent force concept was accepted, when the Cabinet adopted as policy the idea that a weaker democracy could protect itself by threatening to devastate the cities of any potential aggressor, the RAF ceased to issue specifications for long-range heavy bombers. Instead, the cadre force maintained was equipped with medium bombers with a striking range inadequate for any target beyond Paris. The majority of the aircraft in the RAF were general-purpose machines designed to be used as fighter-bombers in colonial operations. Moreover, if the RAF was to play an anti-invasion role and if the torpedo was the weapon at sea, then surely it should have developed efficient armament for this work. But it did not, a point that the 1942 fall of Singapore showed—the one place in which the RAF was specifically charged with this duty.

In fairness to the RAF and to Trenchard, it should be noted that he concentrated much of the limited resources on creating a sound force of mechanics through the Halton School apprentice program and a proper officer cadre through the RAF College at Cranwell. And the RAF emerged victorious from the Second World War because its officer corps, old and new, was able to work in harmony on the operational level with its navy and army counterparts.

In France, Douhet's ideas had been accepted in the early 1920s and a good deal was done then to prepare a bomber striking force for use against any opponent; but in the 1930s, despite the use of French equipment in Spain, the whole conception sagged.

In contrast to the RAF and each other, the French Air Force and the new German *Luftwaffe* were on diametrically opposed paths. Before 1933, the FAF was called the *Aeronautique Militaire* of the army, and in the interwar years its reactive air doctrine stemmed from the requirements of the army as learned in World War I. The decline and fall of the French Air Force was due to a combination of international and national production difficulties, and inter- and intra-service fighting. Diplomatically and politically France supported disarmament in the years until the appearance of Adolf Hitler in Germany in 1933. Up until then, budgets had been very tight due to continuing economic depressions. In 1933, the new Air Minister, Pierre Cot, was able to order 1,010 aircraft, but the industry was on a peacetime workshop basis and could not produce them until modernized.

All through the period, bitter antagonism continued between soldiers who insisted the army needed its own air arm and the Douhetian grand-strategic bomberites in the air service. In the French Air Force, Douhet's supreme influence began to be eroded by Italian Col. Amadeo Mecozzi and the French Assistant Chief of the Air Staff, who both argued for small, fast, maneuverable fighter-bombers able to achieve surprise by flying very low, avoiding combat with the enemy, and then after dropping their bombs being able to fight their way home. While others, notably the Germans, developed these ideas, the French remained torn doctrinally between the concepts of a struggle for air superiority, before the grand battle on the ground took place, or cooperation, and Mecozzi's concept of attack aviation.

Hawker in Britain produced a series of land and naval biplanes powered by Rolls-Royce engines at the rate of 3½ per month from 1929 to 1935: the Fury/Nimrod (0.66); the Hart (ER 0.79), the Fury and Fury II (ER .7), an immensely popular open-cockpit single-seater. The Hurricane (ER 1.94) was essentially a monoplane Fury. (Hawker)

The USS *Lexington* and USS *Saratoga* (foreground), at anchor off Diamond Head, Hawaii, in 1933. The carriers were commissioned in 1929 after the conversion of two battlecruiser hulls under the 1922 Washington Naval Treaty. (Yarnell Historical Collection, Naval Historical Foundation)

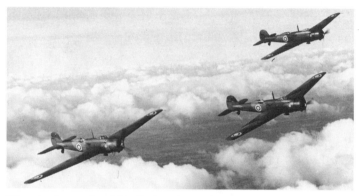

The single-engined Wellesley (ER 5.57) colonial bomber was designed by Barnes Wallis upon his move to Vickers Aircraft, Brooklands, near London, in 1933. Wallis developed the geodetic, basket-weave, metal airframe covered with doped canvas, used also on the Wellington. Three of the aircraft flew non-stop from Egypt to Australia in the 1930s, two of them completing 7,400 miles without refueling. Engine reliability had been achieved by the RAF after secret development trials of all service engines in the 1920s increased their reliability from 300 to 1,700 hours between overhauls. (Vickers)

The long-ranged Sikorsky S-42 (ER 15.5) of the trans-Pacific service of Pan American Airways, 1934. Flying boats required less-expensive facilities than the runways for land planes. (Pan American Airways)

Capt. K. D. Parmentier, First Officer of the renowned KLM DC-2 *Uiver,* and Sir MacPherson Robertson, the organizer of the Great London to Melbourne Race of 1934, the "MacRobertson Air Race." Note the naval legacy in the airman's uniform. The *Uiver* set records in its class of heavy aircraft in the race. (KLM)

The Douglas DC-2 *Uiver* (ER 8) of KLM, a radically new aircraft type. (KLM)

The Boeing P-26 "Peashooter" (ER 0.86) became the standard U.S. Army Air Corps fighter starting in 1934, with deliveries to the 20th Pursuit Group. The aircraft was a popular low-wing monoplane, and each machine had its own pilot and a crew chief. (USAF)

These P-26 Peashooters were still in America's first line of fighters in 1941; they were just being replaced by Seversky P-35s (ER 3.9) and Curtiss P-36s (ER 1.61) and P-40s (ER 2.5). America was about two years, at least, out of the cycle of fighter development. (USAF)

The P-26A cockpit, seen here from the bottom of the pilot's seat, was remarkably clean and simple. (USAF)

The world's largest and technologically leading air force in 1934 was the Soviet. Here the four-engined Tupolev TB-3 (ER 27) drops parachutists in 1934 maneuvers from over the wings. The Soviets had made remarkable progress from 1922, when they had no air force. The country, being roadless and with few railways, was ideal for aviation. (USAF)

The famous 1935 Douglas DC-3 (ER 19.14), a more stream-lined and higher-powered evolution of the company's DC-2. It became the standard by which other aircraft were judged, and the question of a suitable successor was debated long after World War II. In 2003, some fifty were still in airline service, and more in the various world's air forces. The last USAF DC-3 went to the U.S. Air Force Museum in Dayton, Ohio, in August 1975, and an Eastern Air Lines machine hangs in the National Air and Space Museum in Washington, D.C. (Eastern Air Lines)

The 1935 Grumman F3F-1 (ER 1) fighter for the U.S. Navy. Grumman Aircraft Engineering Company was staffed by naval aviators and became known for the rugged quality of its aircraft. Along with Douglas Aircraft Co., it was a principal supplier of machines for the USN through World War II and into the twenty-first century. (Grumman Historical Center)

European airlines used stewards, and American airlines employed registered nurses as stewardesses—now both called flight attendants—until they got married. Into the 1970s, the airlines maintained the image of attractive young women as *ex officio* salespersons. Here, stewardesses of Boeing Air Transport, the forerunner of United Air Lines, stand before a Boeing Model 80A (ER 2.0) airliner of the 1930s. (Boeing)

Left: The Boeing Model 80A (ER 2.0) was one of the last of the trimotored biplanes. It was soon to be eclipsed by the DC-2 (ER 8) and its larger derivative, the famed DC-3 (ER 19.14). (Boeing)

Due to this great doctrinal uncertainty, the French Air Force entered World War II mentally and militarily unprepared, and very short of modern aircraft. The FAF slowly declined, paralyzed by its vision of the "air menace." It had battled the army regarding tactical support, it had sought independence—granted in 1933, but then it had been hit by the nationalization of the aircraft industry (but not design offices) by the Socialist Popular Front in 1936 and its privatization in 1939. This latter interlude stultified design in a force that was both obsolescent and over-age. The defensive side of the Maginot Line became the mindset, and thus the FAF was run over by the *Blitzkrieg* of 1940. In twenty-one years, *L'Armée de l'Air* went from first to last.

At much the same time, the *Luftwaffe,* forbidden to be an air force, did not emerge until 1935, two years after Hitler came to power. The grounded years allowed the General Staff talents of the old German army to be exercised in planning. As a result, the *Luftwaffe* suddenly appeared upon the scene with doctrine, strategy, tactics, and glider-trained pilots ready to man the new modern aircraft that were rushed out of factories to achieve a psychological surprise. All of this stimulated the RAF, for one, to start a series of expansion plans to rearm as rapidly as possible its first-line force (though without reserves or doctrine). Moreover, by 1939 the *Luftwaffe* had had the benefits of participation in the Civil War in Spain, but the RAF and FAF had not.

The Germans in 1939 were geared for *Blitzkrieg,* which combined air and surface forces; the RAF and the French still disdained that sort of tactical approach.

The important change in the United States came not in the Army Air Corps Act of 1926 but in the MacArthur-Pratt Agreement of 1931 and in the Baker Board recommendations of 1934. The MacArthur-Pratt Agreement provided that U.S. Army bombers would assume responsibility for coast defense, thus freeing the USN for offensive roles, which the new carriers made attractive.

And the Baker Board, though rejecting the idea of an independent air force, did agree to the establishment of the General Headquarters Air Force, which would have central control in order to be able to strike in any direction. These two decisions coincided with the technological revolution, whose first fruit was the Martin B-10 twin-engined bomber (ER 4.19), which had barely entered service before the prototype four-engine Boeing YB-17 (ER 24) appeared. The 1934 Air Corps "Project A" request for an aircraft that could carry a one-ton bomb 5,000 miles was not met, due to cost. In fact, the Army Air Corps was so strapped for funds that the first orders for B-17s were very small; cheaper aircraft were being purchased instead. In 1938, a B-17 squadron intercepted a liner 725 miles at sea to demonstrate the Army's ability to frustrate attacks on the U.S. coast, and the Army and Navy Joint Board supported the Army general staff in saying that nothing bigger or longer-ranged than the B-17 would be needed—a vote of confidence that nearly killed Boeing's B-29 Superfortress (ER 414) of later long-ranging Pacific fame. And thus, when the war came, the United States had no aircraft capable of being a grand-strategic—let alone an intercontinental—bomber.

Doctrinal and technological developments were enmeshed in political problems. For air forces to grow in peacetime they had to convince either military or political superiors, or both, that they could play a more economical role than some other arm in national defense, or that they were the only shield against certain hazards. Unfortunately, these two roles might produce incompatible equipment, and, with only limited funds available, compromise or calculated risk were unavoidable. They led either to general-purpose aircraft most suited to colonial operations, or to an investment in a very limited number of squadrons flying up-to-date craft, supposedly prototypes for an expanded procurement that rarely came. And too often these hand-crafted prototypes proved unsuitable for mass production.

Airline Development and Aircraft Production

Coupled to the interwar years' serious dichotomy between theory and practice were two linked problems: airlines and the aircraft industry. Of all the nations in the world, only the United States probably had the climate, the wealthy population, and the distances to make the development of airlines feasible. Although the Russians lacked a wealthy population, they saw air travel both as a national status symbol and as the solution to the lack of roads and rails on their vast land mass. The Germans, however, had no such outlet for their aerial energies, but the British, French, and Dutch had their empires.

Due to technological problems, costs, distances, weather, and public reluctance—combined in some cases with subsidy problems and mail payments—airline development was slow. Although it was true that by the end of the 1930s both the Atlantic and the Pacific had been spanned, so that it was theoretically possible to fly around the world commercially, the lines were still very small.

In order for airlines to succeed, they needed aerodromes with fuel, food, passenger facilities with hotels, and landing and navigation aids. But airports were regarded as money-losing, noisy liabilities or nuisances. Yet, to the contrary, Claude Grahame-White had established Hendon as the London Aerodrome in 1912 and soon attracted up to 50,000 people each weekend to see the show put on by professional and private pilots. After the war he failed to get it derequisitioned from an official to a private property, and the RAF took over first the shows and then the whole facility.

In the United States, aerodromes needed enabling legislation and to be on one of the lighted airmail airways. The site and development of airports reflected lobbying abilities related to boosterism and public policies connected to economic and national defense necessities. Up to the Air Mail Act of 1926, local initiative was haphazard, but stimulated by the Postal Service, to obtain refueling stops along the airways for private mail contractors. After 1926, those who could afford to fly supported the placement of airfields in their locality, to put their cities "on the map," and they began to see the necessity for professional management. And the need for all-weather runways caused the planning budgets to increase.

President Franklin D. Roosevelt's New Deal from 1933 made relief funds available, and the technological revolutions made federal support of municipal ownership highly desirable. By the time of the 1938 Air Commerce Act, airports and even airfields for personal fliers were recognized as necessary. That view was also supported by the armed forces' search for fields the military could use, both in the Sun Belt from Norfolk, Virginia, south around to about San Francisco—especially as war approached.

In the USSR, airports were less costly, as a design requirement for all Russian aircraft up to the Mikoyan-Gurevich MiG-29 (ER 157) of 1975 was that they be able to operate from grass or snow.

Only in the latter half of the twentieth century did planning permission become a major delaying and deterrent factor worldwide. Earlier, both in spite of and because of the Great Depression, airports came into being.

The rise of Adolf Hitler in Germany and of Franklin D. Roosevelt in the United States coincided with the beginning of the technological revolution. The arrival of all-metal monoplanes with useful economic characteristics took place in the mid-thirties, starting with the German Junkers Ju-52 (ER 6.7, 1929); the Ford Trimotor (ER 3); the American Boeing 247 (ER 3.84, 1932); the Douglas DC-3 (ER 19.14, 1936); and the American Sikorsky S-42 (ER 15.5, 1934), Boeing 314 (ER 109.7, 1941), British Short S-23C Empire (ER 11.8, 1936), and German Dornier Wal Do-26A (ER 98.3) flying boats. These made airlines profitable and affordable.

Lambert Field, St. Louis, was one of the first to get concrete runways in 1928 due to the need for all-weather, snow-clearable facilities for scheduled air transport. And gradually the new airfields acquired terminals, hangars, and plane-watching balconies, as well as blind-landing facilities and radio ranges upon which airliners could home.

In European countries, the state created major airports and provided air routes, and after World War II, air-traffic control facilities. The war itself immensely stimulated the building of concrete runways and permanent facilities, which became available for postwar civilian uses worldwide.

On international routes the airlines held out the carrot of air connections and the stick of backwater status to get airports built. As the size, speed, and range of aircraft increased, less important places were relegated to lesser service. However, growth rates still made these smaller airports attractive, even as this rate slowed annually from 14 percent in the 1950s–60s to 2–4 percent in the 1990s.

In Europe the civil aviation divisions of the Air Ministries regulated, inspected, and investigated; in the United States this was the job first of the Bureau of Air Commerce, and then from 1938 of the Civil Aeronautics Board, which was sunsetted in 1978. In the meantime, American mayors called for airfields as part of boosterism, and independent accident investigation offices began to publish their reports in the name of public safety.

In 1936, airlines in the United States sold more than one million tickets. By 1939–41, civil aviation was here to stay. Included in this were general aviation flying clubs and the private ownership of aircraft, made possible by the arrival of inexpensive, simple light machines such as the de Havilland Moth (ER 0.12), which the young Englishwoman Amy Johnson flew solo from England to Australia in 1930, as the holder of the first British female aircraft engineer's license. Aviation had come of age, and the open cockpit was soon comfortably enclosed.

Strangely, however, when war came on the horizon again in late 1939, air-power leaders, though controlling a highly mobile weapon, failed to understand the role of air transport. Except for the Germans, they still thought of 1914-style trench warfare. Just as in the First World War when an immediate mobilization of skilled workers seriously hampered munitions production, so in the Second—at least in Britain, where the airlines were just being nationalized—both men and equipment were siphoned off to the RAF for other purposes, to indicate again the lack of foresight in peacetime. The German and Soviet air forces, however, being tactical in outlook, had integrated transports into their systems for paratroop operations by the late 1930s.

Fortunately, in the United States, an aircraft industry did exist that was attuned to air transport, and in 1938, stimulated by Anglo-French orders, the relative plethora of available airline managers in 1941 enabled the industry to capture control of the military air transport system, seeing it as a heaven-sent means of acquiring knowledge of international air routes.

In a number of respects, the confusions that had plagued disarmament discussions until 1934 over the ability to convert transports into bombers stayed internationally in the minds of some air force officers. In an unsophisticated way, they continued the peacetime habit of specifying bomber-transports, which were generally neither one thing nor the other. In the 1920s, the differences between bombers and transports were not great, but as airline management came out of the war-surplus era, it began to demand reliability and ease of maintenance, coupled with economy of operation. This led to certification problems, as the testing standards were those of the military, which controlled aviation, and not of the civil operators. But even before the 1930s technological revolutions, the bomber and the airliner were moving apart, for the needs of airline managers were in direct conflict with stated military demands. Airlines had no use for the many things that the military tended to hang on the outside, like bombs and guns, which could cause a machine that might start out with an aerodynamically clean configuration

In the 1930s, at the beginning of the modern simulator industry, the inventor, Edwin A. Link stands with one of the first Link trainer models. The author took his initial test for pilot training in an open cockpit version in 1943, and later in 1944 flew blind, under the hood, of the more sophisticated version. By the end of the twentieth century, simulators could reproduce combat conditions. The great advantage of the Link trainer was that it saved money and lives. (Singer)

Designed as Coastal Command reconnaissance aircraft, the 1936 Avro Anson (ER 2.38) had too limited range, bomb-capacity, and speed. It was soon used as a service trainer and light transport. Aerodynamically perfect for its day, however, it could be landed blind using the Lorenz standard beam approach (SBA). The aircraft shown is in Israeli Air Force livery after the War of Independence of 1948. (Israeli Air Force)

One of the first fighter fruits of the technological revolution, the 1937 Seversky P-35 (ER 3.9) included a variable-pitch propeller, NACA cowling, retractable undercarriage, flaps, cantilever wings, monocoque all-metal construction, and an enclosed cockpit. An initial group of the P-35 was sold to Sweden, but the aircraft were commandeered and sent to the U.S. Army Air Forces in the Philippines in 1941. (USAF Museum)

The 1936 Beech CH-17R Staggerwing (ER 1.1) featured negative stagger with the bottom wing ahead of the top, and a retractable undercarriage. It became a classic. (Beech)

The rugged, heavy-lift 1936 Noorduyn AT-16 Norseman (ER 1.16),with wheels, skis, or floats, proved to be an excellent bush aircraft in the Canadian north. Painted bright training yellow for visibility in white expanses, it soldiered on for years. This one is preserved at the Canadian National Aviation Museum. (Canadian National Aviation Museum)

The crew's compartment on the 1937 Boeing XB-15 (ER 145), gives some idea of the quantum leap in size that took place in the 1930s, and the increasing complexity of instrumentation. This was the largest and heaviest aircraft to have been built in the United States to that date. (USAF)

Only one experimental Douglas XB-19 (ER n/a) intercontinental bomber was built, but its data and features would be incorporated into the generations that matured between 1936 and 1946. The XB-19 was under-powered, as engines lagged behind airframes at this period. (USAF)

The 1937 Vickers Wildebeeste IV (ER 1.7) was a general-purpose aircraft also usable as a torpedo bomber. (Vickers)

The Red (Soviet) Air Force produced the highly maneuverable Ilyushin Il-16 (ER 1.29), which fought in the Spanish Civil War in 1937. In 1984, a former German test pilot told the author that it was the most unstable aircraft he had ever flown—thus making it in many ways an ideal fighter. (USAF)

The Italian Regia Aeronautica enjoyed an undeservedly low reputation in World War II. One of its accomplishments was its 1937 use of the Savoia-Marchetti SM-79 (ER 16.6) bomber, tested in the Spanish Civil War, on anti-shipping strikes in the Mediterranean. (Italian Air Force)

This historical photograph is of interest because it shows the Bristol Blenheim I high-speed bomber (ER 7.28), which was forced upon the RAF by a wealthy former Secretary of State for Air; and it is also of interest for its provenance. The author found the picture in the SHAA archives at Chateau Vincennes, France, in 1987. The Blenheims were identified as aircraft of No. 139 Squadron, RAF, in France during 1939–40. But the scenery was wrong, the aircrew were in shorts, and the hangars in the background were of a standard RAF pattern. Eventually, the setting was traced to No. 84 Squadron in Ambala, India, in 1937. (SHAA)

The Boeing 314 flying boat (ER 109.7) was ordered by Pan Am in the late 1930s for both Pacific and Atlantic routes. BOAC acquired three for its wartime trans-Atlantic services from Lisbon via the Azores to Baltimore. (BOAC)

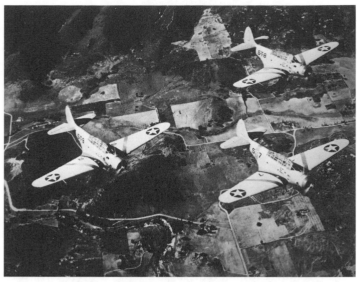

Douglas TBD Devastators (ER 3) in colorful USN markings of the late 1930s. Nearing the end of their operational life, all those committed to the Battle of Midway in late May 1942 were shot down. (USN)

At the Swiss Air Force Meet near Zurich in 1937, the Italian Air Force aerobatic team flew Fiat CR-32s (0.87). The derivative of the C-32 was the CR-42 (ER 1.36), which later fought in the Battle of Britain and in the Western Desert in 1940. (Swiss Air Force)

The highly successful light biplane, the de Havilland DH-82 Moth (ER 0.12) was derived from the basic design of 1924 and remained in service as a trainer in various Commonwealth air forces until after 1945. A DH-82 is seen here on parade with the Arab Legion Air Force. (Royal Jordanian Air Force)

Also seen at Zurich in 1937 was one of the first of the new *Luftwaffe* bombers, the Dornier Do-17A (ER 6.96). (Swiss Air Force)

to lose this during modification to service specifications. Thus, airliners led the way into the economic and technological revolutions.

In the years 1934–45, the aviation world had to learn how to create, build, and maintain—as well as man—ten revolutions: airframe developments, engines, high-octane fuel, all-metal construction, airfields with concrete runways rather than grass, electronics, navigation instead of observation, computers, then jet engines, and nuclear weapons.

Operationally, airlines tended to lead the way in navigation and in night flying, though naval airmen were quite sophisticated in this. Some of the conflicts that developed within air forces during the Second World War came from the interaction of traditional officers with airline personnel. In part, the latter's standards were higher because they had accumulated far more experience and skill in the same time frame. Airlines aimed for an annual utilization per aircraft of some 2,000 hours per year, whereas the military might get 200. Airline men were frequently ex-officers whose ambitions could not be satisfied under peacetime military conditions, and they regarded themselves as professional airmen and the military as amateurs.

Airlines developed cautiously because their survival depended upon fare-paying passengers and freight, and because they were the most heavily supervised of all transportation systems. Moreover, they had stockholders who demanded profits before further investments. They tended to choose those routes on which there was the least competition from ground transport. All over the world, this story was about the same.

Some companies folded as their war-surplus equipment was destroyed and they could no longer raise capital for new machines. Others merged, voluntarily or otherwise, in order to obtain subsidies or mail payments. By 1930, the modern airline system had a basic structure. Then a second generation of small operators moved in to feed the bigger systems and were themselves eventually merged into larger companies. In the meantime,

the main air routes were being pioneered: by the Dutch KLM to the East Indies; Air France to Indochina and Africa; Lufthansa within Europe and into the Soviet Union; and Imperial Airways to South Africa, Australia, Hong Kong, and New York, in conjunction with Pan American, which also operated to South America and across the Pacific. In operating all of these lines, whether they were state companies such as Lufthansa and Air France, or semi-private such as KLM, or subsidized like Pan American and Imperial Airways, political contacts at home and abroad counted for as much as technology. The directors of these companies fought a constant war against international competition and waste, and thus when they had to buy aircraft or run a military air transport service, they tackled the job with "combat" experience behind them.

Airline equipment orders in the 1930s were limited, though in terms of airframe material weight, a large, passenger flying boat of 1935 was the equivalent of a squadron of fighters. For a handful of companies, then, airline orders were more rewarding than military orders. And after 1935, there was a chance of making a reasonable profit on them, while at the same time developing the latest technology with a design team attuned to performance and maintenance economics— points that were not without value in military design and fly-off competitions. But at the same time, the total technological revolution began to bring American dominance with the emergence of the fast Boeing, Douglas, and Lockheed airliners. War gave American manufacturers an additional developmental advantage, but that it was so great was in part Europe's own fault for failing to understand the need for transport aircraft in war.

A close and interesting link between the military, the airlines, and the aircraft manufacturers was the rigid airship. Although Japanese and Italian efforts were limited to blimps or semi-rigids, the Germans, Americans, and British experimented with the more technologically advanced dirigibles. These great streamlined beasts were both successes and failures—civil and military, political and commercial. They might have served as very-long-range scouts and transports, as indeed the *Graf Zeppelin* did, but on the whole they suffered the fate of peripheral weapons in peacetime. Their development was stopped by the deaths of their leading proponents, including Rear Admiral Moffett, in well-publicized crashes, two of which *(R-101* and *Hindenburg)* might not have been fatal had the United States seen fit to export helium.

But the basic problem of these lighter-than-air ships was that they were too expensive, too slow in gestation and development to compete with the technological progress of the airplane, and too unwieldy on the ground. The cost of docking and housing them, as much as anything else, was their downfall, for it limited their use to specific routes, in spite of the apparent lessons of the *Graf Zeppelin's* South American service, which showed that airships could operate trans-oceanic voyages without great investment in ground facilities. Yet for all this, the rigid airship contributed significantly to technological developments in terms of structures and stress measurement, streamlining, and diesel engines.

One other aspect of aircraft production deserves mention. When rearmament began in the mid-1930s, a number of problems arose. First, the ever-changing and thus skaky beginnings of war preparations—rearmamental instability—coincided with the technological revolutions. This meant that on a short time-line, both designers and production engineers had to learn new techniques with new materials. Moreover, as the switch-over from wooden airframes took place, capital costs rose sharply because metal-working machine tools had to replace those of carpenters. And this, in turn, demanded a labor force with new skills at a time when every other defense and new-consumer industry was competing for talent in an evaporating labor market.

For some, the American dominance began to be felt because it was the Yankees who had taken the lead in developing machine tools. The Germans, it is true, had them and presses, but in 1934 they were engaged in their own revolution. They were quietly tooling-up secret aircraft factories, which were putting into production the types that would suddenly, with a public announcement from Hitler in March 1935, boost the *Luftwaffe* from last to near first place among the world's air forces—not so much because of numbers as because of the appearance overnight of what seemed to be a fully trained, cohesive, and coherent modern air force with the latest equipment. The whole emergence of the *Luftwaffe* was a consummate piece of showmanship, and it was effective.

The British and the French thus began a hasty rearmament, continuing to produce the same obsolete types in order to provide production and training experience. The start of rearmament in 1934, after the collapse of the Geneva Disarmament talks in that year, found Britain and France in an awkward position politically, economically, doctrinally, and technically. Pacifist movements divided Great Britain. And a severe social-political rift took place in France, while the newly decreed, independent *L'Armée de l'Air* had to make doctrinal concessions to win the approval of the Chamber of Deputies; the FAF thus ended up with the compromise bomber-combat-reconnaissance aircraft.

The RAF was still ordering biplanes, but new designs reflecting the technological revolution would appear in the 1936–37 period. Both the RAF and the FAF were short of fighters, but at least the RAF had a defensive doctrine proved in the 1920s air exercises. The French saw an "air menace," but not the means to defeat it. In fact in 1937, they approached Britain about having the RAF defend France.

Not until 1938 did the French aircraft industry begin to produce modern aircraft, and even then the FAF lacked the aircrew and mechanics to make them operational. The Air Ministry in London, on the other hand, had begun to pump out expansion schemes and orders starting in 1934 and had also begun a shadow factory scheme for new production, managed by automobile makers with aircraft industry guidance, and established west of a theoretical bomb line, beyond the reach of the Germans. And later Lord Nuffield, the auto magnate, was brought in to manage the Civil Repair Organization to rebuild damaged and salvaged warplanes.

Critical to the expansion of aircraft production and to the air forces was the competition for man and woman power. The men were more essential, due to the services' needs for mechanics and the army's need for soldiers. Ultimately this led to a fight to break the seven-years' apprentice approach to training and to dilute both industry and the armed services with short-course technical personnel supervised by experienced "masters."

The technological revolution increased the development time for a fighter to four years, six for a medium bomber, and eight for a heavy bomber. Thus, when war broke out, the RAF was by no means fully modernized—the heavy bombers not becoming operational until mid-1941. At the same time, the number of types in production or in service had to be pruned from fifty-nine to a more manageable figure. An acute crisis had come in September 1938 when the politicians gave away Czechoslovakia at Munich, and when Fighter Command was defenseless between the phasing out of the old biplane fighters and the introduction and working up of the new Supermarine Spitfires and Hawker Hurricanes. Both the French and British would really have liked to have waited into 1942 before going to war, as would the Nazi navy.

Though the Air Ministry had given Rolls-Royce and others cost-plus-10-percent development contracts, the British aircraft industry as a whole was never stimulated fully to give up its old ways and to go on a three-shift working schedule throughout the war. The French industry never had such a chance, as it was pillaged by the German occupation of 1940–44. German industry, on the other hand, was early on a war footing.

If the industries benefitted increasingly from the technical reports published on their testing by such establishments as Langley in the United States, Villacoublay in France, Farnborough in Britain, Rechlin in Germany, and the TSAGI-TSIAM complex in Moscow, mechanics' tools proved to be an Achilles heel in the RAF until mid-1943 in the Far East. This was coupled to the shortage of spares, due to lack of conceptualization of the nature of war on the part of finance officers who would not approve such gross expenditures.

It was another five years before the fledgling American aviation industry received orders from its own government, though it managed to get through much of the first part of its own rearmamental instability with British and French orders and financing. Meanwhile, the Soviet Air Force had initiated its five-year plans from 1928, and was busy turning out tactical aircraft, some of which were still copies of Western designs, but others that were ahead of them. Much the same thing happened in Japan, except that Japanese designers took over from the European machines they had imported and began to produce their own long-range, high-performance aircraft for the incidents in China that led up to full-scale war, and other possible actions. In all these developments, skilled management became as critical a commodity as raw materials, machine tools, and know-how.

At this same time, the revolution or conversion of airfields from omni-directional grass to concrete runways (made necessary by weather, increasing aircraft weights, and high usage), in turn created the need for earth-movers and for runway-laying machines to spread very large quantities of concrete. War would then force a requirment for additional and widely dispersed facilities across the country for both aircraft and personnel, as well as the development of portable airfield surfaces, such as the perforated-steel-plate (PSP) of World War II. In the late 1930s, an airfield took five years to build, by 1944 less than five days.

The gradual improvements in wireless telegraph (W/T) and radio telephone (R/T) communications was followed from the mid-thirties by the independent development of radar by the

U.S. Navy, the Royal Air Force, and the *Luftwaffe*. Still in its infancy in 1940, radar only really became effective in 1942–43 when it was developed also into navigational sets, which allowed aircraft to fix their own positions and, with another set, to bomb through cloud cover or to detect surfaced U-boats. The vital link for air defense was operational vectoring from the ground, a central control function. Computerized bombsights, as well as the jet engine, did not become operational until roughly 1944.

In this study of the history of air power, the low level of peacetime aircraft usage during the interwar years must not be overlooked. And the peacetime use of aircraft in military maneuvers resulted in artificial statistics, for there was no absence of long-term professional pilots as well as skilled professional maintenance. Both of these factors thus led to a failure to find flaws in the then-current aviation machinery. Modern accident analysis can be used to show that when pilots fly a small number of hours per month, as they did before the war broke out, they are much more accident-prone, in contrast to wartime, when intensive aircraft and aircrew usage became the rule. The one grim advantage of crashes, in terms of technical progress, was that they did dispose of obsolete aircraft that would not otherwise be retired and replaced.

For a long time in the 1920s and 1930s, crashes started with engine failure, and pilots were then blamed for improper use of throttle and then bungling a forced landing. Only in the 1930s did accident investigation and adamant pilots reveal airframe failures due to either material defects or mechanics' errors.

On the other hand, the rate of engine failure, which had been one for less than three hours flying in World War I, was raised in the RAF in the 1920s to one about every 1,700 hours, making pilots much more comfortable on colonial operations over hostile tribes. (Lindbergh's 1927 trans-Atlantic flight was another proving of reliability.) In peacetime, military aircraft usage involved limited numbers of any one type, and thus often no more than enough for one squadron were ordered, with a few spares. Manufacturers, able to count on only a trickle of government orders, still tended to hand-build most aircraft. Thus, peacetime aircraft factories were design establishments with workshops attached, and flaws were ironed out by the shop foreman or the armed service. When in the late 1930s rearmament began and demands for aircraft rose from 1½ per month to 600, at a time when amateur management and unskilled workers had to be employed in the midst of technological revolutions, errors in mass-production multiplied. The many modifications and masses of paperwork had to be passed on to production establishments in "shadow"—hidden—and in other factory locations that were no longer simply across the corridor from the designer's office. Moreover, spares needed were not calculated until after eighteen months of flying. These problems had a significant effect on the war to come, as did the fact that squadrons tended to develop their own flying techniques, with a consequent lack of uniformity throughout the service.

Small air forces in the interwar years had troubles surviving, especially if they, even more than the European powers, faced no apparent enemies. This led to the few available airplanes often flying on survey and forest-fire missions, and to problems of leadership. In Australia, for much of the period, two officers alternated as Chief of the Air Staff, one being posted overseas when the other was in command.

On the other hand, the 1920s and 1930s saw the emergence of small airline companies, which began to make money with or without state subsidies. And once the post-1935 all-metal aircraft appeared, then Imperial Airways and British Airways (1936) in England, Air France, Lufthansa, SwissAir, Aeroflot, KLM of the Netherlands, Qantas of Australia, South African Airways, Pan American (PAA), United (UAL), American (AA), Eastern (EAL), Trans World (TWA), Canadian Pacific (CPA), and Trans-Canada (now Air Canada), and others

The Interwar Years

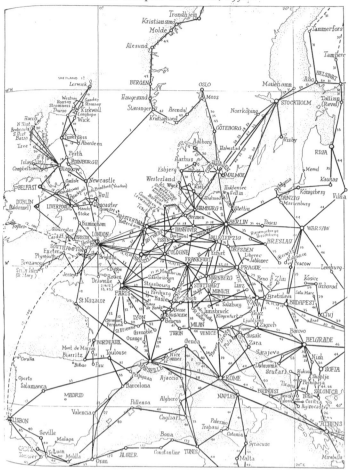

The European Air Routes, 1938

In spite of bad weather and excellent rail service, the European airline network was quite sophisticated by 1938, in part as a result of the introduction of more comfortable, modern airliners, some with all-weather and night-flying capabilities, such as the Lufthansa Ju-52 (ER 6.7). *(The Aeroplane)*

Italian light bombers of the 1938 Breda BA 88 type (ER 9) are here drawn up for inspection before war was declared. (Italian Air Force)

The Fairey Fox (ER 0.716) was a radical design in 1926, built around the Curtiss D-12 motor. Sir Hugh Trenchard, Chief of the Air Staff, Royal Air Force, wanted many of these fighters, but was only allowed to buy one squadron because of domestic pressure. This example is one of a small number bought by the Swiss Air Force and used until about 1938. (Swiss Air Force)

Entering operations just before the war began in 1939, the Morane-Saulnier MS-403 (ER 1.6) was the best of the new 1938 French Air Force fighters. However, shortages of aircrew and mechanics made the force less than effective. This example is a Swiss license-built D-3801 (ER 1.78) of 1944, preserved in the Swiss Transportation Museum at Luzern. Another example is in the French Air Museum at Le Bourget, France. (Postcard)

The early models of the Boeing B-17 Flying Fortress (ER 25.8, B-17B; ER 75.98, B-17G) suffered heavily in early operations from inadequate defensive armament and too optimistic a reading of their superior speed. The more widely used versions, from the E model on, had thirteen .50-caliber guns, and their ammunition was equal to the bomb load carried; but they still lost heavily when unescorted in the realities of 1943 modern air war. (USAF)

C. L. "Kelly" Johnson, the famed Lockheed Aircraft Corp. designer, is shown here in 1938 working a test flight shortly after arriving in Burbank, California. He created the famed "Skunk Works," (named after a building in the "Lil' Abner" comic strip), from which everyone, including the president of the company, was banned. His last product from that secret establishment was the stealth, Mach 3 SR-71 Blackbird (ER 2,040).

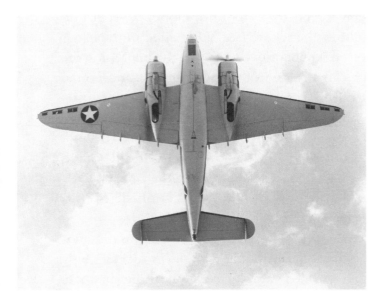

The famous Johnson plan-form that would be used from the Lockheed 18 Hudson (USAAF A-28) (ER 14) through the P-38 Lightning (ER 8, P-38J) and the Constellation airliners (ER 114, C-69; ER 124, L-749; ER 595.8, L-1649). These machines and their derivative, the PV-1 Ventura (ER 23.2), had a dangerous power-on snap-roll stall, to offset which slots, visible here, were inserted into the outer wing panels to increase airflow at low speeds. (Lockheed)

An early Kelly Johnson design was the Lockheed 10A (ER 3.17) of Trans-Canada Airways, a fast, small, passenger liner. (Lockheed)

The Grumman F4F Wildcat (ER 3.9) of 1939 was a rugged prewar folding-wing, monoplane, shipboard fighter. (It was called the Martlet in the Royal Navy Fleet Air Arm.) The F4F remained on operations throughout World War II. By the time later models deployed to the Pacific, the pilots had 450 hours in the plane and regarded it as good as the F6F Hellcat (ER 12.2). (Grumman)

The Short S-23 Empire flying boat of Imperial Airways/BOAC in wartime markings (ER 11.8). The Sunderland (ER 63) was a military derivative. (BOAC)

gradually took off. World War II boosted some of these lines and curtailed others. The United States benefitted the most due to the mobilization of air transport in 1942, an action that had been made possible by the 1936 arrival of not only the Douglas DC-3 (C-47, ER 19.14) but also of the new Curtiss C-46 Commando (ER 36) and of the four-engined Douglas C-54 Skymaster (ER 122) and the Lockheed C-69 Constellation (ER 114). Other factors contributed to their worldwide use.

RECORD-BREAKING

The interwar years also saw a number of interesting specific developments in civil aviation. Record-breaking, for one, was an area in which the future of military aviation was preceded by about a decade.

In 1919, the Schneider Trophy contests for high-speed seaplanes were revived. These soon became international events. In 1923, the U.S. Navy entered a team with full official backing, and the French navy followed suit, though less enthusiastically. The Americans used Curtiss racers incorporating the radical new Curtiss D-12 in-line V engine and won with a speed of 177.38 mph. The contests then seesawed back and forth until the British, using Supermarine aircraft flown by a special RAF high-speed flight, ended the contest by winning the trophy for the third time in a row in 1931, with a speed of 340.6 mph. Just after that event, one of the Supermarine S-6Bs (ER 0.496) was flown to a world speed record of 407 mph, using a specially developed engine that gave 2,530 hp. In 1939, the Germans attained a record of 469 mph, flying a Messerschmitt Bf 109R "Racer" (ER n/a).

Other races, of course, were held, and the reasons for entering them were twofold: they attracted great publicity; and in a dull period they provided considerable excitement—especially as a running commentary could be given on the new public radio systems, and the races could be seen in newsreels at local cinemas. In theory, the winner brought in orders to the manufacturer and recruits to the services. But a more important reason for racing was the chance to prove engines and airframes under something like operational conditions. The Schneider Trophy aircraft led directly to fighter designs used in the Second World War. Experience was gained with monoplanes before the world's air forces were willing to accept them, and engines were boosted to horsepowers that would not become operational for another ten years or more. Contests for prestige provided a way in which both manufacturers and the armed services could put pressure on governments to fund experimental work.

Experimental work, of course, was the heart of peacetime air forces, because it enabled them to keep up-to-date, so that when a war might start, their equipment would match that of the enemy. The real problem lay in balancing an operational aircraft with a much better one on the designer's drawing board. To do this, money was put into prototypes, whose fate often rested in the hands of a test pilot or two and upon the impression the machine made in flying past the ground-bound top brass. In some air forces, however, the new machines had to pass aerial handling by senior officers, with results that were sometimes fatal to both. In other services, each mediocre aircraft arrived with a case of champagne, and the aircraft's evaluation was based more on its alcoholic than its octane rating.

Equal to speed in importance at this time was altitude, for the fighter with the greater climbing performance always had an advantage. In 1920, the Americans captured the altitude record at 33,000 feet; by 1933 it had been pushed up to 43,000; and in 1938 it went to the Italians with 56,000 feet. By 1942, photo- reconnaissance aircraft were operating at 50,000 feet. The benefits from pursuing these records accrued mostly in the area of cold-weather technology and meteorology, pressure suits, and oxygen systems. All of these were important to aviation medicine, in general, and to fighter, photo-reconnaissance unit (PRU), and bomber technology specifically, though for a long time not nearly enough attention was paid to crew comfort and flying fatigue.

Yet, in view of the avowed strategies of the British, American, and Italian air forces, and of their need to protect shipping, the records they should have been most interested in were for range. In attempting to span the greatest distance non-stop, men and machines faced many of the problems that bomber and ocean reconnaissance crews would have to combat. Long-range flight called for absolute reliability of engines, economy of operation, comfortable crew positions, and excellence at both day and night navigation. The machine used also had to be capable of lifting very large quantities of fuel. The first postwar attempts in 1919 were to cross the Atlantic and to reach the outer colonies of the European empires, and these experiments, mostly with war-surplus aircraft, focused on the long-distance record. In 1919, the British fliers Capt. John Alcock and Lt. Arthur Whitten Brown crossed the North Atlantic from Newfoundland to Ireland in a modified Vickers Vimy IV (ER 0.95). In the same year, the airship *R-34* (ER 700) flew to New York and back to Britain. In 1922, two intrepid Portuguese aviators crossed the South Atlantic in a single-engined seaplane. In 1925, the French held the record with a flight of 1,967 miles; by 1929 they had raised it to 4,911, but in 1938, the RAF captured it with 7,158 miles, an achievement made the more remarkable by the fact that the two Wellesley aircraft that accomplished this non-stop feat were single-engined, as was the Soviet aircraft, which apparently flew over the North Pole to California.

The 1924 flight of the U.S. Air Service Douglas World Cruisers (ER 3.07) averaged 72 mph for 365 flying hours in 125 days for 26,345 miles using five planes, fifteen engines, fourteen sets of pontoons, forty-two sets of wheels, and many propellers, as well as 27,000 gallons of petrol in two-gallon cans, 2,900 gallons of oil, and 480 different spares. Logistics required the placement of 91,800 gallons of gasoline and 11,650 gallons of oil either en route or on U.S. Navy or Coast Guard ships. The whole was a classic example of what could be done by advanced intelligence, planning, and inter-departmental cooperation.

The Italians, with their genius for showmanship, also undertook long-range mass-formation journeys. Gen. Italo Balbo led a massed formation of twelve Savoia-Marchetti S-55 flying boats (ER 15.7) across the Atlantic and back. The Italians also participated in polar flying and in giving aerobatic demonstrations, at which they excelled.

But again, peacetime and display formation tactics did not always prove as valuable as they were thought to be. What looked wonderful at an air display became vulnerable in combat, and it took real warfare to bring about more effective deployment. In fighter squadrons, the symmetrical V ("vic") of three was replaced with the German functional pair and a two-pair finger-of-four in the Spanish Civil War (1936–39). Bombers tended to group into defensive "hedgehogs" or flying boxes. In any case, apart from formation, the validity of a defensive system depended upon its firepower *vis-à-vis* opposing fighters and upon the provision of adequate close and distant fighter escorts.

The Private Eagles

As important as official flights were those by privately supported individuals, some of whom were lost at sea or in accidents. Among those were Sir Alan Cobham, who surveyed British Empire routes in a de Havilland DH-50 Moth; Bert Hinkler, who flew a light plane to Australia in nineteen days from England; and above all Charles Lindbergh of the United States, in May 1927, who flew a thirty-three-hour non-stop solo flight from New York to Paris in the single-engined Ryan aircraft, the *Spirit of St. Louis* (ER 0.48). Not only did Lindbergh's personality make for solid public relations in a depressed hero-hungry world, but aeronautically he proved the reliability of the air-cooled radial engine. He was a meticulous man who planned most carefully. And another pilot of note was the Frenchman Antoine de St. Exupéry, who wrote about his pioneering of airmail services in South America.

In addition to Anne Morrow Lindbergh and others, women aviators such as Amy Johnson of Britain, Amelia Earhart of the United States, and Hélene Boucher of France made their names in the romantic days of 1929–35, after which Hollywood stars took over the glamour roles. But there was a cluster of women who became pilots and went on to fly behind the lines in World War II, ferrying the same aircraft men flew in combat; and in the USSR, females became fighter pilots and other aircrew. As the industry accelerated, it once again began to employ women in substantial numbers, as did the armed services.

OPERATIONS

Fortunately, and perhaps ironically for their technical progress, some air forces were allowed to participate in occasional wars. In the conflicts of the 1920s, generally only one side had aircraft; but in the 1930s, several real tests took place.

The wars of the 1920s were mostly colonial skirmishes in which a European power—Britain, France, Italy, or Spain—equipped with a war-surplus squadron or two engaged in reconnaissance and punitive sorties with general-purpose aircraft against rebellious or over-exuberant tribesmen along the frontiers of valuable imperial holdings. The effects of these actions may well have been overrated, even though the British use of air policing was one of the major innovations in aviation and economics politically, and even though operations from Aden in southern Arabia went on for some forty-five years (a fact that raises some question as to their effectiveness). The British exercised air policing in Somaliland in 1919, and

then, to relieve the army and the Exchequer, took over in Iraq, Aden, and the Northwest Frontier of India—but not successfully in more populated Palestine. The process was usually a combination of observation and intelligence, political suggestion, warning leaflets or loudspeakers, and finally bombing and strafing, which generally produced more dust than damage. In addition to the general-purpose two-seater fighter-bomber and single-seaters, these actions also saw the use of twin-engine heavy bomber-transports, whose most spectacular action was the evacuation of the British colony from Kabul, Afghanistan, in 1928.

Although the RAF had twenty years of experience in air-control operations in the colonial theaters, it failed to translate these experiences into doctrine by 1939, and thus went to war unprepared for army cooperation/tactical air operations.

Air control, most useful in relatively barren areas where the locals could be seen, was exercised by the French in North Africa (Algeria) against the Rif in the Atlas mountains, in mandated Syria against the Arabs, and in Indo-China. The Spanish also used aviation against the Rif in Morocco.

Ethiopia

In many ways, the Italian campaign in Ethiopia in 1935–36 was also simply a colonial operation, as it pitted a modern army and air force against a feudal, medieval country. Yet in spite of the fact that the Italians enjoyed overwhelming air superiority and employed poison gas, and in spite of the internal dissensions of the Ethiopians and their faulty ground tactics, it took the Italians eight months to conquer the country and another year to finish pacifying it. And all this occurred at a time when the *Regia Aeronautica* was at its peak with new equipment and a fine professional force in its ranks. The use of gas aroused considerable ire, but it was not particularly effective in the field, and modern operational research analysts would probably argue that it was an inefficient weapon. Certainly, airborne gas was not favored by other air forces because it was easily protected against, in addition to being heavy to carry and awkward to dispense accurately.

Much more significant for the use of air power were two other conflicts, the wars in China and Spain, of which the latter was really known to Western advocates of air power. The Italian campaign in Ethiopia, however, was not as noteworthy.

China

The Manchurian Incident of 1931 coincided with the emergence of aircraft designed and built by the Japanese themselves. In the events that followed, Japanese air power was of first-class significance. In subsequent actions against China, the Japanese had things much their own way, for the sky held few Chinese fighters and virtually no bombers. The reasons for this were the old Chinese warlords, who constantly eroded the central control of Chinese forces, coupled with graft and inefficiency. In addition, many Chinese pilots were mercenaries who had arrived in the Far East claiming to be aces, but who, as U.S. Gen. Claire L. Chennault later found, could wreck a whole air force in a day by themselves.

Basically the lessons must be drawn from the Japanese side. With superior aircraft and airmen, they quickly dispatched the opposing air force by a combination of swift bombing attacks upon airfields and brisk fighter battles. Once freed from opposition, Japanese bombers engaged in grand-strategic raids against Chinese cities. At the same time, however, the Japanese tended to become over-confident, with the result that occasionally the remnants of the Chinese Air Force could strike a blow; on one occasion they caught Imperial Japanese Navy fighter and bomber squadrons drawn up in neat rows on a Chinese airfield and ruined nearly all 200 aircraft. And when in 1939 the Japanese found themselves compelled again to fight the Soviets along the northern Manchurian border, as they had off and on since 1929, they made little progress and were forced to fight a defensive air war to maintain the status quo on the ground at Nomohan.

Nevertheless, in the meantime, the Japanese had been getting valuable experience. Starting in the summer of 1937 they had undertaken long-range raids of some 1,250 miles in which naval Mitsubishi G3M (Type 96) (ER 34) Nell aircraft bombed the Chinese positions around Shanghai to support a beleaguered Japanese marine garrison there. Based on Kyushu and Formosa, the Nells made long over-water raids in many kinds of weather, and the Japanese learned that neither Nells nor carrier-based bombers were immune to enemy fighters, and that they must have cover. In one raid, when the carrier *Kaga* launched a strike of twelve Aichi D3A (Type 99) Val bombers (ER 3.5), they missed their escort and eleven were shot down. The *Kaga* was at once ordered home to take on a full complement of Mitsubishi A5M (Type 96) Claude fighters (ER 0.15), and thereafter her escorted bomber formations were not molested.

After a series of air battles in late 1937, the Chinese moved their bases out of range of marauding Japanese fighters; but the Japanese countered by setting up advanced refueling fields so that their fighters could make very-long-range sorties, thus achieving the advantage of surprise and again catching the Chinese on the ground, as the latter had failed to develop an early-warning system. Naval aircraft also acted in a tactical role for the army, and naval airmen came out of the war with two convictions: that naval aircraft could operate over land, and that the key to success was command of the air. Moreover, naval airmen argued that the special demands they had made for range were justified. Range capability gave them a greater radius of action than had so far been considered by others, a factor especially important in the Pacific and in China where targets were scattered over vast distances. But the younger officers who had done the fighting still faced frustrating conservatism in the High Command of both the

The Vultee BT-13 Valiant "Vibrator" (ER 0.75) of 1940 was the basic trainer flown in the second stage of the three-step training program for USAAF pilots, at each stage of which a high washout rate occurred due to the abundance of trainees and an incorrect training philosophy. (USAF)

By 1940, the cockpit of a fighter (here a Curtiss P-40) had become much more complex. (USAF)

The Westland Lysander (ER 2.6) was a STOL aircraft designed for the Army Cooperation Command. Fitted with an all-flying tailplane and high-lift leading-edge slats and trailing-edge flaps, it was highly maneuverable and could fly very slowly. However, it was too big for its role in contested skies.

A pilot of the U.S. Army Air Corps (the USAAF in May 1941) putting his Stearman PT-17 (ER 0.33) yellow and blue primary trainer through a roll. After Pearl Harbor in late 1941, the red bulls-eye in the roundel was removed to avoid attacks by avid "Jap hunters."

Asked by the British to build additional P-40s, North American Aviation Inc. responded with a challenge that within ninety days it could produce a much better machine, the P-51 Mustang seen here (ER 5.14, P-51A, 1943). This prototype is now in the EAA Museum at Oshkosh, Wisconsin. Fitted with an Allison engine, the P-51 was initially limited to low-level attacks. However, the suggestion was made that a Rolls-Royce Merlin engine be fitted, and this made it the supreme World War II fighter for high-altitude and long-range escort missions. (USAF)

The standard American fighter in 1941 was the Curtiss P-40C (ER 2.5, P-40B, ER 7.3, P-40F), with an Allison engine unsuitable for combat above 15,000 feet. But thousands were ordered of those in production and of improved variants, thus keeping the company very profitable throughout the war, but unable to successfully develop a new generation to compete with the North American P-51 Mustang (ER 9.63, P-51D) and the Republic P-47 (ER 8.1, P-47D). At low level in 1942, well-trained pilots could outmatch the German Me-109 (ER 1.24) or the Japanese Zero (ER 7.89). (USAF)

Flying schools were also established at much more humble facilities such as this one at Manhattan, Kansas. Built with Works Progress (later Works Projects) Administration funds in 1936 at the urging of far-sighted local businessmen, this hangar is still in use in 2003. (Riley County Historical Society, Manhattan, Kansas)

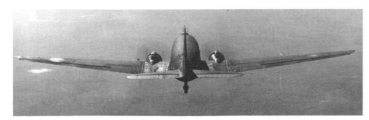

The author took this photograph of a No. 48 Squadron, RAF, Douglas C-47 Dakota (ER 20) over Burma in the fall of 1945.

As the USAAC expanded rapidly in the early 1940s, civilian flying schools were introduced, such as this one at the Grand Central Air Terminal in Glendale, California, where instructors and cadets are lined up in front of their Stearman PT-13s (ER n/a) for inspection. (USAF)

A Northrop A-17A (ER 2.4) sprays "gas" on U.S. Army troops during the Louisiana maneuvers of 1941—a misplaced idea of the effectiveness of gas attacks. Allied air forces resisted the idea of an Army Cooperation Command or tactical air forces, but the Germans and Soviets embraced them. (U.S. Chemical Warfare Service, via Edgewood Arsenal)

The North American AT-6 Harvard (Texan) (ER 1.59) was the favored advanced, British Service School trainer for single-engine pilots. It has also been a much-desired private aircraft for warplane buffs and could still be seen at the EAA Air Show at Oshkosh, Wisconsin, in 2003. Here, in 1947, a Royal New Zealand Air Force pilot gives an aerobatic demonstration at low level.

navy and the army, which continued to insist that the air weapon was auxiliary and not of itself a prime instrument for victory.

Japanese bombers striking the withdrawn Chinese airfields were suffering high casualties, but in late 1938 a new Mitsubishi became available. The Zero (ER 7.89), a sleek monoplane fighter with long-range fuel tanks, gave the bombers continuous escort, even all the way to Chunking, starting in May 1940. It would be another eighteen months before Claire Chennault, the former American fighter pilot, observing these actions from the ground, would begin to have his revenge.

All his life Chennault had been a latecomer. He had been dispatched to China after being retired from the U.S. Army Air Corps. The author of *The Role of Pursuit Aviation* (1935), he had a shortened career in the bomber-minded Army Air Corps. In 1934, an American air mission had been forced out of China by Japanese pressure on Washington. Four years later, Chennault arrived in the theater, inherited a "Keystone Cops" air force that managed to write itself off in training accidents. He settled down to observe the Japanese and establish an early-warning network, while waiting for diplomatic, economic, martial, and physical impediments to a new Chinese Air Force to be removed.

In 1940 it was decided to build the Burma Road, and in 1941 President Franklin Roosevelt declared for all-out aid to China. But not until the end of 1941 was the idea of defending the Burma Road accepted, and one hundred Curtiss P-40 Tomahawk fighters (ER 2.5), declared by the British to be too obsolete for use in Europe, were made available. In the meantime, General Chennault had been allowed clandestinely to recruit experienced pilots in the United States. Both fliers and crated aircraft were in Rangoon, Burma, when Pearl Harbor was struck on December 7, 1941. What Chennault then proceeded to prove was that a professional air force, even with outdated equipment, when properly led with an understanding of the enemy's tactics and weaknesses,

could first fight a defensive battle and win it and then go over to the offensive. Forced to operate on limited funds and matériel, Chennault made his outfit economical, efficient, and effective, because he could not afford to have it be otherwise. He put into practice the ideas he had written about, which showed that the bomber was unlikely to get through if opposed in the air unless properly escorted—a lesson the Japanese had already learned from the Chinese. Chennault made plain that early warning prevents surprise and that a defense against attack is always possible if properly undertaken. His study of the Japanese saved many American lives in the Pacific theater, but his work could also have been usefully applied in Europe, where bomber losses were unnecessarily high until the arrival of proper escort fighters in 1944.

The Spanish Civil War

The war in Spain, from 1936 to 1939, was seen in the West as the most significant combat experience prior to World War II. On both sides were professional airmen and modern equipment, some sent officially and others voluntarily. In Spain, however, air power was not decisive, even if the neutral press, just as in China, played up horror stories of bombings of civilians and the glories of aerial combat.

One of the more significant roles of aviation in the Spanish Civil War came at the very beginning, in 1936, when a fleet of German Ju-52s ferried Gen. Francisco Franco's Nationalist army from North Africa to Spain to begin the huge task of defeating the Republican rebels.

In addition to the Spanish Air Force, three regular air forces fought above Spain: the Soviet, the Italian, and the German. From elsewhere came volunteers, though the British, French, and American governments remained strictly aloof. The French, however, did supply aircraft, and thus at least to that extent their equipment was tested in war.

The Soviet air contribution to the Spanish Civil War was politically involved. Because of mistrust of those sent abroad and a general suspicion of air force personnel, those sent to Spain from mid-1936 onward were captains and above. They flew the highly unstable Polikarpov I-15 (ER 0.39) and I-16 (ER 1.23) fighters and the fast Petlyakov PE-2 (ER 11.71) twin-engined bombers. Their commander, General Smushkevich, had succeeded Alksnis, the commander-in-chief of the Soviet Air Force who had been executed in 1938.

The Soviets had about 1,500 aircraft in Spain for some two years, of which at any one time perhaps a third were serviceable. Soviet personnel gained much experience in the Spanish conflict, but the air force's showing was not high, in part due to Nationalist possession of the German Messerschmitt Me-109 fighter (ER 1.24), which was easily the best combat machine in Spain. Its appearance in quantity in the summer of 1938 caused Stalin to withdraw his air contingents. At home, the Soviet aircraft industry found it hard to explain its failure to develop a comparable fighter, except that it was not so much design as production know-how that was the hindrance. The other Soviet lesson was the inaccuracy of their bomber forces, a problem that was not theirs alone. Even the much-vaunted German Condor Legion had the same troubles in Spain.

The *Luftwaffe* became involved in Spain shortly after it came into the open as the revived German Air Force, and Hermann Goering was determined to use Spain as a real testing ground. Germans who had been running training establishments in the Soviet Union and who had themselves done a post-graduate course with the Italian *Regia Aeronautica* in 1935 were sent to gain experience. And for the Germans, their time with the *Regia Aeronautica* was of value, for the *Luftwaffe,* whose historical section had been forced to work quietly and had been unable to publish, had forgotten a great deal. In Spain, the German Air Force fought primarily against Soviet machines. At first, its Henschel HS 123 (ER 1.10) biplane fighters were outclassed by the newer Soviet Polikarpov I-16s with retractable undercarriage; and the German Ju-52/3m transport-bombers were too slow. But

by 1938, the Me-109 was on hand as a fighter and the Heinkel He-111 (ER 19.9) and the Dornier Do-17 (ER 6.96) as bombers, either of which could out-run most opposing fighters.

What nearly defeated the Germans at first, however, were their own tactical formations, which made no use of the lessons of the First World War. In tight formations, so beloved for exhibitionism in peacetime, there was no room to maneuver and too little time to look around for opponents while holding an exacting position. Thus the German fighters quickly went back to pairs, with two pair to a finger-of-four, and a total of twelve aircraft to a squadron. A loose formation, this was far more flexible and much less easy to surprise. Using the force tactically, the Germans quickly developed a forward-air-controller system so that aircraft could be vectored in visually to targets in front of the troops. If anything, the Germans in Spain gained a reputation for ruthlessness and efficiency, and perhaps never more so than in the bombing of the market town of Guernica, in which the object was to try out the bombing of cities rather than to break a strategic bridge. The attacks started with fighters strafing the crowded marketplace, then methodical high-explosive bombing, and at last a deluge of incendiaries. Out of some 10,000 people, 1,600 died, mostly civilians. International charges of immorality did not improve the image of the Condor Legion.

In Spain, the new modern aircraft permitted the Germans to perfect their tactical doctrine and their whole concept of war, to allow them to ram through a victory on the ground and in the air for their greater objective of *Lebensraum* and self-sufficiency. On the other hand, the French High Command regarded the Spanish Civil War as an aberration and ignored its lessons as passed on by its *Deuxieme Bureau* (Intelligence).

The Italian contribution, like the German, started with helping Franco consolidate the Nationalist position on the mainland by ferrying troops over from Morocco. Like the Germans,

The Interwar Years

too, the Italians were able to use their bomber-transports to good effect to keep supplies flowing and machines airborne. At the same time, their bombing raids acted as a blockade of the southern Spanish ports. Ironically, the Germans failed to understand the real significance of this aerial blockade and thus lost the economic Battle of Britain in the spring of 1941.

ATTITUDES AT THE OUTBREAK OF WAR

The first period of peace in air-power history to cover a whole cycle from demobilization to rearmamental instability, the interwar years 1918–39, provided many lessons for the future. Retaining the memory of an unnatural stalemated war, air forces tended to forget that the most effective conflicts are those of mobility, in which basic equipment must be constantly adapted to new uses in both a technological and tactical chess game.

Those air forces that were best prepared for the Second World War were those that had experienced their showmanship attitudes destroyed by the realities of combat. And the most effective air forces were the tactical forces that had the power to make decisions on the surface by striking at the immediate military threats.

Yet, it was not easy in peacetime in a highly political, economy-minded situation to gain support for even obvious short-term goals. To be successful, air forces had to play peacetime politics as a mixture of economics, public relations, and fear. Airmen tended to be outspoken in their enthusiasm for air power and to overlook the fact that indirect action can be as effective as, and much cheaper than, direct. It can be argued, of course, that this was the game being played by the democracies whose grand strategy was essentially reactive. But those whose move is based upon the enemy's taking the initiative must be provided with technologically current equipment and ideas in the hands of professionals. Whether or not this requires numerical superiority is a moot question,

as is the problem of determining what is enough defensive power and how nearly ready it is. The answers have to be found in planning that takes into account both grand-strategic desires and political, economic, and diplomatic, as well as military, realities. Readiness may well be conditioned not only by the supply of money but by whether or not the logistics plan is in step with grand strategy, if indeed the two have been linked at all. Even when there is centralized control, policies may not be executed centrally or soundly, especially if there is neither the doctrine nor the aircraft, armaments, and crews to carry them out.

All of these are closely tied to intelligence of enemy plans and abilities, which in their turn must be analyzed without wishful thinking, as must the preparation of one's allies. In the period before the Second World War, Allied eyes were fixed on Germany and Japan, but neglected to look at Britain, France, Poland, Czechoslovakia, or Italy. Moreover, air forces were generally so offensively minded that they failed to consider defensive measures adequately, or to understand the limits of production of aircraft and spares, aircrew, and mechanics.

By the time peace ended in 1939, the air weapon was very much more sophisticated than it had been in 1918, due largely to scientific and technological developments. But mentally a significant disparity existed between those air forces that saw their role as strategic and those that regarded themselves as supplementary to a surface service. As events were to show, the latter—the tactical air forces—could often destroy the forces in the field before grand-strategic or strategic bombers could have a paralyzing effect. By 1939, air power was no longer ancillary; it was a force in itself, but not by itself.

A Mahanian assessment of the aviation countries in 1939 finds that Russia was recovering from the Spanish Civil War and the Stalinist purges, was embroiled in a winter war with Finland, was still an aviation power, but was led by a paranoid leader who had just signed a non-aggression pact with Germany and destroyed Poland.

Germany was geared up to fight short wars with standardized models, but was unprepared for a long war, either in aircraft production, raw materials, or defense of the Third Reich.

Italy had already passed her economic peak and would suffer accordingly.

France had avoided civil war, but her air force lacked self-confidence, mature political guidance, and was well short of the needs of total war mentally and physically.

Britain was barely ready for a defensive war; it had a rapidly increasing aircraft production and the men and mechanics gradually to man the RAF, but was short of tools and spares, as well as a Bomber Command lacking the ability to find, strike, and damage targets in Germany. Not until May 1940 would Britain find a war leader in Churchill.

The United States was plagued by neutrality, but had a potential warrior in Franklin D. Roosevelt, and her aircraft industry was already expanding rapidly, as a result of Anglo-French orders. The Air Corps still had to solidify usable doctrine, but the U.S. Navy had carrier doctrine and was getting modern aircraft.

The new player was Japan. It was not an air nation in 1918, but with almost a decade of war in the Far East, it was honing plans for a South Asia Co-Prosperity Sphere. Japan's weakness, like Britain's, was dependence on overseas oil, and like Germany's, lack of imagination of total war.

CHAPTER 4

THE SECOND WORLD WAR: LAND-BASED AIR POWER

In the years 1934–45, the doctrines that existed were put to the test of war and its infrastructured demands. In this the Germans, Russians, and Japanese came off best because their theories of war related to their needs and to the power then available, whereas the British and the American theories had not been costed out in respect to requirements. Later in the war, the Anglo-American air services both adopted tactical doctrines and practiced them effectively, while at the same time striking the enemy homeland with forces that both destroyed works on the ground and defenders in the air. Only the Soviets still maintained a super-efficient strictly tactical air force to complement the ground armies, as they had been in 1941.

PREPARATION AND PROGRESS— EQUIPMENT, TRAINING, COMMAND

In many respects the story of air power in the Second World War is one of continuity, both from prewar peacetime and with the peace that followed. The war started in the middle of rearmamental instability, and wartime equilibrium was not reached until 1942–43; by the autumn of 1944, demobilization was already beginning. It was a time of almost continuous change, of growth, and of constant technological progress, and it was also a period of history that gave rise to myths that die hard.

The impact of Soviet thought-control and of Stalin's ideas resulted in a falsification of Russian aviation history that did not begin to be adjusted until the fall of the USSR in 1991 and the opening of the archives. It will be well into the twenty-first century before more correct works will appear in either Russian or other languages.

In analyses of the conflict, too much importance has often been placed on the more spectacular events and too little on the sinews of war. Too often the tale has been of the excitement of battle from the outsider's view, and too seldom of the realities, the boredom, and the long quiet applications of power. Moreover, in the historical study of air power in the Second World War, the emphasis has been at best strategic and rarely grand-strategic. While it can be argued that the Pacific and the war at sea in general are separate subjects that can be treated in a parallel chapter, it can also be shown that the use of air power over land must be treated as a whole. In particular, the use of Allied air power over Europe, especially the so-called strategic air offensive against Germany, must be assessed in terms of the total objectives of the Allies and the resources at their disposal. And this must also be contrasted with the Soviet and German use of air power in the vast, flat Eastern theater with its lack of accessible grand-strategic targets.

In all of these evaluations, the principles of war can be and should be applied. That they have not been has been due both to the narrow vision of many writers and to the insistence of airmen that theirs was a new world. The use of air power was, of course, governed by the vision of its leadership and the willingness or failure of air staffs to accept the judgments of those who had seen combat or life firsthand. During the latter part of rearmamental instability, a struggle continued in the effort to convince the leadership that air power could not do what it purported to do, and "*homo lagiens,*" the human lag factor, came into play once again. At the same time, what had been learned in peacetime carried over into the war years. Those air forces that had the benefit of combat experience moved ahead rapidly and successfully. Yet, those that had started late and suffered early defeats, such as the Chinese, American, Soviet, and British, by learning the hard way, perhaps ultimately learned better. They also operated, of course, from protected arsenals out of reach of an Axis that lacked long-range grand-strategic bombers with fighter escorts.

Just as the First World War saw tremendous strides in technology, so did the Second. Two air forces, the German and the British, started the war with some biplane fighters, but ended it with a few jets. The British started with 500-pound bombs and ended with 22,000-pounders. Speeds rose from 300 to 600 mph, and fighting heights rose to 30,000 feet; in exceptional cases heights reached 50,000 feet.

The whole problem of locating the enemy began to be solved. While relative speeds in combat remained much the same, overall speeds were rising, and it became vital, especially at night, to be able to identify friend and foe. Visual signals were developed, first pyrotechnics, then lights, and finally a radar pulse called IFF (identification, friend or foe). And where in 1939 an intercepting fighter pilot might be given an approximate course, height, and location of the enemy, based upon ground observers' sightings, by 1945 he was vectored onto his airborne target by a ground controller or by his own radar navigator, whose information was reliable enough to place him in shooting position. As the RAF learned in 1944 to provide night-fighter escort in the bomber streams (a lesson the Japanese in the Far East had learned earlier in daylight raids), identification became still more critical.

The war saw the development of techniques for marking targets at night and for controlling the bombers operating over them, using combinations of radar, pyrotechnics, and radio-telephone, worked both from home bases and by Pathfinder aircraft on the spot. Such achievements were major elements in the ultimate effectiveness of the bomber offensive against Germany.

Much more than the 1914 air war, this one was fought on the ground. It was not merely a war of flying equipment, it was a struggle between competing industrial systems. Design and production were important, but equally vital were fuel, materials, machine tools, and manpower. Forced once again to consider the total production picture, all air forces went back to the salvage and repair operations so cheerfully abandoned in peacetime, with the result that up to 35 percent of some air forces were composed of rebuilt machines and equipment. This was a war, too, of technicians in metallurgical, medical, and radar laboratories, on direction-finding and listening posts, and on airfields.

The airfields became immensely important as the new heavier planes developed from the technological revolution of the 1930s could no longer be operated off grass, but required concrete runways. Constructing the standard three-runway airfield involved moving some 30,000 tons of materials, just for the runways, not to mention revetted dispersal areas, bomb and fuel dumps, hangars, machine shops, stores, and sick and living quarters. And such fields could not be produced overnight in the fluctuating campaigns that took place, other than along the English Channel line.

At the beginning of World War II, the RAF was equipped with the 1937 Gloster Gladiator (ER 1.1), the last of its biplane fighters, which was still in action in Greece in spring 1941. W. G. Carter, who designed this aircraft in the later 1930s, had as his next project the 600 mph Gloster Meteor (ER 15.3). This Gladiator is in the RAF Museum at Hendon, London. (Stuart Howe)

The 1938 Junkers Ju-87 Stuka (ER 2.22), was the much-feared German dive-bomber, which spearheaded the *Blitzkrieg* in France and sank ships in the Mediterranean. It remained in tactical service on the Eastern Front throughout the war. This example was captured from the *Regia Aeronautica* by the RAF. The Ju-87 once preserved in the Museum of Science and Industry in Chicago is now at Oshkosh, Wisconsin. (Source unknown)

A wartime German painting of a Dornier Do-17 Z2 (ER 6.96) over Moscow, from the captured German art collection of the USAF.

The 1939 Junkers Ju-88 (ER 13.4) was an impressive, multi-purpose aircraft, in part due to Hitler's demand that all German bombers be able to dive-bomb. This D-1 example was captured in North Africa and flown back to Wright-Patterson Field in Ohio, where this photo was taken while the aircraft was being tested. It is now in the USAF Museum. (USAF)

The mainstay of the German fighter force throughout most of the 1939–45 war was the 1939 Messerschmitt Me-109 (ER 1.24),sometimes now known as the Bf-109. It was a rugged machine with a very cramped cockpit. This example was landed by mistake at RAF Manston during the Battle of Britain. (Stuart Howe)

A Hawker Hurricane I (ER 1.94) for the Yugoslav Air Force being tested over the English countryside in 1939 with a wooden two-bladed fixed-pitch propeller, which in more side-on photos appeared to curve forward due to tipspeed lift. (Hawker-Siddeley Aviation)

Thus, a whole new organization had to be created to manufacture portable airfield materials and manage the rapid movement of entire landing grounds so that air support was always close to the battle front. In the Italian theater and in the Pacific, aircraft carriers were even used as airfields for air cover until bases could be established within the newly won beachheads.

In such a technological war, aircrew also became of prime importance. Recruitment was rarely if ever a problem. Many were willing to become airmen because of aviation's myth and image, and as opposed to the draft. But even with lowered wartime physical and educational standards, not all were taken. Training depended upon the availability of planes, fuel, facilities, airspace, instructors, and syllabuses.

The British and the Americans were fortunate in that they had vast air spaces in suitable weather belts, which were close to fuel supplies; training could be carried out in Canada and the United States as well as in South Africa without molestation by enemy intruders and without the penalties of fuel shortages. Moreover, the Allies did not make the German mistake of using instructors on hazardous operations. They did, however, suffer from the need to make use of instructors without war experience.

While systems varied, in 1940 British fighter pilots had 150 hours of experience before entering combat, and by late 1944 airmen such as myself were getting 275 hours before they received their wings and 400 by the time they reached a squadron. By December 1944, the RAF had a year's supply of aircrew on hand, and the training program was being slowed down. While the Americans used a three-stage system to the award of pilot's wings and then further schooling before assignment to an operational squadron, the RAF used a two-stage program. After preflight school, American cadets were given instruction and soloed in primary trainers, then moved to basic, and finally to advanced aircraft with variable-pitch propellers, retractable undercarriages, and radio aids. Meanwhile, for bombers, other members of the crew went to specialist schools and then to a gunnery course before reporting to an operational training unit for crewing and training on the type of craft to be used in combat. By mid-war, pilots were getting instrument-flying instruction in Link trainers, while others were given work in primitive simulators. In the RAF, crews selected themselves; in the USAAF, they were assigned.

The *Luftwaffe's* failure to anticipate pilot losses and replacement needs meant that when in 1944 the loss rate was 1,700 monthly, the replacement pool was supplying nothing like that, even though OTUs had been eliminated so that neophytes with one hundred hours went straight to squadrons to be trained as they entered combat.

The technological revolution of 1934–45 also affected other aircrew and ground crew. Observers were replaced by trained navigators, and they in time were ultimately developed into radar-navigators. Bomb aimers had to shift from simple line-of-sight devices to the complex Norden bombsight, which needed a vulnerable straight run into the target, or to the British Mark XIV gyro bombsight, which could drop accurately even when the aircraft was doing evasive turns. In addition, the new, more complex aircraft needed flight engineers, and larger planes required more defensive gunners in power turrets. On the ground the engine fitter and airframe rigger and air mechanic had to be replaced by a team that included armorers for guns and bombs, radio and radar technicians, parachute riggers, and the like. To change a single engine on a B-24 took sixteen men twenty hours. Toward the end of the war, RAF Bomber Command suffered from unserviceability caused by a lack of radar mechanics in a society with few radios at home. And not to be lost sight of was the need for frequent inspections, from a daily to a 100-hour check, to a complete overhaul at 300 hours.

Once a crew had completed six operational sorties it was regarded as invaluable, and all air forces became increasingly anxious to recover downed aircrew as well as aircraft. Air/sea rescue

The 1939 Macchi 200 (ER 1.7) was the major Italian fighter from 1939 to 1943. In addition to the *Regia Aeronautica* markings, the machine is shown in North African desert camouflage at the U.S. Air Force Museum in Dayton, Ohio. (Postcard)

A scene from the 1969 movie *The Battle of Britain* shows 1939 *Luftwaffe* Heinkel He-111s (ER 19.9) on an airfield in northern France. Actually, like the Me-109s also used in the film, these are postwar Spanish Air Force machines equipped with Rolls-Royce Merlins, instead of their original German Junkers Jumos. (Confederate Air Force Flying Museum)

The 1940 Douglas Boston (ER 15.5, Boston III) was one of the designs stimulated by the $500 million pumped into the U.S. aircraft industry during 1938–40 by the French and British purchasing commissions. The remains of a dead French officer found in the crashed prototype caused a political incident in the neutral United States. The Boston was a fast and effective light bomber used on offensive sweeps over France in 1941 and 1942. (Douglas)

Gen. Kurt Student, commander of the German airborne forces that landed on Crete in May 1941. This first successful overseas airborne invasion in history so decimated the German paratroops and the flying instructors, who had been pulled from training units to pilot the Ju-52s, that German air transport failed at Stalingrad in late 1942. (Source unknown)

The 1941 Martin B-26 Marauder (ER 24.6, B-26C) was one of the bold new second-generation USAAC designs. Its wing area was so small that it was known at the time as the "flying prostitute," because it had no visible means of support. But its 2,000 hp engines were powerful enough that it could fly on just one—though if an engine was suddenly shot out, it would do a flick roll. Older pilots were apprehensive and distrusting of such a radical, new machine. (USAF)

Ellington Field, Houston, Texas, in 1941, shows the revolution from omni-directional grass fields to concrete runways and hardstands. Parallel runways enabled twice the amount of flying to take place as long as the weather cooperated, as it usually did in the Sun Belt. At the time this photograph was taken, the field was still under construction.

German designer Kurt Tank's very successful fighter, the Focke-Wulf Fw-190-A3 (ER 3.39), entered service in 1942. Visibility from the cockpit was noticeably improved by the clear canopy and by the raised position of the pilot versus that in the Me-109. (USAF)

The rugged and powerful Republic P-47D Thunderbolt (ER 8.1) was the original mainstay of the USAAF's Eighth Air Force Fighter Command until the P-51 Mustang (ER 9.63) took over those duties. The P-47 excelled as a fighter-bomber in both Europe and Southeast Asia with its six .50-caliber machine guns and two 1,000-pound bombs. (Confederate Air Force)

Air Chief Marshal Sir Arthur Harris, when made Air Officer Commander-in-Chief of RAF Bomber Command in 1942, soon demanded 40,000 bicycles to save the time of his skilled mechanics in moving around the spread-out airfields. The USAAF similarly used bicycles, seen here scattered outside a Nissen hut and washing facility.

Col. James H. Doolittle of blind-flying fame led the retaliatory strike following Pearl Harbor. After special training in naval short takeoff techniques, he led his men in their North American B-25 Mitchell bombers (ER 23) from the USN aircraft carrier *Hornet* to strike Tokyo and other home island Japanese targets, shaking the enemy's complacency in April 1942. (USAF)

This excellent photograph shows why the Spitfire was often considered the most beautiful fighter of World War II. The Spitfire IX entered the service in 1943 with four 20 mm cannon in place of the eight .303-caliber machine guns, and with a two-stage turbo supercharger that enabled it to outclimb enemy fighters above 12,000 feet. (ER 1.9, Spitfire I, 1938; ER 2.63, Spitfire IX, 1943; ER 3.5, Spitfire XIV, 1944)(Vickers)

On March 1, 1935, Hermann Goering (1893–1946) was appointed Commander-in-Chief of the Luftwaffe, a position he held until May 1945. Goering was responsible for the expansion of the Luftwaffe. (Photograph 183 / H 29 948, courtesy Deutsche Bundesarchiv, Koblenz)

teams were developed, using special amphibians or high-speed launches, and on the east coast of Britain two large airfields, Manston and Woodbridge, were established that were essentially enormous concrete areas (3,000 x 250 yards) where badly damaged aircraft could be crash-landed and assisted by special rescue crews. Much work was also done to develop means of homing lost and strayed aircraft by vectoring fighters in to guide them. For airmen fighting over their own territories, recovery was a less serious problem; for them, new aircraft could be more critical. But for those airmen who landed in enemy territory, escape rarely succeeded, and the vast majority spent the remainder of the war in prison camps eating precious little food.

The air war depended, much more than its proponents for some time realized, on the gathering of immense amounts of economic as well as military intelligence. For effective grand-strategic bombing, precise details of an opponent's economic and business resources, inventory, and habits were necessary, as well as an awareness of his military installations and maps by which to locate targets. The air weapon was a rapier, not a sledgehammer. It had to be aimed at small vital spots and thrust in quickly, sometimes repeatedly, to be effective. For that to be done, air commanders had to know economic anatomy, and their sword arms had to be highly trained, well armored, and accurate; and they had to know how to feint by evasive routing.

In reality, however, the Allied bombing and targeting intelligence was quite different. The RAF's Sir Arthur Harris was convinced that for area bombing at night all he needed was a list of German cities and their industries. On the American side, the newly created (1940) intelligence division sought economic information on precision targets and was influenced by the special knowledge of the people recruited. Unlike the weather in the American Sun Belt, that over Europe frustrated the accuracy earlier achieved with the famed Norden bombsight.

Like the RAF, the U.S. Army Air Corps—in 1941 called the U.S. Army Air Forces (USAAF)—greatly overestimated the size of the German Air Force, though this was to its benefit regarding Franklin Roosevelt and war plans. And the cycle was right, so that the USAAC/USAAF's new aircraft—except the B-17 and the P-40—were on the cutting edge. But the Air Corps had underestimated the lethality of GAF fighters and flak.

Modern war ran on oil. Japan conquered what she needed, Germany and Italy did not. But Japan had failed to consider how to carry the oil to the refineries and fronts. Tankers sailed alone, and their calls for air cover only led to Allied aircraft homing on them. In 1945, lack of fuel meant untrained pilots in the air.

The Allies learned very quickly, and coupled to their productivity they beat the Germans at their own tactical air force/armor game of mechanized warfare. From 1941 to 1943, the USAAF was learning how to be an effective tactical air force (TAF); it improved the system in Italy and made it effective from D-Day on in northwest Europe. By 1944, the Germans were on the ropes from bombing, and the TAF was free to roam over the battlefield and to the rear.

From 1941, German air power was limited—part of the disadvantages of success—and declined to impotent in late 1944. With it died the myth of German invincibility.

Barbarossa—the code name for the June 1941 Nazi attack on the USSR—showed the Russians that they needed to rebuild the air arm and employ it and tanks in a new way. Stalin understood the need for aircraft and tanks, to enable the infantry to fight.

By 1943, Soviet tanks and aircraft had reliable two-way radios as did British and American machines, and thus the Soviets revised their tactics to gain local air supremacy, to use aircraft as part of the battering ram.

By 1942, each of seventeen Soviet air armies had 800–900 aircraft; by 1943, they averaged 1,500; and by 1945, the consolidated air armies had

2,500–3,000. In May 1945 the Red Air Force had over 11,000 front-line aircraft.

The Soviet Chief of Air Staff Novikov insisted on a few types, which could be upgraded and fielded without disrupting production lines. Mobile teams repaired aircraft in the field, as they did the tanks. Temporary airfields, dispersed and hidden aircraft using camouflage, and deception—an old Russian fighting ploy—also allowed surprise.

In 1941, the *Luftwaffe* had 2,500 aircraft in the East; in 1944, it had only 1,700—and these were obsolescent because of frozen designs and too many variants and prototypes. The *Wehrmacht* in June 1941 had 21 panzer and 119 foot, horse-and-cart divisions. The Germans had never thought of the consequences if the *Blitzkrieg* of 1941 failed. Yet the pace and distance in Russia had reduced the panzers by November 1941 almost to impotence. The cold—the great Soviet ally—was such that German Air Force mechanics froze to aircraft upon which they were working. The GAF in the East suffered shortages of spares and replacement engines, fuel, and lorries. Rough grass airfields caused wastage of aircraft and crews. Air leaders had failed to foresee the attrition that even a weak opponent could impose, and before losses could be recouped, the new Red Air Force was in the field, and its better models came to dominate the GAF.

At the start of hostilities in 1939, the warring air forces could be ranked in terms of their re-equipment. The Germans were reaching their peak and basically fought the war with what they had in production. The Italians had peaked in 1937 and though some of their equipment was excellent, such as the Macchi 202 (ER 2.25) and Fiat G-50 (ER 1.3) monoplane fighters, by 1940 these were already becoming dated. Little was done to modernize the Italian Air Force because the economy was overstrained. Both the French, in a very small way, and the British, were in the midst of re-equipment programs, but these were not expected to be completed until 1942. The Soviet Air Force was just undertaking to re-arm itself after the Spanish and Finnish experiences; it was already in 1941 moving factories east of the Urals, in part to supply its Far Eastern air force facing the Japanese, who like the Germans were about at their peak in 1939. And the United States, though possessing advanced airliners, was between re-equipments. The naval air force was in fighting trim, but the planes of the U.S. Army Air Corps were nearly obsolete and Congress was still being stingy. In 1939, President Roosevelt's proposed 50,000-aircraft program was still a year away.

The world's leading land-based air force was the German; the leading naval air force was the Japanese. In fighters this meant the Messerschmitt Me-109 and the Mitsubishi Zero. Both were low-wing single-engined aircraft with a top speed of about 350 mph, a ceiling of 30,000 feet, a radius of action of 300 to 1,000 miles (the Zero was designed especially for long-range missions), and an armament of cannon and machine guns. Both air forces possessed dive-bombers and twin-engine bombers. In the former category were the Ju-87 Stuka and the Aichi Val, single-engine aircraft capable of carrying a 2,000-pound bomb load, but vulnerable to fighters when not in a dive. The German Heinkel He-111 introduced during the war in Spain was a fast, streamlined twin-engine bomber, indifferently armed but carrying a 5,500-pound bombload at 225 mph for 670 miles at 25,000 feet. The Japanese Mitsubishi G4M (Type 1) Betty (ER 41) was in the same class.

By the end of the war, the United States air forces possessed probably the world's best equipment, although the Soviet Ilyushin Il-2 Shturmovik (ER 3.7) ground-attack aircraft was in something of a class by itself. The North American P-51D Mustang fighter (ER 9.63) was outclassed only by the German and British jets just becoming operational. The P-51, with its 1,450 hp engine, maximum speed of 437 mph, and a ceiling of 40,000 feet, could bring six .50-caliber machine guns and ten five-inch rockets or two 1,000-pound bombs into action over a range of nearly 1,200 miles from base. The U.S. Navy's Grumman F6F Hellcat (ER 12.2), with a slightly higher horsepower and a considerably higher weight, was somewhat slower; but its gull-winged Vought-Sikorsky F4U Corsair (ER 13) was equal to the P-51. Except for the U.S. Navy's reliable Douglas SBD Dauntless (ER 5.84) and less popular Curtiss SB2C Helldivers (ER 10.36), attack aircraft were largely rugged fighters turned fighter-bombers and armed with bombs or rockets as well as 20 mm cannon. Bombers, which because of their bomb loads had been considered "heavies" in 1939, had by 1945 become medium bombers; the North American B-25 Mitchell (ER 23) and the versatile de Havilland Mosquito XI (ER 30) were the best representatives, with variations ranging from level bombers to anti-shipping aircraft fitted with up to a 75 mm cannon.

Moreover, the Mosquito had replaced the German He-111 and Do-17 of the Spanish Civil War as the unarmed bomber that could outrun fighters. In the heavy class were the British Avro Lancaster (ER 103), which could carry up to a 22,000-pound bomb, and the American Boeing B-29 (ER 414) with its stripped performance of 367 mph at 30,000 feet with 16,000 pounds of bombs over a range of 2,600 miles.

Vastly complicating the logistics problems of the war in the air was the great increase in weight and complexity between 1939 and 1945. The He-111 had an all-up weight of 25,000 pounds, whereas the B-29 weighed 135,000. Even fighters more than doubled in size from the approximately 5,000 pounds of the 1939 Spitfire to the Mustang's 12,000 pounds. Weight was by no means the only measure of change. By the end of the war, a Lancaster carried the Mark XIV gyro bombsight and radar for navigation and defense, not to mention a large number of machine guns, though these were not very effective, and photo-flash devices both for photographing the impact of the bombs and for defense against fighters. All of this meant a drastic increase in the number of man-hours needed to produce aircraft, and the creation and training of much larger ground crews. At the same time, as enemy defenses became bet-

ter, up to 25 percent of the RAF Bomber Command force sent out on any night might be lost or so badly damaged as not to be available for operations the next day. This caused a great need for spares and led to the development of techniques for handling the supply of parts on an estimated replacement basis, and ultimately to breakthroughs in maintenance techniques.

In looking at serviceability figures for 1939–40, the RAF during the Battle of Britain had only 59 percent of training aircraft, 75 percent of fighters, and 82 percent of Bomber Command available. And in continuous operations, that dropped in Bomber Command to 60 percent for most of the war due to enemy action, modifications, rebuilds, and shortages of skilled personnel who had to work in the open.

In 1943, the USAAF knew that to keep a 300-strong aircraft force in the air required 1,200 in the field; yet 80 percent of Eighth Air Force (USAAF) heavies were out of action the next day due to battle damage, as compared to 25 percent of RAF night heavies and below 5 percent for Mosquitoes. By fall 1943, the Eighth Air Force had proved that the doctrine of unescorted grand-strategic bombing was bankrupt; losses could not be sustained. The German Air Force had superior defensive weapons in range, as well as radar and ground control. And at the time, it was estimated that at a 3.8 percent loss rate, only 36 out of 100 aircrew would live to return to the United States.

The whole question of making better use of what was available led to the creation of a scientific organization concerned with operational research, whose personnel studied all aspects of the war in the air. At first these "boffins"—operational scientists—were unpopular with commanding officers and others, but as the value of their work came to be recognized, they were increasingly in demand. All this led to another dilemma: more and more, instead of attempting to solve their own problems, commanders called for a boffin to do it for them. The result was a shortage of these scientists, who were diverted from finding longer-range solutions. Even worse, commanders began to rely upon the scientist to make judgments that were not within the boffin's competence or responsibility. And not only boffins had influence. Even more than in the First World War, staffs included sharp civilian minds with no military career at stake who, with their wider experience of the world and use of forceful logic, disputed, sometimes dominated, and often guided the thinking of senior commanders. All of these influences varied, of course, within different air forces, in accordance with national characteristics as affected by traditions, and according to combat losses, accidents, and personalities.

Nor must it be forgotten that the use of air power built up very gradually. Constant aerial activity could be misleading to observers on the ground. In actuality, only 17 percent of the bombs dropped on Germany by the Allies had been delivered before 1944; and in the Battle of Britain, when Air Chief Marshal Dowding was protecting the whole nation from a German aerial onslaught, he had only about 600 fighters and 930 pilots available, when he should have had more than 1,200 pilots—at least two per aircraft.

Much less than in the First World War were aircrews of World War II thrown continuously into combat if flight surgeons could prevent it, and if operations did not call for it. The whole concept of tours of duty helped limit the time during which aircrews were subjected to the tensions of combat. American heavy bomber and fighter crews were unwilling to continue in combat as they approached the 200-hour sortie mark. Recognition of this factor had its advantages in an air force with a growing pool of trained personnel, for it meant that those with combat experience could be phased into either the staff or into the training command to provide the no-nonsense reality that such systems were apt to lack when staffed for too long by people wedded to established—even peacetime—procedures. And those eager to prove their manhood could be given the chance.

The geometric increase in the use of air space led to the evolution of flying control. At training airfields an officer stationed at the downwind end of the field watched for safety's sake as machines came and went. Sectors of the sky and satellite airfields and ranges were approved for various activities. In operational theaters, especially as radios became available, flying control was closely allied to sector control fighter direction, as at sea to the combat air patrol (CAP). On transport operations, aircraft were tracked en route via position reports. At bomber airfields the recovery of machines was gradually comprehended as a vital matter, so that an airfield and its facilities did not belong to the local commanding officer, but were a part of the larger picture. By 1943, RAF Bomber Command was beginning to insist that flying-control officers were the ultimate authority on the air side. And when crews were briefed, they were filled in on diversion airfields, and, in the event, were notified where to land simply by a code letter. Peacetime intervals for landing were shortened from minutes to ninety seconds. In addition, homing aids were provided and air/sea rescue alerted to try to recover as many invaluable aircrew, if not aircraft, as possible.

During World War II a proprietary attitude of flying control regarding airfield use had evolved into a system designed to save both aircrew and aircraft, complete with homing aids of various sorts. Postwar, flying control developed into a worldwide air-traffic control system handling over-flying, takeoff and landing patterns, and air routes in the vicinity of airports.

The success or failure of air power in the war was not merely a matter of equipment and command; it was also intimately linked to anti-aircraft defense, which was sometimes an air force responsibility, as in Germany, but more often an army charge and which thus necessitated liaison at all levels. Regardless of who was in command, anti-aircraft forces—ack-ack, flak, or AAA—became increasingly larger, not just around forward airfields but around manufacturing centers and in

WWII Land-based Air Power

defensive belts. This was particularly important for rapidly advancing armies and at sea, where sailors tended to shoot first and ask questions afterward.

Throughout the 1939 war, air power remained both a constant presence and a special force, and its capabilities were often overrated by its friends and underrated by its enemies.

Blitzkrieg carried its air support with it, as did the Soviet counter campaign, because the aircraft involved could use impromptu grass airfields.

By the time the Western Allies counterattacked all over the world, they had the advantage of perforated steel plate (PSP), so they could lay new airfields anywhere in short order, or they could rehabilitate captured enemy bases as in Italy and France. They had airfield construction battalions and servicing commandos to refuel, rearm, and repair aircraft until the squadron ground echelon arrived.

Not only did these bases allow the rapid forward deployment of the tactical air forces, but also in the Pacific the advance of heavy bombers. In the latter theater, as in the Mediterranean in a more limited way, escort carriers were employed as advanced fields until fields ashore could be secured.

During the war, ferry and transport services built upon prewar, especially trans-Atlantic and trans-Pacific pioneering, to develop landplane routes so vital to postwar air transport—part of the linkages between air arms and civil aviation via the aircraft industry.

The Allies won in the air in 1944 due to overwhelming supply of aircraft and aircrew and the use of escort fighters, as well as a sophisticated support system.

THE AIRCRAFT INDUSTRIES

The aircraft industries in the major powers—Russia, the United States, Britain, Germany, and Japan—were very different in the Second World War. They were governed by national char-acteristics, the nature of the government, available resources, and planning based upon the anticipated nature of the coming war.

The Russians and Japanese realized that they did not have the technical, organizational, and material resources to create an effective grand-strategic striking force and thus concentrated on tactical air.

Allied aircraft production benefitted from planning for a long war, from the mobilization and allocation of resources, and from the coordination of the whole Office of Planning, Programs and Statistics—a lesson learned in Britain from the history of the Ministry of Munitions, 1915–19. Moreover, efficiencies of mass production and the improved learning curve saw the man-hours needed to build a B-24 drop from 40,000 in 1943 to 8,000 in 1945.

Aircraft production was the major war effort in Britain, Germany, and the United States; it involved the largest number of civilian firms and licenses and allowed Allied air superiority to be decisive by 1945. The British were most impressed by U.S. mass production, and postwar by German training. British observers saw the U.S. system of simplification, standardization, and specialization as great virtues, as translated into mass production and management methods.

Aircraft production depended very much on a nation's citizens. Both men and women had to be employed and cajoled or ordered to where shortages appeared. The newcomers met resistance in factories from established, unionized, skilled labor, but dilution was essential to productivity and led to the breaking down of skilled tasks into those that unskilled workers could handle efficiently. The demands meant that the aircraft industries went onto first a two-shift and then a three-shift, round-the-clock work week, though not in Britain. Everywhere, however, the aircraft industries competed for manpower, whose allocation, as in World War I, became critical.

Production could be disrupted by bombing, notably in Germany and Japan, and by invasion, as in Poland, France, and Russia. In the latter from July to December 1941, 1,523 enterprises were moved east in 1.5 million railway wagon loads, employees and all. Even so, a remarkable restoration of order and output occurred. This owed much to Soviet planning, a legacy of 1914, and meant that the government was prepared to deal with crisis.

From July 1941, Aviaprom, located on the Volga near the Urals, was responsible for aircraft production. This was part of the "industrial cabinet" plan to create production in a resource-scarce economy and get control over manufacturing above all else, while at the same time safeguarding manpower for the military. But improvisation and emergency measures had to give way again to centralized planning after mid-1942, and in November a Manpower Committee took over. By 1943, Russia had a single national economic plan again—simple, economical, efficient, and productive. The goal was 22,000 aircraft for 1942, of only five types, but 25,000 actually were produced. And labor output on a two-shift system rose two to three times, due to automation and standardization in mass production.

Half the Russian labor force were women, who worked twelve to sixteen hours a day in appalling conditions. The allowance of one pound of bread per day was a fifth of the British workers' rations. But the Slavs did not revolt because it was the life they had known since the 1890s industrialization. Propaganda and pride in achievement, and hatred of the Germans, coupled to mass mobilization in a brutal total war, made the system work.

In the United States, a land of abundance well removed from the war and with no tradition of war industry, war production needed a broad political support. What enabled President Roosevelt to ask for a 50,000-aircraft program was the fact that since 1938 the Allies had ordered $500 million worth of aircraft, and thus the American factories were geared up. In July 1941, FDR requested a plan, but this was not completed until the end of the year when new Allied demands became known. In four

years, 1941–45, the United States was catapulted into the arsenal of democracy and produced 297,000 aircraft. In one year America became a military economy, and in 1942 produced 47,000 aircraft versus the Axis 27,000, because the United States was a community of industrialists who liked to meet technical challenges.

Franklin Roosevelt revived the World War I experience of industry associations to enable businessmen to manage the economy through the War Board, Controlled Materials Plan, and the Manpower Commission. Eighty percent of orders went to the one hundred largest businesses well versed in mass-production. And thus Ford Motor Company volunteered to mass-produce B-24s at a new plant at Willow Run, Michigan, with a 5,450-foot-long assembly line covering sixty-seven acres. Each B-24 had 1,550,000 parts of 30,000 different types. By 1943, ten bombers each day were rolling off the line, and in 1944 one aircraft every sixty-three minutes

The American economy boomed with consumer goods, and had food still available, as compared to Russia; however, America also experienced 5,000 labor strikes. Economic opportunism in a voluntary system worked.

But Germany also had a formidable economy, hard to destroy from the air. Yet the regulated economy was not as productive as that of the United States, averaging only 10,000 aircraft per annum for 1939–41. Plans were not matched by reality, for the rational Germans had an economic system full of rivalries and bureaucratic meddling, dominated by military modifications.

Aircraft production, the responsibility of the utterly unsuited Ernest Udet, could have been saved by the former Managing Director of Lufthansa, Erhard Milch, but he was excluded in 1939 from input and direction. Udet was a failure as a technical director and the cause of internecine fights between aircraft manufacturers. Thus the *Luftwaffe* suffered from stagnant production and from lack of successful new operational models. Its older models were phased down, and factories

Table 2. Labor Employed in the Aircraft Industry, 1939–44[1]

Country	1939	1942	1944
United Kingdom	973,000	1,526,000	1,440,000
United States	200,000	471,000	2,102,000
Germany	1,000,000	1,800,000	unknown
USSR	350,000	unknown	750,000
Japan	unknown (1941, 236,000)	343,900	756,246

[1]From R. J. Overy, *The Air War, 1939–1945* (New York: Stein and Day, 1980), 171.

Table 3. Aircraft Production, 1941–44[1]

Country	1941	1943	1944
United Kingdom	20,100	26,200	26,500
United States	19,433	92,196	100,752
Germany	11,766	25,527	39,807
USSR	15,735	34,884	40,241
Japan	5,088	16,693	28,180

[1]From tables compiled for Enzio Angelucci, *The Encyclopedia of Military Aircraft, 1914 to the Present* (Edison, NJ: Chartwell Books, 2001), Plate 175.

were taken up with producing unviable machines. From November 1941, Milch was in charge, yet it took him two years to recover; by then Allied aircraft production dwarfed Germany's. Bombing of the Fatherland then took aircraft to defense, and by 1944 the GAF in Russia had only 300 fighters and 300 bombers spread over 1,350 miles.

At one point, no fewer than 425 variants of aircraft types were in high-quality production in Germany, but with too much innovation. Chaos without a plan came from a Junkers abhorrence of U.S.-style mass production. The Germans preferred technical sophistication to production numbers.

Only in December 1941 did Hitler, impressed by the Soviets' simplification, increase efficiency and mass production on modern principles, and only in spring 1942 did he appoint Albert Speer to manage the whole centrally planned and nationalized economy. By 1944, forty-two aircraft types had been reduced to five. By 1944, three giant factories produced Me-109s at 1,000 per month, as compared to the former 180 in seven factories. Industrialists now ruled without military interference, though until the spring of 1944 Hermann Goering kept control of aircraft production. Real mass production was only just being realized when bombing began in earnest in February 1944, which ironically forced dispersion of the newly centralized production facilities. And, thus, German aircraft production peaked in September 1944. By then, 25 percent of the workers were foreign forced labor in squalid conditions, and were resented by German workers. Food supplies declined and area bombing made for homelessness; many workers spent hours in shelters, and absen-

Leaders of the Allied air offensive against Germany at RAF Bomber Command, High Wycombe, in 1943: l to r, Gen. Henry H. "Hap" Arnold, Air Chief Marshal Sir Arthur Harris, and Gen. Ira C. Eaker, before Eaker was transferred to the Mediterranean. (USAF)

Aircraft could not be kept serviceable and in the air without the ground crews who had to work in the open in all weather. This picture lacks representation by the Women's Auxiliary Air Force, for they were very much a part of the maintenance force in 1943–1945. (Canadian Forces)

An RAF Bristol Beaufighter X (ER 22.7) shown here in invasion stripes for D-Day, June 6, 1944, was a formidable development of the original 1940 night fighter. With five-inch rockets, it packed the punch of a light cruiser, and its sleeve-valve engines and long mufflers made it so quiet that the Japanese called it "Whispering Death." (Source unknown)

By 1944–1945, the premier RAF heavy bomber was the Avro Lancaster (ER 103). Its unsuccessful twin Rolls-Royce Vulture-engined Manchester was changed to four Rolls-Royce Merlins. Unlike U.S. bombers, with their vertical bomb bays near the center of gravity, British "heavies" had a long bay, which allowed them to carry and drop a mix of incendiaries and high-explosive ordnance. This Lancaster carries "Monica" in the streamlined ventral blister, the defensive radar upon which German night fighters unfortunately could home. An example is at the Imperial War Museum at Duxford, United Kingdom. (Royal Air Force)

One reason the USAAF abandoned painting daylight aircraft was not just to save weight, but because it was known from the Battle of Britain that aircraft at high altitude (above 20,000 feet) gave off contrails if conditions were right, causing the hot exhaust to condense into ice crystals. Here, two B-17 Flying Fortresses (ER 101 for ferry range; ER 75.98, B-17G) signal their presence. PRU pilots constantly watched in their rearview mirrors for the telltale trail, then changed altitude to become almost invisible again. (USAF)

Operations on airfields in the Italian theater were plagued by dust in summer and mud in winter. Here, a Consolidated B-24 Liberator's nosewheel has collapsed, and it has come to a troublesome stop off the runway. More than 18,000 Liberators (ER 103) were built, but the aircraft never achieved the recognition of the B-17. (USAF)

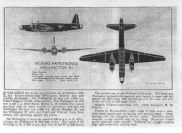

IFF (identification, friend or foe) in the Second World War became of vital importance. It was taught with three-view silhouettes, slides, and models. Shown are the cover and a sample page from a popular paperback published by the leading British aeronautical journal, *The Aeroplane* (1911–67). The author was a supernumerary aircraft recognition instructor and tutor while getting his wings in Canada during 1943–44.

This airport cartoon by the author, dated June 17, 1944, shows the typical Royal Canadian Air Force field layout—this at No. 3 Service Flying Training School Calgary, where the winds were variable, often delaying landings. The pilot in aircraft No. 8143, in flight is saying to his crew, "That's O.K. . . . By the time we get down, they'll be using it again." (Robin Higham)

Called a Cessna Crane (ER 0.6) for the RCAF and an AT- 17 Bobcat for the USAAF, the aircraft was known as the "Bamboo Bomber" because of the nature of their construction. The protruding main wheels ensured minimum damage in case of a wheels-up landing. The author earned his brevet (wings) on this type in October 1944 at Calgary, Alberta. (Cessna)

Flying-control facilities became necessary during World War II with increased numbers of aircraft operating in limited airspace, or when returning aircraft needed to be landed as soon as possible. Control-tower designs have evolved from a mobile caravan at the end of the runway, as used by the USAAF during the war, to facilities such as this at Dulles Airport, Washington, D.C., in 1976, when the Concordes began service. (Air France)

Air bases in Britain, where land was at a premium for agriculture and housing as well, were more compact, with barracks dispersed. The longest runway was into the prevailing southwest wind. In 1947, when longer runways for jets were necessary, it was found that the new, heavier jets were less affected by crosswinds, and thus the three-runway airfield design had been costly. (William Laing, Ltd.)

The Soviets let women fly combat, but the Allies limited them to transport, ferry, and training duties. Here in 1944, Women Airforce Service Pilots (WASP), carrying their 25-pound seatpack parachutes over their shoulders and walk out to the planes they will deliver within the continental United States. (USAF)

The JB-1, built by Continental Motors, was an almost exact copy of the famous German V-1 Flying Bomb, and was one of 1,200 built in the United States in 1944 so that the U.S. Army and Navy could learn about them. The V-1 was effective both as a weapon and as a psychological threat. (USAF Museum)

By 1944, the Northrop P-61 Black Widow (ER 83) was one of the radar-guided night fighters over Europe. The bulbous nose held the radar with the four .50-caliber guns mounted atop the fuselage. (Northrop)

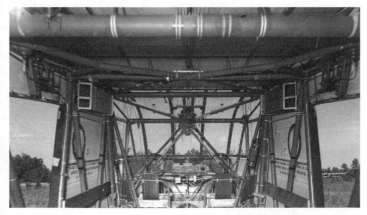

The simplicity of the expendable Waco CG-4A is quite clear here. Apart from enemy action, the biggest danger to the glider was on takeoff when, if the pilots failed to skim the ground, the tug released the nylon towrope, which would recoil through the windshield. As a copilot in a C-47 Dakota, the author kept his right hand over his left shoulder, ready to instantly jettison the glider if the tug could not get airborne. (USAF)

Preserved at the National Air and Space Museum in Washington, D.C., are two of Hitler's secret weapons—the twin-engine Me-262 (ER 9.92), the world's first operational jet fighter, and the Me-163 Komet (ER 6.7), a rocket-powered interceptor that was a pilot-killer. The Me-262 might have challenged the Eighth Air Force earlier than 1944 if Hitler had not insisted that it have dive-bombing capability. (Ronald C. Carriker, via NASM)

USAAF Douglas C-47 Skytrains (Dakotas) and Waco CG-4A gliders assembled for takeoff on an English airfield before Operation Market Garden, in September 1944. A C-47 (ER 20) could tow one Airspeed Horsa or two Wacos. (USAF)

Geofrey de Havilland believed that the simplest design with fewest innovations worked best. For 3½ years, the Mosquito—the "wooden wonder"—was the fastest operational aircraft in the European theater. Designed to carry four 250-pound bombs, this Mosquito PR 45 carried a 4,000-pounder or a very long-range fuel tank. In 1945 it had an ER of 75.86 versus the 1942 Mosquito Mark VI's ER of 30—a remarkable wartime growth. (de Havilland Canada)

teeism soared. From 1944, only fear of the *SS*—the elite *Schutzstaffel*—and of the Red Army kept production going, but in steady decline. The German economy fell between the command system of Stalinism and free enterprise, and it squandered its resources in internal indecision and conflict.

German fuel requirements in 1938 had been 44 million barrels of oil, while the United Kingdom needed 76 million, Russia 183 million, and the United States 1 billion barrels. Roughly 60 percent of the German total (28 million barrels) came from imports, and 3.8 million barrels from domestic sources. Germany was in a precarious position and synthetic plants never produced more than 2.8 million barrels. Rumania exported 13 million barrels to Germany in 1941, and the same in 1942 and 1943. But the August 1943 Ploesti air strike destroyed 50 percent of Rumanian refining capacity, and thus deliveries in the first half of 1944 dropped to 7 million barrels before additional raids halted further production and the Red Armies came.

High-octane petrol was limited by a shortage of steel for refineries and of manpower. Nevertheless, synthetic aviation fuel on hand went up from 10 million barrels in 1938 to 38 million in 1943. By then, it amounted to 50 percent of the fuels from all sources. Total fuel rose from 45 to 71 million barrels at the same time. And, thus, fuel was not a serious problem until early 1944. Farmers obtained more fuel as horses were requisitioned. Meanwhile, alternate lower octane fuels also added 8.2 million barrels by 1943.

Air attacks on synthetic fuel plants on June 30, 1944, to January 19, 1945, cut the output for aviation by 90 percent. The industrial czar, Albert Speer, recognized that if plants were not repaired and if reserves were consumed, Germany could no longer conduct a modern technological war. One effect was that the training of pilots was cut to one-third the normal hours.

In an industrial war, the Germans had failed the test. Strategic bombing passed it.

BLITZKRIEG AND AIRBORNE CAMPAIGNS

The term *Blitzkrieg,* while normally associated with German mechanized operations in the years 1939 through 1941, can be equally well applied to some Allied operations in the sense that it consisted of a combination of armor, infantry, and air power providing a fast striking force. It is thus used here, in connection with the Wave cycle of development. The Germans were shifting from rearmamental instability to wartime equilibrium in their *Blitzkrieg* operations by the summer of 1940, whereas both the Western Allies and the Soviets were still rearming until late 1941 or early 1942. In the development of tactical air forces cooperating with ground forces, the most significant change after wartime equilibrium had been reached was in terms of numbers and power of weapons systems. For this reason, then, little is said of either Allied operations in Italy or after D-Day, or of Soviet support of the Red armies after Stalingrad, because in terms of historical lessons or techniques these contribute little to what can be gleaned from earlier operations. The same comments apply to the development of air transport support operations. The Germans set the style; others simply improved on and massed it.

Europe and North Africa

Although the war in Spain was a testing ground for air power, it did not see the realization of *Blitzkrieg* tactics. These were first made evident in the German Polish campaign at the end of summer of 1939, but the dazzling speed of that performance led unbelievers to discredit evidence of such tactics in favor of other more acceptable and traditional explanations for the German successes. This was a mistake for which they paid dearly in the early summer of 1940.

The secret of the German *Blitzkrieg* lay in meticulous planning coupled with lightning strikes to unbalance the opponent and render his control over the subsequent battle ineffective. The model was provided by Allenby at Megiddo in 1918, when he used aircraft to isolate Turkish headquarters while cavalry and armored cars broke through to the rear. The success of his tactics was capped with the aerial ambush of the retreating Turkish forces, as noted earlier.

German successes generally followed the same pattern, until the tables began to turn in late 1942 when the Americans, British, and Soviets came on the field with escalated versions of the same system. But the Allies were never able at that stage of the war to accomplish what the Germans had at the beginning—that is, to knock out a whole nation by a surprise stroke, succeeding before any counter grand-strategic air bombardment could take effect. Moreover, the German technique combined both military action and psychological warfare, so that the will to resist was half broken before the war started.

The Japanese employed somewhat the same tactics, but in the jungles and undeveloped terrain over which they operated, armor was generally omitted. Their *Judo Blitzkrieg*—sharp, quick blows—used air power to strike at Allied air bases and naval power, so that surface, usually amphibious, forces could get ashore and pad swiftly to their objectives.

In both *Blitzkriegs* the objective was a short, quick victory to obtain economic resources and to destroy existing political and military organization.

German *Blitzkriegs* can be divided into two phases. The first was a series of brilliant successes from Poland in September 1939 to Crete in May 1941; the second was the campaign in the Soviet Union.

Poland

Having taken the Rhineland, Austria, and Czechoslovakia without a shot, Hitler selected as his next victim Poland, recreated in 1919 out of eastern Germany and western Russia. The usual propaganda campaign was mounted, and the Poles were thus warned that they were on the list. This saved them for a few days, for although Hitler struck without warning, they were already forearmed. All serviceable Polish Air Force units had been withdrawn to special landing strips, but unserviceable and obsolete machines were left visible on the old airfields. For the attack on Poland, the *Luftwaffe* could deploy 648 bombers, 219 dive-bombers, 30 ground-attack planes, 210 fighters, and 474 other aircraft. Of these, some 285 were lost to enemy action in the 28-day campaign, and an additional 279 were damaged. To oppose the Germans, the Polish Air Force could muster initial establishments of 159 fighters, 36 medium bombers, and 84 reconnaissance machines. Of these and aircraft in reserve, the Poles lost 333 in the first two weeks; the remaining 116 were flown to internment in Rumania on September 17.

The Polish campaign did not proceed as the Germans had intended. The plan was to destroy the Polish Air Force on the first day, next to help the German army attain its objectives, and, then, when time could be spared, to go after the Polish aircraft industry. The one major question was whether or not Goering could stage the massed attack on Warsaw that he intended to use as a devastating blow, not against the Polish people as such, but against the military, aircraft industry, and communications targets with which the area abounded. After one day's delay due to fog over eastern Germany and Poland, on September 2 the *Luftwaffe* swarmed over Polish airfields, meeting little opposition in the air and cratering runways, blasting hangars, and destroying aircraft on the ground. Not until the third day did the Poles rise from their new lairs. But the Germans had already won the battle for air supremacy, though they did not know it. Their attacks had severed Polish communications so badly that orders did not reach squadrons in intelligible fashion. The Poles had achieved surprise by their concealment of usable aircraft, but the Germans had negated it by disrupting the control system.

The Germans had done more than they needed to do, however, and less well than they imagined. A secret assessment made after the campaign showed that the damage to the abandoned airfields was superficial and that runways could quickly be filled in again. Even worse, the attacks on the aircraft factories had been too effective, and thus these facilities were not available to the Germans.

Nor did the rest of the Polish campaign go smoothly. Polish anti-aircraft fire was accurate and heavy, and German aircraft had to be ordered not to fly low except when necessary. Moreover, Hitler was most anxious to take Warsaw before the Soviets could, for they had also attacked Poland, reached it, and thus put on the pressure for its destruction. But for this sort of attack against a city, the *Luftwaffe* was not prepared. While Stukas could be used effectively enough with high explosives, deprived by effective anti-aircraft fire of the expected low-level bombers, the air commander had to use Ju-52 transports to drop incendiaries, and these literally had to be shoveled out of the doors. After a longer struggle than anticipated, heavily defended Warsaw was eventually forced to capitulate in one day.

Yet, it was not in the air battle over Poland that the *Luftwaffe* really contributed so much to victory, for the Polish Air Force, though gallant, was inferior and soon disrupted. It was the *Luftwaffe*'s aid to troops on the ground that was so significant. The German Air Force was the eyes of the army, with 25 percent of its machines reconnaissance aircraft as well as its long-range artillery. Using the lessons learned in Spain, the *Luftwaffe*'s field commander, von Richthofen, placed forward air controllers with the leading army elements so that Stukas could be directed onto defensive pockets and strong points. The German communications system worked because it was direct rather than routed through channels, as planned.

Norway

The Norwegian operation in the spring of 1940 was not part of the German grand-strategic plan, but it became necessary from their point of view because of British interference with German iron-ore shipments from Narvik and merchant shipping sneaking along the coast, together with an Allied plan to seize Narvik and occupy Sweden. In this respect, then, the German action was a spoiling attack to disrupt Allied intentions. This in itself did not make it unusual; what did was the way in which air transport was used as the instrument. Moreover, the Germans were willing to take risks, whereas the Allies, as often in the war, were too cautious and too prone to assume that the Germans were as fuzzy in their thinking as the French and British were in theirs. The Germans minimized risks by better planning, by taking the psychological initiative, and by intelligence.

Four Norwegian airfields were to be captured by German paratroopers, who would have twenty minutes to do the job before reinforcement transports began to land. And thus an air-transport commander was appointed who was to make certain that the 500 transports operated smoothly in and out of the four airfields. But, as in the attack against Poland, this phase of the German plan did not go according to schedule. Although the Messerschmitt Me-110s (ER 6.0) sent to suppress the anti-aircraft defenses at Fornebu-Oslo airfield moved through the thick fog on the Norwegian coast, the cruiser *Blucher,* carrying the assault infantry, was sunk near Oslo by gunners from a Norwegian fort, and the transports were thus held up. The first wave of paratroopers had been turned back by bad weather, but the second wave of transports were able to land with the Me-110s as soon as the local Norwegian Gloster Gladiator fighter aircraft (ER 1.1) had been defeated. Reinforcements were at once ordered up by X Air Corps Headquarters in Hamburg, and on the evening of April 9 they took the Norwegian capital. Stavanger airfield was seized by paratroopers who were shortly reinforced by airborne troops.

Small risks, in terms of numbers, were taken, but the prize was great. By the time the British reacted and put troops ashore on April 14, the Germans were well enough established for the Allied landings to be untenable. Norway belonged to the Germans for the rest of the war and furnished them with valuable air bases for attacks on the British Home Fleet at Scapa Flow, and later for strikes against convoys to Russia.

Norway was just at the extreme range of British naval fighters based on northern Scotland, and at this stage of the war the British had neither the doctrine nor the escort carriers to use as floating airfields. The Germans won in Norway because they took boldly calculated risks and had the air transport fleets with which to carry them out— and because the British were still using a reactive strategy that allowed the Germans the initiative. It must be admitted that the Norwegians helped nobody with their intransigent neutrality, and the British were unprepared to act in bold disregard of niceties to save the greater objective. In addition to being at that time involved in a Continental commitment in France, they were not yet geared up mentally or physically to fight the war that was being forced upon them. And their ideas of invading Sweden to stop the Germans were farcical.

The Attack in the West

The next *Blitzkrieg* was more conventional, and still shockingly effective. In a matter of weeks the Germans took Holland, Belgium, and France. The techniques were much the same as before, but with some interesting added touches. On May 10, Ju-52s left Cologne towing gliders that landed inside the key Belgian fortress of Eben Emael. The troops had practiced the operation for seven months, and it went like clockwork; once again a complete surprise was achieved and the enemy taken from the rear. Other gliders disgorged their

teams to seize key points and hold them until infantry could arrive, as they had done in Denmark in April.

Included in the attack on Holland and Belgium was another decisive blow at a principal city, in which speed was emphasized, as it had been at Warsaw and Oslo. In Holland, a country easily flooded so that troops would be confined to single elevated roads or rail lines, speed was especially vital to prevent the sluices from being opened. But surprise and secrecy were essentially lost in early 1940 when a staff officer carrying the plans made a forced landing in Belgium; and with the mission compromised, the Germans switched to a variant. Although hampered by the flatness of Holland, which made the target airfields difficult to find, as well as by stubborn Dutch resistance, the Germans managed to take the vital bridges across the New Maas river in Amsterdam by flying seaplanes directly up to them and seizing the bridgeheads. Almost simultaneously, airfields on the outskirts were bombed, and paratroopers dropped outside their perimeters to make the defenders face outwards. However, Ju-52s landing on the fields were torn apart by obstacles placed on the runways, and other airborne attackers got lost or could not land on the fields already choked with wrecks. But eventually an infantry force hemmed the Dutch defenders into a triangle to the north of the vital pass through the center of Rotterdam. There on May 14, occurred a tragedy that was caused by a combination of communications and historical difficulties.

The Dutch colonel commanding refused to capitulate in the face of what he regarded as a ruse, and by the time he was undeceived, the destruction of the city was under way. German communications, as so often at this stage of the war, were too elaborate, and no frequency had been established by which General Student, the airborne leader, could speak directly to *Luftwaffe* aircraft overhead. As a result, precious time elapsed, and try as he would he could not stop a one hundred-plane demonstration raid that had been scheduled that morning for 1500 hours. It was only after fifty-seven aircraft had dropped their bombs from 2,300 feet that the leader of the formation saw the red Very lights fired by the general himself and halted the raid. Then history took over. The old timbered city was an oil and margarine trading center. The Dutch lacked adequate fire-fighting equipment, as did any city of that time. The fires that had started grew quickly out of control, and most of the old city burned while the Dutch capitulation was taking place. Allied propaganda made a great deal of another Nazi outrage, but the Germans have truth on their side. Despite the tragedy of not being able to stop the raid in time, and in spite of what analysts—especially wartime propagandists—have said about it, the operation itself was no more immoral than the use of artillery by both sides at that time and place.

From the German point of view the major disaster of the attack on Holland was that it consumed 310 of the 430 transports employed; and as these were mostly flown by instructors from bomber training units, the chain-reaction effect upon German operations was out of proportion to the value derived. In effect, the Germans suffered something of the same loss of experienced pilots that plagued the Japanese after the first seven months of the Pacific war in 1941–42.

The operations against France were yet another example of the *Blitzkrieg* technique. Here, once again, *Luftwaffe* bombers flying at tree-top height struck at dawn on May 10 at seventy Allied airfields. Although they were not always successful in destroying the fields, the surprise was unnerving. In fact, the Allies were in poor condition to fight. The French Air Force had started to deteriorate in the early 1930s, and its condition had steadily worsened, in spite of the development of some promising new designs.

L'Armée de l'Air was handicapped by the late start to rearm, and thus France did nothing in the 1936 Rhineland crisis. The FAF had already been psychologically beaten by the *Luftwaffe* during

Chief of the Air Staff General Vuillemin's visit to Germany in August 1938, which led directly to the French, and British, appeasement at Munich in order to buy time.

The French Air Force was handicapped by an organization that tied units in peacetime to particular regions, but whose war stations were somewhere else under a new command that had not existed even in cadre before hostilities. No radar existed, and the French had few DCA *(defense contra avions)*—anti-aircraft artillery—not surprising considering that northeast France had 200 airfields, which were a logistician's nightmare, especially once the campaign became fluid.

Modern aircraft came from the French factories from 1938 on, as funds (credits) were suddenly, at last, made available to the Air Ministry. It was true that the FAF had more modern aircraft in June 1940 than in September 1939, but it lacked propellers, engines, radios, and armament, as well as aircrew and mechanics, which forced machines to be stored all over France. In other words, the FAF in May 1940 was still a cadre, not a fighting force. And it lost 410 aircraft in combat, 202 bombed on the ground, and 230 by accident due both to inexperienced aircrew and unproved designs. Moreover, in 1939, only 40 of the FAF officer pilots were under 24 years of age, whereas 1,148 were 35 or older. And they lacked the unity and *esprit de corps* of a team.

The French Air Force was not only defeated in the air, but by its own methods on the ground. Factories were rolling out aircraft and these were accepted, though incomplete, and sent to storage units. The result was that although manufacturing of modern types would have kept up with operational consumption and wastage, only twenty-two serviceable aircraft per day were delivered to units as compared to the thirty-two produced and required. Casualties among aircrew and mechanics could not be replaced. Thus, by June 5 the FAF had about ceased operations and was thinking of continuing the fight from North Africa. But those aircraft and crews that did cross the

Mediterranean found themselves impotent for lack of spares and fuel.

After the Armistice, in July Chief of the Air Staff Vuillemin asked his commanders for an assessment of what had gone wrong. They responded that the FAF was short by two-thirds in personnel, aircraft, and logistics. In July 1940, the FAF commander in the field believed that *L'Armée de l'Air* should have had 500,000 personnel and 7,000 aircraft. It actually had 166,000 officers and men, and 1,370 aircraft. Commission G, based on reports from the participants, sought to lay bare the reasons for failure and to establish a base, to prevent a recurrence. That action, during the German occupation, and the rule from Vichy, restored the FAF's spirit, even though it shouldered much of the blame for the catastrophe.

Anglo-French relations were not always open, and neither partner was really sure of what the other possessed. The French had only 186 bombers, of which 11 were modern, 549 fighters of which 131 were obsolete, and 377 reconnaissance aircraft of which 316 were outdated.

At FAF request, RAF Hawker Hurricanes (ER 1.94) were stationed in the French sector to provide fighter support. Even worse than the fact that this spread British fighter strength very thinly behind the front, neither of the two British bomber types available could survive as flown in the face of German fighters unless escorted, and there were not enough Hurricanes to do that. The Fairey Battle (ER 5.46) was a three-seat single-engine light bomber with a structural weakness, weighing twice as much as a Hurricane but powered with the same engine. In the first three days of the campaign, the Battle averaged a 70 percent loss rate, yet it was expected to make tactical daylight sorties. The Bristol Blenheims (ER 7.28) fared not much better because they were flown at 12,000 feet instead of on the deck. To supplement these machines, Bomber Command in Britain had 200 heavy and medium bombers of the Armstrong Whitworth Whitley V (ER 21), Vickers Wellington (ER 30), Bristol Blenheim, and Handley Page Hampden (ER 17.56) types, making a total of 544 bombers for all European operations.

But even more than the technical inadequacy, theoretical considerations on the Allied side posed problems, for though there had been public debate in Parliament and about Billy Mitchell, air power had never found its J. F. C. Fuller or its Liddell Hart. Moreover, there was no overall RAF commander-in-chief to coordinate operational control. The Chief of the Air Staff was then only the adviser to the Secretary of State for Air. And the Air Officer Commander-in-Chief in France lost his communications center on the first day of the attack, May 10, 1940.

No one was sure that air power could stop a fast-rolling ground offensive, nor were they sure where to strike to attempt to do so, the lessons of 1918 having been ignored. This was not only an Anglo-French point of contention, but also one between the War Office and the Air Ministry in London. The French did not want bombers used except possibly directly on the battlefield, because they were afraid of retaliation. Some British airmen argued for their use tactically, others for grand-strategic attacks against the heavily concentrated German industrial targets in the Ruhr, and yet others for an attack on oil. The whole problem was that no one really was sure what results could be obtained and the commander-in-chief of Bomber Command was not at all convinced that his Blenheims should be used at all. Nor did he believe that his airmen could find targets such as airfields, let alone hit them. The only aircraft in France in which anyone on the British side had any confidence were the Hurricanes, and of these only ten squadrons were available to face some 1,200 German fighters. Moreover, British fighters still flew in unmaneuverable, vulnerable V formations from airfields sited once again for a 1914–18 war.

The fact is that the Allies simply were not prepared to face the concentrated German fighter force, nor did they grasp the lightning nature of *Blitzkrieg*. This kind of war required highly skillful, ruthless, hard-hitting bombing of key passages or bottlenecks in repeated escorted raids. The Allies had neither adequate reconnaissance aircraft nor an anti-aircraft gun that could equal the German 88 mm dual-purpose flak gun nor their quad 20 mm vehicle-mounted cannon. In addition, air superiority had to be established to protect airfields and aircraft that could be concentrated on the enemy's armor, motorized columns, and supply lines. Attacking the industrial base of a *Blitzkrieg* army was unlikely to be of much use, as the Germans planned carefully and the whole operation was designed to be well supplied up front from forward depots. Given their whole system, it is scarcely surprising that the Germans rolled over a France commanded by generals who thought in 1918 terms and were backed by a population with low morale. In part this was due to General Gaumelin's having sought to prepare France for war, yet he was not a battlefield commander.

The one mistake the Germans made was in halting their tanks outside the Dunkirk area. It was there for the first time that they had begun to run into British air superiority, as the *Luftwaffe* had not moved up fast enough. When von Richthofen did advance his groups, many were at half their normal thirty-aircraft strength after two weeks of intensive operations. (In addition, the Germans normally considered that 10 percent of any unit would not be available due to maintenance problems.) At this point Hermann Goering, never reticent, suggested to Hitler that the tanks be held back while the *Luftwaffe* finished off the surrounded Anglo-French forces. For 2½ half days the tanks sat idle, and on one of these days, Stukas and artillery combined to complete the fall of stubborn Calais. On May 26 the Germans launched an all-out attack on the Dunkirk bridgehead, but as it was within range of fighters based in Britain, air cover could be provided and was. In addition, with several days of bad weather, and after only 2½ days of attacks during the nine days and nights of the evacuation, the *Luftwaffe* was withdrawn and switched south, resuming its normal support tac-

tics until France fell. It had defeated the Allied air forces, except over Dunkirk, and helped ruin their armies. The operations, while expensive, were effective and well worth the price.

The campaign in France in 1940 saw the *Luftwaffe* applying its numerical superiority, strategy, and tactics very much to the detriment of the Allied air forces. The latter's airfields were constantly under attack, their logistic arrangements disrupted in part because the French had eleven or more types on 200 aerodromes in the northeast alone. The German Air Force, too, had the advantage over the French Air Force in bombers that were faster than French fighters and fighters that could swarm over Allied formations, while neither the French nor the British had radar to alert them. An effort to have French twin-engined aircraft shadow large German formations on June 3, with their running commentary rebroadcast from the Eiffel Tower, came to naught, as the Germans with their superior radio jammed the signals, which never reached the defensive squadrons.

The Balkans and Crete

The next German *Blitzkriegs* were into the Balkans. A German military mission protected the vital Rumanian oilfields around Ploesti against Soviet advances. In late March 1941 Yugoslavia was attacked, Belgrade bombed, and the country overrun when a change of government refused German protection. And this was the beginning of a campaign designed to eradicate the sore in the Axis side created by Mussolini's ill-fated attempt to conquer Greece.

British reaction to the opening of an Italian Balkan Front was to send a token RAF fighter and bomber force to support the noble Hellenes, the last free opponent on the Continent. London had grandiose plans for the Greek front, but Athens and Cairo were realists. Unfortunately, they were overruled in early March, and the ANZAC (Australian-New Zealand Army Corps) force was sent to Greece.

Hitler, with his intuitive eye for grand strategy,

saw as early as November 1940 that the island of Crete was the key to the whole area. No sooner had the Italians attacked Greece than the British occupied Crete. But just as the British underrated German energy and thoroughness, so the Germans overrated the British. Hitler feared that the British bombers based in Crete, or more likely in the Salonika plain of Greece, would be a threat to the Ploesti oilfields. He, therefore, had proposed an airborne operation against Crete. Nothing was done about this over the winter while preparations for the invasion of the Soviet Union moved ahead, but it was decided to clean up the Greek campaign even before the British landed there in March, to secure the German flank for the invasion of the Soviet Union. Thus, once again the Germans worked to an extremely tight timetable and relied on the momentum of surprise, experience, and organization to carry them through, though delayed by a late thaw.

The campaign in Greece was short and decisive. It was an ideal area in which to use air power, for road and rail networks were almost nonexistent and the defenders were constantly hampered by the terrain. The Germans were not able to strike at key bridges, disrupt traffic by bombing and strafing the closely packed columns on the few roads available, nor destroy aircraft on their landing grounds. British intelligence knew the *Luftwaffe* had a four to one advantage. The British army wanted its own air force, as the RAF was still wedded to grand-strategic bombing without the money to do it.

The one secret weapon that the British had from mid-March was ULTRA and the decrypts of German signals. The Germans should have been aided by the British lack of an efficient early-warning system, which by April 1941 caused the RAF, virtually the Greek air force, to quickly lose its effectiveness and with relatively small loss to the Germans.

The whole Greek campaign was a repetition of France the year before, though German Air Force attacks on troops were not as frequent as the victims claimed. The limited range of the Me-109 only allowed it to reach Larissa from Monastir and return. Not until Larissa was taken did the *Luftwaffe* fighters and Stukas have the endurance to attack the enemy heading south to the Thermopylae Line. And the British managed to disengage at night and evacuate, all except those caught at the Corinth Canal by the airborne landings, though the remnants evacuated out of Kalamata to Crete, again at night. The British Commander-in-Chief Middle East regarded his grand intervention in Greece as a deception of London's Churchill, and thus he conducted a quick withdrawal, after being forced to land more troops than he intended, due to the German attack being delayed a month by heavy snows in the Balkan passes. The analysis and lessons of the campaign in France had not yet reached the British headquarters in Cairo.

On April 21, while the Greeks capitulated, Hitler assented to the completion of the campaign by an airborne assault on Crete. But he specified that this must be done by the airborne and paratroop divisions alone, and that it must be completed by mid-May. Mussolini was persuaded to agree—although he was inclined to accept the German General Staff's appraisal that Malta was the more vital target, lying as it did across the supply routes to North Africa—and the formal order was given on April 25. But it was not until May 14 that the assaulting forces were ready, and by then the airborne division, unable to move south by road from Rumania, had been replaced by an elite mountain division that had never participated in airborne operations.

The irony of all these delays was in the fact that if the British had been able to put Crete into fighting order in the first place, they would have had some three weeks in which to reform and rearm the troops that had been evacuated from Greece. Moreover, if they had built airfields on Crete, and if they had had modern medium bombers or had even used the Blenheims available effectively from the lessons in France, they might seriously have disrupted the German preparations. The passes in the Macedonian mountains were jammed with panzers going north and troops trying to get south, and the airfields were clogged. Unfortunately, on the British side almost everything was missing—except ULTRA—including almost all radar, which was vital to provide the necessary early warning against attacks on Crete. But this was merely an extension of the tragedy of involvement in Greece, the blame for which must be laid at Churchill's door. He failed to understand that the Middle East Command was a vast theater (the distance from Salonika to Nairobi was five times the length of the British Isles), and that paper figures of numbers of squadrons were highly unreliable when vast distances and many campaigns were involved.

To add insult to injury, the campaign against Crete had to be delayed by the Germans for a number of reasons. First, the 500 Ju-52s used for the Greek campaign had to be returned to home bases for overhaul. It is a tribute to German efficiency that this was completed and 493 returned to Greece between May 1 and 14. Unfortunately, no fuel had arrived because the Corinth Canal bridge, though taken by German paratroopers, had been dropped into the canal and the tankers could not get through. After the fuel was transferred into 560,000 45-gallon drums, it had to be taken over abominable roads to the airfields. Even worse, as the RAF had discovered earlier, Greek airfields were composed of either mud or dust. The *Luftwaffe* experienced the dry season; after one squadron took off, well over a quarter of an hour had to elapse for the dust to settle before another could proceed. For all that, on the morning of May 20, hot, tired, sleepless, and dirty, the Germans took off for Crete. The RAF had missed its chance to catch them on the ground.

The Germans' initial wave of 53 gliders and 5,000 paratroopers planned to seize the western airfield of Maleme, but the British had quality intelligence and, despite a heavy pre-attack bombing, most of their concealed positions were intact. As a result, during the first day, the Germans were unable to seize the airfield, although enough anti-aircraft guns were silenced for a substantial German force to be scattered on the ground. Late in the afternoon, in much disorder due to the mess on their own airfields in Greece, where landing aircraft had collided and losses far exceeded the seven Ju-52s shot down over Crete, the second German wave dropped near the other two British airfields. General Student had intended that these be diverted to Maleme, but his staff was unable to get through on the telephone to the squadrons before the aircraft took off. Thus, the second wave arrived in droplets and was unable to capture either Retimo or Herakleion airfields. By nightfall the British held a very narrow advantage. It might have been greater if the desperate German seizure of the vital hill overlooking the airfield at Maleme had met a counterattack, for the paratroopers were out of ammunition and were only saved the next day by the arrival of a single Ju-52 that landed on the nearby beach with a supply. By May 21, *Luftwaffe* aircraft controlled the air, as none of the British airfields was tenable and fighter cover could not be maintained from Egypt. Then at four in the afternoon, General Student's mountain division was successfully landed on Maleme airfield in a desperate stroke, at the cost of eighty transports. At last the Germans had a beachhead on the island. The Royal Navy beat back the seaborne reinforcements that night, but was forced the next day to withdraw, lacking air cover and nearly out of anti-aircraft ammunition. Although the battle went on until June 1, it had been decided by the night of the May 22.

The irony of what had occurred at Crete is that it was the last great German airborne operation. It had cost the Germans too many aircraft and too many elite troops to be repeated. Moreover, once again, as in the west in 1940, the cream of the bomber-instructor crop were lost, and the impact of this was felt all through the remainder of the war. Even more than this, the decimation of the transports in part had hampered the speed of movement of the panzers in the Soviet Union;

this was especially critical because the campaign there opened a month later than planned, not so much a result of the Greek campaign as because of the slow spring thaw that made the ground too soft for tanks until June 22. The cost of the delays would be made plain at Stalingrad in late 1942.

But it is also ironic that Crete convinced the Allies that airborne operations were a prerequisite to success, and men and equipment were therefore diverted to airborne forces. The argument against this policy is that it plucked the best men out of regular units and isolated them in special contingents that were rarely used and, when they were, suffered high casualties.

The *coup de main* airborne tactic was valuable on occasion, perhaps, but it had to be used within clearly defined rules. Basically these were that the units had to be dropped precisely on time and on target and that they had to be relieved within no more than two or three days. Moreover, they had to have air cover and instant resupply, even in those few days. And lastly, as the Allied Arnhem-Nijmegen operation showed in 1944, and as the history of war has all too often demonstrated, such a fragile force could only be committed successfully on the basis of accurate intelligence. In Crete, for instance, the Germans found that the hilly nature of the ground resulted in units landing out of sight of one another while being dominated by hidden defenders. And at Arnheim the British landed on top of a panzer division at rest. Intelligence would have avoided these incidents.

Consequences

As an extension of the *Blitzkrieg* technique, little need be said here of the German thrust into the Soviet Union. The mistake made was simply to attempt on a very broad front what had succeeded on narrow fronts without allowing time to build up the necessary air striking and air-support forces. In each of the previous campaigns, the Germans had been able to strike decisively on the ground straight at the enemy's capital, while receiving support from aircraft based at airfields established be-

fore the campaign started. In each case, moreover, the blitz had lasted no more than four weeks over limited distances, yet even so, *Luftwaffe* units were reduced to something like half their normal strength without allowing for the effects of battle fatigue. The *Luftwaffe* of 1939–41 was a tactical rapier, not a heavy two-edged saber, and it was not backed by an aircraft industry geared for a major war. The fact that it lacked a strategic bomber was no longer a real issue. After 1941, *the Luftwaffe* was placed on the defensive in a war that would last another three years and that would make great calls upon it both in many far-flung battle fronts abroad and in defense of the Third Reich at home. Though it survived to the end, it lacked the stamina to achieve victory.

In early 1942, the *Luftwaffe* was in serious trouble because of failures in leadership, matériel, and training. The stresses of the 1940–42 campaigns had not allowed a correction of its deficiencies or the ability to reorganize. Factories were still on single shift, as they had been since 1935. The *Luftwaffe* lacked doctrine for a multi-front war and failed to understand the need not only to supply current requirements, but also to make quantum leaps in technology.

The *Luftwaffe* also had to fight the *Wehrmacht* over advanced technology, as in the case of the V-I versus the A-4 rocket, which by December 1943 was critical to both sides, when the V-I flying bomb became a cheap weapon that diverted 50 percent of the Allied bomber effort.

One special advantage that German generals enjoyed until the middle of the war was a personal aircraft. In transport planes they had the means of getting to and from the front without loss of time, and in the Fieseler Storch (ER 0.15) they had the inestimable advantage of being able to move about the front rapidly. The Storch was the ideal plane because of its short takeoff and landing characteristics, simplicity, and the excellent all-around visibility it afforded its passenger. More than this, German generals like Rommel were willing to use it.

In June 1942, just as in the Pacific where the Battle of Midway marked the turning point of the Allied fortunes, so in Europe a subtle change took place. The Germans ceased to advance into Egypt or to break past Stalingrad, and American forces joined the Battle of the Atlantic and arrived in Britain, where RAF Bomber Command had finally begun to receive its four-engine heavy bombers and to believe the unpalatable facts that its PRU people had been trying to point out for two years—that it could not find targets! Disappointing as it may be to some patriotic readers, it must be noted that the Allied tactical air forces owed their successes in the years to come to learning from the Germans, to intelligent leadership, and, above all else, to the arrival in the war zone of adequate matériel and men.

Allied Tactical Air Forces

The change was visible first in the Middle East. There in 1942 Air Chief Marshal Sir Arthur Tedder, closely in touch with the Chief of the Air Staff in London by both official and unofficial means, was at last beginning to receive modern matériel. No longer did his pilots have to face the Me-109 in obsolescent Curtiss P-40F Kittyhawks and battle-weary Hurricanes; they now had Spitfires. The Westland Lysander (ER 2.6) was replaced as an observation plane by the Kittyhawk, and the Bristol Blenheims and Martin Marylands (ER 16.8) gave way to Martin Baltimores (ER 14.9) and North American B-25 Mitchells. And at last Tedder had not only radar to prevent surprises and vector his defenders to hostile raids, but also an organization that could leapfrog squadrons up and down the battlefield so that troops could have continuous air cover. Even the faithful Wellingtons used for strategic attacks on Axis supply ports were supplemented with four-engined British and American bombers. Thus, when Montgomery opened his offensive at El Alamein in November 1942 he was supported by a mobile tactical air force the likes of which the British had never before possessed. Moreover, the Western Desert

Air Force was a socially self-sufficient force, very efficient at movements and camping. And the concurrent Allied invasion of North Africa was similarly blessed. In the wide-open spaces of the Western Desert, aircraft were hampered only by rain, dust, and mined enemy airfields. Montgomery's advance moved at such a pace that the tactical air forces could always keep the pressure up and at certain bottlenecks could get their revenge for similar German maulings in earlier campaigns.

As a result of the German successes with gliders, the Allies built large quantities of both light Wacos and heavy Horsas and some Hamilcars, the latter of which could carry a tank. Horsas were towed all the way from Britain to North Africa for the landings there, but the physical endurance required of the crews and their passengers was so excessive as to blunt their efficiency. In the later Sicilian campaign of July 1943, the airborne operation was also badly handled: the crews had to assemble their own gliders; the tug crews were unfamiliar with navigation in blacked-out, radioless, and maritime areas; recognition signals were lacking; and night landings were attempted. Army commanders overlooked a fact that the Germans had learned by 1940, namely that the glider was a special weapon with its own limitations.

At the fortress of Eben Emael, in Belgium, the Germans had been guided to the dropping point by a line of lights within Germany, and the arrival of the gliders had been timed for dawn's first emergence so that they could see the very precise landing zone and each other. At Sicily, not only were the gliders dropped all over land and sea in the dark, but lack of liaison caused the assault-force ships to open fire on the gliders as they passed low overhead, with the double result of casualties to the airborne and the alerting of the defenders. By D-Day in Normandy, a year later, the Allies had learned a great deal; they also had the advantage of staging from nearby main bases in Britain. They were successful due to careful planning and intensive training, and to the development of radar

President Franklin D. Roosevelt's special envoy, W. Averill Harriman, and Soviet generals await the arrival of the first shuttle-bombing mission from Western Europe at a clandestine Russian wartime base. Cooperation with the secretive Joseph Stalin was never easy. (USAF)

Air operations on the Eastern Front rarely were flown above 3,000 feet, and most were down on the deck, as seen in this poor-quality original Soviet photograph. The bulk of the Soviet air armies were equipped with the Ilyushin Il-2 Shturmovik (ER 3.7) two-seat attack plane. Casualties were as heavy as in infantry units, but the aircraft was rugged, repairable, and easy and cheap to produce. (USAF)

The 1941 Petlyakov PE-2 (ER 11.71) was a long-range Soviet fighter and light bomber used extensively on the Eastern Front, where massive Russian air armies of up to 4,000 aircraft operated in close support of ground forces. (USAF)

landing beacons that could be planted as a guide for gliders and paratroop transports homing in the dark, as well as excellent PRU photos.

Allied tactical air forces owed most of their success to the development of matériel and techniques and to the masses of aircraft available. From April 1944, the Allied Expeditionary Air Force had 2,000 fighters and 700 medium bombers engaged in the transportation attack plan in France, by which the Normandy area was isolated from the rest of German-held France. And despite the misgivings and protests of the commander-in-chief of Bomber Command, the 1,000 four-engine heavies he possessed were also on call. The Allies could not disguise the fact that they were going to assault northern France, but they achieved tactical surprise with the use of sophisticated electronic deception. Once ashore, they quickly laid down perforated-steel-plate airfields so that air cover could be based close behind the front lines. Already in earlier campaigns, as Allied air power became plentiful and fuel no problem, British forward air controllers had developed the "taxicab-rank" system: fighters and fighter-bombers orbited just behind the front line and were called in whenever a target appeared. The reaction time from call to strike was thus cut to minutes.

One innovation in France in the summer of 1944 was that the USAAF's Ninth Air Force protected the right flank of the Allied advance to the east after the breakout, by stopping German forces from western France from interfering and by forcing their surrender.

The Allies had learned well from the Germans. If there is one criticism of the German technique, it is that generals became too prone to call upon air power rather than using artillery and risking tanks. The result was that in front of some generals, villages were so destroyed by bombing that bulldozers had to be sent in before the troops could advance. Too much available firepower, then, has disadvantages, as its profligate use is apt to slow rather than speed the advance, especially when controlled by a general who is unwilling to take risks. The Allies had also learned well from the Germans that air power and ground-based armies must cooperate. The successful model was worked out first in the Western Desert, where the RAF tactical commander had his headquarters alongside that of the army General Officer Commanding, so that in both planning and execution at high and low levels there was proper liaison.

In July 1943, the U.S. Army *Field Manual 100-20* made air and ground forces co-equal. But in July 1944, Gen. Omar Bradley's COBRA (coastal, battlefield, reconnaissance analysis) operation at Falaise in Normandy showed that without mutual agreement and training, heavies used in tactical roles were dangerous to their own side.

The improvements in training, technology, and experience surprised even the Air Officer Commander-in-Chief of Bomber Command when his force was used in daylight attacks between March and September as a tactical air force under Supreme Headquarters Allied Expeditionary Force (SHAEF) orders.

The Sicilian and Italian campaigns revealed that air power was not necessarily able to dominate the battlefield under some circumstances. Allied air power did not prevent the German evacuation of Sicily, nor did it prevent the Allies from coming close to disaster after the amphibious landings at Salerno and Anzio. And it was not able to open the Cassino bottleneck, where the Germans held the high ground around the famous monastery. While it could make things difficult for the Germans in the limiting terrain of Italy, where supply lines ran within narrow grooves, it was not able to open the way for the infantry because the ground favored the defense. Rather than an aerial "Operation Strangle," the way to have won in Italy might have been to have mounted the Operation Anvil invasion against northern Italy instead of into southern France; but such a suggestion involves a very complex set of "ifs" outside the scope of this work.

Once ashore in northern France, the Allies rapidly laid PSP airstrips, which gave them both rapid turnaround for tactical sorties and the means to bring in necessities from Britain. As the armies advanced, they not only harried the retreating enemy but also, with the help of the airfield construction teams (Royal Engineers and RAF protected by the RAF Regiment), resurrected captured airfields. The Germans realized the vital nature of this work, and in the Battle of the Bulge at the end of 1944 made concentrated attacks on fighter-bomber wings on forward airfields.

Meanwhile, in the fall, the Allies had overreached themselves at Nijmegen and Arnheim, where at the latter the airborne could not hold out until the ground spearhead arrived, in part because the British had landed on top of a panzer division at rest, due to poor intelligence. And bad weather then limited both resupply and close air support.

The Eastern Front

The German war against the Soviet Union pitted Hitler against Stalin. Operation Barbarossa opened on June 22, 1941, against the ill-prepared advanced Soviet airfields, which might not have fared so badly if Stalin had accepted warnings from the West. As it was, the Russians lost some 1,300 obsolescent aircraft the first day, which proved a blessing in disguise. Though the *Blitzkrieg* was as effective as in France, the Soviets could trade space for time, while being led by a determined, blooded, and internally powerful commander in Stalin. Pressed back to the gates of Moscow and Leningrad and to the Crimea, once winter set in, the USSR made a comeback.

On the Eastern Front, the turning point in the war was the revival of the Soviet Air Force in the winter of 1941–42. The Soviet aircraft industry had been moved behind the Urals, to put it beyond German reach; and, as the Soviets began to put into practice the lessons of the Spanish and Finnish wars, modern matériel was on its way. The farther the Germans advanced, the longer were their lines of communication and the tauter they became. The Cretan campaign had seriously

depleted their air transports, of which only 500 were produced in 1941, and the onset of winter found them without adequate clothing, oil, or other equipment, or even the experience with which to cope with severe winter flying. Eventually the Soviets built up equipment to levels technically comparable to those of the Germans, but far superior in numbers; their transport system became adept, and they were aided by the Western Allies both directly in the form of some 2,000 fighters and indirectly by the so-called strategic air offensive against Germany and by the pressure of Allied attacks in Italy and France.

The Soviet air services had emerged from the desecration of the civil and the Polish wars (1917–22) in a parlous state. Fortunately, the new USSR lacked effective enemies, while at the same time being seen as a pariah. Thus, the Russians on the one hand concentrated on bringing a new generation of aircraft designers into being through special colleges and technical schools; and on the other hand they included the air arm in planning from 1924, and in the sensible five-year plans started by Stalin from 1928. By 1934, the Soviet air services were the largest and most advanced in the world. They had also benefitted from the clandestine liaison at Fili with Germans, where *Blitzkrieg* tactics were thought through. Moreover, the Soviets had enough aircraft that they could undertake full-scale maneuvers and a war in the Far East at Nomonhan, and one in Spain. There, in 1936–37, they dominated; but when the new German and Italian machines came into action, the Soviets withdrew. They then launched the 1939–40 war against Finland, in which they did poorly. But it was a warning that was heeded. Although after purging the Red Air Force leadership in 1938 and refusing to accept British warnings in early 1941, and thus losing the obsolete aircraft in the opening days of the German Barbarossa attack, Stalin's air force was coming up again with both new designs and new factories.

The vast *Blitzkrieg* into the USSR undertaken by the Germans in 1941 and 1942 was turned about by the Soviets starting as early as the winter of 1941. They used their space, time, and winter weather to their advantage, and by late 1942 had gone over effectively to an offensive that by mid-1944 gave them undisputed control of the air over their advancing tank armies. Because of distances and a lack of suitable targets within striking range, grand-strategic bombing accounted for only 0.02 percent of the sorties flown. By far, the vast majority of the effort of the VVS—the Soviet Army Air Forces (*Voenno-vozdushnye sily*)—was in air superiority, tactical support strikes, and escort missions.

Just as in other theaters, so also on the Eastern Front, the evolution of air forces is to be seen. Hampered by its many theaters, the *Luftwaffe* gradually lost control, but it was never totally eliminated, even though vulnerable at every turn. It was ground down, but it did not collapse. In contrast, the VVS, which was dealt a "Pearl Harbor" blow at dawn on June 22, 1941, recovered, modernized, and learned new management techniques, including a reorganized Staff of the Supreme High Command (the *Stavka*), to became a highly effective, if massive, fighting organization. Some of the changes were on the way, as noted, in any case—as a legacy of the Spanish Civil War, the Stalinist purge, the dismal Finnish war, the move of the aircraft industry east of the Urals, and of the normal cycle of design changes. War made their implementation imperative.

Notable in the development of the VVS was the active role played by women, not merely in ground support roles as in all the Soviet forces, but also as combat pilots and crew. In 1942, the Soviets recruited and trained three aviation regiments manned by women and used them successfully until they were rapidly dismissed in 1945. These were the only women allowed to fly in combat, and in some cases were assigned up to fourteen flights per night in Polikarpov PO-2s (ER 0.999).

In addition, among the more interesting and productive ideas of the reorganized VVS was that base maintenance and logistics organizations should be separate from that of squadrons or regiments, so that the operational aircraft and their air and ground crews (170–200 persons) could be switched quickly from one front to another. This was gradually developed during the war to such an extent that by the spring of 1945, 209 regiments could be accommodated on 290 airfields within 65 miles of the front after an advance of over 1,200 miles and still fly the maximum sorties desirable. At the same time, command structures had been modified as the VVS had recovered from the devastation of June 1941, which largely saw material rather than personnel lost. As the reserves accumulated and trained personnel came forward to man the new fighters, bombers, and attack aircraft, regiments could be increased from ten aircraft to twenty, and more, and could operate in larger formations. At the higher levels, this meant that whole air armies controlled by Moscow (*Stavka*) were created with such effectiveness that by the end of the war as many as three armies might be assigned to a single front under one overall air commander. No longer would this commander simply be the air adviser to the army group commander, but rather would be charged in full to gather reconnaissance intelligence, wage offensive action to gain air superiority, and provide maximum support for the tank armies in both the preparation and the execution of ground operations. In 1942, these air armies had about 950 aircraft each, sometimes still in a composite force of fighter, attack, and bomber regiments; by 1945, each contained up to 3,000 aircraft of one class, such as the Ilyushin Il-2 Shturmovik.

The most important Soviet aircraft, and indeed air arm, of the war was the Shturmovik. Created independently of the contest for such a machine, it was a simple to produce and maintain ground-attack airplane. Its heart was a rugged armored "bathtub," containing the engine, pilot, and fuel tank, to which was attached a wood and metal airframe. *Stavka* deleted the rear gunner, but the position was reinstalled at the demand of the squadrons.

When war broke out in June 1941, some 800 Shturmoviks were sited on squadrons. After the factories got back into production east of the Urals, the Shturmoviks came off the line at the rate of 3½ per hour. By the end of the war, in the attack on Berlin, 4,500 Il-2s were in support of the Red armies on that front alone.

Based twenty miles behind the front, the Il-2 stayed below 3,000 feet and ranged not more than twenty miles ahead of the Red Army. Rugged in that intense environment, it was extremely effective as flying artillery. The units using it also took heavy casualties, especially the rear gunners, exposed to both German fighters and ground fire; they were killed at the rate of four per pilot. In all, 36,000 Shturmoviks were produced, but casualties ran at 70 percent from all causes.

Training and tactics went hand in hand. By October 1942, first the fighters and then the new Il-2 Shturmovik ground-attack regiments adopted the pair and the finger-of-four formation learned by the Germans in Spain. The best personnel and machines were concentrated in the newly designated elite Guards units and sent to do battle against the best of the *Luftwaffe*. In this they were helped by the arrival of the new fighters, the Yakovlev Yak-1 (ER 2.36) and Yak-9 (ER 4.14) and the Lavochkin La-5 (ER 2.8), which were the equal of the Me-109s, especially at the low levels at which the Soviets operated over the flat steppes. Soviet bomber losses were high due to poor training, lack of maps (except for the leaders), and the fact that almost all targets were in frontline areas heavily defended by flak.

Though not noticeably operating on interior lines, the Russians did have the advantage of defending their own territories and of being closer to their sources of supply than the invaders were to theirs. While the attrition of aircraft was high from all causes, many damaged machines crash-landed on their own airfields or behind Soviet lines. Airmen were recovered and returned to operations, and the machines salvaged and rebuilt.

One sign of maturity was that the management of the armed forces was run in something of the same manner as Stalin's well-known five-year plans for the Soviet economy and development, which were themselves closely linked to defense. An offshoot of this was that the supreme headquarters, the *Stavka,* controlled the allocations of air resources, and by mid-1942 was holding about 40 percent of the VVS as a central reserve *à la* Duval. These air resources were switched to whichever front required offensive or defensive support, thus satisfying the principles of war— mass, mobility, and surprise. This became most apparent on November 19, 1942, when Stalin took the Great Patriotic War, as the Russians called the 1941–45 war, over to the offensive in the campaign against the ill-fated Germans lodged in Stalingrad. By the battle of Kursk in July 1943, the VVS had grasped the initiative and could achieve local air superiority at will. By 1944, it could have it anywhere, as the Germans could no longer parry air armies that had such a surplus they could mount "hunter"-fighter and, by Stalin's order, ground-attack operations whenever it suited them.

The Longest Front

Even though the Soviets had carefully built their air armies one "steppe" at a time, from mid-1944 on they were faced by the fact that their ground organization could not keep up with the rapid pace of their tank armies. Thus, occasional halts were necessary to allow the air arm to catch up and re-site itself for the next great leap forward, as before the final battle of Berlin.

Readers and historians in the West have too often tended to overlook the fact that by 1945 the Soviets had thirteen air armies in operation. Each of these armies had a formidable armada of aircraft, supported by flexible logistical and maintenance battalions. And they were supported, ultimately, as well by the aircraft industry, which produced some 137,000 aircraft between 1941 and 1945, to which must be added some 14,000 supplied by Allied Lend-Lease. In addition, the VVS destroyed some 77,000 *Luftwaffe* aircraft, or about 57 percent of the GAF's machines, for the loss of about the same number of its own. And all of this happened in a country where a large part of its prewar industrial and agricultural base area was overrun and occupied by the invading enemy. Luckily for the Allies in World War II, space, time, the Russian winter, and Hitler's optimism and lack of long-range planning were on the Soviet side.

From 1942 onward, the Russian front had a low priority in German Air Force supply, with the result that the Germans were outnumbered as much as five to one in the Soviet Union, and their less experienced personnel flying older equipment were operating there. After 1944, when the Soviets gained air superiority, the German armies were without eyes or much tactical support. Yet counter to the claims of air-power enthusiasts, they fought on for nearly two years after they lost their air cover, for instance, still operating the small, rugged Stuka to the end of the war.

The immense challenge for the Red Air Force in 1945 was to switch its vision from a tactical air force to one to counter the Cold War threat of United States and United Kingdom grand-strategic bombers and the shorter-lived French *force de frappe*—strike force.

Asia—The China-Burma-India Theater

In terms of its future impact, the Allied campaign in Burma (1942–45) was both an innovation and the precursor of that in Vietnam (1962–72). Although it was true that in the victory in France in 1944 the U.S. Ninth Air Force had been employed to shield General Patton's right flank, in Burma the air forces were used both to shield and to supply the Allied ground campaign. In addition, air evacuation of casualties was developed to the fullest, and helicopters were employed. It was also the campaign to study for the future, because it was a peripheral or forgotten war, last on the list for all the normal fighting perquisites, including mail for the men's morale, as well as being a theater in which air power had to answer to many

masters located anywhere from a thousand yards to thousands of miles away. Airfields were scattered over many miles of jungle, and both supply and navigation were difficult in an area of few landmarks. Yet the lack of railways and roads, and the expense of building highways in a country notorious for its high rainfall, made air supply essential. Even without the jungles, the country was nearly impassable because of mountains and rivers, and the bridges that did exist were major targets, as the weakest links in the transportation chains.

When the Burma campaign opened in late 1941, the British were being driven out of the country into India, and the Chinese back into their homeland. The year 1942 was not an auspicious time for the Allies to begin a buildup in the forgotten theater. Apart from the competition of the European, Pacific, and North African areas, India was plagued with its own troubles. It was unusually hot and humid; malaria was prevalent, and Mepacrine and Atabrine pills were not yet freely available. The unusually heavy rains caused landslides on the road to the British advanced garrison-base at Imphal. The breakdown of the talks on Indian independence led to a slow-down of airfield construction work, which in pre-bulldozer days was bad enough anyway. The 30,000 tons of fill for runways was dug with shovels, stones were broken by hand, and all was moved in head-carried baskets or by ox carts by a patiently lethargic people.

Construction of airfields was plagued by endemic disease, inexperienced medical officers, and commanding officers who ignored sickness, local merchants, the niggardliness of the government of India and its bureaucracy, and by lack of trained engineers. Nevertheless, the rate of opening new airfields was the same as in the United Kingdom. On top of this, at the end of the retreat from Burma in 1942, only five British squadrons and ten airfields were sited in India, a subcontinent the size of Europe. Most of the British equipment was obsolescent, to be polite, yet it had to be used until the end of 1943, when the last Curtiss P-36 Mohawks (ER 1.61) were withdrawn and the first PRU Spitfires were just beginning their sorties.

The first major operation in the theater was the original Chindit expedition, which was supplied by Douglas C-47 Dakota IV aircraft (ER 19.14), rarely needing escort by the Hurricanes because of the scarcity of Japanese opponents. This expedition terminated as the monsoon broke in June 1943, but it had shown the value of an air transport force. At the end of 1941, the British had decided to develop such an organization, and a plan was put into being in March 1942 to provide 215 airfields, internal air services in India, and a viable flying-control system. At the end of nine months, five airfields were finished. By November 1943, however, a modified program found 140 two-runway fields, 64 with one runway, and 71 fair-weather airstrips completed, with a further 15 fields still being built. Radar had been installed and ground-observer units established. In late 1943, Southeast Asia Command (SEAC) was organized and the British and U.S. Army Air Forces merged. By this time, more than forty-eight RAF squadrons and seventeen USAAF transport squadrons were in the SEAC. Even so, this force was hard put to contain Japanese thrusts, which by coincidence began almost simultaneously with a British drive down the Arakan coast. Success or failure hung on the ability of the Allies to supply their units by air and to shift troops rapidly from the Arakan front to Imphal when the need arose, even if it meant cutting into the Hump airlift to China, over the Himalayas, to do so.

In early 1944, when the Japanese outflanked the British advance down the Arakan coast, the British troops were ordered to stand and fight in a "box," where they were supplied by air until the relief forces reached them. That this was possible can be credited both to imaginative gambling on the part of the High Command and to the arrival in the theater of Supermarine Spitfire VIIIs (ER n/a), which were able to seize control of the air. Taylor-

craft Auster (ER 0.13) light aircraft, later in the campaign replaced by light American types, evacuated the wounded at the rate of 300 per week, immensely raising morale. At the same time, long-range bombers harassed the few Japanese airfields at night. The Japanese siege of Imphal in the northeast was broken by a 758-sortie airlift of a whole division from the Arakan in an operation reminiscent of the German use of railways before Tannenberg in 1914. At neighboring Kohima, the garrison was wedged into a hilltop only 400-by-500 yards, yet planes flying at 200 feet managed to keep them supplied, some canisters even being so accurately dropped as to kill the recipients because the chutes had no time to open! Needless to say, some of the supplies benefitted the enemy.

At Imphal, the situation was so critical that 30,000 support troops were flown out of that box together with the hospitals. The Allies were able to do for the British and Indians in Imphal what the Germans had not been able to do for themselves at Stalingrad. In part, the success was a matter of scale; in part it was because the defenders kept six airfields in their hands; and in part it was due to the Japanese lack of air power or the knowledge of how to interfere effectively. Throughout the siege the British were able to maintain fighters on the fields in daylight, flying them out for rest, maintenance, and safety at dusk. In the absence of radar, standing fighter patrols were used over the entrances to the valley to keep Japanese aircraft out. In the eighty-day battle, the RAF lost two Dakotas and a Wellington while supplying 275 tons per day. One corollary of the airlift operations was the development by the Americans of a conveyor-belt conception of the handling of supplies, a system that saved time in many ways.

In between the Arakan and Imphal battles, in March 1944, the second Chindit operation was airlifted into Burma. This was a most significant new development in that 10,000 riflemen were taken into a single airstrip in Burma—"Broadway"—that had been opened up by bulldozers landed in gliders only the night before. Conditions at Broadway were such that the original lift was canceled for twelve hours, but that night the first two transports into the airstrip were piloted by the American and the British general officers. Thereafter, an aircraft landed or took off from the single two-way strip every three minutes all night.

The Japanese detected and bombed an adjacent landing ground, but they did not discover Broadway for a week, even though it was 150 miles behind their lines. In the course of the campaign, five airfields were created, and one hundred airstrips were established for casualty evacuation. Helicopters used any open patch as needed. All resupply flights were made at night, as the columns were beyond escort-fighter range, but fighter-bombers and Mitchell B-25s provided air support, guided to targets by RAF officers with the troops and by smoke grenades fired onto the enemy positions at the crucial moments.

In the north, American Gen. "Vinegar Joe" Stilwell used airborne troops to capture the Myitkina airfield for his Chinese troops. The siege of the town took seventy-nine days, but seventy-five Dakotas, the equivalent of 1,200 2½-ton trucks, kept his force supplied; the aircrew used were less than half the equivalent force of truck drivers.

Another innovation, again presaging Vietnam, was that in the advance through the Valley of Death to Tamu, the roadway was sprayed with DDT from the air to keep down malarial mosquitoes.

To disrupt Japanese river traffic, especially on the Irrawaddy, mines were sown by aircraft, while in daylight much of the river, road, and rail network was patrolled by Bristol Beaufighters (ER 22.7), known to the enemy as "Whispering Death," because of the silence of their approach, especially in comparison with the B-25s. These aircraft destroyed all the motive power and bridges on the Burma railways, forcing the Japanese to import scarce locomotives from elsewhere. The "Beaus" also did well when compared to the wooden Mosquitoes because of their all-metal construction, which kept their flaps from being blown away in rough weather or on water-soaked runways, or their wings from coming unglued in the humidity.

The final triumph of air supply in Burma was the advance of the British XIVth Army to Rangoon, in spite of both the threatened withdrawal of the American transport squadrons and the monsoon. Taking a calculated risk, the seventeen squadrons, including two Canadian of the combined Anglo-American air-supply force (600 aircraft), kept 300,000 men on the move in the race down-country. That they succeeded was due in no small measure to the effectiveness of the air cover supplied from new fighter strips and old Japanese airfields. So rapid, in fact, was the advance that the bombers were ordered not to destroy bridges for fear of holding up the attackers. Even so, some 8,000 bridges were attacked by aircraft, which ranged as far as 1,400 miles from their bases, using Azon TV-guided bombs.

The whole reconquest of Burma was not accomplished without some headaches. The army came to regard air supply as the norm and began to demand greater and greater loads. The principal problems, apart from the overworking of aircrews (who often made three trips per day, totaling twelve flying hours, over the Arakan mountains to the front), were the failure to see that perishable cargoes cleared airfields before they rotted; failure to ensure that items were not flown in that were available locally behind the front; failure to land incoming transports ahead of the takeoff of routine tactical patrols; and, lastly, failure to see that transport crews had food and rest while aircraft were being unloaded.

The final air campaign in SEAC was to have been a combined airborne and amphibious attack on Penang to seal off Singapore at the base of the Malay peninsula. But the Japanese surrender, September 2, 1945, V-J Day, forestalled it.

Success in the Southeast Asia Command was a matter of the right combination of ingredients in a tight schedule. As an adjunct to SEAC, the Hump route to China had always to be considered, but its problems were not peculiar, and once adequate aircraft and crews were available, its operation was routine, even though the international personalities and the weather involved may have made it seem otherwise. Tonnages rose from 29,000 in August 1944 to a peak of 74,000 in July 1945.

The Japanese failure in Southeast Asia was due to the air force being subordinate to the army, which failed to think strategically. Even allowing for stretched resources, it had failed to attack the Allied airfields, in contrast to long-ranging Beaufighter harassing sorties against the Imperial Army's bases, railways, and water transport.

SEAC was the forgotten, low-priority theater. Its major campaign did not begin until 1945.

AIR POWER AND NATIONAL DEFENSE

Periodically during the Second World War air power was called upon to defend the homeland of one of the belligerents. The ensuing battles were frequently a sobering experience for both sides.

The Battle of Britain

In 1940 Hitler needed to knock Britain out of the war so that he could get on with his other plans, and Goering claimed that this could be done by allowing the *Luftwaffe* to destroy the RAF before an invasion force crossed the English Channel. The British had radar defenses along the arc facing France and Germany, with controllers who could vector in defending fighters by radio. But, although the British had considered the defense problem, they had never developed long-range fuel tanks to allow their fighters an extended patrol at fighting altitudes. Therefore, a great deal depended upon the ability of radar and ground-observer warnings to give sufficient time for the squadrons to climb to height. The RAF had learned from the early French campaign: aircraft were dispersed on the forward airfields, and flexible communications and command centers as

well as elaborate early-warning systems were created. More than this, the commander-in-chief of Fighter Command, Air Chief Marshal Sir Hugh Dowding, was one man who had in the First World War had understood the need to rest aircrews. Thus when the forward airfields began to take a pounding, he withdrew squadrons out of range and rested them while new pilots were assimilated.

It has been argued, however, that keeping the ground crews on station would have been far more efficient, as well as having had special servicing commandos at forward landing grounds to service any aircraft that needed fuel and ammunition, as in North Africa in 1942. One could also suggest that only pilots needed to be withdrawn for rest, not whole squadrons. But squadrons thrived as a family.

The first phase of the Battle of Britain had opened with the Germans attacking coastal convoys to bring out RAF fighters. Dowding refused to rise to the bait, but Churchill forced him to assign six fighters to cover each convoy. While this was acceptable for morale—and perhaps necessary, since the "coal-scuttle brigade" of small coastal steamers was being attacked within sight of the coast—it hardly helped defensive preparations because it put hours on machines and fatigued pilots. What probably saved Dowding here more than anything else were the poor, wet weather, which limited the Germans to sporadic raids, and the fact that the Germans themselves were not ready.

Hitler was an offensive gambler and neither he nor Goering was willing to get involved in long campaigns. They understood the nature of war too well, but not what to do when the opponent refused to give up. Only on July 21, 1940, did Goering order planning for the attack on Britain, which was to be carried out with a three-day knockout blow in early August.

On August 12, the *Luftwaffe* launched a series of attacks, initially against the south coast radar stations and then against fighter airfields. But they ran into two difficulties apart from weather. First, their timing was bad. The early fighter-bombers eliminated some of the radar stations, but the bombers did not show up until about two hours later, after the stations had been repaired and the defending fighters were once again ready for combat. (Carrier commanders in the Pacific judged this better.) Second, the Germans did not know England enough, even though well briefed, and in some cases mistook one airfield for another, so that several training fields were plastered with bombs, while nearby fighter stations were unmolested. British airfields had been built to standard patterns, and such a mistake was understandable, especially in a countryside with too many landmarks.

A number of fighter airfields were hard hit, however, especially by the German fighter-bombers whose arrival had been ignored by radar controllers; the fighter-bombers were not distinguishable on radar from fighters, which Fighter Command had been under orders not to engage. During prewar exercises against the fleet at anchor and to test Fighter Command, the British had found that low-level attackers invariably got through undetected.

But a third problem for the Germans was the inadequate range of the Me-109 escorts, due to insufficient fuel capacity. Nevertheless, attacks continued during August, and major battles raged over southern Britain as the RAF adopted the strategy of first intercepting the high escort and, once it was in a dogfight, sending in other fighters to hit the bombers. Both sides made claims that were about three times as high as the real losses; but in any case, the Germans could not replace their wastage as rapidly as could the RAF, because their monthly production rate was about 200 fighters, compared with the British 475, of which only 90 were Spitfires and Hurricanes. In addition, *Luftwaffe* aircraft lost over Britain were not recoverable, whereas many British machines could be salvaged.

British aircraft needing more than quick repairs at first were set aside and a new machine al-

lotted. It was not until Lord Beaverbrook at the new Ministry of Aircraft Production ordered civilian mobile repair teams into the field—something the Air Ministry had not really considered—that large numbers of aircraft off-charge came back into the inventory. In addition, both sides supposedly were getting short of pilots, in spite of the fact that British pilots generally parachuted back to their own territory, even if shot down.

In an attempt to improve their poor showing in Goering's eyes, the *Luftwaffe* removed its older wing leaders and put the top squadron commanders in their place. This improved morale, and a shooting competition began; but the move did not settle the arguments between the bombers and fighters as to the best method of protecting the attackers, or, in fact, of accomplishing the destruction of the RAF.

The fighter-bombers might have held the key to the problem. Incredibly some of the key RAF fighter-control rooms were not only above ground but on airfields. If the *Luftwaffe* had realized this, it might have paralyzed the whole system by systematically destroying these nuclei with swift fighter-bomber thrusts. Indeed, the Germans did decide in the new phase of the battle, which opened on August 24, to make an intense effort to destroy the RAF fighter stations with groups of fifteen to twenty bombers protected by sixty fighters. By thus striking at airfields, they had a chance of hitting the sector control rooms, which the Germans had assumed were in underground quarters.

In order to be more effective and save wear and tear on pilots already flying five missions a day, the scattered German fighter squadrons were clustered onto fifty airfields in northeast France and Belgium. At this point, if the British had used their defensive imagination and had been less concerned about the German cross-Channel invasion barges, they might effectively have used their night bombers to attack these air concentrations, on the principle that if bombs were dropping, pilots would get little sleep and mechanics could do no maintenance—even if nothing was actually hit. Moreover, the *Luftwaffe* was so accustomed to operating with air superiority that it was not attuned to the enemy's need for defense. That the British did not attack airfields was again due to the lack of an RAF Air Officer Commander-in-Chief who could order Bomber Command to help Dowding; to the refusal to employ the Blenheims, as their New Zealand AOC in France believed they could be used in low-level vics of three; and to the failure to think offensively at the fighter level. Later, in 1941–42, fighter sweeps—"rhubarbs"—over France failed because the Germans withdrew their fighters out of range. Surprise and concentration on the objective had been forgotten.

On August 31, the British lost thirty-seven fighters, and the Germans sixty in melées over the bombers. The *Luftwaffe* believed, however, that it had passed the crisis. In the first week of September, the RAF appeared to have slackened its effort, though No. 12 Group, RAF, had switched over to two-squadron wings instead of individual squadron attacks. But, then, in retaliation for an attack on the outskirts of London, an area Hitler had forbidden, the RAF hit Berlin; on September 5, Hitler ordered the attacks switched to London, and Goering took over personal command of the Battle of Britain. These events were critical, for the British were down to about a two-week reserve of fighters.

The mythology of the Battle of Britain is that Air Chief Marshal Dowding was short of pilots and aircraft. Actually, he had 924 pilots throughout the battle, but was short on commissioned pilots. The shortage of aircraft was due not to losses, which equaled production of Spitfires and Hurricanes, but to failure to salvage and repair disabled machines, as noted. Moreover, Dowding in Fighter Command had roughly 600 Spitfires and Hurricanes to face a total of 2,500 *Luftwaffe* aircraft, of which about 850 were Me-109s and Me-110s.

The Germans might have won the Battle of Britain if they had continued to attack RAF airfields. On the other hand, given its limited re-

sources at the time and continued British withholding of fighters from the front lines, as the Germans were later to do in France, the *Luftwaffe* might still not have achieved victory. The answer is one of the tantalizing "ifs" of history that would be interesting to "game" out. Some German generals have criticized Goering for starting the battle too early, instead of saving the *Luftwaffe* for its usual *Blitzkreig* support of invasion forces. They claim that Goering's plans were made without consultation, that they were unrealistic, and that they violated the principles of surprise and concentration. But the panzers could not cross the English Channel and seize aerodromes.

The massive attacks on London by as many as 625 bombers were designed once and for all to get RAF Fighter Command committed and destroyed before bad weather set in. The climax of this operation came on September 15, when Air Vice Marshal Keith Park, who commanded the critical No. 11 Group, Fighter Command, in southeast England, made the decision—with Churchill sitting next to him—to commit all his reserves. The defense was successful because the exhausted German fighters could not escort a new wave before two hours had elapsed, by which time the RAF was ready once again.

The *Luftwaffe* was discouraged. It had fought longer and harder and with greater losses than ever before, and yet, according to German estimates, the enemy could still field 300 fighters at a time. That Sunday afternoon battle resulted in a jubilant British claim of 185 Germans shot down (the actual number was 56). It was a psychological victory and a propaganda coup. Hitler had already decided upon an attack on the Soviet Union; Britain would be tormented by bombing, but was out of invasion danger once and for all, though this would not be recognized in London until spring 1941 due to greatly overblown estimates of the size of the *Luftwaffe*. The battle petered out in November, partly due to aircrew fatigue, but Hitler left a fighting enemy in his rear to his later regret.

One of the successes of the Battle of Britain

was the Air Ministry's account of the event by that title, published in Britain in the new paperback format in 1940, and 1941 in the United States; the book sold over one million copies in Britain, Canada, and America.

In the night-bombing attacks that followed the Battle of Britain, the Germans ingeniously fashioned radio beams along which their bombers could fly until they intercepted a second beam over the target, upon which they dropped their bombs. The British responded with ground anti-aircraft defenses, beam-bending, and the development of night fighting. The last was at first crude, making use of Douglas A-20 Havoc (ER 15.3) light bombers equipped with searchlights to illuminate the enemy for the accompanying Hurricanes. But the real solution was found in the Bristol Beaufighters, with airborne interception (AI) radar, vectored onto an intruder by a ground controller, and carrying a powerful armament including 20 mm cannon, which entered squadron service in fall of 1940. When the Mosquito came into action in January 1942, the RAF had a fighter that was faster than anything flying at night against Britain for the rest of the war.

Axis Air Defense

The Germans and the Japanese were hampered in air defense by their disbelief in its necessity and by old concepts in handling the problem. These restrictions were particularly acute in Germany where in the late 1930s defensive thinking was tied to the Siegfried Line with an Air Defense Zone West. It was a cordon system patterned on World War I trench-type warfare. It provided for a defensive anti-aircraft belt through which bombers would have to fly, attacking and returning, if they were below 23,000 feet. But it was ineffective, for the British approached from the sea to the north in an end run. The line was backed by a very few squadrons attached to geographical zones, and it was not until 1943 that the Germans developed anything like an effective radio vectoring system to put fighters onto enemy aircraft,

in spite of having radar in 1939. Even after that, they suffered from difficulties with air defense to the end of the war. A major weakness came from the short endurance of their fighters: the Me-109 had only seventy-five minutes, half of which it needed for a climb to fighting altitude.

The experimental German radar had spotted the first British raid on Wilhelmshaven on the day war was declared, and fighters were dispatched. But if the early sorties of 1939 taught the British that daylight attacks were fatal and that night operations were the solution, the Germans did not get the message from their own successes. When British night raids started in earnest in the autumn of 1940, the Germans could not counter them. The failure to develop a night-fighter system was due in part to over-confidence on Goering's part, in part to divided command structures and zone defense systems with rigid boundaries, and in part to poor technical direction.

Again, it was 1943 before the Germans began seriously to try to deal with night raids, at a time when British attacks were having an adverse, though by no means critical, effect upon home morale. Night fighter types were developed, such as the Me-110 (a radar-modified, heavy, day fighter) and the bomber- variant Junkers Ju-88 (ER 13.4) and Dornier Do-217 (ER 30.2), equipped with radar, but they suffered from lack of ground direction, altitude, range, speed, and trained crews. RAF tactics at this time were confusing, first because of the system of individual raiders flying to their own schedules, and then—after the Cologne thousand-plane raid of May 1942—because a whole massive short stream of raiders would be routed evasively and would pass over the target in a very few minutes. And the RAF was by then being equipped with Pathfinder and radar-bombing equipment so that it could mark targets and operate in weather for which the German night fighters were unfit.

The low tonnage of the Allied grand-strategic bombing program gave the Germans the chance to perfect their defenses. But if the Germans were given a great deal of forewarning, they were not in fact forearmed, and a drastic escalation of their fighter and war production only took place from mid-1943 onward, reaching its peak in September 1944. In this rush to make good neglected defenses, the Germans were forced—by their own stubbornness and by the usual run of failures incident to any attempt to develop new matériel hastily—to mass-produce the old tried and true designs, the Me-109 and the Focke-Wulf Fw-190 (ER 3.39). But these aircraft had already been out-developed by the Supermarine Spitfire IX (ER 2.63), let alone the newer American fighters, the Republic P-47D Thunderbolt (ER 8.1) and the North American P-51D Mustang (ER 9.63). The new spectacular German fighters, the rocket Messerschmitt Me-163 Komet (ER 6.7) and the jet Me-262 (ER 9.92), caused alarm but came too late, and had constant engine problems. Moreover, even they were hampered by the German fighter-control system that was sometimes jammed by the Allies, or interdicted by German-speaking Allied interlopers giving contrary instructions, or frustrated by the use of "window"—chaff—the radar-reflective foil strips dropped by Allied aircraft.

On the ground the German defense system consisted of the anti-aircraft "boxes" around vital targets. This scheme was acceptable as long as the British tackled only a limited number of precise militarily important targets. But once they abandoned these for the bigger urban complexes that were more easily hit—and that ironically did not always contain important factories—then the demands for protection far exceeded the means available, at a time when German operations in the Soviet Union and North Africa were calling for increasing flak protection and U-boats were also being flak-armed. Flak belts were set up along the northern German coast and in the Netherlands, but the British often managed to achieve surprise, even after crossing the belts, by evasive routing and a choice of targets. From February 1942 to May 1945, flak accounted for 1,345 of the British bombers brought down, and night fighters for 2,278. The rest—2,072—were lost for a variety of operational reasons from bad weather to engine failure to low flying, plus 112 in known collisions. Of the 297,663 night and 66,851 day RAF sorties dispatched, 13,778 were damaged: flak accounted for 8,848 and fighters for 1,228. Flying accidents, and others including icing, damaged 3,159, of which 876 were writeoffs.

After the early American daylight raids suffered some very heavy losses in 1943, the Anglo-American leaders changed tactics. The U.S. Eighth Air Force was rested while long-range day-fighter escorts were developed. The pause paid off with the launching of the new daylight attack system in "Big Week," of February 1944. By plunging deep into Germany, the daylight raids compelled the enemy to fight. Once they rose to the bait, they found themselves facing not only the close escort but also increasingly large roving hunter-killer groups who were not content to tackle fighters approaching the bombers, but who, by early 1945, were often willing to drop down on the deck and assault anything that moved, with one pass only. This decimated the German fighter force and badly affected its morale.

Moreover, the short range of German fighters meant that if they were withdrawn to airfields out of range of P-51s, which could escort bombers to Berlin and back, they could not reach bombers attacking targets in the Ruhr and the like. Attempts to resolve these difficulties by using parts of the famed *autobahns* as airstrips were frustrated as Allied armies came into closer range, so that even their tactical fighters could swarm over the defender's airfields, salvage depots, and supply trains. Through technological development and an indestructible arsenal in the United States, as well as with the benefits of historical lessons, absorbed albeit with reluctance, the Allies were able to do to German air defense what the Germans had not been able to do to the British. The RAF night effort went into a higher gear, made possible at last by adequate number of aircraft and trained aircrews as well as by sufficient airfields, but limited by manpower.

WWII Land-based Air Power

One interesting example of the power of the defense and the failure of offensive air power can be seen in the survival of Malta.

The Siege of Malta

Lying some sixty miles off the Sicilian coast and athwart the Axis supply routes to Africa, Malta instead of Crete should have been eliminated in 1941, as some Germans realized. Yet the Axis powers failed to launch either an all-out air attack or an airborne invasion, even before the Russian campaign drained off the necessary forces.

The minuscule island of Malta was a strategic spot on the British air route to the Middle East after Italy declared war on June 10, 1940, and after France and its North African colonies fell two weeks later. It was also a base for submarines and anti-shipping forces interdicting the Axis supply route from Naples to Tripoli. That it survived on very short rations was due to the naval and merchant-ship efforts to keep it supplied, to the effectiveness of the combined fighter and anti-aircraft defenses, to indomitable commanders, and above all to the willing determination of the population, which was presented a George Cross, the highest award for gallantry to a civilian.

The Cabinet in London miscalculated that the French fleet would stay in the alliance and guard the convoy route through the Mediterranean. But those ships sailed to Vichy's Toulon, and thus it was left to the Royal Navy to see that Malta was supplied. For air defense, the RN had two pilots and three obsolete Gloster Sea Gladiators (ER 1.1).

Malta is a limestone island with solid buildings and catacombs; casualties were light from bombing. Convoys still arrived, but aircraft fuel had to be allocated weekly, as the siege began. In the meantime, Hurricanes were flown in off carriers, but in November 1940 preparations were not precise and nine out of fourteen ran out of fuel short of Malta. Then a PRU Beaufighter spotted the Italian fleet in Taranto, and photographed it. These prints went to HMS *Illustrious* for the successful attack the next night, November 11, 1940.

But in January 1941, the *Luftwaffe* arrived in Sicily and the attacks began in earnest. Then in February, Me-109s appeared, to seek air superiority, while the bombers attacked the three small airfields and knocked out the anti-shipping bombers parked on them. The attacks upon the city of Valetta only hardened the Maltese hatred of the Axis. Yet, the chance to attack Crete distracted the *Luftwaffe* in May 1941, though the *Wehrmacht* High Command, concerned about supplies for Gen. Erwin Rommel's *Afrika Korps,* wanted Malta seized. The touch-and-go battle of Crete convinced the Germans that Malta could only be invaded with absolute air supremacy.

After fresh convoys arrived in the summer, Malta's defenses and offensives were strengthened, and submarines and forty bomber sorties almost cut Rommel's supply lines. In response, the *Luftwaffe* returned to Sicily in force, concentrating on Malta's dockyards, quays, and airfields. But the RAF struck and destroyed thirty-five German and Italian aircraft on the ground at Castel Vetrano, Sicily. However, in the next two months, Malta was bombed by about 2,000 Axis sorties and her defense and offense were crippled, much to Rommel's benefit. The British army was set to work to fill in bomb craters and built 170 revetments for fighters, usually at night, and especially along the taxi strip connecting two of the airfields. Nevertheless, often only four to six Hurricanes could be sent up by the controller to deal with large enemy raids.

In February, Hitler decided to seize the island by Operation Hercules. Italian and German hesitation regarding invading Malta had to do with the many stone walls, which were a natural barrier to gliders. Then Tobruk fell to Rommel, and Hitler decided he should go to Cairo, and thus Operation Hercules was cancelled; the defense on Malta was still too strong to risk an assault. At the same time, London agreed to send Spitfires, and on March 7, 1942, they were in action over Malta. But the March convoy was devastated by the *Luftwaffe,* with the last two ships sunk in Valetta harbor. Starvation loomed on the horizon. Malta was getting more bombs than London during the Blitz. The morale of the desperate fighter pilots sent out piecemeal from the United Kingdom was suffering from the lack of squadrons to which to be loyal. Moreover, indiscriminate bombing was killing civilians and wrecking one-third of the 300-some churches on the island. It was now a war for existence for the besieged. The tired governor was relieved, and his replacement, Lord Gort, was made governor, commander-in-chief, and supreme commander of Malta.

Aerodromes were regularly bombed four times daily. Only twenty to thirty serviceable RAF fighters faced some 600 German and Italian foes. Prime Minister Churchill appealed to President Roosevelt for the means to deliver masses of Spitfires. The carrier USS *Wasp* was loaned, and two full Spitfire V squadrons (forty-seven aircraft) were ferried to the western Mediterranean north of Algiers, where they were flown off at dawn on April 20, landed, refueled, rearmed, and manned by veteran pilots; they then took off to meet the next enemy raid and two more that day.

Though heavily bombed, the aerodromes were ready again for action the following day, with the help of the infantry. But of the forty-six Spitfires that had actually arrived, only six were serviceable after 400 tons of bombs hit the island. Malta needed one hundred Spitfires per month, and thus the *Wasp* was used weekly for eight weeks. Meanwhile, Malta bled the German Air Force, two-thirds by anti-aircraft.

On May 7, Lord Gort arrived and at once insisted that when the Spitfires were received, they had to be ready to scramble within twenty minutes—the blast pens (revetments) being stocked to do so. The Germans missed their chance. Hitler had misjudged the timing. On May 10, the *Wasp* and *Eagle* flew in fifty-nine new cannon-armed Spitfires. Within ten minutes they were again airborne. Air superiority was regained. But could the Royal Navy resupply the island? The bombing slacked off, which helped.

Yet the path was not always smooth. Air/sea rescue had plucked 123 RAF pilots out of the sea during 1940–43, and 55 Axis pilots. And in late May, short rations had caused dysentery among the pilots. In the meantime, Beaufighters and their ground-control intercept (GCI) station took over night defense above the anti-aircraft's 12,000-foot ceiling. Constant reinforcements of Spitfires were provided to help assure that the first convoy in three months would dock.

Alarmed by Malta's offensive power against Rommel's lifeline, the Axis struck in July again at the three airfields, at heavy cost, as the Allied defenders now had enough Spitfires to tackle incoming raids near Sicily. By the end of July, Axis raids had petered out.

London's habit of cleaning out and sending unwanted pilots to Malta resulted in their high attrition because of lack of experience. But one of these pilots turned out to become an ace in short order—the Canadian "Buzz" Beurling. Yet, Malta was saved at this time as much by soldiers and by the ground crews' ability to repair and maintain the aircraft as by the skill and determination of the fighter pilots. About three Spitfires were lost daily. In mid-July the Air Officer Commanding, Hugh Lloyd, was replaced by Air Vice Marshal Sir Keith Park, reprieved from Training Command after his victory in the Battle of Britain as AOC of No. 11 Group. What he needed most was fuel, as stocks were low. Everything now depended upon the convoy lifeline.

In mid-August the essential relief force battled through under air protection. Four merchantmen made port at Valetta and the precious tanker *Ohio* was hauled in by two destroyers lashed alongside. Malta, down to fourteen days of fuel remaining, now had three months more lifeblood. But the losses had been heavy, even though the *Luftwaffe* refused to work with the Italian navy.

Park went on the offensive with now "unemployed" Fairey Swordfish (ER 1.4) pilots flying Hurribombers over Sicily to break up enemy airfields in a reversal of roles. This "forward plan" saved Malta more damage and raised morale.

Beaufighters began night-intruder operations over Sicily and the toe of Italy, while Bristol Beaufort (ER 19.6) torpedo-bombers forced the North African convoys to hug the Greek coast. And over one hundred RAF fighters now had working radios and 20 mm cannon. In addition, to save food, civilians not part of the defense effort were evacuated to Gibraltar or Egypt. Spitfires were manhandled, not taxied.

The *Luftwaffe* bomber offensive started again on October 11, 1942, as Field Marshal Kesselring sought to neutralize Malta to support Rommel. Solid controlling and excellent shooting broke up the attacks off Sicily, even as the German Air Force escorted a few Ju-88s with sixty to seventy fighters, though some got through to the island. By October 21, the battle was over. Kesselring's losses were too high, and he dropped the idea of invasion.

In the battles of 1942, the RAF destroyed upward of 1,000 enemy aircraft, with a British loss of 195, and 106 pilots; anti-aircraft had brought down another 182 Axis machines.

Malta, the second great defensive air battle, had also saved the Western Desert, and General Montgomery would return the favor after El Alamein in November, when the capture of Martuba airfield opened the way for air cover of a convoy to Malta, arriving on November 20 with 50,000 tons of stores. Malta now went on a round-the-clock air and naval offensive.

British Spitfires graduated from carrying two 250-pound bombs to two 500-pounders, and dive-bombed. Fitted with long-range fuel tanks giving 5½ hours endurance, they interdicted the flow of Ju-52s to and from Tunis, as the Allies closed in.

By March 1943, supplies were normal and the siege was over. A total of 1,660 air attacks had killed 1,386 civilians. By July 1943, nearly 600 aircraft were operating from Malta's five fields. Malta was the rock upon which the Axis in the Mediterranean foundered. And the siege of Malta showed what full service cooperation and civilian steadfastness could do, and what a thorn in the side of the enemy such a redoubt could be.

Defense against the V-Weapons

The one place in which the cordon defense worked fairly well was in the Allied shield of Britain against the V-1 flying bombs. An outer belt was established in which the fighters had full rein, while inside this were fighter, gun, and balloon barrages. The speed of the defense system proved effective, but equally important was the overrunning of the launching sites by advancing Allied armies after D-Day. On the other hand, no defense was found against the V-2 stratospheric rocket, but in one sense little was needed. The V-2 was spectacular but, as long as it was limited to a conventional one-ton warhead, it was not exceptionally dangerous because it buried itself so far into the ground on impact before exploding. Nor did it pose a problem to civilian morale because unlike the V-1, it was not visible or audible until after impact. A more sustained barrage of attacks upon a population in a more jittery state might have had another effect. The V-1 and V-2 forced the Allies to reconcentrate forces from anti-aircraft in the United Kingdom to fighters on the Continent, and to resupply armaments on a route 200 miles through France rather than risk an ammunition ship in Antwerp, another V-2 target.

But the psychological aspect of these weapons has been overplayed; V-weapons affected both sides. They caused the British to deploy forces to defend London and to seek out launch sites on the Continent. However, the Germans lost, as the V-weapons not only complicated procurement politically, but it is estimated that the program cost the German Air Force 24,000 fighters not produced.

Intruders

Both sides engaged in operations that have since developed more significance. Intruding—mainly at night, but also with small fast aircraft by day—while not a major operation, was one that was never given the emphasis it deserved. The Germans began the practice in 1941 and kept it up on

In addition to the fleet carriers (CV), the Allies built carriers on light cruiser hulls (CVL). The CVLs could keep up with task forces or with escort flat-tops (CVE), which were employed with convoys or as floating offshore airfields during amphibious operations until landing strips ashore could be established. CVEs were also employed as aircraft transports. Here, a deck load of Lockheed P-38 Lightnings (ER 8, P-38J) and Republic P-47 Thunderbolts (ER 8.1) are on their way overseas. (Lockheed)

Except for the African American fighter pilots from Tuskegee Army Air Field, Alabama, and their ground crews in the Mediterranean theaters, American armed forces were segregated before President Harry S. Truman's 1948 Executive Order integrating them. Here, trainees stand before a Curtiss C-46 Commando (ER 36) before being sent overseas as support troops. (USAF)

Maj. Gen. Claire L. Chennault (third from left, standing) was a dedicated professional fighter leader forced out of the U.S. Army Air Corps by the bomber boys and exiled to China. He studied his opponents before he had a big force, to his advantage, and by 1944, when he was Commanding General of the Fourteenth Air Force, he had experienced pilots and P-51 Mustangs. (USAF)

Restored warbirds of the Confederate Air Force in Harlingen, Texas. From top to bottom: Curtiss P-40F (ER 2.5) in Flying Tiger markings; Mitsubishi A6M Zero (ER 7.89); North American P-51 Mustang (ER 9.63, P-51D). All three served in the Pacific. (Confederate Air Force)

Ground-crew trainees for Curtiss P-40 Warhawk (ER 2.5) units were non-integrated, all-white in World War II. The USAAF and the USN did a solid job of creating training organizations and the legacy of their audio-visual and other practices are still with us. (USAF)

Flyboys with fifty-mission crush caps could always "shoot a line" to impress the ladies. Here, Lt. Col. (later General) Robert Falcon Scott (left) and a fellow flier with a pair of American nurses in India. Note the winter and summer uniforms: the Eisenhower jacket on Scott, and the famous leather A-4 on the other officer pilot. (Col. Luther C. Kissick/USAAF)

Evidence of wastage and consumption—two Royal Australian Air Force (RAAF) "erks" hold the badly shot-up rudder that they have just removed from a Supermarine Spitfire or a P-40 Warhawk somewhere in the Southwest Pacific. (Source unknown)

A very low-level photograph taken by a U.S. plane whose shadow is on the right of a Japanese navy Mitsubishi G4M (Type 1) Betty torpedo bomber (ER 41) on an airfield near Rabaul, Papua New Guinea. Adm. Isoroku Yamamoto was riding in such an aircraft when he was shot down by Lockheed P-38 Lightnings (ER 8) from Guadalcanal in April 1943. (USAF)

A late model of the Lockheed P-38 Lightning (ER 8, P-38J of 1944) demonstrates why it was called "the fork-tailed devil." The design provided excellent all-around visibility and a lethal concentration of firepower in the nose. Charles Lindbergh taught pilots in the Southwest Pacific how to stretch endurance from 3.5 to 11 hours using high boost and low rpms. (Lockheed)

Carrying over what he had learned in Europe, Gen. Curtis E. LeMay, the new commander of the Twentieth Air Force, stripped the guns from his B-29 bombers so that they could carry a heavier load of incendiaries. He sent them in under cover of night to devastate inflammable Japanese cities. The atomic bombs were only the *coup de grâce* to what the 4.5 incendiary bomb and USN submarines had done to bring the Japanese Empire to its knees. (USAF)

A Seventh Air Force North American B-25G Mitchell bomber (ER 23) fitted with a standard U.S. Army 75 mm field gun is harassing a Japanese destroyer on an anti-shipping strike in which skip-bombing from low level was also used. (Note the open bomb-bay doors.) (USAF)

Dramatic night photos were part of engaging the public and airmen about the air force. Here, a P-63 King Cobra (ER 3.85), the unusual 1943 Bell aircraft with the engine mounted behind the pilot, used in the Southwest Pacific in 1944, demonstrates the firepower of its cannon and machine guns. Pilots did not like it at first because of the mid-mounted engine, but as so often was the case, with training, they found it to be an effective weapon. A P-63 is preserved at the U.S. Air Force Museum at Dayton. (USAF Museum)

By the time the Kawanishi N1K1-J George (ER 6.24) appeared for the home defense of Japan in 1945, the island kingdom was short of fuel and trained pilots, a weakness that went back to the successes over China in the late 1930s. Then in World War II, the devastating loss of senior fliers in the battles of the Coral Sea, Midway, and the Philippine Sea, combined with an inadequate vision of wastage and consumption in a war in the Pacific, left the Imperial Japanese Navy without experienced pilots. (USAF Museum)

The fully pressurized interior of the B-29 Superfortress meant that the crew did not have to wear oxygen masks or cold-weather clothing. The curved nose Plexiglas caused some problems for pilots in lining up on the center line of the runway when coming in to land. However, the bombardier had a wonderful view in the center of the nose, even if his back parachute was somewhat uncomfortable on the long hauls to and from Japan. (USAF)

Maintenance on the temperamental 2,200 hp engines of the B-29 Superfortress in primitive field conditions allowed only minimal use of specialized equipment such as the truck-mounted derrick. (USAF)

Building large enough bases for the B-29 Superfortress in primitive China proved to be a daunting task as bulldozers had to be driven in over the Ledo Road across Burma. Yet, with the employment of up to 30,000 local laborers, bases in India and China were built as fast as in Europe. However, B-29 operations from China were unsuccessful because all fuel and ordnance had to be flown in over the Hump—the Himalayas. (USAF)

As insurance against the failure of the rival Boeing B-29 Superfortress (ER 414), Consolidated Aircraft Corp. was authorized to build the B-32 Dominator (ER 378). Production took place at Fort Worth, Texas, and although authorized in 1940, only fifteen reached the Pacific theater before V-J Day, September 2, 1945. (USAF)

Col. Paul W. Tibbets, captain of the B-29 Superfortress *Enola Gay* (ER 414), shows his aircraft to Fleet Adm. Chester W. Nimitz (left), CINCPAC, and Gen. Heywood S. Hansell (center). The *Enola Gay* would carry the first atomic bomb from Tinian Island in the Marianas to Hiroshima, Japan, in August 1945. (USAF)

The 1946 Hawker Sea Fury (ER 11.95), with a tailhook, was the last piston-engine design to enter Royal Navy Fleet Air Arm service, intended for the Pacific War. It became a favorite of postwar air racers in the United States. This naval version of the Tempest II (ER 15, Tempest V, 1944) was not as long-legged as its land-based version. (Hawker)

A British Gloster Meteor (ER 15.3, Meteor III) being tested in the United States after 1945. In 1946, it broke the World's Airspeed Record with a flat run at sea level of just over 600 mph, or roughly 30 percent faster than the late war single-seat fighters. Learning to land the Meteor was a difficult experience because of the very slow spooling-up of the jet engine compared to a piston engine. (USAF)

a nuisance scale throughout the war. Intruders generally took advantage of the fact that night bomber crews were tired after their long sorties and thus were not vigilant once they had reached the British coast. They also made use of the British Drem landing system, which put an oval of lights around each airfield as a pattern that aircraft in the circuit followed.

Counter-intruder work was made the more difficult by the number of aircraft in the area at the time, but was helped by the installation of IFF radar in British aircraft. The RAF itself also engaged in both day and night intruder operations and fighter sweeps over northern France, which caused the Germans to draw back their aircraft to airfields out of range. Such operations were combined with train-busting and other nuisance work, and the whole stepped up into a major assault in the transportation plan that preceded the D-Day landings. Night intruders, increasingly more active as radar became more sophisticated, harassed returning German aircraft and disrupted training. As Mosquitoes became available, they increasingly undertook special pinpoint raids to destroy key buildings and generally to keep the enemy defense on the *qui vive*. Their accuracy became legendary and they proved extremely hard to counter, for they often flew below radar level, hugging natural contours, and were for some time faster than enemy fighters.

Not only did Mosquitoes operate as part of the Pathfinder Force (PFF) of Bomber Command, but late in the war they also flew in the bomberstream to attack enemy night fighters, thus making the *Luftwaffe* night airmen much more nervous.

The Far East

In the Far East, air defense was hampered by the lack of radar and by long distances over either jungle or water, in which early-warning communications were sketchy, so that the defenders had little notice of approaching raids. The 1942 Doolittle raid showed Tokyo that Japan was not immune, but no serious effort was made to create defenses. It was not until spring of 1944 that the Japanese High Command realized that the B-29 Superfortress, then in China, would pose a threat to the home islands. And then the Japanese had only some 400 fighters on hand to deal with an aircraft that was much improved over the B-17 Flying Fortress (ER 101, B-17E) used in Europe. On top of this, rivalries between the Japanese army and the navy were such that home defense could not be properly coordinated, each service tending to keep its aircraft to protect its own bases and factories.

Like the Germans, the Japanese suffered from the decline in pilot training just when heavy, fast, well-armed fighters like the Mitsubishi Raiden J2M3 (Jack) (ER 6.96) were coming off production lines. The result was that training and operational accidents took a greater toll than did American gunnery. The Japanese navy's new Kawanishi N1K1-J Shiden (George) fighter (ER 6.24) did well as long as a nucleus of aces were left to fly it, but they were soon killed. Thus, by the end of 1944, Gen. Curtis E. LeMay, commanding the American Twentieth Air Force, was in a position to consider a gamble: remove almost all the armament from his B-29s and to send them in low at night, so that they could carry the maximum load of incendiaries to Japanese cities.

Japan had never expected nor planned for air attacks; it lacked the radar-controlled flak of the Germans, and most of its buildings were of highly inflammable materials. In 1945, the whole problem was intensified by the arrival of the American carrier task forces off the coast of the main island, with their combat air patrols equal in strength to the whole Japanese home fighter force. Japan was defenseless even before the atom bombs appeared.

Strategic Air Offensives

No discussion of the use of air power in the Second World War can avoid that emotion-packed topic, strategic—or more correctly grand-strategic—bombing.

The French Air Force had been converted to Douhet's grand-strategic bomber way of war by 1930. This concept then became the part of Socialist politics, resulting in purges and counter-purges of the commanding officers, to the point where by 1939 the Douhetian doctrine in the French Air Force had been destroyed. But the fear of the German air menace had not. The result was that Gallic bombers were relatively few and obsolescent. Raids on Germany, it was believed, would bring retaliation against the heart and soul of France—beautiful Paris. The result, put simply, was that French bombers were not a factor in the nine months before France surrendered in June 1940.

The Germans never really developed a doctrine of grand-strategic-bombing, and after the *Luftwaffe* failed in its attempted grand-strategic campaign against Britain, it reverted largely to a purely strategic and tactical role as an adjunct of the surface forces. In some cases, German airmen struck at capital cities as strategic and grand-strategic objectives of surface attacks; such targets were bombed because their destruction could have an immediate effect upon the battle in progress and hasten victory. The 1940 German attack on London had started as a strategic bomber offensive, an extension of the tactical strikes against British airfields that were intended to prepare the way for an invading German army. But Hitler had decided by November to invade the Soviet Union and had withdrawn the invasion troops, and the Battle of Britain gradually degenerated into a grand-strategic campaign. German tactics shifted to night attacks on industrial centers and ports, but German intelligence was not good and it paid little attention to photo-reconnaissance materials (in contrast to meticulous use of such intelligence in land campaigns).

Slightly more effective bombing of the ports, particularly the London and Liverpool docks, in the spring of 1941 might have brought British surrender at fairly small cost, by preventing the unloading and dispersal of the incoming supplies, and might thus have fulfilled the airmen's dream of victory through air power alone. Docking facilities were in short supply, railway junctions were vulnerable bottlenecks, and industrial centers were being attacked, in raids that received much critical attention in English propaganda, as U-boat attacks on convoys had reduced imports. If the Germans just missed winning the war in the late summer of 1940 when they almost had Fighter Command down, they also again just missed in the spring of 1941 when their grand-strategic bombing of industry was having its effect, and they had almost jammed the docks to a standstill. At that critical moment, the bombers were switched over to the attack on the Soviet Union. Yet the Germans had nearly won victory in Britain without a single "strategic" bomber.

The *Luftwaffe* had been compelled in 1940 to wage a limited war both because its units were well below strength and because orders from on high limited targets to shipping in the Channel. The Germans also claim that the real reason lies in the fact that the *Luftwaffe* had no heavy bomber and that its best machine, the twin-engine Ju-88, had been made over into a dive-bomber. Ironically, having for the usual public relations value developed the Ju-88 into a record-breaking aircraft, military experts then loaded it down with so much operational equipment that its speed dropped from close to that of a Hurricane to some 100 mph slower, and its range from a 1,100-mile radius of action to about 600.

It is true that the Dornier Do-19 (ER 15.3) and Junker Ju-290 (ER 18.6) heavy bombers had been abandoned after German bomber-proponent General Wever's death in 1936, but even if these aircraft or the Heinkel He-177 (ER 30) had been available, there is no guarantee that they would have enabled the *Luftwaffe* to beat Britain in 1940. Neither the intellectual makeup of Hitler and Goering nor the targeting system used could guarantee success. The German economy was not geared to produce the number of heavy bombers or engines that were needed; providing the crews for them would have taxed other air operations;

and night-flying tactics and techniques were not developed.

The British grand-strategic bomber campaign had its roots in the air mythology of the 1920s, as noted; although from Munich on, the High Command knew how weak was the British counter-strike deterrent, and fear of retaliation led to its being used only for leaflet-dropping in the "phony war" period between September 1939 and May 10, 1940, when nothing happened. But by the end of the summer of 1940, the British should have faced up to the basic question of what was to be their grand strategy. And the answer to this should have considered making the best use possible of the available and foreseeable air power according to the principles of war, especially protecting the lines of communication, securing the base, concentration, surprise, and economy of force. War calls for hard, clear decisions; too often they are not made.

When the war began, the Wave pattern, or cycle of development, found the British some way back in rearmamental instability. The heavy bombers needed for an independent bombing campaign were still in the prototype stages and would not be available in strength until 1942, nor would airfields upon which to base them. Both tactically and in terms of technical developments, wartime equilibrium was not reached until well after the thousand-bomber raid on Cologne in May 1942. Demobilizational instability set in late in the war when the number of possible targets began to shrink rapidly and it became more and more difficult to employ the one-hundred-squadron force of heavies by then in existence. (It was also limited by manpower shortages.) This introduces, then, an additional facet of the Wave cycle model, that demobilizational instability may be brought about in part simply because there is no longer a job for a particular force to do.

The British deterrent in 1939 had not proved credible, except to the British themselves. By September 1940 it had obviously failed, and the immediate necessities were defense of the United Kingdom, full production in the island arsenal,

security for the lines of communication, victory in the overseas wars, containment of Germany, and neutralization of the uncommitted. After the Battle of Britain, defense of the country demanded primarily air defense against night raids. Full production could be assured only if the sea lanes were secured, so that raw and manufactured materials, including machine tools, could reach Britain. This meant that as much air power as possible had to be diverted to winning the Battle of the Atlantic before the Germans had enough U-boats at sea to make really effective use of their newly won bases in France and Norway.

Security of the sea lanes was also coupled to the problems of ending the campaigns overseas, notably in North and East Africa, advancing political stability in the Middle and Near East, and bringing Italy, as the weaker partner in the Axis, to her knees. To secure these overseas areas and ultimately to defeat Italy would contain Germany and frustrate her westward ambitions, while ensuring British strength to meet any eventual return to the West by Hitler. And finally, it was necessary to win victories in order to impress neutrals, to keep them either benevolent or at least passive. Of these the most important were Turkey, Spain, Portugal, Sweden, and the United States.

The six tasks demanded of British grand strategy were formidable enough without taking on another World War I-style continental war of attrition, which is what the air offensive against Germany became before 1944. In terms of bombers produced and tonnages dropped in Europe 1939–45, the German total was 17,498 aircraft, which dropped 74,172 tons, or 4.2 tons per aircraft in such sorties. The Anglo-U.S. side had used 130,620 bombers, which dropped 1,996,036 tons on Europe, or 15.3 tons per aircraft in multiple sorties. Bombing advocates promised more than they could deliver due to organizational and technical problems.

The qualification "before 1944" is essential, for only 17 percent of the tonnage of bombs dropped on Germany by the British and American air forces was delivered before 1944. If the object had been to stimulate the German war economy and to encourage the Germans to fight, no better technique than the clumsy air offensive of 1940–43 could have been devised. It is historically akin to the methods used at Gallipoli in 1914–15 to prepare the Turks for an assault; and it had little adverse effect upon the German war effort, which did not begin to go into high gear until 1942 and did not reach its peak until 1944.

With the benefit of hindsight, it is clear that the German hit-and-run tactics should have been used. The Mosquito was an ideal weapon. Fast, cheap, using fewer engines than heavy bombers (two versus four) and a smaller crew (two versus seven), and devastatingly accurate in its attacks, it also had a very low loss rate (2 percent versus 5 percent on average for Bomber Command) and a much better availability on the morning after a raid (95 percent versus 75 percent). Moreover, the Mosquito was a precision bomber able to strike at exactly the key targets that the economic planners most wanted to hit, such as oil and communications bottlenecks, and it could be used as a guerrilla to strike when and where the enemy least expected it. Unfortunately, Churchill, itching for action, sanctioned the Air Staff's large-scale, heavy-bomber offensive.

The history of the bomber offensive against Germany is both difficult and simple to describe—difficult because of the immensity of operations and their technological impediments, and simple because the patterns when seen from a distance are quite clear.

The first operations in 1939 quickly produced lessons that, because they were wrongly interpreted, had a lasting effect upon the war. The Wellingtons sent out in daylight by the RAF contained only power-operated turrets, and the theory was that if the aircraft flew a properly tight formation, enemy fighters could not attack effectively. Unfortunately, theory overlooked the fact that even the Wellington's tail turret contained first only two—later four—.303-caliber machine guns with which to face the 20 mm cannon of the

attacking fighters that quite outranged it. Moreover, the Wellington was vulnerable to attack from abeam, as German pilots quickly observed. At first, higher RAF commanders were simply convinced that the pilots had failed to maintain formation. But they soon learned differently, and the immediate result was the limitation of the then "heavy" bombers to night operations.

With the 1940 attack in the West, bombers were put onto oil and transportation targets in hopes of slowing the *Blitzkrieg,* making the *Luftwaffe* pull back fighters to defend the Fatherland, and compelling it to divert bombers to attack Britain. But as little damage was done by these very light raids, the German High Command sensibly ignored any protests and concentrated on quick victories in the land campaign. It is highly doubtful whether or not German morale, in spite of the wishful thinking of their opponents, would have cracked at this stage in a police state with a skillful and well-financed internal public-relations (propaganda) machine in control of the media. In fact, belief that a nation's morale can be cracked has to be analyzed dispassionately and without inbred prejudices about political and other systems.

Following the German attack on Croydon, the British Cabinet desired retaliatory bombings of Germany, starting with a token raid on Berlin. This compromised the limited strength of the RAF by diverting it from oil targets. The commander-in-chief of Bomber Command in May 1940 had suggested limiting attacks to special targets in heavily populated areas in order to save bombs. After the German attack on Coventry on November 14, 1940, the policy of a twin attack on oil and morale was accepted. But the damage done was minimal. These early raids were capable of delivering only about one hundred tons of bombs at a time, and a bomb was only about two-thirds explosive and one-third casing. Some 60 percent of the bombs dropped on cities such as London had landed in open spaces, and another 10 percent were duds. The inaccuracy of British bombing began to be revealed by PRU photographs in November 1940, and eventually it was decided to follow the German precedent and make use of incendiaries with just enough high-explosive bombs to keep the firefighters in their shelters until the flames took hold. The effectiveness of these early raids was further blunted, however, by the desultory way in which the bombers reached the target; for while a raid might drag on for several hours, it violated the principles of war by not concentrating force in accuracy, weight, or time. And the whole effort was enfeebled by the constant necessity to call off aircraft for the Battle of the Atlantic, which was after all the fundamental conflict.

Bomber Command proposed in early 1941 that it go back again to attacks on transportation and morale, inasmuch it could not hit oil. The Cabinet agreed, but a month later a special study of the PRU photos versus bomber claims—the Butt Report—showed the Cabinet that the aiming error was something like five miles. Under those conditions there was little hope that Bomber Command could hit anything smaller than a city. The immediate response was to sanction area attacks. Again, the comment must be made that the whole grand strategy was wrong. Area attacks, while perhaps justifiable as retaliation, were a complete violation of the principles of war strategically. They vitiated forces rather than concentrating them against the decisive point, they were uneconomical of force, and they strengthened the enemy will to resist and inoculated him against later onslaughts. But area attacks were an end-product of RAF thinking about cracking enemy civilian morale that dated back to 1917–18 and to colonial wars.

The best solution to the effective use of Bomber Command in the attack on Germany or, for that matter, elsewhere with the same aircraft and crews, was the 1942 development of the Pathfinder Force. Leadership was given to D. C. T. Bennett, sometime RAF pilot turned professional navigator. The author of one of the standard air navigation textbooks and the holder of a long-distance record, Bennett was a professional air-man rather than a professional officer. The PFF went through many of the usual problems associated with establishing an elite organization. Other commanders jumped at the chance to dispose of not their best but their worst crews. While some of the latter proved to be bright and were simply regarded as troublemakers by sluggish commanders, others were duds who were promptly returned to their units. Gradually, Bennett built up a force of elite crews that were specialists in locating targets and who could handle the new electronic gear that enabled them to place their pyrotechnic markers accurately at night. In addition, the Master Bomber concept was instituted, according to which the bomber stream was commanded by a senior Pathfinder orbiting the target area who could call for new markers and give radio corrections to the arriving aircraft, in order to keep bombs falling as close as possible to the aiming point. A nucleus of adept and experienced crews enabled a large number of the inexperienced to concentrate on the target; and, thus, by vastly improving Bomber Command's aim, the arrangement enabled it to develop economy of force.

At the same time, the Butt Report led to the appointment of Air Chief Marshal Sir Arthur Harris as Air Officer Commander-in-Chief of Bomber Command. Harris, who had many of the solid qualities of Haig, took charge at a time when Bomber Command was at last building up to a force of 500 bombers of the Wellington and Whitley types. In addition to the beginning of Pathfinder operations, Harris had two other advantages. He enjoyed close relations with Churchill, with whom he occasionally spent the weekend, thus by-passing the usual chain of command, and his experts began to work with those in the Ministry of Economic Warfare concerned with the German economy. In the spring of 1942, Bomber Command began to recover its reputation with a series of raids on German cities, culminating in the massive thousand-plane attack on Cologne on May 30. If not an outstanding military success, this was at least of considerable propaganda value.

Harris was always one to emphasize efficiency and the exploitation of new weapons. He had conducted night-flying sorties in Iraq in 1924. As the head of planning in the Air Ministry, he had in 1934–36 urged development of the heavy bomber. He lamented the state of RAF air navigation and opposed the dissipation of aircrew on ground duties. After he became Air Officer Commander-in-Chief, Bomber Command, he demanded 40,000 bicycles to save the time of ground crew getting about on airfields.

Harris had seen flying control in the United States in 1938 and understood its value. The development of flying control in RAF Bomber Command came about because of the necessity of preserving resources and was opposed by those who wished to retain their precious authority. Thus officers were appointed to manage flying control and were invested with supreme authority.

A system, called Darkie, further enhanced flying control by enabling lost or disabled machines and crews to be recovered. Important in all this was the backing as well of the technical vision of the High Command.

It took almost four years of war to build up Bomber Command to become an effective force and two years for the Eighth Air Force. When Harris came in as AOC-in-C of the RAF campaign, his arrival coincided with that of the 1936 heavies—the Short Stirling (ER 72), the Handley Page Halifax I (ER 54), and the best of them, the Avro Lancaster I (ER 103).

What was not realized until the heavies arrived was the amount of training that aircrews needed first in operational training units (OTU) on Wellingtons and then at heavy conversion units (HCU) to learn how to handle aircraft that were twice as heavy as the OTU machines. And not only had ground crew to be trained, but also aircrew and ground crew had to be briefed on new equipment, which was to make Harris's force by 1944 far more skilled and accurate than in 1942. Air navigation, for example, which finally became a specialty in 1942, soon involved the electronic aids Gee, by

which a position could be fixed if the aircraft at altitude was in "line of sight" of the master and two slave stations; Oboe, which had greater range; H2S, which enabled the navigator to "map read" and bomb through clouds; and, finally, the Pathfinder pyrotechnic target marking system controlled by a master bomber broadcasting directions.

In February 1942, on average, the RAF could lift 510 tons of bombs; by January 1944 that had risen to 3,047, and a year later to 5,264, due in large part to a nearly all-Lancaster force, even allowing for a little over 60 percent serviceability (availability). In February 1942, the RAF had 224 heavy bombers; in January 1945 it had 1,873. And whereas 1,000 sea mines were laid in 1941, 16,000 were dropped in 1944.

At this time, the RAF also experienced the effectiveness of its night bombing, which had been enhanced by closing up aircraft on takeoff and in the stream in order to pass over the target after evasive routing so rapidly and heavily that the defenses were swamped. In 1942, over 1,400 tons were delivered in ninety minutes; in 1944 that had risen to more than 3,000 tons in the same time. An offshoot of this efficiency was the need to be able to land returning bombers much more rapidly, so that they no longer straggled in all night.

To counter the very effective German night fighters, by 1944 Mosquitos not only intruded against German Air Force airfields, but also flew in the stream as invisible escorts. Also by 1944, Air Chief Marshal Harris had 128 airfields and 3,804 aircraft, in spite of consistently having his resources posted to overseas campaigns or diverted to Coastal Command or Admiralty targets. In the end, only 45 percent of Bomber Command's effort was devoted to industrial-city targets, and that in spite of his forces being assigned to the Supreme Allied Commander of SHAEF from March to September 1944.

More so than the Eighth Air Force's attacks on Germany, Bomber Command's were made a moral issue even before the end of the war. It was forgotten that the German Blitz against Britain in

1940–42 had caused 42,000 civilian casualties, and the V-weapons in 1944–45 some more.

The Allied bombing of Germany caused an estimated 410,000 deaths of men, women, and children in the Third Reich. In contrast, the RAF suffered 55,000 dead, wounded, and missing, as well as 10,000 POWs during those sorties.

Modern war switched the burden to civilians, not just in direct victims, but also in the constant strain of the lack of services to provide for daily needs and new lodgings, and the psychological strain of long hours in air-raid shelters, working in bomb-damaged facilities, and worry about the fate of relatives and friends.

The argument is correctly made that the grand-strategic air offensive against Germany was a second front aiding the USSR by tying down enemy resources of men and women to the extent of 1,125,000 people employed to clear away bomb damage and to supply replacements of material items, as well as to repair gas and electrical services and railways. By 1944, 75 percent of the *Luftwaffe* fighter force was on home defense and 889,000 personnel were manning the flak, searchlights, and radar defenses. Factories lost many man-hours and suffered from as much as 25 percent absenteeism. It has been estimated that in 1944 Germany could have produced 96,000 aircraft, but actually only managed to make 36,000. And, thus, 55,000 RAF casualties spread over a six-year campaign was a small price to pay, and compared favorably with the 200,000 of the early D-Day campaign in 1944. The average size of Bomber Command during the war was 125,000 men and women.

It was in mid-1942, just as the RAF was working up its strength, that the first elements of the USAAF's Eighth Air Force arrived in Britain to join the fray. Equipped with the much-vaunted Norden bombsight, their accuracy was reduced by European weather (60 percent clouded), and the necessity for a long straight run-in at a fixed altitude increased the vulnerability of the bomber to flak. Although they made a small strike on Rouen in northern France on August 17, 1942, the ne-

cessity of building up for the Operation Torch attack on North Africa in November prevented the Eighth Air Force from being effective until mid-December. It was at last allowed to move from attacks on the French coast to Bremen and Kiel, as P-47 Thunderbolts arrived in Britain in January 1943, though they did not become fully operational until late summer in an escort role, due to engine and radio failures.

Although it would still take another year to make the combined Bomber Offensive devastatingly effective, Hamburg in July 1943, with its 40,000 dead, showed what could be done. In October, Kassel also experienced a firestorm delivered in twenty-six minutes, which disabled 20,570 out of a population of 225,000.

At the Casablanca Conference in January 1943, the Allied heads of state called for the "Pointblank" uninterrupted air offensive against Germany. This was a great political gesture, but the means of carrying it out were still unavailable—not an uncommon dilemma facing military commanders. In theory, the attack was to be a combination of massive RAF night area raids and precision USAAF day attacks. In fact, apart from the destruction of Hamburg, the scheme fizzled not so much from the inability of the Eighth Air Force to gain air superiority over Germany as on the intolerable losses when its bombers moved beyond the range of their escorts.

The most disappointing of these raids were those on Schweinfurt of August 17 and October 14, 1943. That time had elapsed before both these raids took place was due to the fact that if used intensively, neither the bomber force nor its fighter escort was able to operate for more than about a week continuously. This meant that targets could not usually be demolished, only damaged, and the Germans were warned as to which industrial targets needed to be dispersed and given time to undertake this.

For the twin attacks on the Schweinfurt ball-bearing plants and the Messerschmitt works at Regensburg of August 17, 376 B-17 Flying Fortresses were dispatched, of which 315 attacked the target and dropped 724 tons of bombs. But sixty of the attacking force, or 19 percent, were lost. The claim that 288 enemy fighters were shot down was greatly exaggerated; the Germans actually only put up some 300 fighters—a number far below the four to one ratio they believed necessary to defeat the American bomber force—and they lost only twenty-seven. Attacks in the second week of October cost the Eighth Air Force 148 aircraft and about 1,500 men. But the German fighter leaders, at least, began to realize that they had to prepare to meet the long-range escorts that the Allies would now be bound to introduce. Hitler was still insisting that the bulk of fighter production go to the Eastern Front and the Mediterranean, and he and Goering opposed Adolf Galland, the German fighter leader who urged that the new jet Me-262 be pushed rapidly. Thus, when in February 1944 a much augmented USAAF returned to German skies with P-51 Mustang escorts, the beginning of the end of Nazi air power was in sight. The Germans, weakened by the 1943 attacks and with inadequate defensive aircraft, could not thwart the bombers, let alone the fighters.

Nor did the Germans in a lack of defensive imagination realize how vulnerable the Mustangs were as they entered European airspace with their rear fuselage tanks full, which made them unstable and likely to tumble if forced to maneuver before that fuel was consumed.

Meanwhile, in March to July 1943, the RAF had fought the Battle of the Ruhr, followed a few weeks later by the combined assault on Hamburg. When continuous attacks created the firestorm that destroyed the center of the city, ironically new industry was located on the periphery. And when jobs were burned out in the core, workers went to the very industries that were short of people, but most essential to the war effort.

In May, the Dams attack took place. Although ten out of nineteen aircraft aborted or were shot down, the Mohne and Eder dams were breached and Wing Cdr. Guy Gibson became a household hero in Britain.

But by fall 1943, the German defenses once again had the upper hand, and the night offensive was approaching a crisis. In the Battle of Berlin, from November 1943 to March 1944, losses rose to 9 percent and then at Nuremburg to 11 percent, losses that were concealed by the Operation Overlord diversion. But by then, the new aluminized explosive additive had increased the lethality of bombs ten-fold.

By September 1944, the RAF was able to bomb with pinpoint accuracy eighty oil, transportation, and tank-production targets, though Harris wanted to keep up the demolition of industrial cities.

In January 1945, the Allied combined air forces were ordered to undertake Operation Thunderclap, to aid the Red Army in the East by demoralizing and creating disorder in German cities, and to hamper *Wehrmacht* moves.

The last Bomber Command raid of the war was by 126 Mosquitoes on Kiel, May 2, 1945. However, the Battle of Germany was virtually halted in the spring of 1944 by the need to deal with targets behind the proposed Allied beachhead in France. After some very strong political fighting within the Allied High Command, it was finally agreed that General Dwight D. Eisenhower, as Supreme Commander, should have control over not only the Allied Expeditionary Air Forces but also over Bomber Command and the Eighth Air Force. The plan to destroy transportation targets in France was the work of Eisenhower's Deputy, Air Chief Marshal Sir Arthur Tedder. The directive Eisenhower issued in March 1944 essentially used the Allied air forces independently, as had been intended in 1918. Bomber Command attacked cities, and also transportation in France, with an accuracy that surprised its commander-in-chief; the Eighth Air Force was assigned the destruction of the *Luftwaffe,* while the Allied Expeditionary Air Forces generally softened up northern France and disrupted German supply routes in the Low Countries. The end result was virtually a dislocation of the German ability to respond. Heavy bombers were even used over the battlefields, churning up the ground on which German tanks would find themselves impotently isolated by craters. Thereafter, the bombers provided on occasion an extra punch for tactical forces, until released by the Supreme Commander in September.

At that time they went back to oil and morale targets, but the feeling existed, nevertheless, that Berlin should be demolished to aid the Soviets. The arguments between the oil group and the morale-busters lasted into 1945, when it was finally decided to make Dresden a psychological object lesson, with tragic consequences for the many refugees packing the city.

On February 13–14, 1945, the Allies, as a matter of military necessity said the Command, wished to be certain that a German collapse, already becoming visible, would occur before Nazi nuclear weapons could be used. Dresden was hit to aid the advancing Soviet armies, though oil remained the top-priority target. Dresden was low on the German defenses, as it had escaped attacks. Harris elected a two-punch attack, which caught the civil defenses in the open. The firestorm out of the center of the old city was devastating. The post-raid press release emphasized that it had been a terror raid on a population center, which set off the long line of accusations that Harris resented. Nevertheless, the debate has continued. It had been the policy in Whitehall, the seat of British government, to attack population centers; afterward, Churchill asked that the policy be reviewed. The validity of the Dresden target has been argued ever since, with a greatly scaled-down number of casualties.

Economic Intelligence in the Strategic Air Offensive

Both the British and American so-called strategic air offensives against Germany and the U.S. Army Air Forces attacks on Japan had suffered from a lack of proper economic intelligence. At first, highly inaccurate and consequently seriously damaging to areas surrounding military targets, grand- strate-

gic bombing was used as a sledgehammer, often wastefully and blindly. The reason for this can be found partly in the misinformation or lack of information concerning the capabilities and actual performance of the bombers; partly in the argument that war workers were combatants in a modern industrial conflict; partly in the fact that once a vast heavy-bomber force had been built up, its leaders were unwilling to keep it idle; and partly in the belief of the air forces that they had a "mission" to smash evil. For some two years the British had refused to believe photo-reconnaissance evidence that their average bombing error at night was five miles; in any case, economic intelligence was only gradually assessed as indicating that the key targets were small, compact, specialized industries such as ball-bearing plants, synthetic-fuel refineries, and transportation bottlenecks. In Japan, as the U.S. Strategic Bombing Survey pointed out, the vital and easily broken rail network was largely ignored, although destruction of its few vital tunnels would have been decisive.

A technological argument could have been made for German grand-strategic strikes against Russia, relative to the rate of Russian industrial development and to the Stalinist five-year plans. Because the Russians industrialized late, they had the advantage of being able to utilize large power plants and other complexes. In the West, however, the slower growth over a longer period of technological innovation resulted in smaller, scattered factories. Thus, ironically, while the Russians benefitted from the lateness of their modernization, conversely they were more vulnerable to precision attack. Fortunately for them, no one in the German Air Force appreciated this.

Although it is important not to overlook the seesawing technical battle between the attackers and the defenders, it must be recognized that the grand-strategic air offensives against Britain, Germany, and Japan resulted from intellectual political battles fought out at the higher-direction levels throughout the campaigns. In a war supported by new technology, oral evidence was no longer acceptable; airmen had to justify their claims by photographic and additional means, and these were tested by economic and other intelligence units not under their control. In this respect it should be noted that Allied intelligence assessments of German aircraft production were highly inaccurate. Until mid-1942 they had estimated the average German monthly aircraft production at 1,575, whereas the actual rate was 880; by 1944, they erred too far the other way—1,870 compared to the actual 2,811. Also unreliable were the RAF's overestimate of the GAF in 1940–41 at 14,000 aircraft. As this affected grand strategy, Mr. Justice Singleton was appointed to investigate, and in March 1941 put the total closer to 4,500.

To further clarify the growth of bomber power in Europe in the first thirty months, we can look at the RAF's annualized sortie rate, which was 1,962 per month (a sortie being one aircraft sent out). In 1944 alone, that rose to 13,904 per month and the tonnage dropped by the RAF rose from 0.842 to 3.2 tons per sortie. Some 85 percent of Bomber Command sorties and 95 percent of the tonnage dropped was in the period February 1942 to May 1945, 45 percent of it on seventy cities and some small towns. The RAF loss rate for sixty-eight months was only 2.1 percent, even though 7,122 aircraft were lost with 43,786 aircrew killed, 4,000 injured, and 10,000 POWs. Non-operational accidents caused the loss of 8,349 aircraft and 4,095 crew.

Bomber Command aircrew casualties totaled 55,000: 47,268 killed or died as prisoners of war; 8,195 killed in flying or ground accidents; and 37 killed in battle on the ground. Another 9,838 survived as POWs, 4,200 wounded in aircraft that returned from operations, and 4,203 wounded in flying or ground accidents, for total aircrew casualties of 73,741.

In the 2,074 days/nights of the Second World War, Bomber Command lost 8,953 aircraft on operations (grand-strategic bombing, Résistance operations, and Mediterranean flights). On 71.4 percent of the nights and 52.5 percent of all the days,

RAF Bomber Command flew a total 307,253 night sorties and lost 7,953 aircraft (2.6 percent); on the 80,163 day sorties, 1,000 were lost (1.2 percent, or of the 387,416 sorties flown, 2.3 percent lost, an average of 4.3 aircraft and crews every twenty-four hours). Daylight losses were deceptively low, as most occurred in 1944–45 when the Allies had air superiority. Operational crashes were generally less than half a percent, except for Vickers Wellingtons (0.72 percent), Bristol Blenheims (0.81 percent), Armstrong Whitworth Whitleys (1.43 percent), and Avro Manchesters (0.95 percent). In contrast, of all the Me-109s built (some 35,000-plus), two-thirds were involved in takeoff or landing accidents.

Air Chief Marshal Harris suffered near disgrace after the war for his Bomber Command casualties, which were higher than the losses of other services. But he was the AOC-in-C for three years as the six-year grand-strategic campaign reached its peak and victory. Most of his casualties were over enemy territory, in contrast to Dowding's in the Battle of Britain. Moreover, a lot of bad feeling came after the war when Harris refused ennoblement unless his vital ground crews received the 1939–45 Star with clasp. Unfortunately most people, including those in high places, did not know the unending harsh conditions in which the ground crews had worked outdoors in all weather.

Further Consideration of the Air Offensive against Japan

The bombing of Japan, another important Allied strategic air offensive, has received less than its due in most historical accounts. Reasons for this have to do with the vastness of the Pacific theater and, on the Allied side, the partners involved, as also with the state of technology and the fact that the campaign, outside of the 1942 Doolittle raid flown off a carrier, was not launched until suitable islands for air bases had been captured and the fields created in 1945. The weapon of choice was the new B-29 Superfortress, which just had the fuel for the 2,500-mile trip from Guam to Honshu, and return. Whereas the air war in Europe had taken almost six years, that against Japan lasted only six months. During this latter campaign, 414 B-29s were lost, with 2,251 crew members. In the same period, 2,251 B-29s had landed back on the fields at Iwo Jima, saving 24,761 officers and men. But 200 newly arrived P-51 escort pilots were killed in their bivouac on Iwo Jima by infiltrating Japanese infantry.

The U.S. Twentieth Air Force's attack on Japan was ineffective due to technology, training, and weather. The Twentieth's commander, the very aggressive Curtis LeMay, had been transferred from the Eighth Air Force in Europe. A bold tactician, LeMay now decided that B-29s could go unarmed, carrying incendiaries instead of their defensive guns, and flying at low level at night.

This adoption of RAF tactics was not because of the daylight defeat, but followed in the trail of the pattern of bombing tactics. The advantage here was that LeMay's force could be highly destructive with firebombs in wooden Japanese cities. Thus, at the end of February 1945, LeMay inaugurated incendiary attacks that destroyed 178 square miles of some sixty-six built-up urban centers and forced one-seventh of the Japanese population (8.5 million people) to evacuate after leaflet warnings. This campaign focused on Japanese war-making capacity, while the RAF over Germany had aimed to undermine the morale of war workers. The U.S. approach, it was hoped, would also shield it from charges of indiscriminate attacks, even with A-bombs.

What was not known until the campaign started from the Pacific end was that weather, almost more than the Japanese, became the major opponent. In the few operations launched from China, where all supplies—including POL (petrol, oil, lubricants) and bombs—had to be ferried over the Hump, the jet stream was discovered, which affected returning bombers. In the Pacific, on the long over-water flights, a B-29 had to escort the P-51s for navigational purposes. With thunderstorms en route, the fighters were separated from the bombers and even some of the bombers themselves did not have enough fuel or navigational skills to get back to Iwo. Rescue submarines saved a number of invaluable aircrew, mostly offshore of Japan.

By this time in the war, the Japanese air forces were like the *Luftwaffe* a few months before, down to new pilots too poorly trained to contend with the enemy's new more powerful fighters just becoming available, let alone to combat the enemy's powerfully armed B-29s flying at high altitudes and protected by the long-range P-51s—not to mention the arriving U.S. Navy carrier raids.

The B-29s, in addition, had the advantage of LORAN (long-range navigation) and other electronic navigational gear. They were helped by the fact that underwater radar-equipped (sonar) USN submarines were already bringing Japan to her knees, and that two atomic bombs, on Hiroshima on August 6, 1945, and on Nagasaki on August 9, made it very plain that the end was near.

In the meantime, Japan was also being heavily hit by carrier-based warplanes, including those from the British Pacific fleet, which were for political-diplomatic reasons limited to targets on other than the main island.

That the Pacific campaign appears to have been more quickly successful than those in Europe must certainly in part be attributed to its lateness in the scheme of war—the groundwork had been laid, the big battalions mustered, and the skills and weapons honed. The atomic bombs were the icing on the cake, which saved a ground invasion of the home island of Japan.

LAND-BASED AIR POWER AT SEA

Further to complicate the matter of choosing targets during the last nine months of the European war were the many parties to targeting, from Tedder at the tactical end to the commander-in-chief of the USAAF in Washington, not to mention the British Admiralty, faced again with another new U-boat menace technically far more serious than any heretofore. And in a sense, this once more brought home the fallacy of not winning the Battle of the Atlantic before tackling Germany itself. Although Harris can be lauded for his single-minded devotion to the bombing of Germany, he can be condemned for his unwillingness to recognize the need to win the Battle of the Atlantic first. He fought constantly with the Admiralty over targets, always resenting the diversion of his force from what he regarded as its prime goals. Naval officers may have argued that the way to defeat the U-boats was to let them attack well-defended convoys, but proper use of air power also dictated attacks upon U-boat assembly slips and servicing pens, nearly all of which were easily identifiable targets because they were located on shorelines. That these attacks were not decisive until late in the war was due to the paucity of effort, puny bombs, the lack of concentration, and the inadequacy of the attacks before 1944, except at Hamburg in mid-1943.

The Battle of the Atlantic, continued from the 1914 war, was also an oscillating technical battle, which the Allies won in mid–1943 but would have lost again in 1945–46 due to the arrival of the new fully submersible Type XIX and XXI U-boats.

Many similarities can be found between the Battle of the Atlantic and the Battle of Germany; both were three-dimensional. In one, convoys faced U-boats; in the other, escorted bombers faced fighters. In each, the method by which a battle was won was to lure the hunters to the cargo carriers to be destroyed. This tactic failed when the defenders were weak, but was successful once the close escort was supplemented with hunter-killer groups and with direct attacks on the enemy's bases. And just as the convoys benefitted from direction-finding wireless fixes that located their chattering enemy, so the bomber groups also depended on intelligence that located defending fighter formations. Just as the convoys began to benefit from long-range air patrols or planes flown off escorting carriers, so the bombers over Germany benefitted from pathfinding and other ac-

tivities, even to the extent at times of decoy raids. Although the effort to locate and destroy the U-boat was slow, an interchange between night-fighter and anti-submarine warfare crews might well have proved highly rewarding, and still might. The problem remains essentially the same: protect, seek, find, destroy, and "think outside the box."

The destruction or harassment of shipping by land-based air power was a constant feature of the war around Europe and was practiced with varying success by German, Italian, and British airmen. The sea has marks for those who are vigilant, and crews learned to get the feel of the weather and to read the surface. The Germans, after some successes in the North Sea, settled down to make *Luftflotte X* the major anti-shipping force, and the personnel who manned its torpedo-carrying He-111s became highly efficient. The Germans quickly learned that attacks on British coastal convoys were often risky if fighter escort was present, yet they and their Italian allies soon found profitable targets in the Mediterranean and then in the north—around Russian convoys. They mauled the Russia-bound ships so badly in 1942 that between July of that year and March 1944, when air escort became available, only one convoy was run. The German Ju-87 Stuka was effective in the English Channel and even more so in the clear Mediterranean, but it remained highly vulnerable to fighters. In general, the Germans used the He-111 and the Ju-88, especially when the weather was bad and the attack had to be made at low altitude. The Italians used the Savoia-Marchetti SM-79 torpedo-bomber plane (ER 16.6). No one found the high-level bomber of much use, except as a diversion, for ships could turn away when they saw the bombs released.

The British at first used a twin-engine torpedo-bomber, the Beaufort; but because it was as vulnerable as most medium bombers were to the increasingly heavy flak that German coastal convoys threw up, as well as to fighters, its place was taken by its stablemate, the Beaufighter. The latter was heavily armed and highly maneuverable;

it could also carry both a torpedo and rockets, when these came into use in 1943. Thus, it had a punch like a light cruiser at ten times the speed.

The response of all sides was not only to arm convoys and their escorts heavily, but to develop other defensive devices such as kite balloons, towed in the First World War also, and flame-throwers, as well as looser steaming formations better suited to violent evasive action in air-sea battles. It was in attacks on shipping that the Italians proved most brave and very adept, but they dropped out of the war just as their equipment became obsolete.

From 1941, combatants had an increasing tendency to use fighter-bombers or rocket-firing fighters against the many small coastal vessels that dotted the European shipping lanes. These were not worth a torpedo and were too hard to bomb, but were vulnerable to rocket and cannon fire. Moreover, offensive sweeps by fighter-bombers flying low were hard to spot on radar and harder to defend against. The one blessing, apart from an opponent's air escort, was the inaccuracy of the attackers. Torpedoes were tricky to drop, had to be aimed carefully, and depended for their accuracy on the guesses and calculations made by the attacking crew, who had also to resist the tendency to jink on the approach. Rockets only required that the aircraft be held steady for a few seconds and could be aimed by firing the guns until hits on the target were observed. A similar advantage had been conferred on the heavy bombers over land when the British Mark XIV gyro bombsight became available, allowing the bombs to be dropped while the aircraft was taking evasive action.

The use of land-based air power at sea was perhaps best demonstrated by aircraft from the island of Malta. PRU Marylands and Spitfires from there kept watch on Italian shipping, and their photos and reports enabled the RAF and the Royal Navy to attack Italian supply ships almost constantly. Although the cost of maintaining Malta was high, the damage its ships and aircraft did was more than worth it.

But from the German and the British standpoints in the Battle of the Atlantic, land-based air power played yet another role, that of long-range air patrol. German Focke-Wulf Fw-200 Condors (ER 46) scoured the Atlantic shipping lanes seeking British convoys after the fall of France. The British retaliated with fighters shot off catapults on merchant ships, then with escort carriers. By 1943, the U-boats were largely left to seek for themselves or relied on radioed intelligence.

On the other hand, the British had started the war woefully inadequately equipped to patrol their lifelines by air, in spite of the lessons of the First World War. Although Coastal Command, which controlled land-based air power at sea out of Britain, was established in 1936, it had few suitable aircraft in 1939 or 1940. Even machines it could have had were squandered in ferrying supplies to Norway, or in the bomber offensive against Germany. Its Short Sunderland flying boat (ER 63) had only an 800-mile radius of action in an ocean 3,000 miles across. On top of that, Britain's Irish bases had been largely given away in 1938 by a well-meaning Prime Minister. Air patrols with Whitleys and Hudsons were started from Iceland, but it was not until 1942 that long-range Consolidated PBY Catalina flying boats (ER 16.6) and very-long-range (VLR) B-24 Liberators (ER 103) began to become available. Thus, not until an air base was established in the Azores under the Treaty of 1393, in conjunction with greatly increased escort-carrier and hunter-killer forces, was the air gap over the middle of the Atlantic closed. Before that, aircraft proved invaluable in patrolling close to convoys, keeping U-boats down so that they could neither sight shipping nor send out intelligence.

In May 1942, the RAF established a radar offensive against U-boats in the Bay of Biscay. This was a strategic air offensive properly designed to harass and destroy U-boats in transit between their own bases and operating areas along the convoy routes. To counter it, the Germans developed long-range patrols of Ju-88C heavy fighters, but these had little effect, as the faster and better-armed, very-long-range Liberators and Mosquitoes were introduced over the Bay. The battles developed in intensity in 1942 and reached a climax in 1943. Once British aircraft, equipped with radar and powerful airborne Leigh lights, located U-boats on the surface at night that were charging their batteries and attempting to make a quick passage, they dropped down, illuminated the surfaced submarine, and attacked. When the Germans countered by developing a radar detector, the British switched wave-lengths. In July 1943, aircraft sank six submarines in the first twenty-one days of the month, and destroyed nine more in the last seven days, in a combined offensive with hunter-killer surface forces. For all of this to be possible, well-trained crews and the right weapons were required to make the system efficient.

At first anti-submarine warfare suffered from a lack of suitable bombs and depth-charges, from poor aiming techniques that failed to allow for the movement of the U-boat while the depth-charges sank to their pre-set level, and from the general paucity of aircraft. By 1943, aircraft were available in sufficient quantities that as soon as a sighting was reported, additional aircraft could be vectored in. Thus, when U-boats took to traveling in company and fighting back on the surface, their defense could be disoriented by attacks from various directions simultaneously. The U-boat's quad 20 mm guns could also be stymied by the fire from the .50-caliber guns on Liberators and Flying Fortresses, and eventually silenced by the arrival of the Mosquito with a 57 mm cannon and rockets. The submarine only had to be holed once for that to be fatal.

The Battle of the Atlantic was in its last 2½ years dominated by Allied air power. Of the German and Italian submarines sunk during the six years of the war, surface forces alone accounted for 285½, land-based aircraft 245½, ship-based aircraft 44, and a combination of surface and air forces 53. In addition, 64 were destroyed by bombing at their bases. But these figures alone do not tell the whole story, because the escalation of air effort was such that while in the first three years of the war surface vessels sank sixty-one and assisted in seven cases, aircraft accounted for only nine. In 1942–43, when the Battle of the Bay of Biscay was on, aircraft accounted for 88½ kills compared with 75½ for ships, and 16 combined sinkings. And in the last two years of the war, aircraft destroyed well over half the submarines sunk in the European theater.

Bombing raids steadily grew more accurate and concentrated: in the first three years of the war, two U-boats were destroyed as they were being built; twenty-six more were disposed of in the next two years; and thirty-six were destroyed in the final year of the conflict. In other words, attacking assembly plants was only effective when the raids were continuous and the aiming of sufficiently destructive bombs accurate. Air attacks at sea were less costly in losses of aircraft and highly skilled crews, and far more effective, for although the onslaught of the U-boats was continuous, when attacked, they could only retaliate after they had surfaced. Even the adoption of the snorkel, enabling them to travel submerged, did not shield U-boats fully from the better radar by then in use. Moreover, U-boats and their crews in port ceased to get a respite in their massively reinforced pens when RAF bombers could deliver Tall Boy 12,000-pound and Grand Slam 22,000-pound bombs that penetrated over twenty feet of the pen's reinforced concrete roof.

The air war at sea was at all times strategic or grand-strategic and dependent for its effectiveness upon the tactics, equipment, training, and flexible response of the leadership. In the case of the Battle of the Atlantic, it was for both sides a grand-strategic campaign vital to victory or defeat. The Allies won a definite success because they were able to mobilize and concentrate their forces and because the Germans had not developed the concept of air cover and long-range reconnaissance for their navy.

Ironically, the bombing of Germany and Japan, their unconditional surrender, and banning of their armed forces enabled them to rise as economic powers after 1945, unhampered by the need to spend upon defense until the Cold War Soviet threat changed their status. In the meantime, they benefitted from aid packages such as the Marshall Plan.

ANALYSIS

In answer to the airmen's complaint that they were never allowed to use air power properly, the critic is tempted, after considering the Second World War, to reply that the trouble is that they were allowed to use it improperly.

The victor in most campaigns was he who could move most rapidly and who observed the principles of war in regard to protection of the base and the lines of communication, concentration, economy of force, and surprise. Many opportunities for airmen to have won the war went unrecognized or unheeded. In most cases, decisions affecting these opportunities had been made in peacetime.

As Wave cycle theory shows, actual declarations of war seem to come partway through the period of rearmamental instability, so that the force that is better prepared at that moment has the better chance of winning quickly. But the Second World War showed all too clearly that preparation must include the gathering and use of intelligence. The Germans, tactically oriented, were prepared to deal with Poland and France, and even Norway, but they were insufficiently educated where England and the Soviet Union were concerned. As continual campaigns eroded the German momentum, when wartime equilibrium set in late in 1942, the *Luftwaffe* suffered because the German economy was still not in high gear; the air force was trying to win with designs that came from the early years of rearmamental instability.

Although the British put a temporary stop on their own developments for some months during the Battle of Britain, they continued to balance quantity with quality, so that they kept the technical edge sharp. The Japanese made the mistakes of the Germans, and the Americans and the Soviets followed the British pattern.

Yet decent equipment without intelligent doctrine and qualified crews was not enough. Modern war requires the mobilization of manpower, management, and methodology. It is an organizational business in which the human problems can become paramount. Thus, on the German side, were the problems of Goering, Udet, and Hitler; the British had Churchill and Harris; the Americans had the heirs of Billy Mitchell.

The war showed the effectiveness of tactical air forces over land and sea and the ineffectiveness of the deterrent weapon. Early bombing offensives were highly inaccurate and costly, and because tactical air forces, operating at much lower altitudes over both land and sea, were much more accurate, it can be argued that they were a far better investment than high-level bombers. Yet, operational research helped to increase accuracy; and, in fact, when high-level bombers were employed in tactical roles, their accuracy surprised even the commander-in-chief of RAF Bomber Command, who had come to believe that they could only hit cities.

The war showed also that no weapon could be used continuously without modification in tactics and that senior commanders had to understand a weapon's limitation. Thus, the Stuka had its heyday, but it soon became the victim of fighters unless moved to less well-defended targets. Paratroopers and airborne operations were acceptable only if they achieved a *coup de main* with minimum losses and were not expected to fight against fully equipped ground forces for more than about twenty-four to forty-eight hours. Another lesson was the extreme value of a transport service that had sufficient useful aircraft to be able to resupply an army on the move. Moreover, as aircraft ceased to be first-line, they could be usefully employed in both training and tactical roles. Bombers that became too vulnerable for offensive operations were used in operational training units and as glider tugs or transports, or were assigned to ocean patrols. Fighters became fighter-bombers and personal transports. An aircraft designed for one task might be more successful in another; or, conversely, equipment that seemed wonderful in peace might prove of more limited combat use.

The problem in war was to make the most effective, rather than the most showy, use of what was available. To this end, the work of the operational research scientists was enormously useful; their contributions, foreshadowed in the 1914 war but generally neglected in peace, were many. And behind these boffins were the experts in the laboratories, who developed better theories and better weapons, and the factories that produced the equipment.

But even though this was a technological war, outside the main European theater much of it was fought with the equipment at hand. In more distant theaters, as even in the Soviet Union, the side that did not have air superiority was not necessarily the side that caved in at once. In several theaters, neither side had aircraft to cover the battlefield, let alone the back areas, so that even if defenders had no air cover, unless it was in a naturally channeled area such as Greece, they could counter with dispersion and anti-aircraft fire. Tactical air forces were ordinarily at their most effective when they could make continuous attacks upon an enemy caught by geography in a pass, at a river crossing, or in some other bottleneck—though in Italy and Burma, geography could frustrate air power.

Another way of looking at air power is to see it as both a guerrilla and a counter-guerrilla force. In the Battle of Britain, German fighter-bombers were guerrillas, and an RAF counterstrike plan against enemy airfields could have been. In the Battle of the Atlantic, RAF Coastal Command played a counter-guerrilla role, while its coastal anti-shipping forces were guerrilla. The Allied grand-strategic bombers were guerrilla in their evasive routing and selection of targets.

At almost no stage of the war was air power alone decisive. It was most effective when combined with surface forces, except in those cases where it had a distinct advantage over its opponent, as in the war at sea, and it excelled in its capacity for continuous observation and destruction. It was used at its best in fast and sometimes repeated random thrusts at a vital target, thus clearing the way for surface action; but at other times, its use was superfluous.

Ironically, the economic effect of bombing cities was in the long run the opposite of that anticipated. By destroying German and Japanese urban areas and initially forbidding the defeated nations to rebuild their armed forces, the victors forced them to start afresh and concentrate their energies. Their very modernization has created economic nations that increasingly challenge the victors. Tactical air power created no such bogeys.

Conclusions

The massive destructive—not always effective—uses of air power in World War II left a number of legacies.

The amount of resources poured into the Allied grand-strategic bombing campaigns both stimulated and debilitated British and American economies, to the detriment of the former. After five years of war, the end product was a shrinking force of one hundred heavy-bomber squadrons in RAF Bomber Command, whose technical complexity rendered them increasingly unserviceable due to shortages of skilled manpower. Ultimately, the RAF was only able to administer the *coup de grâce* to an already tottering enemy.

On the plus side, however, the grand-strategic air campaign against Germany spun off the benefits that helped civil aviation to grow like a hothouse flower after 1945—radar, air-traffic control, trained aircrew, reliable engines, concrete runwayed airfields of the first construction revolution, as well as an aviation-educated public. Even the manufacturing of bombers had converted the industry from cottage to modern industrial establishments.

The U.S. Army Air Forces did not face the limitations on manpower that the British did, and had access to far greater resources and a technically minded people. Moreover, America's need to ferry bombers to overseas theaters created a worldwide network of airfields, as well as the ability to reach and use them, that was vital to the postwar growth of U.S. air transport, especially when coupled to the monopoly on twin- and four-engined transports, which the war had created.

The other national air forces of the 1939–45 period lacked either suitable targets for a grand-strategic doctrine and effort or the political will to allocate the research, or lacked the materials needed to create a bombing force. This was true also of the U.S. Navy.

What the Second World War showed very clearly was that the bitter prewar arguments about army cooperation had significantly delayed, in most countries, the development of the more effective tactical air forces. While the British, French, and Americans argued, the Japanese and American navies developed aircraft-carrier task forces, and the Germans and the Russians created *Blitzkrieg* air arms, integrated into the armies and capable of allowing decisive engagements—especially in the Eastern theater, where operational art integrated tactical air forces into deep battle.

Although tactical air forces did not emerge supreme from 1939–45, they did have a large impact upon military thinking in the postwar years. However, in Britain and America, and later in Russia, they did not have enough impact to overcome the influence of the "bomber barons," which lasted well into the 1960s because nuclear weapons and increasingly long-range aircraft brought global targets into the crosshairs.

The creation of tactical air forces meant the production of masses of fighters and medium bombers and swarms of mechanics, though fewer aircrew. Mass production and modification helped produce almost perfect aerial tools. And the demands of tactical air forces for airfields led to the second airfield construction revolution—the PSP three-day wonder.

Tactical air forces and fighters won decisive victories in the Battles of France and Britain, Pearl Harbor, Midway, and the Philippine Sea, not to mention in *Blitzkrieg* and on the Eastern Front. Part of their effectiveness came from the development of new weapons, part from sheer numbers and trained pilots, and part from the development of command, control, communications, and intelligence at all levels, as well as an understanding of the assets and limits of their use.

CHAPTER 5

THE SECOND WORLD WAR: SEABORNE AIR POWER

The air war campaigns in Europe were characteristically long and drawn out; the strategic air offensive against Germany, for example, dragged on for nearly six years. Even the operations of tactical air forces consisted of a fairly endless series of raids and sorties. Rarely, if ever, was there a clearly defined air battle in which it was plain to both sides that one had won and the other lost.

The situation at sea was very different. Naval battles rarely lasted over four days, and on most occasions much less than that. Clearly one side thought it was the winner, and generally it was right. But it was the very brevity and decisiveness of battles at sea, as well as the fact that the carrier actions meant a new kind of warfare, that makes these conflicts of such interest. A number have to be examined and described in some detail, in order to draw up a balance between the coverage generally given by historical analysts to separate air forces and that given to naval air arms. Though naval aircraft used fewer bombs than land-based aircraft, the task forces wielded by carrier admirals were often as powerful as the land-based armadas.

Land-based air power played a significant role throughout the war at sea, and some of the lessons of the Battle of the Atlantic and the early Mediterranean conflicts have been earlier analyzed. By 1943, the Battle of the Atlantic had reached the plateau of wartime equilibrium, and the use of very-long-range (VLR) landplanes and of escort aircraft carriers had become an accepted tactic.

The Atlantic-Mediterranean area and the Pacific theater were on the whole scenes of entirely different naval aviation operations, and analysis of them provides different historical lessons. In the Atlantic-Mediterranean area, which included the North Sea and the northabout route to the Soviet Union, Allied naval air power contended with Axis submarines and shore-based aircraft, but not with Axis carriers. In the Pacific, there was little Axis submarine activity, nor did the Japanese respond in the air to the devastating U.S. Navy undersea craft; but the Pacific was the scene of much carrier action between rival fleets. In both oceans, escort carriers were employed for amphibious operations, and this was perhaps the greatest unity between the two theaters.

THE ATLANTIC-MEDITERRANEAN AREA

Throughout the interwar years, Liddell Hart and others had been stressing that the appropriate British role was not to fight on the Continent, where England did not have the manpower to compete, but rather to make use of maritime mobility to strike at times and places of her own choosing, forcing the enemy to expend his energies guarding against threats that in guerrilla fashion might materialize in any one of a dozen or more places. Capt. S. W. Roskill, the official British naval historian, has noted that it was a blessing in disguise when the British were thrown off the Continent. Unfortunately, many of the advantages thus gained were frittered away by Prime Minister Winston Churchill's insistence on action, which led to the wasteful Greek campaign, the loss of an advanced base in Crete, and the virtual impotence of Malta, not to mention the diversion of resources to the air offensive against Germany.

A really effective British naval strategy was handicapped by the prewar resistance to air power, a prejudice that was reinforced by the traditional outlook toward both submarines and aircraft, displayed in the writings of the Royal Navy's one influential prewar thinker, Adm. Sir Herbert Richmond. The Admiralty was reluctant to develop aircraft carriers at all, and particularly unwilling to build them instead of battleships. More than this, not until three years after serious rearmament started in 1934 did the Air Ministry hand over control of the design, development, and production of naval aircraft for the Fleet Air Arm. As a result of such attitudes and organization, the British fleet entered the war with too few carriers carrying too few aircraft of too old designs.

In addition, British tactical doctrine was more attuned to peacetime maneuver displays than to the facts of battle. The umpires and commanders on maneuvers were usually gunnery officers, thus the power of the air arm was heavily discounted— and British ships were therefore not equipped with strong anti-aircraft armament. Fliers had not been compelled to change their rigid flight formations to random courses that would distract the gunners. Moreover, despite the fact that torpedoes were regarded as the principal ship-killing weapon by both the Fleet Air Arm and the Royal Air Force, little work had been done to develop gliding or homing torpedoes (the latter in part because submarines were also distasteful to gunnery officers)—or "black-boxes," the aiming devices that

would enable torpedoes to be dropped accurately with the minimum run-in.

A further limitation was Admiral Richmond's idea that if but a few vessels of any one type were available, they should not be hazarded. Thus, it could be concluded, carriers should be used in anti-submarine and anti-raider sweeps in the open ocean but kept out of the narrow seas in which they might be attacked by shore-based aircraft. Yet, because naval aircraft would then only be employed against ships at sea, not enough thought was given to fighter or carrier defense.

The Continental powers were not much interested in carriers. The Italians really had no need for them within the confines of the Mediterranean because they had bases on both sides of it, as well as in the Dodecanese Islands. Moreover, in Italy the Air Ministry came into being in 1922, and aviation was thus placed firmly in the hands of a third service. The Italian navy was not able to free itself, and perhaps did not entirely want to, from an Air Ministry that enjoyed the close support of the dictator. In 1939, France had one aircraft carrier, the *Béarn,* but little concept of what to do with it. In Germany, a start was made toward a carrier with the laying down of the *Graf Zeppelin,* but as aviation was under the control of Hermann Goering's *Luftwaffe,* no aircraft were developed to the operational stage for naval use other than those for catapulting from cruisers and battleships. It is fair to say that in the European theater at the beginning of the war, those who had carriers had little doctrine, and others had not yet come to appreciate the significance of the use of air power at sea. By the time France fell in June 1940, only the British were left with operational carriers.

On the whole, European naval aircraft were inferior to those of the United States and Japan at the outbreak of war and generally remained less efficient than American aircraft. Nevertheless, by 1944–45 many of the machines in British carriers were of U.S. design. The reason for this was that only the United States and Japan had major naval

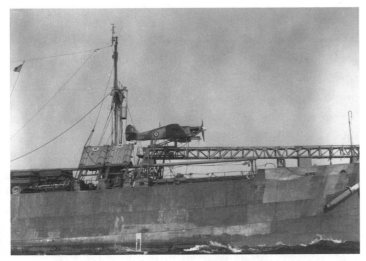

Before the availability of escort carriers (CVE), several innovations were developed to protect merchant convoys in the Atlantic. One was the installation of a flight deck over the grain carriers from which anti-submarine warfare Fairey Swordfish (ER 1.4) operated, since submarines submerged when aircraft were seen. Another was the merchant aircraft-catapult ship, or MAC. The Hawker Hurricane (ER 1.94) was commonly used to counter the *Luftwaffe*'s long-range Focke-Wulf Fw-200 Condor (ER 46). More successful in scaring off the Germans than in shooting them down, the poor pilot had either to try to ditch close to an escort or parachute. In either case, a lack of thermal suits meant that death was likely to come before the whaleboat. (G. J. Goulet/ Department of National Defence/National Archives of Canada)

The last flying Fairey Swordfish (ER 1.4), belonging to the Fleet Air Arm Museum at Yeovilton, United Kingdom, clearly shows the torpedo, arrester hook, and the custom of flying the ensign (in slower aircraft up to 1945), though usually only on the ground. The Swordfish of 1934 was operational throughout World War II; its slow speed was an asset in chasing down German E-boats (motor-torpedo) in the English Channel and the North Sea. (British Airways)

The Consolidated PB2Y Coronado (ER 43.56) flying boat originated in 1936, but was not delivered until 1940 due to constraints. The Coronado was not used by the U.S. Navy for patrol work, but most of the 210 built were converted to transports in order to haul freight to the Pacific theaters. (Convair)

Cdr. Minoru Genda was the assistant Imperial Japanese Navy attaché in London in 1940. Immediately after the successful Fleet Air Arm attack on the Italian fleet at Taranto, he gathered as much intelligence as he could and returned to Tokyo. There, Adm. Isoroku Yamamoto placed him in the group planning the subsequent attack on Pearl Harbor. Yamamoto had felt that Rear Adm. Chuichi Nagumo was the wrong man to lead the Hawaiian attack, as he was not a risk taker and had failed to launch additional strikes to destroy the USN fuel reserves and workshops. (Imperial Japanese Navy)

The Grumman F7F Tigercat (ER 26.8) was developed from the unsuccessful 1938 XF5F to meet the U.S. Navy's need for an all-weather fighter capable of operating from carriers at night. It was started in 1941 in order to be available for the 45,000-ton Midway Class carriers. The F7F was the Navy's first tricycle undercarriage aircraft, and the first shipborne twin-engined aircraft. (Grumman History Center)

air arms that were free to purchase designs specifically manufactured to meet their own requirements. In Britain until 1937, purchasing for the
Fleet Air Arm was handled by the Air Ministry;
naval officers lacked experience in writing specifications, and the three or four companies that had
specialized in naval aircraft had received so few
orders that they, in turn, lacked the necessary
expertise to produce new types quickly at a time
when aeronautical technology was going through
the revolution from fabric-covered biplanes to all-
metal monoplanes and the like. Even more than
the RAF, the FAA suffered from the fact that its
operational requirements, which had to be included in specifications, lacked a sense of the future of warfare; and there was no encouragement
for designers to risk limited resources on advanced
conceptions. The creation and acceptance of new
equipment requires imagination both within and
without the services.

The Royal Navy entered the war with a force
largely composed of biplanes, a number of which
were conversions of RAF models. It had a relatively
new, though already obsolescent, torpedo-spotter
reconnaissance machine in the single-engined
Fairey Swordfish biplane (ER 1.4), which remained
operational throughout the war, and a small quantity of modern machines in the form of the Black-
burn Skua (ER 2.9) and Roc (ER 2.9) monoplane
dive-bombers and fighters. Later the Fairey Fulmar (ER 4.4) and Firefly (ER 11.5) were added.
The first single-seat monoplane fighters to reach
the Fleet Air Arm were ex-Battle of Britain Hurricanes converted in 1941 for use off merchant-ship
catapults and from carriers. These were followed
by Supermarine Seafires (ER 3.5) and by the delivery of Grumman F4F Wildcats—which the British called Martlets (ER 3.9)—from America, and
later by Vought F4U Corsairs (ER 13) and Grumman F6F Hellcats (ER 12.2). On the whole, in European operations, what British carriers needed
were fighters to provide a defensive umbrella over
the fleet and convoys. Offensive striking power was

less important, but also less available. Most British
torpedo-bombers were not successful in attacks on
surface ships with air protection. They generally
could be used against ships in harbor only by exceptional tactics, such as in the well-executed night
raid by carrier-based planes at Taranto, Italy, in
November 1940. At the end of the war, suitable
aircraft were just beginning to come from British
manufacturers but, apart from the Fairey Barracuda
(ER 5.57), the majority of these never saw action.

In other European air arms, the same problems
arose. Naval aircraft were in most cases standard
land types adapted for work at sea as torpedo-
bombers and for mine-laying duties.

Three important changes took place in the
equipment of naval aircraft in the European area.
The first was the increase in gun armament from
two machine guns to eight, or to 20 mm cannon—or in the case of American aircraft, to .50-
caliber machine guns instead of .303s. The second
change was the introduction at the end of 1941
of radar (then called ASV, air-to-surface vessel) in
naval aircraft. The third change was the arrival of
rockets, in 1943. To these might be added the development of escort aircraft carriers, and such
other improvisations as merchant vessels fitted
with a fighter on a catapult and flight decks on
grain and other merchant aircraft carriers (MAC
ships) that enabled aircraft to be taken to sea for
local ASW patrols near convoys.

The increase in gun armament paralleled that
on land, and gave naval fighters a better chance
against their shore-based opponents. It had been
decided early in the 1930s that the speed of air
combat gave aircraft so little time to fire that with
two machine guns of the type then used, they
could not destroy an opponent. The British solution was to increase the number of guns; the American solution was to use the .50-caliber machine
gun. Most European nations, however, favored
the installation of cannon, which, while firing at
a slower rate, could use explosive shells, any one
of which could cause severe damage. The British

eventually followed this trend, but it was not until 1943 that cannon-armed naval Fairey Fireflies became operational. In the meantime, the Fleet Air Arm's opponents were usually the cannon-armed German Me-109s or Italian Macchi 202s (ER 2.25), or the less well-armed biplane Fiat G-50 (ER 1.3) or Fiat CR-42 (ER 1.36).

In multi-seat aircraft of all European powers, the rearward defensive armament had failed to keep pace with the increase in firepower of fighters. Most aircraft used over the sea had a single machine gun fired by the observer. The only aircraft that were difficult to attack were the British Sunderland flying boat, though it only had .303-caliber machine guns, and the American B-24 Liberator and B-17 Flying Fortress, which were used on long-range patrols by Coastal Command, and possibly the German Ju-88C. The German Focke-Wulf Fw-200 Condor and Heinkel He-111, the Italian Savoia-Marchetti SM-79, and the British Bristol Beaufort and Handley Page Hampden were all easily shot down from the rear, as was the British Fairey Fulmar fighter-reconnaissance machine, which carried no rearward guns. On the whole, more formidable was the American Grumman TBF Avenger torpedo plane (ER 10.5) with its power-operated, twin, .50-caliber turret and ventral gun position, but few of these aircraft saw air-to-air combat in the Atlantic-Mediterranean theater.

Experiments with airborne radar had started as early as 1939, but when the war broke out, there was an acute shortage of experimental and production facilities. Radar began to appear on ships only in late 1940, and not until early in 1941 could aircraft on patrol use it tentatively to spot both submarines and surface ships. As time went on, radar use increased, thus stripping vessels on the surface of the veil of darkness or fog. Installation of radar on ships had the potential to prevent surprise attacks from aircraft and gave defending carrier fighters a chance to scramble and gain altitude to intercept. This was particularly important in defending against the German Ju-87 Stuka dive-bomber, which was very vulnerable when not in its dive. The early, not entirely reliable, radar sets with a range of under fifty miles only gave less than a five-minute warning; in such cases, fighters could only be scrambled if they were already spotted for launching. Fortunately for the British carriers, the Germans had no experience with carrier operations and failed to time their strikes to catch the carriers at their most vulnerable—with aircraft landing on. British carriers also were saved on a number of occasions both by skillful handling and by the box construction of their armored flight decks. Once small escort carriers (CVE)—"baby flattops"—were being used to support amphibious assaults in late 1942 and afterward, even these CVEs were equipped with radar, and casualties were light. No British carriers were lost to enemy air attack in European operations, and only the old carrier HMS *Hermes* to the Japanese, off Ceylon in the Indian Ocean, though five had been sunk by U-boats and one by an internal explosion.

Experiments with rocket projectiles for aircraft began in 1941 in Britain; in 1943 tests were completed and naval aircraft began to use rockets at sea. These weapons had a number of distinct advantages: they carried as much explosive as a three-inch or five-inch shell; they had no recoil, so that they could be fitted to almost any aircraft; and they were simple to use with the pilot merely aiming the aircraft. After their adoption, the torpedo, with its need for intricate calculations and a perfect low-level approach, was much less often employed. Moreover, rockets allowed older aircraft, such as the Fairey Swordfish and Albacores (ER 3.17), to be used against E-boats—German motor-torpedo boats—and other small craft that were either not worth a torpedo or of too shallow draft for one to be effective. In addition, the weight of eight rockets was not as difficult for the less experienced new pilots to handle as was one torpedo; and the simplicity of aiming the rockets also cut down the training required of aircrew, when compared to the height and speed restrictions for using torpedoes. Less use was made of rockets in the Pacific than in the Atlantic because Pacific naval aircraft were employed not so much against coastal shipping and submarines as against enemy fleets with their well-armored ships.

In the European theater, the carrier—in spite of increases in the power of the aircraft in its striking force—remained of small potential as compared to land-based forces. The fleet carrier, even when equipped with American naval aircraft, could generally only launch a maximum striking force of some thirty-six to forty aircraft. In the case of HMS *Ark Royal* in 1940, this meant eighteen fighters and eighteen torpedo-bombers. In the Pacific, larger forces were operated, both because the carriers were bigger and carried sixty or more aircraft, and because doctrine and availability caused carriers to be operated in company. Thus, striking forces of a hundred or more aircraft were common at the beginning of the war, and a combat air patrol might number well over 400 by 1945.

In both theaters, carrier actions were few and far between, but they could be of great significance, especially when surprise was achieved. But as carriers became more effective striking forces, their targets developed better protection.

Warship defense underwent a change as a result of experience. In the interwar years, navies largely dominated by gunnery specialists held the traditional view that aircraft were not a great menace, and as a result, the anti-aircraft armament of most warships was quite light. In the Royal Navy, some obsolescent light cruisers were fitted with high-angle guns, but these were not of a rapid-fire model and their crews were exposed to enemy strafing as were the crews of the multiple pom-poms—the batteries of short-barreled anti-aircraft guns. Not envisaging the potential of air attack, designers provided insufficient stowage for the large quantities of anti-aircraft ammunition needed, nor was enough attention paid to fire discipline in this sort of action. The result was that for some time, especially in the Mediterranean, ships ran out of ammunition within forty-eight

hours at sea if kept under continual attack, and cruising formations did not allow sufficient room in which to maneuver and clear fields of fire.

As experience taught its lessons, new gun designs provided semi-automatic high-angle fire from turrets that fully protected the crews. Larger magazines with a higher rate of delivery also were incorporated, the number of anti-aircraft guns was increased, and new steaming formations were adopted, including those that kept the carrier covered while operating her aircraft. Most of these developments were British, for they were then the only country using seaborne aircraft. But their opponents also learned. High-level bombing, except as a diversion for low-level torpedo- or dive-bombing attacks, was largely abandoned because so few hits were obtained. Land-based units became far more skillful, and attacks on merchant ships in particular became much more of a menace as new techniques were developed by low-level combined anti-shipping forces.

Operationally, the Atlantic-Mediterranean war can be divided into two major phases. In the first, Italy was an opponent, and the period is characterized by fleet-carrier actions as surface forces achieved most of the U-boat kills. In the second phase, from the opening of the Mediterranean to the Allies in 1943 to the end of the war, hardly any spectacular naval actions took place there, for even the battleship *Tirpitz* was eventually sunk in a Norwegian fjord by RAF Lancasters. Naval air work was limited to convoy escort, amphibious support, and attacks on enemy coastal shipping.

In terms of the Wave pattern cycle of development, the war against Italy to the end of the North African campaign was the period of rearmamental instability for Britain, in which innovation and organization for war were still active. Wartime equilibrium set in well before Italy left the war in September 1943, and it can be suggested that the instability of demobilization began as the major British fleet units were transferred to the Far East in late 1944.

In the early days of the war, Winston Churchill,

newly returned as First Lord of the Admiralty, decided that the carriers then available could play a critical role in the trade war at sea. They would act as the core of a hunter-killer group of four destroyers that would be stationed at the great junctions of the sea lanes, where large masses of shipping passed on their way to or from home ports. This was starting from where things left off in 1918. It was a logical development that was later on gradually taken up elsewhere, especially by the U.S. Navy, when escort carriers became available from 1941 onward. But on the first occasion, the result was a dismal failure, for *U-29* struck first and sank the large old carrier *Courageous*. At the same time, the new *Ark Royal* was on anti-submarine patrol in the North Sea, where she was attacked by *U-39*, which missed and was sunk for her pains. Meanwhile, the *Ark*'s aircraft attacked *U-30*, but two of the three dived too steeply and the crews ended up as prisoners aboard their intended victim, which escaped to Germany. A few days later, the *Ark Royal* barely evaded a 2,000-pound bomb. Shortly thereafter, the Admiralty detached her to join the force-hunting raiders in the South Atlantic. Some time later, after the sinking of the pocket battleship *Graf Spee,* the *Ark Royal* returned to the Home Fleet in Britain.

The invasion of Norway illustrated the possibilities and the hazards of naval air power. The British commander-in-chief decided to make an attack on the German cruiser *Konigsberg* berthed at Bergen. His original intent was to use aircraft from the carrier *Furious,* but because she had been attacked by land-based bombers that morning, instead he ordered Skua dive-bombers based in the Orkneys, north of Scotland, to strike at the limit of their range. This they did, and with four bombs put *Konigsberg* on the bottom. Other dive-bomber attacks were not as spectacular, but were equally useful. *Furious* and *Glorious* tried to provide fighter protection for units ashore, but with only a squadron of Gladiator biplane fighters and one of Swordfish torpedo-bombers apiece, their obsolescent aircraft were spread too thin to accomplish much.

And far to the north, the British battleship *Warspite's* Swordfish spotting airplane did invaluable work in detecting German destroyers lying in ambush in Narvik fjord.

One further achievement preceded the final disaster. *Glorious* was sent to fetch off two RAF fighter squadrons from Bardufoss, in northern Norway. The Gladiators successfully flew on, but a proposal was made to abandon the Hurricanes because no modern high-speed monoplanes had yet been landed on a British carrier. However, the pilots, with the typical love of airmen for their aircraft and disciplined reluctance to abandon them to the enemy, asked to be allowed to try to land on the *Glorious.* They were successful, without tailhooks! But this most important achievement was merely the prelude to misfortune, for shortly afterward, the *Glorious* ran into two German battlecruisers and was sunk.

The Norwegian campaign showed that carriers could be operated along an enemy coast that was not too heavily defended by airmen trained in naval tactics. But a carrier was extremely vulnerable if she was not escorted by a surface force at least as strong as any that might be sent against her, especially if she was unable to fly off a strike against her tormentors. Moreover, the complement of aircraft in general was too small, and British carriers were at this date operated not as a task force but rather as ferries.

In fact, this was a role they continued to play in the campaign in the Mediterranean and Middle East. The older carriers made a number of trips to the West African coast with Hurricanes, which were then flown onward in a series of hops over 3,000 miles across Africa to Cairo. On other occasions, carriers penetrated the Mediterranean until they were just west of Sicily, when they flew off RAF fighters to reinforce Malta. The risk was justifiable in view of the imperative need to defend that base, a permanent thorn in the Italians' side, but indirectly these reinforcing operations cost the Royal Navy the carriers *Eagle* and *Ark Royal,* both sunk by U-boats.

WWII Seaborne Air Power

Meanwhile, the fall of France in June 1940 caused the British to attack the Vichy-French fleet at Mers-el-Kebir, near Oran, North Africa. When the French battleship *Strasbourg* escaped, with a destroyer escort, *Ark Royal* sent Swordfish in pursuit. The six aircraft failed to score any hits, and after a skillful approach, the still-inexperienced torpedo-bomber crews in the second group dropped their six torpedoes at dusk from outside the screen and also did no damage. The next morning they redeemed themselves with a perfect attack in line astern out of the sun—there was no radar yet—upon the beached battleship *Dunkerque.* Through surprise, more than six hits were obtained.

Taranto

By far the most spectacular and successful British naval air attack was undertaken by aircraft from the new carrier *Illustrious* off southern Italy. The mission went forth with a few additional machines from the *Eagle,* which had been forced to remain behind by a leaky fuel system resulting from near misses. The plans for the attack on Taranto, had been laid before Italy entered the war on June 10, 1940, but time was needed for practice and reconnaissance and for fitting long-range tanks to the Swordfish, so that they could make the round trip from their launching point 180 miles south of the Italian naval base. Then *Illustrious* had a hangar fire that damaged some aircraft, and the next date chosen proved to have no moon. With better trained crews, this would not have been a hazard; as it was, the safety of flare-dropping was questioned. Finally, November 11, 1940, was chosen.

Six Italian battleships were anchored in Taranto harbor. *Illustrious* was detached from the main fleet and sailed to the launching point. The initial force of twelve Swordfish set out at 8:30 P.M., followed by nine others—all that were available—an hour later. In the first wave, six aircraft carried torpedoes, four bombs, and two flares. Clouds split up the formation, but the flare-droppers accurately lighted up the eastern edge of the harbor, and then dive-bombed and fired the oil-storage tanks. The leading torpedo machine was shot down, but the others evaded the barrage balloon cables, ran in with their wheels thumping the tops of the waves, dropped their loads, and damaged the two large battleships and one smaller one. The second wave was equally successful, and *Illustrious* withdrew without being molested. On the next morning, RAF photographs showed two battleships beached and a third and two destroyers damaged, for a loss of two Swordfish.

Spirits in the Fleet Air Arm soared, and its officers hoped that at last the navy would recognize its worth and stop confining its operations largely to the enemy in the open sea. But even the new British carriers had only a small striking power. When *Indomitable* joined the fleet at the end of 1940, she carried only ten Albacore biplane torpedo-bombers and thirteen Fulmar eight-gun monoplane fighters.

Late in March 1941, various units of the Italian fleet sortied in three groups, one of which contained the battleship *Vittorio Veneto.* The British fleet—including three battleships, the aircraft carrier *Formidable,* and four cruisers—put out from Alexandria on March 28, and a dawn air search was launched. It was apparent that the advancing British cruisers were about to be caught between two powerful enemy groups, and a strike of six Albacores escorted by two of the new Fulmar fighters was launched by *Formidable.* Just as the enemy was sighted, the Fulmars were forced to break off and attack two German Ju-88s that appeared on the scene, but the Albacores dodged to within 800 yards and managed to make one hit on *Veneto.* The enemy ships turned for home, but the British commander was not going to let the Battle of Cape Matapan peter out. He dispatched another strike to slow down the Italian battleship, successfully achieving surprise because the *Veneto* had stopped evasive action, believing the attack to be over. A third attack was sent in at dusk, but by then the Italian cruisers had closed on their wounded comrade, and the anti-aircraft fire was so intense that the British were forced to abandon their traditional peacetime maneuver of attacking in formation and to let every aircraft approach on its own. While the *Veneto* was not again damaged, the cruiser *Pola* was hit and stopped dead; the Italian admiral departed with the *Veneto,* leaving two cruisers to guard the *Pola.* All three cruisers were surprised and destroyed by the British fleet later in the night.

To prepare for an expected night surface action, the carrier *Formidable* had been detached to operate off to the side of the line of British ships. After destroying the Italian cruisers, one British ship suddenly illuminated the *Formidable* with a sweeping searchlight. Only quick action by a gunnery officer prevented her destruction by eager British gun crews, who assumed that any vessel out of the line was an enemy. The incident illustrates the danger inherent in carrier operations in confined waters. The decision to keep the *Formidable* in company may have been influenced by paucity of escorts, the presence of numerous enemy units, the short range of the Fleet Air Arm aircraft of the day, the fleet's fear of lack of air cover in daylight, and the traditional military principle of not dividing forces. However, she should have been detached with escorts for the night, with orders to cruise safely to the east and rejoin at daylight. But it is also valid to note that Adm. Sir Andrew Browne Cunningham was aware that he might have a long stern chase to sink the *Veneto,* and that by morning he would be so far to the west that the carrier could not have caught up; in the meantime, she would have been exposed to surface attack during the night and aircraft and submarines the next day.

The Grecian and Cretan campaigns that followed in April through June 1941 saw a complete change in the situation in the Eastern Mediterranean. The British were expelled from their ill-advised, deceptive Balkan intervention, and the Germans and Italians under the fresh leadership of Rommel were able to sweep them out of Cyrenaica, leaving them only the bridgehead at the Libyan seaport of Tobruk, which was a naval liability. Crete might have been held if sufficient carriers and naval aircraft had been available to supply fighter cover over the island and strikes against the German air bases in Greece and Rhodes, but at this point the only carrier in the Eastern Mediterranean was the *Formidable,* and she was short of aircraft. Thus Crete was lost because the British lacked the means of defeating an airborne invasion in the air, they were unprepared on the ground, and they had insufficient naval striking power.

Meanwhile in the western Mediterranean, the *Ark Royal* had been involved in the Battle of Cape Spartivento. There the situation was similar to that at Cape Matapan, but the less experienced naval aircrews were not as effective. A more important example of the use of naval air power took place, however, in May in the North Atlantic.

Sinking the *Bismarck*

Alerted to the fact that the new German battleship *Bismarck* and her escorting cruiser *Prinz Eugen* had sailed for Norway, the RAF attempted to locate them. After one successful PRU effort, low clouds and fog enshrouded the powerful task force, but the news that they were at sea was finally signaled by a Fleet Air Arm aircraft that crossed the North Sea and made a detailed reconnaissance of the Norwegian fjords at 200 feet. On May 22, 1941, the Home Fleet sailed. The carrier *Victorious* was just working up to operational status with a cargo of crated Hurricanes for Malta. These were hastily off-loaded, and the only naval aircraft available, a squadron of Swordfish and two flights of Fulmars, were taken aboard. The *Bismarck* was sighted in the Denmark Strait northwest of Iceland and shadowed by a newly radar-equipped cruiser. The battleship *Prince of Wales*—still with builder's crews on board—and the battlecruiser *Hood* attacked. The *Hood* was sunk by radar-directed gunfire and the *Prince of Wales* damaged, but not before a shell had ruptured one of the *Bismarck*'s fuel tanks. The only hope of slowing her down were the Swordfish on the *Victorious*. Smashing through miserable weather associated with a cold front, the carrier launched her aircraft at ten at night. The Swordfish sighted the *Bismarck,* swung out to make a proper approach, then lost her. Redirected by the *Prince of Wales,* they flew in clouds until their radar indicated a ship. They dropped down, only to be facing a still-neutral U.S. Coast Guard cutter. However, the *Bismarck,* visible a short distance away, at once opened up with her radar-controlled guns. Each of the three flights then made separate attacks, strafing the ship with their machine guns as they passed over her on their way back to the *Victorious.* One hit was achieved.

As the aircraft returned to the *Victorious,* the homing beacon on the carrier broke down and they passed her. Her captain took the risk, in U-boat waters, to use direction-finding radio to home the aircraft, and a searchlight as a visible beacon.

The *Prinz Eugen* had already left the *Bismarck* to refuel, and shortly after the attack, the *Bismarck* shook off the shadowing cruisers. A search of the area was begun by the Home Fleet and another force, including the *Ark Royal.* By May 26, the *Bismarck* had entered an area in which PBY Catalina flying boats from England could search, and it was one of these, guided by orders from Coastal Command, that found her. Fourteen minutes after the Catalina was driven off by gunfire, the first two *Ark Royal* Swordfish and another Catalina took up shadowing. Again, as in the case of the *Vittorio Veneto* at Matapan, the prey was too far ahead to be caught by the fleet, especially as the British battleships and cruisers were running low on fuel and fighting heavy seas. Once more, therefore, an air strike had to be laid on.

While the aircraft were being ranged on deck and armed, the cruiser *Sheffield* was detached from Force H to the south and sent to close the forty-mile gap between the *Ark Royal* and the *Bismarck.*

Unfortunately, the pilots were not informed of this move, and thus when the fourteen Swordfish were literally tossed into the air from their carrier's heaving deck, they expected the first ship they would see to be German. Because of clouds, they were using their ASV radar, and when a ship appeared on the screens, they maneuvered, dropped out of the overcast in line astern, and attacked. Eleven dropped their torpedoes before the *Sheffield* was recognized—though an unmistakably British design. She barely managed to evade these "tin fish," and in response to the last aircraft's transmission, "Sorry for the Kippers," sent a reply that caused some marvel at her signalman's ability to spell the captain's expletives!

With aircraft on shadowing duty and three crashes when the first strike returned, as the *Ark Royal*'s stern was pitching some fifty-six feet, a second strike was readied. Fifteen aircraft were flown off with strict orders to contact the *Sheffield,* which would give them the course to the target. Dusk was approaching; cloud cover over the *Bismarck* was at 700 feet, and there was danger of icing. By accident rather than by design, the attack was split up and the Swordfish approached in bunches from various points. Again, as at Matapan, a hit was scored by a straggler who came in after the *Bismarck* had stopped firing. Another hit aft crippled the steering gear. To be sure of her demise, Swordfish fitted with long-range tanks were flown off to relieve their consorts, and the *Bismarck* was kept under surveillance until after two the next morning, when a destroyer flotilla took over. At dawn, the *Ark Royal* again flew in a strike, but by then British battleships were in action and the *Bismarck* was on her way to the bottom.

Within a matter of months, Fleet Air Arm crews, flying obsolescent aircraft with bravery and distinction, had materially contributed to victory in important battles. But in both the Matapan and *Bismarck* engagements, they had not been opposed in the air. When they were, the result was not as successful, for pure bravery is no substitute for competitive equipment.

The Channel Dash

Late in 1941, the damaged *Ark Royal* was torpedoed and sunk in the western Mediterranean while on tow to Gibraltar. The aircrews were sent back to Britain to re-form, and they were doing so when the German battlecruisers *Scharnhorst* and *Gneisenau* staged the daring dash up the English Channel. The cruisers had been sheltering in Brest, together with the *Bismarck*'s consort, the *Prinz Eugen*. On February 11, 1942, the Germans had left Brest at night, contrary to Admiralty assumptions. Radar breakdowns in patrol aircraft and other lookout failures caused the British to be ignorant of the move until the vessels were well up the Channel under an umbrella of shore-based fighters—and even then intelligence reported a convoy rather than warships. By that time, the Germans were passing through the Straits of Dover, but the ex-*Ark Royal* Swordfish squadron had moved to Kent. With six aircraft it hurriedly took the air and formed up under a Spitfire escort, which had trouble keeping contact because of the differences in speed. Within twenty minutes the enemy was sighted, but the Swordfish had to face not only the intense, radar-directed naval anti-aircraft fire but also Me-109 and Fw-190 fighters, which the small Spitfire escort was unable to overcome. Despite their immense gallantry, none of the Swordfish scored a hit, and less than two complete crews survived, as all the aircraft were shot down. It was not until the Germans reached the Dutch coast that the *Scharnhorst* struck twice and the *Gneisenau* once on mines laid by RAF aircraft.

The Channel dash clearly indicated, if the actions in the Mediterranean had not, that warships could operate within range of shore-based aircraft if plans for their use were skillfully made and if they had adequate fighter cover. It also clearly indicated that the neglect of naval aircraft in the interwar years had come home to roost in Britain.

After a public inquiry, the Admiralty was granted greater priority in production of naval equipment, and some Spitfires were converted to Seafires for use on carriers. But producing a fine aircraft takes time, and no one in Britain had that. The solution was to get American aircraft; the U.S. Navy had been consistently developing carrier types, and production lines were swinging into top gear. Thus, the Royal Navy at last, as a result of a national humiliation, was to be equipped with competitive aircraft. At the same time, the Admiralty finally recognized the importance of carriers. It now demanded fifty-five, and since neither resources nor time was available to produce that many immediately in Britain, again the solution was in part to obtain them from the United States under Lend-Lease.

After the Channel dash, fleet actions in the European theater were non-existent, if attacks on the *Tirpitz* by Lancasters and the sinking of the *Scharnhorst* by surface vessels are overlooked. British escort carriers operated in support of amphibious operations in which they were equipped with modern aircraft, or with convoys where they met with little air opposition.

Conclusion

If the air war at sea in the European theater was largely a British story, it was because only the Royal Navy was operating carriers there in fleet fashion. British carriers were not generally employed to lend support for ground operations, except for a few CVEs during Italian operations in 1943, as were Japanese and American carriers on occasion. The explanation for this lies in geography, because of the closeness of European shores; in the fact that most European naval aircraft were inferior adaptations of land-based equivalents; and in psychology, because the Europeans were much more conservative than the aggressive and better-equipped American naval airmen, who had much earlier won a major position in their navy. The exceptions, and they are few, would be the Royal Navy's raid on Taranto and attacks on the *Bismarck*. Later, in the Far East, the Fleet Air Arm was used more aggressively.

The Pacific Theater

The proximity of land and the U-boat menace in the European theater conditioned attitudes toward tactics and equipment; the vastness of the Pacific, however, produced a different kind of naval air war. The forces were much larger, the distances much greater, and the engagements, though fewer, were usually of more significance. Submarine attacks on Allied convoys were few, and the incidental Japanese response to American submarines came from surface rather than air craft. Perhaps equally important, the Pacific air war was fought by teams trained in carrier-versus-carrier concepts.

One of the reasons for the success of both the Japanese Army Air Force and the Imperial Japanese Navy Air Force was that these were veteran fliers honed in combat in China, and in the former case also versus the Russians. Against these elite forces were arrayed in the Philippines, Malaya, Singapore, the Dutch East Indies, and Burma, newly fledged inexperienced pilots in mostly obsolete aircraft. The exception was Claire Chennault's American Volunteer Group out of China, the famed Flying Tigers.

Part of the Japanese aviation success was psychological shock. Though warned by their air attachés in China, the Allies regarded the Japanese as inherently inferior and failed to recognize the excellence of their designs and their professionalism. The major Nipponese weakness was planes without armor and self-sealing tanks. However, the long-range Mitsubishi Zero was a very nimble fighter, though one that could be out-dived by heavier Allied aircraft. On the Allied side, the Brewster Buffalo (ER 4.42) was better than its inexperienced pilots, but became a scapegoat.

Japanese success in 1941–42 was also due to meticulous planning and training, speed, and improvisation, as well as clear objectives. They also enjoyed at least a three-to-one superiority in numbers, let alone quality, and they were not hampered by a doctrinal need to obtain air superiority. Surface and air forces worked together to achieve success as Allied ineptness played into their hands. At Clark Field in the Philippines, for example, aircraft were still lined up for inspection hours after the High Command knew that Pearl Harbor had been attacked.

Over China and in Manchuria, the Japanese learned through the Battle Lessons Committee how to hone their air weapon into *sentai,* or groups, of homogeneous aircraft and how to cooperate with the other service. As losses were light, experienced army and navy fliers and leaders could strike fast and far during 1941–42. But the Achilles heel was that the High Command had not anticipated the needs, consumption, and wastage of long and widely spread campaigns and thus dissipated limited resources, including the merchant navy support force.

This failure affected pilot resources, which were 3,500 army and 2,500 Imperial Japanese Navy pilots in 1941, augmented by roughly 5,200 new men annually in 1942 and 1943, versus over 10,000 killed in those two years. And the numbers of casualties increased as the fighting grew heavier. In contrast, the U.S. Navy had a rapidly expanding pool that was started in 1934. By 1944, a Gruman F4F Wildcat squadron went out to the Pacific with each pilot having already 450 hours on type. They were opposed by IJN pilots with only seventy hours total. The Japanese naval pilot attrition rate simply led to even less experienced fliers being thrown against U.S. pilots, who had fewer accidents as well.

Ironically, due to declining aircraft production, Japan had 8,000 more pilots than aircraft for them to man at the end of the war in August 1945. Production was affected by uncoordinated allocation, which caused one factory to close down for want of parts while another had them in storage.

Carrier war in the Pacific had been anticipated in 1919 by Adm. Sir John Jellicoe of the Royal Navy, whose plan of Imperial defense had called for carrier fleets to be stationed at Singapore, in

Australia, and in western Canada. But the opponents in the Pacific had modern carriers and aircraft, skilled personnel, and doctrine that had been evolved for nearly two decades. And, if the Japanese did score brilliantly in their carrier-based preemptive strike against the United States at Pearl Harbor on December 7, 1941, they failed to find any of the American carriers.

Both sides, therefore, started with something like parity, to which has to be added the immense American advantage of holding the key to Japanese coded messages. Both sides rapidly developed their tactics, but in the long run the superiority of the American arsenal and its pool of airmen proved decisive. Industrious as they were, the Japanese were unable to turn out carriers to match those of the U.S. Navy; and they made the same mistake as did the Germans in freezing aircraft design too soon, letting the development of the next technical generation lag and as a result sacrificing quality to quantity. More than this, they failed to take the attack upon their own shipping seriously and thus suffered the fate Britain nearly did in 1917—starvation by submarine blockade.

The Pacific was a vast oceanic area in which naval forces steamed and flew with the same sort of freedom from restrictions that armored forces found in the Western Desert during 1940–43. And in this great spatial combat zone, the Japanese attempted a cordon defense. This failed, resulting in the defeat of an island naval power by a continental power, a reversal of the situation in Europe. That the Anglo-American alliance was in many ways a continental one, of course, might be argued. But it also can be argued that Japan, Britain, and the United States were all maritime powers. In this case, Alfred Thayer Mahan's criteria for sea power also apply, and in the Second World War only the United States did not have to worry about home defense.

The Pacific Ocean theater, besides being many times as large as Europe, was sparsely inhabited. Apart from the Southeast Asian peninsula and the East Indies, and their adjacent archipelagoes, what land existed was mostly in the form of islands or atolls whose names are far larger on Pacific Ocean maps than their physical being. But because of this scarcity of land, the Pacific was an ideal war theater in which defenders could hold fortified atolls and attackers could sweep the ocean reaches. It was an area that the Japanese were rumored, and indeed believed, to have fortified, though we now know that they had not. They relied instead on delivering a *coup de grâce* that would leave them invincible behind great oceanic reaches, just as the Russians hoped to use space to save themselves.

But the weakness of this strategy was the same in the Pacific as that which the Germans had found in the Soviet Union, and that which the French military engineer Vauban had discovered more than two centuries earlier on the borders of France: that forts are traps unless mobile forces exist to plug the gaps between them.

And thus the vastness of the Pacific became a liability rather than an asset for the Japanese. Elements that particularly contributed to this disadvantage were inadequate aircraft and facilities for refueling and resupplying at sea, and the destruction of the Japanese merchant marine. These elements were available to the Japanese, but they failed to exploit them sufficiently because they did not foresee the kind of war they were going to have to wage.

The Pacific was particularly suited to air operations, for the weather, though occasionally breeding typhoons, is rarely as severe as that in the stormier Atlantic. Carriers in particular did not have to fight ice or green water over the flight decks, and although clouds and squalls happen to have played a fair role in the great air actions of the oceanic war, this was in part, perhaps, because commanders deliberately sought to use them as cover until at the end of the war radar negated such tactics. But it must also be remembered that the radius of action of American carrier aircraft was only 175 miles at the start of the war and not over 300-odd at the end; and even though long-range patrols could be flown from land, scouting over

The growing size and complexity of naval fighters is well illustrated here in 1944 with the F6F Hellcat, where a constant-speed propeller is being installed while four other workers assemble ancillary equipment, and a forewoman supervises. (Grumman Historical Center)

The famous Douglas SBD Dauntless (ER 5.84) served throughout the 1941–45 war in the Pacific. Small and highly maneuverable, the SBD would start its dive at 20,000 feet and pull out at 3,000. Note the "Swiss cheese" double flaps, which solved stability and fire problems in the prototype. They had been suggested to designer Kelly Johnson by a visiting engineer from the National Advisory Committee for Aeronautics (NACA) at Langley Field, Virginia. (McDonnell Douglas)

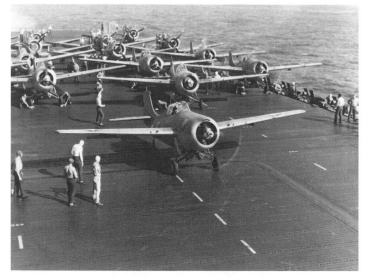

Grumman F4F Wildcats (ER 3.9) prepare to take off from the wooden deck of a USN carrier in the Pacific, 1942. These wooden decks were both a fire and splinter hazard, unlike those of British carriers, which were armored and could withstand *kamikaze* attacks later in the war. (USN)

The Vought-Sikorksy F4U Corsair (ER 13), the "bent-wing bird," was a fearsome aircraft in the 1940s. The gull wing was adopted in order to use a sixteen-foot diameter propeller, to absorb the power of the new 2,000 hp radial engine. The U.S. Navy declined to operate this machine from fleet carriers for much of the war during 1941–45, but the Marines flew it off CVEs. The F4U was considered the finest naval fighter of the war, and some argue that it was even better than the P-51 Mustang. The aircraft shown here is over Korea during 1950–51. (USN)

The Grumman TBF Avenger (ER 10.5) was just coming into service at the Battle of Midway in May 1942. Here, the aircraft carry the intermediate war markings of the white star in a deep blue circle, without as yet the white bar. The Avenger proved to be an excellent torpedo-bomber. (USN)

The Grumman F6F Hellcat (ER 12.2) incorporated the lessons learned at Midway and was the U.S. Navy's standard fleet fighter later in the war. Note the wide-track, rugged undercarriage as compared to the F4F Wildcat. Although the F4F had a lower ER in 1940 (3.9)—as well as the later F4F/FM-2 Wildcats (4.94)—its late-war pilots thought it was the equal to the Hellcat, evidence that purely statistical Efficiency Ratings are only part of the quality equation. (Grumman History Center)

The F4F Wildcat's narrow undercarriage made landing it more hazardous than the F6F. It was vital that a crash on the flight deck be cleared as quickly as possible, and thus an aircraft such as this Wildcat would be shoved over the side as rapidly as possible. (Grumman History Center)

In July 1942, the U.S. Navy decided that it needed to evaluate helicopters, and thus borrowed an early U.S. Army model (ER n/a), seen here in 1944 landing on a Liberty ship's special helipad while being watched by the evaluation committee. (Sikorsky)

anything like the whole area, as was done in the Mediterranean and the Atlantic, was impossible. The importance of code-breaking and what is now called SIGINT—signals intelligence—is evident.

The size of the Pacific theater and the fact that the Allies agreed that success there was secondary to winning the Hitler war, made progress in it slow. The *Judo Blitzkrieg* Japanese strategy, based on the land and traveling light, was a plan they could follow by staging under an air umbrella as they did down the mainland and island chains to their southwest. In comparison, the very nature of the road from the U.S. continent dictated an American football approach by a series of power plays, often passing, but backed by a formidable logistic bench and training system. And these national approaches and philosophies are reflected in the equipment employed.

Throughout the Pacific war there was surprisingly little change. The Japanese, long accustomed to operating unopposed over China, had not been forced to think of technological change, and this especially affected their naval aircraft and carriers. By the time it became clear that their aircraft, which had been successful in the opening phases of the war, were becoming obsolete, the loss of experienced pilots, shortages of materials and fuel, and the bombing of the home islands prevented quantity production of new models.

The U.S. Navy entered the war just at a period of changeover in equipment, so that most of the aircraft in service in 1941 either represented a new generation or were shortly due for replacement. The standard American shipboard fighter, the Grumman F4F Wildcat, was slower and heavier than the Japanese Zero, but faster in a dive. It was generally replaced in 1943 by the F6F Hellcat, which had been under development when war was declared, but which, with the benefit of combat-experienced pilots' advice, was rushed out to the fleet in some fourteen months and remained the major fleet fighter for the rest of the war. The Vought F4U Corsair was also in the development stage in 1941, but it took thirty-two months to

reach combat and was at first regarded as unsuitable by the U.S. Navy for carrier operations—though the Marines flew them off of CVEs. Both of these fighters used 1,850 hp—or higher—engines and although the Hellcat was very maneuverable, its speed was only about 380 mph compared to the Corsair's 420-odd mph. The Japanese Zero could never match this high speed and, as noted, suffered from a lighter armament and lack of armor or self-sealing tanks. The Japanese made a fatal mistake in not developing a replacement for the Zero until 1945, when it was too late. Nevertheless, Allied pilots retained a healthy respect for the Zero, which was a first-class dog-fighting aircraft.

War at sea quickly showed that level bombers were useless. Thus, the attack machines soon fell into two types and were even in the prototype stage at the end of the war, moving into a single type. Basically the U.S. Navy was equipped with the Douglas SBD Dauntless (ER 5.84) dive-bomber, which was just coming into service in 1941 and which remained the principal dive-bomber until 1943 when the heavier, less attractive Curtiss SB2C Helldiver (ER 10.36) appeared. The SBD, however, remained in service until the end of the war. The Japanese equivalent was the Aichi D3A (Type 99) Val (ER 3.5), which had a fixed undercarriage, and was succeeded by the Nakajima B5N (Type 97) Kate (ER 5.24) with a retractable undercarriage.

Again, in terms of torpedo-bombers, the United States was lucky in its timing. The old Douglas TBD Devastators (ER 3) were wiped out at Midway, as were the first of the new Grumman TBF Avengers (ER 10.5), but the latter were modified and remained standard throughout the war. They owed some of their longevity, of course, to the fact that the Hellcats controlled the air. The mainstay of the Japanese attack forces was the twin-engine Mitsubishi Betty (ER 41) bomber, which could not be operated from carriers. Here, too, as in other fields, a lot was due to American production.

The U.S. Navy had started the war with 514 fighters and ended it with 13,940, out of a total of some 40,400 serviceable aircraft. It might also be noted that the USN's loss rate was remarkably low. Of 2,360 planes of all types, lost by all causes, only 664 were to enemy aircraft, whereas the United States claimed to have destroyed over 8,600 of the enemy (which with an "adjusted" divisor of three would equal some 2,867 Imperial Japanese Navy planes actually shot down). In fact, the IJN lost 96 percent of its aircraft in the first eighteen months of the war.

In terms of aircraft carriers, the United States again enjoyed the advantage. Japanese carriers were generally lighter and smaller, though those of neither side were well armored, or even well armed at first. What gave the United States its particular edge, apart from a highly efficient production and training system at home, was the fact that it was just shifting to new carrier designs in the early 1940s and that many of these were able to benefit from combat experience while still building. And although each battle seemed to reduce the strength of the Japanese aircrew pool, it had the opposite effect on the Americans, who had anticipated needs and wastage in an expanded aviator training program begun in 1934.

After Midway, in June of 1942, moreover, the U.S. Navy enjoyed the advantage, and though not operating on interior lines, it could choose the time and place to strike. It was able to wait and to train its personnel; and after it managed to get through 1942, its technical advantages in terms of new aircraft, carriers, radar, and rockets constantly widened the gap over its opponent. The standard 27,000-ton, 30-knot Essex Class fleet carrier was indeed a formidable ship, with its 80 aircraft capable of striking some 200 miles.

The Wave pattern or cycle of war can be seen in the Pacific even more clearly than in the Atlantic-Mediterranean. U.S. rearmament was in full swing at the time of Pearl Harbor and continued until after Midway. Even for some time after that, the U.S. Navy was still building up; neither tactically nor in terms of equipment did it enter the period of wartime equilibrium until the

middle of 1943. On the other hand, because the Japanese had already been prepared by their operations in China, entering the Second World War with an experienced fighting force, wartime equilibrium began earlier for them. However, it contained so many disasters that demobilizational instability and defeat followed soon after. The U.S. Navy, preparing to assault the Japanese home islands, did not enter the instability of demobilization until in mid-1945 when Japanese surrender became likely.

The Japanese at first could claim prestige as anti-imperialists who had defeated the white colonialists. They possessed the power that comes from war budgets, and they started the war with a wealth of combat knowledge, not only in the air but in logistics as well, which the Americans had yet to acquire. In a country on a war footing, whose government was controlled by military factions, it was easier to conceal intentions than it would have been in the United States at that time. The result was that the planning for the attack on Pearl Harbor was accomplished in great secrecy.

Pearl Harbor

The Japanese fleet was able to assemble out of public sight, to study models of Pearl Harbor, and finally to sail off across the unused reaches of the Pacific to the launching point for the attack without being spotted. Intelligence agents in the Hawaiian Islands enabled the Japanese to be well informed of the U.S. Navy and its habits—well enough to know that a Sunday morning attack was most likely to catch the Americans unprepared, as indeed earlier U.S. Navy maneuvers had demonstrated in 1932 and 1938. The attack itself was a brilliant combination of the use of the three-dimensional capabilities of the modern navy, such as German Vice Adm. Reinhard Scheer had tried to develop in the raids that led to Jutland in 1916. But in this case, the Japanese main fleet was composed of carrier task forces rather than of battleships. The success of the strategy and the tactics (which the British had tried to develop in the First

World War) of attacking the enemy in his own harbors was much enhanced by the relatively poor U.S. anti-aircraft defenses both at Pearl Harbor and on the ships themselves, not to mention difficulties caused by the Sunday closing of ammunition lockers and of the one new, untried, U.S. Army early-warning radar set.

In tactical evolution, the Japanese surprise attack, based upon the 1940 British Taranto model, was well coordinated. Six aircraft carriers escorted by two battleships, three cruisers, and nine destroyers comprised the task force, ahead of which twenty-seven submarines were deployed in the Hawaiian area. Intelligence relayed to the Japanese on December 6 showed that eight American battleships were in harbor, but that the carriers USS *Enterprise* and USS *Lexington,* the real prizes in the mind of carrier commander Adm. Chuichi Nagumo, were not. He decided to risk an attack, nevertheless, and at 6:15 A.M. he launched 183 aircraft (a sharp contrast to the eleven initial Swordfish that had attacked Taranto). A study of history would have reminded American commanders of the 1904 surprise Japanese attack on Port Arthur—now Lushun, China—but in spite of a war warning from Washington, the Hawaiian commands were on nothing more than a sabotage alert. Nor was complacency ashore dispelled when half an hour after Admiral Nagumo had launched his preemptive strike, a patrolling destroyer sank a midget Japanese submarine off Oahu, Hawaii. And insufficient attention was paid to a radar sighting because the set was new and those in charge too junior to assess the significance of their information, or to demand access on a Sunday morning to those who should have been able to evaluate the radar image.

Although December 1941 was a time when visual recognition was still a prime requisite of safety—as the war in Europe had already demonstrated to those who cared to note its lessons—the arrival of formations of aircraft from the north was ignored, until at 7:55 A.M. when bombs began to spatter battleship row. The easily spotted high-level bombers and dive-bombers were sent in first, in a ruse already practiced in the clear Mediterranean skies. Before they came into action, but while lookouts and gunners still concentrated on them, torpedo-bombers skimmed in over the calm surface of the anchorage and unloaded their deadly "fish" straight into the anchored battleships.

The first combined Japanese attack was a perfect surprise, and in less than thirty-five minutes it effectively eliminated the U.S. Navy's Pacific battleship fleet. The second wave of 170 fighters and bombers did far less damage and received the brunt of the IJN casualties. The loss of U.S. aircraft on neighboring airfields was devastating, as they had been mostly drawn up in neat anti-sabotage rows. For a loss of only 29 aircraft, plus some that crashed in landing on their carriers, the Japanese destroyed 311 American aircraft, leaving only 79 serviceable. They sank two battleships outright, and caused three to need major repairs.

Looking back at the event now, it is evident that the raid was both a success and a failure. Tactically it was a partial success in that it did put the American battleship fleet out of action for a while and it did seriously weaken the air forces at Hawaii. But Admiral Nagumo can be faulted on tactical grounds, and the Japanese High Command on strategic and grand-strategic counts. Nagumo's fault lay in his failure to reflect upon his own actions. If he could carry out a successful strike with only two battleships in a force of carriers, why should not the Americans do likewise? By failing to hit the cruisers and destroyers in the harbor, he left the basis for a future American task force. Moreover, after the two strike waves, he still had some 300 aircraft available; and because Japan was risking all to prevent America from interfering with her planned expansion into Southeast Asia until it was a *fait accompli,* he should have risked more than he did. His intelligence people should have been able to provide him with some information on the whereabouts of the *Enterprise* and the *Lexington*. And even if they did not, the *En-*

terprise's planes came in to land in the midst of the attack on Pearl Harbor, so he knew that she was somewhere around. In fact, she was returning from supplying aircraft to Wake Island. Nagumo had at least a three to one ratio of aircraft compared to that of the *Enterprise,* and about a two to one margin with his six carriers, as compared to the two American carriers. Moreover, he had two battleships in company, where the Americans had none. If he had flown off scouts, they should have located the *Enterprise* alone, and he should have destroyed her.

As a result of his omission, Admiral Nagumo granted the U.S. Navy a number of services. He removed the older battleships from the main fleet, and caused the Americans to go over to a carrier strategy, divorcing their striking forces from the lethargic and under-armed battleships. He caused the older battleships to be relegated to the much more efficient role of fire support for amphibious operations, thus sparing aircraft from a task for which they were really not as effective, especially at night. It was only later in the war that the new fast battleships of the 1936 and later programs joined the USN carrier task forces as floating anti-aircraft batteries and as command ships, a role for which they were well suited because their heavy armor made them far less vulnerable than the volatile carriers to bomb and *kamikaze* hits. Furthermore, Admiral Nagumo's attackers neglected U.S. Navy repair facilities and oil tank farms, thus leaving the recuperative ability intact. Nagumo's staff was not able to persuade him to pass through the islands and deliver additional strikes to finish the job.

From a strategic point of view, the attack on Pearl Harbor can be faulted because the commander was not briefed on the need for sacrifice to achieve the desired political end. The Japanese did not require carriers for their conquest of Southeast Asia as much as they needed absolutely to destroy the American power to retaliate. Moreover, having decided to enact what would be regarded as an immoral blow by important segments of world opinion, the aggressor had to succeed or be placed in double jeopardy. Nagumo hit the mule-like American people over the head with the proverbial two-by-four. He got their attention, but not in the way he had intended—an ill-considered grand strategy on the part of the Japanese High Command, for it aroused a people hitherto divided internally and united them. It has been argued that Admiral Isoroku Yamamoto made a mistake when he appointed Nagumo, for Yamamoto knew the United States from firsthand experience as a student and naval attaché, and was aware of its potential.

In terms of the use of air power in the Pearl Harbor attack, it must be admitted that the conception was excellent. Air power is at its most economical and effective when used in a preemptive strike that abides by the principles of war. But war entails risks, and the impression is that the Japanese were, like Jellicoe at Jutland, unwilling to take the risk of being decisive. The following June Battle of Midway is often regarded as the turning point of the war; it may be suggested that Midway only made obvious the failure of Japanese grand strategy.

The fate of Japanese expansion was settled at Pearl Harbor, after which they proceeded to jump down through the whole of Southeast Asia to New Guinea and up the Indian Ocean to the Burmese gates of India in a campaign that was in many respects perfectly conventional. Air support was only of decisive importance because the Allied matériel facing the enemy was scarce, badly out of date, or ill-handled.

Fateful 1942

During 1942, the Americans made a number of basic decisions that were to govern the whole of the war in the Pacific. Most important of these was the installation of Adm. Chester Nimitz as Commander-in-Chief of the Pacific Ocean (CINCPAC) areas in Hawaii, and Gen. Douglas MacArthur as Commander-in-Chief of the Southwest Pacific (CINCSWPA) in Australia. The basic strategy decided before the end of 1941 was to hold the Hawaii-Midway-Fiji line and to strike at the Japanese when possible. As a consequence of this, the U.S. Asiatic Fleet, combined into the Allied ABDA (American, British, Dutch, and Australian) organization in the Netherlands East Indies, was sacrificed. Its loss is of interest to the history of air power only insofar as it demonstrated the dangers of operating within range of enemy airfields without fighter cover and without means of undertaking aerial reconnaissance, especially in waters unfamiliar to the captains involved. At the same time, a very considerable blow was dealt British prestige in the Far East when, as a prelude to the loss of Malaya and Singapore, the battleship *Prince of Wales* and the battlecruiser *Repulse* were sunk by Japanese planes on December 10, 1941. These two ships were the victims of indiscretion, lack of air cover, and of faulty prewar planning.

Malaya

It had largely been assumed in Britain that a Far Eastern war could not be fought at the same time as a European conflict, and that in the event of hostilities in the Pacific, the main fleet would proceed to Singapore. Unfortunately, Admiral Jellicoe's astute 1919 recommendation that a Far Eastern Fleet should consist heavily of carriers had not been accepted. Thus, when war did strike at a time when the Royal Navy was heavily involved in the European theater, the Admiralty had only one carrier to spare. And to add bad luck to bad planning, the *Indomitable,* then on trials in the West Indies, ran aground, and thus there were none.

Further complications compounded the problems. In the interwar years, political economy had dictated accepting the cheapest solution to the defense of Malaya, in Southeast Asia. The result was that the naval defense of the area had been relegated to torpedo-bombers. But when war came, the machines on hand were not only out of date, to put it mildly, but their reinforcement was to be from India (which had none anyway) via a series of airfields scattered down the Malayan peninsula and outside the army's defensive plan.

The first Japanese move at this time was to land near the neck of the peninsula and endanger the British reinforcement airfields. It was in response to this threat that Vice Admiral Phillips gallantly, but foolishly, took to sea. Shadowed early on by long-range Japanese aircraft, he had no air cover and was attacked in the classical multi-directional manner, not in Royal Navy rigid peacetime fashion. Whereas prewar Fleet Air Arm attacks had been limited to precisely structured formations, the Japanese were out to sink ships, not to impress visitors or gunnery-officer umpires. The *Prince of Wales* and the *Repulse* were quickly dispatched by Japanese aircraft that came in from all directions, making it impossible to employ the old naval counter to destroyer-type attacks generally delivered from abeam by swinging toward the enemy, to comb the tracks and let the torpedoes slide harmlessly by.

Admiral Phillips's action gained him nothing but a grave, and he took none of the enemy with him. He had failed to learn the elementary lessons well demonstrated by the previous operations in both the North Sea and the Mediterranean. But his error was greater than this. A commander has in the last resort two alternatives. He can ignore his orders—though when this means being accused of an unwillingness to fight, it is a psychologically loaded choice—or he can resign his command if his judgment is not acceptable to the higher command. Even allowing for very great pressures upon him psychologically, and knowing what the Japanese had done at Pearl Harbor, Phillips's action was unwise; but more than this, it was bad strategy. Possessing the only Allied capital ships in the western Pacific, he should have preserved his force to provide punch for the ABDA fleet then being formed. In the series of surface actions that followed in early 1942, the weight of shells hurled by these ships should have been decisive in the engagements between Allied cruisers and Japanese forces protecting invasion convoys. Moreover, though in fact the Japanese sent Admiral Nagumo and his carriers to attack places like Rabaul during this period, the presence of a strong Allied force would have acted both as a greater deterrent and as a greater bait to the enemy, and possibly would have delayed the sweep down the East Indies. Of course, it is perfectly possible that the Japanese would more swiftly have mobilized their strike forces and have dealt the same blow to the two ships at a different time and in a different place. But by then, if the *Prince of Wales* and the *Repulse* had been operating within the ABDA fleet, they would have been surrounded by better anti-aircraft support. Lacking air power, Admiral Phillips should have beaten a strategic retreat and fought instead on another more propitious day.

It is ironic, as noted, that the Japanese inflicted the damage they did upon the Royal Navy, because it was former RNAS officers who had gone out to Japan to give that country's naval airmen their initial training between the wars. And one of the major factors in the Japanese success was the reluctance of their opponents to admit to themselves that the Japanese were experts, or at least their equals. Not content with letting the Japanese prove off Malaya that they had learned well, the British further allowed them also to sink scattered units in the Indian Ocean, including the old carrier *Hermes*, which was caught unescorted south of Ceylon. That no further disasters occurred was due to the withdrawal of both sides.

Before the initiative shifted to the Americans in mid–1942, several crucial battles took place while the U.S. Navy was girding for the contest and before it had the ships, planes, and men to organize the decisive weapons that it employed to win the Pacific war. Besides the submarine force, which did to Japanese shipping what German U-boats failed to do to Anglo-American merchantmen, the two great American weapons, wielded by Admiral Nimitz and General MacArthur in

coordination but in a sense under one Supreme Commander, were the fast-carrier task forces and the amphibious landing forces. The one employed air power as its striking weapon; the other used air cover to enable it to operate with impunity within range of enemy air bases. Both established their power on carriers, though the first objective of amphibious forces was generally to obtain an airfield ashore from which U.S. Marine and Army Air Forces aircraft could operate. Both made use of mobility and surprise, and concentration and economy of force, to penetrate the cordon enemy defense.

Although, as has been suggested, the Japanese had already passed the decisive point with their attack upon Pearl Harbor, they could still have retrieved the war. The Americans were desperately short of carriers, and, although the *Yorktown* was ordered from the Atlantic to the Pacific, shortly after she arrived, the *Saratoga* was torpedoed southwest of Hawaii and put out of action for a crucial five months. Fortunately for the U.S. Navy, the Japanese submarine fleet, to everyone's surprise, proved to be nearly impotent. The *Saratoga* was allowed to limp 2,500 miles back to the West Coast without being finished off.

At this time, Admiral Nagumo's carriers were off in the Southwest Pacific aiding landing operations. As a counter, and to protect Samoa, the first American offensive operations were launched with carrier strikes against the Gilbert and Marshall islands. Though small affairs, employing only one carrier in each case, they were psychologically wise offensive operations, and their effect was more than might have been expected in that the Japanese government promptly ordered two of Nagumo's carriers home for defensive patrols, thus reducing his strength by a third.

An examination of the distances from American bases and a war game should have shown that the U.S. Navy was far too vulnerable to undertake large-scale attacks on the Japanese mainland, even though the famous Doolittle raid on Tokyo was launched from a carrier on April 18, 1942. One problem for the Japanese was that they had little means of gathering intelligence about an enemy whose main bases were so far away. But just as the Allies tended to underestimate Japanese abilities, so, too, the Japanese overestimated American power. Home governments and headquarters always seem to inflate their own importance and the destructiveness of their enemy. At the same time, they fail to warn the population that some attacks are to be expected, but that results might be minimal. Instead, their elaborate statements about the invulnerability of the homeland result in greater alarm when attacks occur, and this rebounds upon them in terms of political pressure for greater security. In turn, this detracts from the concentration of resources for winning the war. And thus did it occur with Japan. On the other hand, Americans rejoiced at then Lt. Colonel Doolittle's brilliant strike against the enemy's capital and have overrated its effects.

The Coral Sea

The Doolittle raid was followed by an attack from the *Lexington* and *Yorktown* air groups against a Japanese landing force on the northeast side of New Guinea. Although surprise was achieved by launching from south of the island, few ships were found. As was so often the case, by the time news of the Japanese landings was relayed to the strike forces, the enemy vessels had pulled back, their mission accomplished.

Much more important at this time was the Japanese reconsideration of their strategy, now that they felt they had achieved most of their objectives in much less time than expected and with far fewer casualties. They were still bogged down in China, however, and had a vast perimeter to defend. After arguments between the army and the navy—and more importantly within the navy itself between the admirals at sea and the naval general staff ashore—the Japanese conceded that it was vital to destroy American carriers. The April Doolittle raid supported the admirals' conclusion,

led by Yamamoto, and it was agreed that strikes should be made against Midway and the Aleutians. But at the same time, a decision had already been made to undertake a modest campaign to isolate Australia. Considering the resources of the day and the immense length of Japanese supply lines, it can be argued that the two grand strategies were incompatible when undertaken concurrently. On the other hand, reviewing their successes to date, the Japanese had reason to believe that they could do both.

The first move was an attempt to isolate Australia by taking Port Moresby, New Guinea, in order to neutralize northern Australian airfields. At the same time, the intent was to also take Guadalcanal, as a step toward seizing Samoa, thereby severing the route to the United States. For the execution of these plans the Japanese sent six naval forces southwest, including a carrier task force and a covering carrier force. The Allies had the advantage of access to Japanese enciphered messages, but the air forces in the area were under two commanders-in-chief many thousand miles apart. General MacArthur controlled land-based air from Sydney, while Admiral Nimitz controlled naval air from Honolulu.

As soon as Nimitz learned of the enemy's plans, he dispatched the *Enterprise* and the *Hornet,* hastily rearmed after the Tokyo raid, to join the *Lexington* and the *Yorktown* already in the area. The latter two carriers were merged into one fighting formation with a single screen under a peculiar command arrangement: during air operations, Rear Adm. Aubrey Fitch exercised tactical command; the rest of the time, seniority gave control to Vice Adm. Frank John "Black Jack" Fletcher. The Americans were fortunate on that evening of May 6, when they finally merged and were refueling the carrier groups, that Vice Admiral Takagi's task force had turned back at dusk when only seventy miles away.

Such flukes were to be typical of the ensuing Battle of the Coral Sea. Bad weather, fog, and poor inter-service communications hampered both sides. On top of this, a mistake in coding caused Vice Admiral Fletcher to launch an air strike against a force that turned out to be only two cruisers and two destroyers, instead of the two carriers and their escorts that he had expected to find. However, as luck would have it, these ninety-three planes discovered the 11,000-ton carrier *Shoho* and sank her with one lightning blow. Fletcher flew no more strikes that day, awaiting enemy attacks and news of the other two enemy carriers known to be in the area.

The Japanese also had their share of misreporting, and in consequence mistook the U.S. Navy oiler *Neosho* for a carrier, wasting some time in attacking it. The cruisers that Fletcher had detached to stop the amphibious thrust aimed at Port Moresby were attacked not only by the Japanese but also in error by the U.S. Army Air Forces, but they survived both strikes. Meanwhile, these diversions had cost the Japanese the best part of a day, and they decided to gamble on a night attack on the American carriers. Of twenty-seven aircraft dispatched, nine were shot down by American fighters vectored in by the new radar from the carriers lying invisible under low clouds. The six pilots who returned to the *Takagi* reported the American carriers only fifty miles away (actually they were ninety-five), but neither side dared a night surface attack.

The next day, each side spotted the other at 0800 hours, but Vice Admiral Fletcher was under clear skies whereas the enemy was in the bad weather zone, and U.S. Navy torpedoes were less successful than those of the Japanese, which were remarkably accurate. Nevertheless, the carrier *Shokaku* was caught in the open between rain squalls, and a well-coordinated dive- and torpedo-bombing attack put her out of action. The Japanese air strike force was intercepted by only three fighters, however, and the independent maneuvers of the two U.S. carriers, not accustomed to working together, allowed the *Lexington* to be struck by torpedoes and bombs. Although she recovered all her planes, and Rear Admiral Fitch

had forty-nine aircraft serviceable compared to Takagi's nine, ruptured fuel lines and a faulty vertical aviation gasoline storage system caused internal explosions, and the 33,000-ton *Lexington* was abandoned and sunk. The *Yorktown,* having recovered most of her own planes, was unable to take on those of her companion vessel. Erroneous reports by Japanese pilots that both American carriers had been sunk caused the Japanese to retire, and thus Vice Admiral Fletcher got safely away.

Although the Japanese had won a tactical victory in the Coral Sea, strategically they were now checked, as they lacked the forces to continue their drive southward. Because of aircrew losses and bomb and torpedo damage, neither surviving Japanese carrier was fit for the important Battle of Midway, which followed less than a month later.

Crucial Midway

The Coral Sea was the first true carrier versus carrier battle in history, but the Battle of Midway would surpass it in importance. Here, again, the Japanese undertook elaborate planning and made use of a number of forces and objectives. Such multiplicity helped confuse both sides, but the Americans kept a clearer eye on their objective of destroying their opponent's carriers. If the Japanese vision was not as sharp, they can at least in part be excused, for they believed that they had sunk both the *Lexington* and the *Yorktown*. And they were unaware that the Allies had their code. Thus, the Japanese did not know that the U.S. Navy realized that American carriers could be safely brought from other areas to counter the Midway and Aleutians operations. The Japanese attack in the Aleutians at this time was part of a complex plan to engage American forces; although weather in the Aleutians was abominable, the Japanese sent two carriers there, thus leaving only five at Midway. Yet, as an aerial operation in itself, the Aleutian campaign has little to add to a general history of air power.

The Japanese had planned to cause the U.S. fleet to steam through lines of submarines (*à la* Jutland in 1916), entice them into the air net, and finish them off with the main battle fleet. Admiral Yamamoto himself was to command the battleships, and it was a battleship admiral's plan. Deprived (or shed) of their battleships, the American admirals had to think differently.

What the Japanese did not achieve, and what frustrated their attempt to take Midway—which would have given them a base from which to maintain a surveillance of Hawaii—was surprise. Instead, Admiral Nimitz was able to get three carriers—the *Hornet, Enterprise,* and *Yorktown*—across the vital Japanese early warning zone before the enemy submarine patrols were established, and these carriers then assembled 300 miles to the northeast. On Midway itself were some thirty PBY Catalina long-range-patrol flying boats, together with some seventeen B-17s, twenty-six obsolescent fighters, and thirty-four attack planes manned by pilots direct from flight school. Essentially, the only modern aircraft were six newly arrived Grumman TBF Avengers. In addition to an air search by PBY Catalinas, with a radius of 700 miles, nineteen U.S. submarines on lookout and ambush duty were stationed west of the island.

On June 3 the main Japanese invasion force was spotted, but except for a night torpedo attack by radar-equipped PBYs, it was ignored. American commanders suspected that the enemy carriers were coming in from the northwest under a weather front, as indeed they were, in a mobile force under Nagumo. Just after daylight on June 4, 1942, a PBY spotted the 108 attacking Japanese aircraft, which were shortly picked up on radar. Within minutes, a PBY found Nagumo's carriers, the *Kaga, Akagi, Soryu,* and *Hiryu,* and radioed a sighting report, which however placed the enemy forty miles southeast of their actual position. Nevertheless, because of the warnings, most aircraft based on Midway were in the air, either patrolling, on their way to attack the enemy, or providing fighter defense. The attack damaged ground facilities, and of the twenty-six fighters, only two were serviceable after its conclusion.

Midway's counterattack hit Nagumo's force just as he was about to launch a second wave. However, the uncoordinated thrusts did no damage and expended almost all Midway's attack aircraft, but the delay imposed upon the Japanese enabled the *Hornet* and the *Enterprise* to close to within the 175-mile range of their torpedo-bombers. The *Yorktown,* which was forced to steam into an easterly wind to recover her planes, turned west and, thirty minutes after the others, launched half her aircraft; two hours later she sent out another search for more Japanese carriers. The attack by the Midway planes confirmed the Japanese flight commander's report that another strike was needed against the island, and Admiral Nagumo ordered the torpedoes replaced by bombs on the planes for the second wave. While still in the midst of the changeover, he was attacked by an American submarine, and shortly afterward his first-strike planes returned. He had just started to retire northward when the planes from the U.S. carriers appeared.

But lack of coordination hampered this first attack by aircraft from the *Hornet* and the *Enterprise.* Many of the planes ran out of fuel, having had to search for the enemy. Some made it back to their own carriers; others attempted to reach Midway, and many were lost. Some never saw the Japanese carriers, although the torpedo-bombers, of an obsolescent design, ran directly into the enemy fighters that had come down to destroy the TBFs from Midway. The American dive-bombers, however, arriving overhead during the melée, took advantage of the confusion below to bomb accurately. SBDs of the *Enterprise* caught the *Akagi* and the *Kaga* with flight decks loaded with aircraft about to be launched, while the *Yorktown* group, arriving later, hit the *Soryu.* The Second World War carriers were extremely volatile because of the high-octane fuel used by the aircraft, and neither the American nor the Japanese ships had armored flight decks. Caught at their most vulnerable, the three Japanese carriers were soon flaming wrecks; the fourth, the *Hiryu,* was some distance to the north and remained unscathed. The division of

Japanese forces then proved fatal, for the two carriers in the Aleutians and the one that had been kept with Yamamoto and the main body of the fleet, though called to the scene, could not reach the battle in time to redress the balance.

The *Hiryu* launched a strike against the *Yorktown,* the one his carrier's scout had reported; and the *Hiryu's* attacking force was spotted only fifty miles from the American ship. The *Yorktown* at once launched all aircraft on deck and waved away those coming in to land. Although twenty-eight fighters were at hand, the Japanese made three hits on the *Yorktown,* and in a second strike hit her port side with two torpedoes. Without power to shift fuel or counter flood, she was taken in tow toward a repair base. For once the Japanese did the proper thing: a submarine was ordered up, which, after a lengthy search, found the *Yorktown* and sent her to the bottom on June 7. Ironically, just as the *Yorktown* was suffering her second attack, one of her scouts spotted the *Hiryu* only some one hundred miles away. An attacking American force of bombers set the Japanese ship on fire and worked over her escorts.

Only toward evening on June 4 did Admiral Yamamoto, still not directly involved in the battle, learn that three American carriers were in action, not one, as he had thought. At this point he called off the invasions of Midway and the Aleutians. Adm. Raymond Spruance, then in tactical command of the U.S. forces, was aware that heavy enemy units might be in the area, and, of course, did not know that Yamamoto was now retiring. Spruance moved to be in a position to support Midway in case of invasion, but on June 5 there was little action. Two Japanese cruisers that had collided in the night were spotted and attacked by dive-bombers from Midway, but with no damage; and later in the day B-17s dropped eighty bombs on a destroyer but missed it. Striking forces from the *Enterprise* and the *Hornet* had a fruitless day and had to be recovered after dark. Because most aircraft had never before landed on at night, Admiral Spruance ordered the carriers illuminated; he well recognized that the handful of experienced combat crews he had were priceless leaders for the future. One of the damaged Japanese cruisers was eventually sunk, but the day ended peacefully. Spruance retired to refuel and to rest his depleted aircrew, and so ended the battle.

Midway was the most decisive engagement of the naval air war in the Pacific. By conducting an offensive defense and by a judicious retirement, Admiral Spruance achieved a major American victory. He enjoyed a certain amount of luck, from possession of the Japanese cipher to the timing of his strikes against the opposing carriers. The Japanese carrier commanders were unlucky in their timing and in their lack of radar, which even in its primitive 1942 form had forewarned the American carriers and had enabled them to fly off their combat air patrols.

Yamamoto had made a number of crucial mistakes. His forces were dispersed in such a way that they were not mutually supporting. Dispersion is valuable where forces of different types are present, especially in an amphibious assault force; but it can be argued that he should have used the main force of the fleet as a screen for the carriers, and that greater dispersion of the carrier forces, as in the American case, would have prevented an attack on all of them at once. The argument that Yamamoto should have been aboard a carrier is faulty. Both Fletcher and Nagumo were forced to transfer their flags to cruisers from their carriers, which were the volatile prime targets of attackers. Later in the war, even Admiral William F. "Bull" Halsey shifted his flag to a well-armored, more secure "battlewagon" to avoid losing control when in action, though here it may be granted that the new TBS (talk-between-ships) system enabled him both to interview returned pilots and to keep in constant touch with his captains.

Midway provided many lessons for the U.S. Navy. It showed that the old attack bombers were far too vulnerable to fighters, and that the new torpedo-bombers, the TBF Avengers, could not continue to use the old peacetime tactics of the long run-in at low level. To remedy these defects, combat survivors, who knew the lessons of actual battle, could now translate them into doctrines and tactics, and their experience could be useful in the design of new aircraft. At least one firm, Grumman, had specialized in close liaison with the U.S. Navy; the TBF was one product of this, and another was shortly to be the F6F Hellcat. Another important technological fact reinforced at Midway was that U.S. torpedoes were faulty, as had been claimed by American submariners and others.

From a doctrinal standpoint, the Battle of Midway emphasized again the lessons of the Coral Sea: the need for better scouting and communications, and for better early-warning radar and quicker interceptions, as well as for more powerful anti-aircraft batteries on the screening forces. It also revealed the need for more coordination in attacks so that dive- and torpedo-bombers could complement each other in distracting the enemy's defenses, though it was obviously desirable to have a fighter escort if possible.

Midway was both a tactical and a strategic American victory. Not only did it cost the Japanese 4 carriers, 322 aircraft, and 100 first-line experienced pilots, but it gave them their first defeat in centuries, prevented their capture of Midway, and ended the expansive phase of the war in the Pacific.

The Lull, Mid-1942 to Mid-1944

Nevertheless, the results of the Battle of Midway did not usher in a dramatic change. Both sides had to lick their wounds, and operations in the Southwest Pacific as well as in North Africa stretched American resources, so that at times up to the end of 1942 only one American fast carrier was in the Pacific.

Thus, in some ways, airstrips ashore again became important, especially in the Southwest Pacific, where photo-reconnaissance showed the Japanese building an airfield on Guadalcanal. That vital point was included in invasion plans for the Solomon Islands; but in terms of the history of air power, the operations around Guadalcanal, while hot and fierce, offer no new lessons. Enemy submarines were for once very active, sinking the carrier *Wasp* and sending the *Saratoga* home again for repairs. The *Hornet* was sunk after the Battle of the Santa Cruz Islands, not by air attacks, torpedoes, or shells, but by the Japanese after the ship had been abandoned and the enemy was unable to take her in tow. During this period the Japanese carriers operated from their main advanced base at Truk, in the Caroline Islands, a central position from which they could deploy on internal lines. But by the end of 1942, the U.S. Navy was getting escort carriers that could provide air cover both for convoys in the battle zones and for amphibious landings, thus freeing the fast carriers to seek and destroy the main enemy forces.

At the conference in Casablanca in January 1943, the Allies generally agreed that the Pacific would be an American war to which the British would contribute by driving the Japanese out of Burma and by teaming up with MacArthur in the western Pacific Celebes Sea. Within the theater it was decided that the main task would be to drive the Japanese out of the central Pacific by a series of offensives staged through Pearl Harbor. The Aleutians and the Southwest Pacific campaigns were thus to be secondary. This grand strategy was undoubtedly correct. The Aleutians were neither in great danger nor of great military importance, and they were in fact abandoned by the Japanese in 1943. The Southwest Pacific was twice as far from the United States as the central area, and it appeared to involve a series of slow and costly island-clearing amphibious assaults. In fact, of course, MacArthur soon developed a by-pass system in the Southwest Pacific, and Yamamoto's attempt to mount a special air offensive against the Americans and Australians, using shore-based naval aircraft, failed. Allied air power staged several successful operations in the Southwest Pacific during 1943, shooting down Admiral Yamamoto in an action that made brilliant use of intelligence and timing, sinking convoys and their escorts, and

By 1944, U.S. Adm. Marc A. Mitscher alternated with Adm. William "Bull" Halsey in command of the American fleet at sea in the Pacific. Mitscher had been successful in the Battle of the Philippine Sea, willing to take the risk of illuminating his carriers so that planes returning from the last long strike against the retreating Japanese could safely land aboard when low on fuel. (U.S. Naval Aviation Museum)

USN pilots of May 1945 prepare for a mission, dressed in the flying gear of the day, complete with parachutes and lightweight, cloth, summer flying helmets. These men were very well trained, and by that late stage of the war had far more hours in their logbooks than their Japanese navy opponents. (Roy Seligman)

An example of ordering two different aircraft for the same requirement in case of failure is the Martin Mauler (ER 31) of 1944. This attack aircraft had the new 3,000 hp engine, four 20 mm cannon, and fifteen hardpoints, allowing for the carriage of three torpedoes or an assortment of other ordnance. It entered service in 1947, but was superseded by its rival, the Douglas AD-1 Skyraider (ER 10.12). (Martin)

attacking from carriers with better radar, better anti-aircraft fire, and better-trained crews than the Japanese could provide. Apart from improved equipment, better communications and control, and accurate concentration of aircraft in support of tactical forces, however, the Southwest Pacific campaigns offer no new lessons once the patterns were set.

Even in the central Pacific, where the fast-carrier task forces played a major role in the disruption of Japanese defenses, techniques and tactics quickly became stabilized. American success was due to well-trained personnel manning a plethora of equipment, while directed by some of the best minds in the business, more than to innovation. To tackle this area of small atolls in an immense sea, the Fifth Fleet (so officially named in early 1944) was organized, beginning operations in the fall of 1943. Essentially it was composed of two classes of fast carriers, the 28,000-ton *Essex* Class, which included the new modification of a port-side elevator, and 14,000-ton light fleet carriers of the *Independence* Class, which were converted light-cruiser hulls. By the time operations began, the Fifth Fleet consisted of six heavy, five light, and eight escort carriers; twelve battleships, fourteen cruisers, forty-six destroyers, and a support force of twenty-nine transport and supply vessels, the whole commanded by Admiral Spruance of Midway. At its head was the fast-carrier task force of four task groups, each containing two heavy and two light carriers, escorted by about twenty surface vessels. Apart from the amphibious element of the Fifth Fleet was its land-based air force, drawn from the U.S. Army, Navy, and Marines, which was used for advanced photo-reconnaissance and bombing missions and then for operations ashore after an airfield was captured.

The key to the whole concept, apart from the American industrial production, was logistical management through the service forces. It provided mobile bases for repair and resupply and ultimately extended refueling at sea to a full re-plenishment service that enabled the carriers to stay in the battle line for weeks on end. By 1944 the system was so refined that every day one of the four carrier task groups withdrew from the task force to be resupplied. The replenishment group was itself rotated on station.

The central Pacific campaign began in the fall of 1943 with American carrier strikes against the Gilberts and Marshalls that caused the defenders to fire off a lot of ammunition they could not replace and to withdraw their bombers that had been annoying Allied bases in the Ellice Islands. On the whole, attempts to fend off American attacks on the Gilbert Islands and Wake Island, and against Rabaul in late 1944, cost the Japanese too many carrier aircraft and crews, so that when the amphibious attacks in the central Pacific took place, the Japanese defenders were severely crimped.

By 1944, American carrier task forces were being used like panzer units, in the sort of *Judo Blitzkrieg* warfare that the Japanese had earlier adopted, reaching out in thousand-mile jabs throughout the Japanese-held Pacific atolls. In many ways, the Japanese made the same mistakes in the oceanic areas that the Allies had made in Poland and France four years earlier. They assumed that natural barriers were on their side, and they failed to organize a highly efficient, well-trained counterattacking force. At first American strikes were simply designed to destroy as much enemy air power as possible; but in each case this was only the prelude to a later attack. In the oceanic campaigns, as in Europe, it was not necessary to occupy all the space—control of key routes and key points was sufficient. Time and again the Americans merely occupied certain single islands, causing the Japanese to pull back to a new line. Moreover, the U.S. Navy was not hampered by a formal command structure as rigid as that of the Japanese, so that flexibility was possible. In the latter part of 1944, complete forces were shifted from the central to South Pacific commands while en route; and the attack on Leyte was moved up after Admiral Halsey's discovery that the Philippines were not heavily defended, and after President Roosevelt listened at Pearl Harbor to the arguments of Nimitz and MacArthur. In addition, some of the planned island-hopping campaigns, as well as the invasion of Truk, were eventually abandoned.

The "Mariana's Turkey Shoot"

The Battle of the Philippine Sea, commonly known as the "Mariana's Turkey Shoot," took place in the spring of 1944, and it afforded important lessons. The successful American seizure of the Marshall Islands, aided in part by the 750-plane Task Force 58 under Adm. Marc A. Mitscher, followed by the effective neutralization of Truk by carrier strikes, had shown that the U.S. Navy's roving panzer forces could effectively operate well within the enemy's defensive perimeter. It was decided in March, therefore, that the central Pacific forces should jump 1,000 miles to the west and take the Marianas. This would open up a direct route to Japan, provide airfields from which the new long-range four-engine B-29 Superfortress bombers could attack the Japanese home military-industrial complex, provide bases for other forces to attack economic communications within the Nipponese empire, and, hopefully, pose such a threat that the Japanese would be forced to come out and fight.

The ensuing battle was a classic case of a siege; on a condensed timetable, that is what the amphibious assaults were. The Japanese had called for a relief expedition, but heavy attrition of their naval air power in previous campaigns, together with a chronic shortage of fuel and the American domination of the air, prevented the relieving force from getting the additional support it might normally have expected. The Japanese force was thus unable to crush the American besiegers in a vice, as planned. At this stage of the war the lighter, less complex, and less heavily armored Japanese aircraft had about a 200- to 300-mile range advantage over their American counterparts. However, their airmen were badly trained, for like the

Germans at the same period, they did not have the fuel to spare for flying training, and the constant presence of American submarines off Borneo, where fuel was available, kept the tankers in the harbors. Also, the Japanese central Pacific commander was lost in an air crash shortly before the campaign started, and his replacement insisted on the old tactics of a divided force. While it was true that the American Task Force 58 under Spruance cruised in five sections, no one group was more than fifteen miles from any other, so that they were mutually supporting. In contrast, the Japanese forces in five groups were one hundred miles apart, and attacks on the van—the lead—could therefore not be beaten off by forces from the main body.

Every commander hopes to solve all his problems in one brilliant coup; the mature realize it is very unlikely to happen that way. Admiral Mitscher's task as commander of the carriers was basically to destroy enemy carriers, but he also knew he must recover as many of his own trained crews as possible, because carriers without aircrews would be merely empty symbols of power. Deciding between the two courses was to give him some difficult moments. As overall commander, Admiral Spruance understood Mitscher's desires to pursue the Japanese carriers but correctly overruled them, because his primary mission was to secure Saipan and Guam for grand-strategic reasons. Both Spruance and Mitscher knew they might be shuttle-bombed by Japanese planes operating from the carriers to Guam and back again.

Tactically, the Battle of the Philippine Sea was a display of what properly handled carriers combined with radar-vectored fighters could do under bold, mature leadership. The two commanders fought a classic offensive-defensive battle while at the same time containing the besieged. Hellcat fighters on June 19 shot down aircraft that attempted to take off from Guam and destroyed arriving reinforcements. When radar reported the approach at 150 miles of the first Japanese striking force, the American carriers first flew off 450 fighters as a massive combat air patrol—somewhat reminiscent of Air Vice Marshal Lloyd's use of the newly arrived Spitfires at Malta on May 10, 1942. The carriers then launched the bomber and torpedo planes to orbit out of trouble and attack the defenders on Saipan. The result was that the Japanese attackers were driven off with losses, while the American defenders were able to use the carriers as Sir Hugh Dowding had used forward airfields in the Battle of Britain, so that fighters could be refueled and rearmed in series. When the enemy paused to regroup, radar-vectored fighters were stacked above them and sent in for the kill. Of 430 Japanese attackers, 330 were shot down or suffered operational accidents. At the same time, two American submarines got into the Japanese van and torpedoed two carriers, both of which eventually blew up and sank. The one thing that was in the Japanese favor at this point was the wind, which forced Admiral Mitscher to turn his carriers away from the enemy every time he wished to launch or recover.

Spruance was as yet unable to verify that the two reported enemy fleets had joined, and it was not until 4:00 P.M. on the May 20 that a reconnaissance plane spotted the enemy again. After a strike was launched, it was discovered that the position the pilot had given was sixty miles out, and because of heavy radio traffic the correction was delayed. Mitscher, however, having taken one bold decision followed with another. Rather than recall the first strike, he canceled the second and headed at full speed up the track of his fliers in order to recover as many as he could. The strike found the enemy, sank one carrier, and set fire to two others, but by then low on fuel it set course for the fleet. Mitscher turned on all lights and fired illuminating star shell. Pilots with poor fuel discipline landed in the sea, but many made it aboard any carrier they could reach. Mitscher then searched farther back up the attack track and in the end recovered 160 of the 209 airmen in the strike. The combination of patience and boldness

paid off. The Japanese eventually lost three more carriers and most of their trained aircrews, a blow from which they never really recovered.

Leyte Gulf

Although American carrier-borne aviation would eventually operate off the very coasts of Japan and would engage in strategic attacks against naval bases, airfields, and military-industrial targets, these operations were in most respects similar to those conducted from Britain, as a kind of fixed aircraft carrier off the shores of Europe. The last great battle of interest in the naval air war in the Pacific was that of Leyte Gulf, with its famous "Bull's Run," in October 1944.

By autumn 1944, the Japanese were confused by a trick of American organization. When Admiral Halsey commanded the fast-carrier task force it was known as the Third Fleet; when Mitscher commanded, it was the Fifth. Its subdivisions were accordingly TF-38.1 or TF-58.1, 58.2, and the like. But the Japanese, no doubt confused also by the ability of the U.S. Navy to keep the seas for weeks because of its mobile replenishment system, thought they were facing two major fleets.

The Japanese response to the seizure of Saipan and Guam in the Marianas was to prepare another plan similar to the one that had led to the Battle of the Philippine Sea. The *Sho-Go* plan called for land-based planes to devastate enemy forces while surface and air fleets were held ready for the *coup de grâce*. In fact, the plan failed before it could be properly launched. Halsey's raids in the China Sea and other attacks had destroyed over 1,000 planes in the two months preceding the Leyte landings. In addition, submarines had concentrated on Japanese tankers to such an extent that the fleet could not operate as a unit from the home islands, but had to be based where fuel was available, with all the consequent problems of disunity, distances, and disoriented communications. Battleships were at Singapore, light forces in the Ryukyus, and carriers in the Inland Sea. Yet Adm. Soemu Toyoda, the supreme Japanese naval commander, had to fight, because if the Philippines were lost, the empire would be cut off from Japan itself.

Forced this time by economic geography and logistics to operate initially in three groups, the Japanese still failed to combine for one concentrated thrust. The two main attacks were to be made by Japanese surface forces; the carrier force, with hardly any pilots well enough trained to be able to land on, was simply to be a decoy for Halsey's Third Fleet. As a gamble intended to seriously damage the American fleet, the *Sho-Go* plan almost succeeded, but it could not have stopped the overall American offensive. By this stage of the war the American side was developing super-abundance of matériel, whereas the Japanese did not have the air power left to exploit a victory if they achieved one.

The Battle of Leyte Gulf essentially consisted of three parts: the classic defeat of the southern Japanese force in Surigao Strait by American battleships under Adm. Jesse B. Oldendorff; the confrontation between Japanese Adm. Takeo Kurita's center force and first Admiral Halsey's and then Adm. Thomas C. Kinkaid's carriers; and the success of the Japanese decoy carriers that pulled Halsey away from San Bernadino Strait and uncovered Kinkaid. In terms of the history of air power, the first phase can be ignored. In the opening of the second phase, Halsey's scouts discovered Kurita heading into the Sibuyan Sea in the central Philippines. Third Fleet carrier task forces were ordered to close formation, and strikes were launched at once on October 24. Admiral Kurita's battleships, without air cover, were forced to retire, and the super-battleship *Musashi* was sunk. When darkness fell, it looked as if Kurita was beaten. Meanwhile, by launching all fighters and retiring under a rain squall, the one American carrier group spotted by the Japanese avoided damage, while its experienced pilots shot down all but twenty of the attackers. Admiral Halsey was not aware of enemy carriers in the area.

Unfortunately, this was the first time the Central and Southwest Pacific forces had operated in conjunction, and a certain lack of clarity in orders became evident. Admiral Nimitz's operations plan specified that Halsey's primary duty was to protect the invasion forces *unless a major portion of the enemy fleet could be destroyed,* when that was to become his primary target. Kinkaid, however, to whom a copy of the orders had been sent, was under MacArthur's direction, and he had armed his ships simply for the support of invasion forces and not for a possible naval engagement. Thus, his carriers had large supplies of anti-personnel bombs, but few heavy bombs or torpedoes. He was convinced that Halsey's role was entirely to protect him against enemy naval forces, and when he intercepted Halsey's preparatory signal for the formation of a battleship group to be detached from TF-38 in case a surface engagement developed, he incorrectly assumed that such a group had been formed and was being left to guard the exit from San Bernadino Strait. This was to lead to subsequent trouble and to a postwar verbal battle.

On the evening of the October 24, the main force of Japanese carriers was located, Halsey construed their appearance as part of a plan to make a pincer attack on Leyte Gulf, and he was at once determined to break it up. The southern Japanese force obviously could be handled by Admiral Oldendorff, and Halsey's pilots assured him that Kurita in the center was retreating after being badly damaged. To avoid being shuttle-bombed, Halsey, who could not close the Philippine airfields as Mitscher had shut down those on Guam, elected to move out to meet the enemy carriers. Thus, he was drawn out of position, as the Japanese desired. He took with him the battleships that Kinkaid mistakenly assumed were to be left on guard as a separate Task Force 34, and the message informing Kinkaid of his decision to go north was unfortunately ambiguous to the reader. No thorough air coverage of San Bernadino Strait was maintained, therefore, for fear that during the night Kinkaid's planes would be shot down by Halsey's. And Kinkaid's patrols, like the RAF's at the time of the Channel dash in 1942, just happened to miss the enemy ships as they sortied. Halsey for his part, convinced that Kurita was no threat and that the carriers were, continued north despite new evidence that came in during the night that Kurita had turned about. As a consequence, when early on October 25 Kurita sortied into the Pacific, Kinkaid's only shield was a force of light carriers providing close support for troops ashore. Halsey's Task Force 34 had in fact been formed by then, but it was to be a clean-up group to pounce on cripples left after air strikes against the northern Japanese carrier force.

Halsey finally received a message sent off 2½ hours earlier by Kinkaid, asking for confirmation that TF-34 was backing his light forces at the mouth of San Bernadino Strait. Halsey's *"Negative"* was a real shocker. Receiving further cries for help, he ordered Adm. John S. McCain's group, then refueling, to proceed at once to Leyte Gulf, while he kept on after what he believed to be the bigger threat. To add to Halsey's difficulties, and to illustrate a commander's problems in modern war, Nimitz had been listening in from Hawaii to the flow of signals. He now asked Halsey, *"Where is, repeat, where is Task Force 34? The world wonders."* The latter sentence had been added by the enciphering, but Halsey did not know this. He made the difficult decision to turn TF-34 about and dash south in the infamous "Bull's Run," taking with him one carrier group as air cover. Mitscher continued his attack on the northern Japanese force and finished off all but one of the enemy carriers there.

Meanwhile Kurita, never able to establish radio contact with the northern group, did not know that he had a clear field. With a force that still consisted of four battleships, eight cruisers, and eleven destroyers, he was more than a match for the escort carriers and amphibious support vessels of Kinkaid's right flank. However, mistakenly thinking he had come upon fast-fleet carriers, he failed to destroy the slow small force that should have been at his mercy. Instead, attacks by defending destroyers and continuous harassment by carrier planes caused Kurita to sheer off after sinking only one small American carrier for a loss of three cruisers. Almost simultaneously, *kamikazes* made the first of their attacks, sinking the American light carrier *St. Lô* and damaging two other escort carriers. Faulty intelligence lured Kurita away to tackle a non-existent American force, and he then came under attack from Admiral McCain's carriers, just then coming into reach. He sensibly retired.

The Battle of Leyte Gulf was frustrating for both sides. Neither had the chance to annihilate the other. The Japanese were plagued by faulty intelligence, and the U.S. Navy proved to be susceptible to misunderstandings on the command level in a joint operation by two major forces. Leyte Gulf also emphasized the need for clear communications, especially when commanders have been actively engaged in major operations for several days. If Halsey had been allowed to follow his plan to the north, Japanese military leaders might not have continued to resist civilian and imperial pressures for peace, because they would have had nothing left with which to resist.

On the American side, all naval forces should have been placed under Admiral Nimitz's operational control to provide singleness of purpose, not with one fleet controlled by Pearl Harbor and the other by Brisbane.

ANALYSIS

Although not all U.S. Navy admirals in the Second World War were airmen, they grasped the significance of the aircraft carrier because Pearl Harbor gave them no other choice. British Adm. Tom Phillips demonstrated only too clearly off Malaya in 1941 what happened when air power was discounted, and the Japanese provided the lesson of the fate of a service whose able chief is shot down. All of these things can be seen behind the strategic and tactical lessons. The Americans in the Pacific fought essentially an offensive war, and from Midway on sought to use sea and air power strategically, as Liddell Hart and Fuller had urged Britain to do with a maritime rather than a continental policy.

On the tactical level, the war at sea showed how formal peacetime tactics are tested by the accidents of weather and war. Peacetime maneuvers should at least periodically be structured only to the extent that an "enemy" is delineated for planning purposes, so that new tactical methods or lessons can be discovered. The Pacific conflict was a flexible air war in which it was possible to employ *Blitzkrieg* and even *Judo* tactics to win dramatic victories through imaginative planning and timing. An ability to take a calculated risk and the sense to withdraw on occasion to fight another day were also essential. Like the war in the Western Desert, this was truly unlimited mobile war in which air power was used essentially as a tactical striking force to obtain strategic and grand-strategic ends.

The defeat of the Imperial Japanese Navy Air Force showed that the lessons learned from ma-neuvers and in minor wars could be misleading, especially when they did not strain logistics.

The war over China had never really tested serviceability. And the IJNAF both benefitted and suffered from the technological revolution at sea after 1937. Because the air war over China was so much in its favor, casualties were light and thus training was not expanded. Moreover, with the sea a safe haven, supplies and replacement parts flowed smoothly from the home islands to the fleet. However, after December 7, 1941, new demands, increased wastage and consumption, and distant island air bases strained the mercantile marine transport system. Then came the attrition at Rabaul. On top of this, the personnel policies that did not allow rest and recuperation (R&R), continual labor in humid tropics, the abandonment of ground crew when withdrawals took place and the loss of other skilled personnel in the carriers sunk in 1942 and 1944, the lack of air/sea rescue units, the *bushido* code—the warrior's code of conduct, and the lack of radar control through combat intelligence centers all doomed the Imperial Japanese Navy Air Force in the last year of the war.

CHAPTER 6

CHANGES—MILITARILY, POLITICALLY, 1945–2003

Major phases in aviation development have derived out of technical advances, war, and demand. The first had occurred in 1917, when finally aircraft technology, training, and tactics came together to produce a force that could influence the battlefield. The second phase started in the mid-1930s with the technological revolutions, which by 1943 allowed the fielding of a very different type of air force than in 1934, one that could hit harder, had better-trained aircrew, and was at last capable of grand-strategic impact. A branch of the developments of the 1935–45 decade was that of air transport, which reached up to the jet stream in pressurized machines that could carry passengers and some cargo on long over-water or over-land flights. The third major phase began with the introduction of the jet engine and the computer, navigation and communications improvements, radical change in POL, and in airports. Noise and the closeness and size of airports became a concern as the numbers of passengers grew exponentially and cargo became not a war-surplus matter but a major source of revenue.

Cultural changes were also significant after 1945. Although the French and the British armed forces with the colonials had already become integrated before 1939 (I served in a multi-racial, multi-cultural RAF in 1943–47), the U.S. forces were not desegregated until by President Harry Truman's Executive Order of 1948, which pioneered the change in America. By the 1970s, gender also had become a civilian issue, affecting especially the terms of employment of airline attendants—then called stewardesses—and finally coming in the 1990s to the admission of women to combat flying.

All of this meant changes in structure and organization as aviation pioneers passed in the 1960s, and later in the 1980s as nationalization took a back seat to privatization in airlines and industry where there was a constant pressure for international mergers. By 2000, privatization was affecting service training. For air forces, as the power and lethality of individual planes increased, their number in the air force decreased; in contrast, even as airliners became increasingly more efficient, the growth of business demanded yet more seats and cargo space, and even new corporate aircraft.

While aeronautics was coming of age, science was rapidly accelerating and combining with engineering. Yet the gap would remain between scientists and the engineers on one side and humanities on the other.

A continuing problem for airmen until the 1960s was the rapid obsolescence of technology due to the advances in research and development (R&D). Piston-engined aircraft advances had stabilized by 1946 as a result of the onset of aerodynamic compressibility and the approaching sound barrier. The new rocket and jet aircraft crossed that barrier, and advances continued until a plateau was reached in the late 1960s. Thereafter, development of new supersonic types of warplanes continued—though only the Anglo-French British Aircraft Corporation/Aerospatiale Concorde (ER 4,262) and the Soviet Tupolev Tu-144 "Concordski" (ER 4,970) emerged as airliners, together with well-financed fighters and spy planes. However, this development was at ever-rising costs due to the complexity and miniaturization of electronics, computers, and increased lethality of weapons, which made the single-seat Republic F-105 Thunderchief (ER 132) of 1960 more powerful than the thirteen-man B-17 Flying Fortress of 1941. Moreover, aircraft life was extended to several decades, due to modifications and complete rebuilding, in part because neither crews nor airframes flew many hours.

In airliners, the turbo-prop and the pure jet became so costly that airlines had to amortize them over fifteen years rather than over four to seven. And although a residual secondary market largely of charter and freight operations remained for the smaller aircraft, the required modifications, operating costs, and thorough rebuilding to extend the life of the craft meant that the market was limited—until package transport services went airborne in the 1970s, shortly before noise restrictions limited night operations. By the twenty-first century, the second bid for a U.S. supersonic transport (SST) had collapsed, and the future of commercial aviation looked to be in very large long-range aircraft such as the proposed but abandoned Boeing 747-XX, which was revived as the "quiet" 747-400 (ER 8,760) and the proposed successful Airbus A-380 double-deckers (ER 10,907). At the same time, short-haul jets such as the British Aerospace (Bae) RJ-146 (ER 115, RJ-146-200) competed with turboprops on routes/sectors as short as 250 miles. Below that stage, in Europe by 2000 the airlines were forced to make alliances with the railways, whose high-speed TGV (Train á Grande Vitesse)-style expresses made better time

between city centers than could aircraft and ground transportation in spite of high-speed links.

Essential to air services have been airfields, whether the 12,000-foot single runway military fields, as opposed to the triangular layout of World War II; the multiple-runway commercial airports such as Midway, in Chicago; or the original London Heathrow (LHR) layout. Heathrow started with 2,800 acres in 1944, whereas Denver's new 1995 airport had 21,000. Yet technology in the air and on the ground has kept Heathrow the busiest airport outside of the United States. What has most inhibited the growth of airports has been planning permission and democratic populace demands in technological and commercial decision-making, as at Amsterdam's Schipol Airport in the late 1990s and at Hong Kong's Kai Tak somewhat earlier, the latter resulting in a vast new airport, like Munich II, located well outside city limits.

An important consideration regarding the location of military facilities was their local economic impact. RAF Chivenor, for example, in 1992–93 contributed £14.7 million in wages and salaries and £379,000 in local purchases, even though much of its consumables were imported into the area, as well as £300,000 in local investments, all of which with the economic ripple effect amounted to roughly £21 million. The latter figure gave pause to base-closing thought.

THE NUCLEAR AGE

August 1945 marked a watershed in aeronautical history. The two atomic weapons dropped on Japan had far more overall destructive power than any bombs used before. Although the immediate damage done in particular areas might not be as great as that from incendiary raids, one aircraft was now lethal enough to obliterate a city, and the long-term fallout might be significant.

And the moral issue continued. The bombing of urban areas remains a topic for fervent national and international debate. The extent to which the ordinary citizen can be considered a combatant during wartime has not been determined. If that citizen makes munitions or raises food, is he or she a legitimate target for enemy aircraft? Furthermore, is war ever moral, even a so-called just war? On whose side is God, if there is one? And why does war always degenerate to the lowest level, unless it is short and for limited objectives?

The atomic bombs ushered in a revived burst of thinking about grand strategy, in which much of the published work came from the hands of American civilians either in quasi-private establishments such as the USAF-sponsored RAND Corporation or in academic institutions. Belatedly in 1958 the Institute of Strategic Studies was set up in London to concentrate British and other minds on international strategic problems. And within governments, the work of military pundits, whose position papers never reached the public, began to assume more and more significance as technological decisions were made that committed a nation to a certain course years before the public could speak to the point. By the late 1960s, a tendency appeared to be emerging, in the United States at least, to recognize the real perils of such procedures, and to call for public discussion of immensely expensive and potentially dangerous systems as the anti-ballistic missile (ABM), once again promoted in 1999. That such discussion could take place was due in part to the rise to power of politicians who had served in the Second World War, to the enormous interest in these matters by the mass media and the defense industries, and to the genuine and lobbying attempts of all to explain the problems to the general public.

Economists, political scientists, sociologists, and other academicians found themselves concerned with the subject of defense, not always for purely professional reasons. Even more important, suffering from guilt over the atomic bomb and the secret consumption of vast government funds for defense research—and perhaps horror-stricken at the power for annihilation they had created

and doubtful of the rational nature of man—scientists were talking in public about the consequences of their work. The debate began with the Oppenheimer-Teller squabble in the United States over the hydrogen bomb, and it gradually coalesced with many other problems whose side effects, such as the risks of air pollution and lack of civil defense in the cities, were becoming too evident to be ignored. In Russia, Stalin—until his death in 1953—pushed the nuclear program under the pervasive influence of anti-imperialist Socialist dogma and fear of outsiders. U.S. saber-rattling in the wake of the Great Patriotic War only exacerbated the situation.

But for the history of air power, 1945 was significant in many other ways than atomic. The jet engine posed new problems in aerodynamics, metallurgy, flying, public relations, and expense, though it simplified that of fuel. It pushed the whole aircraft, not just the tips of the propeller blades, up to and beyond the sound barrier. Demands for far more sophisticated metals, for much more exacting flying procedures, for new runways and airports, for better electronic aids, and for noise suppression to encourage better public relations created greatly increased costs. Weights and costs had risen about six-fold between the two world wars; then in the twenty years after 1945, weights again increased about six-fold, but costs rose thirty-fold, very largely because the old rule-of-thumb and intuitive design methods, and hand crafting, simply could no longer be risked. However, the increases were offset by revenues, as many more people and much more cargo flew and defense budgets escalated.

By the Second World War, aeronautical manufacturing had become one of the major defense industries. It remained a key economic factor after 1945; although military orders fell off drastically in Britain and America for a few years, they were revived for the Cold and Korean Wars (1947–91). The air budget peaked in 1962 in Britain, but continued at a very high level in the United States partly due to inflation, even after the Soviet Union collapsed in 1991. Soviet spending on air defense and deterrents had remained high from 1945 onward, eventually helping to bankrupt the country in 1991. Soviet design bureaus came out of the Great Patriotic War (1944–45) free to work without responsibility for manufacturing, which itself was related to unemployment.

In all three countries, the demands of civil aviation provided the industry with a better basic market than had existed before the war, but with rising costs and limited design staffs the problem increasingly—for both nations and companies—became one of choosing the correct economic course. After 1945, such choices required teamwork: success or failure depended upon astute analysis of the future in political, economic, social, technological, diplomatic, military, and even ideological terms.

These teamwork approaches were slow in coming. Neither firms nor nations could afford to make mistakes, though it can be argued that even mistakes provided employment and useful technological spin-off. The critical stage at which the cost of developing and producing a single product could bankrupt a firm was reached by the mid-1950s, when Bristol Aeroplane Co., a major British firm, had to be rescued by Cabinet order. The aerospace industry—as it began to call itself—fell into difficulties that evolved from long domination by certain individuals, neglect to reinvest profits in research, and failure to merge into larger groups with stronger capital structures. Manufacturers who had long relied on government financing found they could not get airlines to bankroll them during the several years it now took to develop a new airliner and ready it for service. And the airlines could well argue that there was no reason why they should, for they needed to turn over their own limited capital at least every ten months in order to make enough money to pay for the new aircraft they had on order. Operating in an industry with a 14 percent per annum growth rate, the airlines had enough difficulties of their own to solve, for the long-haul lines did not have real money-makers until the arrival of the big jets in 1958.

In France, a long series of five-year plans began to recreate the aircraft industry, the first fruits of which entered military service in the 1950s. Later came the Sud Caravelle III of the 1960s and the Airbus machines of the 1980s.

The impact of nuclear bombs precipitated a very costly expansion of the aviation-electronics defense industry, not to mention certain naval aspects. This tended to force attention on almost impossibly expensive projects to the neglect of those possible. The power of the hydrogen bomb in particular became such that by the end of the 1950s it was becoming apparent even to policymakers that it was not likely to be used, but would remain a stand-off threat—a threat that might, as the film *Dr. Strangelove* showed, lead accidentally to an atomic holocaust. Doubts remained about the use of nuclear ballistic missiles, which by the end of the 1950s were replacing manned bombers. These doubts were intensified in the 1960s by Red China's development of its own nuclear weapons system. Nevertheless, the principles of war still applied—and would even if the whole system were moved into space.

The atomic bomb certainly had solved the problem of the inaccuracy of area bombing. But by 1962 the Cuban missile crisis made clear that neither side could afford to use nuclear missiles because of the pervasive fallout, in addition to the actual destruction. And thus began the long, international diplomatic *démarche* to destruction of nuclear weapons and the reversion to the conventional, while at the same time particular countries of the world were attuned to deterrence.

Wide recognition of the deterrent concept is at least as old as Machiavelli's sixteenth-century doctrines, and it was understood by leaders well before that. The concept is sound as long as it is credible to the potential aggressor, convincing him that the cost of an attack would not be justified by the potential gain. However, it became evident that when nuclear deterrent existed only in massive form, not balanced by conventional forces, the opponent would decide upon a nibbling strategy, which has been much harder to combat, even in psychological or propaganda terms.

Yet, no government could afford to be so imprudent as to neglect the protection of its national vitals, or at the very least the creation of a dependable deterrent.

Under any circumstances, the arsenal base, the deterrent, and certain lines of communication have to be protected, even if this function is left to another friendly power. Circumstances change, of course, and the end of the 1960s saw European nations outside of Russia, and possibly France and Britain, becoming less concerned about the chances of an all-out war and consequently limiting defense in reality to frontier protection and peacekeeping. Unfortunately, it has been a rule of human behavior that nations have only agreed to disarmament in terms of those weapons that have become obsolete or have been thought to be so, or that have become too expensive to operate. When this concept is coupled to the sixty-year cycle of technologically acceptable performance, as seen in the Plateau theory, the question is raised whether grand-strategic bombardment may be fading from the political scene as a viable weapon, and the emphasis shifting to more acceptable means with less costly ends. In this, the Persian Gulf War of 1991 was an aberration, as attacks upon Baghdad were only strategic in terms of range, though grand-strategic in intent. In Afghanistan a decade later, grand-strategic and tactical were combined.

What nuclear theories of war did initially was to cause the Western powers, notably the United States, to overlook the vast possibilities for escalation of guerrilla warfare in the underdeveloped areas of the world, where latent social problems could easily be made kinetic by effective leaders backed with small cadres of properly equipped personnel. Having tried the use of massive pressure over Berlin in 1948 and having been foiled by the Allied Airlift, then having failed again in Korea, the Communists gave up appeals to the use of force in favor of appeals to the people. The odds against the Communists were almost reversed by the inability of Western powers to use their superior technology against packets of guerrillas. Their failure to understand the nature of the wars being fought, and their lack of rapport with the people who wished to liberate themselves were part of the problem. For the Communists, the cost of such actions was usually negligible, though Afghanistan (1979–89) was the exception.

The decision-making machinery tends to be too slow in its response to realities, especially in peacetime. Thus nuclear policy-making in Britain was just reaching its peak in 1957, with the publication of the White Paper, *Cmnd. 124, Defence: Outline of Future Policy,* assuming that next major conflict would be a three-day war. The British report emphasized nuclear-tipped rockets for deterrence, even proposing that fighter aircraft would "in due course be replaced by a ground-to-air guided missile system." But, in fact, the Suez Crisis in 1956 had made it obvious that what were needed were conventional forces able to deal with minor powers. Even before that, the 1954 retreat of the French in Indochina had shown the way wars were likely to proceed. It involved a misunderstanding of the nature of modern civil wars, which are essentially negative preemptive operations, and of insurgent ideological rebellions or revolutions linked to local grievances—what also had caused the American over-involvement in Vietnam. Bosnia, in 1996, showed NATO and the United States to have had a somewhat better strategy by then, but the 1999 Kosovo bombing was not decisive.

A great weakness of air leaders, especially in the United States, has always been to assume that defense was irrelevant and unimportant and thus to downgrade the enemy's ability to deny penetration of his airspace and to destroy his invaders. In addition, leaders have overlooked the significance of uncertainty and inaccuracy embedded in World War I artillery calculations of probability of hits, and have ignored the weather and climate as factors.

The greatest USAAF enemy during 1941–45 was the combined effect of the two older services, the U.S. Army and the U.S. Navy, as the struggle for an independent air force was the main objective. After the war, the deterrent role of the USAAF/USAF was assumed with isolationist vengeance against what was thought to be the immoral, heathen Communists of China and the USSR, a mental legacy of the nineteenth century.

But the struggle—the Cold War—did not work out that way. China did not have suitable targets that might be "nuked," and the Soviets had both distance and defenses, as well as real experience of war. Thus, while the Cold War became a stand-off militarily in favor of an economic and ideological engagement, the real wars proved to be those limited or short conflicts in which tactical air forces had to cooperate with surface and naval forces, including air, in counter-guerrilla struggles such as Vietnam (1963–72). The Persian Gulf War of 1991 was another "real" war, and a limited engagement involving tactical forces.

The Cold War, meanwhile, persisted, and although it seemed that for a while in the 1970s relations between the United States and the USSR—two super powers—would warm somewhat, by the early 1980s they were once again more frigid. In part this was due to the seesaw of technological advantage. The USSR had unveiled the Tu-26 Backfire (ER 2,930) swing-wing long-range bomber at a time when the USAF's North American XB-70 Valkyrie (ER 19,800) had been sent to the U.S. Air Force Museum and the Carter administration had canceled the North American B-1 Lancer (ER 6,279) follow-on in favor of jet-powered cruise missiles. At first, those with their eyes only upon prestige failed to see the flexibility provided by the cruise missile and its almost guerrilla threat to as vast a land mass as the Soviet Union. Conversely, the Soviets, having witnessed the ease of movement of the U.S. threat from one sea to another began to demonstrate their usual ability to copy from the West not merely in rocket-powered intercontinental ballistic missiles (ICBM)

on submarines, but also in the development of the helicopter carriers *Moskva* and *Kiev,* with evidence that full fleet carriers might appear in the 1980s to challenge U.S. domination of the high seas. The subsequent election of Ronald Reagan as U.S. President put a priority back onto defense, and the B-1 bomber was reinstated with an order for one hundred. Yet, at the same time, a willingness existed to resume disarmament negotiations. In the end, the Soviets launched two super-carriers, but could not use them because the Union of Soviet Socialist Republics broke up before they were completed and because U.S. superiority and will, among other things, had impacted the USSR disintegration.

MILITARY POLICY, ORGANIZATION, AND EQUIPMENT

It is against this paradoxical background of developing the biggest and best offensive weapons, while at the same time looking toward peace and disarmament, that air power has evolved since the Second World War. Similarly paradoxical, the so-called American strategic bomber developed into an eight-engine jet monster of 500,000 pounds all-up weight, used for strictly strategic or tactical missions in Vietnam and the Persian Gulf. On the other hand, the McDonnell F-4 Phantom fighter-bomber (ER 236.4) was developed from a tactical weapon into a respectable (by 1945 standards) heavy bomber that was sent on grand-strategic missions. Moreover, because no enemy possessed aircraft carriers from 1945 until the 1960s, the U.S. Navy found its expensive carrier aircraft diverted away from naval operations into long-term use in tactical support for the U.S. Army and Marines ashore, and in grand-strategic strikes at the enemy heartland, nuclear grand-strategic warfare threats, and peacekeeping.

The use of carrier aircraft in tactical support, while effective, is not necessarily justifiable in terms of the wear and tear on specialized military forces that may better serve national interests by being applied elsewhere. The policy has meant cluttering carriers with large aircraft for a questionable mission, while they might better be armed with strike forces suited for anti-submarine warfare or suppression of brushfire conflicts—minor limited wars—until regular army and air force units can become operational from shore bases.

The post-1945 period also saw the rapid development of the air-support arms—logistics, maintenance, and transport. Because of vast distances and the accelerated pace of modern diplomatic and military events, the use of air transport became increasingly important to military operations. Airlines in the early 1950s were able to convince the armed forces and merchant shipping companies of the economies of sending personnel by air, as opposed to having them out of action for weeks while traveling by train or ship. And as transport and strategic usage rose, maintenance became more of a problem, demanding skilled mechanics at a time when the armed forces were hard put to meet the competition from civilian airlines.

Aircraft were becoming highly complex and needed specialists to adjust their increasingly sensitive and sophisticated gear. Nations faced with a real shortage of manpower, such as Israel, realistically and sensibly opted for much simplified aircraft requiring less time-intensive training—and with maintenance problems reduced by the removal of over-sophisticated equipment—as well as the use of reservists, as in Sweden, and skilled women in many roles.

One of the curses of peacetime in most air forces tends to be the escalation of the age of responsibility, which shifts from the twenties to the forties, and a consequent growth in the requirements for placing command in the hands of an aging elite. Such a system leads to greater turnover in the lower ranks and an over-expenditure on education not really needed by those whose real proficiency should be in the flying arts, as in the airlines. A large proportion of the budget is thus expended on salaries and broadening of education rather than on training. This is not to suggest that war is good, or that armed forces should be composed of automatons, but rather to clarify that leadership becomes ossified during long periods of peace, while the tendency is to over-educate junior officers in non-essentials rather than to continue to train them for the straightforward business of operations. On the other hand, it must be recognized that higher technology demands far more complex staffs to manage and service it.

The effects of peacetime could be seen in the problems facing the U.S. Air Force in Vietnam as opposed to Korea. In Korea, plenty of Second World War pilots were still available; but in Vietnam, these had shrunk to a group largely composed of lieutenant colonels and above who were flying because of a shortage of some 3,000 pilots. Retention rates of pilots were low because by the mid-1960s the airlines—with nineteen new jets each week joining commercial fleets in America alone—were desperate for aircrew; they could pay better salaries and offer married men a stable career of very little risk.

Another peacetime curse, generally eliminated in wartime equilibrium, is the constant modification of equipment and routinization of methods and techniques. In the 1960s, the armed forces and the airlines benefitted from the development of a methods branch closely allied to the computer; but at the same time, the mere volume of business, space, and paper tended to clog the system, which was run by people unwilling to abandon old procedures. The advantage of occasional wars, or of losses instead of profits, is that they allow a quantum jump forward toward solving accumulated problems by the use of an efficiency sword on the tightly pulled Gordian knot, as the airlines were forced to do between 1989 and 1996. Having to lay off personnel, however, is not a sign of strong management, though the national practice of increasing personnel in times of plenty has to be pared.

The post-World War II revival of the deterrent

theory, with nuclear bombs, once again put the war's bomber commanders in the sphere of influence, if indeed they had ever left it in the American and British air services. The first evidence of this came with the late 1940s battle over the Consolidated B-36 Peacemaker bomber (ER 2,042, B-36B) in the United States between the newly independent U.S. Air Force—as of September 1947—and the U.S. Navy, both now subordinate to the new Department of Defense. The USAF took the view that the atomic bomb could solve any difficulties that diplomacy could not handle. The U.S. Navy was supported by the Secretary of Defense in its view that while a deterrent was important, eventually ground troops would have to be committed, and this would require both a tactical air force and protected logistical support. Moreover, naval officers, with their long years of experience in quasi-war situations, recognized the need for forces to cope with brushfire wars, and they regarded as unsound the USAF demand for control over all aviation. But in budgetary battles, the siren call of the USAF seemed so simply logical that it won many supporters. After all, was it not cheaper?

The battles of 1946 were revived again in 1948. The USN asked for newer and larger carriers, in part so that naval aircraft could carry atomic bombs. The USAF took this as an attempt to usurp some of its powers and responded with a journalistic campaign in favor of the B-36. The new Secretary of Defense, James V. Forrestal, sided with the Air Force, refused the carriers, and fired the Chief of Naval Operations, Adm. Louis Denfeld. The battle continued in the corridors of the Pentagon, until the Korean War brought liberalized budgets.

Some of the arguments were affected by the fact that the Soviets, extremely conscious after the Second World War that they did not have adequate air defenses, proceeded to put a maximum effort into the development of both radar and other air protections, as well as the atomic bomb. The result was that on May Day 1949, the Russians were able to display Mikoyan-Gurevich MiG-15 jet fighters (ER 20) that vitiated the argument claiming the B-36 to be impervious to hostile defending forces. In fact, for those who were not blinded by their faith, the lessons of the 1943 Schweinfurt and Regensburg raids were plainly written on the wall of history: bombers cannot always get through with acceptable loss rates. The British, for example, had jets that could reach the B-36 in eight minutes from radar-warning scramble and could fly at 540 mph at 30,000 feet, compared to the B-36's 370 mph. At this same time, congressional hearings caused charges of influence to be bandied regarding the $6 million B-36. Nevertheless, despite all the controversy, the B-36 remained in service until 1958. But better solutions to the delivery of grand-strategic strikes appeared in the all-jet air-refuelable Boeing B-47 Stratojet bomber (ER 992). It was as fast as current fighters and could operate with atomic bombs or conventional weapons from the bases that had been acquired around the Soviet Union either by treaties with the North Atlantic or Southeast Asia (NATO or SEATO) Treaty Organizations, or through arrangements opened up by Korean War spending.

Even before the B-36 controversy had fully run its course, the declining order-book situation in the American aircraft industry had begun to worry manufacturers and political leaders. In 1947, President Truman appointed the Thomas K. Finletter Air Policy Commission to study America's place in the aviation world. In its 1948 report, *Survival in the Air Age,* the Finletter Commission pointed out that a scientific-technological revolution was endangering the safety of the United States and that it was imperative that the U.S. Air Force start immediately to build a modern organization. It was claimed that in 1947, 44 percent of U.S. Navy aircraft were obsolete, and that in 1948, 95 percent of USAF aircraft were still Second World War types. The Commission was unhappy about recommending a seventy-group air force, but felt it had to do so, while at the same time urging that other roads to peace be explored—once again the ever-present paradox. After considerable discussion, by mid-1948 Congress and the President had agreed to a sixty-six-group force, which was just being built when the Korean War started.

In both the United States and the USSR, the air services were regrouped. In the USAF, the Strategic Air Command (SAC) was created at Omaha in 1948 under Gen. Curtis E. LeMay and became both the instrument of policy and a major military political force. But SAC did not control Civil Defense. On the other hand, in the USSR the responsibility for the integrity of Soviet territory lay with the Voyska PVO Strany (Troops of the National Air Defense) from 1941 to 1982, and thereafter with the Voyska PVO (Air Defense Troops), which controlled surface-to-air radar and air defenses, interceptor aircraft, and civil defense, and which after 1945 concentrated on downing USAF and RAF high-flying bombers that penetrated Soviet airspace. Surface-to-air missiles (SAM) were one of the by-products. And the system changed after 1949 as NATO did.

The Strategic Air Command was dismantled in 1992 in favor of two new commands, Air Combat and Air Mobility, which also superseded Tactical Air Command (TAC) and Military Airlift Command (MAC). The former SAC headquarters at Omaha became the Joint Services U.S. Strategic Command. These developments recognized the final rise to power of tactical airmen in the wake of a series of limited, peripheral wars.

With the need to speed decision-making in a global atmosphere, USAF headquarters was streamlined in 2001 and a new deputy chief of staff for warfighting was added to modernize and integrate command, control, communication, and computers—called C^4.

The British also were concerned with the grand-strategic bomber and developed three types, all jets, eventually to replace their piston-engined Avro Lincoln bomber (ER 160), which had entered service in 1945 and remained operational until 1955. The new V-bombers—the Vickers Valiant (ER 652), Handley Page Victor (ER 527), and Avro Vulcan (ER 653)—showed a progression away from conventional aircraft. The Valiant was the first into service and, although it had swept wings, it was reasonably conventional. The Victor had a crescent wing and a high-altitude performance equal to that of a fighter. The most radical of all was the delta-winged Vulcan. But what was often overlooked by those discussing strategic bombing was that although these aircraft were under development in 1947, neither the Victor nor the Vulcan joined squadrons until 1956, the year of the Suez Crisis. And the Valiants, after flying only 2,500 hours each, were withdrawn in 1965. Yet strategists talked as though the bombers existed long before they were in fact operational. And distance restrictions were still a serious factor.

In 2002, the RAF envisaged as well that it would have a capability gap in 2008 when its three Jaguar GR3-A squadrons would be phased out, before the new Eurofighter was established.

It was true that after the Second World War the major air powers benefitted from the British development of aerial refueling, but for this range-extender to be effective, safe refueling rendezvous had to exist. At one time a British proposal had been put forth simply to send crews on suicide missions into the Soviet Union, because there seemed no other way of reaching vital targets. A common error at the time was to credit the Soviets with a whole force of a type just because one or two were flown over at the annual Tushino airfield display. And just as in early World War II, when the RAF had greatly over-estimated *Luftwaffe* strength, during the Cold War the Western allies similarly portrayed the Soviets as more the aggressor than they proved over time to be, often for political funding reasons at home. Fortunately, containment rather than conflict was the rule until and after suitable striking forces were developed.

Much more speculative for a long time were the roles that France and China were to play. After Charles de Gaulle once again took the reins of power in 1958, France moved to develop her own *force de frappe,* a nuclear capability that would give her a say in international affairs. Her aircraft industry had been quietly working to produce fighter-bombers and small-strike aircraft such as the Dassault Mirage IV (ER 65), able to deliver nuclear weapons. Yet where France stood as a military-diplomatic force remained in doubt in the 1960s.

At the other end of the world, the Chinese seemed to have developed nuclear bombs, but rather than moving toward long-range bombers, they appeared to be headed directly to ballistic missiles. As to Chinese intentions, analysis of these rather depended upon whether the foreign observer believed that China was essentially a paper dragon, more afraid of others than intent on aggression, or real.

The advent of ballistic missiles, foreshadowed by the German V-2 rockets of the Second World War, started arguments in both the technological and military communities. The discussions ranged around the solid- versus the liquid-fueled rocket, with the solid-fuel spokesmen gradually winning out in the early 1960s for both airborne and seaborne missiles, and even for those in silos, because the solid-fuel rocket could be fired instantaneously without going through a time-consuming topping-off process. The arguments also revolved around the morality of using nuclear weapons. Whether or not people liked to ponder the unthinkable, pundits like the American Herman Kahn argued that they had to do so and to decide just about how many millions of people could be sacrificed in a nuclear exchange. By the end of the 1960s this had evolved into a new argument over whether or not the Soviets were deploying the anti-ballistic missile (ABM), and whether or not the Americans should. What made the argument particularly difficult to resolve was the prospect of a battle in space between two robot systems, each of which was now capable of polluting the atmosphere with deadly fallout that might kill millions, while still leaving the chance that at least one warhead would get through, especially if fitted with multiple independently targeted re-entry vehicles (MIRV).

A long gap existed between the evolution of nuclear deterrent theory and the availability of the hardware. Second World War rocket developments and subsequent advances made in aircraft design, gyro-stabilizing systems, radio, and radar made ballistic missiles possible; but developments in the immediate postwar period were restricted by several factors, among them relocation of the German expert teams to the United States and the USSR, and restricted budgets. And in the United States, at least, the core of the German team went to the U.S. Army rather than to the Air Force. But the lag was also due to the fact that air-breathing missiles rather than rocket-fueled ballistic missiles were more popular with military decision-makers. Another well-concealed fact was that the USAF had only six crews during 1947–48 that could bomb-up nuclear strike aircraft. Not until 1954 did the miniaturization of inertial guidance systems and the arrival of the thermonuclear (hydrogen) warhead, which provided greater punch for a smaller space and weight, make possible a strike by unmanned missiles, with fair accuracy, on a target some 5,000 miles away. Even so, in spite of the impetus given the American program by the Soviet launching of the Sputnik I satellite in 1957, it was 1958 before the first Atlas missile was test-fired; and the so-called missile-gap situation was one of the issues in the American presidential election of 1960.

Meanwhile, the Soviet Union and the United States had developed intermediate range missiles (IRBM) with a radius of about 1,600 miles. The intercontinental missile had become operational in the 1960s, and the U.S. Navy's Polaris submarine-launched ICBM had enlarged its range by its ability to be moved into firing positions closer to the targets. Starting with a range of 1,200 miles, the improved Polaris A-3 was credited with 2,875 miles by 1969. As a counter to this development, the Russians accelerated their sophisticated oceanographic research, concentrating on anti-submarine warfare measures and developing their own missile-carrying and killer submarines.

Changes—Militarily, Politically, 1945–2003

Other nations engaged in experimental rocket programs and atmospheric and spatial exploration, but only the British attempted to rival the two major powers in the 1950s. Their Blue Streak air-launched stand-off missile was canceled before it was test-fired, however, and instead some attempt was made to use American Thor IRBMs. But by the end of the 1960s the British had dropped out of the race, opting for U.S. Polaris missiles on their underwater craft.

In the USSR and the United States, work on anti-ballistic missiles continued, and whether they would be successful would depend upon the amount of money expended in research and upon the political forces their supporters could muster, as much as upon the technical know-how of the manufacturers and operators involved. History has shown, however, that an antidote to any weapon can be found if enough money and effort is put into the task. At last, in the 1991 Persian Gulf War the Americans claimed—erroneously—that when the Patriot missile shot down Iraqi Scuds, the ABM had become reality. An ABM system was still an issue for the twenty-first century.

To some extent, the two super-powers had recognized by 1961 that the dangers of nuclear war probably outweighed the advantages; thus they established the "hot line" between Moscow and Washington and used it effectively during the 1962 Cuban missile crisis and the 1967 Arab-Israeli War to neutralize a conflict, even between themselves. The original impetus for the hot line came, however, from a political scientist's observations that a nuclear holocaust could be started by an unknown, or *nth,* power, lobbing a missile from a submarine into one of the major cities of the two super-powers, in the hopes that they would, like the two mythical sleeping giants, knock themselves out and leave the world to others.

The hot line was in addition, of course, to elaborate peripheral radar defenses set up by both sides, including the well-known Canadian-American DEW (distant early-warning) line across the Arctic facing Russian missiles launched on a great-circle route. By the later 1960s these systems had been extended to satellite surveillance, yet ironically the warning time remained about the same fifteen minutes it had been in 1939, until 1969, when the United States claimed its MIDAS spy-in-the-sky would give it thirty minutes. In the 1950s, SAC developed an airborne-alert system, under which some of its aircraft and a command ship were always airborne.

Both the Soviet and the American air forces pressed for the development of new manned bombers in the 1950s. Various attempts had been made to develop an atomic ship, and then, when that proved not to be very practical, to produce a large supersonic bomber to take the place of the aging B-52s as well as of the world's first supersonic bomber, the Convair B-58 Hustler (ER 2,508). Production on the B-58 stopped in 1962, however, because the aircraft was unpopular with the USAF "high brass." By 1960, two prototypes were under construction, but North American's two-ship XB-70 Valkyrie program was held to a testing level; one crashed, and then in early 1969 the survivor was cancelled. The manned-bomber lobby still continued in action, but with ballistic missiles able to reach any target in the world, the arguments for a manned super-bomber, other than a very expensive test vehicle for a supersonic transport, began to appear unsupportable. The manned bomber could no longer make the most meaningful and economic contribution. Then, early in the 1970s the United States had evolved the Triad concept of land- and sea-based missiles that were given added flexibility by the B-1 Lancer, a low-level supersonic strategic bomber. As noted, President Carter's canceling of the B-1 delayed production, and only one hundred would enter service in the 1980s, to be followed in the 1990s by a mere twenty of the Northrop B-2 Spirit stealth flying wing (ER 2,877.6). In the meantime, the Soviets had developed the Tu-26 Backfire bomber.

By the end of the 1960s Vietnam was, indeed, showing that the wars of the future were increasingly likely to be local affairs in underdeveloped areas, and tactical aircraft would be able to carry sufficient force to do the job if properly assigned. Even more importantly, Vietnam and the Arab-Israeli War of 1967 showed that how conventional aircraft were handled was what ultimately mattered, and that generals needed a really sound understanding of the strengths and weaknesses of air power, of the limitations under which it operated, and of the people and terrains that composed the zone of contention. These wars began to show, as did modest budgets in the smaller powers, that more attention needed to be paid to simpler, less sophisticated, but more usable aircraft than to B-52 bombers and F-4 fighters. In a sense, war had come full cycle to another aspect of the Second World War—the tactical. Aircraft like the old reliable Douglas AD-1 Skyraider (ER 10.12) were needed, which had a remarkable bomb- and rocket-load, great endurance, and the ruggedness to operate off relatively primitive fields. Built at the end of the 1945 war, the Skyraider proved to be irreplaceable in the later 1960s. In its stead were flown aircraft that lacked its basic qualities in one way or another. Eventually a number of replacements were accepted, including the twin-jet light Northrop F-5 Freedom Fighter (ER 82); it was sold originally to air forces that could not afford the F-4E Phantom and adopted with reluctance and then enthusiasm by the USAF, whose fighter side tended to be dominated by the "air superiority" group. Others in the same economic fix, such as the Australians and the Israelis, opted for the French Dassault Mystere IV (ER 16.4) and Mirage, though the Australians were also talked into a few expensive General Dynamics F-111FB Aardvark figher-bombers (ER 1,189), which the British for their part finally quite rationally canceled as unsuitably expensive for their needs.

The Communist equivalent of this pattern was the export of the MiG-17F (ER 26.6), MiG-19 (ER 48), and MiG-21 (ER 14.2) to various smaller countries and to be license-built in China, to be followed much later by the MiG-29 (ER 157) and the Sukhoi Su-27 (ER 174).

Evidence of the great advances made in the 1950s and 1960s was seen in the 1970s when the Lockheed F-104 Starfighter (ER 68), carrying Sidewinder air-to-air missiles, could reach 80,000 feet and by a pitching maneuver hit targets at 100,000. However, that action caused them to flame-out and lose pressurization, with the pilot only saved by his anti-G suit. But a deadstick landing because of inability to relight the engine meant starting a final approach at 40,000 feet!

The Sidewinder missile, developed after World War II by an unfunded team at Naval Air Station China Lake, California, is a classic example of a weapon, still in production in 2000, whose creation and perfection was done *ad hoc* without bureaucratic guidance or much funding.

Meanwhile, by 1988, development time had stretched to the point where the newest European fighter prototype had just flown, but would not enter service until 2003—this compared to development time of ninety days to four years for a World War II fighter. And the lightweight Northrop F-20 Tiger II (ER 88), designed to be available in quantities for medium-budget powers, was shelved because it was not impressive enough and the USAF would not buy it—thus no one else would.

This same attitude killed the Israel Aircraft Industry's Kfir (ER 57.83), an advanced fighter based on a U.S. engine and Middle Eastern combat experience, but later manufactured by South Africa.

By the 1960s, the success of air-to-air missiles such as the Sidewinder, Sparrow, and others caused both airmen and designers to believe that dogfighting was obsolete and that guns and air-combat maneuvering (ACM) were unnecessary weapons and skills. Thus the F-4 Phantom was only fitted with guns during the later Vietnam War when experience showed that even the best missiles proved only one-fifth or less as reliable in operation as in tests. And the LTV Aerospace Corp. F-8 Crusader fighter (ER 68) (originally F8U) with its guns similarly had a better kill rate than missiles—this compared to other fighters versus MiGs.

Combat often forces the "reinvention of the wheel," and prognosticators find past history haunting them. Thus combat experience in Vietnam as well had proved the gun still essential and fighter versus fighter dogfights still possible, in spite of missiles. Although missiles have evolved to become much more reliable, identification problems, counter-measures, and skill have negated them. In the 1991 Gulf War, French Dassault Mirage F-1s (ER 54.7) had to be sent home to avoid confusion and suicide, as the Iraqi enemy also had them.

In the post-1945 era, electronics of combat aircraft have also evolved, to become much more reliable, miniaturized, and computerized. By 1988, simulators could be used not only for flight training, but also for air-to-air combat scenarios. And although none of this was cheap, it was safer and less costly than losing valuable personnel in accidents or combat.

As for military engines and aircraft, some new shapes have emerged, but in many cases performance seems to indicate that bigger may not be so much better. Numbers and training, rather than design, may still be the real clue, unless a stealth paint as much as stealth technology makes a real breakthrough. Certainly it is true that the B-1B has a radar signature less than .016 percent that of the venerable B-52, and the stealth bomber is calculated at only .003 percent of that of the forty-year-old SAC warhorse now destined to remain in service to 2045. On the other hand, the twenty B-2s in the USAF inventory are so sensitive that they cannot stand out in the rain! And proportionately, the expense of military electronics equipment for stealth offense and defense, as well as special coatings, makes a B-1B, for example, cost $280 million versus the $130-odd million for a 747.

Interestingly, of the 744 B-52s built, 97 re-mained in service at the end of 2000, and only 75 will be available by 2007 due to the 1993 START II (strategic arms reduction talks) treaty between the United States and Russia. Early in the twenty-first century, warfare was calculated by the Pentagon at one incident per decade, but like many such predictions, it has been immediately subject to modification.

Equally critical is the number necessary to maintain a certain size force. In 1993, the Belgian Chief of the Air Staff pointed out that 120 General Dynamics F-16 Fighting Falcons (ER 113) were required in order to have a force of 72 aircraft. He needed eighteen extras for training (the F-16B), and the electronic refit program would immobilize twenty aircraft. In addition, with a reduction in permitted flying hours to 14,000 per year, higher attrition could be expected, amounting to another ten aircraft over the service life of the seventy-two.

The lightweight F-16, one of the most prolific designs of the postwar era, was conceived in the 1960s and put into production in 1974. While not yet exceeding the F-4 Phantom II's 5,000 copies, the F-16 has undergone a more complete metamorphosis in its nearly thirty years, with more than twelve block derivatives (ER 113 for the A/B; ER 304 for the C/D Block 50). The aircraft was radical with its fly-by-wire (computer-initiated) controls and blended wing body, which produced a fighter with both long range and agility at reduced cost. Furthermore, the miniaturization of electronics and rapid advances in engine technology have meant that the F-16s coming off the line now are very different from those of 1974. In the competition against the Dassault Rafale (ER 336) and the Bae EF 2000 Eurofighter Typhoon (ER 107.4) in 1999–2000, the F-16 received 210 orders. These orders have boosted major sensor avionics and powerplant improvements, including installation of the equivalent to the LANTIRN (low-altitude navigation and targeting infrared for night) laser system pod in the nose of the F-16 for better aerodynamic efficiency. Other modifications and developments have been combined for non-recurring and recurring cost savings, making the new combined systems cheaper.

By 2003, new modems were allowing the F-16, with its glass cockpit cathode-ray displays, to become a "system of systems" in an advanced-capability cockpit. And by agreement with Israel Aircraft Industries (IAI), the new F-16s will have the Elta Electronic Industries SAR (sythetic aperture radar) pod, giving the Fighting Falcon an all-weather, high-resolution, real-time reconnaissance capability. In addition, Lockheed Martin, which absorbed General Dynamics, is offering more than one hundred different external stores options.

The F-16 started out at 33,000 pounds (15,000 kgs) and by the year 2000 had reached 50,000 pounds (22,700 kgs); but as this has cut range, the conformal fuel tanks (CFT) above the wings have been introduced, extending the range again to 800 nm (1,480 kms). At the same time, fuel efficiency has permitted the installation of the 32,000-pound-thrust engine, which gives 34 percent more power than in the F-16A/B; but the new engine is not available for export models yet. Mid-life upgrades (MLU) are being applied to the 3,000-odd older models still in service, including updated wiring to keep them flying to 2015–20. And the aircraft may continue "to be grown" after that. In 2002, Lockheed-Martin was awarded a contract to maintain the F-16s of the U.S. Air Force and of twenty-three other countries for the next twenty-three years.

Much bigger than the original F-16, the McDonnell Douglas F/A-18E/F Hornet (ER 124.4) has two General Electric F-414 after-burning turbo fans, 25 percent more powerful, for its 18 percent higher takeoff weight of 66,000 pounds, but it lands 10 knots slower, in spite of a 30 percent greater touchdown weight of up to 9,020 pounds (4,100 kgs). At zero-fuel, the aircraft weighs 31,900 pounds (14,500 kgs); the single-seat E models carry 14,685 pounds (6,675 kgs) of fuel. Fuel flow in cruise is 2,180 kgs per hour, yet the Hornet gets airborne at 146 mph (125 kn) after

roll of only 1,200 feet. Maximum speed is 913 mph (780 kn). On the other hand, the F/A-18E/F can fly at an angle of attack (AOA) of 48 degrees nose up at 70 knots. Its fly-by-wire system is quadriplex-redundant—any one of four computers can take over—so that it can automatically compensate for battle damage; it also has low-observability features to decrease the radar signature, and chaff and towed decoys for self-defense.

The new four-nation Eurofighter—of Britain, France, Germany, and Spain—due in service in 2003, indicates some of the reasons why the comparable Japanese and Indian fighters are five years behind schedule in development. By mid-2000, Eurofighter Typhoon prototypes had flown more than 1,300 hours, with 1,200 still remaining. They had three types of software programs being integrated. When Typhoons join the German Air Force, it will retire the RSK MiG-29 Fulcrum and later its F-4 Phantom II (ER 370) aircraft. In the meantime, the Norwegians have decided not to make a decision for purchasing the Typhoon until 2010. Political and industrial pressure on the Netherlands was being maintained to keep it within the joint-strike-fighter (JSF) sphere. Meanwhile, biennial updates of the software in the Typhoon have been promised over the aircraft's thirty- to forty-year life, with direct factory-to-squadron spares replacements, perhaps in packs for out-of-theater deployments. In addition, part of the aircraft's component-repair workforce at the factories may be by military service personnel. All this calls for a whole new way of management thinking.

Due to delays to the new European transport aircraft, the RAF began a seven-year lease of McDonnell Douglas (now Boeing) C-17s (ER 2,505) in 2001. The size and range of the machine enabled a dismantled Tornado fighter from the Falklands air defenses to be flown back to the United Kingdom for maintenance and repair, with one stop to refuel at Ascension Island, instead of being ferried with a need for aerial refuelings and support aircraft.

Changes—Militarily, Politically, 1945–2003

Navies, too, underwent changes post–World War II. Aircraft carriers were their mobile airfields. Almost all carrier improvements were confined to the American and British navies, as these were the service organizations developing advanced equipment until Soviet carriers began to appear in the 1960s. In all, the battle against the rival air force caused the adaptation of technology to become "cost effective." In the U.S. Navy, the yardstick by which performance was measured was the ability to hit Russia, and traditional roles were neglected. Larger and stronger flight decks as well as better handling facilities were required for postwar jet fighters. The steam catapult, the deck-edge elevator, the angled deck, and the mirror landing system were produced, all British innovations, followed by the radar lock-on approach tracking and television supervision through island- and deck-mounted cameras.

Yet, both the old and the new carriers were not vastly more efficient: a 60,000-ton *Forrestal* Class carrier was able to launch four aircraft per minute, while keeping tankers overhead for returnees short of fuel. Jets meant that strikes were faster and that handling had to be more precise on the part of deck crews and pilots. The first American operational jet squadron roosted aboard the USS *Saipan* in May 1948 flying McDonnell FH-1 Phantoms (ER 33.5). With a top speed of 479 mph, a weight of 10,000 pounds, and a ceiling of 41,000 feet, they were the precursors of the F-4 Phantom IIs of the Vietnam War, which in turn were aircraft bigger than a DC-3, weighing 50,000 pounds and capable of 1,400 mph. The last significant development in carriers, apart from helicopter ships, was the nuclear-powered *Enterprise* Class, with a flight deck 1,040 feet long (twice the 1922 *Langley's*), an extreme beam of 252 feet, and a full-load displacement of 85,350 tons. Some, indeed, have wondered if the super-carrier was not a case of putting too many eggs in one basket.

While carriers were modernized, their aircraft continued to age. Thus the U.S. Navy found by 2003 that the maintenance cost of the fleet's aircraft was such that retirement was the best option for the future—the Grumman F-14 Tomcat (ER 463.6, 1990s) to be retired in 2007, followed by the F/A-18C/D in 2019.

The Soviets also began to undertake carrier development, but by the late 1960s the nucleus of their force was still the helicopter ship *Moskva,* useful for brushfire wars. Not until the 1980s did they begin to build full-scale carriers, and shortly thereafter the collapse of the Soviet Union scuttled their use and led to attempts to sell them to India and China.

The development of helicopters after the Second World War showed no startling innovations until 1968, when the rigid rotor machine capable of aerobatics and speeds of close to 300 mph was demonstrated. Igor Sikorsky had shown the first successful helicopter in 1944, and it was adopted for air/sea rescue. In the Korean War, the "whirlybird" came into its own in mountainous terrain, bringing casualties back to MASH—Mobile Army Surgical Hospital—units. With new lifting capacity, thereafter the air cavalry concept came into being, and thus "choppers" played a large role in mobile warfare in Vietnam, accompanied by newly developed gunships to provide mobile fire support. Helicopters were also used to supply isolated artillery fire posts.

At sea, helicopters not only flew guard for carriers and other air activities, but ferried Marines and supplies ashore and were a key part of the anti-submarine warfare (ASW) organization.

With the time required to locate and rescue downed aircrew critical, especially in places such as Afghanistan and Yugoslavia, combat search and rescue (SAR) helicopters were by 2003 being refitted to be able to pinpoint downed crew members more rapidly while also defending the rescue craft.

In civilian use, the helicopter became an adjunct of police departments, road traffic control, forest-fire fighting, medical evacuation, crop spraying, and city-center-to-airport shuttles.

As lifting capacity increased, due to service demand to move artillery, air cranes became available not only to the armed services but also to help with offshore oilfield rigs, in such tasks as the positioning of telecommunications apparatus on roof and mountain tops, and in logging. Piston engines were replaced by gas turbines, and some progress was made with rotor technology, but not much in noise suppression.

Much neglected was the convertiplane, which should have played a major role in anti-submarine warfare, as it had considerable range advantages over the conventional helicopter. Only after 2003 was the Boeing V-22 Osprey (ER 164.5) perhaps going to enter U.S. Marine service. But even more significant was the general failure to exploit the new gas-turbine engines for the development of short takeoff and landing (STOL) aircraft, which were basically machines that used modern power and construction techniques to deliver the same short-field performance as aircraft in the 1920s, but with much greater weight and safety. The Saab JA-37 Viggen (162.7) jet fighter represented a STOL solution for use from roads through the Swedish forests.

Ironically, one of the reasons for the slow development of the STOL aircraft was that it was unsalable to air forces whose leaders had their eyes focused on the bigger and better sonic boom. Yet for both airlines and the military in many parts of the world, the STOL aircraft was the most practical solution to a roadless area filled with small clearings. Of all the aircraft manufacturers, de Havilland of Canada most realized the STOL aircraft's possibilities, with its quiet gas-turbine engine, partly because of the long use of airplanes in the bush of the northern backwoods.

And a further irony was evident. By the early 1960s it was becoming hard to find any engineer for STOL work with experience of propellers. Yet at the same time an active, working market was found for Fiberglas copies of such old reliable piston-engine machines as the Ford Trimotor, an aircraft at least thirty years old, for gas turbines had the great advantage of quiet operation.

The other development of the 1960s was the evolution of the vertical takeoff and landing (VTOL) aircraft, which used vectored thrust to lift off and then for forward flight. The Soviets followed the lead of the Hawker Harrier (ER 75), also manufactured for the U.S. Marines by McDonnell Douglas. The Harrier was designed to operate out of concealed locations or on ships, and it proved its versatility and value in the 1982 Falklands War.

INTELLIGENCE

Overflight of rival territory was important—whether by balloon in the 1950s over the USSR, by U-2 flights, or by peripheral patrols, as in 2001 off China—and intelligence gathered was only as good as its quick and skillful analysis and the relaying of the findings to the decision-makers.

In the 1960s, the film from the USAF's Corona satellites still took four to five days to get to Kodak in Rochester, New York, for processing, and then move for onward transmission to the National Photo Intelligence Center.

At first the cameras used were developments of the World War II K-24, but by the time the Corona satellites were orbiting the globe in the 1960s, highly sophisticated KH cameras that faced both forward and back gave stereoscopic images. They provided 36,000 feet of high-resolution images that could be ejected from the satellite in one or two buckets. No wonder the USAF called the 1960–72 project Corona Harvest. In fact, satellite imaging was so plentiful that film was discarded without any system of saving random sets for historical comparison, as the RAF's PRU interpreters had done at Medmenham, England, during 1940–45, and from which their comparisons revealed the new German V-2 rocket. From all the 1954–60s imagery, the analyses managed to deflate the missile gap myth of 1960—one of the points upon which John F. Kennedy was elected, that America was behind the USSR.

And here Richard Nixon had been helped by

the unknown desire of the Kremlin to slow the arms race in the face of the rise of Red China, eventually leading to both a post-Vietnam rapport with Moscow, an ABM treaty, and a new relationship after 1972 with China.

In the meantime, from 1969, when the Russian Tu-26 Backfire was first spotted, the Central Intelligence Agency and the Defense Intelligence Agency, both in Washington, disagreed as to the bomber's capabilities. The USAF said the Tu-26 was a threat to the continental United States and that view prevailed. This assessment, presented at the strategic arms limitation talks at Geneva—SALT II—stalled the discourse until 1979. To resolve the CIA-DIA dispute, President Gerald Ford had the National Intelligence Estimates prepared by two teams—one from the Soviet perspective, and one from the American. In the past, the dispute concerned whether only hard data or whether ideology, strategic doctrine, and national character should play a part. And also of issue was the nature of the 1970s Soviet civil defense program.

However, subsequent intelligence coverage of the USSR had to be cut so that money could be siphoned to develop the KH-8 and KH-9 high-resolution satellite imagery covering a swath up to 360 miles wide, needed from 1984 for arms control and verification, and by then television/video oriented.

By 2001, in the Afghan War, for the first time intelligence products were being fed directly to aircraft on operations, so that the crew could visualize a target well before they could actually see it. This required matching U.S. Navy P-3 SIGINT with U-2 and AC-130 data and feeding it to B-52s, F-14s, F-15s, and F-16s.

THE ROYAL CANADIAN AIR FORCE

An example of what has happened since 1945 is the story of the Royal Canadian Air Force (RCAF). Immediately postwar, the missing pilots and aircrew were traced and exhumed, and monuments erected; but no history of World War II was written due to the lack of vision of the Air Council in Ottawa. Yet the RCAF had half of Canada's defense budget. A history did not begin to appear until 1980, with the first volume covering 1939–45; at that time, the RCAF was the third largest Allied air force, with 210,000 personnel at the peak in March 1944. The RCAF history project, however, was canceled for economy after the third volume.

In the RCAF, destruction of World War II surplus and reduction of personnel reached 12,000, a level below the 17,000 who had been killed or died in the war. But the Korean War brought expansion to 46,000 and a nascent aircraft industry. Canadian defense was focused on the Soviet Cold War threat over the Arctic, with air supply of ground counter-forces. This led to the formation of Tactical Air Command in 1953, but it was disbanded in 1959 when the Canadian army decided air transport was only needed under Air Transport Command. After 1946, another task was undertaken, that of surveying possible airfield sites in the Arctic archipelago. A search was made for the true magnetic North Pole as air routes began to overfly the ice cap. Photographing and mapmaking were required, until the task was completed in 1957 when the squadron concerned switched to Arctic intelligence related to the Cold War.

As a legacy from the 1939–45 war, Search and Rescue (SAR) was equipped with radar that could locate enemy submarines or ships in distress. Helicopters were added for remote areas, together with survival gear, equipment, and rations under International Civil Aviation Organization (ICAO) agreements. Aid to the civil power was another important activity in flood and other disasters.

In the Korean War, No. 426 Transport Squadron of the RCAF was ordered on short notice to open a trans-Pacific service in cooperation with the USAF's Military Air Transport Service (MATS), sending five aircraft weekly to and from Japan using a rotation of only six aircraft, which meant 155 hours per month per crew. This was reduced by

MATS to 110 hours as more crews became available. The service made 599 round trips before it was discontinued in 1954.

North American F-86 Sabre Jets (ER 31.4) were ordered in 1949 to replace the older de Havilland Vampires (ER 8). The Sabres were built in Canada for home defense or NATO commitments; but the first twenty-six pilots were operationally trained by the USAF in Korea, where they flew fifty-mission tours compared to the one hundred for USAF fighter pilots. At first, men experienced in World War II were sent, but then the need to have qualified junior pilots changed priorities.

The Cold War saw Avro Lancasters recovered from storage, refurbished, and used for RCAF reconnaissance, east and west coasts, until in 1955 Lockheed P2V Neptunes (ER 115) could replace some, to be followed in 1958 by the Canadair CL-28 Argus (ER 574) in the Maritime Air Command. The threat of a Soviet Air Force attack on Canada called for a home defense force of nine fighter squadrons, while the much more vulnerable RCAF squadrons in the United Kingdom needed another nine, upped in 1951 to twelve. The first six squadrons went by sea, but the later six flew across via Newfoundland, Greenland, and Iceland. By early 1955, the RCAF had a whole air division in France and Germany. It was the golden age of the RCAF's largest fighter force, when the air force as a whole had 55,700 personnel.

In 1961, Canadair began supplying the first of 1,791 Lockheed F-104 Starfighters to the RCAF and its allies, but at the same time the Avro CF-100 "Clunk" (ER 90) was withdrawn from NATO and the twelve squadrons of the 1st Air Division reduced to six. The CF-100s were a single-seat nuclear strike force that reduced the USSR's options to nuclear war or to none at all. These individual-mission pilots were 3,600-hour veterans, married, with two or three children. By 1972, the nuclear weapons had been withdrawn. In the 1980s, when the Avro CF-18 Hornet (ER 124.4) began to come on line, it was strictly a conventional and reconnaissance aircraft.

Because maneuver space was limited in West Germany, NATO pilots were trained in Canada starting in 1951. By early 1957, 4,500 pilots and navigators from ten NATO countries had passed through the Canadian program, when it was then reduced to serve only Norway, Denmark, the Netherlands, and Germany.

Meanwhile, the air defense of North America was worked out jointly with the U.S. Air Force, which had free passage over Canada. After the Soviet atomic bomb test in 1949, the threat was seen as no longer remote, and radar "fences" were erected and updated to match jet bombers and then intercontinental missiles. In the air, an organization arose, similar to the "clubby" Royal Auxiliary Air Force in the United Kingdom, flying older aircraft until 1955, when F-86 Sabres were introduced. But since 1945 the RCAF had realized it needed a long-range Canadian-built jet interceptor with great temperature tolerance and a 650 nm radius of action. The result was the Avro CF-100.

The RCAF's Ultimate War Plan of 1952 had envisaged the need for a 300,000-man force of 116 squadrons; but even such a force would let 70 percent of an attacker's aircraft through, and that was unacceptable in a nuclear age. Thus, a deterrent force had to be the responder. The CF-100 began to reach squadrons in 1953. The planned successor, the Avro CF-105 Arrow (ER 223.2) was beyond the Canadian budget and was cancelled in a loudly debated move in 1959. The successor McDonnell/Canadair CF-101 Voodoo (ER 252) was never fitted with its nuclear weapons, even though the pronouncement of the death of the nuclear bomber was premature. Nor did the RCAF's Boeing Bomarc-B SAM work out well, even with the DEW line radar, which also raised questions of Canada's sovereignty, especially as Canada became even more integrated into the North American Air Defense Command (NORAD) in 1958. The USAF commander at Colorado Springs, or his Canadian deputy, could order the RCAF into action. In the 1962 Cuban missile crisis, Canadian forces were put on full alert without Cabinet consent. The politicians then reached a critical point after fence-sitting, when the retiring USAF NATO commander declared that Canadian refusal to put "nukes" on the Honest John missiles in Germany would be in violation of treaty commitments. This split Washington and Ottawa and led to Canadian parliamentary elections. However, by 1972, the obligation to carry the warheads had been diplomatically disposed of, except for the question of arming the CF-101.

Elsewhere and contemporaneously the RCAF had been involved in United Nations peacekeeping, both as long-range airlift and by in-theater operations, in New Guinea, Yemen, and Lebanon, as well as in the Congo. In the latter, the commanding officer had to direct operations in eight languages! Another peacetime activity was the use of aerobatic teams to show off the RCAF at home and abroad, as epitomized in the Snowbirds, with new pilots and old jet trainers.

In the usual worldwide pattern of failed evaluation of pilot and aircrew needs, the RCAF released 500 experienced aircrew in 1965 as an economy measure, only in the next year to have to try to get them back from the airlines.

Meanwhile, in 1964, the Canadian Defence Force—the army, navy, and air force—emerged as a single service in a green uniform, with the National Defence Act of 1967 officially uniting them in 1968. The RCAF simply became part of the defense forces, as the Canadian Air Force. In 1970, when the last aircraft carrier, HMCS *Bonaventure,* was paid off, the naval defense force was left with only helicopters.

In parallel action, since 1945 the Canadian army had also sought its part in air matters to ensure that its needs would be met. This led to air-portability concepts—everything should be movable by air— and to the Canadian Airborne Regiment, which was short-lived. The army also sought to get air observation post (AOP) Taylorcraft Auster XIIs (ER 0.09), and they acted as the eyes of the Canadian Division in Korea. All of this necessitated low-level, nap-of-the-earth flying, for which the joint training center in Manitoba was ideal. In 1975, Air Command re-emerged because the single-defense-force concept did not work, and in 1985 distinctive air and naval uniforms were re-introduced.

The Cold War, 1947–91, was costly, especially in equipment; and, thus, RCAF personnel were ever more tightly stretched at close to 90,000. Bases were closed and units shrunk. The re-equipment promised in 1985 did not receive approval, and only fifteen to eighteen CF-18 pilots each year were being trained. Much was privatized, including a return to the World War II concept of civilian elementary flying training schools (EFTS), as well as other non-operational activities.

As the Cold War receded, the joint RCAF/ USAF Pinetree radar line across Canada and the DEW line were closed, but arguments over a toxic waste legacy at air bases and radar stations have persisted. Low-level roles even before that were hazardous in a CF-104: of 750 Canadians who flew them, 37 were killed; 84 ejected successfully, and 7 did not. When the 138 new CF-18 Hornets were delivered from the United States, they formed three squadrons in NATO and four at home in Canada. The NATO squadrons had been disbanded by 1993, but had to be called back to Europe to participate in the post-Yugoslav uncertainties in the Balkans and in Bosnia in 1998.

Meanwhile, in the Persian Gulf War of 1991, the twenty-four Canadian CF-18s flew 2,700 hours and undertook fifty-six radar strikes, the first Canadian operational war sorties since 1945.

By the year 2000 and beyond, the question was again what role should the costly Canadian Air Force play in an unstable world?

THE DECLINE OF AIR FORCES

In 1996, Poland decided to cut its air force by the year 2005 to 230 aircraft from 352, it personnel to 41,000 from 53,500, and its radar sites from to 175 from 300. But SAM units would rise by one to forty-three. The MiG-29s were expected to last until 2016; and helicopters were moved to the army.

In 2001, the Italian Air Force decided to lease thirty-four McDonnell Douglas F-15 Eagles (ER 187), as it had earlier twenty-four Panavia Tornadoes (ER 72), to replace its aging F-104 Starfighters until the Eurofighter Typhoon would become available to it in about 2010.

Norway, in 2001, elected to scale back its air force to meet peacetime demands for a smaller air service and command structure by 2005. Ten F-16 Fighting Falcons will be stored, leaving a front-line force of forty-eight.

In 2001, the Royal New Zealand Air Force had to scrap its combat wing of seventeen Douglas A-4K Skyhawks (ER 26) and sixteen Aeromacchi trainer/strike aircraft. It was left with Lockheed P-3 Orion (ER 794.2) maritime patrol aircraft and Lockheed C-130H Hercules transports (ER 344, C-130B); personnel was reduced from 1,100 to 750 by 2003. Royal Australian Navy pilots would no longer be trained in New Zealand. Maritime air patrol was expected to be contracted out.

In 2002, Sweden had to close its bases F-16 at Uppsala and F-10 at Angelholm, causing a re-evaluation of the training system; only eight bases and a joint-services headquarters were left for the Royal Swedish Air Force.

The Belgian Air Force, early in 2002, lost its independence when it became the army air component with six squadrons of seventy-two F-16 Fighting Falcons. Twenty F-16s in storage were to be kept to sustain the seventy-two operational until 2015. All of the Belgian armed forces were reconfigured for humanitarian operations based on a 1991 budget: 75 percent for salaries, 20 percent for training, and 5 percent for procurement. By 2015, according to the 2001 Belgian plan, the country's armed forces will be shrunk from 44,000 to 39,500 personnel in a single organization with Tactical Air Command absorbed into Command Operations Air (COMOPSAIR). Senior officers will belong to an executive branch, and twenty-five establishments will have been closed. Air force logistics will become an army responsibility.

Hungary in 2002 opted to lease Saab/Bae Systems JAS 39 Gripen (ER 78) for twelve years, as opposed to used F-16s. Industrial costs would be offset 100 percent, with 30 percent being direct. Nevertheless, funding problems had cut the original order of thirty-six to fourteen.

On the other hand, the 1991 cancellation of the U.S. Navy's proposed Curtiss A-12 Shrike led to lawsuits, first settled in favor of Boeing and General Dynamics and then reversed in federal claims court. The contractors decided to appeal the $4.4 billion judgment against them.

Clearly the trend to reduction was evident by 2003. Air forces that faced no immediate threat and had no peacekeeping role would shrink for political and economic reasons and would possibly disappear or be absorbed into a regional force, such as the European Community (the former European Union).

THE MILITARY AIRCRAFT INDUSTRY

Before World War II, the international aircraft industry had concentrated upon military orders with a growing airliner sideline and a smaller general aviation component.

The 1939–45 war had, of course, seen a vast expansion of the industry and the demise or destruction of its factories in Germany, France, Poland, Italy, and Japan. In the free world, the United States became dominant. After 1945, the British industry declined, and the French rose from the ashes. The USSR maintained a modernizing industry as part of employment policy; and China, Canada, and Brazil entered the marketplace. What stimulated growth and advances was the jet engine.

The Jet Engine

Though belated, Hans von Ohain in Germany and Frank Whittle and Frank B. Halford in the

United Kingdom had already been at work on jets before the war. The U.S. Navy and the U.S. Army Air Corps, however, were not interested, thought the ideas impractical, had failed to follow the subject in spite of an international conference in Italy in 1935, and had neither funds nor vision, especially in the key headquarters staff. The United States finally became involved when in 1943 Gen. Henry H. "Hap" Arnold saw the initial film of the Gloster jet prototype test and turned the American ability to apply science to the task. He selected General Electric, with its electric-power and supercharger experience and its metallurgical knowledge, and Bell Aircraft to build America's first jet aircraft, the P-59 Airacomet (ER 5.94), which was a failure due to a shroud of secrecy and a refusal to work with NACA—the National Advisory Committee for Aeronautics, which deprived Bell of the necessary high-speed wind-tunnel design data. The U.S. reputation was saved by Kelly Johnson's Lockheed P-80 Shooting Star (ER 27, P-80C/F-80C), an independent outside effort by a skilled designer.

By 1945, the Whittle centrifugal and the Halford, General Electric, and Westinghouse axial-flow engines were running and had been tested at the NACA facility at Cleveland.

Pratt & Whitney was tooled up for immense piston-engine contracts, which were cancelled when the war ended. Pratt & Whitney and Wright had been excluded from the jet scene by General Arnold's selection of Bell, and now saw a government laboratory competing with them in research, invention, and development. In addition, as the Cold War developed, the possibility arose that the Russians, too, would benefit from both British and German research.

The companies' response to the publication of results of their investigations by governmental laboratories was to invest heavily in their own wind tunnels and testing devices to keep their work proprietary. Unlike piston engines, jet-engine parts could only be tested on a running whole. That made test facilities vital. And in the United States in the late 1940s, the issue of proprietary rights versus national security was a problem then arising.

U.S. companies also sought to get ahead by buying samples of the latest British engines, such as the Rolls-Royce/Whittle Nene, which was also sold to the Soviets—and to the NACA Cleveland Laboratory, the only time NACA had obtained an engine that way. The Nene forced some Americans to realize that funds had to be used more wisely and a better product had to be produced. But not all companies had the expertise and management comprehension to do this. Curtiss-Wright Corporation tried to run before it could walk with the Armstrong-Siddeley Sapphire engine, thus losing the confidence of the USAF.

The Korean War changed American engine production so that jets became the preferred propulsion, although large airliner piston engines would be manufactured until the Douglas DC-7C went out of production and service in the 1960s. By 1953, Pratt & Whitney had designed its own highly successful J-57 (JT for airliners) axial-flow engine and would soon rival GE as the premier American jet-engine maker and compete with Rolls-Royce in the international field. Then the de Havilland Comet I (ER 183.5) crashes put the Americans in the catbird seat to power the Boeing 707 (ER 1,733, 707-320) and the Douglas DC-8 (ER 1,517). At the same time, the U.S. defense companies benefitted from both Korean and Cold War orders, while the British suffered from lack of long-delayed test facilities.

The origin of the jet-engine revolution, which was ultimately mated to airframes to create the jet aircraft, was very different in Britain, Germany, the United States, Japan, Russia, France, and China.

In both Britain and Germany, research and development was encouraged in theoretical as well as practical matters. Both the British and German governments sponsored experimental contracts on a cost-plus basis and had by the mid-1930s jet engines in primitive development. Thus by the early part of World War II, both the Germans and the British had engines and airframes in process, notably the Messerschmitt Me-262 (ER 9.92) and the Gloster Meteor III (ER 15.3), which would be operational in 1944. Once the basic principles were understood, then progress was much more rapid, especially when established firms were brought in to undertake production.

The U.S. Navy, having won the Pacific air war, and in 1945 having ninety-nine carriers of all types, and 29,125 combat aircraft, suddenly found itself without a role. The result was that manpower departed just at a time when technologically the world was changing to jets, guided missiles, and atomic weapons, and angled decks, steam catapults, and mirror-landing systems on its carriers. Although eventually the USN did work out a carrier role in the army-navy-air forces defense triad, including the use of nuclear bombers, in both Korea and Vietnam its flattops were used as almost stationary mobile airfields, and naval aviators were hazarded in ground-support missions. The aircraft also became more complex and expensive, so that maintenance was even more critical than in the Pacific war. This, of course, affected manufacturers as costs climbed. Congress was skeptical, missions were controlled by the White House, and all were criticized as the military-industrial complex.

France was eliminated from the industrial field until after 1945 by its defeat in 1940 and the German plundering of the aircraft industry. The Russians were too busy building tactical low-level aircraft to get involved, until they captured the German scientists in 1945. And the Japanese lacked resources and perspicacity, as did the Italians, to come through beyond prototypes before the war ended in 1945.

Thus, national perceptions of science, bureaucratic mind sets, national policy, and funding, as well as individual talent, determined the great engine and aerodynamic leap forward. And, as noted, Hitler's insistence that the Me-262 also be a dive-bomber sufficiently delayed production so that the Allied bombers and piston-engined fighters could still hold the skies over the Fatherland.

In any war, an air force is only as good as the mix of all its parts, including its commanders—especially when the service is being used as an instrument of policy, which involves political, diplomatic, military, economic, scientific, technological, medical, social, and ideological questions. Many of these factors impinge upon and are brought together in the aircraft industry in peace and war. These complex and often personal relationships, as much as product excellence and management skills, are important, as was to be seen in the fall of Curtiss-Wright between 1946 and 1956.

The USSR

In the Soviet Union the aircraft industry passed along a rather different path than in the West, because the Second World War had shown that the Soviet air forces possessed a number of serious weaknesses. In particular, they were vulnerable to the sort of grand-strategic attack that Anglo-American forces had been using due to the positioning of their infrastructure. Thus, postwar the Russians set out first to build a defensive fighter force and then to develop grand-strategic bombers. In this work they were greatly helped by the fact that four-fifths of the German aircraft production facilities had fallen into their hands, including crates of new but short-lived (ten to twelve hours) axial-flow jet engines (of poor metallurgical quality), together with the specialists to design, produce, and maintain them. (Their British engines, in comparison, were high-quality centrifugal types that provided the MiG-15 over Korea with highly competitive performance.) More than this, the Soviets managed to get most of the German rocket scientists with their experience in high-speed aerodynamics. In 1946, the Soviet grand-strategic bomber force was once again reactivated and given the Tupolev Tu-4 (ER 414), a copy of the American B-29 Superfortress, until turboprop and four-jet bombers were available to carry the atomic weapons the Soviets produced in the 1950s.

The Soviets also knew they needed to develop air transport, for they had seen how successfully the Germans had switched their air power on the Russian front through the use of this. Aeroflot, the USSR's monopolistic airline, had the routes upon which to employ transport aircraft, ironically in part because industry had been scattered east of the Urals as well as rebuilt in traditional areas, thus necessitating bureaucratic travel. While the usual struggles for financial allocations went on between groups favoring one particular type of aircraft or style of fighting, as they did in other air forces, the Soviets had the advantage over the United States in that they did not have two almost equally matched services—like the USAAF and USN— carrying on an annual battle for the financial pie. Rather they had a *Luftwaffe*-style set of forces on the ground and in the air under one commander-in-chief.

The supply of Soviet aircraft to Communist China and the satellites, while at times of benefit in keeping the aircraft industry employed, also saw a number of types manufactured abroad under license agreements alone. Central control over the aircraft industry appears to have provided somewhat clearer direction than in the West, though in the Western countries the close ties between industry and government indicated that the interlocking military-industrial complex may, in fact, be principally controlled. In a nation dedicated to state management as was the USSR, however, allocation of resources, including manpower, was clearly centralized, and there was little place for rival projects. Permanent design teams were kept grouped about a few successful designers such as Tupolev, Mikoyan-Gurevich—"MiG," Sukhoi, Ilyushin, and Antonov until after 1991. Although many Soviet civil aircraft appear to be virtual copies of those produced in the West, this is not true of its fighters or bombers—except for the Tu-4; the bombers have also spawned airliner designs.

On December 26, 1976, the Tu-144 "Concordski" made the world's first commercial supersonic flight at 1,553 mph from Moscow to Alma Ata, Kazakistan. But the aircraft was not a success, and after a time as a freighter and the loss of one at the Paris Air Show, it was taken out of service until the twenty-first century, when a survivor was employed in Russo-U.S. high-speed tests.

By the late 1960s, the Soviets were feeling the loss of the Chinese market, as the latter had shown themselves capable of stealing the latest Soviet designs, such as the MiG-21 sent in 1966 to North Vietnam, or of producing new aircraft themselves. The repercussions of the Sino-Soviet split of their aircraft industries were only partially apparent by 1970. What was clear was that as the needs for the defensive fighter and the grand-strategic bomber were replaced with missiles, the Russians began once more to pay greater attention to ground-attack aircraft and to helicopters.

In the years 1971–91, three worldwide patterns in aircraft production can be noted: generally competitive bidding, as in the West; state-managed private enterprise; and total state direction, as in Russia.

The Russian trend was to continue to produce aircraft to keep design teams and factories busy, because costs were not as important as full employment. But one result was that the aircraft turned out were not as salable abroad as those of the West, and it was also noticeable that the Soviets were more hesitant to make their most recent military types available to even their satellites.

It was significant that in the upheavals of the 1991 fall of the USSR, and with the attempt in Russia to shift to a consumer economy, the design bureaus suddenly found themselves forced to link up with the factories that had made their production aircraft. And the factories found that they had to hustle for business. In these circumstances, with strictly limited finance, few new designs reached the test phase, and the sale of others was not helped by the poor showing of Russian material in Africa, in Iraqi hands in 1991, and in Serbian fists in 1999. Lower wages in Russia, as a result of the now market-driven economy, did not thus translate into significantly lower-priced competition.

The collapse of the Soviet Union and its breakup into the Commonwealth of Independent States (CIS) caused a dramatic shutdown of the military aircraft industry. Production virtually ceased. Civilian airliners received Western electronics and engines, and the former Eastern bloc countries went their independent ways—or, as in the East German case, became reincorporated into Germany, and thus became a Western country. Its air force was merged into the *Luftwaffe,* and by 2003 the former Eastern bloc would be brought into NATO and the European Community.

Aeroflot during this time saw passenger numbers drop 85 percent in Russia and the CIS countries to 28 million, and only slowly recovering by 2003. Exports dropped sharply, except for Mil helicopters.

Aviation technology has always been linked internationally, and if enough manpower and money is managed correctly on the same matter, similar or ingenious solutions are likely to appear. Although by 1998 some Russian aircraft types had Western electronics and engines, on the whole the aircraft industry lacked the finances for survival. Consolidation and overseas sales had to be exploited, but without success. One of the arrangements being worked out in 1998 was to supply South Korea with Sukhoi fighters as an offset to debts Russia owed that country.

And, later, in 1999, although Kosovo showed the Russian Air Force that it had to rearm for diplomatic reasons, and led to small orders to such manufacturers as Sukhoi, MiG-MAPO, and Mil, civil orders over the last decade of the twentieth century plummeted as passenger traffic fell; the civil factories sold less than thirty jet airliners in the five years from 1995 to 1999 inclusive. Help did not come from the U.S. Export-Import Bank, but from the Russian government granting leasing companies legal status. It was hoped that this would siphon off airframes that had sat on the assembly floors since 1990.

But under President Vladimir Putin, the industry was by no means dead; it was being re-organized for modern realities. Aeroflot began to order again, and Russia was by 2003 turning out aircraft such as the Ilyushin Il-96-300 (ER 2,045) freighter with Pratt & Whitney engines, and the Tupolev Tu-204 (ER 563), which is being offered with Rolls-Royce jets. On the other hand, Aeroflot effectively canceled the Il-96 freighter by leasing Douglas DC-10Fs (ER 2,988, DC-10-30).

By 2002, the Russian Air Force was looking for a follow-on next-generation fighter to the MiG-29 and Su-27/30. For the competition, a complex pair of entwined RSK MiG and Sukhoi alliances were being assembled, both of which have built the others' designs. Sukhoi had created a holding company as part of the process of converting four state industries to joint-stock companies, and at the same time, the new Su-35 (ER 173.6, Su-27, 1983) multi-role fighter was being delivered to the Indian Air Force.

In 2002, RSK MiG was working on a modified MiG-29 for both shipboard use and as a multi-role combat aircraft in both single and dual-seat versions with glass cockpits. The engines were to have a time between overhaul (TBO) of 1,000 hours and a life of 2,000, and the new aircraft would now carry 11,220 pounds of fuel versus the older MiG-29's 9,680 pounds. The MiG-29M was competing again for orders in Malaya against the F/A-18.

The Russian aviation industry had twenty-three factories in 2000, too many even for the former USSR's needs, with many building a variety of designs. But just as the design bureaus had shrunk in number in the 1990s, so, too, did the factories. One had dropped out to build agricultural tractors. Even cheap labor had not allowed the Russian aircraft industry to succeed, with capital losses occurring, due to corruption or naiveté, or both, when factories were privatized.

Recognizing that the European and American markets had been lost, in 2000 the Russian government proposed a full inventory of the industry, privatization of some major factories, certification of foreign aircraft in Russia only after other countries accepted Russian aircraft certifications, and an import tax on all foreign aircraft for which there was a Russian equivalent. In addition, Moscow was to take diplomatic and economic steps to boost exports.

The overhaul of the Russian defense industry, by the beginning of 2002, was focused on consolidating by 2010 some 1,600 enterprises into fifty state-controlled holding companies, and only these would be funded for research, development, and production. This would drastically cut over-capacity and all its ills and the huge debts accumulated during the 1990s. The move further consolidated the Sukhoi manufacturing firm and provided a single marketing organization instead of each factory doing its own. The loser, of course, would be the local tax base.

Russian aerospace sales under President Putin had begun to increase in 2001. Sales of between $4 and 5 billion, following $3 billion in 1999 and $3.7 in 2000—second only to the United States—included more than thirty Sukoi Su-27UBKs and Su-30MBKs to China, with sales pending to Iran, Latin America, and Africa.

Russia's aim has been to develop markets other than India, China, and other long-term customers. By 2000, Brazil had signed fighter and launch pacts with Russia and the Ukraine. The Brazilian link will lead to comprehensive trades in many fields, including agriculture and nuclear power. A Brazilian fighter contest was to be settled on both the best price and the best technology-transfer terms, and one of the winners was the Sukhoi Su-35.

By 2001, the Russian aircraft industry had orders for almost 500 Su-27 "Flankers," which with RSK MiG-29s amounted to roughly 80 percent of Russian combat aircraft business. About the same number were operational in the USSR, Southeast Asia, and Africa, thus producing a healthy demand for spares, maintenance, and upgrades, yet with the need for new products after 2010. The Russian engine makers were also being forced into an amalgamation, called NPO Saturn, to be strong enough to compete with the

West and to be able to develop and supply the fifth-generation engines made by a new 35,000-strong workforce; the engine derivatives are also widely used in ground applications.

Also typical of the industry at the time was Russian helicopter specialist Mil, which had been in the doldrums in the 1990s, entering bankruptcy in 1998 due to lack of orders. Private investors struggled for control until President Putin stepped in during the first years of the twenty-first century, allowing the company to begin to raise cash. Russia owns 31 percent and Sikorsky 9.38 percent of Mil. But the company still has to improve lifetimes of both helicopters and engines. Because they fill a niche, the Mi-8/17 (ER 2.56) family of thirty-passenger or four-ton freight helicopters have sold 7,000-plus to fifty-seven countries, while the larger Mi-26 (ER 21.32) with a twenty-ton payload has also been exported to five countries.

As 2003 approached, it was evident that Sukhoi was the leading Russian design and manufacturing consolidation, with MiG and Yakolev likely to be squeezed out, the former especially because it had lost its talents. A lack of commercially skilled personnel had affected the entire industry, except perhaps for those in Aeroflot's international division. The former state airline had lost all of its regional lines to the new Commonwealth of Independent States.

The new government did not understand market regulation and concentrated upon safety; the new airlines had little investment and no long-range strategy. The result was an overall drop in passengers from 160 million in 1990 to 53 million in 1999.

And by the end of 2001, the September 11 terrorist attack in New York City had affected Aeroflat's international line to the extent of 100,000 lost passengers per month with revenues down $18 million. The burden of flying was placed on its aging Tu-154Ms and newer Boeing 737s.

Elsewhere, the venerable Soviet-built Tu-154 (ER 393.8) airliners were also being phased out in the twenty-first century. Malev Hungarian Airlines made its last Tu-154 flight in March 2001, after twenty-nine years of operating the type. Residual value was about $400,000 each for the last five aircraft.

In 2001, however, the Il-96 was revived with Pratt & Whitney engines and Rockwell-Collins electronics; it had earlier died, following ten years in gestation. As the all-Russian Il-96-400, it has begun to sell in both passenger and freight versions.

Also in 2001, as Tu-204s became available, they were to replace Tu-154s at Krasair over the next four years, with ten Tu-204s planned by 2005 and also ten Tu-214s (ER n/a), the purchase buoyed by profits. In late 2001, Russia made its first export sale of Tu-204s—to China, five Rolls-Royce-powered examples, with options on a further ten. It was a deal brokered by Sirocco Aerospace of Egypt, which had the exclusive license and was to set up a bonded spares store and a Tu-204 simulator in China.

And Aeroflot also had begun, earlier in 2000, to build alliances. By the end of that year, four Russian airlines had finally been linked together, at Domodedovo Airport, Moscow. The alliance had 177 flights, with 97 aircraft of 12 types, operating on 44 routes, carrying 1.46 million passengers and 46,000 tons of cargo.

In all, during 2000, Russia's 300 airlines flew 21.76 million passengers. Aeroflot enjoyed an 11 percent increase on domestic routes, and though it had dropped "international" from its logo, it was expected to join the Delta-Air France Skyteam alliance. Unlike those in the United States, the major airlines in Russia improved, while the regionals declined.

By 2003, then, Russia—like France in 1950—was beginning to emerge again as an aviation player.

China

China did not have an aircraft industry before 1949. The story of how the country got to that date and what has happened since is inextricably blended with China's political and military history. The beginnings can be traced back to 1921 when post-1918 European and American salesmen saw a potential market. However, sales were fitful and oscillated between Soviet and American types until, about 1934, Stalin concentrated upon rearmament in the West and against Japan's adventures in the East. Americans filled the sales vacuum through Hong Kong until the Japanese cut off that source.

The situation in China was both an international struggle and an internal civil war between the Nationalist government in Nanjing and the warlords, and also the Communist Party (CCP). Chiang Kai-shek, who had been part of the 1912 overthrow of the imperial government and the establishment of the Republic of China, regarded the Communist Party as the country's main threat. Given the geography, distances, and lack of roads and railways, Chiang viewed an air force as a necessity. And the battles against the Japanese over Shanghai in 1932 drove the lesson home. Thus Chiang bought aircraft abroad and encouraged foreigners to establish companies in China.

From 1926 to 1929 an international arms embargo had been in place against China, but armament was a lucrative business and the prohibition was withdrawn. The availability of arms enabled renewed civil war in South China in 1936. By 1937, the Nationalist Air Force had been the catalyst in unifying the country. But this worried the Japanese and brought on hostilities once again, forcing the Americans to limit assistance of instructors and aircraft to the Chinese Air Force. However, the American aircraft industries needed sales to China to offset the Great Depression and to save a national military resource.

In the second half of 1937, the Chinese Air Force held its own, but then the United States pulled back and prohibited Americans to fly for China. The CAF thus turned to the USSR during 1938–40. U.S. commercial interests remained active in the south of China, but the isolationist U.S. State Department imposed an embargo on exports to the country. And then the deteriorating

Igor Sikorsky, the pioneer Russian American aircraft designer, arrived in America in 1919 as a result of the Russian Revolution, with the goal "to construct aircraft," as his passport noted. He is pictured here in his later years, with one of the Sikorsky Aircraft "direct-lift" helicopters. (Sikorsky Aircraft)

Young Chinese female aircrew in winter flying gear. The aircraft is a North American AT-6 Texan (Harvard) (ER 1.59), another legacy from the Nationalists and the U.S. Fourteenth Air Force stay in China. (People's Liberation Army Air Force)

The Red Chinese Air Force—the People's Liberation Army Air Force (PLAAF)—inherited in 1949 a motley collection of Nationalist planes, including North American P-51 Mustang fighters (ER 9.63, P-51D) and North American B-25 Mitchell bombers (ER 23). (People's Liberation Army Air Force)

PLAAF pilots in the 1950s. (People's Liberation Army Air Force)

The PLAAF also inherited Soviet Il-2 Shturmovik attack aircraft (ER 3.7). (People's Liberation Army Air Force)

PLAAF pilots run to man their MiG-15s (ER 20). This was a Soviet design, exported to China and manufactured there from 1958 as the F-2. Chinese and North Korean pilots had flown the MiG-15 against USAF North American F-86 Sabre Jets (ER 31.4), but had suffered from their poor training. (People's Liberation Army Air Force)

License-built F-2s (MiG-15) over the Chinese countryside. Sometimes the enemy was the USSR, and at other times it was Taiwan. At this period, PLAAF pilots were not considered very aggressive. (People's Liberation Army Air Force)

The *Kiev,* a Soviet helicopter carrier of the l960s. In the oscillations of international developments, the first Soviet response to the new 1950s threat of the U.S. Navy's aircraft carriers was the Kuril Class of helicopter carriers for anti-submarine, anti-Polaris missile threats. The normal delays in creating and funding new technologies led to the new 1990 ocean-going fleet carriers being caught in the wind-down of the USSR. One of the carriers actually completed was sold to India; others were scrapped. (USN)

Almost contemporaneously with the advent of the Cold War (1947–91) came a dramatic change in the shapes in the air, stemming from German wartime work in high-speed aerodynamics and German and British work on jet propulsion. The Cold War and the "hot" war in Korea (1950–53) saw a quantum leap forward in performance, and an eagerness to find out what the other side was doing. One result was the capture of this Soviet MiG-15 (ER 20), now exhibited at the San Diego Air Museum. (San Diego Air Museum)

One way for the West to gather intelligence was to take photographs of new aircraft flown in the annual May Day parade in Moscow. But the Soviets knew this, and thus they presented prototypes well before the production machines were operational—a game of intellectual ping-pong. Shown here is the Sukhoi Su-7 (ER 82) in 1961. The Su-7 was the size of a Douglas DC-3 or a Vickers Wellington, but could do Mach 1.8. (USN)

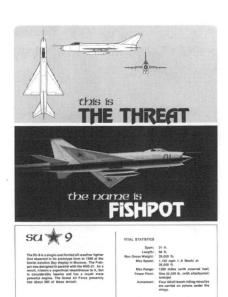

The Cold War encouraged aircraft manufacturers to seek orders, and one way to do so was to make the public and Congress aware of the enemy threat, as in this McDonnell Douglas ad of the late 1960s, featuring the 1956 Sukhoi Su-9 (ER 64.26).

The Soviets did not fall fully into the jet age, but sensibly adopted the turboprop because of its more economical operation at lower altitudes, especially for oceanic surveillance sorties. Here, a Tupolev Tu-20B (ER 2,652) is shadowed over the Mediterranean by a USN McDonnell F-4 Phantom II (ER 370). Note the immense counter-rotating propellers. (USN)

Another Tu-20 is this time being escorted by an LTV F-8 Crusader (ER 68). The cockpit windows give an indication of the size of the aircraft. (USN)

The Tupolev Tu-18 (ER 2,594), NATO code-named Badger, was a contemporary of the British V-bombers, and shows it in the buried engines in the wing roots. The aircraft was used for long-range sorties over the Pacific and elsewhere. (USN)

Initially seen at Tsushino airfield in Moscow, in 1961, the Tupolev Tu-22 (ER 477) was the first of the Soviet Air Force large aircraft to have rear-mounted engines and a fixed refueling probe on the nose. The fuselage was area-ruled—"wasp-waisted" for low drag—as in the USAF's Convair F-106 Delta Dart (ER 212.5). The Tu-22 had an all-moving slab tailplane, evidence that the Soviets monitored Western developments and adopted innovations. Though supersonic, the Tu-22 still had a multi-wheel undercarriage suitable for grass airfields, always a Soviet Air Force requirement. An F-106 is preserved at the U.S. Air Force Museum in Dayton. (USN)

The Mikoyan-Gurevich MiG-21 (ER 14.2) was not only built in quantity in the USSR from 1957 on, but it was also widely exported to Communist satellite states. Many are still in service in 2003, either in their original form or updated and uprated. The parachute seen in the photo was used on many aircraft from fighters to the Boeing B-47 Stratojet (ER 992) to shorten the landing run. This aircraft belongs to the Soviet Air Force Kerelian Wing. (Source unknown)

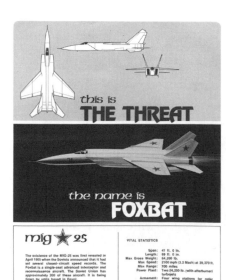

The MiG-25 (ER 179) was a mid-1960s high-altitude interceptor and low-level strike aircraft capable of nearly 2,000 mph (Mach 3). It claimed several records, including carrying a payload of 4,409 pounds to over 98,000 feet, and was deployed to Egypt for a while. (McDonnell Douglas)

A Red Air Force Kaman Ka-25 helicopter (ER n/a), first seen in 1961, was evidence that the free-turbine machine was still in production for both military and civilian use. (USN, 1971)

Also seen in 1961 during the aggressive Kruschev era was the Myasishchev M-52 (ER n/a), here accompanied by two MiG-21s. The M-52 was not a success, and after two were built the designer was appointed head of TsAGI, the Russian aeronautical technical institute. In contrast, the MiG-21 was very successful. (USN)

By the 1980s, the Tupolev Tu-26 Backfire B (ER 2,930) was in production, and used for maritime reconnaissance, here being escorted over the Baltic by a Swedish Air Force JA-37 Viggen (ER 162.7). (Royal Swedish Air Force)

Another view of the swept-wing supersonic Tupolev Tu-26 Backfire. (Royal Swedish Air Force)

Games of "chicken" were played all over the world between Communist air forces and Western surveillance and intelligence-gathering planes in international air space. This photograph was taken by a Norwegian Air Force aircrewman, and shows a MiG-29 Fulcrum (ER 157) just before it collided with a RNAF patrol plane. (Royal Norwegian Air Force)

The new Sukhoi Su-35 (ER 173.6, Su-27, 1983), is shown taking off at ILA '96—the International Aviation Exhibition (*Internationale Luftfahrt-Ausstellung*)at Berlin-Brandenburg. In the post-Soviet world, the Russians have been eager to let Westerners test-fly their aircraft in hopes of sales. The Su-35 is a formidable challenge to fighters such as the McDonnell Douglas F-15 Eagle (ER 187), General Dynamics F-16 Fighting Falcon (ER 113, A/B models), and Grumman F-14 Tomcat (ER 129), all of which are a generation older, though later models have vastly increased performance. (ILA '96 photo by Chris Sorensen)

European situation, due to German aggression, caused the Soviets to withdraw. Thus, in 1941, President Franklin D. Roosevelt began Lend-Lease of matériel to China and that led, along with the U.S. oil embargo against Japan, to the Japanese assault at Pearl Harbor.

Parallel to the Nationalist approach was that of the Chinese Communists. The Chinese Air Force was "founded" in 1924 by Chang Qiankon and Wang Bi at a time when the Communist Party of China and the Kuomintang had a united front. Chang had gone to the USSR and had studied the Red Air Force until 1940, and up to the following year the USSR had supplied credits, arms, and aircraft.

Air operations in China had been going on since at least 1937. They were confused by the Japanese invaders fighting the Nationalist Chinese, who were gradually assisted by the American Volunteer Group, and who were in turn also fighting the Chinese Communists. After Pearl Harbor, the Ledo Road from Burma was supplemented by the airlift over the Himalayas—the "Hump"—with matériel for the Chinese and the Americans, and by USAAF manpower and aircraft. The AVG became the USAAF's Fourteenth Air Force, commanded by the renowned Gen. Claire Lee Chennault. The Fourteenth Air Force eventually operated from airfields behind the Japanese—who controlled only cities, ports, and railways—and attacked Shanghai. But these AVG activities were stopped by a Japanese ground offensive. B-29s of the USAAF's Twentieth Air Force were based briefly in Chiang Kai-shek's China, but the supply process was so tedious that they were soon moved to Pacific island bases within striking distances of Japan itself.

The Chinese Civil War, 1945–49

After 1945, U.S. forces withdrew from China and Chiang and the Communist leader Mao Tse-tung fought a civil war that ended in 1949 with the Nationalists withdrawing to Formosa (Taiwan), thus ending a struggle that had begun in 1927.

When the Soviets in 1945 liberated Manchuria, China's northernmost region, they gave Mao the beginnings of an air force, and the U.S. Marine Corps protected the Nationalists on the coast around Beijing until June 1946, making little use of their F4U Corsairs.

For its part, the Nationalists, the Kuomintang Party (KMT), were well equipped with wings of P-51 Mustangs, P-47 Thunderbolts, P-40 Warhawks, B-25 Mitchells, B-24 Liberators, C-47 Skytrains, and C-46 Commandos. Nevertheless, by 1947 the People's Liberation Army (PLA) under Mao was gaining the upper hand. But as in other civil wars, it was not the combat aircraft, but the transports that were significant in a land that was the size of the United States, but with poor non-riverine supply lines.

General Chennault returned to China under United Nations auspices to organize and fly AVG relief sorties, until the contract ran out, and then Civil Air Transport (CAT) was created to support the KMT. But CAT's problems were primarily fuel and maintenance, for the enemy had few anti-aircraft weapons. The PLA, however, took cities and airfields and the CAT was pushed back to Kunming. As defeat became evident, the CAT and its rivals, including the China National Aviation Corporation (CNAC), flew their aircraft to sanctuary in Hong Kong and eventually to Taiwan. The U.S. Central Intelligence Agency helped Chennault buy CNAC, and in 1952 he finally got the aircraft out of Hong Kong to Taiwan. The CIA-CAT relationship would become significant in the future.

The People's Liberation Army Air Force

In 1941, Chang returned to his homeland where he served as a maintenance expert and eventually deputy commissar of the People's Liberation Army Air Force (PLAAF). The real basis for the PLAAF was the founding of the air force engineering school in 1941, by the CCP's Central Military Committee, and three years later an aviation section, both run by Chang and Wang. Not until the Japanese surrender in 1945 were aircraft available for the school, together with technicians who stayed on to train some 560 personnel, including 126 pilots.

In the next eleven years, the PLAAF grew, especially after the start of the Korean War, when it acquired modern Soviet aircraft including the MiG-15. Air divisions and anti-aircraft regiments were established, the latter under a new air defense headquarters, which also controlled searchlights and radar to defend cities from Nationalist attacks from Taiwan during 1949–50.

When in 1949 the Communists gained full control of China, the PLAAF had a logistician's nightmare—159 foreign-made aircraft of 21 different types spread across 542 "airfields." Most of the 220 pilots and 30 navigators were of the CCP, but most of the 2,373 ground crew were former Nationalists, and a mixed 100 were Japanese. (Other sources give 2,302 personnel, 113 aircraft, 1,270 aircraft engines, 40,910 tons of equipment, 40 airfields, and 12 factories, nearly all damaged.)

The PLAAF acquired some of the machines left behind by the Nationalists, new aircraft manufactured in former Japanese factories in Mukden and Harbin, Manchuria, and Soviet MiG-15s paid for with gold. Soon the PLAAF had a sizable equipment cache from which to patch the 200-odd KMT P-51s and P-47s.

The Korean War, 1950–53, subsequently stimulated the establishment of PLAAF command and airfield repair organizations, to acquire enough aircraft for twenty-eight divisions and to gain combat experience. As in the case of the RAF in the Great War, the PLAAF was on such sound lines that it was still using the same structure in 2003. And the veterans of the Korean War commanded the PLAAF through the 1980s. By 1953 the PLAAF had MiG-15 fighters and Il-28 (ER 37) bombers. Five of the bases north of the Yalu had each been capable of handling 300 MiGs.

Ordered to go on the offensive, but denied targets in South Korea for fear of reprisals, and lim-

ited by the one hundred-mile radius of action of the MiGs, Gen. Liu Yalou, commander of the PLAAF, began secretly to build airfields inside North Korea with radar coverage and control, which extended well across the 38th Parallel. The ground-control intercept (GCI) at Andong in China could take care of MiG Alley. By 1955, the new airfields were defended by 785 anti-aircraft guns, 1,672 automatic weapons, and more than 300 searchlights effective up to 30,000 feet, weather permitting. However, the U.S. Far Eastern Air Force (FEAF) B-29s, based in Japan, were able to make the new airfields unusable so that the Communists never had effective air support.

The PLAAF used the Korean War to blood its pilots, rotating them through in a three-month combat cycle and then sending them for R&R, in which to mull over what they had learned. However, since the USAF F-86 Sabre Jets had the upper hand, the PLAAF suffered for the good of China, due to inexperience and in spite of Soviet tutelage. Battles with a first-class air power, they learned, were very expensive. From an optimistic viewpoint, maintenance on the ground benefitted a good deal from the experience. The war taught the Chinese the need both for political commissars to maintain morale until victory, and the need for technical superiority. As a result, by 1953, the PLAAF training system had become one of the best in the world.

In June 1950, the United States had inserted the carrier *Valley Forge* into the Formosa Straits to prevent a KMT invasion of the mainland. However, the KMT in Taiwan benefitted from the Korean War as it distracted Beijing, and by 1954 the Chinese Nationalist Air Force (CNAF) had two Republic F-84G Thunderjet wings (ER 78, F-84F), in addition to F-51s and F-47s, as well as B-25s and B-24s. In 1954, a duel over control of the nearby islands of Quemoy and Matsu was calmed by the presence of two U.S. Navy carriers.

During 1949–53, the PLAAF had supported the pacification of Tibet by using six C-47s and C-46s to drop supplies to the troops making the difficult uphill advance, helped by a few Soviet Il-12s. In all, fifty-one tons were dropped. The air force also went after bandits in Sichuan and Gansu provinces during 1952–53.

In 1954, China reorganized the PLAAF along Soviet lines under a new Ministry of National Defense. The anti-aircraft forces were then also brought under air force control, and the next year the PLAAF was made the equal of the People's Liberation Army (PLA) and the People's Liberation Navy (PLN). The air force now totaled 149,000 personnel in a fully integrated establishment. However, two administrative and operational structures remained intertwined into the twenty-first century, with six regional headquarters and eleven major functional departments in Beijing replicated in the regional setup. The PLAAF was designed for air defense and not for ground support.

At this time, to counter the Nationalists' aggressiveness, the People's Republic of China (PRC) placed 200 modern Soviet aircraft on five airfields. But that was the extent of their defensive posture because the air force lacked an organized intelligence system, had never worked with the other services, could not fly in bad weather or navigate over water, and did not have a wartime logistics system. This was then the only time other than in Korea that the PLAAF became involved in ground-support activities.

In 1958, with the U.S. distracted by Lebanon, the PLA attacked the Nationalist-held offshore island of Quemoy with the intent of interdicting the Nationalist resupply routes and thus causing Quemoy and Mattsu to surrender. The action was also designed both to probe U.S. intentions and to aid the start of Mao's Great Leap Forward. In preparation for this new campaign, command and control was established in Fuijian province, command philosophy was set, and the fliers trained under realistic conditions with the help of political commissars. The Soviets supplied new MiG-17s and radar. The Nationalists countered with their new F-86Fs escorting RF-84s, and the U.S.

Seventh Fleet inserted four carriers into the area to prevent a PRC invasion of Taiwan. Due to a shortage of parts, the PLAAF fighters flew only once every four days. Nevertheless, large air battles developed and on September 24 the first use of an air-to-air missile in combat occurred when the KMT air force used Sidewinders to down four MiGs. Neither side bombed the other's airfields, but C-46s supplying the islands were ambushed by low-level MiG-17s after their escort had been decoyed away.

In 1960, CNAF flights began over the People's Republic of China. The CIA had arranged for the CNAF to get two Lockheed U-2 Gray Ghosts (ER 45) to make the 3,000-mile round trip to the PRC's Lop Nor nuclear development site in Sinkiang and the test range in Kansu. The first U-2 was lost in 1962 and the second in 1963, but they were replaced, as were another nine, up to 1974, that had been shot down. In 1979, the United States recognized the PRC and broke off diplomatic relations with Taiwan. By 1981, America was co-manning a Cold War post at Lop Nor to listen in to the Soviets.

On the whole, the PLAAF had continued to lack offensive spirit and the ability to coordinate with the surface forces. Nevertheless, it was by 1959 a major military air force with a permanent presence in South China. But at the same time, Mao's new hostility to the USSR cut off its sources of instruction and supply—setbacks that still affected the PLAAF into the twenty-first century.

The PRC Aircraft Industry

The real birth of modern aviation in the People's Republic of China dates from the Communist Mao's victory in 1949. The 1949–53 plan was to train 25,400 technical personnel and to expand the PLAAF to 290,000, which was done. By 1954, some 3,000 aircraft were in the inventory and 6,000 pilots. The formative phase had begun in 1951 and, after the Great Leap Forward, lasted until 1961. Control of development was under the Communist Party, and the guiding ethic was self-reliance.

Great faith was placed in the importation of Soviet aviation technology, and much emphasis was placed upon both the training of cadres and upon enticing former Nationalist specialists to serve Mother China. The process adopted was cautious, but sensible: first, to salvage some 750 aircraft and to practice the manufacture of parts by creating the spares with which these derelicts could be returned to service; from there, to design aircraft in time for the Great Leap Forward, as experience was accumulated.

Repair factories with professional skills, equipment, and materials were scarce. What was really needed was an industry to produce a large number of aircraft, but such a complex needed not only factories, but also research facilities and schools. However, before this industry could even take off, the Korean War broke out in June 1950 and revealed the extent of China's overall vulnerability. This greatly stimulated Chinese defensive efforts. New aircraft were vital, and with Soviet assistance, the Ministry of Heavy Industry was placed in high-priority charge with Chairman Mao's full approval. By 1953, 1,626 machines of sixteen types were available; a five-year plan was in place, and 143 projects were underway, including new jet fighters and engines. Three years later, accessories factories were begun, which enjoyed the latest technology and machinery. The Shenyang Factory within a year had 13,000 people producing jet engines.

By 1958, thanks to excellent Soviet tutelage, Chinese aviation was able to become independent, with a workforce of 100,000 producing piston-engined trainers, jet engines, and machine tools. Not only had recruits from the KMT and new workers been trained, but the government directed that educated persons were to join those being transferred from other defense industries. As the whole PRC educational system was improved, more personnel became available. Spares, always such an important weakness, were now built by factories devoted only to their production, in which accuracy and management were emphasized. By 1953, enough spares had been accumulated that a new Yak-18 could be assembled; it flew in 1954.

At the same time, work on the license-built J-5 (ER 26.6, MiG-17) proceeded so rapidly that the first flight took place in 1956 with a Chinese-built engine. As a result of solid government support, China had reached the ranks of the world's foremost aircraft manufacturers—Britain, France, the USSR, and the United States. In 1956, Mao agreed to a twelve-year plan to develop scientific research and development, so that the PRC would have the ability to design, develop, and produce its own advanced aircraft. Again skilled personnel were transferred and wind tunnels built, and shortly a light Chinese jet trainer appeared, with a new indigenous engine.

But in July 1960, the Soviet Union abrogated all contracts—the People's Republic of China aircraft industry was left completely on its own. But it met the challenge through scientific training institutes and soon was producing materials and accessories. The policy of adjustment, consolidation, replenishment, and improvement led to the realization of these goals.

By 1961, the industry had produced 767 fighters, 238 trainers, and 41 transports, and missile production had been started.

In the second five-year plan, factories were built across China to disperse the largesse, but this time expansion was far too fast and the dilution hurt the industry. Both proposed supersonic fighters, the East Wind 106 and the 113, had to be canceled. Capital projects were under-funded, delayed, and of inferior quality; scientific management was weakened; and quality control lost. The introduction into the industry of Communist self-criticism proved to be self-destructive.

However, as the nascent Cultural Revolution of 1965–69 spread, in those same years, when a strong focus was placed on making the PLAAF operational, development projects were cut to one fighter, one trainer, and one transport, and the other ten projects canceled or slowed dramatically. A step-by-step approach was taken to implementing batch production of the MiG-21. Within two years only two engine and two airframe factories existed, with the ancillary electronics industry being heavily revamped. In times of economic hardship for the defense industry, the Minister urged cadres to pull together and thus infused a new spirit into the industry, while at the same time protecting it from ideological pressure so that it could be creative. This resulted in a careful management approach from standards, to plans, to tooling, to batch production. Inspections led to needed modifications and even rebuilding, to achieve quality once again, all guided by the "Seventy Rules" published by the Central Committee of the Communist Party of China. Even technical problems such as buffeting in the MiG-19 were being solved.

By 1964, when the Ministry of Aviation Industry came into being and a new strategic plan was developed to meet both defense and industrial needs, the workers were also being informed of what was needed and great progress was made. The complexity of the new aircraft could be seen in the fact that the J-5 needed 7,632 different parts and the J-6 (ER 48, MiG-19) 12,319, all of which had to be created out of new super-alloys developed by the metallurgical industries. By Chinese boast, in the mid-1970s the Chinese Rolls-Royce Spey jet engine contained better materials than the original 1957 British version.

In the meantime, on May 14, 1965, the 76-ton Xi'an H-6 (ER n/a), a heavily modified Soviet twin-jet bomber design, had completed an atomic-bomb delivery test. This was followed by the Y-7 (ER n/a), a fifty-passenger airliner, and in 1969 by the arrival of the Q-5 (ER n/a) supersonic attack plane that had been started in the late 1950s as the Nanchang A-5—a MiG-19 derivative—then abandoned, completed by workers on their own time, and accepted by the PLAAF after its own tests and further modifications. The start of production in 1969 indicated that the Nanching

Aircraft Factory by then had a capable and powerful design team.

The MiG-21 was worked over first into the J-7 (ER 40) and then, after 6,000 suggestions and 11,000 wind-tunnel tests, developed into the supersonic high-altitude Shenyang J-8 (ER n/a). The Chinese used a philosophy that Geofrey de Havilland had pioneered in the West—to make the correct combination of the available new technologies rather than to design a whole new machine. The J-8 flew in the midst of the Cultural Revolution, which masked the fact that a new era in Chinese aviation was beginning.

Thus the Red Chinese concentrated on building up both defensive fighter and tactical bomber forces, while developing their technological know-how as rapidly as possible. The result was a regeneration whose significance must not be overlooked. The Chinese tradition of craftsmanship together with patience appeared to be creating an efficient modern force manned by young personnel who were not being lured away by Taiwan Nationalist cash offers. PLAAF personnel available for the periodic battles over North Vietnam and South China seemed to support this, although there were reports, too, that a struggle continued within the air force between the "professional" officer corps and the militia reserve officers. By the 1990s, the Chinese were becoming more internationally aggressive, notably over the sea, while on the other hand air transport was burgeoning with foreign airliners and arrangements to participate in manufacturing with Boeing and Airbus.

On the military side, the development of the PLAAF was plagued by the problems associated with its readiness and combat effectiveness. It was also affected by relations with the two superpowers. In 1968, the USSR began to mass forces in Mongolia, and armed clashes on the China border led to a rapprochement with the United States in 1972.

That the PRC had made such progress was—as in France after World War II—that Premier

Zhou Enlai and the government in Beijing kept a direct oversight of aviation. At the same time, the government insisted that all intellectuals in the industry dress in padded-blue outfits, just like any other worker, and the Premier promulgated "Fourteen Rules" to govern their conduct.

Despite the political turmoil, by 1976 seven new types of aircraft had been developed, which in some cases even had all-weather performance. These developments occurred during a time when the top political and managerial leadership had been maltreated unto death, procedures abolished, and anarchy allowed to reign. Products were warehoused because they were defective, and the PRC aviation industry was on the brink of bankruptcy. Planning had been sacrificed to arbitrary orders for the development of up to twenty-seven new types in 1971 alone, set against impossible goals. These circumstances had delayed the perfection of the J-7 by a decade, and other types took even longer and were never certificated. Thirty others were stopped halfway into the development process, and the money wasted. Time lost could never be made up.

Because of the actions of Lin Biao, made Minister of Defense in 1959, and the "Gang of Four"—the quartet of officials, including Mao's wife, who dominated the political scene during the early 1970s—over one hundred construction projects were started in the mountains and other unsuitable places, where there was no room for runways, no labor, and no raw materials. No feasibility studies had been done, and not even geologists consulted. It was all a terrible waste of resources, manpower, and money, resulting in the disruption and destruction of the aviation educational system. Standards disappeared, and professionals became in short supply.

Premier Zhou Enlai and the vice premier, Deng Xiaoping, were especially concerned as the PRC's defense was being laid bare. Thus, it was from 1972 that the government both insisted on the return to inspections to restore quality and be-

gan importing the Rolls-Royce Spey. In 1975, Vice Premier Deng Xiaoping led criticism of the leftists and at once set about a drastic management reorganization within the industry so that factories could produce what was needed, restore quality, and at the same time ensure the livelihood of the workers.

By 1975 the industry was back on a firm, rational footing. The year appeared to be a peak in the ten years of turmoil, but the leftists again pursued the Cultural Revolution to the detriment of aviation. However, they were on the wane as the Gang of Four had been eliminated, to be replaced by Socialist modernization, much to the benefit of the national economy as well as of the aircraft industry.

By 1979, scientific research again was able to produce the current generation of aircraft, to develop the next, and to begin to study the successor. Foreign trade was emphasized, and in 1982 the PRC Ministers approved the coordination of the development of military and civil aviation, in order to achieve independent design and production, combining the supply system for both domestic and foreign needs, as well as to economize on management. The industry was urged to break through in the development of new products for the PLAAF, the airlines, and for export. And these desires guided the industry from then on, while the Ministry of Defense began to take a new view of the threats to the PRC from the USSR, the United States, and Taiwan.

The factories had been purged between 1978 and 1982 of the Gang of Four's "bad characters," so that by 1982 quality had been restored, along with political unity and stability. Inferior items had been dealt with both at the factories and on PLAAF airfields; inspectors and customers were once more back in charge, as evidenced by the fact that only 58.7 percent of new engines in 1978 were acceptable. From 1982 to 1985, product replacement was accelerated by reorganization and reformation. Younger, more knowledgeable, and professional personnel were brought in. The average age of managers dropped from 53 years in 1981 to 46.2 in 1985, at which time 72 percent had a higher educational background as opposed to 20 percent in 1981.

Quality management was combined with cost effectiveness and economic accounting to measure efficiency, which was also rewarded by institutions and establishments being allowed to keep 40 percent of any profits they made. By 1985, the aviation industry had 222 certified directors, 33,731 middle managers, 11,627 scientific officers, and 60,537 professional managers, all trained since 1983. Productivity since 1978 had gone up 28.4 percent and value 73.8 percent. The best R&D minds were focused on producing aircraft for the 1990s and beyond, into the twenty-first century. In 1978, with half the industry lying idle, 95 percent had been military production. By 1986, civilian production in twenty-nine provinces and cities accounted for 61.2 percent—but, as the Chinese pointed out, excluding the province of Taiwan. Before 1981, Chinese airlines flew mostly foreign aircraft. In 1981, Deng Xiaoping proposed that they should use locally built machines. By 1985, the Harkin Y-12II (ER n/a) as well as the fifty-seat Harkin Y-11 were in service. In April 1986, construction started on license-built McDonnell Douglas MD-82 150-seat jets (ER 439, MD-87), at the time new Chinese turboprops were also coming off the assembly lines. Increasingly, there was international cooperation and exchanges of personnel, not only with American organizations, but with Swedish, German, Japanese, Italian, and Hong Kong companies.

In 1987, the PRC defense sector was brought into the mainstream of the national economy. Civil production became the main task as China shifted to a planned commodity economy.

In the 1990s, Chinese airlines grew rapidly using McDonnell Douglas, Boeing, and Airbus products. By the twenty-first century, the same phenomenon of airline progress in China as elsewhere in the world was taking place.

In the meantime, sophisticated systems for the PLAAF aircraft had been started back in 1977 when Shenyang began developing a fly-by-wire system. Progress speeded up with the use of a J-8II (ER n/a) fighter and, from 1992–95, with computer-controlled foreign technology inputs. A parallel program was also underway at Chengdu for its J-10 (ER n/a) fighter. The first photo of the PLAAF's Chengdu J-10 fourth generation fighter was leaked on the internet in 2001, though it had flown in March 1998. It had originated in the late 1970s as a defense against Soviet fighters such as the MiG-29 before 1991, and had Israeli design and fly-by-wire inputs, Russian engine concepts, and international systems.

Details of the J-10 began to emerge in 2002, but it was unclear whether many would be produced. Similar to the canceled Israel Aircraft Industries Lavi (ER 2,940), and though Israel denied involvement, the design was believed to be based upon Lavi data. Both the Chengdu J-10 and India's new light combat aircraft have experienced difficulty with their fly-by-wire systems. Having no indigenous engine available, the aircraft was to be powered with the Russian Lyulka Saturn AL-31F at 22,500 pounds, as in the Sukhoi Su-27 and Su-30.

Concurrently, at this time, China was also developing the new XXJ, as identified by U.S. Navy intelligence, a multi-role stealth aircraft, probably to be in service in 2010 and to be joined by the new Shenyang J-8II offensive fighter, to build up a strike force quickly. Chengdu had also been developing the J-7MF (ER n/a), another development of the MiG-21, created in conjunction with Pakistan. The J-7MF had a heads-up display (HUD) and Doppler radar, with a 45 nm (80 km) range, and pylons for a three-ton load. Its advanced nature can be judged by a range of 1,625 nm (2,600 km), maximum Mach 1.8 speed at 52,500 feet, and a 2,145-foot (650 m) takeoff run. The more advanced FC-1 had initial problems, in part caused by disagreements between China, Pakistan, and Western governments over the supply of missions systems. In addition, the military side of the Chinese aircraft industry previewed in late 2000 both unmanned aerial and unmanned combat aerial vehicles (UAV and UCAV) for surveillance for combat, as well as unmanned helicopters.

Yet, the Chinese aviation industry still cannot handle sophisticated fighter orders. In 2002 the Russian factory in Amur received a $1.5 billion order for an additional forty Sukhoi Su-30MKs to the forty on hand, with another forty-aircraft order expected later.

The PLAAF, 1976–

In 1976, the year that both Mao and Zhou Enlai died, the People's Liberation Army Air Force was restored to favor. Deng Xiaoping became the power behind the throne, and soon titular head. In 1978, China was again set on the road to modernization. The PLAAF was so weak, however, that it was kept on the defensive. But by the mid-1980s the new doctrine of "People's War in Modern Conditions" moved from the idea of drawing attackers into the vastness of China to using mobile forces to counter any attacker on the borders—even to the use of modern nuclear weapons, as China had developed a hydrogen bomb in 1967. Still, the dragon could not afford a war with the USSR, and thus it was content in this decade to shop abroad for modern weapons.

In the 1981 military exercises, the PLAAF was heavily involved, including the control of army's airborne troops. In 1985, Deng declared that a major war was unlikely and reduced the armed forces, with the assumption that a local rather than a "People's" war would be dominant in a conflict. Local Rapid Reaction Units (RRU) were formed, for which the air force received new equipment. In 1986, an Army Air Corps, mainly of helicopters was created, but the inventory was far too few for the geographic spaces involved.

In the 1980s, the PLAAF was forced to raise its own food and engage in light industrial production, which both diverted it from its primary tasks and encouraged corruption with the lure of a potential source of money. After the Tiananmen Square tragedy in 1989, the army managed to re-polish its tarnished image left from the 1965–69 Cultural Revolution.

The traumatic events of the very early 1990s, including the collapse of the USSR and the Iraqi's lack of success with their Soviet weaponry in the Persian Gulf War, forced Beijing to consider a new strategy. The United States had made clear to the Iraqis, and to the world, that a revolution in military affairs (RMA) had occurred, in which a "system of systems" had played a key role. This used command, control, communications, computers, and intelligence—C⁴I—together with precision use of force, while simultaneously undertaking concurrent tasks: immediate comprehensive battlefield assessments, explicit mission assignment, and dominant battle-space knowledge.

It was thus evident to Beijing that the synergy had fundamentally changed, and it was technologically difficult, very expensive, and required a new bureaucratic management style. It was evident that U.S. technological vulnerabilities as seen in the 1991 Gulf War and in the seventy-eight day 1999 campaign in Kosovo—with limited results in spite of the lessons of the Gulf, but over a very different terrain—had caused the Chinese experts to believe that the concept of a People's war—as in 1949—was still valid. Others argued that for nuclear war, China needed a network-centered, computer-linked, high-speed command system. A third group argued for retaining existing weapons and simply focusing on disrupting the U.S. command system by targeting its satellites and computers—a low-cost defense. Yet another school argued that China should abandon the laws of war and strike at the U.S. fear of high casualties by using terrorism and manipulation of the environment in an unlimited manner. Even so, although in the 1990s the Chinese defense budget rose four-fold, it did not keep up with inflation.

By 1993, the Chief of the Air Staff was at last a pilot, cadets were getting 250 hours flying in three years of schooling, and pilots were flying

125 hours per year, this last barely enough to maintain competence. With 470,000 officers and men and 5,000 aircraft, the PLAAF had become one of the larger air forces in the world. By 1999, the twelve corps and thirty-six fighter, seven bomber, six attack, and two transport divisions were being consolidated, as were the various regional air commands, to be able to provide united campaigns in wartime. The newly independent PLAAF now operates under a clear written doctrine based on the U.S. land-air concepts. And the PLAAF has learned from Vietnam about firepower, maneuverability, and electronic control, and that the USAF is still much concerned about air mobility and airlift capacity. The PLAAF is afraid that such could end a war before its air service could get started.

Defense has shifted from border fighting to deep strikes into enemy territory, much as the Israeli Air Force has demonstrated. Yet, all that is necessary to enable China to make effective use of this new grand strategy may not be available until 2010 to 2020, judging by the methodical past developments.

The rapid rise of the learning curve, however, must not be discounted. And not to be overlooked is the fact that even though some 6,000 obsolete Chinese aircraft were scrapped in the 1980s and more in the 1990s, the PLAAF will have only an estimated 2,344 total aircraft in 2005 and will still be employing Shenyang J-6s and J-7s in low-level strike roles. (By contrast, the USAF by 2014 will have only 170 bombers—and only 130 of these operational.) Chinese air defense is much more being left to SAMs, because the PLAAF is still too small for the army with which it has to cooperate.

After the Gulf War, the PLAAF began night flying in bad weather, and practiced low- and high-altitude attacks and emergency mobility maneuvers. Tactical ranges were established and support organizations capable of supply, maintenance, and repair in the field were developed to accompany mobile forces.

By 2003, the fourth generation of PRC aircraft, developed with Israeli and Soviet assistance, were beginning to enter service. But at the same time, Russian Su-27s were bought, together with a license to manufacture more, as well as Su-30s and transports. In addition, air-refueling capabilities were under development, and an integrated air-defense system was being added. Information warfare systems and anti-viral computer-component security—asymmetrical warfare for both defense and offense—were in process, while the old skills in camouflage and deception remained honed. Yet, two weaknesses were still present: the unwillingness of Chinese pilots to push their planes to the limits, and the shortage of spares for foreign-bought aircraft.

At the beginning of the twenty-first century, the PLAAF was still wrestling with the age-old dilemma that had so driven the French Air Force in the 1930s: how to provide forces to give tactical support to ground troops, to launch independent air campaigns, and to defend the mainland. And the same difficulties remained but, as we have seen, may well be overcome by hardware, force structure, personnel, education, and training. Analysts were divided in 2002 as to whether an Asian arms race would occur when prosperity returned to the area.

China's Airlines

In 2002, Beijing authorized the China Aviation Industry II (AVIC II) directive, to select a family of thirty- to fifty-seat regional jet airliners. Annual projections show a need for 1,900 passenger jets by 2020, with an increasing number being regionals. Meanwhile, the earlier directive, AVIC I, is developing seventy- to ninety-seat airliners and is ordering also from Bombardier of Canada, Embraer of Brazil, and Fairchild of the United States. Beijing's approval of such contracts is required.

Concurrently, Chinese regional carriers urged the government to review tax policy on imports, as the regionals have to pay a 23 percent levy on aircraft under twenty-five tons (50,000 pounds) versus the large airlines only paying 7 percent on their imports. The tax imposed in 2001 was seen as trying to force foreign manufacturers to open factories in China.

With the Chinese government urging the regional airlines to buy turboprops and small jets, Embraer by 2002 had sold more than fifty there. And Fairchild-Dornier was considering building the fifty- to sixty-seat 328 jet (ER n/a) in China. The Chinese government itself was ready to finance an indigenous seventy-seat aircraft.

On the other hand, in order to "punish" the United States for the Hainan incident, when a PLAAF jet collided with a U.S. Navy Lockheed P-3 Orion, China was in 2001 negotiating an order for up to thirty-two Tu-204s in order to tighten an industrial alliance with Moscow and to snub Boeing.

One reason by 2000 for revamping Chinese airlines, the Chinese Civil Aviation Administration (CAAC) reported, was to improve an industry with over-capacity, ruinous price wars, heavy debt, and poor services. The services earned $96 million, but had high fuel costs. The real culprit, however, was discounted tickets without a database. Air China has been burdened, as the state carrier, with unfunded political obligations and a vast route network. Yet China Southern Airlines carries twice the number of passengers and China Eastern nearly 900,000 more than Air China's 8,056,000. Part of the problem was Beijing's buying of aircraft without reference to airline needs. In addition, Air China is an unlisted company on the securities exchange, whereas China Southwest and China Eastern Airlines have stockholders. And market rules have also been ignored in the allocation of schedules.

In May 2000, the CAAC consolidated thirty airlines into twenty, in three groups, headed respectively by Air China, China Eastern Airlines, and China Southern, with Hainan Airlines still independent, but slated for transcontinental services in 2002. Yet, overseas services were still unprofitable, and some in China argue that they should be handled only by one carrier. The remaining independent airlines, some municipal-owned, have criticized the new groupings to be for administrative convenience and not for market rules, assets, and carrier performance. And the actions of the State Council, they fear, will not be helped by China now being in the World Trade Organization.

As Chinese airlines expanded into the twenty-first century, they also began to experience shortages of aircrew. Hainan Airlines has hired foreign pilots to fly the 737-800 (ER n/a) and has paid industry wages.

By 2002, China Cargo Airlines was well established at Shanghai's new Pudong International Airport with seventy warehouses, each of 32,000 square feet, on 166 acres, at a cost of $145 million. In 1996, Pudong had been a rice paddy. In the twenty-first century, with four runways, it will be one of the world's larger airports with also some of the better access facilities, but a shortage of skilled cargo handlers.

China was rapidly becoming one of the great manufacturing centers of the world by 2002. The limitations of the U.S.-China bilateral agreement were being eliminated, and UPS (United Parcel Service) was admitted to the market with Chinese airlines reciprocating. In the meantime, Hong Kong had already become the busiest air-cargo airport in the world, at 2.2 million tons in 2000, because all roads lead there.

Outside of China, the picture in Southeast Asia was complicated for 2001 by the move to open the skies in order to attract more free-spending tourists to Vietnam, Cambodia, and Laos.

CHAPTER 7

POST-1945 MILITARY OPERATIONS

In the second half of the twentieth century, aviation came of age. Military operations continued the prewar roles of colonial peacekeeping and national security deterrent. The active operations were all of the limited sort either in force or area. Their success depended upon the professionalism of the air forces involved, equipment, supply, and sources and evaluation of intelligence.

The Soviet war in Afghanistan (1979–88) was the continuation of a long series of British and Russian forays into that hostile region, and with no better results in nine years than to prove that guerrillas can still beat technology to a draw in suitable terrain, especially if supplied with weaponry from a safe refuge in Pakistan.

The Falklands/Malvinas War of 1982 in the South Atlantic was most interesting in that both sides fought at the limits of their range. In theory, the most dangerous weapons were Exocet missiles, but this might be disputed if thicker-sided ships had been engaged. Moreover, the results for the British might have been quite different if, instead of the Argentinians, the combatant had been Israelis, with their flair for adaptive tactics, who had flown their Mirages and A-4 Skyhawks against the Harriers and the Royal Navy's last World War II armored carriers.

As it was, the Soviets, like the Americans in Vietnam, swallowed their pride and withdrew from Afghanistan; and the British are stuck with a sheep pasture that is a hostage to Argentine fortune.

The long, dragged-out Iran-Iraq war of 1978–88 repeated the lessons of the past. On the Iranian side, the highly sophisticated air force was largely deprived of its pilots and command structure by the revolution that had ousted the Shah in 1979, ran short of spares, and was unable to maintain and operate sophisticated weaponry. On the other hand, it countered the lack of airmen by creating a missile force and returned to the tactics of the Germans of 1944–45 by aiming long-range rockets at Baghdad, the Iraqi capital, for psychological effect. Meanwhile Iraq, with a trained air force and with access to new aircraft and spares from the USSR, used its limited air power sparingly, though it, too, engaged in raids against the enemy capital, Tehran, and other cities. In a stalemated war evocative of the First World War, air power gave neither side the advantage for victory. Ironically in the subsequent Persian Gulf War of 1991, the Iraqi Air Force voluntarily flew itself to internment in Iran.

And after the terrorist attack on the World Trade Towers in New York City on September 11, 2001, and the Pentagon in Washington, D.C.—plus the plane downed in Pennsylvania—resulting in just under 3,000 civilian casualties, America and an international anti-terror coalition attacked the terrorist network in Afghanistan, using its massive air power to disperse the ruling terrorist-sanctioning Taliban.

AIR INTELLIGENCE

On and off throughout the Cold War period incidents had developed over lost and snooping aircraft. Electronic eavesdropping has been a favorite means in intelligence gathering, using aircraft, ships, and permanent stations. The most spectacular of the episodes involved the shooting down of an American U-2 spy plane over the heart of the Soviet Union in May 1960, an incident that was used by the Soviet Premier as an excuse for calling off the Paris Cold War summit conference. Although in this case the pilot was employed as a civilian, U.S. President Dwight Eisenhower took the unprecedentedly honest step of admitting that he had known of the overflight.

Yet such flights were not new. The Germans overflew Britain before the Second World War, and used the airship *Graf Zeppelin* to scout British radar defenses. And the British sent a specially equipped civilian aircraft over Germany. Nevertheless, airborne spying has become big business, with the Lockheed SR-71 Blackbird reputed to cost $24.7 million each. This strategic reconnaissance plane cruised at very high altitude, near 100,000 feet, and at Mach 3 speeds. It was highly effective—so much so that after being withdrawn from service and donated to museums, it subsequently, in 1993, had to be recalled and refurbished for use over Iraq, which U-2s were still overflying in 1997.

Questions remain, however. Does the destruction of a spy plane cost the defender more than he gains? And, is the spy overflight system, "illegal" as it may be called in an area of international relations, not in fact a safeguard of peace rather than a liability? Yet, spy overflight is not a perfect solution, for the 1991 Persian Gulf War showed that reliance upon instant transmissions and satellite computer-enhanced images was all very well, as long as cloud cover did not intervene.

Supplemental to electronic intelligence gathering are the unmanned aerial vehicles—the UAVs—whose operational rise was pioneered by the Israeli Air Force and Swiss agricultural intelligence firms. The machines are relatively inexpensive and provide a long loiter time and high-altitude immunity to interception, as well as real-time video transmission of data, combined with global positioning (GPS) facilitation. In April 2001 a Northrop-Grumman Global Hawk UAV (ER n/a) crossed the Pacific non-stop in twenty-four hours, monitored—but not controlled—from Australia. Of course, photographic televised relay and electronic intelligence is only as good as the assessment of its interpreters and the ability to influence decision-making. However, by the 2001 Afghan War, the UAVs were a very important component of C^4I, and one that demanded interservice coordination and compatibility. By 2003, F-16 pilots would find themselves "flying" in ground cubicles, controlling armed UAVs. The 1914 cycle was beginning to be repeated. And by 2003, as well, the $16 million Global Hawk UAV could stay at 65,000 feet for thirty-five hours while transmitting radar and video images to troops on the ground.

An additional application of the unmanned aerial vehicles became the security surveillance of urban areas, using small, six-inch-wing UAVs, a product made possible by the steady miniaturization of electronics and power sources in the last half of the twentieth century.

BERLIN AIRLIFT, 1948–49

During the post-1945 period, a time that has been punctuated with a number of heated incidents of interest to the history of air power,

The quantum jump in the size of aircraft during the technological revolution can be seen in the comparison of the World War II B-29 Superfortress (ER 414), started in 1940, and the Consolidated B-36 Peacemaker intercontinental bomber (ER 2,042, B-36B), begun in 1941). The B-29 had a range of 4,100 miles, whereas the B-36 had a range of 10,000. The B-36 was the early mainstay of SAC, but due to a shortage of technicians, very few could be bombed up with nuclear weapons at any one time. (USAF)

The innovative Northrop flying wing of 1941 was developed as both the piston-engined XB-35 (ER 117.3) and the jet-engined XB-49 (ER n/a). Although production contracts were eventually procured, the aircraft had all been canceled by late 1949. It has been suggested that Northrop was too innovative for the Pentagon, another example of the fate of genius that afflicted people such as the British designers F. G. Miles, James Martin, and Barnes Wallis. Eventually, the flying-wing design was revived as the basis for the stealth B-2 Spirit (2,877.6), of which only twenty were built in the 1990s, and a few of which saw service in Afghanistan during 2001–02. (USAF)

The de Havilland Vampire (ER 8) stemmed from a 1941 British Air Ministry specification for a second jet fighter. True to de Havilland tradition, the aircraft was made of wood. These Swedish Air Force fighter-bombers have the one-piece Plexiglas canopy, showing that this version is pressurized. Performance improved rapidly as the Goblin engine was refined. (Royal Swedish Air Force)

The United States received the first Whittle engines in 1943, and the Bell Aircraft Corporation XP-59 (ER 5.94) was designed to use them. As in the case of early Soviet designs, they were mounted in the lower fuselage. The XP-59, now in the National Air and Space Museum, was a conventional aircraft and had a poor performance. But Larry Bell soon went on to sound-barrier breaking, high-speed, experimental machines. (USAF)

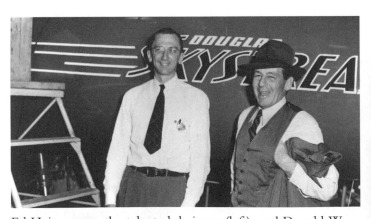

Aircraft such as this Grumman SA-16A Albatross (ER 50) are still needed for the search and rescue role, and the ability to land and recover downed aircrew. Designed to a 1946 U.S. Navy requirement, the Albatross remained in service until the early 1970s, when it began to be replaced by helicopters. One of its key features was the ability to be airborne for almost twenty-three hours, as a result of its under-wing fuel tanks. (Grumman History Center)

Ed Heinemann, the talented designer (left), and Donald W. Douglas stand by the D-558 Skystreak (ER n/a) in 1947 at Muroc Dry Lake in California. The D-558 was one of a series of aircraft designed to approach and pass the speed of sound. The D-558-I set a world speed record of 650 mph in August 1947. (McDonnell Douglas)

The D-558 Skystreak here shows the high-mounted tailplane necessary at the time because of the "tube" of the jet engine extending from nose to tail, and the short, straight wings with slight dihedral for stability. (McDonnell Douglas)

The DH Canada DHC-1 Chipmunk (ER 0.16) of 1946 was the first all-Canadian designed aircraft and was a very popular trainer, manufactured also in Britain and Portugal. (DH Canada)

Lt. Gen. and Mrs. William A. Tunner with one of the children taken out of the western sector of Berlin during the 1948–49 Allied airlift to the safety of a "vacation" in West Germany as a part of Operation Kinder Lift in the summer of 1948. General Tunner had run the Hump operation to China in World War II and commanded the Berlin Airlift, which was not only a successful response to the Soviets' challenge to peace, but indicative of the humanitarian side of U.S. Air Force activities. (USAF)

Airborne early warning (AEW) became very important in the Cold War of 1947–91 and onward. Lockheed EC-121 Super Constellations (ER 422) were adopted from the airliner and fitted with a large, self-supporting radar dome housing a rotating antenna. The capaciousness of the civil design allowed for the many electronics stations that were needed. (Lockheed)

The period between the end of the Second World War and the outbreak of the Korean War in 1950, when jet fighters first fought against each other, was transitional. The workhorses were piston-engine machines from 1945, often those that had been ordered during World War II but delivered too late for service. The Douglas AD-2 Skyraider (ER 18.2, AD-6, 1952) was ordered in 1944 as a carrier-based dive- and torpedo-bomber, the first American single-seat aircraft in that category. It could carry as much weight in bombs as a B-17G Flying Fortress (ER 75.98).

As the need for aerial refueling became part of first SAC's and then the USAF's policy in general, so the need for tankers developed. This is the 500th KC-97 Stratofreighter (ER 564) delivered by Boeing. The aircraft had an all-flying boom that coupled with a probe on the receiver aircraft. The KC-97 was developed from both the B-29 Superfortress (ER 414) and its derivative the B-50 (ER 603). The KC-97 used the same airframe as the Boeing 377 Stratocruiser civilian airliner (ER 423). (Boeing)

The Boeing B-47 Stratojet (ER 992) was a design break-

through similar to the de Havilland Mosquito (ER 30). Begun in late 1943, its creation was heavily influenced by the German work on swept wings that Boeing personnel saw immediately after World War II. The first B-47 flew in 1947, and entered service in 1951. By the 1950s, the aircraft was considered a weapons system. When production ceased in 1957, SAC had about 1,800. (Boeing) the first of these was a diplomatic incident in which power was exercised and a struggle of wills ensued. On June 24, 1948, the Soviet Union decided to close the Allied surface routes to occupied West Berlin, with the apparent intention of taking the area by starvation. To the Soviets' surprise, the Western Allies responded at once with an airlift. Here the training of the RAF and USAF in the Second World War paid dividends, especially as the commander of the airlift was the same Gen. William Tunner who had managed the American Hump supply to China.

Apart from Soviet harassment during the operation, the major problem was the weather. But new developments, especially the radar ground-controlled approach (GCA), enabled aircraft movements to reach 1,000 daily at the three Berlin fields in use. By the time the airlift ceased in October 1949, 2.3 million tons had been carried in 277,728 sorties. That this was possible was in part due to the plethora of air-transport companies flying war-surplus machines, for whom the airlift was a "shot in the arm."

The Berlin operation showed that the Western Allies were prepared to use air power to stand their ground and not to be intimidated. By the mid-1950s, the supply of these aircraft had dwindled away, but gradually in the 1960s a surplus of large piston-engined and jet aircraft became available that could be chartered when needed and whose working capacity was many times greater than that of the aircraft used in the 1948–49 airlift.

The Korean War, 1950–53

Only some nine months after the cessation of the Berlin Airlift, the Korean War broke out. It presented a number of novel circumstances, as the first war in which jets tangled. The air operations in the war, however, did not really contribute much to air-power concepts other than to prove once again that slow bombers cannot operate in daylight in the face of fast fighters, and

that speeds in a dogfight remain relative. What was new and frustrating was the sanctuary in Red China from which the Communist air force flew, and the tacit stand-off between the Chinese and the Americans that limited the war to the airspace over the peninsula south of the Yalu River and north of the Pusan perimeter. Most grand-strategic bombing was ruled out because both sides were vulnerable.

In June 1950, the United Nations forces were caught badly off balance at first, but their quick recovery resulted in the destruction of the North Korean Air Force at a time when the Soviets were just helping to reorganize the People's Liberation Army Air Force. The result was that the Soviets had *carte blanche* and a chance to test their planes and pilots against the Americans. Quickly finding in November and December 1950 that MiG-15 jet fighters were more than a match for the F-51 (P-51) Mustangs and the jet F-80 (P-80) Shooting Stars of World War II, the USAF brought in the new F-86 Sabre Jet.

The Soviets and the Chinese had the immense advantage of early-warning radar that allowed them to climb from airfields north of the Yalu to 50,000 feet and then to swoop from out of the sun onto USAF planes, attacking targets just south of the river. USAF tactics had to be short and sharp, as even with long-range tanks their aircraft were low on fuel. But the American pilots had the benefit of radar gunsights, and the kill ratio for the remainder of the war rose and the Soviets were in their favor. The Chinese Air Force was badly beaten.

Affecting the Korean War was logistics. In 1946, two Victory ships were needed to carry 15,000 tons of cargo from San Francisco to Japan and return, using 14,000 barrels of oil. In Korea, 3,000 C-54 flights were needed to carry the same cargo, consuming 1,140,000 barrels of high-grade aviation fuel for the round trips, plus eight ships to carry refueling supplies, greater man hours for servicing and operating, highly trained crews and extra refinery capacity for high-octane gas, as well as maintenance and storage costs. Later jets made quicker trips with greater capacity and used low-grade fuel.

Because it was mentally attuned to Europe, the USAF thought the Korean War was an aberration—fighting at a fixed line, with the enemy operating from a sanctuary, and without victory. Actually, it was an example of the point that previous wars need to be studied, for, ultimately, Korea had a lot in common with the Western Front of 1914–18.

The Korean War consisted of five phases from June 25 to September 15, 1950, when the South Koreans and the Americans were forced back from the 38th Parallel to the Pusan perimeter:

- from MacArthur's September 15 end-run landing at Inchon to late November;
- when the Chinese intervened and caught U.S. forces out in north field;
- from early 1951 to the re-establishment of the line along the 38th Parallel again;
- from mid-1951 to the end of the peace talks at Panmunjon after the bloody stalemate in the mountains.

Two things made Korea a hard place in which to fight—the mountains and paddies terrain, and the fact that most weather came down from the north and thus could not be accurately forecast by the Allied meteorologists. Heavy rains in July made for both humid and muddy ground-fighting.

How the air war needed to be fought depended upon the vantage point of the personalities involved. Key figures commanding the USAF during 1950–53 would later have senior responsibilities in Vietnam, notably Gens. Curtis LeMay and Jacob E. Smart. The Air Force entered the Korean War with a strategic-bombing doctrine that would not work because the MiGs and most of the important industry to be targeted were in the prohibited zone north of the Yalu River, which marked the northern boundary of North Korea. Thus, the USAF had to reinvent the tactical doctrine that had served it so well in the ground campaigns in the Second World War, notably in Italy. This meant they had to cooperate with the Army and Marines and interdict enemy resources behind the front.

However, air commanders did not like being in a tri-service war and complained that they spent 40 percent of their time shooting down the ideas of their sister services. In part this was a mindset that had been nurtured by the B-36 controversy and the 1948 "revolt of the admirals," the opposition to giving the USAF the dominant role with the B-36. The revolt also stemmed from the USN's successful carrier leaders needing to find a new Cold War role. Much as in France in 1934–40, the U.S. Army and the USAF were at loggerheads over close air support versus striking the enemy homeland. Earlier, as the USAAF, the Air Force had spent part of World War II fighting the Army for independence, and after having just achieved it in 1947 was afraid that it would lose that as well as its tactical air role. The Army, for its part, envied the Marines with their own dedicated air support. Not until mid-1952, when personal visits between commanders had started, were cordial relations developed, and not until 1953 did the new UN Supreme Commander in Korea, Gen. Mark Clark, impose a joint staff.

From 1947 to 1953 the USAF was being reorganized into functional commands, as the RAF had been during 1936–38: Strategic Air Command, Tactical Air Command, Air Defense Command, and the overseas theater commands supported by Air Materiel, Air Proving Ground, Air Training, and Air Transport Command, backed by the new Air University at Maxwell Air Force Base, Alabama.

The service had shrunk from the 2,253,000 at V-J Day in September 1945 to 303,600 in May 1947. And in addition to this erosion, the USAF lacked a coherent military strategy, as AFM-1 (Air Force Manual-1), *United States Air Force Basic Doctrine,* was not promulgated until 1953. Concurrently, targets were divided, on the prewar conception, into those that could be destroyed by precision bombing and those that were too large (i.e., urban complexes). Those large targets would have to be given General LeMay's incendiary treatment or leveled with an atom bomb; precision targets were wastefully too small for such armament.

Where generals stood in the issue depended upon their wartime experience, but Chief of Staff Hoyt Vandenberg and the State Department were opposed to urban-area attacks, as being most likely to stir up hatreds and bring on guerrilla warfare. On the other hand, Bernard Brodie of The RAND Corporation and Yale University argued for using leaflets to instill fear of threatened attacks.

After General LeMay had organized the Berlin Airlift, he was sent to revitalize the Strategic Air Command, while at the same time Tactical Air Command was downgraded to planning, until critics from the Army, Navy, and the press succeeded in having it reactivated. But at this time, neither Tactical Air Command nor anyone else saw the role of the new jets as anything but interceptors, yet by 1953 they would become the best fighter-bombers. It was thought that with all the propeller aircraft gone, Tactical Air Command would have two years after an atomic war started to recreate itself as a ground-support force.

The Korean War, however, was another case of war not coming when, where, or how planned. Thus, after the conflict broke out on the peninsula, coordination of tactics, techniques, and technology were necessary to achieve accurate destruction and efficiency. Emphasis was put upon guided missiles as cheaper and more accurate weapons. Tests showed that by using missiles as opposed to free-fall bombs, the hit rate could be raised from 50 to 96 percent, and that without well-trained B-29 crews, thirty-three rather than four 1,000-pound bombs would be needed to take down a bridge span. The 12,000-pound Tarzon guided bomb was abandoned as not cost effective—it cost too much to do too little.

Enemy flak in Korea was another challenge. With modern automatic weapons, aircraft were vulnerable below 2,500 feet. Yet when forced up higher, fighter-bomber hits on pinpoint targets

dropped from 11 percent in 1952 to 4 percent in 1953. The U.S. Navy, therefore, reverted to dive-bombing from 5,000 feet, in order to pull out at 3,000. Night bombing was no more accurate, for one hundred bombs were needed to kill 1.8 trucks, with a hit having to be within fifty feet to do damage. The cause was lack of Douglas B-26 Invader (ER 25) units in the United States, so that crews arrived untrained at operational squadrons. Even when the Invaders managed an average of four trucks a night, the enemy was not affected. Additional erosion of accuracy was caused by poor maps, lack of target photos, old World War II munitions until 1952, and the fatigue of crews who had to bomb-up their own aircraft. SHORAN—short-range navigation, a radar plotting device—was available, but its maximum range was only 200 miles at 25,000 feet.

Another disturbing factor in the campaign were accusations that the United States was using germ or biological warfare, in spite of the fact that the Far Eastern Air Force had no such capacity. In the end, in 1953, after Stalin died, the Soviets exposed the falsity of the claims, ironically just as the United States began to get the capability. In the meantime, U.S. Army and Air Force relations were soured by the U.S. Army's Chemical Warfare Service. Actually, the USAF thought atomic bombs preferable.

The Korean War continued to escalate, into 1953. At that time, the U.S. Navy was concerned that MiGs and Il-28s could sneak under their combat air patrols and attack the carriers. The USAF had only 176 F-86 Sabre Jets facing 700 MiGs; officials worried that the North Koreans might make a surprise attack on the USAF assets that were crowded on the few air bases. The USAF did not have sufficient engineers to disperse the F-86s.

And while Washington was considering expanding the war to bring results at the peace talks, it was unaware that the Chinese commander had 1.35 million troops in North Korea and was preparing his own offensive. With the idea that the USAF would be the single strategic offensive instrument of the war, the decision was made to destroy the dams that irrigated the rice crop, to deprive the enemy of 250,000 tons of food. Once again it was not the successful breach of the selected dams by fighter-bombers that surprised intelligence, but the speed of the recovery efforts. At this same time, the USAF violation of air space north of the Yalu indicated that the United Nations might widen the war. Actually, these were unauthorized incursions in which the aircraft pair left "upstairs" had assumed the leader's call sign, in order to deceive UN controllers while the other pair hunted.

By the end of the war, the UN forces had lost 110 aircraft in air-to-air combat, out of the total of 409 lost. The Allies claimed 838 MiGs destroyed, 149 probables, and 936 damaged. Applying the divisor of three, it is likely that the actual results were 329 destroyed and 312 damaged. In addition, the U.S. Navy lost 1,248 aircraft, only 564 by enemy action. Of the 17,000 tons of bombs dropped, roughly 10,000 were aimed at 110 supply centers, 2,000 more on strategic industrial targets, and an equal number on airfields, leaving North Korea a devastated landscape in which nearly every family had lost someone to bombing.

Just as it was observed that the USAF considered the Korean conflict aberrant, so in 1954 as the B-29s left the inventory, FEAF Bomber Command reverted to SAC and its self-confident view of general war. The lessons of air power in limited wars were seen either as irrelevant or something to be ignored. Even the commander-in-chief of Tactical Air Command in 1954 had voted for adopting the nuclear role, and thus the F-84 Thunderjet was followed by the large F-105 Thunderchief, which was unsuitable for both air combat and tactical roles, and ended up being employed in Vietnam as a small grand-strategic bomber against North Vietnam. The USAF confidently believed that if it was prepared to fight NATO's anti-Soviet battles for Europe, it was in a position to handle brushfire wars as well. President Kennedy tried to change this thinking, but by 1964, 75 percent of the higher-ranking USAF officers came from SAC.

American strategic bombers, mostly B-29s, hammered at Communist targets while tactical aircraft, many from carriers offshore, flew the usual interdiction raids along and behind the front. One lesson that had to be learned—and it should have been realized earlier—was that the multitudinous Asian peasants with messianic leadership had the perseverance to rebuild overnight the damaged bridges and railways, or to make by-pass embankments. Moreover, inefficient as it might be by Western standards, these people were willing to move slowly at night and to hide by day in order to bring supplies forward. Western intelligence officers took some time to understand that conventional assessments could not be applied to people who used feudal methods. And the over-optimism of USAF bomber zealots, who believed they could cause the North Koreans to retreat to the Yalu without ground attacks, remained a continuous problem.

The North Koreans and their Chinese allies became willing to sue for peace only when they found that they could not maintain air bases south of the Yalu. Without these bases, and with the equipment then available, they could not launch attacks against the UN beachheads and ports, nor keep enemy air forces from dominating the air over North Korea.

The Korean War showed the USAF that it had to relearn from past experience. It was fortunate in 1950–53 that its leaders and fliers were still largely those who had fought the Second World War. But obviously there was a need to accelerate the production of its histories and special historical studies so that future generations would not overlook past lessons. Included in this was the need to document current experiences, so that lessons could be disseminated in the future.

Interestingly, with the later Vietnam conflict the USAF concluded that Korea had been a fluke; it had been possible to use strategic air power for tactical purposes only because that particular situation demanded it, that lavish tactical air support would not be available to ground troops in the future because tactical air forces would have to spend most of their time fighting for air superiority, unlike over Korea, and that the Navy would never be as free again to use the seas for mobile air bases. Therefore, it would be fatal for the USAF to model itself on what it thought was the successful mix used on the Korean peninsula—suicide in an air force without a massive grand-strategic bomber wing and without an air-superiority force with which to hold the skies.

In these concepts the USAF leadership was correct, within limits, for Korea showed that interdiction behind the battle line was most effective because it caught the enemy when he was both concentrating his forces and engaged at the front. Strategic bombing had to take the place of grand-strategic, because industrial targets lay beyond the Yalu, out of bounds, and thus the war had to be fought over the army's battleground. Air-superiority lessons had to be modified because the narrowness of the battlefield enabled sweep tactics to be employed against the Communist air force, whose pilots did not really understand or exploit the advantages of their machines. The USAF can complain that neither Gen. Douglas MacArthur, in proceeding northward, nor Gen. Matthew B. Ridgway, in maintaining a static position on the 38th Parallel, appreciated the limits and the advantages of air power. MacArthur was defeated when he attempted to range beyond the area in which air power could control the enemy's logistical system and give sufficient direct tactical support to troops at the limits of their supply lines. Ridgway failed to allow the UN air forces their freedom over North Korea in mid-1951 for fear of disrupting truce talks—which in fact dragged on for two more years—without recognizing that interdiction without a ground battle could not win. In other words, as the air-power proponents now admit, air forces alone cannot win wars, the 1991 Persian Gulf and 2001–02 Afghan experiences, and 2001–02 Afghan experiences notwithstanding.

The USAF had been most concerned about another war in Europe, yet history had ironically forced it to fight in the Far East, where both the opponents and the geographical conditions were quite different. But precisely because the USAF was prepared to fight on its preferred European battlefield, and in part because its strategy called for a massive nuclear retaliation if it did so, it was most unlikely that a conventional war would break out there. Yet the USAF had evolved its doctrine from the European area, and had expected the Army to use its artillery to the full. The U.S. Marine Corps, on the other hand, had derived its doctrine from the Pacific campaigns in which light infantry was thrust ashore with the support of its own tactical air forces, while the U.S. Navy flew high cover. The operation could expect little artillery support other than that supplied by naval guns afloat. In Korea, the U.S. Army demanded the Marine system, and it worked because of the air superiority enjoyed by the UN forces as a whole. When after the war the USAF denied the concept of a U.S. Air Force role in ground support, the Army went ahead and developed its own air force of helicopter gunships and tactical airplanes, especially in Vietnam.

In Korea, a Joint Operations Center had been devised that effectively concentrated all the air units available to handle crises on the front. The adoption of the "Mosquito" forward air controller (FAC) system, using the World War II North American AT-6 Texan (Harvard) aircraft (ER 1.59), was considered impractical for the future, and it was assumed that the identification of targets would be placed in the hands of jet fighter-bomber Pathfinders or be done by radar. Yet in Vietnam in the 1960s, the use of light planes for forward air controllers remained, once again, vital and effective.

For a smaller air service such as the Royal Australian Air Force, the lessons from Korea were limited to the action of its No. 77 Meteor Squadron. That experience re-emphasized that aircraft capabilities must be matched to specific roles, that versatility and flexibility were of value, that the next war might not be a major war, that a hot war could provide a core of combat-experienced officers for the next thirty years, and, finally, that Australia needed to train to USAF standards and to rely on the United States and no longer on Great Britain.

The most dramatic and long-range effect of the Korean War was the expansion of the U.S. Air Force from 42 wings in 1950, to 95 by 1953, with a goal of 143; at the same time, the budget of the services was allocated on the basis of the role to be played so that the Air Force came out with the largest funding. The Eisenhower policy—"New Look" at defense—only reduced the number of wings to 137, in view of the nuclear ratio with Russia. Backed up with a "massive retaliation" strategy, this expansion deterred the Communists from overt actions.

VIETNAM, 1950–75

Effectiveness of intelligence and covert action was well demonstrated in the way in which the French were ousted from Vietnam. Granting that the French strategy of holding fortified posts was wrong and that their military commanders on the spot for political and economic reasons worked with one hand tied behind their backs, the Vietnam operations showed that, unlike in Burma in 1944–45, the mere use of air transport alone could not counter guerrilla tactics in a civil war.

The 1954 fall of Dien Bien Phu amply demonstrated that the French had learned nothing from Crete or other Second World War battles. From 1950 onward, paratroopers were dropped into hopeless last-ditch engagements. Attempts to counter the Viet Minh seizure of the jungle highlands with napalm and rockets meant useless shooting into the dark, green foliage. When in April 1953 the French attempted to set up air bases in the Plaine des Jarres, 500 miles from Hanoi and 1,000 miles from Saigon, they mortgaged all their air transport. At Dien Bien Phu they repeated mistakes made in Burma by trying to maintain an airfield surrounded by a ring of hills dominated by the enemy and his anti-aircraft guns. That the United States was able to do the same later in 1968 at Khe Sanh remains a puzzle, unless it is assumed that the Communists used their threat to the base as an attrition tactic or a feint—perhaps they realized that the Americans had immense air superiority, centralized control, and the ability to resupply and reinforce by air.

As in many peripheral and even in some major conflicts, air superiority in Vietnam was irrelevant, especially if the enemy air force was virtually impotent, his anti-aircraft powerful, and much of his movement at night or in bad weather. If defensive fighters could make the attackers jettison their bombs to be more maneuverable, then they had saved the target and won.

The U.S. part of the Vietnam War (1963–72) was primarily an air war, with 8,000,000 tons of bombs dropped. But except for Linebacker II against Hanoi in late 1972, the USAF ignored the lessons learned there. However, nearly twenty years later, in 1991, the Persian Gulf War was fought under very different conditions and circumstances, but by leaders blooded in Southeast Asia; the one hundred-day victory in the Gulf War had a cathartic effect.

In general, the successful suppression of guerrillas demands a ten to one manpower ratio and has to be handled on the ground. Air power can only be effectively used if it is able to spot and spoil, and if it is backed up by intelligent ground support that denies the guerrillas sustenance and wins over the local population, as well as ultimately the dissidents, by honest political and economic reforms. The object is peace and prosperity, and massive destruction is not a solution. Air power cannot make reforms, as both Cyprus (1955–59 and since 1963) and Malaya (1948–60) have demonstrated. Moreover, the jet is seldom the answer. Helicopters and STOL aircraft are needed, for the targets are small and relatively slow-moving, the expense of pacification continuous, communication essential, and the patience of the taxpayers touchy. In other words, although air power can support such conflicts to a degree, it is much better employed in open limited wars.

The Vietnam War in many respects bears out these points. Although air power was heavily used, the war dragged on because the targets were not large enough or concentrated enough for it to be really effective. The few genuine targets, primarily contained in the Hanoi complex, were placed off-limits until the war escalated, and such a technique destroyed the value of air power's sudden physical and psychological impact. Moreover, as in Korea, a sanctuary was created, north of the demilitarized zone, which by order of the U.S. President was also off-limits when peace talks were anticipated. And a second sanctuary existed in Red China (the PRC).

As in the Spanish Civil War, outside military leaders appear to have seen the Vietnam War as a great place to test equipment and theories. Certainly the war showed that the air-superiority fighter, when used for tactical purposes, had many disadvantages. Designed for high-speed combat at high altitudes against missile-equipped opponents, USAF jets were found highly vulnerable to small-arms ground fire at low altitudes, as almost the whole of their cubic content contained critical equipment and was unarmored. The result was that North Vietnamese peasants armed with automatic small arms with simple sights were knocking down or damaging Mach 2 fighters and fighter-bombers. In many cases the lessons of the Second World War had been forgotten: unarmored aircraft with vulnerable fuel tanks and hydraulic control systems were put out of action by random hits. Fleas bite tigers.

In many ways Vietnam was a colonial war reminiscent of British operations in Iraq up to 1920, with cumbersome ground forces gradually superseded by air forces. Ironically, part of the original escalation of ground forces in Vietnam was to protect massive air bases made possible themselves by the lack of enemy air opposition. The absence of an opposing air force shows starkly in the figures for enemy aircraft shot down: only sixty-one MiG-17 and twenty-five MiG-21 confirmed claims between July 1965 and February 1968. Interestingly, twenty-five of these credits went to single-seat F-105 Thunderchiefs, the rest largely to two-seat F-4 Phantoms.

The USAF had been present in Vietnam from 1950 when a Military Aviation Advisory Group (MAAG) was established at Saigon and mechanics sent out to keep loaned aircraft flying. In 1954, after the Cold War Paris Peace Accords, President Eisenhower was fearful of the domino theory, that if one state fell the rest would follow, and thus used the creation of the Southeast Asia Treaty Organization (SEATO) to assert the protection of the new state of South Vietnam.

In May 1959, North Vietnam decided that because elections to unify the country had not been held in 1955, it would handle the situation by force. Viet Cong units began to infiltrate into the South. The U.S. counter was to send in Special Forces to train the Army of the Republic of Vietnam (ARVN) and to replace the worn-out Grumman F8F Bearcats (ER 12) with twenty-five USN Douglas AD-6 Skyraiders (ER 18.2); but these were soon grounded by lack of spares.

When President John F. Kennedy had taken office, he had endorsed a counterinsurgency plan, but the 1954 Geneva Accords prohibited the use of jet aircraft. The USAF thus began to train combat crews at "Jungle Jim," Eglin Air Force Base, Florida, and the Farm Gate support force was sent out with RF-101 PRU planes operating from Tan Son Nhut air base at Saigon and Don Muang at Bangkok. By 1962, a USAF general was in command of four detachments in Southeast Asia and Operation Ranch Hand defoliant spray sorties were being flown over the highlands. However, at this time the USAF was very concerned not to harm civilians. Rules of engagement began to be expanded from one page to many with—as a legacy from Chinese intervention in Korea—tight control from Washington.

U.S. air raids against the north, which started with retaliation for the "claimed" 1964 Tonkin

Gulf attack on a USN destroyer, were escalated into a full-scale offensive in March 1965. But rather than use air power as it should have been used—in a series of short, sharp, guerrilla surprise, grand-strategic surgical strikes at Hanoi and the critical war-making industries, airfields, and docks elsewhere in North Vietnam—the air offensive was launched as a drawn-out series of raids by fighter-bombers that were gradually stepped up until attacks on Hanoi itself were allowed. By then, of course, the Communists were ready with a thicket of anti-aircraft guns and surface-to-air missiles. Nor did the bombing slow down the flow of men and supplies to the south. The rate in fact almost doubled from 4,500 men per month in 1965 to 7,000 in 1966.

By the end of 1967, the U.S. had lost 3,000 aircraft in all areas, including 1,401 planes and helicopters in action and 1,555 to various operational causes, though a loss rate of only 2.18 planes per thousand sorties, as opposed to 3.5 in Korea and 9.5 in the Second World War. In both of the latter cases, however, there was air opposition. The Communists increased their SAM missile forces and at first saw increased success, but U.S. airmen discovered that by keeping low and taking evasive action they could avoid the missile; however, this often placed them within range of the effective ground fire. The USAF developed SAM-detection and jamming gear, and pilots found that when the aircraft made sharp turns, the SAMs could not follow. The Soviets claimed the SAMs were 50 percent effective; the U.S. indicated that only 2 percent made kills.

Much of the successful American use of F-105s depended upon air refueling out of SAM range. This enabled F-105s from neutral Thailand to bomb North Vietnam. However, the threat was ever-present that such dependence could critically endanger strike forces faced with enemy interception of the vital but highly vulnerable tankers.

For the RAAF, the Vietnam experience saw only thirteen aircraft lost and fourteen personnel killed by all causes in 331,000 sorties by a force of some sixty-five aircraft. These were basically transport helicopters, and thus the lessons for the defense of Australia were limited, though the armed forces became ever keener on these airships. In 1986, the army proposed taking over the RAAF's helicopters—a perennial move by ground forces worldwide. Of interest as well, the RAAF had only fifty-six sick out of 50,000 personnel in seven years—a rather amazing statistic.

The RAAF was in Vietnam as a token presence, as opposed to their greater representation in Malaya. The Martin B-57 Canberra (Intruder) light bombers (ER 146.7, B-57B) were sent to Vietnam because they had become surplus to requirements as the RAAF rearmed with the F-111 Aardvark.

America's use of aircraft carriers off Vietnam gradually began to be seen as expensive and wasteful, and in 1968 they were ordered to slow down their operations when the USS *New Jersey,* the only battleship in commission, arrived off the coast. And although the extensive use of the carriers had been costly, the policy helped to iron out the "bugs" in the system. The Navy realized that it needed the slower, longer-ranged, more heavily armed LTV F-8 Crusader (ER 68) or the two-seat Grumman A-6 Intruder (ER 84.5) for many roles, rather than the sophisticated and expensive McDonnell F-4 Phantom II (ER 370), which should essentially have been reserved for air-superiority work. Moreover, with many airfields available ashore, carriers were less essential.

As in Korea, grand-strategic bombers were used for strategic missions. By February 1969 some 105 B-52s from the Strategic Air Command were flying about 1,800 sorties a month from Guam (2,000 miles from the battlefields), Okinawa, and Thailand. Most of the raids were spoiling attacks in which large tonnages of bombs were dropped over suspected areas of enemy concentration to hinder organization of divisions for battle. The 750-pound bombs used created hazards to both health and the economy. The craters could not easily be filled in, and the stagnant water in them bred malarial mosquitoes; in addition, bomb splinters so damaged trees as to cause the lumber industry to lose two hours per day repairing saws at the mills. This was hardly the way to win over the populace. And the high cost of such operations, which amounted to air-freighting high explosives over great distances, raised sound arguments for a shorter response time by a larger tactical air force operating from local fields.

The credibility of bombing operations in Vietnam coincided with a growing public interest and awareness in Anglophobe countries of the Second World War bombing attacks upon Germany and Japan. By 1971, an argument was raging as to whether or not the six million tons of bombs dropped upon an area the size of Texas—three times the tonnage dropped upon Germany—was either effective or justifiable. Interestingly, more than half this tonnage was dropped by fighter-bombers such as the F-105, which carried as much as a B-17 of 1944. Opponents of bombing cited the ecological and physical devastation; and proponents cited the disruptive effect upon enemy operations and the salvation of friendly ground troops, especially at places such as Khe Sanh, where 6,000 Marines held off 25,000 attackers.

The most interesting development of the Vietnam War was undoubtedly the successful employment of helicopter air-cavalry tactics, first suggested in August 1957 by Gen. James M. Gavin, an airborne commander of the Second World War. Helicopter fuel systems were vulnerable to ground fire, but the casualties to helicopters were at first surprisingly light. The U.S. Army estimated in 1969 that about 18,000 combat sorties were flown per helicopter lost. Helicopters provided great mobility and enabled infantry and artillery to be switched quickly from one area to another. The air-mobile concept was based upon an acceptance of a certain degree of vulnerability, and it succeeded because of surprise and flexibility, enabling troops to be moved around even in actual battle, without long vulnerable supply lines. And in a manner reminiscent of the picquets used

to guard hilltop flanks on the Northwest Frontier of India, fire-support bases were established on hilltops rather than around airfields, as the French had so fatefully done at Dien Bien Phu.

It can be argued that helicopter losses were light considering their intense use, but a case can also be made that this was only possible because of the lack of enemy air opposition. However, helicopters may prove to be the best anti-guerrilla weapon armies possess. In most such operations the enemy is unlikely to have aircraft that can challenge control of the skies, unless supported by an outside power—though anti-aircraft guns and rockets are another matter. In addition, the removal of casualties to base hospitals via helicopters is quick, helping to raise the morale of even isolated units.

The U.S. Army viewed the Vietnam experience as equivalent to a nuclear war, in that pockets of the enemy and not the seizure of terrain would be the objective. The helicopter was adapted to carry out firepower, mobility, logistics, and communications roles. Helicopters gave the Army the mobility and concentration with which to hit a numerous enemy with limited forces; and provided that the U.S. Air Force could keep enemy fighters out of a twenty-mile area behind the battlefield, the air-cavalrymen were convinced they had a battle-winning weapon, especially when gunships became available.

By 1971 this vision of victory began to look less certain, for the Viet Cong and the North Vietnamese had at last realized that helicopters were vulnerable to small-arms anti-aircraft fire and rockets. Vietnamization—using the local people—had offered them a greater chance to lure in or decoy helicopters by broadcasting commands in pidgin English on helicopter frequencies.

Yet much as they were a benefit, during the years in which "choppers" were used in Vietnam, the operations were not cheap. By early 1971 more than 4,200 had been lost, 45 percent shot down. At that time, helicopter losses were running at the rate of three per day, out of a force of 3,500 machines—

about a four to three ratio to losses of fixed-wing aircraft—and 71 percent of the aircrew and passenger casualties had occurred in helicopters.

A different aspect of the Vietnam War that caused controversy was the use of herbicides. The technique of airborne spraying of the countryside with defoliants, to expose enemy movements and ambushes, could be supported on military grounds; air surveillance, though perhaps less accurate, was certainly far cheaper and quicker than ground patrols. The precedent for using herbicides had been established in Burma in 1944, but the chemicals had caused damage both to rubber trees and to the ecology in general, and their use in Vietnam raised again the problems of public relations, not so much in the battle area as at home in a changed climate of opinion, as well as in neutral countries. And this had become an important consideration when so many had voting rights in the United Nations. By December 1968, the subject of defoliants had split the membership of the American Association for the Advancement of Science.

A lesson from Burma also initially overlooked by the military was bridge busting with television-guided bombs. The tactic and technology was re-invented for Vietnam, another example of waste caused by not being familiar with history.

And, as the RAF had learned in World War II, the defense of airfields was not a popular job with the soldiers; thus, the RAF Regiment had been created. In Southeast Asia, air-base defense became a vitally important matter in all areas, for the Viet Cong and the North Vietnamese Army could strike anywhere at any time, and frequently did so from very close outside an airfield's perimeter fence, using mortars. The first such attack used only about seventy-five rounds in minutes to destroy five B-57 Canberra bombers and to damage others, and to cause seventy-six casualties. Based upon excellent—even inside—intelligence, planning, and control, such attacks took less than twenty minutes; North Vietnamese and Viet Cong sappers—demoltion commandos—needed only thirty to sabotage American aircraft. Stand-offs, sapper raids, and sabotage all aimed at the destruction of matériel, not causing casualties.

Although more difficult to defend, urban air bases already existed, and new bases were frequently not sited with any thought to defense. Because the USAF lacked soldiers, it had to create its own security police and train them in the three-zone (inner, middle, and outer perimeter) static- and mobile-defense concept. Protection of air assets was usually added to these duties, and the whole area outside the perimeter commanded by the local Republic of Vietnam Armed Forces (RVNAF) wing commander for linguistic simplicity. Not until after the Tet Offensive in 1968 did the USAF Pacific Air Forces (PACAF) impose a local base defense requirement complete with armored vehicles, radios, heavy weapons, and small-unit training. In the end, ten security police squadrons were present in Southeast Asia, another thirteen worldwide.

Another problem in the Vietnam War was that by 1969 1,697,000 tons of matériel were being brought in by sea annually, along with 48,000 tons by air. But such a flow overwhelmed men and facilities—thousands of tons were lost, misplaced, or unaccounted for. Thus, special teams were sent on temporary duty to establish viable accounting, inventory, storage, and issue procedures. In addition, special rapid area-maintenance (RAM) teams were used to repair 885 damaged aircraft, to fix 88 for a one-time flight to a repair depot and 123 for shipment to such, and to cannibalize 29 unrepairable machines. Teams were sent to train Vietnamese mechanics and to install computers, along with engineers to build revetments. A 400-man RED HORSE team—of rapid engineer deployable, heavy operational repair squadron engineers—was also sent to build roads and repair mortar-attack damage.

Similar to the mushrooming of construction and supply needs were those of ordnance. There, too, straight-through shipment from the United States was initiated, with ships pausing only briefly to refuel at Subic Bay in the Philippines. This cut the transit time from 150 to 30 days over a 10,000-mile line.

South Vietnamese Air Force (SVNAF) pilots proved adept at flying the AD-6 Skyraiders, but not at night as the aircraft lacked landing lights and serviceable artificial horizons. Yet night was the Viet Cong's (VC) favorite time to strike, and thus flare-dropping from C-47s started, which stopped the attacks. In the meantime, by spring 1962 the commander of the USAF Seventh Air Force had a tactical air-control system in place and could manage all air assets. And, based upon British experience in Malaya, a strategic hamlet pacification scheme was established.

Earlier in 1962, Military Assistance Command Vietnam (MACV) had opened and insisted that all U.S. Army helicopter operations have fixed-wing air cover. Liaison officers were attached to all ARVN units. After 462 ambushes in eight months, CINCPAC, the overall theater commander, made air cover of all operations mandatory. The next year saw no more entrapments. The American military also realized that processing of PRU films took far too long in a guerilla war, and thus the RVNAF got more aircraft from the United States and regional Vietnamese processing centers were established. USAF pilots relieved SVNAF pilots so that they could fly the new North American T-28 Trojan fighters (ER 5.8). The U.S. Army then received helicopter gunships and the new Grumman OV-1 Mohawk turboprops (ER 12.4). At the end of the year, Washington approved the National Campaign Plan, but it proved inadequate, and USAF assets in-country had to be doubled to be able to fly more sorties. These, however, were limited by the lack of effective air-ground communications and of SVNAF forward air controllers. Meanwhile, the Viet Cong had learned from their defeats and were building deep bomb-proof dugouts. By mid-1963 the Farm Gate forces were suffering from the shooting down of their T-28 and B-26 aircraft and declining serviceability. Strategic hamlets were falling to night attacks because they could not call up flare-dropping air-

craft or could not get through at all on the radio nets. Increasingly the Army of the Republic of Vietnam turned to U.S. Army gunships for emergency support.

In November 1963, with the revolt against President Diem and his murder, the Viet Cong attacked in Saigon. Political uncertainty reigned, but out of it emerged Gen. Nguyen Cao Ky who made sure that his air force was not placed under local army commanders. Further losses came as both the T-28 Trojans and B-26 Invaders had to be grounded and scrapped because of wing failures. The new Commander-in-Chief of the the the Pacific Air Forces (CINCPACAF) Gen. Jacob E. Smart, of Korean experience, urged that the 1954 Accords no longer applied and that B-57 Canberras be sent. However, Washington believed that the South Vietnamese must control their own destiny and delivered only additional AE-1 Skyraiders (ER 10.12). In May 1964, Secretary of Defense Robert McNamara, ordered the USAF only to train the South Vietnamese Air Force, who were to fly the additional Skyraiders.

Also at this time, in Saigon, the Military Assistance Command Vietnam and Military Assistance Advisory Group (MAAG) were amalgamated. Gen. William Westmoreland assumed command, and the new CINCPAC was Adm. U.S. Grant Sharp. Shortly thereafter, the U.S. Army, U.S. Air Force, and South Vietnamese Air Force operations centers were co-located, with emergency support being obtained through the latter due to language necessities. A few days later, the Tonkin Gulf attacks occurred, and the U.S. Congress authorized President Lyndon B. Johnson to aid South Vietnam to defend its independence and territorial integrity. Soon thereafter, the President accepted the recommendations of the ambassador in Saigon, Gen. Maxwell Taylor, and air strikes were authorized into Laos to disrupt the flow of men and arms from north to south. Subsequently, the Viet Cong decided that they were strong enough to shift from insurgency to conventional war.

Up to 1957, the USAF was training 5,726 pilots annually; but this had been phased down to 1,300 in 1962, just as the World War II cadre left the service and as airline demand was accelerating. Squadrons deploying to Vietnam had only 1.25 pilots per aircraft, and the shortage was exacerbated when in 1965 the Air Force Chief of Staff decreed that a tour would be limited to one year. The acceleration of the war in Southeast Asia caused pilots to finish their tours ahead of time. And, thus, 3,000 pilots were withdrawn from administrative jobs, and a 30 percent reduction was made in professional schooling. Other pilots were gathered from the earlier-than-planned phasing out of some Strategic Air Command and Air Defense Command squadrons, the pulling out of some Air National Guard advisers, holding reservists in for an extra year, putting navigators instead of second pilots in the rear seats of two-seaters, and expanding the Air Training Command's (ATC) undergraduate program. By 1971, ATC's program was compressed from 53 to 48 weeks, and from 240 to 208 flying hours. All of these measures, undertaken belatedly, finally remedied the shortage of fixed-wing pilots just as the war was terminating.

The helicopter course also had to be shortened, as the 700 students available in 1965 were less than half the number needed. The forty-three week course was shortened to produce ninety pilots every twelve weeks. In all, ATC trained 22,948 pilots up to the last year of the war, when 10,250 were graduated. The crews formed from this production had to be trained in nearly a dozen different types, and once they were combat-ready, they still needed survival training. In 1965, 720 completed that, rising to 11,000 in 1968.

The need for technical personnel was equally important. For their support, a whole new system had to be worked out. In 1961 few roofed facilities were available in Southeast Asia, and thus Air Force Logistics Command (AFLC) had to supply twenty-four mobile maintenance vans and outfit aircraft flying out with 300-day mission-support kits, which were periodically replenished from the depot at Clark Air Force Base in the Philip-

pines. However, this support chain involved too much unloading, storing, and reloading; and, therefore, in late 1962 Saigon became the main supply base, with fifteen ships steaming out weekly from the United States and going into demurrage in the Mekong River until they could be unloaded. An attempt was made to abandon aerial supply, but the number of "not operationally ready—supply" incidents (NORS) rose rapidly.

Also needed at this time were new and expanded air bases. Four were added to, and four more built in 1965, but shortly eleven more were needed. To overcome the gravity of the supply situation, Operation Bittertwine became the largest logistics activity since Korea. Procuring, packaging, packing, and shipping was done without the usual requisition forms. Each "package" contained enough material to support 4,400 men in tents; packages for temporary buildings followed, and, finally, civilian contractors to complete runways, operational buildings, and base housing. In eighteen months, 1,500 packages containing 346,000 different items were shipped for four bases in South Vietnam, and two in Thailand.

Then on March 2, 1965, Operation Rolling Thunder began, an intensification in the bombing of North Vietnam, designed by political minds to force the North Vietnamese to their knees. Rolling Thunder was intended to raise morale in the south, to penalize North Vietnam for supporting the Viet Cong, and to reduce infiltration from the north. President Johnson had to personally approve each mission and to ensure that civilian casualties were minimal, while also giving the Chinese and the Soviets no reason to intervene. F-105s, B-57s, and B-52s were used, dropping twenty-five to thirty tons of iron bombs each, as well as Boeing KC-135 Stratotankers (ER 1,769) under strict controls. However, the attack was blunted by the mid-October to mid-March monsoon. As the Rolling Thunder USAF aircraft dropped down to avoid SAMs, they took automatic small-arms fire, but until 1966–67 they did not have to worry about MiGs, nor radar around Hanoi. Subsequently, however, Hanoi had one of the world's heaviest and most sophisticated air-defense systems, including air-raid shelters for the population. And after 1966, North Vietnamese fighter aircraft carried their own electronic counter-measure (ECM) pods.

The U.S. Air Force and U.S. Navy were handicapped at this time by the lack of surprise, resulting from Washington's insistence that planes avoid sanctuary and other sensitive areas, as well as civilian casualties; and they were impeded by a weather system that made the best operational time a little bit on either side of midday. The short tours of duty of USAF crews, as opposed to the USN's longer-duty approach, meant that many USAF aircrews were inexperienced in-theater. And the U.S. assignment of "route packages"—the six divided geographical areas of North Vietnam, which the U.S. had established—made targets more predictable for the enemy. In addition, LBJ's frequent bombing pauses let the Viet Cong regroup and the North Vietnamese Army repair. Only in April 1967 were MiG bases permissible targets, and then the enemy flew well out of range to Red China.

In the three years and nine months of Rolling Thunder, 304,000 tactical sorties and 2,380 B-52 sorties were flown, and 643,000 tons of bombs were dropped on North Vietnam. In late 1971 when the North Vietnamese Air Force (NVAF) had 250 MiGs, of which 90 were MiG-21s, 1,025 sorties were flown against their bases. In the final eleven-day 1972 battering of the Hanoi and Haiphong area, twenty-six aircraft were lost, fifteen of them B-52s.

From 1965 to 1972 the North Vietnamese Army began attacks upon U.S. establishments in South Vietnam. The United States no longer talked of withdrawing, and Military Assistance Command Vietnam was authorized to use USAF aircraft without the required South Vietnamese Air Force observers whenever the SVNAF could not respond to emergency calls. By the end of May 1965, 50,000 American servicemen were in-country. Air power began to be used massively,

with the U.S. Navy and Marine Corps joining USAF B-52s in strikes.

In 1966, U.S. troop strength had risen to 385,000 with Korean and ANZAC forces added. Jets now arrived by squadrons. By 1972, the trans-Pacific reinforcement system had been perfected to the point that the 4th Tactical Fighter Wing at Seymour-Johnson AFB, North Carolina, departed within seventy-two hours of being warned. Some 400 tons of cargo and 854 personnel moved in thirty-eight Lockheed C-141 Starlifters (ER 1,470), while four C-130s carried the servicing personnel to handle the thirty-six aircraft at stops en route. The F-4 Phantoms flew in cells of six and were refueled several times en route in their eleven-hour non-stop to Hickam AFB, Hawaii, accompanied by KC-135s all the way. The first eighteen F-4s flew to Guam the second day and on to Ubon, Thailand, the third day, followed twenty-four hours later by the another eighteen F-4s. All thirty-six started flying combat sorties on the third day in Thailand. By 1972, SAC had 168 jet tankers and 285 crews and could perform up to 130 air refuelings in each day in Southeast Asia. SAC also had 54 B-52s at U-Tapao, Thailand, and 117 on Guam.

Since they first went into action in June 1965, targets for the heavy bombers had been personally selected by General Westmoreland. By 1966 they were equipped for direction by the new Combat Skyspot radar, which enabled ground controllers to guide them to targets and drop the bombs. This reduced planning time and allowed diversions to targets of opportunity while the B-52s were en route, or to scramble the six-plane alert force on Guam.

In the meantime, the enemy had begun using the classic tactic of sending in a small assault to draw in defense reinforcements and then to ambush them. At the battle of Suoi Da in October–November 1966, 2,300 tactical sorties were flown in support, 3,300 tactical airlifts were made with 8,900 tons of cargo, and 11,400 men were airlifted

The McDonnell F2H Banshee (ER 34), the second of the St. Louis company's shipboard jets, was initiated in 1945 to provide the U.S. Navy with a fighter-bomber. Production ended in 1953, after the Korean War showed that a larger, more powerful aircraft was needed at a time of rapid evolution. (McDonnell Douglas)

The ease of servicing the new low-slung jets is obvious here with an F2H Banshee. (McDonnell)

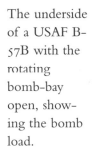

The underside of a USAF B-57B with the rotating bomb-bay open, showing the bomb load.

By the time the English Electric Canberra PR-9 became the Martin B-57A Canberra (in background), aircrew had to wear high-altitude G suits to prevent bends and blacking out. (Martin)

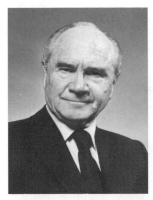

"Mr. Mac," James McDonnell, Sr., the driving force behind the success of the St. Louis McDonnell Aircraft Corporation, the designer and manufacturer of advanced aircraft. He eventually took over the famed Douglas Aircraft Company in an inevitable consolidation of the industry in the 1960s. (McDonnell Douglas)

One of the rare adoptions of a British design by the American services, the English Electric Canberra PR-9 (ER 305) became the USAF Martin B-57 Canberra (ER 146.7, B-57B). It made its first delivery flight to Martin in Maryland in 1951, the first jet to fly non-stop westbound across the North Atlantic. For U.S. service, the crew was seated at first side-by-side, but in the B-57B, they were in tandem, and that aircraft was fitted with a rotary bomb bay in which the weapons were mounted on the door itself. (Martin)

With the Cold War heating up in the late 1950s, Martin and General Dynamics produced two new versions of the Canberra, the RB-57D and E (ER 185), both fitted with a much enlarged high-altitude wing and larger engines so that the machine could fly along Soviet borders and perhaps penetrate Soviet airspace. (Martin)

Aside from Grumman Aircraft Engineering Corporation, the other leading builder of aircraft for the U.S. Navy was the Douglas Aircraft Company, whose Ed Heinemann opted for the smallest machine possible. Based upon the World War II research of German designer Alexander Lippisch on delta wings, Heinemann proposed a modified shape to maximize the performance of a short-ranged shipboard interceptor, which started life with a 5,000-pound-thrust engine in 1948. However, due to development failures in the engine, the F4D Skyray (ER 42), which first flew in 1954, went into service with a 14,500-pound afterburning power plant. (McDonnell Douglas)

Another late-war design that came into postwar service was the Grumman F8F Bearcat (ER 12), later very popular with air racers. (Grumman History Center)

The Lockheed P-80 Shooting Star (ER 27, F-80C) was a sleek jet fighter. Designed by Kelly Johnson starting in 1943, it was the first operational USAF jet fighter. An asset in the Korean War, one of its strengths was the ease of field maintenance (here an engine change exposes the Whittle-style de Havilland H-1 engine). Johnson settled the details of the P-80 in one week, and proposed a 180-day construction schedule, but he actually delivered the prototype in 139 days. (U.S. Army)

The Vickers Supermarine Swift (ER 15.2) of 1952 was one of the less successful early jet fighters, and the subject of a Parliamentary inquiry. It was the first swept-wing RAF fighter, and the first with powered ailerons in 1954. (Vickers)

The follow-on aircraft to the F2H Banshee (ER 34) was the F3H Demon (ER 61), now carrying air-to-air missiles. Intended to prove that seaborne fighters could match their land-based counterparts in aerodynamics as well as in structural and propulsion advances, the Demon was hamstrung by the failure of its Westinghouse J40 engine. However, its legacy was passed to both the U.S. Navy and the U.S. Air Force, as well as to the Royal Air Force and the Israeli Air Force. (McDonnell)

A two-seat trainer version of the Lockheed P-80/F-80 Shooting Star was called the T-33. The low-level pass seen here is being made by an aircraft from the Japanese Self-Defense Forces. (Lockheed)

Left: The Lockheed C-130 Hercules (ER 344, C-130B) evolved from the 1951 USAF decision that in the future all transports would be turbine powered because of the crew savings that would result. The Hercules was the first medium-sized transport to be designed as a weapons system. Entering service in late 1956, the aircraft is a classic example of a sound and versatile design that has been steadily improved by modifications and sometimes by rebuilding. The aircraft seen here is in Egyptian service, and the type was still in production at Marietta, Georgia, in 2003. (Lockheed-Martin)

By 1955, the *Luftwaffe* had been revived as a NATO air force. Symbolically, at Luke AFB, Arizona, in 1957, the German World War II ace Maj. Erich Hartmann received his fighter school graduation certificate from former Flying Tiger Col. Warren H. Higgins. (USAF)

The challenges of the Korean War caused a demand for the creation of the North American F-86 Sabre Jet (ER 31.4). The F-86 had been started in 1944 for the U.S. Navy, but was ordered by the U.S. Army Air Forces after UN fighters and bombers had encountered Soviet-built and manned North Korean and Chinese opponents near the Yalu River. When postwar German research was available, the design was changed to create the USAF's first swept-wing bird. The F-86 had a pressurized cockpit, but still had the same reliable Browning .50-caliber guns. By late 1950, modifications included power-boosted controls. (North American Aviation)

The North American F-100 Super Sabre (ER 90) was evolved from the F-86 and was the first fighter in the world capable of supersonic level flight. Along with the prototype, 110 were ordered, and in 1953 one was flown to the last low-level speed record of 755 mph. (USAF)

In September 1950, with Korean War funds available, the USAF accepted the Republic Aviation Corporation proposal that the straight-wing F-84 Thunderjet (ER 27.8; ER 78, F-84F) be revamped with swept wings to get higher performance. The aircraft first flew in 1952, and eventually 2,715 were built, some of which went (under the Truman Doctrine) to the Royal Hellenic Air Force in Greece. (Royal Hellenic Air Force)

One of the alternate solutions to the jet was the turboprop. This is a Canadair CL-44 Yukon (ER 710.5) cargo and maritime reconnaissance plane developed from the Bristol Britannia (ER 517). It was also used as a long-range transport. (Canadian Forces)

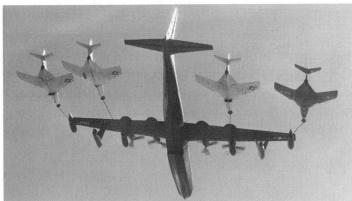

The Convair R3Y Tradewind (ER 504) weighed twenty-four tons. With four 5,500 hp turboprops, it could get off the water in thirty seconds. In 1956, it demonstrated for the first time the ability to refuel several jet fighters at once from its drogues. Probing here are Grumman F9F Cougars (ER 24). (Convair)

A French Navy Breguet Atlantique (ER 429) and a Grumman S-2 Tracker (ER 15.6), two developments in the maritime surveillance and anti-submarine warfare field. (Source unknown) in and out. The enemy lost 1,100 men and 2,000 tons of rice.

In 1966 air power was much enhanced by the development of effective forward air controllers, who spent time in their areas; by technology-enhanced night reconnaissance; by the use of cluster bombs and their bomblets; by delayed action bombs that penetrated tree cover before detonating at ground level; and by the use of AC-47 and AC-130 USAF gunships for hamlet protection at night.

During 1967, U.S. forces in Vietnam rose to 486,000 who were supported in combat by bombing of the enemy within 27 to 77 yards from their front line. A lull also occurred, while North Vietnam's General Giap re-formed with fresh Soviet help. Yet, by November, General Westmoreland thought that the South Vietnames were winning. USAF personnel were flying fifteen sorties per man.

Early in 1968, Khe Sanh was attacked as the North Vietnamese attempted to break through the demilitarized zone. The U.S. air response was Operation Niagara, in which Air Force General Momeyer became the manager of all USAF air assets, including the new C-130F Airborne Battlefield Command and Control Centers. In spite of the bad weather, but with the assistance of Skyspot radar, 110,000 tons of bombs were dropped on the besiegers in the surrounding hills. A few days after Khe Sanh was invested, North Vietnam's Tet Offensive struck thirty-six provincial capitals in the south, five autonomous cities, twenty-three airfields, and some district capitals. While most of these were defeated in two or three days, the Battle for Hue lasted several weeks. Estimated losses were 45,000 North Vietnamese and Viet Cong, but also 14,000 civilians killed, 24,000 wounded, and a further 627,000 made homeless.

The Allies won in the field, but it was a political disaster for Lyndon Johnson, about to run for another term. He sent additional troops and encouraged the speeding up of transferring the burden of the war to South Vietnamese shoulders. He then halted all bombing north of the 20th Paral-

lel. The North Vietnamese did attend peace talks in Paris, but at the same time strongly reinforced their units in the South. The North Vietnames Army and Viet Cong again opened an offensive in May.

After Richard Nixon won the presidential election, he accelerated Vietnamization, and by 1970 the first USAF units began to be withdrawn. Nixon then pressed for peace, invading Cambodia to gain time for a withdrawal, and by the spring of 1972 called for massive bombing of North Vietnam to urge the North toward a resolution. The Linebacker I operation concentrated major air attacks on North Vietnam from May 8 to October 23, 1972. After a pause late in the year, the Linebacker II operation was initiated for eleven days of nearly non-stop bombing, between December 18 and December 29, for the first time targeting sites within and around Hanoi and Haiphong, along with munitions and fuel sites and infrastructure. Peace agreements were finally signed in January 1973.

Linebacker II was almost immediately interpreted as reflecting traditional air-power doctrine. Sound application of air power, it was thought, had forced Hanoi back to the table, and thus, proponents concluded, it could have won the war years earlier and saved thousands of lives. However, by the late 1980s this view began to change, for the original interpretation was based upon informed guesses and not upon North Vietnamese information. The eleven-day attack in 1972 needed to have been compared to those of World War II and to the reactions of those political leaders affected.

In truth, by the end of the short, crushing campaign, the U.S. had run out of targets, having eliminated the enemy air defenses and transportation; and there was no industry to destroy. What North Vietnam needed at this time was to get the United States out of the theater so that it could renew conventional war.

By the late 1980s, American thinkers were reconsidering limited wars and tactical air forces and saw the traditional application of air-power doctrine in the Vietnam War as dysfunctional. North

Vietnam did not have the industrial heartland upon which the philosophies of Douhet, Mitchell, Trenchard, and LeMay had focused, any more than Marxism was applicable to Russia or China in 1917.

The coincident ending of the Cold War, and a realization that the United States would fight different wars in the future, helped deflate the emphasis and interest in strategic (or grand-strategic) bombing. This was reflected in the new 1992 issue of *Air Force Manual-1*, concerning U.S. Air Force doctrine.

The assessment of the use of air power in the Vietnam War was originally made more difficult by the fact that at the time of writing of the 1972 edition of the USAF guide, the war had not ended and emotional factors could not be eliminated from any estimation of its results. The enemy's evidence was not available, and even if written, was likely to be just as biased as some of that from the Allied side. The use of air power was entangled with the whole war strategy in such a way that it had become hard to unravel valid air historical experience from invalid because of political overtones and considerations, if not blunders.

The use of air power in Vietnam was vastly complicated by the political position. Although the American viewpoint is now different from that of 1965 when the Rolling Thunder bombing campaign on the North was initiated, on the whole, at that time, honest men were trying to make honest decisions. The slow escalation of Rolling Thunder can be attributed, perhaps, to an excess of political science and not enough military realism. And the Ranch Hand defoliant programs, which later came under ecological criticism, were originally a scientific solution to a battlefield problem. Perspective on the whole war has been distorted by complex political and emotional responses, and it seems quite clear that the old lessons should have been heeded, which indicated that involvement by outsiders in a civil war is a kindness to no one.

The military felt at the time that the politicians formulated Vietnam policy, and then the generals were asked how it could be carried out—a situation that too often has happened in the past. Unlike the balance of military and political objectives achieved in the Second World War, an incompatibility of objectives existed in the Vietnam conflict. It can be argued that although airmen found themselves involved in the consensus process that had become modern American policy-making, airmen who had grown up in the First World War were well aware that air power alone could not win wars, especially counterguerrilla operations.

One of the legacies of the conflict in South Vietnam until the 1975 collapse was the U.S.-trained South Vietnamese Air Force. It had had to take over the role of lavish air support for ground forces, by then accustomed to massive USAF and Allied help. The need for defense against North Vietnamese MiGs and helicopter support had made the American air forces the last to withdraw under the Nixon phasing-out of the Asian land war in 1972.

In retrospect, in Vietnam grand-strategic air power was at last used properly, when President Nixon had decided on the Linebacker II strategy. At last mass was used to strike offensively at the decisive point while at the same time demonstrating economy of force in pursuing a clearly defined objective. As in World War II, not only were iron bombs dropped in North Vietnam, but evasive routings and times were employed so that maneuver helped achieve surprise and maintain security. And, as many had thought, the same operation, carried out much earlier, in 1965, would have had far greater impact.

The story of the Vietnam War by 2003 is less shrouded in emotions and media as well as national security problems, making a fully rational analysis easier to complete than in earlier years. But the traumas, myths, and antagonisms were not dispelled until America's 1991 Persian Gulf War victory. It does seems clear that over the course of the Vietnam War, air power was hampered by the fact that three U.S. presidents considered themselves constitutionally and actually qualified to play the role of commander-in-chief, and that modern communications enabled them to do so. Presidents Eisenhower, Kennedy, and Johnson were determined not to lose the Cold War to the Communists, but also wished to succeed at the least official cost and involvement. Ironically, that cost was great.

And it must not be overlooked that the Joint Chiefs of Staff, under Secretary of Defense Robert McNamara, had acquiesced in the political decisions, allowing the politicians to make military decisions as to targets. The result was a quasi-air war in which aircrews were endangered, for the advantage was given to the enemy defense.

The U.S. manner of waging war in Southeast Asia was essentially imperial—the Americans took over—and this destroyed the confidence of the Vietnamese in their own abilities, including trust in their own air force. Moreover, when a victory was achieved over the enemy's Tet Offensive in 1968, for domestic political reasons the American leadership threw it away by failing to claim it and to follow through, in order to win the elections at home. The best grand-strategic weapon the U.S. had was the B-52, but it was held on a tight leash until President Nixon made the decision to use it against Hanoi, seven years after U.S. involvement began in 1965.

It can also now be pointed out that the American approach was the normally profligate attitude so common to U.S. activities before the Arab fuel embargo of 1973 and sharply escalating fuel prices. Essentially five American air forces were operating in Vietnam: the U.S. Navy, both from carriers at Yankee Station in the north, for grand-strategic raids with tactical aircraft against Hanoi, and from Dixie station in the south, in tactical support of those ashore in the Delta; U.S. Air Force F-105s and later F-111s from Thailand, also in grand-strategic roles; jet and piston-engined aircraft flying from bases in-country; the U.S. Marines Corps; and the U.S. Army helicopters. And there was also the South Vietnamese Air Force, not to mention the enemy. In justification of these large forces, it is true that enemy attacks on the enormous airfields occupied by land-based units in-country did require large garrison counter-forces, though nothing compared to what might have been needed if the North Vietnamese had been able to use an offensive air force.

Looking back, we can see that this presence of numbers had lulled the Americans into a false sense of security, for they had too many aircraft on the ground in vulnerable dispersals, and they placed too great a reliance on operations in which aerial refueling was a key ingredient.

Much like other wars, the war in Southeast Asia showed that the most modern weapons may not be the most reliable and that operative lessons and technological/mechanical links with the past must not be forgotten. Still much valued was the C-47, a 1936 design, as both a cargo carrier and a gunship, and the U.S. Navy's 1944 A-1 Skyraider, with its weight-lifting ability, reliability, simplicity, and loiter time.

India-Pakistan, 1965 and 1971

One curious war of the post-1945 period was the inconclusive armed clash between India and Pakistan in September 1965. Essentially a Second World War campaign, it was fought without grand-strategic purpose, without much imagination, and in the end without effect. The air role was strictly limited to ground support, and the results were on the whole misconstrued due to the fact that reporters generally failed to divide claims of aircraft downed by at least a factor of three. As in other battles earlier, once this was done, the losses on each side came close to the figure acknowledged by the loser. Both sides suffered severe wastage of their ammunition and fuel, as well as other equipment, and fighting was largely brought to a halt by supplier powers imposing an embargo on arms shipments. If any lessons can be drawn, they are that countries entirely dependent for their supply of arms upon the outside world should very carefully weigh the odds and the objects of going to war. The object in this case was confrontation, not victory.

Tactically aircraft of both sides flew under radar screens. The Pakistanis, having only one enemy but two fronts, were able to concentrate their aircraft and thus ease their maintenance problems; the Indian Air Force, with a wider variety of aircraft and the possibility of Chinese intervention, faced more complex problems. Yet both in the air and on the ground the Pakistanis discovered that the Indians had the advantage in numbers, though both sides found that it was the simpler, older, and more familiar equipment that was easier to maintain and operate. Air forces especially tend to become oversophisticated to the extent that the equipment exceeds the abilities of the humans assigned to it—a kind of technological Peter Principle.

Although as in the past each side claimed many enemy aircraft at the time, losses actually were limited. The great distances made concentration on airfields sensible, while other operations focused on aiding or blunting ground attacks. From both a political and a defense view, Pakistan benefitted in 1971 by the loss of incompatible and indefensible East Pakistan.

Much was made of the fact that Pakistan had American F-104s (it actually had only twelve) and that the Indians had MiG-21s, yet these aircraft never met in combat, and air superiority was never made an issue; what did happen after the war was that, with American aid cut off, the Pakistan Air Force had to buy French and Soviet aircraft and thus become more polyglot than was desirable. Nevertheless, it appeared that the Pakistan Air Force, with its more aggressive spirit, emerged with a strengthened ego from the hostilities, while India, already upset by the Chinese invasion of 1962, was left with losses of some seventy-five aircraft to the Pakistanis' nineteen. As in the case of the Arab-Israeli conflicts, the smaller—and of necessity—better-trained air force proved once again that it could stand up to a much larger combatant and, if pilot morale was high and maintenance

efficient, could inflict disproportionate losses. The whole "war" was so short that no more lessons can be drawn from it than from one annual maneuver, nor with any more safety.

Pakistan had the disadvantage, from the partition of India in 1947, of being essentially two small Muslim states separated by Hindu India. But East and West Pakistan were hardly compatible, and in 1971 the East became Bangladesh. An airlift using Pakistan International Airways 707s via Colombo, Sri Lanka, delivered three divisions to Bengal, but civil war ensued. India and Pakistan went to war. The Indian Air Force had 735 aircraft to the Pakistani 240. Both sides obtained reinforcements of modern aircraft.

The Pakistan Air Force had tried to emulate the Israeli success in the 1967 war and use a preemptive strike at Indian airfields to disrupt its larger opponent. But the dusk effort was too small; the Indian Air Force had all night to make repairs and retaliated in kind. In East Pakistan the IAF bombed the major air base at Dacca as a prelude to intervention, while air strikes from the Indian carrier *Vikrant* in the Bay of Bengal hit others.

On October 16, Indian B-57 Canberras attacked West Pakistan and fighting ensued on the ground in the east and in the air in the west. At this time, the Indian Air Force had 625 operational aircraft to the Pakistan Air Force's 210. The IAF now had 175 MiG 21s and 150 Su-7BMs (ER 82) and some 160 Folland Gnats (ER 12.8), 100 Hawker Hunters (ER 18.6), 60 Canberras, and 40 Mysteres. The Pakistan Air Force had acquired 70 Chinese F-6 (Mig-19) and 20 Dassault Mirage III (ER 84.2, Mirage III/50) and some 90 additional Canadair F-86 Sabre Jets (ER 31.4) bought from West Germany via Iran; the PAF also had built or enlarged airfields. The December 3 PAF preemptive strike against eight IAF airfields was too thin to be effective, and by the next morning the IAF was able to counterattack ten airfields in East Pakistan. Meanwhile, in the Bay of Bengal the Pakistan navy lost its leased U.S. submarine *Ghazi,* as it lay in wait for the Indian carrier

Vikrant, which flew 160 sorties against targets ashore. The Pakistan Air Force base at Tezgaon was neutralized, and India's invading forces had air support. Constant air action continued in the west, including light planes requisitioned for patrols. Jordan loaned ten to sixteen F-104s, of which four were lost by the PAF.

The Indians then began to use helicopters to move troops forward as the Pakistan Air Force in the east had ceased to exist. In the west, ground operations were supported by the IAF with steady losses on both sides, but the IAF had airborne warning and control system (AWACS) support from a high-flying Soviet Tupolev Tu-114 (ER 1,977). By December 15, Dacca had fallen and Bangladesh came into being.

In summary, in this highly compressed war of less than two intensive weeks, the Pakistan Air Force flew about 2,840 sorties in the west to the Indian Air Force's 4,000, about half of which were ground support. Actual losses were probably forty PAF to sixty-five IAF, most to guns. Apart from the loss of indefensible East Pakistan, the conflict was a stand-off in which, once again, old reliable aircraft bore the brunt of the battles and proved most maintainable. This was also a struggle over airfields, but neither side in the west succeeded in eliminating the opponent's bases.

THE ARAB-ISRAELI WARS, 1948–

The Arab-Israeli Wars carry very clear-cut lessons. By scavenging and purchase of war surplus, the Israeli Air Force emerged from a covert to an overt force in the 1948–49 War for Independence. By 1956, the IAF was on a solid professional footing with some jet fighters and a sound concept of the feasibility and the sensibility of air power in strategic and tactical roles, operating from central bases.

In 1956 the Anglo-French drive to recover the Suez Canal was combined with an Israeli desire to secure the Sinai, in order to provide a buffer against an aggressive nationalist Arab Egypt and the Royal Egyptian Air Force (REAF). The IAF had British Supermarine Spitfire IXs (ER 2.63) and Dassault Ouragan (ER 11.5) jet fighters, as well as the P-51 Mustang; the REAF had Soviet MiGs and British de Havilland Vampires. To make up their weakness in the air defense of their cities and lack of roads, the French offered the Israeli Air Force fighter cover and Nord NorAtlas 262 transports (ER 29). Israeli strategy was to give the Egyptians a setback, to clean out the Gaza guerrilla camps, and to clear the Arab forts preventing free Israeli use of the port of Eilat. By a combination of air transport, paratrooper, and ground-support efforts, the Israeli Air Force enabled positions to be consolidated while the Royal Egyptian Air Force was neutralized. This coincided with the Anglo-French attacks upon Egypt, the RAF containing the REAF and the French Air Force destroying the REAF's bomber force in a long-range penetration to Luxor.

The British in 1955 had evacuated Egypt but retained logistic matériel and the defense of the Suez Canal. However, they foolishly refused Egyptian Gen. Abdul Gamal Nasser new arms, and thus he turned to the Czechs and the Soviets of the Communist Eastern Bloc. When the West refused aid for the crucial Aswan Dam, he nationalized the Suez Canal. Plans were then set afoot for a joint Anglo-French-Israeli invasion of Egypt, of which the IAF's 1956 war was the prelude.

The Anglo-French attack started with ineffective bombing raids from high altitudes by B-57 Canberras and the new Vickers Valiants. Moreover, Allied photo-reconnaissance estimates concerning the Royal Egyptian Air Force, supplied by the U.S. Air Force, were twice those of the ground-based Israelis.

The RAF role using bombs was to strike airfields and destroy the REAF. Because of U.S. disapproval, the Valiants did not bomb on the first day, and Soviet instructors evacuated REAF aircraft both to Luxor and to Syria and Saudi Arabia. The RAF bombing from 45,000 feet followed World War II practice at night with low-level Pathfinders marking the targets. But the tonnage dropped on fifteen airfields was only sufficient to have destroyed one. Wishful thinking is a poor substitute for substantiated calculations.

Much more effective strikes were flown by British carrier planes, Canberras, and French F-84F Thunderjets, carefully avoiding causing civilian casualties. Some of these sorties were based on Cyprus and some on Malta. But for transport operations, the RAF was terribly short, having only twenty-seven aircraft for the paradrop at Port Said airfield to start the invasion. They were reinforced by naval aircraft.

The capture of the Suez Canal was frustrated by international pressure for a cease-fire and by irresolution in London and hostility in Washington. What should have been a swift *coup de main* was vitiated by poor intelligence assessments, diplomatic pressures, and indecision, as well as lack of suitable forces for a proper application of surprise in a preemptive assault.

The 1967 Six-Day War

Understanding the forces involved, the Israelis waited for nine years. The failure of the United Nations allowed the Arabs to make aggressive moves in the hopes of either cutting off Israel from access to the eastern seas or forcing the Israelis into attacking.

The Israelis chose to make a preemptive strike in June 1967. The vulnerability of the Arabs was revealed by the drastic way in which Israel improved upon the 1956 Sinai campaign. The whole Israeli plan was based upon precise timing, hard training, accurate striking power, understanding of their own limitations, and proper intelligence, including an accurate psychological assessment of their opponents.

The dawn Israeli strikes were launched before the Egyptians customarily were ready for work,

and in a surprise move the IAF swept in low from over the sea to the northwest. Within three hours they had attacked sixteen airfields with special bombs and cannon fire. Within two days the Arabs had lost 333 aircraft on the ground and 95 in the air, and thus the Israelis had no need to fear either bomber attacks on their homeland or tactical interference with their armies. The strikes employed the principles of concentration, economy of force, and surprise, as well as simplicity; yet flexibility was maintained by ground controllers who could have switched aircraft to new targets as needed. All targets were hit from as low and as close as possible to avoid misses and decoys. Dibbler bombs were dropped from 100 feet to disrupt concrete runways, and cannon were used at ranges of about 100 yards, yet in both cases, the aircraft flew at speeds of 500 knots. And prior to battle, training had been limited in order that virtually 100 percent availability of aircraft could be achieved.

The Israeli aircraft were then switched to direct support of the army, and the result was *Blitzkrieg* at its best. No attacks were made on civilian centers, so that Arab politicians had the least cause for creating a general will to war. In fact, the Israeli forces have inherited a legacy from the Second World War and polished it to perfection in an arena that is still in many ways the Western Desert. They maintained the initiative by the acquisition of U.S. aircraft, when French sources were closed, and by refusing to sign the nuclear non-proliferation treaty.

The Israelis won a classical campaign, but they found themselves facing a guerrilla war, the logical reaction for the Egyptians and their Soviet advisers. When Israel countered sneak infantry raids with jet strikes against guerrilla bases and deep into Egypt, the Russians shifted from fighter defense to the development of SAM sites. Israeli strikes at these were effective until a cease-fire was imposed that allowed the Egyptians to carpet their side of the Suez Canal with SAMs. By 1971 it looked as if a stand-off had been reached that in turn might lead to a peace settlement if the defense had made the offense too costly. But knowing Israeli determination and tactical ingenuity, and given the religious nature of the nationalistic conflicts in the area, nobody could bet on it.

The Yom Kippur War of 1973

Electronics has also been at the heart of air warfare in the Middle East, where drones have replaced manned aircraft in the deadly SAM-belt reconnaissance flights or as decoys to enable the SAMs to be destroyed. Yet, Soviet and American equipment continued to be tested there at the tactical level.

The Yom Kippur War in 1973 followed on the period of Arabic electronic guerrilla war. In this encounter, the Egyptians started with the advantage of surprise, but the Israelis reacted with their usual battlefield flexibility on top of their rapid mobilization. The Egyptian SAMs were cleared out by surface forces and then the Isaeli Air Force was unleashed, resulting once again in a rapid victory for a country that cannot afford a long war.

Gradually over the next few years the Israelis not only made peace with the Egyptians but were supplied with ever more sophisticated U.S. aircraft and systems, until by the 1980s they had both the McDonnell Douglas F-15A Eagle and the General Dynamics F-16 A/B Fighting Falcon. Then they once again showed that surprise could be achieved in launching a daring strike across Arab territory to destroy what they claimed was an Iraqi nuclear bomb plant at Osirak. The small force of F-16s flew a very tight formation that gave a radar signature of an airliner, and its spokesmen chattered in Arabic for a complete deception. Partly out of fear of other such attacks and partly because Iran ceased to be an ally after the revolution, the United States became involved in loaning AWACS aircraft to Saudi Arabia and in the sale of F-15 Eagles to Arab countries as well as to Israel.

In 1982, Israeli air power again proved its competence in the invasions of Lebanon, when drone decoys were used to enable Syrian SAMs to be taken out, thus once again giving the IAF freedom to operate in support of the ground forces. But when they reached Beirut and the Palestine Liberation Organization (PLO) refused to surrender, the Israeli Air Force was largely powerless and the war reverted to a tank and infantry affair, but with the Israelis refusing to get mired in house-to-house urban warfare.

The First Gulf or Iran-Iraq War, 1980–88

In the incredibly complex politics of the Muslim Arab world, compounded as they were after 1950 by both revolutions and coups on the one hand and by the Cold War on the other, not to mention the presence of the Jewish state after 1948, there were many strange bedfellows.

The 1980–88 war clearly showed lack of comprehension of the use of aircraft. Iraq feared Iran's intentions in the wake of the Islamic Revolution that deposed the aviation-minded Shah, and thus Iraq went on the offensive and invaded Iran in several places after air strikes against ten airfields. But a sloppy attack and hardened shelters deflated the effort. The Iraqi Air Force had 350 operational aircraft, the Iranian Air Force a few less, but lacked spares. The helicopter ratio was 165 to 600. Both sides continued strikes behind the lines and made large claims, but neither supported the troops engaged in the fighting style of World War I.

Both sides bombed the respective capital cities—Baghdad and Tehran—and both attacked oil; but by early 1987 stalemate had been reached and even philosophically radical Iranians trained in Russia had little effect. Concurrently, Iran's sophisticated U.S.-made Grumman F-14 Tomcats gradually declined from fifty-five in 1980 to five in 1988, due to shortage of spares and poor maintenance. Attacks on shipping were a new feature in this war, but were not pressed home or effective. In the meantime, the Egyptians resupplied Iraq's MiG-19 and MiG-21 losses. Late in 1983, Iraq used napalm and mustard gas, and then loosed five Dassault Super Etendard IV (ER 32.4) fighters from France, whose Exocet missiles appeared to be aimed at international tankers and caused Western concern.

In a new offensive in the so-called "War of the Cities," both sides used gunships well in defense to blunt enemy offensives. Then in March 1984 the Exocets began to hit neutral tankers at the Iranian oil depot at Kharg Island, to which Iranians responded in kind; and to this the Saudi's responded with F-15s. By the end of 1984, sixty-seven major tankers had been attacked, though they survived; but early in 1985 eleven tankers had to be scrapped. Later in the year, Iranian rocket-armed helicopters attacked from the Rostam fuel platform down the Gulf. By this time the Iranians were benefitting from covert U.S. aid, including Hawk missiles, 707s, and parts for F-4 Phantoms. In late 1986, Iran fired Scud-B missiles into Bagdad, and in 1988 Iraq shot up to forty SS-12 missiles at Tehran. Jordan and Saudi Arabia offered Iraq F-5 Freedom Fighters and crews; and in addition to 24 MiG-29s, the Iraqis used 113 Mirage F1s.

The tanker war flared and both the Western allies and the Soviets placed warships in the Persian Gulf. One was the cruiser USS *Stark,* which was heavily damaged by Iraqi Mirages. The Iranians installed Chinese Silkworm missiles near the choke-point Straits of Ormuz, and the Kuwaitis re-flagged their tankers under U.S. or USSR registry and appealed for USN convoys. The USS *Guadalcanal,* a helicopter carrier, was brought in to sweep mines in August 1986. But as the U.S. Navy was short on mine-sweeping gear, the Royal and French navies were called in also. The war escalated, and 178 tankers had been hit by 1987. In 1988, with tensions still high in the Gulf, the cruiser USS *Vincennes* by accident downed an Iran Air Airbus A-300, with two SAMs, due to lack of response to radar queries and plotting confusion.

Suddenly, on July 19, the Iranians accepted a UN resolution for a cease-fire. Iraq continued to fly PRU sorties for several more weeks into 1988

before the war was regarded as over. Then, in December, Pan Am Flight 103, a 747, was downed by a bomb over Lockerbie, Scotland. At the time it was thought to be in retaliation for the *Vincennes* incident, but by 2000 two Libyan operatives were on trial in a Scottish court in the Netherlands for this case of terrorism. One was convicted.

The First Gulf War was a stalemate, but it had important international repercussions at a variety of levels, even if it saw no great aerial lessons.

AFGHANISTAN, 1979–88

Outside powers intervene in Afghanistan at their own peril. The mountain-and-desert terrain is ideal for defensive and offensive guerrilla and partisan operations of the hardy, ingenious, and independent people, and very difficult for armies and air forces. Internal politics have always made for a political situation that was built on sand. In the 1970s, this led to a military coup, followed by Soviet intervention in a land where the air force had already been converted to modern Soviet arms. By 1979, some 5,000 Russian advisers were in the country, which was plagued with local revolts. For a while the in-fighting and consequent lack of coordination among the rebel factions enabled the government in Kabul and its Soviet backers to keep a shaky upper hand. During the summer of 1979 the Soviets prepared to invoke the treaty of 1978 because not only of instability but also for fear of the rising Muslim tide all along the Soviet borders. At the same time, the Russians wanted their traditional goal of warm-water ports in the Persian Gulf, for which pressure could also be applied to Iran, and the United States could be embarrassed by having to embrace the Pakistani dictator.

The invasion began with the Soviets flying in troops to seize the Kabul airport and deploy along the road into the capital. The American reaction was to scour the world for surplus Russian arms that could be supplied to the guerrilla *mujahideen,* who had declared a *jihad*—a Muslim holy war—against the invaders. Initial Soviet tactics were a failure, and the operation was rethought, including much increased use of air power, especially helicopters, of which some 300 were in use by 1981. By then the Soviets had 100,000 men and 400 aircraft committed.

The Russians began to lose aircraft to ground fire and to guerrilla attacks on their air bases. Bombing and strafing campaigns were launched in conjunction with cordon-and-sweep operations in which paratroopers were used, again with variable success. Attacks upon refugee camps over the border in Pakistan and on the *mujahideen* lines of communication bringing in ammunition from the south helped persuade the United States to provide more aid.

For the Pakistan Air Force these armed incursions posed especial difficulties, as the mountains shielded enemy aircraft until they debouched into Pakistan air space. Denied U.S. AWACS planes, the Pakistanis had to fly constant patrols. And the rules of engagement only allowed PAF fighters to attack if they were sure the hostile victim would fall in Pakistan. The United States aided with F-16s, but the 1985 adoption of the Pressler Amendment to the Foreign Assistance Act of 1961 denied them spares, as Pakistan had by now become a nuclear power, as had arch-rival India. The PAF learned to have parts made at home.

The Russians and the Afghan army next tried to advance up valleys, protected by a circle of six Mil Mi-24 (ER 3.2) gunships, called in one at a time by a forward air controller on targets of opportunity, much as the old RAF taxicab rank had operated in late World War II. As in the past, when the floor of the valley was gained, the rebels reasserted their presence from the high ground, and the invaders were forced to withdraw. But in 1982, the Soviets had some success in cooperation with the Afghan government forces in the plains. A subsequent campaign saw a faster tempo, with airlifted troops blocking the exits from the valleys as those on the ground advanced, supported by hel-

icopters. Forced high up the mountains, the *mujahideen* were ineffective. But, having achieved their objectives, the government troops then scorched the valley floors and withdrew before winter.

In 1983, the rebels increasingly were able to use SAMs, and thus the Soviets had to employ flares as decoys. By the summer, the *mujahideen* had antiaircraft guns, and Russian and Afghan air forces lost more aircraft both in the air and on the ground. In 1984, the Russians brought in more aircraft, and carpet-bombing of valley floors was undertaken by Tupolev Tu-16s (ER 2,594) based within the Soviet Union. Special Russian air-assault forces (the VDV) were also organized, and as many as 2,000 soldiers at a time were moved in. This tactic opened up the roads that were so often the scene of ambushes, but the new forts and garrisons on the valley floor were constantly harassed by the rebels.

The next Soviet action, mounted directly from the Soviet Union, was to relieve the pressure on forts close to Pakistan, to destroy guerrilla supply dumps, and even to attack their camps in neutral Pakistan. By 1985 the Soviet forces in Afghanistan were backed by 40,000 more in their own country. But the rebels, though split into many groups, were receiving heavy U.S. aid, as well as Soviet-made shoulder-fired SA-7 missiles. The battle seesawed as the rebels countered with Stinger SAMs. The air forces retaliated with laser-guided bombs to penetrate the caves hiding the guerrillas. Some of the fighting might have been more decisive on the part of the rebels if only they could have unified.

The Russians by mid-1987 were losing 150 men per month, and the Soviet leader, Mikhail Gorbachev, offered to withdraw. The rebels, now equipped with British Blowpipe missiles, simply fought harder; and in spite of strong air support, by October, after having lost some 500 helicopters, the Soviets began to retreat. The real impetus came in March 1988 with the Soviet Air Force flying in ammunition, stores, and even helicopters for the Afghan government, with return loads from

Kabul of troops. A UN mission arrived in Kabul in May, and a full-scale Russian withdrawal began. The Afghan government left behind soon collapsed as the rebels swarmed in. But having won a victory, they squandered it again by internal feuding. However, Afghanistan was a major step along the road to the dissolution of the USSR in 1991.

The nine-year war in Afghanistan generally showed that in such mountainous terrain, inhabited by a determined, well-led guerrilla force or forces with access to modern outside arms and accustomed to enduring hardship in favor of freedom, even the most contemporary armaments were not sufficient to bring victory to an invader dabbling in a civil war. From all accounts, the Soviets never grasped—as the British had—that victory in mountain war goes to the force occupying the heights. When the Soviets did try to seize peaks with small helicopter pickets, these did not last long. The Soviets never grasped that probably the only real way to success would have been to deliver large numbers of troops to the heights above the guerrillas and keep them well supplied, working down on top of the enemy that would be hammered between an airborne force and troops advancing up the valley floor, all equipped with high-angle guns and with fighter-bomber and gunship support.

THE PERSIAN OR SECOND GULF WAR, 1990–91

The legacy of the Iran-Iraq War was that Iraq's Saddam Hussein had the world's fourth most powerful army, and his ego demanded constant triumphs and his regime steady outside threats. Thus, in the summer of 1990 he abruptly invaded his rich neighbor, Kuwait, formerly a part of Iraq. The United States and Saudi Arabia responded with Operation Desert Shield, a massive show of support to prevent Saddam from advancing into Saudi Arabia; but it was also a front behind which the movement of men and support matériel and weapons could be set in readiness. Key to this whole effort was the putting together of an Allied Coalition, excluding Israel, for the fear was—correctly—that Saddam would then declare a Holy War against the Jews and fracture the Coalition. Indeed, after the war—Desert Storm—started and Saddam aimed missiles into Israel, great diplomatic pressure had to be exerted on Tel Aviv and Jerusalem to keep the Israelis passive.

Fortunately for the Coalition, Saddam was a politician rather than a strategist. He failed to strike southeast from Kuwait before the Coalition could build up, and he especially neglected to trump the air bases already existing in Saudi Arabia. Nor did he attempt to strike at the carrier task forces in the Persian Gulf and the Red Sea with any of his 550 aircraft.

As a result, this war became an eighteenth-century aberration in which each side was given time to prepare, and the Coalition was allowed to choose the time and place of the one hundred-day air assault, which began on January 19, 1991. It is unlikely, except in peacekeeping efforts such as over Bosnia, that two major military opponents will ever again allow each other so much time.

The Coalition's strategic objectives in the Persian Gulf War were to prepare for a ground campaign, to eliminate Iraq as a threat to both Israel and Saudi Arabia, to obliterate nuclear, chemical, and biological threats, to destroy Saddam's ability to control his forces, and to destabilize his regime.

Before 1990, the U.S. Navy and the U.S. Air Force had rather different approaches to threats to peace. Two aspects of this were that the U.S. Navy had a much better idea of the dangers its carriers might face, and its EA-6A Intruders had a broader electronic-jamming capacity than the much larger USAF EF-111A Raven. The EA-6A could deal with both Western and Soviet-made radars, air-defense linked communications, and early warning systems. The U.S. Navy also had the updated F/A-18 Hornet, and the USAF used the EC-130H. However, due to the need for suppression of enemy air defense (SEAD), strike capabilities were severely blunted. The Navy did not have a stealth aircraft, but the USAF had acquired the Lockheed F-117A Nighthawk (ER n/a), which could fly at very low levels almost invisibly at night and seek out ground-control intercept stations, making the enemy fighter forces impotent, especially on moonless nights when the backup optical systems were useless.

After the first night's attacks, the Iraqi air-defense system did not respond, perhaps for lack of spare parts, never plentiful under the Soviet manufacturing system. The three antiquated Iraqi Ilyushin Il-76 AEW aircraft (ER 898) were useless. At the same time, the Soviets withdrew their technicians in deference to the Coalition. On the other hand, the Iraqis had learned deception well from their tutors, and were adept at painting simulated damage on buildings and runways. This ruse often deceived Coalition analysts—perhaps too eager to believe in success.

French-made Roland missiles had protected Iraq's airfields and other important sites and were effective against their attackers. Just before the strikes, the Coalition had located all Iraqi radars, some by feints, which caused them to be switched on. The radars were attacked by low and slow helicopters, which did not show up on the screens. The helicopters used laser-guided weapons effectively to open the way for the bombers and Tomahawk missiles to then take out the long-range radars. The Tomahawks especially could knock out inactive radars, since the missiles were targeted by coordinates. To get at the volatile Roland missile sites, the RAF used air-launched anti-radar (ALARM) munition parachute decoys, and when the radars came on to search for the Tornadoes, they were swatted by missiles. Within two hours the Iraqi air-defense system was down, with the loss of only one F/A-18. The Iraqi army still retained its low-level defensive system, but it was with the troops in the field and, thus, there was no need for the Coalition to challenge it.

Interestingly, Saddam had failed to learn one of the basic lessons from the 1940 Battle of Britain—

his ground-control intercept stations were above ground for political reasons. And because they had been built by foreign contractors, the Pentagon had copies of the plans.

The attack had opened with the modern night mixture of cruise missiles and stealth aircraft, and daytime strikes with both laser-guided munitions and reliable iron bombs.

The RAF had the anti-airfield role because it had trained under NATO to defeat Warsaw Pact forces by sneaking in under radar with nap-of-the-earth high-speed passes across the fields, dispensing JP 233 runway-busting bombs; and this they did in Iraq. They also had the role because the Coalition was short of hardened-shelter penetrating munitions and the range to hit the northern airfields, to which the Iraqi Air Force had withdrawn.

The RAF attack on the airfields and the attempts to destroy Scud launchers used forty Tornadoes, in Operation Granby. These aircraft flew 1,500 low-level sorties and nine were lost, some flying into terrain. But after two weeks, the hardened shelters were hit and the Iraqi Air Force decamped to Iran where it was interned. Saddam did not trust his airmen, nor they he. But the loss of his air force cost him his eyes.

Yet, the nature of the war in general must not be obscured by what happened and what was demonstrated in the conflict. As the analysts could not be sure that all air defenses had been destroyed, SEAD forces were kept with strike units. B-52s flew at only 500 feet to make the initial low-level attacks, as the Iraq terrain is relatively flat. Predicted losses based upon Vietnam figures were 2.6 to 3 aircraft per thousand sorties, but only the U.S. Navy approached that rate because it flew in the low-level flak. Other Coalition forces averaged only 0.9 or 40 aircraft in 50,000 sorties.

Electronic reconnaissance was vital, and the U.S. Navy continued its prewar Soviet-borders work using older carrier aircraft based ashore for 6.5- to 8.5-hour flights. Threat warnings and other intelligence was passed directly to USAF aircraft.

The U.S. Air Force began planning a strategic bombing campaign in August 2000, but a predicted shortage of armament and of precision-bombing forces cut the target list that was presented to President George Bush at the end of the month. Operation Instant Thunder had been based on the current anti-Soviet plan, but had to be modified for the lack of Third World data. Digital maps had to be made of Iraq, to be able to program the Tomahawks. However, recalling Vietnam, no one wanted Washington to designate targets. The Gulf conflict was going to be a professional war.

By the time the plan reached the Coalition's Commander-in-Chief, Gen. Norman Schwarzkopf, it was a phased approach: seven to ten days to destroy the air defenses, one day against Kuwait targets, and then a thirty- to thirty-nine-day softening of the main enemy lines before the ground attack. General Schwarzkopf deleted the attacks on Kuwait.

As in the Japanese bombing attacks off Malaya and RAF Bomber Command attacks over Germany, assaults on Iraq were to come from many directions; as over Germany, they were to drop massively. This meant a major scheduling of aircraft from many bases in three-dimensional space, plus time, only made possible by computers. Exceptional air-traffic control and frequency coordination were necessary. One commander issued daily computer-generated tasking orders. Unlike the Vietnam War, no predictable "route package" flights were planned, and in any massive air operation, the fear of collisions was ever present.

As the air tasking orders (ATO) were too rigid and precise for the carriers, which needed flexibility, ATO assignments were flown out twice each day. The ATOs were rigid in part because they were based on the European Plan, but one result was that they could not cope with mobile targets. Thus, in part because of the shortage of tactical PRU aircraft, "kill boxes"—free-firing zones—were established over mobile targets, but with only limited strike time allowed. And because the Rockwell OV-10 Bronco reconnais-sance aircraft (ER 4.76) were shot down, F-16 Fighting Falcons—"Fast FACs"—had to be used. However, over the desert, as opposed to over the Southeast Asia jungles, the F-16s worked.

It is important to note that the complex air tasking order is only usable when the USAF holds the initiative because of air time needed to complete it. Complacency and arrogance may be a factor in another war. Furthermore, ATOs had generated the wrong statistics, as they counted sorties and not targets destroyed, and bomb-damage assessments were not reliable until confirmed on the ground. Here again, due to USAF shortages of RF-4 PRU aircraft, the U.S. Navy did the bomb-damage assessment flights.

In between satellite passes, the Iraqis had time to cover bomb damage and to paint on decoys. To fill the gap, two JSTARS (joint surveillance target attack radar system) aircraft under test were dispatched to the Persian Gulf where they could analyze data without having to download it to ground stations. One weakness of JSTARS, however, was that it could not identify Scud missiles on trailers versus empty trailers. And, therefore, some ten percent of the sorties flown were Scud-hunting and they were a failure.

The lethality of the 2,000-pound bombs used in 1991 was no better than in 1945, but accuracy was much improved. However, Tallboy or Grand Slam bombs were lacking, which could penetrate to Saddam's deep bunkers. Only B-52s could have delivered such bombs, and only the F-111 could carry the 5,000-pound GBU-28, making one of the lessons of the conflict the broader mix of weapons required. In 2001–02, these deep-penetration munitions would be essential in Afghanistan and were available in 2003.

Apart from the shortage of RF-4 Phantoms for bomb-damage assessment, the USAF also had the weakness that its tankers had been purchased for a short-range rather than a long-range war, and they also had the disadvantage in that they were not compatible with the drogue-and-probe air-refueling system employed by the USN and the

RAF. And the RAF tankers were also more popular, as they could refuel three fighters at a time. Some USAF tankers were altered to accept the RAF system, and then it had two incompatible refuelers!

In terms of losses, the Iraqi Air Force lost forty-three aircraft in combat, mostly from Sparrow missiles or the ineptness of their own pilots. The other 151 aircraft were lost when they fled to Iran. Of the sixty-two Coalition machines lost, thirty-three were by flak; seventeen had no cause listed for twenty-seven days in action. The largest losses were eight RAF Tornadoes by flak and one by a cause unknown. At least one of these was from ground impact on a low-level Scud hunt.

The boastful Saddam Hussein was certain that his elite Guards regiments would stop any Coalition thrust. He was not prepared for the skill, determination, and accuracy of Coalition air attacks, 30 percent of which came off U.S. Navy aircraft carriers. While a CNN television team was broadcasting from Baghdad, these attacks were destroying his infrastructure—though they could never hit him.

The Americans, whose leadership had been bloodied in the Vietnam War, were from the level of the President down determined to avenge the defeat in Southeast Asia. From a technical and purely military view, the Persian Gulf War was a resounding success, restoring faith in the U.S. armed forces. The planning of the air war was meticulous, the electronics and satellite imaging was excellent (except when bad weather prevented the spies in the sky from seeing), ever more powerful and accurate munitions were delivered, and maintenance was such that there was a 95 percent availability/serviceability rate.

But from a grand-strategic position, the war was a failure. The ultimate purpose of the war appears to have been merely the liberation of Kuwait and the immediate defeat of Saddam and his forces, not the settlement of peace upon the Middle East. Whether or not the Coalition forces should have been ordered to seize Baghdad in a costly street-fighting campaign—or could have done so given the support, reserves available, and the threat to politics at home from high casualties—or whether or not the Coalition should have insisted on the surrender of Saddam and his henchmen is still open to debate. What is true is that the U.S. Army's in-theater commander-in-chief was allowed to make the peace, a task for which as a soldier rather than a diplomat he was not qualified. Political leaders had failed to realize that commanders of *instruments of policy* are not *policy-makers.* Former British Prime Minister Margaret Thatcher noted later that the Coalition had lost—President Bush was in retirement in Houston, Texas, but Saddam Hussein was still ruling in Iraq eight years after the war. In the political world of the Arabs, Saddam came out the winner; David had survived the onslaught of Goliath.

The long-term failure of the 1991 Gulf War has been one of matching means to ends and the congenital inability of politicians to make hard, realistic choices when dealing with peoples inured to violence. A similar failure would be evident in air actions in the Balkans in the late 1990s—though such an air strike had worked with Ghadaffi in Libya in 1986.

The Gulf War was seen by the USAF as a test of the theory that air power alone could win a war. The fallacy of this approach was that it could not work well against a dictatorship or against an urban complex. Hitting civilians in Baghdad, Iraq's capital, would only have escalated the support for Saddam's war among his people. In the end, only twenty-nine buildings were destroyed in the city, though one was claimed to be a shelter containing 400 civilians. That incident allowed Saddam to aver that the Coalition was inhumane. Saddam, of course, in spite of his uniforms, was neither skilled in the art, nor the planning, nor the execution of military command. He did not understand the elements at his disposal, and hence his air force was ill-trained, starved of funds, and not to be trusted. But, on the other hand, Saddam Hussein was a master political grand strategist who aptly made the point that if he survived, he would be the victor. The Coalition, hypnotized by what it saw as a potentially revolutionary war, failed to heed that the ultimate objective had to be the elimination of the Iraqi leader and his cronies.

A great deal of "hype" was heard at this time about the wonderful revolutionary air war. And it did involve immense planning, as well as the coordination and integration of target packages of some twenty aircraft of the U.S. Navy, U.S. Air Force, and Coalition allies. All of this was managed via giant television screens in the command bunker in Riyadh, Saudi Arabia. And on the whole it worked very well.

However, a variety of problems were evident, as old as air warfare. Weather had prevented satellites from seeing and transmitting data, and cruise missiles and F-117s could not operate in rain or fog, or in the smoke from the Kuwait oil fields, which were fired. Intelligence was inaccurate (560 of 800 targets incorrectly assessed) and not always timely, due to clogged lines and simple human faults. The sortie rate of 3,000 to 4,000 per day was more than command, control, and communications—C^3—could handle in real time.

A great deal of public discussion covered the use of "smart" weapons, and television showed over and over again the same strikes; but the reality was that of the over 88,000 tons of bombs dropped, only 7 percent were smart weapons, and of these only 60 percent struck within acceptable accuracy tolerances. The vast majority of the ordnance dropped was iron bombs, much as in World War II, with an accuracy of only 25 percent. B-52s were used to bomb the elite Iraqi Guards regiments, but did very little physical damage, though the psychological impact was an important element. And although 109,500 sorties were flown in four weeks, inaccuracy rendered about half of them ineffective. Only half of the total were bombing missions; the others were for refueling, defensive patrols, and escorts.

The faulty intelligence meant that early in the war the thirty-five main Iraqi Air Force fields were not fully destroyed, that by the end of the war four out of seven nuclear sites were still untouched, and chemical and biological warfare (CBW) plants, whose products were most feared, were essentially undamaged, many having been moved into underground bunkers.

The original war plan had envisaged Iraq being vanquished in a few days by the air onslaught. In fact, the air assault lasted six weeks and the ground war only four days.

In the meantime, the Iraqi Air Force refused to parry the initial attacks, which were designed to hit its C^3 organization and force countermeasures that would have revealed the location of enemy radars to the Coalition forces with their ALARM munitions.

This was a highly complex war, as a glance at the Cause and Effect Cube, seen earlier, can suggest. Saddam was playing a long-range grand-strategic game as befitted a ruthless politician with absolute control. The Coalition faced not only the difficulties of holding an assortment of Europeans, Americans, and Arabs together, but also the failure to have a plan that would end animosities in the area. This was complicated by the fact that the collapsing Soviet Union saw its client state humiliated, particularly in the area of air defense, a Russian specialty.

The Coalition consumed munitions so rapidly that the Desert Storm ground attack had to be launched while friendly forces were at their peak. By the end, the USAF was down to a three-day supply of bombs, and other shortages existed, which played a role in the decision not to drive into urban Baghdad.

While generally the Coalition forces were located in and about Saudi Arabia, others were also operating out of Incirlik, Turkey. Part of those forces had to be sent home for safety reasons, as both the Iraqis and the French Air Force flew Mirages, and it was feared that Coalition machines would be shot down by mistake.

Saddam launched some 200 Scuds from mobile launchers that were hidden by day and moved

During World War II, very few navies in the world had oceanic capabilities. By 1950, it became obvious that the anti-submarine warfare teams of the immediate postwar era were being overpowered by the development of fast nuclear submarines. The U.S. Navy, therefore, requested designs for aircraft that could carry air and undersea search equipment, transport the weapons needed to destroy enemy submarines, and be able to operate off carriers. The result, from Grumman, was a series of aircraft. In the forefront is the standard S-2A Tracker (ER 15.6), and in the rear is the E-2 Hawkeye (ER 61.2). (Grumman History Center)

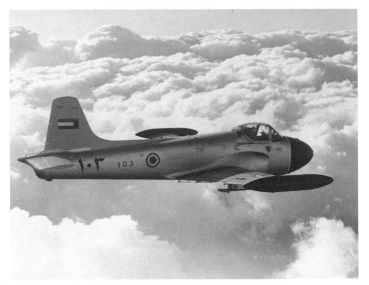

The Hunting (Percival) Jet Provost (ER 7.2) was a British variant of the piston-engine trainer developed originally by Hunting-Percival. A number of lesser air forces found that a combined trainer and attack aircraft was what they could afford for internal security and training. This aircraft, in 1962, was about to be delivered to Kuwait. (British Aircraft Corporation)

The Canadian-built de Havilland DHC-6 Twin Otter (ER 4.2) was a very successful bush and commuter aircraft, also adopted by a number of military services. Seen here is an Argentine navy plane. (de Havilland Canada)

The Canadian de Havilland DHC-5 Buffalo (ER 51) was a further development of the successful DH Canada line of light transports. Assigned to many tasks, this one was with air/sea rescue, and was also sold to the USAF as the United States did not have a small- to medium-aircraft production capacity. Capable of carrying 14,000 pounds off a 700-foot airstrip, it was a true STOL aircraft with almost three times the up-lift of the Douglas C-47 (ER 20). (de Havilland Canada)

The French aircraft industry made a remarkable recovery from the ashes of 1944. As early as 1954 the Dassault Ouragan (ER 11.5) was operational and was being proven by the Israeli Air Force in the Middle East. An Ouragan is preserved at the U.S. Air Museum at Dayton. (Avions Marcel Dassault/Israeli Air Force)

Much more successful than the contemporary Swift was the Hawker Hunter (ER 63), the mainstay of RAF Fighter Command from 1954 to 1960. This was a versatile fighter-bomber, as the loads displayed in the photograph demonstrate. (Hawker-Siddeley)

Of the three British V-bombers, the Vickers Valiant (ER 652) was the most conventional and least successful, each of the aircraft flying only 250 hours annually in the ten years before being withdrawn in 1965. Based upon a 1948 specification, the Valiant joined squadrons in 1955. The V.1000 civil airliner, derived from the same basic design, never went into production. (Vickers)

The second V-bomber was the crescent-winged Handley Page Victor (ER 527), shown here as a tanker refueling two 1959 English Electric Lightning fighters (ER 134). In the Falklands War, the Victor refueler was a vital part of the shuttle-bombing from Ascension Island, and in ferrying aircraft to that South Atlantic base. (Ministry of Defence, Crown Copyright)

The third V-bomber, the Avro Vulcan (ER 653), proved to be both innovative and a success. Its delta wing was a rugged design for high or low penetrations; it was highly maneuverable, being slow-rolled at the Farnborough Air Show; and at high altitude its wing enabled it to turn inside fighters. The Vulcan shown here is equipped with two Skybolt missiles, and is in formation with a USAF Strategic Air Command Boeing B-52 Stratofortress (ER 6,336). Both aircraft are preserved at Offutt AFB in Bellevue, Nebraska. (USAF)

The Folland Gnat (ER 12.8) was a late 1950 design to provide a small, agile, and less-expensive fighter. The RAF bought a few, the Norwegians used it, and India manufactured it. (Ministry of Defence, Crown Copyright)

The Hawker Sea Harrier (ER 75) of 1957 was eventually adopted by the U.S. Marine Corps as the AV-8, a truly VTOL machine. It fought effectively for the Royal Navy and the RAF in the 1982 Falklands campaign, and by 2003 had not yet been replaced. (McDonnell Douglas)

The McDonnell F-4 Phantom II (ER 370) was a supersonic fighter-bomber. But the original specification was changed to make it a high-altitude, long-range fighter, and the gun armament was removed in favor of missiles alone—which the Vietnam War would prove was a mistake. From 1958, eventually more than 5,000 were produced. The version shown here belongs to the Japanese Self-Defense Forces. (McDonnell Douglas)

Viewed from below, the F-4 Phantom II clearly shows its developed features—twin jet engines, air-to-air missiles, heavy ordnance and fuel loads, variable intakes, and leading-edge maneuvering slats. (USN)

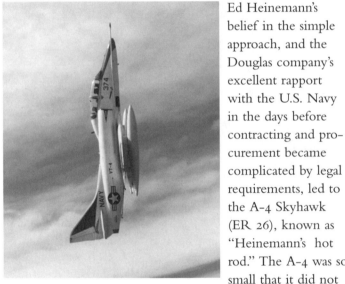

Ed Heinemann's belief in the simple approach, and the Douglas company's excellent rapport with the U.S. Navy in the days before contracting and procurement became complicated by legal requirements, led to the A-4 Skyhawk (ER 26), known as "Heinemann's hot rod." The A-4 was so small that it did not need folding wings. Work commenced in 1952, and more than 3,000 had been produced by 1975. (McDonnell Douglas)

This plan view clearly shows the modified delta wing, leading-edge slats, trailing-edge flaps, and the rear-fuselage speed brakes of the Douglas A-4 Skyhawk. (McDonnell Douglas)

The Lockheed P2V (ER 115) was the latest development of the Neptune patrol aircraft. These early 1950s versions had a lengthened rear fuselage to accommodate magnetic anomaly detection (MAD) equipment for anti-submarine warfare. (USN)

The two auxiliary jet engines seen under the wings of the P2V Neptune give additional takeoff power and high speed over a target, as well as the capability to fly on jet power alone. Note also the wingtip fuel tanks to increase the range and loiter time on patrol. (USN)

The new jets were significantly noisier than the older piston-engine aircraft, and thus in peacetime, relations with local communities had to be considered. Because the running up of engines for tests caused complaints, test cells such as this one for the Lockheed F-94 Starfire (ER 24.7) had to be developed to muffle the sound. (Lockheed)

The Northrop F-89D Scorpion (ER 74) was proposed in 1945, and became the first two-seat, all-weather USAF fighter jet. Between 1949 and 1956, 1,056 were supplied. The wingtip tanks were an integral part of the design, and a total of fifty-two 2.75-inch rockets were mounted in their noses. The aircraft not only had airborne interception (AI) radar, but also had an autopilot to rest the pilot on long patrols, especially at night. (USAF)

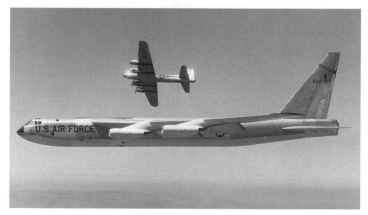

The Boeing B-52 Stratofortress (ER 6,336) was conceived in April 1948 and began entering SAC in 1955. Essential to meet the specification was air-to-air refueling. The sharp contrast in the size of the 1935 World War II B-17 Flying Fortress (ER 101, B-17E) and the B-52 is clear in the photograph, as in their ERs. (Boeing)

The distinctive swept wing of most jets in the 1950s is clearly visible here in this B-52 Stratofortress, as is the eight-engine layout totaling 89,600 pounds of thrust. By 2003, a single engine could supply better than 100,000 pounds. (Boeing)

Development of a supersonic bomber design was started by Convair in 1949, and the first B-58 Hustlers (ER 2,508) entered the service in 1956. Here, it is soon to be refueled by the Boeing KC-135 Stratotanker (ER 1,7 69). (Convair)

to firing positions by night. The locations of the hits in Israel were kept secret, but eventually Patriot anti-missile missiles were loaned to that country, and deployed in Saudi Arabia as well, with variable success. However, the Patriots were a start on a defense against missiles.

In the Gulf War, a lesson from Vietnam, much in the minds of senior commanders who had been bloodied there twenty years earlier, was that the media involvement would be controlled. Thus, press pools were set up, as in World War II, of which the media complained.

The Persian Gulf War has been oversold as revolutionary and underrated for its diplomatic, grand-strategic complexities. It was, within limits, an excellent example of planning for a peacekeeping action, but it lacked the overall objective of peace in the region. As a result of television and other media coverage, the war's public emphasis was upon the fascinating action, including helicopter assault forces, and that played into the hands of the ferret.

As for the revolutionary air war, assurances were essential, in an age of information-based warfare, that so-called "garbage" was not being in-put, and that data, intelligence, and orders could be transmitted in a timely fashion, whether in large or limited warfare. The 2003 Third Gulf War showed that lessons had been learned.

BOSNIA AND KOSOVO

After the breakup of the former Yugoslavia and the subsequent 1992 declaration of a new Federal Republic of Yugoslavia by Serbia and Montenegro, the always latent tensions between Muslims and Christians in the Balkans degenerated into ethnic cleansing that horrified Europe and America. Serbia, attempting to unite its people in neighboring new republics into a "Greater Serbia," tried to eliminate the Albanians in Kosovo. This led NATO and the United States to seek to keep the peace. In order to impress upon Belgrade the need

for that, a seventy-eight-day bombing campaign was flown in 1999. Much like the 1972 Linebacker II campaign against Hanoi, this did eventually bring Bosnia, part of Greater Serbia, to the table.

But the Balkans were an area very similar topographically to Afghanistan. The targets were too often small and the enemy equipped with highly mobile anti-aircraft missiles. This meant that the strike forces, based in Italy, had to fly higher. Bombing was not always accurate (the mistaken smashing of the Chinese embassy in Belgrade led to an international diplomatic incident), and attacks on vehicles and trains gave the Serbs great propaganda ammunition. Although hailed at the time as a success, by 2000 critical analyses had deflated claims made of accuracy and effectiveness. And in the end, air power alone proved no substitute for troops on the ground in peacekeeping, as in other martial actions.

In the 1995 NATO campaign in Bosnia, Raytheon Tomahawk cruise missiles were found to be very accurate in the limited number used, but the performance of the same company's high-speed anti-radar missile (HARM) raised questions. In the 1995 campaign in Yugoslavia, the U.S. Air Force concluded that its "smart" weapons did not perform adequately—in particular HARM, and in part because Serb radar operators appreciated the threat and stayed off the air as much as possible. All the radar sites destroyed, except one, were hit by laser-guided bombs. Other weapons used in Operation Deliberate Force—the UN and NATO campaign in Bosnia—were not overly successful either. One cause was thought to be the high cost of weapons, which limited live-fire training in peacetime. Another cause was the "frequency interference" experienced by USN and USAF joint-strike forces with different guided weapons, which created electronic guidance failures. This was lamentable in the deep valleys and cloud cover of Bosnia, which challenged pilots to find their targets. Of nine guided-bomb unit (GBU) bombs dropped, four hit, four missed, and one had guidance failure.

For the first time since World War II, German Air Force planes flew operational sorties against an enemy, and that also was true of the Belgian and Dutch in intra-European actions. And for the Northrop-Grumman B-2 Spirit, these sorties were its stealthy baptism of fire.

Rules of engagement in the Balkans, as in Vietnam twenty years earlier, were very difficult as they had been set by political leaders. Nevertheless, during the 78-day Kosovo involvement of 1999, over 900 fixed-wing peacekeeping aircraft flew nearly 4,500 sorties including air defense and combat air patrols. Of the 900, roughly 200 were F-16s. One USAF wing flew 9,000 sorties totaling 40,000 hours, with mission endurance going up from just over two to more than seven hours. Some systems failed at two hours and some after a five-hour sortie. After 200 hours, flight-phased inspections were carried out; but phase times rose much more rapidly than expected, and thus demanded more mechanics. In the air, the more the pilots flew, the better they and the aircraft performed. However, twenty-four-hour coverage of the theater used up the availability of both pilots and aircraft.

In 1999 the Joint Stand-off Weapon (AGM-154A) glide bomb came into use in the Balkans. At the time, it was considered the biggest tactical advance in fifteen years—the weapon of choice against soft targets. It subsequently was used, in 2001, in Iraq from F/A-18s.

NATO Allied Force operations in the Balkans used joint direct-attack munitions (JDAM), with GPS, to make 900-pound iron bombs into precision weapons, as well as GPS-guided and laser-guided cruise missiles. In the war in Kosovo, "kills" of tanks were only verified by one-seventh the number of carcasses. This lack of tactical success led to greater use of cluster munitions, leaving a legacy of 30,000 unexploded warheads. On another level, accurate stand-off weapons effectively damaged the infrastructure.

After the bombing stopped, surveys were made. The RAF was chagrined to discover that less than 60 percent of its bombs hit the target and none from Harriers dropping through cloud cover.

The readiness of USAF Europe (USAFE) was also a concern at this time. In the fall of 2000 it was at 75–80 percent rather than the desirable 80–85. Normally, USAFE and Pacific Air Forces (PACAF) operate at five percent higher readiness than in continental U.S. forces. The commander of USAFE blamed the lower rate on a long-standing lack of spares and by being a bit thin on mid-level maintenance supervision. But the spares shortage went back to before 1995, when USAF leaders began to be aware of a funding shortfall that was only just being cleared at the time of the conflict in Kosovo. The RAF had a similar problem due to doctrine not including logistics.

The air war over Serbia demonstrated both air power's assets and its limitations. Air power cannot be a substitute for strategy. Just as Korea in 1950 was essential to the preservation and future of the United Nations, so Kosovo in 1999 was to the integrity of NATO. And just as Korea remained a conflict without a peace settlement, so, too, have the Balkans. Fighting having ended does not mean that the war has been concluded, nor that its costs have stopped.

The United States, meanwhile, had been reconsidering its overall grand strategy, and this, of course, affected air power. The Pentagon had been envisioning the day the United States might have to fight in two geographic areas. The first application of a two-war strategy involved the Persian Gulf and Northeast Asia and was limited to five U.S. divisions. In 1997, that "bottom-up" view, essentially from the services rather than the White House, was the U.S. policy statement—the Quadrennial Defense Review—that aimed to balance readiness, long-term modernization, and improvement of the quality of servicemen's lives. According to the Review, in order to modernize, further cuts in manpower would be necessary, to have sufficient funding for essential enlisted personnel. This was the basis for the new twenty-first century revolution in military affairs (RMA).

The Review proposed to limit the battlefield to 40,000 square miles, using data gathered real-time, with the updated systems of command, control, communications, computers, and intelligence (C⁴I). Yet, it would be reasonable to assume that in spite of computer-facilitated targeting, precision-guided munitions (PGM) could be hampered by weather and terrain, and the erratic dispersion of enemy forces. Add to this the problem of hacker warfare to destroy the enemy's inter-organization computer networks to neutralize their command structure.

The NATO approach to peacekeeping led to asymmetric war of regulars against irregulars, or guerrillas, in which the enemy counter was to hide, with a concurrent rise of out-of-control gangs, as in the Thirty Years' War of 1618–48 and in Rwanda in 1994, with a high rate of brutality, murder, and rape. The Swiss, however, it might be noted, gamed a solution to this: saturate the gang's area.

The heralded revolution in military affairs is also expected to lead to a revolution in business affairs (RBA) toward better use of resources, such as focused logistics, and including base closings. All of this is embodied in the policy statement Joint Vision 2010, of which the USAF counterpart is called Air Force 2025, with its emphasis not on digitization, but on space and air power.

AFGHANISTAN, 2001–2002

The first Afghan War of the twenty-first century occurred when the United States reacted forcefully to the organized terrorist hijacking of four heavily fueled airliners—two being crashed into New York City's World Trade Center twin towers, one into the Pentagon in Washington, D.C., and another into the ground in Pennsylvania when the passengers attempted to retake the 767. These acts of terrorism were the work of the Al Qaeda organization of Osama bin Laden, a renegade Saudi teaching *jihad* against the United States, with sanctuary in Afghanistan. Very quickly the United States and Britain set up a coalition aimed to counter world terrorism and persuaded other states to give support. An air campaign was launched against the right-wing Taliban ruling party in Kabul and Khandahar in Afghanistan, and against Al Qaeda.

USAF B-1 Lancers largely avoided using Arab bases, and primarily operated from Diego Garcia in the Indian Ocean. A few B-2s flew from Whiteman Air Force Base in Missouri; F-15 Eagles and tankers, including RAF Vickers VC-10s (ER 2,475), flew from the Arabian peninsula; and most of the strike force came from USN carriers in the Indian Ocean. Other air assets as well flew in from Tajikistan. (Whoever would have thought a little over a decade earlier that U.S. forces would be allowed to pass through and fly over Russia and to operate from a former Muslim Soviet republic?)

The air campaign combined with local rebel Afghan forces to destroy the Taliban and Al Qaeda. The result was the installation of a temporary coalition government in the country to try to restore the Afghan state with massive foreign aid. Support of the key state of neighboring Pakistan was critical for the assault on the forces of terrorism. Then in January 2002 Pakistan and India were brought to an alert by warring Kashmiri separatists. Shuttle diplomacy by British and U.S. leaders helped bring temporary calm, but the volatility remained both north and south of the Khyber Pass.

Another aftermath of the "9/11" terrorist attack was that NATO AWACS planes joined their USAF counterparts to fly over the United States in a multi-national security effort.

At the outset of the American retaliation, the media's supposed pundits had suggested that a significant influence on the strategy of the new Afghan War would be the concern that the American public might only stand zero casualties—or at least they believed that had been the perception in Washington since the 1993 debacle in Somalia, when American troops were brutally killed. However, the American people proved to be realistic and resilient as a wave of patriotism and support for the military's role swept across the country.

In the 2001–02 Afghan War, the United States and its allies were aided by the traditional *mujahideen* opposition on the ground, thus enabling special forces to be inserted at first covertly and then overtly. Kabul fell before Christmas 2001 and Khandahar shortly thereafter. An interim Afghan government was established.

Clearly air power had done the job under the new revolution in military affairs doctrine, in part because of the arid nature of the country, and because of its poverty, with one-third of the population having fled to Pakistan. Yet, despite all the initial success and promise for the future of the Afghan state, the fate of Osama bin Laden was still unknown in mid-2003, and a long clandestine war on terrorist factions as well as peacekeeping in Afghanistan was the prospect.

In the meantime, the impact of 9/11 drastically hit the world's major airlines, already reeling, though not so much the regionals. Added to their woes was the withdrawal of war-risk insurance coverage, which given its low-risk nature should be a governmental program, as in World War II (in Britain third-party coverage was supplied by the government).

Defense spending as a result of the Afghan War did rise, and initiatives were begun toward extensive modernization, such as the conversion of 767s to surveillance aircraft and into tankers, the deployment of unmanned aerial vehicles, and a refilling of the arsenals already at their lowest level in fourteen years. USAF readiness, instead of being 92 percent, was in April 2001 only 68 percent. The average age of the air fleet was twelve years, with the B-52s thirty-nine and tankers between thirty-seven and thirty-eight, but the B-2s only six. The sixty-five Boeing F-15C Eagles at Langley Air Force Base, Virginia, were increasingly costly and difficult to keep ready, due to a shortage of spares, and for this reason the B-1B bomber fleet was cut in 2001 from ninety-three to sixty. The

thirty-three withdrawn machines were to get avionics updates and later to recirculate.

In 2000, twenty-three of the USAF's 126 C-5 Galaxy jet transports had been unavailable, and as of the Afghan War in 2001–02, this was still being rectified. The aircraft's global logistics system, which had been drawn down by earlier Allied Force operations in the Balkans, was being streamlined by civilian firms. At this same time, all USAF C-141B Starlifter transports were temporarily grounded after the left wing on one aircraft being refueled at Memphis, Tennessee, had collapsed.

By mid-October of 2001 the air war in Afghanistan was in full swing with the ruling Taliban's high-altitude air defense eliminated. Aircraft above 14,000 feet were immune to attack. They were directed to targets by an air force general of the coalition, using the JSTARS system. The coalition general had the authority to launch weapons against senior enemy personnel and also had deep-penetration weapons such as the 5,000-pound GBU-37 GPS guided bomb. Perfected in Red Flag exercises in Nevada, the air forces fighting in the Afghan War were able to make quick strikes as soon as targets had been observed. After just three days of war, by October 10, the only targets left were those requiring surgical strikes, such as the entrances to cave complexes.

Aircraft carriers launched fifteen bombers and twenty-four F-14s and F/A-18s daily covered by Grumman EA-6B Prowlers (ER 77.3). Boeing (formerly McDonnell Douglas) C-17 transports (ER 2,505) were flown depressurized above 20,000 feet with crews on 100 percent oxygen during 15- to 25-hour sorties. British aid included a submarine-launched missile, Nimrod R1 electronic intelligence systems aircraft, and the English Electric Canberra PR-9 (ER 305) reconnaissance aircraft, as well as tankers and AWACS. The Canadians and Australians also participated. Humanitarian food drops and constant worldwide assurances that this was not a war against the Muslim religion but against terrorism helped temper a volatile Pakistan.

In November 2001, the United States opened

up the additional airstrips in Tajikistan for C-130s and helicopter bases, for better supply to special Afghan groups fighting the Taliban and Al Qaeda forces. At that time fighter sorties were averaging 70–120 daily, depending upon carrier availability.

The Afghan War of 2001–02 forced the U.S. Navy to consider the need for longer-ranged aircraft such as the F/A-18, as well as UAVs with data links and new, larger tankers. By March 2002 the demand for air transport in the war on terrorism was gutting the budget such that training was being shorted. In the United Kingdom this caused a conflict between the RAF's need to stockpile munitions and the Treasury's insistence on lowering defense costs. Lessons of the anti-terrorism campaign and fear of advanced capabilities of small SAM missiles from 2002 also caused the U.S. Air Force to consider equipping the AC-130 with stand-off weapons and even using UCAVs.

NATO supported the air attacks, and its wariness of prolonged bombing was deflated by the shortness of that stage of the war. By mid-November 2001 air-strike packages were returning to carriers, as ground controllers had trouble being sure of targets and avoiding being hit by the enemy. The necessity for 6½-hour sorties wore down the crews, but reduced the strain on aircraft carrier equipment. Iron 500-pound bombs were commonly used to save expenses, and relieved the aircrew from having to program GPS coordinates or to use a laser designator. RAF tankers were praised by USN aircrew for their willingness to adjust, as well as for their time-saving probe-and-drogue refueling system, which had handled three, and sometimes four, aircraft at a time. And F-14s in the Afghan War became forward air controllers, due to the absence of E-3 AWACS, but they could not drop joint direct-attack munitions (JDAM) until refitted with new software. F-14s were also due to be replaced by F/A-18 E/Fs at the end of their tour.

For the war in Afghanistan, the USAF had unveiled new systems: the Northrop Grumman/Israel Aircraft Industries laser-designating pod for the F-16 C/D; the Link 16 data link on B-52Hs to update targeting information en route from Diego Garcia; and the use of unmanned aerial vehicles to laser-designate targets and to attack tanks with Hellfire missiles.

But handicapping the U.S. forces was their failure to keep developing their reconnaissance and surveillance technologies to pursue the enemy leadership on the ground. The newly operational Global Hawk UAV carried 2,000 pounds of payload at above 65,000 feet, and the Predator, another UAV, operated at 25,000 feet and relayed its video intelligence to AC-130 gunships. The arming of Predators was also planned by 2002. At the same time, the AC-130Us were to have their all-light-level (ALL) television subsystem replaced with a multi-spectral, 360-degree field-of-view sensor to meet the most challenging requirements in Afghanistan and of anti-terrorist operations.

After six months in the Afghan War, the U.S. military decided that MASINT (measurement and signature intelligence) was extremely useful in tracking down Taliban and Al Qaeda forces within and outside of caves. In addition, clear benefits were seen from the deployment of contingency response groups (CRG) to possible bases to determine their usable requirements. At the same time, it was determined that data had to be integrated, in order to track terrorists; and the military quickly learned they had a shortage of linguists able to sift through captured documents. The problem of wastage and consumption of stores creating critical shortages in other theaters, was also evident, especially in precision weapons and intelligence aircraft. Yet, mission-capable (serviceability) rates in the Afghan War remained high. Thus, instead of postwar lessons, a team drew ongoing instructional updates.

However, one old lesson resurfaced: in units being worked twenty-four hours, seven days per week, the staffing had to be doubled. Moreover, a larger quantity of ready stores had to be forward for instant operations, and greater communications were essential between airlift and its users.

The 2001–02 Afghan War also showed the need for better radar jammers, and thus Boeing and the U.S. Navy were developing a special F/A-18 (EA-18) for that role. And by early 2002, U.S. Marine Corps AV-8B Hawker-Siddeley Harriers (ER 75) were shifted from the USS *Bataan* in the Arabian Sea to Khandahar Airport. In addition, one hundred civilian Boeing 767s were being converted to refuelers, though over the objection of the Airbus firm, which had wanted to make a competitive bid; as a result, the Pentagon leased the planes.

The Afghan War of 2001–02 was much more costly than the Persian Gulf or the Yugoslav wars because each sortie required a refueling, thus creating tanker-crew fatigue. When working with the short-legged USN aircraft, tanker crews had to fly 5½- to 6½-hour missions. The costs per hour were high for the various types in service: F-16, $9,300; F-15E, $14,800; B-52, $23,100; and B-2, $54,000–$100,000. If estimated on the cost per bomb dropped on a 500-mile radius sortie, costs are shown as: F-16, $12,700 for each of two bombs; F-15E, $9,220 for each of four bombs; B-52, $5,120 for each of 12 JDAMs; and B-1, $3,690 for each of 24 JDAMs. Because the B-2 flew directly from the United States, their operating expenses were so substantial that they only were used for three days.

Writing in 2002, it is too early to be sure of all the on-going lessons from the Afghan War. Like the Persian Gulf War, the value of the U.S. Navy as a super-power mobile carrier task force once again was evident, as were lessons about intensive refueling and the necessity for flexibility and standardization of basic refueling procedures—just as Grenada in 1983 had reminded everyone of the need for compatible radios and channels.

Suppression of enemy air defenses, as in the Persian Gulf War, was a necessity, but quickly ceased to be a factor, and thus Allied air forces had a free range. What was needed in both wars was real-time intelligence.

Perhaps as important as anything else was the need for diplomatic control of a very touchy situation, not just in adjoining Pakistan, but in regard to all factions of Afghans, both in their own country and in Pakistan. Diplomatic oversight also was essential for the delicate and simmering state of Kashmir and its irritation of Indo-Pak relations; for the sensitivities of Arab states, always playing politics; and for the Muslim world in general, as well as for the relations of the western Afghan warlords and Iran with the complexities of tribalism, honor, and insult—in an area where everyone has arms, but not a livelihood.

All in all, however, it remains to be seen whether or not air power in both its military and humanitarian roles can help create a peace and prosperity essential to Kabul's successful transition into the twenty-first century, and whether those who have used air power as an instrument of policy have the will to sustain the climate for a real victory, peace, and trade.

Minor or Colonial Air Wars since 1945

The number of aerial conflicts since 1945, in general, have done more to sharpen the lessons of the Second World War than to provide new ones. Looking at the British and French use of air power in colonial conflicts during the interwar years, the student will probably find that much of what appears to be new in anti-guerrilla warfare was present earlier, with only the jungle and helicopters providing a partially different setting and timing. Instantaneous communication, however, is new and has affected operations, enabling the press to query the President before the pilot returns from a mission and letting armchair generals see the edited battle on their fireside television sets. And while this means that the officer on the spot is more open to instant criticism, it also means that he will get the benefit of better-informed, yet still detached, comments.

In the post-1945 world, air power was used against colonial unrest until the costs of trying to suppress independence movements exceeded the value received from the colonies. At the same time, support at home for imperialism waned in the wake of World War II and in Europe pressure for social programs and a greater sense of equality took precedence. Only the two super-powers had the resources for anti-guerrilla operations, but lack of success either through proxies or with their own forces in these non-nuclear activities also caused them to pull out, especially as former imperial possessions or satellites fractured into early civil wars. Thus, the locus of activities shifted in the 1990s after the fall of the USSR to peace-keeping under the UN flag or to joint command modeled on the Troppau Protocol of 1819, to take collective action to prevent the spread of revolutionary contagion, in the name of humanity—though not in Africa.

The use of air power after 1945 saw military and civil arms often combined in their focus. Militarily the forces employed combined modern fighters, bombers, and PRU aircraft with helicopters, the latter used in multiple roles from transport of men and matériel to gunships. In addition, civil air transports shuttled in troops, arms, and other supplies and evacuated the military wounded, civilians by the thousands, and, finally, the colonial power's withdrawing forces. In all of these air activities firepower, speed, range, and lifting capacity played a part. Airfields were of particular importance as supply bases and maintenance and repair shops, and in the field as advanced landing grounds and gateways to isolated fortified fire bases and garrisons.

Air power as a means of protecting columns on the ground, reconnaissance, and as a strike arm gave mobility and independence, as determined by the nature of the countryside. In desert or open country, air assets were more effective than in mountainous or jungle areas. In either case, both sides had to understand the nature of the topography.

Equally important for the independence movements faced with an airborne opponent was the vastly improving means of defense, especially the availability of SAMs, shoulder-fired portable missiles, automatic weapons, and radar.

Moreover, the effective use of air mobility, including that of paratroopers, and flexibility in the ability to shift efforts, had to be at low-level in order to be effective against not highly visible, small mobile targets. Casualties in the air were generally low, though participants on the ground suffered more severely from aerial weapons, including napalm and herbicides. The highest casualties were usually created by undisciplined armies on the spot, those running into thousands and even millions, especially in Africa where tribal forces came into play in brutal civil wars.

The fact that the post-1945 wars were often fought vicariously meant that extraordinarily complex skeins existed to both overt and covert diplomacy and arms supply, and to the volunteers, mercenaries, and identifiable forces employed, as the campaigns illustrate.

And, of course, in all of the above the supply of food, medicines, and mail for morale were still vital.

Many of the lesser air wars in the second half of the twentieth century have been one-sided, the colonial power employing aircraft to attempt to suppress revolutionaries and guerrillas. This was true in Portuguese West Africa during 1963–74; later in Mozambique, where Lisbon decided the cost of remaining imperial was not worth the benefits; in Yemen, 1945–70; and in Morocco, with the French, in 1975, and earlier in the Rif. In Indonesia, the Dutch inherited the legacy of defeat and Japanese occupation, which ultimately frustrated their attempt to recreate the Dutch East Indies. In many of these cases the terrain was similar to that in Malaya and not suited to the old air-policing methods. More successful were helicopter and airborne operations, and denial of supplies in cooperation with ground forces and civil action.

In other cases, such as Nigeria and the Congo during 1967–70, the Philippines after 1946, and in Latin and South America, both sides were indigenous forces. On a few occasions, as in the

Nigerian-Biafran conflict, outside airlift to the underdog played a part, but was ultimately put at hazard by lack of transports and freelance crews, and by enemy action.

In South West Africa-Angola, during 1961–75, both sides used helicopters and light aircraft, with finally the South Africans moving in to prevent the spread of war into their domain.

Not all of the many wars after 1945 can be covered, nor do they all have lessons to teach in the use of air power. In most cases only one side had aircraft, with its advantages of tactical and strategic flexibility and mobility. In other cases, aircraft proved to be a disadvantage as their noise and visibility to people, such as the Mau-Mau in Kenya, enabled the guerrillas to evade ground patrols.

Some conflicts, however, did possess either a significant air component or have important lessons to offer. In many minor activities in various places since the Second World War, air power has been used in dribs and drabs, mostly in support of ground operations or to impress local dissidents. In such operations, transport aircraft have played an important part, as have helicopters, and sometimes piston-engined, four-engined heavy bombers such as the Avro Lincoln and the Shackleton (ER 215) did bombing, reconnaissance, showing the flag, and even strafing. Transports also evacuated nationals; Sabena, the Belgian airline, lifted over 34,000 out of the Congo and British United some 9,000 out of Aden.

The long campaigns in southern Arabia in the end led to naught for Britain, as the Arabs gained independence. And across the Gulf of Aden, in the Horn of Africa, troubles rumbled on finally to a head until in 1988 the United Nations attempted to restore order, only to fail in Somaliland when ground forces were denied armored personnel carriers and tanks for the task that helicopters alone could not handle.

One of the equations that came into play in the 1960s was the arrival of surface-to-air missiles, which gave the defenders on the ground a potent response to air superiority and air attack, especially when backed at low-level by multiple-cannon, such as the Germans had used in the 1939–45 war. A second influential weapon, especially in Afghanistan, was the shoulder-fired SAM, which guerrillas could tote, hide, and fire most effectively against low-flying fixed-wing aircraft and helicopters.

Africa

The vast African continent, which is divided by the equator, is also split into a number of geographic regions of differing topography, climate, and historical background: North Africa from Morocco to Cyrenaica; Egypt and the Sudan; the Horn of Africa; East, Central, and West or tropical; and Southern Africa.

And although in the twentieth century intense air activity has at times taken place along the northern littoral and on into the Middle East, in the vast reaches to the south, air operations generally have been thin and spread over a number of years.

As the older colonial powers withdrew, the two super-powers, the USSR and the United States, moved in and out as much due to the whims of local policy as of grand strategy. What became notable in the British handling of various colonial crises, civil wars, and guerrilla activity was the flexibility of air power due both to the ferry range of operational machines and the immediate support provided by transport aircraft.

Significant in Africa was the polyglot nature of the forces employed, most of whom, at the air level, spoke English. What is also to be observed is that a little air power went a long way, as in Palestine in 1918.

East Africa, 1947–91

In both West and East Africa, conflicts arose between tribes to whom the artificial boundaries drawn by latitude- and longitude-minded Europeans made no sense. Thus, the Somalis attempted to incorporate into the Somali Republic (from 1960) their kinsmen in both Kenya and Eritrea, with alliances shifting from the Soviets to the

Americans versus common enemies. Famine and disease have been weapons. Mutinies in newly independent states were quelled by British naval air power. Otherwise, little air action occurred other than shows of force.

In the Mau Mau emergency of Kenya, AT-6 Texan (Harvard) trainers converted to light bombers proved noisy and ineffective and thus were replaced in 1953 by Avro Lincolns, which could pattern-bomb suspected terrorist camps. Operations took place in the early morning before clouds and turbulence built up, but the main difficulty was the supply of bombs and the need for delayed-action fuses with drops from below 900-foot ceilings. The other deficiency was post-bombing PRU for damage assessment and as an intelligence infrastructure.

By 1956, the Mau Mau insurrection was over, but had cost eight out of nineteen aircraft in accidents, and 602 members of the security forces versus 10,527 Mau Mau dead and 2,633 captured. The emergency had also cost Britain over £55 million.

The Horn of Africa has been the scene of both tribal and Cold War activity as the government of Ethiopia sought from 1975 to destroy the Eritrean rebels, with limited success in spite of the employment of MiG-19 and MiG-21 fighter-bombers. However, the rebels retaliated with two commando raids in 1986, which between them destroyed some seventy-four aircraft at Asmara. On the other hand, claims were made that the Ethiopians used napalm bombs to fire crops and induce famine.

In Somalia in 1969 the Soviets granted support to the Socialists there in return for an air base and port at Berbera, on the Gulf of Aden. This coincided with the attack in May 1977 on the Ogaden region of Ethiopia, which ironically in 1978 was held by 1,500 Russians and 3,000 Cubans advisers. The Soviet-equipped Somali Aeronautical Corps soon found itself opposed by Soviet-supplied Ethiopian Air Force fighters. Thus, Somalia expelled its 6,000 Soviets.

Meanwhile, the Russians airlifted arms to Addis Ababa in its Aeroflot airline colors from Black Sea bases, refueling in Baghdad and Aden. In 1978, Jijiga was taken after Mil Mi-6 helicopters (ER 13) airlifted seventy tanks to the rear of the city, which was attacked by some seventy MiGs. Although the war officially ended, border attacks continued for years, as did Eritrean efforts, notably again in 2000. In 1981, the United States occupied Berbera as a major Rapid Redeployment Force base.

In the Sudan—Africa's largest country—and Uganda, the air forces were variously equipped with Soviet MiG fighters and Mil helicopters and U.S. Northrop F-5 Freedom Fighters. In the war against Tanzania in 1977, the Tanzania Air Force lost three Xi'an F-7 (ER n/a) Chinese-licensed MiGs to their own SA-7 missiles: amicide and aircraft mis-recognition go hand-in-hand.

The Congo, 1960–64

The Congo air war was the scene of civil rebellion brought on by inadequate preparations for independence. As in other parts of Africa, mercenaries were employed due to the unreliability of the indigenous troops. Some of these white professionals became warlords and the saviors of hostages.

Air activity came from the ingenious use of older types such as the AT-6 Texan (Harvard) and the B-26 Invader, both of which could operate from ill-prepared airfields. And due to problems of overflying some countries, the swift deployment of troops was delayed or endangered; commando helicopter carriers, when within range of the land, proved their worth as floating offshore airfields.

The first significant use of aircraft was that of the *Force Arienne Belgique* (FAB), which repatriated civilians while also moving Belgian troops to key spots. Helicopters plucked whites from remote farms escorted by armed AT-6s and Fouga Magister (ER n/a) trainers, and the AT-6s soon suffered losses. The main concern was to protect the international mining interests in rich Katanga, which had declared independence. The Congo appealed to the United Nations, which then established the *Force de l'Organization des Nations Unies* of the UN Operation in the Congo (ONUC, *Operatión des Nations Unies au Congo*), employing troops from neutral countries. The RAF began moving troops from Ghana, and the USAF moved in other African forces. Irish troops were flown in, and the USSR "loaned" the Congo nine Il-14 transports (ER 16.5). The conflict now became a hot spot in the Cold War.

In the meantime, the Belgian airline Sabena had in a few weeks evacuated the Belgian civilians through Leopoldville, and more had been flown out by C-47 Dakotas of the Royal Rhodesia Air Force (RRAF) from Ndola to Salisbury, while Italian Fairchild C-119 Flying Boxcars (ER 67.5) flew out its nationals. A liaison headquarters was established for air operations, and the Swedish Air Force handled liaison flying with de Havilland U-1 Otters (ER 2.1), U-6 Beavers (ER 4.2), and helicopters.

The situation was complicated by the operations of the African National Congress (ANC) from Leopoldville. The ANC had been a presence in South Africa since the early part of the twentieth century, and was renamed as the ANC in 1923. Its guerrilla arm was trained by Soviet advisers in Angola. And in addition to the ANC complications were the pro-Communist forces, the Katangans' arch-enemies the Kasai Balubas, and the Katanganese gendarmerie. The UN's role seemed to be to attempt to end Katangan independence.

By September 1961, Indian and Ethiopian aircraft were involved out of Leopoldville and Swedish fighter-bombers went to Kaniena; chartered companies flew in supplies, while twenty-seven USAF Douglas C-124 Globemasters (ER 420) brought in troops, arms, and armored cars to Elizabethville for the final UN drive to eliminate Katanga. Despite a cease-fire, fighting continued in 1962 with old USAF T-6s taken out to Africa and assembled by Portuguese Air Force technicians for the Katangan Air Force. Meanwhile, the USAF transports supported the Irish in Elizabethville,

where they were joined by Ethiopian troops whose Shenyang F-6 Mustangs (ER n/a) were little used. However, further Swedish Saab J-29 Tunnan fighters (ER 24.6) arrived in 1963. These, with Indian Air Force Canberras, soon took out the Katangan Air Force. Peace came in April 1964 and four Swedish J-29s flew home, the rest being destroyed *in situ*. The United Nations had withdrawn by July 1964.

Civil war broke out again shortly, and T-6s, as well as USAF Douglas B-26s flown by Cubans, were acquired and used against the Chinese-backed Simbas. The Belgian Air Force was back with C-47s, and armed T-6s, and T-28s were operational. Belgian paratroopers were flown in by USAF C-130 Hercules to take Stanleyville. The Soviets supplied arms via Algerian and Ghanian transports operating into Brazzaville.

Air support of paratroopers and commandos on the ground enabled a final offensive. But the civil war continued with U.S. CIA-recruited pilots replacing unreliable Congolese. The final mercenary attacks into Katanga were driven back by air power, and in 1968 some of the mercenaries were repatriated to Europe by Red Cross-chartered Douglas DC-6 Liftmasters (ER 278). The last rebel leader was hijacked on a flight to Majorca and imprisoned in Algeria, where he died.

The Congo was then renamed Zaire (1972) and in 1977 was attacked by a fresh band of rebels supported by Angola and Cuban mercenaries. Zaire's appeal for help resulted in twelve French Air Force transports flying in 1,500 Moroccan troops, with the United States supplying financial and military aid and the Egyptians offering pilots.

In less than three months the war was over. But in 1978 another coup was attempted from Angola, which took 2,000 hostages while destroying the airfield at Kolwezi. A Zairian paratrooper attack on the airfield on May 16 was a complete failure—60 percent casualties, though they did keep hold of the airfield. The French acted at once to avoid the cumbersome UN process and flew in paratroops from Corsica and Orleans in chartered DC-8s to Kinasha; they were then airlifted in Zairian C-130s into Kolwezi on May 18, followed by Belgian paratroopers and British medical teams. They were all replaced on May 25 by 5,000 Africans flown in by the U.S. Air Force to help the Congolese maintain order. Decisive action using air mobility prevented the massacre of the 2,000 hostages.

The Nigerian Civil War, 1967–70

The Nigerian conflict occurred in another colony, which when granted independence in 1963 soon slid into civil war—again due to tribal conflicts. The Ibos in the east had oil and seceded after an army coup and became Biafra in 1967, with Swiss bank accounts.

Biafra, faced by the newly formed Nigerian Air Force equipped with trainers and transports, started to build its air force by hijacking two airliners. The Nigerians advanced on the ground and were attacked by the four aircraft of the Biafran Air Force, one of which bombed the airfield at Makordu. By August 1967, two B-26s were in action. The Nigerians needed both air cover and close-support aircraft and received these from the USSR in the form of armored trainers, MiG-17s, and MiG-15 UTI trainers. The British "allowed" recruiting of aircrew, and Airwork Ltd. contracted to do maintenance.

Both the CIA and the French supported Biafra, with some eighteen army supply aircraft operating under a dummy name out of Lisbon using time-expired Douglas DC-4s, DC-6s, and DC-7, as well as Lockheed C-69 Constellations. Both sides attacked airfields with moderate success, but thereafter winter weather limited air operations, as did shortage of spares. The capture of Port Harcourt cut off Biafran access to the sea in May 1968, and the Biafran air lifeline suffered from sabotage. By June the Biafrans had just one airstrip and the Red Cross was building another. However, the Nigerian Air Force by then had six Il-28 bombers flown by Egyptian and Czech crews.

Biafra had early on employed a Swiss public-relations firm, which in mid-1968 had mounted a campaign about the poor, starving Biafran people being murdered by the Nigerians. The wellspring of sympathy resulted in relief flights, which only prolonged the agony. The last of the RAF's venerable Avro Ansons (ER 2.38) were bought to fly medical supplies in Biafra, but three of the six crashed upon delivery. All relief flights had to be made at night and included arms.

The Biafrans surrounded and took Onitsha while the Nigerian leader, General Gowon, sought to help his government's image by also filtering in relief flights. But arms continued to be flown in and relief aircraft shot down, with the chartered airlines suffering the losses. A veteran Swede organized a new unmarked Biafran Air Force of light planes flying out of Libreville and the strip at Uli, using two-seat light Malmo MFI-9s known as "Minicons" (ER 0.19). They especially singled out Nigerian oil targets. As the Nigerian Air Force inaugurated night patrols, the Biafra Air Force acquired two British Gloster NF11 Meteors (ER 27.3). But they failed to arrive, and the brokers were indicted in England. Then, in early 1970, Biafra was cut in two and defeated, relief flights flown into Lagos, and the civil war was at an end.

Angola, Mozambique, and Rhodesia/ Zimbabwe, 1961

Nationalist movements in this relatively barren area had no outside bases until Britain and France emancipated their neighboring colonies in 1956. With unrest, the *Force Aérea Portuguesa* (FAP) moved a few aircraft (C-47s and Lockheed PV-2 Harpoons, ER 3.42) to the capital of Luanda. When serious sieges started in 1961, the FAP had only a few transports and utility aircraft in the country, which were used in support roles. A squadron of F-84Gs arrived in June and the Harpoons were fitted to be bombers. Fragmentation bombs were dropped and parachutists employed. Aerospatiale Alouette III helicopters (ER 0.52) were acquired, and the FAP expanded into a regional air force. To counter the Chinese support, the Congo rebels were now backed by the United States to ensure a pro-Western, rather than Communist, independent Angola. More of the fighting took place in the Dembos Mountains, with air strikes and paradrops. The Portuguese Air Force lost five F-84Gs, all in accidents.

In 1965, the United States lifted its arms embargo to let the FAP have some Douglas B-26 Invader bombers, through a private company. With the founding of the southern tribes' UNITA (National Union for the Total Independence of Angola) attacks on the Benguelatt railway, the Congo and Zambia became upset as they needed the line for their copper exports. The war was now triangular—Portuguese, UNITA, and the northern MPLA (Popular Movement for the Liberation of Angola) tribes all against each other.

The Portuguese increasingly used helicopters to avoid the mined roads, as South Africans also entered the conflict, ostensibly to guard the Namibia iron mines. Herbicides began to be used to deny crops to the rebels, and tracts were burned off along the roads to thwart ambushes. But a hearts-and-minds policy and the movement of one million people into strategic villages, along with major offensives, failed in 1970 and 1972. Morale in the Portuguese Army fell. Fiat G-91s (ER 25) were sent in 1972 from Mozambique, but the Portuguese economy could not stand the strain of fighting in three colonies. In 1974, shortly after a coup in Lisbon, Angola was offered independence. Civil war followed, with the major Cold War powers arming their protegés. In 1975, some 300,000 Europeans, Portuguese armed forces, and equipment were flown out.

The arms airlift saw the United States, the Soviet Union, France, and China as suppliers, together with South Africa and Cuba, assembling arms in the Congo. C-130s were used by both the South Africans and others to airlift armored cars and matériel. MiG-17s and MiG-21s were supplied to the MPLA/Cuban forces. The United States, having guessed wrong about which side to support, withdrew, forcing the South Africans to pull back. Once the MiGs became operational, they faced Israeli SAMs and U.S. Redeye missiles. And the MPLA now had Nigerian support. In 1976, the MPLA started to use helicopter gunships against UNITA. The Russians began to use Angola as a base for other operations in Africa with two Tupolev Tu-95 (Tu-20) Bears (ER 2,652) operating out of Luanda by late 1977.

In 1978, the South Africans returned to Angola in pursuit of SWAPO (South West African People's Organization) guerrillas. At the same time, the Angolan People's Air Force (FAPA) had grown to about fifty aircraft, including MiGs, Mils, An-12 transports (ER 204), a C-130, four Nord 262 transports, and two Boeing 707s, the latter six aircraft being operated by TAAG Angola Airlines—*Transportes Aéreos de Angola*. SAMs and the use of napalm also accelerated, as did casualties on all sides. By 1986 FAPA aircraft totaled twenty-three MiG-23 (ER 274), ten Su-22, seventy MiG-21, and twenty-five MiG-25 (ER 179) fighters; seventeen Mi-17 (ER 2.87) and fifty-two Mi-8 helicopters; thirty An-26 (ER 16.8), twelve An-12 (ER 209), and eleven An-2 (ER 2.1) transports; and twenty-five Pilatus PC-7 turbo-trainers (ER 4.83). South African Air Force Mirages had also become active.

Increasingly air bases and airstrips became vital to operations and were the focus of attacks. In their defense, after 1987 Stinger SAMs played an important role. By 1989, South Africa appeared to have withdrawn.

In Mozambique, on the east coast of southern Africa, the Portuguese Air Force had increased its organization with T-6s, Dornier Do-27s (ER 0.76), and a few Alouette helicopters. Bases were established or expanded and acted as units instead of squadrons. As the guerrilla FRELIMO (Front for the Liberation of Mozambique) forces gathered strength, the Portuguese Air Force brought in Fiat G-91 ground attack aircraft, but these were forbidden to assault guerrilla bases in Tanzania and Zambia. However, anti-aircraft attacks from across the border were met by counter-bombing. Once the FRELIMO threatened the railway and obtained Chinese SAMs, the Portuguese decided to withdraw, and in 1975 Mozambique became independent, with a fighting ex-FAP air force of about a dozen machines. In 1977, this was increased with a gift of Soviet MiG-21s. The South African Air Force responded to this threat with a new base nearer Mozambique. Various incursions and counterattacks followed, with the Mozambique People's Air Force receiving some fifty MiG-23s.

In neighboring Rhodesia, the Royal Rhodesian Air Force was the strongest in the region after the South African Air Force. From January to August 1966, Royal Navy carriers threatened Mozambique and checked shipping, but thereafter the blockade of Beira, Mozambique, was by land-based aircraft; Shackletons of the RAF were based in French Malaguay (1972–75). Rhodesia handled its guerrilla problems until in 1970 it was made an independent republic and nationalist pressure rose. When Portugal pulled out, South Africa preferred a stable black rather than a Marxist government in Rhodesia. But the new Zimbabwe government was facing yet another threat, including that from Botswana creating a four-front war.

To meet these, "fire forces" of helicopters and paratroops were deployed, backed by central reserves and new landing strips. As the guerrillas mined attack roads, so the Zimbabwean forces developed more accurate napalm bombs ("frang tons") and 1,000-pound bombs that used the old Western Desert proboscis fuzes to explode them above ground, as well as *fléchettes*—steel darts dropped from aircraft—as in 1914. Lynx helicopters were used in many roles, including flare-dropping at night and as communications links. The Rhodesian Air Force lost most aircraft to SAMs after 1972. By 1978, its strikes attacked guerrilla training camps well within Zambia, Mozambique, and Angola. But in 1979 elections were held, and Prime Minister Ian Smith, a former RAF pilot, lost his position. The new cease-fire ended in 1982, when much of the old Rhodesian Air Force was destroyed on the ground.

In 1987, the Zimbabwe Air Force received twelve MiG-29s. From 1983 to 1986, the Zimbabwe Air Force had a Pakistan Air Force officer as CAS, along with his staff to put the ZAF back on its feet before a native Zimbabwean took command.

In the meantime, arms supply defeated the embargo against Smith's Rhodesia by circuitous air routing and transfers in South Africa and the Comoros Islands, as well as via Oman and the Congo—or from Italy to Beirut to Israel, which exchanged the arms for their used equipment and delivered them to Rhodesia under a Singaporean label. The cargo line Affuetair operated around the world on these flights and often out of Schipol Airport in Amsterdam.

South Africa not only employed her security forces in Angola, but also, and more importantly, against Nationalists within the Republic and in South West Africa (Namibia). The South West African People's Organization had been formed in 1958, and its military arm began to operate out of Zambia in 1965. From then until 1973, the South African Police handled the incursions, with aid of SAAF helicopters. After that, the armed forces took over with Air Commando Impala helicopters and a Mirage squadron in support.

In 1978, a successful airborne attack on a camp was made 155 miles into Angola, supported by Canberras and Hawker-Siddeley Buccaneers (ER 152). By late 1980, the SAAF was flying regular PRU sorties over southern Angola, to counter which the Angolan armed forces set up a defensive belt. The South Africans, in turn, countered this with air and mechanized forces striking hard in 1981 into Angola, destroying SAMs and radar—an operation repeated to destroy guerrilla bases. But in 1982, such successful raids on foot, by vehicle, and with air support faced Soviet-built ZSU-23 quad light anti-aircraft guns and SA-8 and SA-9 missiles. MiGs began to challenge PRU sorties, which were then escorted by new Mirage F1s.

South Africa was not supporting UNITA in Angola. And though by 1988 the Angolan air-

From almost the beginning of aviation, airshows have appealed to the public for their power, escapism, and spectacular nature. The development of aerobatic display teams has almost been *de rigueur*. Here, at Le Bourget Airport, Paris, in 1965, the RAF's Red Arrow team in Folland Gnats (ER 12.8) show off their tight-formation expertise. Trainers have often been favored over fighters because they are more economical and can maneuver in less airspace. Designed as a private-venture fighter, the trainer was ordered in 1957 and was designed to last ten years, or 5,000 hours. (Hawker-Siddeley)

The 1955 Convair F-102 Delta Dagger (ER 63, F-102A) was a delta-winged, tailless interceptor, again with the benefit of postwar research. However, the prototypes encountered significant drag, and thus in 1954 Convair undertook a 117-day crash redesign that incorporated the Whitcomb area rule developed by NACA—the wasp shape, reducing drag by allowing flow over wings-fuselage junction, to by-pass that choke point. This resulted in the F-102A having a "coke-bottle" fuselage. The F-102 was the first USAF fighter designed to be armed only with missiles, an approach that the Vietnam War proved to be illusory. (Convair)

A product of Lockheed's famed Skunk Works, the U-2 Gray Ghost (ER 45) was a very high-altitude, single-seat spy plane for overflying the USSR to gather photographic and electronic intelligence. Pilot Francis Gary Powers was flying a U-2 from Pakistan to Norway when he was shot down in 1960. Although considered highly secret, three-view drawings of the plane had appeared in *Model Airplane News* in 1958. (Lockheed)

In 1960, the USAF decided that it had a requirement for modernizing the strategic airlift capability, and the Lockheed C-141 Starlifter (ER 1,470) was the result. The aircraft, shown here over Marietta, Georgia, was intended to be able to carry 90 percent of all portable U.S. equipment, loaded through the large rear doors, as on the C-130 Hercules. In 1965, the C-141 began a daily cargo service to Vietnam. Thereafter, it flew worldwide resupply missions until withdrawn in 2002 after a wing collapsed while refueling on the ground. This close-out was made possible by the availability of "white-tail" Boeing 767s (ER 1,088). (Lockheed-Martin)

Gen. Curtis E. LeMay, as Chief of Staff, USAF, in the 1960s. He gained operational experience with the Eighth Air Force in England, then commanded the Twentieth Air Force in the Pacific and switched from daylight to night incendiary raids to defeat Japan. During the Cold War, he created the USAF Strategic Air Command, the most significant air power deterrent to ensure peace, though SAC was never called on to make a nuclear attack with either bombers or missiles. (USAF)

Also a product of the Skunk Works and Kelly Johnson's team, the SR-71 (YF-12) Blackbird (ER 2,040) was a very fast and high spy plane. Capable of 2,000 mph (Mach 3), a 90,000-foot ceiling, and a range of 3,000 miles, it was an exceptional intelligence tool in the Cold War. Taken out of service after the 1991 Persian Gulf War, SR-71s had to be refurbished and put back in use in the 1990s. (Lockheed)

This ugly bird is the Grumman OV-1B Mohawk (ER 12.4), the U.S. Army's first turboprop airplane that was to be used jointly with the Marines for battlefield surveillance. However, the U.S. Marine Corps dropped out of the project early on. Mohawks were deployed first to Germany, then in 1962 to Vietnam, where a version could do radar mapping with instant prints. One is preserved in the U.S. Army's Aviation Museum at Fort Rucker, Alabama. (Grumman History Center)

The Republic F-105 Thunderchief (ER 132), known as the "Thud," was designed to be a tactical fighter-bomber, but in the Vietnam War it was used as a grand-strategic weapon. The two-seat version carried a second crew member for ECM (electronic counter-measure) work. Operational in 1959, it was the first supersonic tactical fighter-bomber designed as such. As big as a B-17 Flying Fortress, but with only one crew member, it was a formidable weapon. An F-105 is preserved at the U.S. Air Force Museum at Dayton. (General Dynamics)

A number of jet trainers have found a second niche as attack aircraft. In Sweden, trainers become attack machines upon the outbreak of war. Here, the versatile Cessna A-37 (T-37) Dragonfly (ER 6.14) out of Wichita, Kansas, shows off the variety of armaments that it could carry. (Cessna)

The swing-wing General Dynamics F-111 Aardvark (ER 1,189) was conceived in the early 1960s as a multi-purpose aircraft, with the hope of emulating the success of the U.S. Navy-Air Force F-4 Phantom. However, the Aardvark suffered a number of problems while trying to fly nap-of-the-earth in Vietnam. Originally known as the TFX in 1962, production lasted until a decade later. (Royal Australian Air Force)

The Cessna 0-1 Birddog (ER 0.038) was a spotter, and has hardly changed since 1945. With one or two crew, several radios, and some markers, it was ideal for flying low and slow over villages during the Vietnam War, and then directing fighter-bombers onto a target. (USAF/Cessna)

Engine size grew rapidly in the years after World War II. Compare the Lockheed P-80/F-80 (ER 27) engine pictured earlier with this North American F-100 Super Sabre (ER 90) Pratt & Whitney PW-100 turbo-fan engine of 20,000 pounds thrust. With two of these engines, the McDonnell Douglas F-15 Eagle (ER 187) had a thrust-to-weight ratio of better than one to one, enabling it to climb vertically. (United Technologies)

A mixed flight of a USAF F-4 Phantom (ER 236.4) and West German (Federal Republic) and Royal Canadian Air Force Lockheed F-104 Starfighters (ER 68) fly formation over Western Europe, symbolizing NATO's cooperative nature. (Lockheed)

Higher speeds, altitudes, and G forces led to the adoption not only of ejection seats, but also of means to ensure the safety, comfort, and efficiency of aircrew. Here, a Royal Hellenic Air Force pilot stands by his Northrop F-5A Freedom Fighter (ER 82), with "bone-dome" helmet, retractable visor, oxygen mask and microphone, parachute harness, and flying suit. (Royal Hellenic Air Force)

The two-seat light-attack A-7A Corsair II (ER 101.4) was developed by LTV for a 1964 U.S. Navy contest, one of whose requirements was quick production. Based on the F-8 Crusader, the Corsair II was in squadron service by 1967. Note the probe-and-drogue refueling boom just below the right side of the cockpit. (USAF)

An LTV A-7 Corsair II (ER 101.4) flies over the USN attack carrier *Ranger* off Vietnam in 1969. Note that the *Ranger* is a classic post–World War II angled-deck carrier, able to land jets in such a way that a "bolter," having missed the wires, can take off again without crashing into aircraft parked on the bow or those behind the bridge. (USN)

The LTV Vought F-8 Crusader (ER 68) air-superiority fighter was the last design produced by the Vought Corporation before it was absorbed into the Dallas-based LTV. The Crusader had a variable-incidence wing (shown here in the slow-speed mode for landing on a carrier), an all-flying variable-incidence tailplane, and an energy-absorbing undercarriage for arrested landings. (USN)

The Grumman E-6 Prowler (ER 77.3) is the electronic version of the A-6 Intruder. The A-6 originated in 1957 from a U.S. Navy requirement, learned in the Korean War, for a high subsonic speed, very low-level attack plane, with a long range, that could penetrate under radar into enemy space. The first A-6As were operational in 1963. In all, by 1969, 482 were built and were still in service during the Persian Gulf War of 1991. Rather ungainly looking, nevertheless its side-by-side seating made for very efficient crew work. It was featured in the movie *The Flight of the Intruder* on the Vietnam War. (Grumman History Center)

A Sikorsky S-70 air/sea rescue helicopter (ER 4.14) of the U.S. Coast Guard, in high-visibility markings. (USCG)

Designed as a high-speed, low-level, long-range bomber, the British Aircraft Corporation (BAC) TSR-2 (ER 1,197.5) fell victim to defense cuts and was canceled in 1965 after only three were built. Its demise was premised on the idea that it would be useless by the time it became operational. The cancellation was costly in terms of prestige, pounds, and physical information. Ironically, the decade-older Boeing B-52 Stratofortress (ER 6,336) was by 2003 expected to last until at least 2020 or even 2040. A TSR-2 is preserved at Duxford, United Kingdom. (British Aircraft Corporation)

With its 15,000 pounds of external stores, the Grumman A-6A Intruder's all-up weight was just a little under that of the four-engine heavy bombers of World War II.

In the 1960s, the major air forces found that their manned bombers had to compete with intermediate and long-range ballistic missiles. A logical argument was made that only missiles could successfully penetrate enemy air space. McDonnell Douglas Thor IRBMs (intermediate range ballistic missiles) were emplaced in Britain, but could only be fired if both British and American instructions were given. The Thors subsequently became outdated by the Polaris and Poseidon sea-launched ballistic missiles in the 1970s. (McDonnell Douglas)

Designed for Canadian air defense over the Arctic, the Avro CF-100s (ER 90) were known as the "Clunks" for the noise made when the undercarriage retracted. Some served in Europe as part of the Canadian Forces in Germany. (Canadian Forces)

The 1957 McDonnell Douglas F-101 Voodoo (ER 252) was developed as an air-defense fighter for the North American Air Defense Command (NORAD) with the need for long flights over uninhabited areas. Some 480 were built for the USAF, which released 66 to the RCAF, with whom it shared the NORAD responsibility. (Canadian Forces)

The Italian Fiat G-91T trainer (ER 25) was a derivative of the G-91 fighter, a common pattern. (Italian Air Force)

The impact of the jet was also large upon facilities, as was the changing social climate. This 1963 view clearly shows the two almost parallel runways, wide and long, and the importance of housing for married enlisted as well as officer personnel—even though this was Kamina near Elizabethville in the Congo, home to the Swedish F-22 Squadron. (Royal Swedish Air Force)

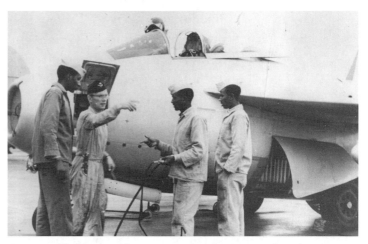

On one of the very few occasions when neutral and unaligned Sweden sent airmen overseas, a Swedish technical warrant officer at Addis Ababa instructs an Ethiopian ground crew on what was to be done before the squadron continued to Zaire in 1961. (Royal Swedish Air Force)

In 1963, Swedish airmen went to the Congo. Here, rugged, single-seat Saab J-29 fighters (ER 24.6) are deployed at Kamina. One of these aircraft is preserved at the Swedish Air Force Museum in Lynköping. (Royal Swedish Air Force)

The Swedish aircraft industry, always closely linked to the auto companies, stubbornly entered the jet field with its own design. Given the special needs for dispersion and concealment, and the shortage of manpower, the Saab J-35 Drakken (ER 35) was designed to operate off country roads, and to be maintained by reservists. A display team is seen here at the 1965 Paris Air Show. Swedish aircraft are preserved at the Air Museum in Lynköping. (Royal Swedish Air Force)

defense system was the most sophisticated Soviet installation outside of the Warsaw Pact, it failed to deter the South African Air Force. The South African Defense Forces (SADF) response was surgical infantry and air strikes. In general, these operations were successful, but it was the political forces and world pressure through the United Nations and sanctions that ended apartheid in 1994 and turned South Africa over to majority rule.

Portuguese Guinea, 1963–74

Portuguese Guinea was a lightly inhabited colony with some impressive rivers. PAIGC (African Party for the Independence of Guinea and Cape Verde) fighters trained in Algeria, Cuba, the USSR, and China emerged in 1963. The Portuguese Air Force had only a few T-6s available, due to troubles in Angola and Mozambique. By 1967, the PAIGC had made twenty-two attacks on airfields that were used as daytime forward bases by the FAP.

An aggressive Portuguese campaign started in 1969 and used napalm, defoliants, and herbicides. A seaborne strike into Guinea recovered downed FAP aircrew. But Nigerian MiG-17s supported the guerrillas, who now had SAMs and other anti-aircraft weapons. The 1974 coup in Lisbon led to independence before the end of the year. Troops went home, and the new Guinea-Bissau benefitted from abandoned equipment.

The Desert Air Wars, 1945 to the 1990s

In 1927, as a result of the success of air control in Iraq, the same technique was extended to South Arabia from the base at Aden by a similar combination of air action and ground levies. Not much attention was paid to the inter-tribal squabbles until after the end of the Second World War, when demonstrations of force using Mosquitoes began in combination with RAF armored cars. Advanced notice by leaflets was given and offending villages rocketed and bombed. Over the years, local forts were attacked, using armor-piercing rockets, and other targets were bombed by Avro Lincolns.

In 1954 and 1955, action escalated and RAF intelligence officers were brought in to select and mark targets for economic attack, with helicopters available for casualty evacuation. In 1957, Meteors arrived to provide PRU for mapmaking and targeting. Maritime Shackletons detached from the United Kingdom were then used for all tasks ranaging from strafing to maritime patrol. In 1960 and 1963, Royal Navy carriers also provided support, as did Army Auster AOP aircraft, and more transport aircraft were added.

In 1962, during the revolution in Yemen, and a detachment of the Egyptian Air Force came to aid the new state in a civil war. This inspired dissidents in Aden to press for independence and undermine the British presence. The main airfield, Khormaksar's single runway, became one of the busiest in the world with both military and civil flights.

A joint operation in 1965 in the Radfan area kept escalating and new airstrips were built, but the Westland helicopters used to lift artillery to inaccessible places suffered from sand ingestion, and operations had to be temporarily suspended. Paratroopers were used extensively along the ridges as light infantry. The Jebel in eastern Arabia having been taken, and the tribes having high casualties, gradually sued for peace. Some 1,700 sorties had been flown, and helicopters had made roughly 10,000 landings.

The British government then decided on independence by 1967, but the actual withdrawal took place a year earlier. Forces were pulled back into Aden and disbanded or taken to the Persian Gulf Trucial states. The RAF then undertook the largest airlift since Berlin in 1948, using Vickers VC-10s of British United Airways and regular service transports, with the last rearguard flown off by helicopter to the HMS *Albion,* with air cover from the HMS *Eagle.*

For the last few years, with the withdrawal east of Aden, military activity had been pointless; but casualties had been light, even if costs had been high.

Even before the British had left in 1967, Yemen had become involved in a civil war of republicans, supported by Egyptians, and royalists; and there was evidence that the Soviets were involved. Arms were supplied from diverse sources including Austria, Bulgaria, China, Africa, and Iran, often by air via Ethiopia.

Egyptians bombed royalist bases in Saudi Arabia, and in early 1967 Il-28s dropped new gas bombs with overlays of mustard gas in five attacks, which killed 195. The Six-Day War forced the Egyptians to withdraw. The royalists then gained support and used their new English Electric Lightnings (ER 134) in ground support to regain their capital of Sanaa, then lost it and regained it again in 1970, when a coalition Yemen Arab Republic came into being.

The 1952–59 campaign in Oman countering the rebels was similar and tied to that in South Arabia and Yemen. Detachments were shuttled in and out and naval aircraft were also involved. The key to ending the war was reconnaissance, air control, and the use of the Special Air Service (SAS) force to take the heights of the Jebel, and this was finally accomplished in early 1959.

In 1961, Kuwait was threatened by Iraq. But it was saved by the rapidity of the British response, which again involved the airlifting of support forces and supplies from such diverse places as the United Kingdom, Germany, Cyprus, Aden, and Kenya, as well as carriers from India. The show of force was sufficient. Useful lessons, however, were learned: the RAF had used VHF radios, and the Fleet Air Arm had incompatible UHF radio sets; the RAF lacked useful radar (its portable SC 787 did not have a height-finding capability); and stockpiles in-theater were needed.

Libya, 1971 and 1976

In 1967 the United States was required to abandon Wheelus Air Force Base at Tripoli and the British El Adem. Libya's Muammar al Ghadaffi had come to power in 1969, and British oil interests were nationalized in 1971. In 1977 he fired into Egypt as a hint against peace negotiations with Israel, and fighting followed, including an Egyptian raid on El Adem. However, Egyptian President Sadat reached a cease-fire.

Libya, 1981

In 1969 Ghadaffi soon forged links with the Soviet Union. Thereafter, there were a series of minor incidents occurred along his boundaries. Acts of terrorism sponsored or based in Libya led to U.S. aid to Tripoli's neighbors and the constant exercising of the U.S. Sixth Fleet in the Gulf of Sirte, leading to the shooting down in 1981 of two Libyan Su-22s by F-14 Tomcats. Ghadaffi's subsequent sponsorship of terrorism resulted in the Palestine Liberation Organization's (PLO) headquarters outside Tunis being struck by Israeli jets flying a 3,000-mile round trip.

A guerrilla terrorist attack subsequently resulted in a bomb in a café in Berlin. The United States decided to exercise the right of self-defense under the United Nations Charter. In April 1986 various U.S. aircraft covered Libya seeking target intelligence: RC-135Ws reconnaissance Stratotankers; the U-2 espionage/surveillance Gray Ghost; and the SR-71 Blackbird, the titanium surveillance machine called the "monster." Tankers were assembled as well as twenty-four F-111s. Because France denied overflight permission, a 5,500-mile trip had to be flown around west of Spain and then down the Mediterranean to Libya and back. The attack had to be coordinated with one from the Sixth Fleet carriers.

The result was a finely orchestrated strike with specific targets, such as aircraft and barracks, though not a full success. Five of eighteen F-111 Aardvarks and two A-6E Intruders had to abort, and significant collateral damage occurred near the targets.

More serious than earlier terrorist bombings, however, was the December 1988 bombing of Pan Am Flight 103, a 747 passing over Lockerbie, Scotland. But after the April 1986 U.S. strike, Ghadaffi maintained a low profile.

The 1986 American raid had shown that assets from many sources could be concentrated quickly and a rapier-like strike delivered with diplomatic effect.

Morocco, 1975

The Moroccan Air Force—*Force Aerienne Royale Marocaine* (FARM)—was supported financially by Saudi Arabia to a total of $1 billion (U.S.) per annum. Aircraft have been used against guerrillas in a number of cases. However, the guerrillas have been quite successful in using SAMs and ground fire to bring down their enemies—a Mirage flying at 20,000 feet was hit by an SA-8 launched from Algeria.

The importance of aviation, even in minor theaters, should not be overlooked.

Algeria, 1947–62

Algeria was the scene of a prolonged effort by the French to maintain order in their North African province—a part of metropolitan France had been heavily inhabited by French *colons*. Rigged elections that denied Muslims their rights led to the outbreak of hostilities in 1954. Air power was ill-prepared for a campaign against the Muslim National Liberation Front/National Liberation Army (FLN/ALN). However, 700 North American T-6 Texans were brought in to Algeria and air command posts were well equipped with radios established, especially in the mountains, while naval air patrols intercepted suspected arms shipments. Helicopters were introduced as assault transports, and these and sophisticated air control allowed the army flexibility of response.

However, during much of 1956–58, the fighting was urban. To stop resupply and the launching of attacks from havens in neighboring Tunisia to the east and Morocco to the west, an electrified fence was erected, patrolled by PBY Catalinas backed up against any breach by air and ground strike forces. One counterattack, unfortunately, in leveling a Tunisian village, hit the school and the church, giving the FLN propaganda materials.

By 1958, tensions were growing between the *colons,* the Muslims, the army, and Gen. Charles de Gaulle's new government in Paris, with the stains of Vietnam and Suez lingering over the whole. A new French general and a new plan aimed to wipe out the FLN/ALN successfully used air intelligence, bombing, and paratroops to surround and destroy the rebels district by district. Some 700 aircraft by then were deployed, but sophisticated ground-based weapons forced the withdrawal of the T-6, and it was replaced with Skyraiders and other armored planes. Large transport helicopters improved the mobility of ground troops, and air assets were made available to ground commanders on a daily basis. Moreover, a sophisticated radio net enabled the new North American F-100 Super Sabre attack aircraft to remain based at Rheims in northern France, flying daily sorties with a refueling stop at Istres.

Operational successes were negated, however, when de Gaulle announced that he would negotiate with the FLN. After a revolt in Algiers, this led not only to the formation of a Muslim negotiating team but also to a French secret army in opposition to the government. The heart went out of military operations, and the commanding general led a mutiny against Paris. But de Gaulle put tanks in the streets and air patrols overhead, and the uprising by the *Organization Armée Secrète* (the OAS) degenerated into a terrorist operation that led to a truce after an Air France Constellation was blown up at Algiers in 1962. Algeria was subsequently granted independence.

The campaign had been expensive, and ended in a retributive bloodbath by both sides. Even so, the French Air Force felt that it had come out of the Algerian civil war with its head held high, in contrast to the debacles in Vietnam and at Suez.

The East Indies since 1945

The successful Japanese defeat of the old Imperial powers in Southwest Asia in 1942 fueled native ambitions for independence. This—coupled to the arms available in 1945, the concern of the

Allies to return the Japanese and to repatriate POWs, and the wish of the United States to allow the free determination of peoples—made the position of the Dutch, recovering from the German occupation at home, very difficult. Thus, in 1950, they turned over the Dutch East Indies to Indonesia. Dutch New Guinea was given up to Indonesia in 1962, which in 1975 attempted to take East Timor, but was unsuccessful, and the fighting lasted until 2000.

In the late summer and fall of 1945, a strong RAF contingent worked with the Dutch army to pull out detainees and POWs, while at the same time ship the defeated Japanese home. The process was complicated by Indonesians, well-armed from Japanese stocks, determined to gain independence from the Dutch. Dutch troops had to guard airfields, as RAF fighters covered both road convoys and evacuation ports. Transports were used to airlift out the former POWs. Some Mosquitoes dropped leaflets to get Republicans to lay down their arms, while others bombed. Conditions were made more difficult by rain and floods that broke up runways already short for the modern aircraft using them. And with spares being scarce, 425 tons weekly had to be delivered for the RAF to Java alone.

Gradually RAF aircraft and units were withdrawn and disbanded as the Dutch took over a deteriorating situation in 1946. However, talks for federation broke down, for the "Indonesian Republic" began to create an air arm with about fifty surplus Japanese aircraft. As the Dutch took over more territory, anti-British feeling arose and the RAF Regiment had to be committed to defend the RAF's two main bases at Medan and Kemajoram, but all British units had left by October 1946.

Although peace was agreed early in 1947, clashes continued, and the arms embargo was violated to bring in aircraft for the Republicans. The Dutch launched attacks on airfields in a police action, which pushed the guerrillas back into the hills and starved them of supplies. Late in the year, a Dutch paratroop attack caught the rebel leaders; but the move was condemned and international pressure in 1949 forced the Dutch to make an orderly transfer of government to Sukarno, who became president of the United States of Indonesia. Dutch air assets were left behind or, in the case of ineffectives such as the Spitfires, were returned to the Netherlands.

From the beginning, Muslim Indonesia had to face rebellions and revolts by minorities living on the 10,000 islands. The population of 100 million would soon become the fourth largest in the world. As the nationalist president tolerated Communists, the United States became concerned, and in 1957 regarded the building of a new airfield in Borneo as a step toward allowing the Soviets into the area. Rebellions subsequently broke out in Sumatra and the Celebes, which were aided covertly from the U.S. air base at Clark Field in the Philippines. President Sukarno ordered arms from the USSR, but political amnesty ended the struggle in 1961.

In 1962, Sukarno claimed Dutch New Guinea and West Irian, sent an invasion force, and the Dutch handed the colony over in May 1963. The ambitious Sukarno wanted to add Malaya and Borneo to Indonesia, as well as the Philippines. In 1962, as a counter, the Malayan Federation came into being, which included Malaya, Singapore, Sarawak, Sabah (or Borneo), and Brunei. The latter was the oil-rich weak link where a coup was attempted. Forewarned, the British flew in Gurkhas from Singapore and by afternoon the position had been restored. Transports even landed at local airstrips, and their troops seized the facilities, much to the surprise of the Kolimantan army, which had started the disruption. The oilfields were retaken, and helicopters from the commando carrier *Albion* supplied needed support ashore. But the jungle allowed the rebels to survive for some months.

Then in 1963, the Indonesians began a series of cross-border raids. Late in the summer a "confrontation" occurred, in which Britons were air-evacuated from Djakarta. Raids escalated in 1964 as the Indonesians acquired MiG-17 and MiG-19 fighters and Il-28 and Tu-16 bombers. An air-defense zone was established around Borneo in 1965, but only a few penetrations were made. Indonesia then raided West Malaya and dropped ninety-six paratroopers at Lobis from a C-130, but they were killed by rocket attacks. Amidst tension, RAF and RNZAF reinforcements were flown in, and Hovercraft were employed. But RAF Gloster Javelins (ER 57.3) were too big and fast to deal with the old B-25 and B-26 Indonesian aircraft. However, in the summer of 1964 Sukarno was toppled by a coup, and a year later in 1966 peace was declared.

East Timor, 1975–2000

East Timor was an ancient Portuguese colony, inhabited by non-Indonesians and coveted by them. After the 1974 coup in Lisbon, a vacuum existed in East Timor, with no one prepared to govern. Civil war broke out between the Timor Democratic Union (UDT), which wanted to join with Indonesian West Timor, and the *Frente Revolutionária do Timor—Leste Independente* (FRETILIN), which was for independence. Indonesia dropped paratroops into the East Timorese capital of Dili from C-130s supported by F-51s, as their Soviet-supplied aircraft were unserviceable. Although East Timor was incorporated into Indonesia, the FRETILIN with its old family networks, continued to resist until it received post-Cold War recognition and support. Neither side had used much air activity in a jungled terrain.

Jungle Wars

Unlike the open spaces of the deserts, the jungle, as in Vietnam, presents a difficult operational scenario for air power. As a result, more than ever the emphasis has to be on political and economic, as well as military, operations on the ground, supported by airlift.

The Malayan Emergency, 1948–60

The Malayan Emergency developed after the end of the 1941–45 war in the Pacific in which the Japanese had shown that Asians had the potential to defeat the European empires. Although the ethnic Malays were not restless, the immigrant Chinese with their Communist connections were. In 1948, after riots, an emergency was declared in Malaya and Operation Firedog began. For the first three years the government was on the defensive as the guerrillas attacked, disappearing again into the jungles. The RAF was ordered to support the inexperienced ground forces, but its assets were limited. Nevertheless, strikes were mounted against camps when intelligence could pinpoint them and when the morning mists burned off and ceilings permitted. But the terrorists soon understood the nature of air power and dispersed. Thereafter, the RAF expended heavy tonnages of bombs on suspected jungle hideouts, with little apparent effect, except to keep the bandits on the move. Heavy bombers were deployed to Singapore and No.1 Squadron Royal Australian Air Force remained on duty there from 1950 to 1958.

The most important development in reversing the situation was the assignment of a Director of Operations who chaired the multi-agency committee that controlled all aspects of the struggle. With the appointment in late 1950 of General Sir Gerald Templar, circumstances improved immensely. At the same time, the RAF was re-equipped with a variety of more modern aircraft, including the long-range de Havilland Hornet fighter (ER 59), withdrawn from Fighter Command in the United Kingdom, which had re-armed with jets. However, operations were limited by serviceability problems and a lack of 1,000-pound bombs. The other major difficulty was getting a quick response to intelligence and accurate marking of targets.

As in Burma in 1943–45, air transport support became crucial for both the resupply of patrols and the maintenance of the hill forts with which Malaya was sprinkled. Air drops extended the in-jungle stays of patrols from four to ninety days. Paratroopers were for awhile dropped in, but as helicopters became available the paras were phased out and regular infantry employed. As with other aircraft, the helicopters suffered from unserviceability due to overuse. In 1953, some of their work was taken over by STOL Scottish Aviation Pioneers (ER 0.58).

Forced to lose their village support by the resettlement program that deprived them of this resource, the Communist terrorists cleared space in the jungles in which to grow crops. As soon as these sites were spotted from the air, they were sprayed to deny the terrorists sustenance. And the terrorists were also harassed by PRU Spitfires and by Austers and Dakotas fitted with thirty-second broadcasting. The combination of ground and air forces resulted by 1954 in the end of the offensive; and for the remaining six years of the Malayan Emergency, mopping up and "winkling out" remaining cells of guerrillas were in order, with a lessened air effort.

In the meantime, the Malayan Auxiliary Air Force had been formed and upon independence in 1957 became the nucleus of the Royal Malayan Air Force.

Perhaps the biggest lesson learned was that a much quicker response to the initial uprisings and sounder intelligence would have brought a much speedier victory.

The Philippines after 1945

The first Huk (Hukbalahap) guerrilla insurrection caught the Philippine government by surprise, and after the United States was involved in Korea and the Chinese were forced on to Taiwan, military supplies dried up. A new approach to win the support of the Philippine people, coupled with effective use of mobile P-51 units supported by C-47s on various airstrips away from Manila, led to a peaceful conclusion in 1954.

Ten years later, Muslim Malays in the Sulu archipelago felt threatened by the Christian government and revolted. The Philippine Air Force no longer had P-51s, but F-86s for air defense. The elderly C-47s were still of use, but clashes were inconclusive. Then in 1968 a Maoist Communist Party created a military wing, the New People's Army (NPA,) and launched attacks, especially with bombs, against aircraft. The Philippine Air Force reorganized for anti-guerrilla operations, acquiring North American T-28 Trojans for counterinsurgency (COIN) work, as well as the new Northrop F-5A Freedom Fighter. But neither had suitable radios for cooperation with ground forces, nor was this deficiency made good until 1989. New transports—Fokker F-27s (ER 16.69, F-27-100) and U.S. Chase-Fairchild C-123 Providers (ER 44)—were acquired, as well as helicopters, for the first time. Maritime patrols had to be increased due to the porous nature of island commerce. But by the end of the 1980s, most of the PAF was grounded due to lack of serviceability, and general corruption in high places.

South of the Border since 1945

The United States application of the Monroe Doctrine of 1823, the Roosevelt Corollary of 1904, and the fear of Communism after World War II guided U.S. policy south of the U.S. border for many years. It led to the major confrontation with the Soviet Union in the Cuban missile crisis of 1962, but did not always play a part in the many conflicts in the Caribbean and Central America, and the few in South America where more stable regimes existed. Notable in these conflicts was the use and abuse of older, war-surplus aircraft and then the gradual introduction of modern helicopters.

Concerned over the domino theory that countries would one after another fall to the Communists, the United States aided the Costa Rican government in 1955 with four P-51 Mustangs at $1 each. But two were lost.

Guatemala in 1954 was another CIA operation, this time involving nine aircraft in support of rebels. However, there was no air opposition as the Guatemala Air Force of the day had only two Boeing P-26 pursuit aircraft (ER 0.86) of 1930s vintage, and eventually the left-wing government fell.

Air action took place along the Mosquito Coast between Honduras and Nicaragua in 1956–58, but it was of little import. In 1969, the "Football War" broke out, as prelude to the 1970 World Cup, between rivals Honduras and El Salvador. The Salvadoran Air Force (*Fuerza Aérea de El Salvador*) attacked Honduran targets, and ground forces entered Honduras. What initially had been called "minor incidents" escalated finally into armed fighting. The conflict resulted in estimates of between 2,000 to 5,000 deaths; a few attacks on airfields, with dogfights between El Salvador F-51s and Honduras F4U Corsairs, caused losses of eight and four aircraft, respectively.

Former British Honduras was threatened by neighboring Guatemala from 1948, and thus British military, naval, and air forces garrisoned or supported the colony until in 1973 it became Belize. The British had to remain, however, and in 1975 the Belize Air Force received five new Hawker-Siddeley GR-7 Harriers (ER 27.7) flown from the United Kingdom and refueled in flight by Handley Page Victor tankers. When the threat evaporated, they were dismantled and flown back to the United Kingdom in Short Belfasts (ER 853). But tensions rose again in 1977, and Harriers were flown across direct, each being refueled eight times en route by one of twelve Victor tankers. Once there, they were flown by RAF pilots from any of thirty-six available airstrips and the Belize Airport. Both Aerospatiale Puma (ER 1.8) and Westland Scout(ER n/a) helicopters were also in-theater with the RAF Regiment providing airfield defense. These were sufficient to ensure peace.

In Nicaragua, internal politics led to the outbreak of civil war in 1979. The *Fuerza Aérea de Nicaragua* (FAN) used its Cessna A-37D and T-28 aircraft against guerrillas in the mountains. The Sandinista rebels seized power in 1980, and in 1981 U.S. President Ronald Reagan decided to support the "Contras," who were opposed to the new left-wing government, which was accused of supplying rebels in El Salvador and of sending pilots to Bulgaria to learn to fly MiG-21s. But only Mil

helicopters and Antonov transports had been supplied, together with anti-aircraft guns and SAMs. The United States used U-2 surveillance planes over the area and enlarged airfields in Honduras, while being concerned about anything being flown in from Libya. The U.S. presence in Costa Rica and Honduras grew, and the conflict continued into the 1990s with a loss of about two aircraft per month.

In 1980 civil war broke out in El Salvador between peasants and the right-wing military *junta*. The United States supported the *junta* with both helicopter and AC-130H gunships, whose crews were trained in Panama. The guerrilla war continued into the 1990s with desultory air support.

Except in Argentina where the air force—the *Fuerza Aérea Argentina* (FAA)—attempted a coup against President Juan Peron in 1955, there was almost no use of air power in South America until the Falklands War of 1982.

The Falkland/Malvinas War, 1982

A dispute over the ownership of the sheep-breeding Falkland Islands had smoldered since 1833. The Argentine military government, which had come to power in 1976, was getting into domestic trouble and thus opted for the classic escape—a foreign war. The seizure of South Georgia and of the Falkland Islands (the Malvinas to the aggressors) occurred in early April 1982. The surprise response was initiated by the pugnacious British Prime Minister Margaret Thatcher, who dispatched a hastily assembled and requisitioned task force, which sailed within days for Ascension Island. While the assault force was being reorganized, a Victor bomber made the 7,000-mile, fourteen-hour round trip from Ascension to the Falklands and back, refueling from tankers four times in each direction. On May 1 the first bombing sortie took place against the airfield at Port Stanley in which twenty-one 1,000-pound bombs were dropped by twenty aircraft, including an Avro Vulcan that would make a fifteen-hour round trip to participate in the bombardment. In the meantime, the task force had drawn near and was able to launch Harrier (VTOL) strikes against other local airfields. Suspecting an imminent invasion, the Argentina Air Force was sent to intercept the task force. However, it found few ships, as it did not have the range from mainland bases to go well east of the Falklands, because it had insufficient aerial refueling facilities for its 110 aircraft. (If the Israelis in a similar situation had been operating the Mirages that they had in their inventory, it is an interesting speculation to know what they would have done.) And although the Argentine Air Force Excocet missiles had enjoyed a great reputation as a result of being used against thin-skinned ships in guerrilla attacks, which had set fires, when used against the armored aircraft carriers *Hermes* and *Invincible* they had little impact.

With the task force in place, reinforcements of Harriers were dispatched from the United Kingdom, 4,600 miles to Ascension in nine hours, and then embarked on a converted merchant ship with a ski-lift ramp to save takeoff fuel. Harriers and helicopters did very well in their many tasks, but the fleet itself lacked long-range radar protection, and as a result four ships were hit by Exocets or bombs, the former because anti-missile gun-laying had not been perfected. The Argentines were no better off, and their carrier, the *25 de Mayo,* returned to port and stayed there.

In the islands, Royal Marine commandos were landed from helicopters to put peripheral airfields out of action. As the invasion approached, Sea Harriers flew not only combat air patrol above the task force, but also were utilized in ground attacks, in addition to naval gunfire. Both Harriers and helicopters were lost in the misty bad weather that foreshadowed the coming of winter in the South Atlantic.

In June, the British invasion seized forward airfields, which enabled Harriers and helicopters to operate close to the front and to provide air cover. The helicopters also carried in supplies and did medical evacuation (MEDEVAC). The nature of the anchorages in sight of the Argentines ashore and the hilly country allowed the Argentine Air Force to make a number of successful attacks on transports. Both sides used extensive small arms and light-caliber anti-aircraft guns. The Argentine Exocets were fired from both the land and from aircraft; and the British defensive missiles were discharged off ships and land with AIM-9Ls in the air.

The Argentine Air Force had planned to fly 505 combat sorties; it actually flew 445 (80 percent), of which 272 (64 percent) reached their targets. But it lost 34 percent of the aircraft flown, and that was 12 percent of its total establishment. The Argentine Air Force also shot down fourteen aircraft and twelve helicopters. Of the 12,454 FAA hours flown, 2,782 were in combat units and 7,719 by transports. Ninety percent of the casualties were career personnel and 10 percent were enlisted.

The short war showed the need of sea power for air power and for well-trained ground troops that could be helicoptered in for the landings, as well as for anti-aircraft systems that could operate at very low levels amidst shipping. The war also re-emphasized the need for spares, maintenance, and logistics, especially after all helicopter tools and spares were lost when the *Atlantic Conveyor* was sunk. At the distances involved, refueling was essential, and the British responded with the rapid conversion of several types, including C-130s, to allow helicopters to be ferried from Britain to the action. But the task force did not have airborne early warning capability, for this, in the form of two Westland Sea King helicopters (ER 4.1), did not arrive until after the surrender.

Although the Falkland/Malvinas War showed that an ill-prepared air force could not do well against a modern force, the matter was in many ways political. The government in Argentina needed a diversionary coup; the government in London needed to rally the country. For peacetime, the British showed commendably rapid mobilization, conversion, and innovation. But winning back the Falklands merely left the colony at risk 8,000 miles from home, the whole being really a matter of prestige.

The Dassault Mirage V (ER 65) of 1967 was the very successful French delta-wing fighter-bomber often exported to other countries as a part of France's major arms business. (Avions Marcel Dassault)

The Swedish Saab JA-37 Viggen (ER 58)STOL all-purpose combat plane of 1971 was designed to operate from roads. It was being phased out in the beginning of the twenty-first century. One is at Lynköping. (Royal Swedish Air Force)

The first Boeing KC-135 Stratotanker (ER 1,769) was delivered to the USAF in 1957 to obviate the difficulty that high-speed jets had in refueling from the old piston-engined KC-97 (ER 564) tankers. In 1968, the USAF then ordered the Lockheed C-5A Galaxy (ER 5,675), seen here in the foreground, as a super heavy transport, of which eventually eighty-one were delivered. (Lockheed Martin)

The Lockheed C-5A Galaxy (ER 5,675) posed a number of problems because of its size. In 1983, Lockheed technicians had to use a hydraulic bucket lift to take them five stories up to inspect the aircraft's vertical stabilizer, as the plane was too tall to fit into the hangar. (Lockheed-Georgia)

The increasing sophistication of modern aircraft is exemplified by two technicians checking the computer-driven systems on a C-5A Galaxy in transit at Rhein Main, Germany, in the 1980s. With engines remaining on the wing for up to five years, airframes had been lifed starting in the late 1950s and components thereafter. Scheduled maintenance includes not only a small number of daily checks, but a precisely timed changing of components, to allow personnel to work in cramped spaces, while keeping the aircraft out of service for as few hours as possible. (Lockheed-Georgia)

The Grumman F-14 Tomcat (ER 129) was selected in 1969 as the winner of the contest to replace a carrier version of the General Dynamics F-111 (ER 1,189). The twin-engine, two-seat fighter was first delivered to the U.S. Navy in 1972, where it has remained the principal fighter ever since. Initially, it suffered from the failure of the selected engine, but was successful with a substitute. (Grumman)

Since its introduction into service in 1972, the F-14 Tomcat, like the F-15 Eagle and F-16 Fighting Falcon, has been upgraded. The late 1990s models of the F-14 had an ER of 463.6 compared to the earlier ER of 129. (USN/Grumman)

The General Dynamics F-16 Fighting Falcon (ER 113, F-16A; ER 304, F-16C/D) is popular worldwide—not just with the USAF—as a versatile, highly maneuverable fighter with an excellent thrust-to-weight ratio. (General Dynamics)

The British Aerospace (Bae) Hawk (ER 13.8, T.Mk1) was designed in 1971 to meet the need by the RAF to rationalize its training programs; 175 were ordered off the drawing boards, and production began in 1974. Performance was better than the expectations, and the aircraft soon reached supersonic speed in a shallow dive. It was the first British aircraft designed throughout to the metric standard, and the first to provide fine visibility for both instructor and pupil. As was the pattern, it was then developed into an attack aircraft. (British Aerospace)

The mid-1970s F-15 Eagle (ER 187) from the McDonnell Douglas factory in St. Louis was developed as an air-superiority fighter, but quickly became adaptable. The Israeli Air Force used it both as a fighter and a fighter-bomber. In the 1991 Persian Gulf War it was used in the attack mode. More recent developments have included extending the range by conformal rather than drop tanks. (McDonnell Douglas)

The North American Rockwell B-1 Lancer (ER 6,279) of 1974 was designed as a replacement for the B-52 Stratofortress (ER 6,336), with the ability to make high-speed, low-level penetrations below enemy radar. But the Carter administration pegged production at only 100 aircraft, one of which was lost early on due to a bird strike. The variable-sweep wing concept of Barnes Wallis's proposed Swallow trans-Atlantic mail plane and of the F-111 Aardvark/Raven was used. The B-1 operated in the 1991 Persian Gulf War, and again as a conventional bomber in the Afghanistan operation of 2001–02 and in Iraq in 2003. (North American Rockwell)

The Northrop F-5E Tiger II (ER 128.2) of 1972 was derived from the earlier private-venture T-38A Talon trainer (ER 22.7) for the USAF. The fighter line was developed for the Military Assistance Program in 1959, providing military aid to foreign countries. The Swiss were amongst the air forces that bought this economical but efficient fighter with two small afterburning turbojets, seen here in slow flight. By 2002, these aircraft were for sale with 800 to 2,300 hours—not yet ready for an engine change. (Swiss Air Force)

The fully armed attack version of the Bae Hawk 200 (ER 14.27). (British Aerospace)

For the expected battle on the north European plains versus the Soviets, the USAF needed a tankbuster. The outcome in 1975 was the Fairchild Republic A-10A Thunderbolt II (ER 26). Too late for the Vietnam War, it saw action in the Persian Gulf Wars in 1991 and 1993. (USAF)

Following on the Concorde SST joint venture, the 1972 BAC-Dassault-Breguet Sepecat Jaguar (ER 55) was another new, multi-role fighter, but intended primarily for the tactical role or as a trainer in the two-seat version. One is preserved at Le Bourget, France. (BAC)

The 1978 McDonnell Douglas (now Boeing) F/A-18 Hornet (ER 124.4, F/A-18E/F) is a dual-purpose fighter and attack aircraft originally developed for carrier use, but which is now in several air forces. The Hornet seen here is in Royal Australian Air Force markings. (Royal Australian Air Force)

For the aerobatic display to heat the spectator's blood, the McDonnell F-4 Phantom II (ER 370) was excellent, but expensive of fuel after the Arab oil embargo of 1973. Pictured here are the USAF Thunderbirds in their distinctive livery. (USAF)

The self-taught British aircraft designer James Martin in the 1939 war had teamed up with Captain Baker, a pilot at Martin, to design several high-performance fighters. However, a variety of reasons, including the crash of the prototype in official hands, led Martin to concentrate on reducing the loss of pilots for both humanitarian and economic reasons. The result was a steady progression of ever-better ejection seats, which by the 1960s allowed escape while the aircraft was still on the ground and at zero speed. (Martin-Baker)

In 1967, the U.S. Navy began to replace the Grumman S-2 line. The Lockheed S-3 Viking (ER 155.4) was selected the next year, and batches were purchased in the 1970s. The S-3s made the first carrier landings for the type in 1973. (USN)

The Panavia Tornado (ER 72) was another development of a European consortium, this time of Britain, Germany, and Italy, hence the multinational markings on this early publicity shot. In 1979, this was another multi-role fighter. In the Persian Gulf War of 1991, the RAF used it as a nap-of-the-earth Scud missile hunter. One is at Duxford, United Kingdom. (BAC)

The Brazilian Embraer Tucano (ER 3.87) was a rival to the Pilatus PC-9 (ER 0.9), adopted as the U.S. JPATS (joint primary aircraft training system) all-service trainer. (Embraer)

Just going into production and service at the end of the twentieth century, the multi-role Bae EF 2000 Eurofighter Typhoon (ER 107.4), a joint effort of the United Kingdom, Germany, Italy, and Spain, is here demonstrated at the ILA International Aviation Exhibition at Berlin-Brandenburg in 1996. (ILA '96 photo by Chris Sorensen).

A Eurofighter (ER 107.4) taxies out at the Berlin ILA in 1996 followed by an Me-109 (ER 1.24) and a Supermarine Spitfire (ER 1.9) of 1943, showing how the size of fighters has increased in half a century. (ILA '96 photo by Chris Sorensen)

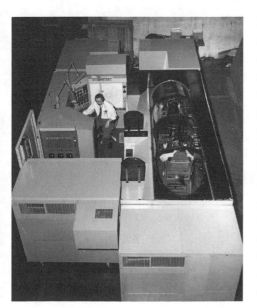

Modern simulators can train aircrew in most situations, and save time and money in qualifying people on type. Note the vast block of computer electronics that make the situations real for the two crewmen in the cockpit. (Source unknown)

The modern Russian fighter is the Sukhoi Su-30, a derivative of the Su-27 (ER 174). Like the USAF F-15 Eagle (ER 187), which it resembles, the Su-30, here in 2001, has a dive brake extended behind the cockpit while it fires its air-to-ground missiles. (Sukhoi)

CHAPTER 8

CIVIL AVIATION

The second half of the twentieth century saw a shift in operations and values from the armed forces to civil aviation—to airlines and general aviation. Several links have been evident, notably the flow of personnel from the air forces to the airlines, whose training costs thus received an invisible subsidy—the internationalization of aviation personnel and equipment; the influences of longer ranged aircraft, radios, and computers; and the connections through the aircraft manufacturers and the ancillary businesses. The latter were specialized and gradually either died or were absorbed into conglomerates. A look at the aircraft industry makes this plain.

AIRCRAFT INDUSTRIES SINCE 1945

At the end of the 1939 war only three large national aircraft industries remained intact—the American, the British, and the Soviet. Of those that had existed in 1939, the French, German, Polish, Italian, Dutch, and Japanese had been expunged.

Demobilization had impacted the American aviation industry in a positive way. Consumer demands for other goods and the increasing need for airlines and private planes, coupled with a government program of selling off wartime factories

for a dollar each had accelerated the move out of the industry by temporary manufacturers. Then the Cold War and the Korean War created a new expansion, allied with the American demand for the best technological developments. Much that was war surplus was junked or sold abroad.

British industry postwar suffered a severe demobilizational insecurity and was still sliding downhill when the Korean War started. Britain was forced to borrow American aircraft for the RAF until production could be re-started in 1951; by 1955 its V-bombers were entering service. In the early 1960s, post-Korean War demobilization again found the British aircraft industry with increasing difficulties and advanced projects were canceled. Government-directed mergers and joint international projects did not compensate for the loss of both the RAF market and overseas customers.

The future of aviation was to be filled with changes, which already had been on the secret horizon in 1939 when World War II broke out: all-metal construction, pressurization, jet engines, electronics and computers, and airfields. Not only were these fundamentals to be vastly refined, from rule-of-thumb to computer-aided design/computer-aided manufacturing (CAD/CAM) and inhuman tolerances, but the industry would be internationalized and then globalized—a process that took about forty years from the Lockheed L-049 Constellation (ER 113) of 1946, to the Boeing 777

(ER 3,845) of 1990. In the process, several generations of managers and workers would come and go, and a socialization of the industry would occur in which minority and women workers—previously unutilized except in wartime—would become welded into teams.

Orders for airliners and business jets would overshadow those for military and general aviation use. Aircraft from gliders to jumbos would become more sophisticated in all aspects. And manufacturers would be reminded that the customer was their commander—he who pays the piper calls the tune still holding true.

Business forces gradually created bankruptcies and/or mergers, so that by 1997 only Boeing (including its acquired McDonnell Douglas) and Airbus outside Russia and China built large jet airliners.

Both the Douglas DC-6 Liftmaster of 1951 and the DC-7 Seven Sea series (ER 526) of 1955 envisaged the aircraft being offered in domestic and long-ranged versions. In Britain, a similar dichotomy was recognized in aircraft to be used for either the Atlantic and the Eastern or Empire routes. Thus, the de Havilland Comet I was to have been followed by the II and the III; and the Bristol Britannia and the Vickers VC-10 were designed in both trans-Atlantic and Empire versions. In the Atlantic format, the ideal was first London-New York non-stop against an 80 mph headwind and then London-Los Angeles on the Great Circle route.

Britain's postwar decline in aviation can be traced to a number of causes. The nation had been spent by two decades of post-World War I depression, coupled with six years of the 1939–45 war. World War II had fatigued managers as well as factories. The advent of the Labour Party to power again did not dispel the dreary attitudes caused by depression and war-weariness, as well as by continued concepts of sacrifice, "utility" goods, and rationing into the 1950s. Moreover, the grouping of companies that had started in the 1930s was not followed through postwar; the Brabazon report of 1942's legacy on postwar civil aircraft indicated too many types and too many engines. In addition, other factors were responsible for Britain's postwar erosion of success and a brain drain to the United States:

- the sharing of technology with the United States, which was also benefitting from the highly advanced German jet and supersonic research;
- the scarcity of capital;
- the lack of a strong laboratory and testing philosophy and system;
- the wrong-headed decision to use only scale models for advanced research;
- the absence of government technical direction;
- the split of aviation between ministries;
- the use of the Ministry of Supply as the purchasing agent for the new airlines, BOAC (British Overseas Airways Corporation) and BEA (British European Airways).

On top of all was the deadening parochial control by the British Treasury, which presumed to make technical financial decisions with little commercial acumen.

Just as in the airlines where there has been consolidation as a result of the relentless pressure of competition (i.e., war), so, too, in the aircraft industry, the competitive nature of the product and of national sales determined survival. In 1945 the Americans were dominant, the British were reviving, and the Russians were an unknown.

In the first twenty postwar years, the British followed the will-o'-the-wisp of prestige aircraft, hypnotized by the twin-types concept of certain aircraft suitable for the North Atlantic and others for the Empire routes. The Americans, however, had learned during the war that an aircraft that could fly across the United States and operate from its hot and high airfields could also span the oceans and fly anywhere in the world. Moreover, as the underdog in aviation from before the war, America was determined to grab the world market. American airliners were designed and tailored to be adaptable worldwide, to the most airlines possible.

British aircraft manufacturers at this time were still hampered by getting their orders through the Ministry of Supply, the successor to the Air Ministry, and the Ministry of Aircraft Production; thus their focus was only on what Britain's nationalized airlines wanted. For many years, the British firms did not charge for design or manufacturing changes. Moreover, they did not coordinate their limited resources, so that despite the fact that the RAF was in the forefront with three V-bomber jets, little communication existed with BOAC to develop the V.1000 derivative of one of these into a long-range airliner. If this communication had existed, the derivative might have been the necessary stop-gap when the de Havilland Comet I, a potential world beater, had to be withdrawn from service in 1954 because of metal fatigue. Instead, the V.1000 was canceled and eventually replaced by the Vickers VC-10 (ER 2,475) and Super VC-10 (ER 2,709), fine airplanes, but commercially unnecessary and too noisy for the environment in which they found themselves in the 1960s. They were banned at Zurich in 1964.

Yet, in the meantime, the British had made a success of the turboprop Vickers Viscount (ER 64) with its Rolls-Royce Dart engines, even breaking into the U.S. market. The cockpit nose section of the ill-fated Comet was supplied to France for the French aircraft industry's first jet success, the long-lived twin-jet Sud Caravelle (ER 281.9, Caravelle 12). Then in the early 1960s the British and the French agreed to their historic collaboration on the supersonic transport, the SST, known as the Concorde, which would enter service in January 1976 and raise the cruising speed from 585 mph to 1,340 mph. But the SST proved to be the perfect example of the plateau effect. Public outcry in the United States over damage to the environment, takeoff and landing noise, and especially the sonic boom basically came to limit the machine to trans-Atlantic routes, where there was

a sufficient growth of traffic and conspicuous consumption to support a luxury surcharge fare. The Concorde, a 1955-concept aircraft, eventually went into limited service in 1976, with thirteen aircraft sold under compulsion to BOAC and Air France. Concorde shuttled across the Atlantic regularly until in mid-2000 yet another tire failure led to the loss of an Air France machine on takeoff at Charles de Gaulle Airport, Paris. All Concordes were grounded for modification until late 2001.

The real story behind the Concorde, of course, was that in many ways it was a smokescreen for two important happenings. On the one hand it represented the decline and fall of the major British airframe industry from lack of private and government foresight, and on the other the determined recovery of French technical supremacy from the ashes of World War II.

In 1940 not only was France defeated, but its aircraft industry was stripped and made the servant of the German manufacturers. Upon liberation in 1944, France emerged years behind the leaders. But fortunately, certain stable members of the industry and the unstable French government—in spite of its coming and going at half-yearly intervals—determined upon a series of five-year plans to recreate the industry as a sinew of great-power status. Just as Britain's Rolls-Royce and Bristol-Siddeley saved the jet engine business, so, too, in France determined companies such as SNECMA worked on engines and Dassault on fighters; and eventually in the 1970s a new multinational consortium called Airbus emerged after thirty years of patient work to challenge the American dominance of the airliner field.

The French success was carefully orchestrated. It also fit the country's socioeconomic patterns in which close links exist between the polytechnical colleges, the armed forces, the bureaucracies, and industry in such a way that passage from one to the other is regarded as natural and beneficial— unlike in Britain and the United States. Moreover, because the French aircraft industry has been an underdog, like the Swedish, it has been innovative. The Airbus A-320 of 1988 (ER 560), for example, was the first airliner in service with side-stick controls and a fly-by-wire system.

Thus, by the end of the twentieth century, Airbus, with its subsonic, economical passenger/cargo airliners, was making money rather than the derivatives of the Anglo-French supersonic Concorde.

The American companies, although the leaders—and with Boeing through consolidations becoming the world's largest producer of airliners—were much more conservative and moved only slowly to the glass cockpit. Moreover, while Boeing still in 2001 led in terms of backlog on the order book, Airbus had by 2000 scooped up half of all new orders. By 2001, seventy-one of the new Airbus A-340-600 (ER 6,330, A-340-300), with 380 seats, were already on order, putting it in direct competition with the Boeing 747. Similarly, the Airbus A-340-500 (ER n/a) competes with the 777-200LR (ER 3,845) at a 15 percent savings in trip costs, with double the cargo capacity and the ability to fly from Singapore to Los Angeles non-stop. Yet one of the reasons for Boeing's continued success was its willingness to reinvent the company, its policies, and practices to win markets. This was evident with the 377 Stratocruiser (ER 423), the 707 (ER 1,733), the 747 (ER 5,989), and more recently with the coordinated cooperative spirit that built and delivered the 777 on time and pre-certificated to both American and European standards, including ETOPS (extended-range twin-jet operational) requirements.

When an organization has a solid design team, financing, and a skilled work force, success is possible—but it takes a very large and powerful consortia. As at Boeing, success has come in part from creating a company "culture" that is oriented to product success and not to national goals. Looking ahead in 1998, Boeing had reorganized the company to be more customer-oriented, friendlier, and simpler in structure. Everyone at Boeing was at last on the same plan. By 2000 the company was delivering 530 airliners each year.

By the time of the 1950s development of the Boeing 707, the manufacturers moved to produce stretched models with a common cockpit and fuselage. From the 1960s onward, stretched versions of passenger aircraft became a normal assumption as data was accumulated, engines became more powerful, and designers more confident and able to use computers for calculations of the sizes of "plugs" in the fuselage both forward and aft of the wings.

The thirty-year evolution from the 735,000-pound 747-100 (ER 5,989) to the 850,000-pound 747-400 (ER 8,760) was unusual only in that a special-performance smaller version, the 700,000-pound 747SP (ER 5,628), was developed early on to allow South African Airways to fly a smaller load of passengers non-stop, Cape Town to London, without having to land and refuel at any Black African airfield—an impossibility then due to apartheid in South Africa. By the 1990s the Qantas 747-400 could fly Los Angeles to Sydney non-stop in 15½ hours.

Not unnaturally the French have emulated the successful American companies. Airbus, like Boeing, is building a family of airliners. Given the fact that airlines fly a variety of routes and need a mix of long-, medium-, and short-range aircraft, the more compatible these types can be, the less expensive the spares inventory; and the smaller the workforce and the less pilot training time, the greater the savings on labor. Thus Boeing's first family of jets in the 1960s included the 707, the 727, and the 737, all with the same cockpit and fuselage cross-section providing up to 60 percent commonality among the 40,000 spare parts required. And starting in 1960, many of these were kept in Renton, Washington, at Boeing's headquarters, to be shipped upon teletype request, or in worldwide spares' pools, thus cutting down everyone's inventory and avoiding money being tied up unproductively.

Sources of supply have increasingly grown "off-the-shelf" and "just-in-time." However, the basic raw materials have a much longer lead time, and, therefore, in 1998 Boeing signed ten-year contracts with five aluminum mills to guarantee stable prices and supplies. This cut Boeing's suppliers from more than seventy-one firms.

In the 1980s, Boeing successfully launched simultaneously the narrow-bodied twin 757 (ER 663) and the wide-bodied 767 (ER 1,088), while closing down its highly successful 707 (ER 1,733) and 727 (ER 641) lines, the latter after selling over 1,800. Meanwhile the variations on the 737 (ER 232) were close to the 5,000 mark in sales by 2003; and the 747-100 was enlarged by 1989 to the 8,000-mile range 450-seat 747-400. The follow-on large twin 777 with two 90,000-pound-thrust engines (ER 3,143, 777-200) came into service in 1995.

In the 1990s, when the CAD/CAM design programs appeared, they had the advantage of being able to present three-dimensional perspectives and of making lofting, the sketching out on the floor of non-dimensional drawings from which full-size templates could be derived. The Martin Company had pioneered an early version of the lofting method in the United States on a floor 30 feet by 150 feet, but this soon gave way to tables, and to photographic templates made directly onto tooling material. The Martin process was used on the P6M Seamaster flying boat (ER n/a) of the mid-1950s.

In 1996, when Boeing acquired McDonnell Douglas, it renamed the MD-95 the Boeing 717 (ER 374). In early 2002, Boeing announced that rather than the 747X stretch, airlines wanted a quiet 747 family, essentially of quality improvements to existing late model airframes, including noise reduction to 777 and Heathrow noise level quota-count classification (QC-2) standards. As Rolls-Royce and General Electric were already working on new engine nacelles to achieve this, the 747QC seemed to have a future.

In the years since the big jets came into service in 1958, the public has tended to overlook not only the enormous commercial influence they have had in shrinking the world by moving people and goods, but also the way in which they and their associated equipment, services, infrastructure have come to supersede military procurement as the backbone of the aviation industry. The most prominent example is the Boeing Commercial Airplane Company of Seattle, which has produced more than 4,000 737 jetliners alone, a number closing in on that of the 5,000-plus F-4 Phantom fighters produced by McDonnell Douglas. The significance lies in the cumulative weight, size, and cost of these machines, the newest and latest of which, the 747-400, in its fully developed 1988 model, sold for $129 million versus the North American Rockwell B-1B at $278 million. But only 100 of the B-1Bs were ordered, in contrast to more than 1,000 747s. Moreover, as the new jets have come into service, their fuel economy has been improved to the point where the 747-400 is capable of carrying a full load of passengers, with below deck a cargo equal to the capacity of a 707 non-stop from New York to Tokyo westbound against the headwind, or on another leg non-stop from Singapore to London. And for these fourteen-hour sectors the aircraft's two-man crew are relieved en route by additional pilots who sleep aboard in a special bunk area.

As prices have risen, the number of aircraft manufacturers has declined. How many major manufacturers will exist outside of the USSR and China by the year 2003 can be counted on the fingers of one hand. Lesser airframe companies will continue to come and go, for a while depending upon breakthroughs in materials, manufacturing methods, size of aircraft produced, and propulsion used. Exchange of technology is such that the four major engine manufacturers—General Electric, Pratt & Whitney, Rolls-Royce, and SNECMA—and their ancillaries in the Western world, all have or have had some commercial relations.

Boeing had announced early in 2001 that rather than develop the Super 747X in response to the Airbus A-380, it would launch the Sonic Cruiser (ER n/a) to carry 250–300 passengers at Mach .98, but given airline interest and new research, transonic speed ranges were also being considered. In mid–2002, the entry into service date was predicted to be 2010–12. Due to economics it was cancelled in 2003.

In designing the Sonic Cruiser, Boeing used computational fluid dynamics (CFD). This proved very close to wind-tunnel results regarding aerodynamic data with a cabin cross-section, which would be comfortable for up to 250 passengers for close to 9,000 miles. The aircraft was to be built of larger parts derived from the joint-strike fighter experience, allowing for less sophisticated production tooling. And by 2003, new research and designs also were tackling the sonic boom problem with computerized innovations, shapes, surface roughness, and possibly off-board energy projection.

One of the tools that Boeing has used to speed up production is the moving assembly line, with time markers showing how long the pause at each work station can be. In addition, the company's portfolio has been better balanced, to 60 percent commercial aircraft and 40 percent military and missile systems, as compared to 80 percent and 20 percent, respectively, in 1991. Revenues doubled in less than ten years. And by 2003, the use of carbon fiber material (CRFP) was showing dramatic advances. The Boeing 777 was 10 percent carbon fiber, whereas the new Sonic Cruiser was to have been 60 percent.

A revised tactic in aircraft sales had emerged in 1999 when Singapore Airlines agreed to sell its fifteen Airbus A-340-300s (ER 6,330) and two on order to Boeing as part of a deal to exercise ten options held on the 777. Then it followed that the American company had also made offers to China Eastern Airlines and China Airlines (Taiwan). What was unusual is that these were not older used aircraft, but some not yet even built. Boeing had set the precedent in its 1984 deal with Kuwait for A-310s (ER 2,248) to be replaced by 767s.

In the twenty years after the Second World War, various European manufacturers came back into business in an attempt to grasp those sectors of the world market in which the Americans lacked a competitive aircraft. But timeliness, reputation, compatibility, and interchangeability of parts are realities and headaches that the companies have had to face, in addition to personality and political problems. In seeking the solution to all of these, in the background has constantly loomed the possibility of merging into American consortia, if the national government would allow such action. The German, French, Italian, Spanish, and Dutch industries have become locked into a European consortium for survival, though much of the success of that depends upon whether or not European politicians can face facts and leave technical negotiations and agreements to those who understand them and have to carry them through.

By 1997 the Dutch Fokker company had declared bankruptcy, and the Swedes had joined a British alliance. And the earlier bankrupted Soviet Union left a legacy of a disintegrating industry. In 1992, 26 percent of the world's airliner fleet had been produced in the Soviet Union, and the annual rate was 150 aircraft per year, plus 300 civil helicopters, 620 military machines, and 390 service helicopters. But rather than the projected 4,000 aircraft and 3,000 helicopters for the 1990s, the actual figures for 1992–2000 totaled 240 aircraft and 400 helicopters. In 1999, only nine civil and twenty-one military aircraft were built—none for the Russian forces—the end result of hasty privatization of 224 of the 315 factories owned in 1991, and of bad management. More consolidation under a new Russian national plan had taken place by 2003.

Although not new in 1988, a significant emerging force in aircraft sales had come to be the leasing companies who were placing orders for as many as one hundred jet airliners at a time. The game being played was to give airlines flexibility in the seat market with aircraft that would last twenty years, while the markets could change more rapidly. But the gamble caused General Electric to have to rescue one such Irish company because its assumptions were over-optimistic and its debts too great.

The Lockheed L-049 Constellation started as the C-69 (ER 114) during World War II, but was then developed into a successful airliner (ER 124, L-749 Constellation of 1947; ER 342, L-1049 Super Constellation of 1954). The clean and graceful lines are evident here. (Lockheed)

The interior of this Douglas C-54 Skymaster (ER 122, C-54A) was comparable to its civilian sister, the DC-4 (ER 83). Note the narrow seats, the sleeping bags in the overhead racks, and oxygen masks above them. (USAF)

Pan American World Airways introduced the Boeing 377 Stratocruiser (ER 423) in 1947, a comfortable double-decked airliner for the long haul across the North Atlantic. (Pan American Airways)

After World War II, the airlines pushed for easier-to-maintain aircraft in order to get more hours per day out of the expensive aircraft and to lower labor costs. Here, Finnair mechanics work on a Convair 440 radial engine, about 1950. (Finnair)

When it went into service in 1951, the Vickers Viscount (ER 64, Model 810, 1962) was a radically new aircraft that soon had worldwide appeal. Its Rolls-Royce Dart turboprops gave it a vibration-free flight that greatly pleased passengers, and its speed equaled that of a Spitfire of ten years earlier. By January 1962, over 460 had been sold. The Dart engines proved to be so good that they were still in service fifty years after launch. (Vickers)

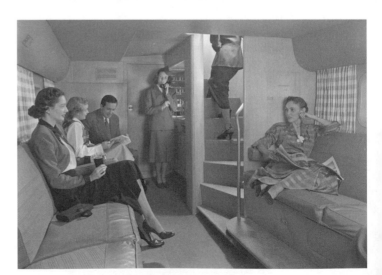

The double-decker Boeing 377 Stratocruiser had space for comfort, such as this lower deck lounge and cocktail bar. Until the introduction of economy- or tourist-class fares in the 1950s, air travel was first-class and rather a luxury; passengers still dressed in their better clothes. (Pan American Airways)

The Bristol Britannia (ER 517, Empire) of 1952 was built in both Atlantic and Empire versions. Fitted with turboprops, it offered a smoother ride than piston-engined aircraft. However, it suffered from engine-ice ingestion problems, which caused flameouts and delayed entry into service on the North Atlantic until shortly before the big jets, thus eroding its advantage. Domestic sales in the United States were lost because the undercarriage could not be redesigned for the aircraft to meet the requirement to turn on its own axis when leaving airport gates. (Bristol)

As the Soviet Union recovered from the Great Patriotic War, and as it began to produce aircraft to counter its Cold War opponents, some of the military types had civilian equivalents. Here, a Tupolev Tu-114 (Er 1,977) seen at Frankfurt-am-Main, Germany, in 1957 clearly shows its military origins; the interior had been fitted out to carry up to 220 passengers. (Frankfurt-am-Main Airport)

Famed engineer Dr. Barnes Wallis in his office at Weybridge, England, about 1959. Wallis had a very wide range of design talents: the painting on the wall shows his Airship No. 9 of 1912; on the bookcase is a model of the geodetic Wellington; and on the desk is a model of the unbuilt supersonic Swallow trans-Atlantic mail plane with sweeping wings, pivoting engines, and a pop-up cockpit for all-around visibility at slow speeds near airports. Wallis also developed the dam-busting bombs of 1942. (Vickers)

The Soviets saw turboprops as a useful, powerful, fast, but more economical engine than the pure turbojet. By the 1960s, they had begun to develop airliners that were not just bombers with seats, though the interiors looked like Victorian passenger trains. The Ilyushin Il-18V (ER 322) of 1962, seen here at Frankfurt-am-Main, Germany, in the 1960s, was one such. (Frankfurt Airport)

This composite photograph to the same scale was made for the author by BOAC in 1962 to show the growth of airliners from the twenty-four passenger Short S-23 Empire C Class flying boat (ER 11.8) of the late 1930s to the 189-passenger Boeing 707-436 (ER 1,733) of the early 1960s. (BOAC)

The 1958 176-passenger Douglas DC-8 (ER 1,517) was so close to the Boeing 707 (ER 1,733) that the choice for the airlines hinged not upon engineering as much as on company reputation and salesmanship. The photo shows the stretched DC-8-61 of Eastern Air Lines. (Eastern Air Lines)

Outside of Europe, the most successful manufacturers are now likely to be China, which is modernizing rapidly and was by the twenty-first century an aerospace power, and a revived Russia. The Japanese have the traditions, skills, capital, and dedication to make their industry viable; the Japanese aircraft industry was by 1971 turning to defense contracts as the country became more independent. Whether this tendency would lead to the kind of suicidal spiral of costs that was engulfing Lockheed and Rolls-Royce in the West in 1971 remained for a while open to speculation, but was resolved in favor of success by the 1990s in part due to Boeing sub-contracts.

Attempts to create an Indian aircraft industry have largely fallen upon the same stony ground as in Britain—the ability to design but the inability to produce. And after the 1939–45 war, a number of leading German experts had emigrated to Argentina, but there, despite a friendly society, little production appeared. In Brazil, however, Embraer gradually succeeded.

An aircraft industry is expensive, complex, and highly sensitive; it must be managed both by its owners and directors, and by the government, with great perspicacity, and it must be well supplied with capital, research facilities, and markets. Few countries can meet these requirements. Some fail because they pursue the prestige rather than the practical aircraft. Indonesia tried with the twin-turboprop N250 (ER n/a), which like the Fokker 100 (ER 182) they endeavored to have built elsewhere. Yet, amidst all of this, Israel and Singapore have succeeded by going also into the maintenance and rebuild business.

The market in Europe for civil airliners was dominated by the United States because of the size of the American industry and the fact that in Europe until the 1970s only the British and French aircraft industries were in any position to produce new machines. For ideological, technical, and other reasons the Soviets could not sell in the West. Russian concepts simply were too Victorian to attract Western customers, and maintainability was uncertain.

Looking back, by the end of 1969, Boeing, Douglas, and Convair had sold 3,421 jet aircraft, whereas the British and the French had delivered only 605, including the Comet I and Comet 4 (ER 520), and the Caravelle. Moreover, the Americans had the advantage of a domestic market large enough within one tariff system and with many customers who needed trans-continental range roughly equal to that required for trans-Atlantic service. In fact, even the European national airlines—BOAC, Air France, Lufthansa, KLM, Swissair, and Alitalia—bought U.S. piston-engined aircraft, and then, starting in 1958, jets for trans-Atlantic services. Their only differences were in cabin staff and meals. SAS (Scandinavian Airline Systems) received its first Douglas DC-9s (ER 49.5) in 1967 and over the years operated seventy-one before the last flight in early 2002. It still has sixty-five of the derivative MD-80 (ER 402) in service.

In the face of the overwhelming American sales successes, catering to airline customers in general, Europe realized that the inevitable international consolidation would follow the domestic rationalizations of the 1930s through 1960s. The symbolic first step was the 1963 Concorde agreement.

Europe had suffered not only from "national aircraft" imposed upon national carriers, with all the costly inefficiency of maintaining and servicing a small number of any type, but also from nationally dictated preferences in such equipment as autopilots and avionics. Moreover, since the manufacturers had limited captive markets, they made little attempt to sell a ready-to-fly product. Thus, the European reputation slumped. Failure to remedy faults rapidly meant that aircraft were soon not competitive with newer rival models, as happened to the de Havilland Comet 4 and the Vickers VC-10, with the Caravelle soon doomed by lack of vision as to market demands. When Douglas brought out the highly successful DC-9-10 (ER 53), it overtook the British Aircraft Corporation

BAC-111 (ER 192, 111-600) to dominate that niche, while Sud, the maker of the Caravelle, centered its effort on the SST.

From roughly 1955 to 1965, before they hit the plateau, many airlines saw the SST as the successor to the 707 and DC-8 jet transports. In fact, it was with relief in the mid-1960s that airlines came to realize that the Concorde was not the next generation but years away, and thus they opted for fuel-efficient long-ranged fan jets such as the 707-336 (ER 1,733) and the jumbo 747-100 (ER 5,989), and then the wide-bodied Lockheed L-1011 Tristar (ER 2,057) and the Douglas DC-10-30 (ER 2,988)—both made for less dense routes than the 747.

In the end, only 200 McDonnell Douglas MD-11s (ER 5,739) were built, the last delivered in March 2001 from a 1966 program that had started with the original DC-10 proposal for a double-bubble (one fuselage atop another) DC-8.

The European response to the American challenge was a 1966 request for proposals based upon traffic-growth predictions that foresaw a need for 200- to 250-seat aircraft capable of design-stretch to compete with the Douglas DC-9 and the Boeing 727 and 737. This led to three consortia—Sud and the new British Aircraft Corporation already on the Concorde, de Havilland and Breguet, and a new German group, Arbeitgemeinschaft Airbus, to investigate returning to civil aircraft manufacture. Pushed by their funding governments, the three agreed jointly to produce a 250-seat medium-haul twin airliner. Rolls-Royce opted out of the engine side in order to supply RB-211s to Lockheed for the 300-seat L-1011, but went bankrupt. Thus, with the Rolls-Royce RB-707 engine now unavailable, the U.S. engine teams at General Electric and Pratt & Whitney both decided to offer engines suitable for a 250-seat aircraft, and these proved also to be those for the 300-seat wide-bodies.

To save money and emphasize their still non-European, nationalist position, the British government withdrew support from the consortia, hoping the French and Germans would welcome their cooperation. Instead, the Europeans went ahead and Hawker-Siddeley Aviation (formerly de Havilland) opted to put up its own money to stay in. Thus, in 1969 the Europeans agreed to support the Airbus, as the aircraft came to be called.

The 1973 Arab Oil Embargo caused a pause in airline acquisitions, and this enabled Airbus to improve its product and sales, saving Sud, which had been part of the original consortia. On-time delivery and after-sales service allowed the Airbus an edge against the tri-jets with their higher fuel consumption and noise. By 1975, the A-300 (ER 1,178, A-300B4) could be marketed against the 727-200 (ER 641). Moreover, tests showed that the stretchable design philosophy was correct, and that the aircraft could operate both medium- and long-haul routes, as well as from hot and high airfields such as Denver, Teheran, and Johannesburg. By the end of the 1970s, the 1967 Airbus design incorporated all the advancements of the recent decade, which were vital as Boeing had changed philosophy and was introducing the 757 and 767. At the same time, the British government switched to full support, allowing Hawker-Siddeley Aviation to become a partner in Airbus Industries, just before HSA and British Aircraft Corporation were merged into British Aerospace.

The engine industry became Europeanized and not largely British, and Airbus by 1980 had captured half of the worldwide 200- to 300-seat market. However, smaller products such as business jets and regional airliners remained national properties. But to compete with the McDonnell Douglas (since 1966) range of DC-9s and the highly successful Boeing 737, Airbus to be viable needed a family of airliners from 130–150 seats on up. This was how the four-engine A-340 came into being, the sister to the twin-engine, long-range A-330, with the A-320, A-319, and A-321 nucleus and with cost-saving cross-certification for aircrew.

Civil Aviation

Airbus, an underdog in 1970, simply had to try harder, which it did. All the way from the original A-300 to the 2001 A-380, the company has been at the forefront of technical innovations. In 1974 the A-300B2 became the world's first twin-engine, twin-aisle, wide-body with triplex power and control systems, an advanced rear-loaded aerofoil, full flight-regime autopilot, and automatic windshear protection. In 1982, the A-300FF was the first two-crew wide-bodied aircraft with all the flight-engineer tasks automated and systems controls in the overhead panels. This airliner also introduced the philosophy of the "dark, quiet cockpit": when systems are activated, the designator light is extinguished, making conspicuous any system inactive or not switched on. The aircraft also had digital flight management. The 1983 A-310 introduced cathode-ray-tube flight instruments and electronic, centralized, aircraft-monitor displays, as well as carbon-fiber secondary structures such as wing fillets, and electrical signaling of the status of secondary controls such as flaps/slats and spoilers. Two years later the A-310-300 saw the introduction of CRFP primary structures for the fin and tailplane, in which there were trim tanks for center-of-gravity control. A further three years on, the A-320 came into service with digital fly-by-wire flight controls with flight-envelope protection and active ailerons, side-stick control in pitch and roll with automatic pitch trim, and CRFP fin, tailplane, elevators, ailerons, and spoilers. In 1993 the A-330/A-340 series (ER 6,330) was provided with a cockpit that allowed cross-training between the two types as well as with the A-320. By the time the A-380 enters service in 2006, it is expected that cross-training for all Airbus machines will take only eight days, thus sharply cutting labor costs.

The competition between Airbus and Boeing is also between crisis management philosophies. The French and European approach is farsighted and frugal, sharing the work in order to conserve skills; in contrast, Boeing appears to be wasteful in severing employment of skilled workers and managers during down times, then recruiting and training again as orders increase—perhaps substantiating the criticism that Americans are profligate of resources.

The demand for regional jets tapered off in late summer 2001 and American Eagle, finding it could not sell its turboprops, decided to retain a limited fleet of smaller Alenia-Aerospatiale ATR-72s (ER 26.5, ATR-42) and Saab SF 340Bs (ER 19). At the same time, United Airlines began retiring its old 727-200s, and replacing them with Airbus A-319s and A-320s.

In the United States, regional traffic was soaring in spring 2001, forcing the hard-hit majors to pay more attention to integrating their second-tier carriers into their total operations as a growth opportunity. Concurrently, Boeing had made a deal with seven Russian companies to develop a regional jet (RJ) to be built in Russia and marketed by Boeing to Russia and the United States.

Meanwhile, in 1980 de Havilland Canada (DHC) introduced the twin-turboprop 37–39 seat DHC-8 (ER 25.9) and stretched it to 50–56 seats in 1986. The company was sold to Boeing, and then in 1992 to Bombardier. The DHC-8-400 (ER 25.9, DHC-8-100) had by then been conceived as a 410 mph 70-seat aircraft, but was not launched until 1995 when the Bombardier (formerly Canadair) CRJ-70 jet (ER 56.8, Canadair 100) also took to the air. Bombardier maintains that forecasts show the need for both the short-haul CRJ-400 and the long-haul CRJ-700.

Entering the already crowded 70-seat regional jet market in 2006 will be the Chinese ARJ21 twin-jet. Fairchild-Dornier, toying with the jet 728 to enter the market, by 2003 had gone bankrupt.

The flight range of business jets also lengthened from 1972 when Garrett, then Allied Signal, and now Honeywell, introduced the high by-pass, fuel-efficient TFE-31 engine, with the 10,000th engine delivered to Learjet Inc. in 2002. Maintenance intervals in 2002 were six times greater than in 1972. At the same time, the 2002 Bombardier Global 5000 (ER n/a) business jet has a range of

4,800 miles with a crew of three and eight passengers at Mach .85; and the Dassault Falcon 900 (ER 222) will be able to fly 6,670 miles non-stop from Paris to Tokyo, or New York to all of South America.

Cooperative jet ownership now allows businesses to benefit from private aircraft at a fraction of the cost of full ownership and to be able to fly to and from airports not reached by scheduled services at a considerable savings in time. Obviously, because of this, United Air Lines and others were by 2003 thinking of countering with rentals their loss of high-end business travelers, whose companies were cutting air budgets up to 28 percent.

A Twentieth/Twenty-first Century Perspective

With the British and French moves to consolidate the aircraft companies into national enterprises, a result has been the emergence of Airbus Industries as a multinational conglomrate with the strength and products to challenge Boeing in the battle for the world's large and medium airliner markets—a head-to-head struggle in which sometimes the deciding factor is ancillary equipment and sometimes financing.

By the end of the twentieth century, the German conglomerate DASA (Deutsch Aerospace SA) and British Aerospace (Bae) were becoming dominant and presuming a merger until Aerospatiale had joined with Dassault and spoiled the idea. But in 2000, European Aeronautic Defense and Space Company (EADS) came into being.

In the United States, Lockheed dropped the L-1011 TriStar and left the passenger aircraft business while still producing the C-5B Galaxy (ER 5,675) and the C-130 Hercules turboprop. McDonnell Douglas gave up the DC-10 (ER 2,967) after failing to win a large USAF order and decided at first to concentrate on the DC-9/MD-80-90 series (ER 435+), then later added the modified DC-10, the DC-11 (ER 5,739), but with limited success. In the meantime, various other mergers saw Northrop and Grumman join and Martin Ma-

rietta and Lockheed, the latter becoming the leading U.S. defense contractor as Lockheed-Martin had already absorbed General Dynamics. Then in the mid-1990s came the merger of Boeing and McDonnell Douglas to make the world's largest aerospace company.

In 1980, the United States had seventy-six companies; by 2000 fifteen had combined into General Dynamics, nine into Boeing, thirteen into Raytheon, nineteen into Lockheed-Martin, and twenty into Northrop Grumman. The costs of new aircraft will undoubtedly cause a further consolidation in the world's aircraft manufacturing companies, as in the engine firms.

Meanwhile Bae's T-45 Hawk jet trainer (ER 33), a British design, was being produced at only six aircraft per year, or half the economical rate. The U.S. acquisition of the Pilatus PC-9/Raytheon PT-6 Texan II (ER 0.9) JPATS (joint primary aircraft training system) was expected to total 782 aircraft, of which the U.S. Navy would get 328. By 2017, a total delivery of 800 was planned.

Since the 1960s, the number of viable military aircraft developed has shrunk significantly, while development times have lengthened appreciably. Moreover, as a result of upgrading of systems and weapons, an aircraft such as the F-16 Fighting Falcon, has been remade again, after thirty years and more than 4,000 copies. Inside it is virtually a new aircraft, due to miniaturization, computers, glass cockpit, and new engine technology. And mid-life upgrades are allowing older models to be brought closer to the Block 60 standard to allow the aircraft to stay in service until 2020. In the meantime, it is 25–30 percent cheaper than the competition, until the JSF (joint-strike fighter) becomes available in 2010.

This allows the F-16 to compete against the new Bae Eurofighter Typhoon, which by 2000 had been more than fifteen years in development but was not to start being delivered to the European air forces until 2003, after 2,500 hours of testing. The Eurofighter was in 1996 the first of the world's combat aircraft to be fitted with an integrated, structural, health-and-usage monitoring system to perform real-time airframe fatigue calculations. Given the compact complexity of modern aircraft, the system holds down man-hour inspection costs. When Eurofighter enters service in 2003 it will have been the most expensive procurement in British defense history, and to maintain it in-service will require a similarly costly infrastructure. The ten suppliers will reduce their support to two levels: operator and industry.

Another competitor is France's dual-role Dassault Rafale, a 66,000-pound naval strike fighter with 3,725 gallons (6,250 kg) of fuel, which gives a maximum endurance of three hours. A high-angle-of-attack aircraft, the Rafale can hold 48 degrees nose-up at 70 knots and do 897 mph (1,435 km). However, the aircraft costs $40 million each, at a production rate of forty-eight per year. The Rafale, by mid-2002 was newly delivered to the French navy, and the fighters were on the carrier *Charles de Gaulle* in the Gulf of Oman for training. They were expected to be operational by 2003.

With a new electronics update in the later 1990s, the venerable Northrop T-38 Talon (ER 22.5), first flown in 1959, was expected to continue to 2020 and train pilots for the Lockheed-Martin/Boeing F-22 Raptor (ER 282) and the future JSF. But in the case of the F-22, delays and congressional fiscal limits were pushing production orders past 2003, leading to manufacturer's instability. The future of the manned heavy bomber in the USAF at the end of 2000 looked grim. The Pentagon appeared to be planning to maintain a 130-strong mixed fleet of B-52s, B-1s, and B-2s for the next thirty-seven years.

At the other end of the scale, the military is being faced with keeping geriatric airframes in service to such an extent that when now phased out as planned, the last Boeing B-52s will be eighty years old. They will be saved, however, not only by rebuilds, but essentially by the gutting and up-dating of their electronics and other capabilities. Others have also received similar treatment.

Variations of the same agenda include the fact that accidents are no longer due to pilot error alone, attested to by the Indian Air Force experience with the MiG. The Indian Air Force, during 1991–2000, lost one hundred MiG-21s in accidents, killing thirty-four pilots—a serious problem, as MiGs make up 70 percent of the IAF aircraft. India's dispute with Russia regarding this has been over the low quality of Ukranian and Eastern European spares, and the refusal of RSK MiG, the manufacturer, to let India assist in upgrades. The Indian Parliament's Public Accounts Committee thus recommended that the MiGs be phased out; and in the meantime, the IAF grounded seventy-two of them.

One result of this problem was that India had consulted Israel Aircraft Industries about upgrades of the MiG-27 (ER 274.7, MiG-23MF) and MiG-29 (ER 157) aircraft, which annoyed the Russians. In the meantime, Israel had a contract to upgrade Polish Sukhoi Su-22s (ER 93.3, Su-17) to be able to carry Western weapons and radar. Some 125 Indian Air Force MiG-25s (ER 179) are being upgraded with new cockpits, navigation systems, and heads-up and heads-down displays. Russia's RSK started the work in 1996, and deliveries are expected by 2003.

In late 2001 Russia and India signed an agreement to produce a fifth generation successor fighter to the Su-30 and the MiG-29 by 2010. India inquired about taking Tu-26 Backfire bombers and perhaps another aircraft carrier. At home, India pushed ahead with an indigenous light combat aircraft (LCA), which took its first flight in mid-2002.

Another aircraft that has been upgraded is the Lockheed U-2S, of which in 1998 the USAF had twenty-seven. Lockheed-Martin indicated it could take over worldwide base support for the U-2 until 2020, with a quarter of the personnel employed in 1998, under a Total Systems Support Responsibility program.

The C-130J of 1996, the workhorse Hercules, had problems with integrating its new electronics and computerized control systems, due to over-optimistic suppliers, and with certificating the aircraft for civil use, as some of the paperwork dating back to 1957 for the airframe had been lost. Certain things also had not been done "by the numbers" over the years.

As the Swiss phased out their Northrop F-5 Freedom Fighters (ER 82) in 2002, the Brazilian Air Force acquired them for Embraer to upgrade to F-5BQs. Switzerland expects to replace all one hundred of its F-5s by 2010 with additional F/A-18s. And Saudi Arabia was also selling its F-5s. Brazil was in the market for forty-eight replacement aircraft, and Dassault was sweetening the arrangement with investment in Embraer.

With global military budgets failing, the gap between the U.S. air arms and the rest of the world's air forces grew in 2002 both quantitatively and qualitatively. Of the world's nearly 90,000 military aircraft, the United States had the primary share, with five of the ten largest fleets of American manufacture, the others being of Soviet make. And although many fighters are becoming decrepit, the modernizations and package upgrades continued to extend service life. In 2002, 889 Boeing (McDonnell Douglas) F-4 Phantoms were still in service, 3,324 MiG-21s, 1,563 MiG-29s, 504 Mirage 2000s, and 3,398 F-16 Fighting Falcons.

And also in 2002, Spain had proposed a step to full European Union integration by asking for a common arms policy, another inevitable challenge to nationalism and national air forces.

In the twenty-first century, the Latin American arms market was reopening with Chile buying F-16s and Argentina considering either F-16s or ten Spanish Mirage F1EEQs—and possibly Israeli Kfirs (ER 57.83), as well as taking upgraded used U.S. Marine Corps F-4 Phantoms.

Israel's sixth purchase of F-16 Fighting Falcons in 2001 added another fifty-two to the fifty ordered in 2000. Lockheed-Martin, as of 2002, had a backlog order book of 247 F-16s, and the production line was to stay open to 2009. The 2002 fighting between Israel and the Palestinians saw the Israeli

Air Force refocus its technology to match its intelligence, using helicopters and UAVs to aid it in street fighting on the West Bank—a struggle that the Israelis had generally to that point avoided. And meanwhile, Israel Aircraft Industries in 2002 beat out Boeing to convert 767s to freighters.

By 2000, RAF British Aircraft Corporation Tornadoes (ER 72) had flown over 4,000 hours each and were being upgraded to last until their planned withdrawal in 2018–20, by which time they will have 8,000–10,000 hours and have completely rebuilt electronic systems and new weapons. The Royal Saudi Air Force was also in 2003 facing the upgrade decision for its Tornadoes, but this was dependent upon stable oil prices. Perhaps to be selected were the new post-Kosovo precision-guided bombs (PGB) and the extended-range version. Eventually, about 2020, the Tornado will be replaced by the Future Offensive Air System (FOAS), which will combine UCAVs, cruise missiles, the Eurofighter, and the JSF F-35.

For many air forces, finances dictated modernization rather than new purchases; and potential opponents were not part of the equation. Yet, the F-22 and the JSF were scheduled for production, and in October 2001 Lockheed-Martin won a $22 billion F-35 joint-strike fighter contract from the U.S. government, with Pratt & Whitney supplying the engines. Nevertheless, the U.S. air services still faced the problem of maintaining their other aging aircraft well past 2003, a long-term financial challenge emphasizing the change and continuity in air affairs.

The U.S. services in the twenty-first century are faced with fleets that will jump in average age from thirteen years in 2001 to twenty-one years a decade later. The basic U.S. Air Force aircraft inventory is composed of 1,300 F-16s already, in 2003, fourteen years old on average, 400 F-15 C/Ds nineteen years old, and 66 A-10s twenty-two years old. All new fighter programs were by 2003 moving into the model Plateau Theory, which made procurement officers nervous: Would there be fewer numbers purchased, or would the

The 140-seat Convair 990 (ER 1,172) of 1960 was the third of the new American jets, and the least successful. It had considerable drag problems that were solved by the addition of trailing-edge speed blisters to accelerate the airflow. Swissair was one of the few who bought it. (Convair)

In 1960, the fifty-six passenger Tupolev Tu-124D (ER 69) began to appear in Europe. The one seen here was operated into Frankfurt-am-Main by Aeroflot, but others were sold to the satellite countries. Built by Russian State Industries, the problem with many of the earlier Soviet types was the lack of spares. (Frankfurt-am-Main Airport)

In 1964, the Boeing 727 (ER 641, 727-200, 1972) began to enter service. It had the same cockpit and fuselage cross-section as the 707 (ER 1,733), but had three smaller engines and was designed for shorter-length domestic routes. One of the great advantages that the U.S. aircraft industry enjoyed until the creation of the European Community in 1993 was a tariff-free market 3,000 miles across, with a wide range of climates and altitudes. (Eastern Air Lines)

The British rival to the American big jets were the Vickers VC-10 (ER 2,475) and Super VC-10 (ER 2,709) that was sold to BOAC and a few affiliates. Pilots liked its handling characteristics, but management objected to it as an unnecessary aircraft. In 1964, as part of a reorganization of the top management, the Air Minister agreed to let BOAC defer some of its order. The aircraft went out of production shortly afterward, and in due course ex-BOAC aircraft were converted to tankers for the RAF. (British Aircraft Corporation)

The 1963 186-passenger Ilyushin Il-62 (ER 1,614.7) seen here compared favorably in looks with the Vickers VC-10 (ER 2,475), its contemporary. It was a long-range aircraft most suitable for trans-USSR routes from Moscow to Vladivostok, for like the United States, the USSR had the advantage of long internal routes. (Ilyushin)

Eliminated from the competition for what became the USAF C-5A Galaxy contest, Boeing used its studies as the basis for a new, much larger transport. What emerged in the later 1960s was an enormous quantum jump that eclipsed the unbuilt Douglas "double-bubble" fuselage DC-8. As the picture shows, the 707 (ER 1,733) was surpassed in size, carrying capacity, and efficiency by the jumbo 385-passenger 747 (ER 5,989, 747-100; 8,760, 747-400), which could carry in its cargo hold as much as a whole 707. (Pan American Airways)

The naval tradition in airline uniforms is seen here with the BOAC captain visiting the 747 cabin mock-up and talking to school children, an especially cared-for passenger group. (BOAC)

In the 1960s, not only did the women's movement begin to push for lifetime careers for cabin staff, including the right to marry and have children without being fired, but airlines with significant overseas routes and traffic, such as BOAC, came under pressure to train and employ women from the geographic areas they served. Here, African women from Nigeria pose in a variety of native costumes in the cockpit while in London for training. (British Airways)

During the long period from 1945 to the 1980s, when most airlines flew either Boeing or Douglas aircraft, food and service were valued highly by passengers. This posed manufacturer's photo shows the interior of the cabin in a Lockheed L-1011 Tristar (ER 2,057). The similarities between North Atlantic airlines led in 1964 to the "great sandwich war" in economy class, because SAS served an ample Scandinavian open-faced version piled high. (Lockheed)

The growth of cargo transport was originally very slow and largely confined into the 1950s to high-value items such as gold or diamonds. With the availability of surplus passenger planes after about 1950, cargo volumes rose rapidly. By the late 1960s, not only were aircraft being converted, but they were also being designed initially and sold as freighters. Here, a Pan Am freighter is loaded with goods on pallets, which preceded the containers used today. (Pan American Airways)

The capacious main compartment of the Boeing 747F (ER 5,989) held 214,000 pounds of cargo on thirteen pallets. These encapsulated shipments were soon replaced by highway tractor-trailer sized containers measuring eight feet wide by eight feet high and as much as forty feet in length. (Pan American Airways)

This UPS DC-8 (ER 1,517) at the Louisville, Kentucky, hub clearly shows the smaller containers used for efficient shipments to a variety of points, and the machinery used for loading them into the aircraft. Federal Express uses Memphis, Tennessee, as its hub. Both central shipping points were sited away from congested and noise-conscious passenger-hub cities. (UPS)

program be eliminated in favor of a cheaper alternative? The joint-strike fighters, meant to counter this, were to be delivered slowly over twenty-one years.

Given production rates for the F-22 and the JSF, the F-16s and F-15s will have to last to 2020 and the A-10s to 2028. Unless funded, many of these airframes will be on a death spiral in less than ten years as maintenance costs rise and flying hours decrease. Because the USAF was not prepared mentally for the demands of post-Cold War peacekeeping efforts, the spares pool had dried up by the twenty-first century. Yet the two-seat F-15E is expected to remain in service until 2033, when it will be thirty-five years old. After thirty-one years of active service in 1992, the U.S. Navy and U.S. Marine Corps retired their last F-4 Phantoms.

With the cost of aircraft support rising at about five percent per annum, programs have had to be developed to determine when such essentials as wiring will begin to break, while at the same time facing challenges such as new SAMs and beyond-visual-range (BVR) combat, never envisaged in the 1970s when most of the machines in the inventory were designed. Some airframes need structural life extensions, and engines in the F-16 had already exceeded 12,000 total accumulated cycles, well beyond design parameters. In the new environment, the A-10 needs data links and target selection to enable it to operate above the capabilities of the new man-portable air defenses (MAN PADS). Fairchild, which made the A-10, no longer exists, and thus a comprehensive integrated remake will be expensive.

As the aerospace industry marches farther into the twenty-first century it faces the dual problems of design and production in a changing paradigm. If there is to be competition without necessarily production, in order to keep the technical edge, it is questionable whether or not private industry can be expected to compete while maintaining neither production facilities nor skills. In the civil sphere, Airbus was in 2002 preparing to reduce workers' hours rather than releasing the skilled staff, to avoid later hiring searches and training time and costs as business revived. And in the former Warsaw Pact nations—Poland, Hungary, Czechoslovakia, and Romania—the dilemma is even more acute, due to limited budgets and soaring dollar costs.

On the commercial side of the aviation industry, however, in 2001 UPS entered into a twelve-year contract with Airbus for ninety more A-300-600 freighters (ER 1,730) with the proviso that A-380s or other types can be substituted at any time. The A-300-600 can handle fifty-ton loads. At the time, UPS had a fleet of 238 Boeing and Douglas aircraft. This twenty-first century arrangement indicates promising future for the aviation industry.

Financing

Financing and leasing expenses represent eight percent of airline costs. After sixty-eight nations signed a treaty in Cape Town in 2001 to standardize financing arrangements, costs were expected to decline because a registration system would protect lenders' assets in airframes, engines, and helicopters.

Very important for the success of aircraft manufacturers and of airlines has been the ability to finance new aircraft. Since World War II, governments have subsidized their nationalized airlines and have given loan guarantees for purchases on credit. Aircraft manufacturers and banks now have philosophically united in the financing arrangements. The United States established the Export-Import Bank to handle loans with only ten percent non-U.S. funding required. By the end of the twentieth century, Europe was also involved, especially to make sales to the emerging smaller nations such as in the Balkans. With aircraft from the 1960s being amortized on fifteen years instead of four, with a 25 percent residual value, twelve-year mortgage loans were seen as too short. (And, of interest, at times the abuses of human rights by particular nations had been raised to challenge financing arrangements.)

A secondary dispute over subsidies has been smoldering since 1995 between Canada, Brazil, and the World Trade Organization over loans for airliner sales. In 2002 the WTO ruled against Canada, and thus representatives were to try to resolve the problem.

As two examples of financing difficulties, in 1946 BOAC could have had thirty Constellations, but the British Treasury, not understanding the dollar-earning capacity of the North Atlantic route, would only allow the airline to purchase six. Thus, these intended purchases were supplemented by the Canadair DC-4M (ER 83) with Rolls-Royce Merlin engines—a "British" aircraft, but actually an eight-year-old U.S. design. Similarly, when in the late 1960s BOAC had money in U.K. municipal bonds, it was not allowed to use these for the Boeing 747s, although no comparable British aircraft existed. BOAC thus borrowed 90 percent of the cost of the 747s from the U.S. Import-Export Bank and the other 10 percent from the Bank of Nova Scotia in Canada.

The whole question of U.K.-U.S. open skies and ultimately of a Euro-U.S. agreement was early in 2002 jeopardized by the U.S. Department of Transportation's demands regarding competitive remedies. Too many slots at Heathrow were thought to be taken away from the One-World alliance partners, American Airlines and British Airways. And thus these airlines withdrew their application for anti-trust immunity. On the other side of the Atlantic, the European court ruled that U.S.-European national bilateral flight agreements were contrary to European Union law. The next step was expected to be a U.S.-European Community bilateral agreement. Independent Virgin Atlantic Airways then demanded that the United Kingdom "join Europe" in U.S.-EC talks.

The Asian airline slump of 1997 for economic reasons was repeated in 2001 when airlines again faced the strong dollar, rising fuel prices, and a downturn in travel and the air-cargo market. In the interim four years the airlines learned not to chase market share at any cost. As a result, Malaysia was back in government hands after having caused international carriers to abandon Kuala Lumpur due to fare slashing. Thai International had a new board imposed by the politicians; and Philippine Airlines was shut down until a new CEO could be appointed, who vastly reduced the network. Two years later Philippine Airlines' fleet had risen from twelve to thirty-four, and four international routes were operating again. Korean Air Lines and Asiana were also again severely affected and reported big losses; and Pakistan International Airlines received government approval for a $319 million rescue package.

In the meantime Alitalia, having failed in 2000 to ally with the Dutch KLM, in 2001 joined Air France, Delta, and Skyteam in arrangements that included passenger and baggage handling, code-sharing, and some maintenance.

In South America, with 80 percent of the airlines on the verge of bankruptcy by 2002, the new movement appeared to be not so much European investment or takeover, but local consolidation, with entrepreneurs controlling not only airlines but also airports. Colombian and Mexican airlines were considering a merger, while the Spanish owner of Aerolineas Argentinas was desperately trying to sell its 85 percent of the troubled carrier.

The chaotic Latin American airline picture was seen likely to be solved by 2003 only through consolidation to create higher revenues and lower costs. Four airlines had failed by mid-2001, and six were teetering. What Latin CEOs foresaw was the need for a common "aviation community" policy, an easing of government anti-trust enforcement, and encouragement of mergers and code sharing.

As a result of the downturn in 2001, coupled to the 9/11 blow, airlines in Latin America were in parlous states with the three Columbian lines merged into one, and elsewhere Aerolineas Argentina and Brazil Varig struggling. However, Mexico ranked fourth in the U.S. aviation market, and its two companies belonged to international alliances. The big problem was a new airport for

Mexico City, which pitted the government against nearby farmers.

Equally as parlous as the airline situation in Latin America by 2003 was that in Africa, where Uganda Airlines had collapsed in 2001. Air Afrique, established in 1961 and owned by eleven member states in West Africa and by Air France, was by 2001 in crisis with two of its Airbus A-330-200s (ER 6,330) impounded by creditors. Liquidation in 2001 was only avoided by the heads of state of the region who recommended an outside accounting firm, a technical and commercial partner, recapitalization, and a financial moratorium.

One result of the disastrous fiscal 2001 was that sources of airline funding dried up. As a result, changes were seen in bank loans, capital markets, state export support, and manufacturers' finance schemes. The question was: how much risk could be taken? Leases became an attractive option. Whether or not labor could be blamed for the airlines' financial crisis, the fact that those costs had risen sharply in the last decade to 2002 could not be overlooked. In 2002–03 fares became too low to yield profits, while labor and fuel costs rose, as had been the case after the Persian Gulf crisis of 1990–91, when recovery took two years.

Added to all of this, the long battle of U.S. travel agents to keep airline commissions was lost in March 2002, when the airlines unilaterally abolished commissions in favor of direct booking on the internet. However, agents responded by passing on their costs to the traveling public in a fee for services.

Privatization has been important since the 1970s, when governments decided to sell off assets to improve their bottom lines. But this has not always been easy. By 2003 the sale of Greece's Olympic Airways and India's Air India and Indian Airlines were still seeking qualified bidders.

Ancillary Industries

Closely associated with the aircraft industry are many adjunct firms. In Britain in the late 1950s, at a time when sixteen airframe and four engine firms were members of the Society of British Aerospace Constructors, 540 ancillary firms existed. Electronics, pressurization and air conditioning, navigation equipment, ejection seats, and the like have all caused their spawning, and these firms create military-industrial-complex problems in each country desiring to build its own aircraft.

Governments are highly unwilling to be dependent upon outside sources for vital parts, and thus pressure is applied to have home-manufactured equipment fitted, even if the airframe and engines have to be bought abroad. But this makes for uneconomical maintenance problems. The costs of spare parts, for example, rose so rapidly when the big jets came into service that Boeing set up a pooling organization around the world. Moves to cut the costs of holding large inventories of spares are being pursued, for who can afford to hold some 40,000 for just one type of aircraft? Thus, the country that wishes to build its own aircraft is faced with either giving them only simple equipment, building only standardized aircraft, or relying for many parts on outsiders. The decision gambles security with economics, not to mention challenging the pilots' unions.

But lesser powers are most likely to continue to be supplied by greater allies; they will have to judge which one is most likely to be able to deliver the goods at a crucial moment. Perhaps the example of the Turkish Air Force in the Second World War, flying British and German aircraft, provides the best equivocal answer—take from both sides!

For the lesser powers, moreover, training forces and facilities must be convertible to tactical use. A short war thus is a necessity, unless resupply is immediately possible. At the same time, stockpiling parts for aircraft and engines with long times between overhauls faces political economies and ultimately parts being lost and having to be made anew. The Swiss Air Force F-5s, as an example, have only needed to change their engines at 2,500 hours, or once each quarter century, based upon normal usage. But parts not purchased with the engines have later to be made at much greater expense. In 2002, the Swiss decided to sell their F-5s, even though they were not yet ready for an engine change.

Personnel

Related to procurement of machines is the need for personnel and their training. Recruiting, often of air force officers with diminished career prospects, has been falling short since the 1990s. In 2001 the British services needed 290 fast-jet pilots annually, but had a deficiency of 45. Part of the problem was that the training by 1998 was taking six years, hopefully to be reduced to three-plus, and was costing $8.2 million per pupil. The shortfall of pilots over-stretches the military services, but as of 2000 was not seen as likely to disappear until perhaps 2012. In the meantime, to save money, training was being privatized, as in the United States, where fee-for-service contracts were in use by 2003, together with advanced simulators for both commercial and military training.

Although by the mid-1960s roughly half of the USAF cadets' flying-training time was in simulators, basic airmanship still had to be taught in the air, and aircraft such as the Raytheon Beech Pilatus PC-9, for instance, was adopted in the United States for JPATS (joint primary aircraft training systems) in all four services.

At the end of the 1980s, the projected and actual supply of qualified pilots, in spite of mergers and layoffs, was seen as a worldwide shortage of 400,000, due to the increasing numbers of cockpit crew needed by new aircraft and the growth of business. This shortage had begun to increase before 1988, and in turn was already impacting the world's air forces, with a severe drain on the smaller services. The Royal Australian Air Force had lost nearly one-third of its pilots and had to develop a high-bonus plan to retain aircrew, which then displeased ground staff. And the Belgians were borrowing pilots from the RAF. This more than anything else appeared likely to make NATO air forces inferior to the Warsaw Pact, regardless of how modern their aircraft. Fortunately, with the collapse of the USSR these NATO pilots now see their action periods as "out of theater," in places such as Bosnia or Africa. It is conceivable that at some time in the future, a European Air Force indeed may become a reality.

In the U.S. Air Force, not just pilots may be in short supply in the twenty-first century. The USAF has a need for 3,000 more engineers to fill a gap in 2007, when that number will leave the Air Materiel Command, to be followed by another retirement bubble twenty years later. To meet this, the graded pay system is being replaced by rewards according to contributions.

The major source of pilots (540 annually) for the USAF is the U.S. Air Force Academy, which interestingly dropped flying training in 1997, placing blame for unsuccessful results on the aircraft. In fact, the problem was found to be poor training of the instructors. Flying training thus was reinstated in 2002, but contracted out.

The numbers gap in the contemporary military services is also increasingly being reduced by the participation and contribution of women, as a result of affirmative action and their innate ability and competitiveness—certainly a positive change since 1945.

Flying safety and concern for the valued pilot resource has always been emphasized; the military services operate high-performance aircraft in demanding roles—and dead airmen do not win wars. Data from the 1980s shows that the RAF's accident rate per 10,000 hours flown dropped sharply from twelve fatal occurrences in 1983 to five in 1986, though it rose to seven in 1987. The cause of the accidents has been evaluated as aircrew error 40 percent, technical defect 17 percent, servicing error 10, natural operating and medical risks 10 percent, other (unknown) 6 percent, and not positively determined 27 percent. Interestingly, each year about 700 RAF aircraft have been hit by birds, with anywhere up to thirty-six minor accidents each year, necessitating a civilian-operated anti-bird program at thirty-six airfields in the

Noting the man on the left, this picture of a Douglas DC-10 (ER 2,967) under construction should be compared with the earlier 1924 photo from Douglas to see the way aircraft have grown in size. (McDonnell Douglas)

The British Aircraft Corporation's BAC-111 (ER 192) was slow in development in the early 1960s because of too small a staff, and thus the aircraft was rapidly overtaken in sales by the Douglas DC-9 (ER 49.5), even though it had been started several years after the BAC-111 design. The BAC-111 here is doing a rough runway takeoff test. (BAC)

McDonnell Douglas tried to revive its fortunes with a refined DC-10 (ER 2,967) called the DC-11 (ER 5,738.5), whose improvements included drag- and turbulence-reducing winglets. The aircraft suited Swissair, but did not save the airline from bankruptcy in 2001. (Swissair)

When the Boeing 707 (ER 1,733) and Douglas DC-8 (ER 1,517) went into service, they were powered by four jets of 12,500 pounds thrust each. The early 747s (ER 5,989) had four engines of 47,600 pounds of thrust each. By the end of the century, the Boeing 777 (ER 3,845) and its Airbus rivals were being fitted with two 100,000-pound thrust engines. In the meantime, starting in the early 1980s, twin-engine jets such as the 767 (ER 1,088) had been allowed to make ocean crossings as long as they were never more than 120 minutes (later raised to 180 minutes) from an alternative airfield in case an engine failed or had to be shut down. Here, a senior service engineer works on a Pratt & Whitney JT9D engine mounted in one of the Rohr-designed nacelles common in the DC-10, 747, and the Airbus A-300. (Rohr)

A Pratt & Whitney JT9D of some 47,000 pounds thrust shows the multi-blade fan of this by-pass jet and the core behind it that provides both power to the fan as well as thrust. (Pratt & Whitney)

The other wide-body, the Lockheed L-1011 Tristar (ER 2,057) was popular with overseas airlines such as Gulf Air. Later, some were converted to tankers for the RAF. Supplying the engines for the L-1011 bankrupted Rolls-Royce in 1971, from which it has since successfully emerged. (Lockheed)

The size of the new Pratt & Whitney JT9D for the Lockheed L-1011 Tristar and the ease with which mechanics could reach it, as a result of the Rohr Industries nacelle, illustrates again the growth in size and power of jet engines and the means constantly taken to diminish labor costs. (Eastern Air Lines)

This photograph of a DC-9 (ER 49.5) was taken before public concern was voiced and government restrictions were placed on environmental pollution. Fuel was still inexpensive. In 1964, however, the British VC-10 had been banned at Zurich for noise pollution. Four versions of the DC-9 were produced for over forty airlines worldwide; the types could accommodate a range of passengers from 70 to 125. Eventually, DC-9 derivatives became the MD-95 (ER 374) and, finally, in 2000, the Boeing 717 (ER 374).(McDonnell Douglas)

The stretched version of the DC-9 was renamed the MD-80 (ER 402) after the takeover of Douglas by McDonnell. Here it is seen in Swissair livery at Zurich. Note the very thin wings set far back. Inside, the aircraft had two seats on the port side and three on the starboard. (Swissair)

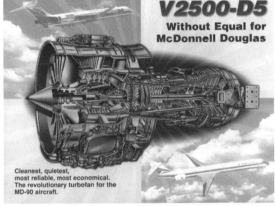

Engine manufacturers were especially concerned about noise and pollution, not just for ethical reasons but also for sales. In addition to reliability (and therefore on-time dispatch), International Aero Engines stressed efficiency, reliability, and the promise of a quiet, "green." environmentally friendly engine. (International Aero Engines)

The immensely successful Boeing 737 (ER 363, 737-200), which was still based on the 707 (ER 1,733) cockpit and fuselage, had sold some 5,000 copies between 1967 and the end of the century. Pictured here is a 737-100 with the original small engines. Later aircraft were fitted lower-slung engines of more powerful thrust, and the cabin was lengthened to carry increasingly more passengers, especially in the new generation (NG 737-500, -600, -700, and -800 versions). This 737 was flying in China in 1988.

One of the difficulties of dispersed production is bringing all the pieces together for final assembly. A solution developed by Airbus, based on the A-300, is the A-300-600ST Beluga (ER 1,730, A-300-600), which can carry the large, awkward parts. (ILA '96, Berlin-Brandenburg)

United Kingdom. The armed services now release accident statistics, if only in limited form, making the seriousness of the topic obvious, as do the data recorders carried in both military and civilian aircraft, which also provide clues as to non-combat wastage rates.

Also important to flying safety has been the ejection seat, designed to save the lives of the very essential and expensive aircrews.

By the twenty-first century, fighter pilots faced a host of new menaces, including laser beams and chemicals, aimed at the human in the airframe. One approach was a new helmet to protect against nuclear, biological, chemical, and G forces, which was to be available to all the U.S. air services in 2006 and would be compatible with cockpits in sixteen aircraft types.

VIABLE DESIGNS

The major problem for the aircraft industries after the Second World War was that the cost of research and development rose so drastically that companies could no longer play with several projects but found themselves increasingly limited to as few as one—and then able to undertake that only with massive government financing or the guarantee of orders of up to first fifty and then one hundred. By the time of the big jets in 1958–60, the break-even point had risen to around 300 aircraft, with a price tag of some $5 million each. Such staggering figures meant that companies that did not very carefully estimate markets, costs, inflation, and research and development times found themselves dangerously close to bankruptcy. By 1995 the Boeing 777 cost $150 million each; however, the company's reputation was such that it had orders for 140 before first flight.

But in the later 1990s, Boeing was hit by a production slowdown caused when parts supplies were out of synchronization with production needs, and work was also out of sequence. Output dropped to just fourteen 737 aircraft per month, but by 2000 was back to thirty-two, and Boeing had a large backlog. What made the business boom was the excellent world economy and the popularity of the 737 and its derivatives.

In July 2000, Southwest Airlines, which estimated its growth rate as 8 percent per annum, ordered 294 more Boeing 737-700s. In addition, 1,000 geriatric jets needed to be replaced worldwide, and would be estimated to total approximately 5,550 aircraft by 2018, some of which would be scrapped and others converted to cargo or package service. Accelerating the trend toward replacement, or elimination, is the airline ideal to operate as few types as possible, and thus the wish to get rid of high-cost "narrow-bodies" and avoid expensive "hush-kitting" of noisy older engines. But hush-kits for older airliners still sell well.

Asia is expected to be the biggest purchaser of wide-bodies once China nationalizes her airlines. But lurking was the problem of what would happen when dollar debts were converted to Euros. Manufacturers in the Euro area have deep loan reserves, and airlines can pay these off with Euro earnings.

Turboprops

The evolution of airliners until recently followed ten years behind military developments, just as operational aircraft had been a decade after record-breakers. Two innovations were basically British: the first efficient turboprop airliner, the Vickers Viscount, which had entered service with British European Airways in 1951; and the ill-fated de Havilland Comet I jetliner, which BOAC had put into service in 1952.

Turboprops proved to be ideal for intermediate routes with a large number of stops, but when developed into larger, prestige aircraft they ran into difficulties because they could not compete against jets that had entered service to stay in 1958. The Lockheed Electra (ER 232) was caught in this dilemma but continued to offer satisfactory service into the 1970s (and into the twenty-first century as a USN patrol plane), while the Bristol

Britannia 100 (ER 517) suffered from the fact that it was four years late entering service and thus was a bare six months ahead in 1958 of the big jets on the highly competitive North Atlantic routes.

Turboprops were developed by the Russians and adopted by the Canadians for over-water patrols and for freight services, and were gradually also employed by the fighting services of other countries for supply-drops and anti-submarine warfare. The turboprop had the advantage of quiet, vibration-free flight and economical fuel consumption, especially at low altitudes, as compared to jets, with whom it competed on airline stages below 350 miles. In the military, loiter time was significantly greater with turboprops as opposed to jets. Twin-engine turboprops developed in the 1980s and 1990s, such as the Saab SF 340 and the Beech 99 (ER 7.12) in the late 1990s, faced the handwriting on the wall as new, small regional jets gained acceptance. And thus the turboprops were switched to the freighter role.

Until 1995, Sweden remained outside the European groups with its military jet and Saab SF 340 and SF 2000 (ER 61.7) turboprop commuter airliners for feeder operation. But economic realities had by 1996 begun to create linkages between Saab and British Aerospace, forcing Saab in 1997 to abandon the SF line in the face of regional jet competition. Other players in the small airliner field were Bombardier of Canada, CASA of Spain, ATR of Italy and France, and Embraer of Brazil—and an attempted entry from the world's fourth most populated state, Indonesia.

In 1988, the future of the unducted-fan (UDF) engine as a commercial proposition for use on the MD-90 series (DC-9s) and other aircraft had started along the classical path of technological innovation. Greatly acclaimed as cutting fuel costs 30 percent, the UDF engine appeared to increase maintenance by 19 percent. The developed high by-pass ratio jets, already reliably in service, proved a safer bet, with an airframe time before check inspections of 25,000 hours (or roughly four to five years). In comparison, only tried-and-true turbo-prop engines, such as the Rolls-Royce Dart with nearly fifty years in service and just starting a new cycle on the Fokker F-50 (ER 45.2), or the well-tried Pratt & Whitney Canada PT-6 and the like, seemed still to have an assured future as turboprops, in spite of a switch to new more fuel-efficient small or regional jets in the late 1990s.

Conversely, the manufacture of the largest jet engines is a major task. Rolls-Royce had to increase production rapidly in 2000–01 to meet the demand for the Trent 500—from 20 engines in 2001 to 150 in 2003, with 550 on firm order. Meanwhile, four test aircraft were to accumulate 2,400 hours of flying time. Across the Channel, engine-maker CFM International, a joint company of SNECMA and General Electric, by 2002 was producing twelve CFM 56-7 engines weekly. And by the end of 2001, the GE-90 derivative engine for the Boeing 777-300ER had reached a thrust of 120,000 pounds, with a maiden flight on the airframe by 2003.

The SSTs

By the late 1960s the world had three supersonic civilian transports (SST) flying or on the drawing boards, apart from military supersonic aircraft. Little was known about the politics behind the Russian Tupolev Tu-144 SST (ER 4,970), but in the West the Anglo-French Concorde faced airline resistance on its economics and severe cost-recovery problems; its basic development estimates had skyrocketed from £150 million in 1962 to £1,000 million in 1971. In the United States, a lengthy competition for the SST design contributed to the financial troubles of Lockheed and Boeing.

The demise of the U.S. SST inspired the Plateau Theory of development. The political dimension was publicly obvious in protest movements against aircraft noise, and the economics appeared to be so tenuous that in 1971 the U.S. Senate refused to provide funding for two prototypes after the government had spent $1 billion on the program. This was a political rather than a

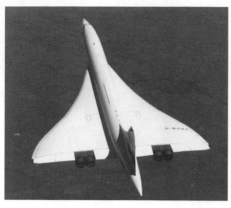

The origins of the Anglo-French supersonic Concorde (ER 4,262) went back twenty years to studies started in 1952. By the 1960s, it was becoming obvious that the costs would exceed what a single company could handle, so the Air Ministers signed the 1962 Anglo-French agreement, which eliminated a possibly disastrous and costly rivalry. While the Concorde was being developed by Bristol/British Aircraft Corporation in Britain and by Aerospatiale in France, the Americans held a design competition that was ultimately canceled in 1969, as the project was affected by the Plateau Theory—the public would no longer support the effort. Concorde ceased to operate in 2003. (British Airways)

In 1981 and 1982, Boeing introduced the single-aisle 757 (ER 663) for up to 233 passengers, and the double-aisle 767 (ER 1,088) for up to 289 passengers. The former had a shorter range, while the latter was ETOPS-cleared (extended-range twin-engine operational) for Atlantic crossings. Due to similarity of cockpit layouts and handling characteristics, the FAA agreed that with minimum training, pilots could be licensed to fly the 757-200, the 757-200PF, and the 767. (Boeing)

Operators such as Scandinavian Airlines Systems (SAS) found that the longer-range Boeing 767-300ER (ER 3,044) served them well on their trans-Atlantic routes. The similarities of the 757 and 767 make them difficult to distinguish. (Boeing/SAS)

The Boeing 767 (ER 1,088) was also immediately sold as a package freighter. Here, Boeing employees greet the rollout of the first for United Parcel Service.

One of the aims from the start of French aviation policy in 1945 was eventually to challenge the American large airliner dominance. Being the underdog made Airbus more innovative. One of the new ideas was the fly-by-wire electronic/computer control, fuel management, and self-monitoring systems, which transmitted to base. The A-300B4 of 1974 (ER 1,178) could carry 330 passengers, and began to provide airlines with a non-U.S. choice. Other members of the family followed, and by 2000 Airbus and Boeing sales in terms of numbers were even. (Airbus)

The similarity of jets is shown by this A-321 (ER 560, A-320-100). Each fresh design tends to incorporate improvements derived from the constant wind-tunnel and other testing to compound the economies of more fuel efficiencies—not to go faster, but rather either to go farther or to carry more revenue-earning payload. (Swissair)

The Airbus A-310-300 is another member of the family from Toulouse, France, though built by the European consortium now known as EADS. The A-310-300 (ER 2,248) burns 5,400 liters (4,426 gallons) per hour. (Lufthansa postcard)

Ecological concerns were strong by 1994 when Swissair changed its livery to use only paints containing no heavy metals, a contribution of chemistry to the environment. This aircraft is an A-310-322 (ER n/a). (Swissair)

The Russian Antonov An-225 (ER 3,387) is a very heavy lifter. For an idea of size, note the man by the starboard wheel in the lower left of the picture. Fewer than ten of the aircraft have been built, and fiscal problems in the Commonwealth of Independent States (CIS) have prevented all from being certified. (Russian State Industries)

The size of the new 95,000-pound thrust engine can be seen here in the Rolls-Royce Trent 800 on the Boeing 777 (ER 3,845). (Rolls-Royce)

When front-line aircraft became less competitive, they were shifted to feeder routes; but the DC-4 (ER 83) even proved too big for that, and thus those surplus machines went to all-cargo airlines. By the 1960s, the venerable, reliable DC-3 (ER 19.14) was becoming too small as passenger boardings rose and so new, more efficient aircraft such as the Fokker-Fairchild F-27 (ER 16.69, F-27-100) came into service. With Dart low-maintenance engines and easy passenger and freight-loading (because it was set low to the ground), the F-27 sold well. This one belongs to the Spanish airline Avensa. (Fairchild)

With the background and demand for bush aircraft, de Havilland of Canada, briefly a Boeing company, was in an excellent position to develop STOL (short takeoff and landing), quiet commuter aircraft for feeder or other routes, which needed either thin or very frequent operations. An early bird in 1959 was the DHC-6 Twin Otter (ER 4.2). (de Havilland of Canada; Tony Honeywood)

technical or business decision. But, in fact, the SST could not compete with the 747, in service since 1969.

Behind the scenes were the struggles of the Boeing engineers to meet the rapidly developing noise restrictions that in their turn demanded a heavier airframe and engines. It was clear that the data was available from Concorde and the SR-71 Blackbird, and thus what was needed was not a test vehicle, but constant design and development using computers and wind tunnels.

By 1967, Boeing was on the proverbial "horns of a dilemma" as it was becoming clear that an SST was not the next generation aircraft, but that the 747 was. The company had not the physical, financial, nor human resources to do both. The SST was an enormous risk for a minimal return, whereas the 747 could be expected to sell well and was not a strenuous quantum leap beyond two sound barriers to Mach 2.5 (1,800 mph). In addition, the 747 engine-yoke mounting problem had to be resolved, and quickly, so that jumbo sales would not be lost. It was Boeing's own money invested in the 747—but not in the SST; and what Boeing did have in the supersonic prototype was returned in government cancellation payments.

In truth, the project was not ready. Supersonic boom or ozone-depletion issues attracted public attention, but the reality was too little technical knowledge existed on the SST and too few usable routes upon which to bet the company.

In fact, these planes appeared to bear out the hypothesis that technological development continues for three generations, or fifty to sixty years, before it hits a plateau caused by political, economic, social, and ideological—not to mention military and diplomatic—resistance. How long the plateau lasts depends upon the development of both a new climate of opinion and a more economically appealing technology usable on viable routes. By 2003 there was evidence that technical breakthroughs might make a supersonic cruiser possible. The environmental discontent at New York in 1975 regarding the Concorde had passed

and has not reappeared, but then the original aircraft was a noisy 1950s design.

Air France and British Airways had placed the Concordes in service in 1976, and despite the surcharge on first-class tickets to fly on the only commercial SST, by 1986 the British Airways planes had made 15,000 Mach 2 flights. The Air France Concordes had carried 620,000 passengers at a 60 percent load factor, of whom 32,000 were on charters. The Concorde-Cunard *QE2* air-and-sea package round trips were very popular. In fact, the Concorde and its small tightly knit staff exuded *esprit de corps;* the Anglo-French group knew each other well.

The Concorde was the first civil aircraft fitted with fly-by-wire controls, later adopted on the Airbus lines. The weak point was the engines, which took more than a decade to get up to a time-between-overhaul of 2,000 hours. The powerplants were controlled by an early computer. In 1986, a likely cause for grounding was considered to be the cost of spares. The stop came in 2003.

Maintenance on the Concorde has been twenty man-hours per flying hour. Most delays (more than fifteen minutes), amounting to about five percent of departures, were caused by the undercarriage—wheels, tires, brakes, and retraction gear. New tires last only forty landings, as compared to a 737's 200. Tested in 2001 to 20,000 three-hour cycles, the Concorde should last to 60,000 hours, or at 1,000 hours per year, until 2036. Safety experts believed in a divisor factor of three for these numbers, but this proved overcautious, and up to 10,000 cycles may be allowed.

By 2003, the likelihood of a new SST in the future seemed to be coming closer, with the U.S. Defense Advanced Projects Research Agency promising contracts to develop quiet military supersonic aircraft with high efficiency and low sonic boom noise.

Fuel

In the good old days of the 1920s, aircraft could be fueled from four-gallon tins. But the 1936 DC-

Table 4. Boeing Aircraft Standard Fuel Capacities[1]

Aircraft	Liters	U.S. Gallons
707–320C	90,299	23,839
727–200 Advanced	30,622	8,084
737–200 Advanced	19,532	5,156
737–400	23,830	6,291
747–200B	198,380	53,372
747–400 LR	228,250	60,258
757–200	43,490	11,481
767–200 ER	91,380	24,124
777–200 ER	171,170	45,189
777–200 LR	195,285	51,555
MD 81	22,104	5,835
MD 11	146,174	38,590

[1] 1 liter = 0.264 U.S. Gallons

3 needed 800 gallons, and by 1958 the 707 required 19,000 gallons; the 1988 747-400 required a total of 60,258.

No longer could a mobile fueling truck do the job. By the 1960s, fuel farms outside the airports were connected by pipelines to aircraft hardstands, and mobile pumps put the fuel up into the machines themselves.

Petrol, oil, and lubricants (POL) have all been refined. Jet engines used highly flammable JP-4, a gasoline derivative, or kerosene. But the very high rpms (10,000 or more) led to the need for synthetic oils and bearings. All of this spawned a very large, worldwide business getting oil out of the ground, refined, or synthesized, and delivered in reliable quantities and at an acceptable quality. The impact of the 1973 Arab oil embargo was high oil prices, which stimulated production and resulted in an oil glut that subsequently reduced fuel prices and then held them steady until 2000. The much more significant long-term result of the 1973 embargo was the technical refinement of engines to give a vastly reduced fuel burn altogether.

Closely related to economical fuel burn has been emissions, which the International Civil Aviation Organization (ICAO) began to monitor under a new set of standards in the 1960s and which were sharpened by the Kyoto Protocol of 1997, leading to new emissions and noise standards in 2000. The studies for the latter included improved air-traffic control management, climb and cruise rules, and charges on users not taxes.

Evolutionary Problems

As most aircraft began after 1939 to fly at levels requiring either crew oxygen or pressurized cabins, air conditioning systems were developed to keep those airborne at up to 60,000 feet at a pressure equivalency of 8,000 feet. The constant pressurizing and depressurization created reversals of stress metal fatigue, such as brought down the Comet I.

Another unforeseen negative development was that the aging airliners concurrently had a new wave of fatigue, corrosion, and noise problems at a time when the independent feeder airlines had been forced to opt for more fuel- and noise-efficient medium-sized airliners. The inefficient machines were thus difficult to sell. In addition, the early 1988 miraculous descent of an Aloha 737 that had lost the top of its fuselage—an aircraft with 89,000-plus twenty-four minute flight cycles—stimulated the grounding of older planes and more orders for new ones. More recently, however, in-air failures have come from explosive or inflammable situations, or flying into terrain, rather than aging machines.

Electronics

Not only in airframes and engines has great progress been made since 1945. Electronics is a field that was in its infancy in World War II, to such an extent that the word itself was unknown. But from radar—GEE (the British pulse, grid navigation aid, so named for the "G" in grid), LORAN (long-range navigation), and their derivatives—electronics progressed rapidly to ground-controlled approaches (GCA) to the fully automatic landing by the late 1960s, in which the aircraft is flown hands-off down the glide slope and landed. This was of great importance to the airlines because what in crude form had been used by the RNAS flying boats in 1917–18, and proved by the British in 1944 but not adopted until 1963, enabled reliable all-weather service—a cost saver.

Coupled with these advances have been those in communications that allowed the elimination of the radio operator from the flight crew because by the mid-1960s the single side-band radio enabled airborne captains to communicate with company headquarters from anywhere in the world. And then it became possible to dispense with the navigator, even for over-ocean flights, as sophisticated inertial-navigation systems (INS) came out of the World War II plot-keeping developments. When the INS is set correctly, an airplane can fly a complex course from takeoff in Alaska to landing in Seoul—though if not done accurately, the plane might get shot down, as happened to KAL 007 over the USSR on September 1, 1983.

By the 1980s, another development with significant potential was in place, the miniaturization of navigation equipment as a result of advances in the computer component industry. This made LORAN available, for instance, to small private aircraft at an affordable price and at an acceptable weight. By the late 1990s, the compact cell-phone-sized global positioning system (GPS) was installed, accurate enough (to within fifty feet) for final approaches. The GPS was so precise that prescribed airways were being superseded by the concept of "free flight," which in the northern hemisphere allowed captains to choose their air routes and altitudes for best economic advantage, using electronic data transmission and computers, from taxiing out to final approach to the gate at destination. But although the hand-held GPS is a great advance in accuracy and miniaturization, it can be affected by atmospherics, other communication systems, and deliberate disruption of the signal.

In 2002, Europe approved its own Galileo satellite navigation system. Immediately it faced the requirement to negotiate the interoperability with the U.S. GPS, which is also commercial.

COMPUTERS AND AIR-TRAFFIC CONTROL

Europe's airports by the end of the twentieth century were struggling to overcome the air-traffic-flow management (ATFM) after the disastrous summer of 1999, when there were a large number of flights to the Balkans. The problem of growth could be seen in the 20 percent increase in flights during 1997–2000—some 500,000. Major delays were caused by France, Switzerland, and the United Kingdom, and at Eurocontrol's upper-air center in the Netherlands, due to airport issues, shortage of parking space, and low-visibility procedures. And also in Asia, Hong Kong's traffic had increased 10 percent to 33.7 million passengers, and Changi, Singapore, had increased 10 percent as well, to 28.6 million, with cargo up 12 percent to 1.7 million tons.

Of enormous and often unseen impact on aviation had been the computer revolution started in World War II with the computing bombsights, moving through to the GPS of the 1990s. But computers have also been a hidden loss-leader in the airline business. Introduced in the reservations systems in the early 1960s, they became both worldwide facilitators and slave-drivers, as well as a means to monopolistic control. What destroyed British Caledonian Airlines was not the cost of new aircraft, but the cost of locking into a computer reservation system, even if probably on a shared basis.

Yet on the positive side, computers also manage aircraft in many ways, from fueling to crew rostering, to maintenance data transmitted (since 1995) while en route to shorten turnaround times. Computers also have become vital in worldwide air-traffic control, especially in the highly concentrated corridors such as the airways in North America, across the Atlantic, and in Europe. But these wonder data machines have themselves been undergoing revolutionary changes, especially when coupled to radar. The result has been built-in obsolescence at a time of escalating budgets, leading to political sleight of financial hand in the United States to keep Federal Aviation Administration (FAA) trust funds unspent in order to appear not to be going deeper into national debt. The not unfamiliar result has been a deterioration of the air-traffic environment.

In 1957, the FAA took over for the Civil Aeronautics Authority (CAA) and had the clout to make the skies safer before the big jets arrived. Towers received modern radar of the day and a lot more authority, as traffic doubled every few years and the skies became filled with civil, airline, and military planes, and airports expanded. This led to understaffing of the FAA's air-traffic control, as five years of training were necessary to educate a controller for the pressure cooker in the tower.

In 1966, the new Department of Transportation took over the FAA, which until then had had direct access to Congress. Budgets subsequently suffered, and the FAA fell behind the 15 percent per annum traffic growth. President Lyndon Johnson's investigative committee wrongly concluded that the peak had been reached and that a decline in air traffic was ahead.

In the early 1970s, much of air-traffic control was tied together in the United States by automated flight-data control systems. This allowed outbound aircraft to be held on the ground until they could be programmed into a destination landing slot. By 1980, identification data on the controllers' radar scopes showed the number and altitude of each flight.

In the late 1960s, the Professional Air Traffic Control Organization (PATCO) came into being in the United States. The 1981 PATCO strike was a mistake in judgment, as such action was illegal and President Ronald Reagan called the union's bluff. Some 10,000 strikers were fired as civil service workers who had violated the law. The remaining air-traffic control personnel were beset by both an extremely heavy work load and disgruntled former co-workers, but 12,000 applications were on file from which to fill slots.

As the summer of 2002 approached, the airlines faced the double whammy of weather and security delays disrupting the air-traffic control system. New technologies were helping, but experienced controllers were skeptical as to a completely effective solution.

By 2003, information technology (IT) had begun a rapid climb in use, and in usefulness, in aviation to help carriers cut costs and monitor customer desires. IT has now become an ever-expanding and enabling area, but it suffers from a critical shortage of skilled personnel and in the airlines requires an investment of 15 percent or more of the budget.

In the twenty-first century, the airlines face the problem of obtaining and retraining pilots, with internet postings making the availability of jobs easier to discern. At the same time, due to economic trends, the airlines were also furloughing these vital personnel. However, cross-licensing of crew on different types such as the various Airbuses gave the companies flexibility. Some 7,000 U.S. airline pilots were furloughed. Then, in 2,000, some 14,000 were hired, and in 2002 some 7,000 more were rehired. Meanwhile, in spite of layoffs, the number of airline maintenance technicians was expected to remain at around 150,000 into 2003. The number of women employed was, by 2003, just above 20 percent of the workforce.

By 2003, the internet was widely used: by suppliers, and for after-sales service, online maintenance, operational data, trading of aircraft, catering, engine repair and ordering, multiple airline travel agency service, and online ticketing (with access to 500 major airlines, 30,000 hotels, and 45 car-rental agencies), as well as for global transport commerce logs from pick-up to delivery, including paperwork.

The importance of the internet may be judged from the fact that in 2002 the USAF created a new portal called *My.Airforce,* which included millions of pages from 28,000 sources and 1,500 web sites, allowing 1.2 million USAF personnel, families, and contractors to have access.

Several companies made a name for themselves by concentrating on the feeder niche. One of the beneficiaries of these enterprises was Pratt & Whitney Canada, which produced the P&WC PT-6 series of turboprop engines. This Saab 340 (ER 19) of 1984 happens to be powered by the rival GE CT-7. The Swedish Saab broke into a number of markets, only to be crowded out by either the desire to consolidate on one type such as the Beech Model 1900D airliner (ER 7.12, Beech 99), or to switch to newer regional jets.

The Saab 340 (ER 19) cockpit is compact and cleanly laid out. Many young pilots started getting their transport hours on commuters, as is the young lady on the right.

Two pilots and one cabin attendant handle the roughly twenty-eight passengers in the Saab 340. Overhead luggage racks hold only briefcases or purses, and thus all carry-on baggage has to be handed in at the aircraft and stowed in the after compartment.

The Brazilian manufacturer Embraer also competes in the commuter field. Foreign manufacturers invading domestic markets face trade barriers in the form of tariffs, although by 2003 a single international certification through reciprocity was being achieved. This is the EMB 120 (ER 156). (Embraer)

The venerable Dutch Fokker company, which had started in the First World War and survived the Second, finally ceased business in the 1990s when it ran out of capital and the government would not make it any more loans. It simply did not have the resources for the expensive development, manufacturing, and certification processes for the F-100 (ER 182), and so sales failed to materialize for what otherwise would have been a fine aircraft. (Fokker)

What started out as the Avro 146 (ER 115) regional airliner became a British Aerospace RJ (regional jet) product after consolidation. Nevertheless, it survived and is still being sold. It broke into the U.S. market with Pacific Southwest Airlines, which purchased the Bae 146-200 (ER 115) one hundred-seat aircraft in the late 1980s. (British Aerospace)

Modern airports such as Germany's Frankfurt-am-Main are small cities of about 40,000 highly productive people who also live in the neighborhood. This sometimes leads to interesting conflicts between a noisy occupation and a desire for quiet at home. Also of much concern is the ability to allow access to the airport, preferably by train as automobiles require roadways and, above all, parking spaces. In this 1990 view, the *autobahn* is in the foreground, then the railway, and, at the top, the passenger terminal. (Frankfurt-am-Main Airport)

The Bonwell-Higham rule is that while passengers increase geometrically, facilities only expand arithmetically. Hence, major airports are always undersized and constantly under construction. (Frankfurt-am-Main Airport)

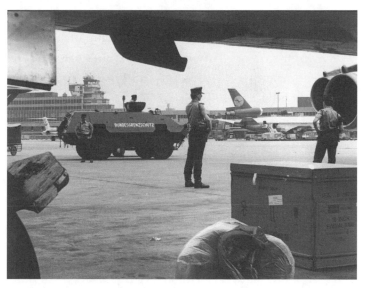

American concepts of freedom were shattered on September 11, 2001, and airport security was seen as a gaping hole. Actually, Europeans and other have long been security conscious. Baggage-matching on the tarmac was in use at Istanbul in 1979, and at Frankfurt after the 1988 Olympics terrorist attack. This 1990 scene of passengers boarding an Aeroflot flight after identifying their baggage on the tarmac has been the custom for more than a decade. (Frankfurt-am-Main Airport)

Armed troops or police have long been found at airports outside the United States and Canada. Again, this is Frankfort in 1990, but it could have been Zurich earlier, after an attack on El Al aircraft—or today. (Frankfurt-am-Main Airport)

Runways and taxiways are the very heart of visible airport operations and cover several thousand acres. Design varies for many reasons. This is Frankfurt in 1990, with the terminal area to the right and the cross runway beyond the main parallel runways. (Frankfurt-am-Main Airport)

Automatic landing systems were perfected in 1944, but not accepted until 1964. They can overcome low visibility and dark of night, but snow must still be dealt with physically. Here, a fleet of plows clears one of Frankfurt's runways. (Frankfurt-am-Main Airport)

In 2002 the U.S. air-traffic control system finally began to use automation to replace voice communication with aircraft, to relieve controllers who were being dangerously overworked or swamped, for in the United States, in June 2001, 4,500 flights were logged daily.

In Europe in 1995, 80 percent of all air movements were by commercial airliners, whereas in the United States they were by general aviation. By 2000, Europe had mandated that all airliners had to have the TCAS II traffic alert and collision avoidance system that had been mandatory for U.S. airlines for thirty years. By 2002, air traffic in Europe had been growing at the rate of 7.4 percent since 1980, straining facilities. With the new Airbus A-340-500 entering servicing in 2003 with flights of up to twenty-two hours versus fifteen hours previously non-stop, authorities were working out new crew duty-time regulations and alertness measurements and warnings.

After education and capital infusion, in 2000 Eurocontrol handled 8.3 million flights using 2,071 airports in thirty-eight nation states. In 2005, European national boundaries will disappear, with air traffic expected to double by 2020. To increase capacity, technical improvements on aircraft are being mandated, which are costly to business aircraft operators—$7,000 to $425,000 per machine. In addition, EC operational regulations will also be a burden.

Forecasting a major change in European air-traffic control was the 2001 winning bid of the Airline Group to take over the U.K.'s National Air Traffic Services. The Airline Group holds 46 percent, employees 5 percent, and the U.K. government 49 percent.

In the spring of 2001, the U.K.'s National Air Traffic Services (NATS) started trial North Atlantic controller-pilot data link communications (CPDLC), and followed way-point reporting in January and voiceless route clearances as an alternative to the overloaded voice channels. At the same time, Eurocontrol's air-traffic control centers introduced the reduced vertical separation minimum (RVSM). Covering flight levels FL290 (29,000 feet) to FL410 (41,000 feet) it opened six new flight levels by reducing separation from 2,000 feet to 1,000. This has been made possible by more accurate height-measuring equipment versus the older barometric altimeter, and has been supported by the cost benefits of lower fuel consumption and fewer delays. RVSMs were first introduced on the North Atlantic in 1997 and have since spread worldwide. About 10,000 flights per day use European airspace, but with 7.4 percent annual growth, RVSMs will only suffice to 2005.

European air-traffic control improvements also took a step forward in early 2002 when the new en route air-traffic control center at Swanwick, United Kingdom, came on line. The French and Swiss already had been experiencing delays caused by certain airlines using Eurocontrols' new central flow-management unit (CFMU) to file flight-plan bookings as a hedge against delayed takeoffs, but failing to cancel the unused bookings. On a day when 10 percent of the plans were not used, 38 percent of departures were delayed.

Due to a shortage of air-traffic controllers, the Germans in 2002 began to hire Irish personnel on two- to five-year contracts.

And in the United States in 2002, the concern was prevalent that terrorist hackers might disrupt the electric-power and air-traffic control systems.

Australian air-traffic control had switched by 1999 to a highly automated system to handle oceanic air traffic. It was regarded in 2001 as the benchmark for high-tech, cost-effective centers, with either Brisbane or Melbourne being able in an emergency to handle the other's load. Managed as a private corporation, its very fiscal success has made it a target for government revenue seekers.

SECURITY, SAFETY, AND ACCIDENTS

In the years since the introduction of the big jets, terrorists with political agenda have realized that a hijacked airliner has both a great media potential for publicizing their cause and for blackmail. This has impacted both passengers and airports by increasing security checks with more sophisticated electronic means and personal searches—all of which has required more airport personnel and secure areas. Security precautions in the air have included armed guards and locked cockpit doors, at least in the United States. Boeing, using its savvy and resources, scooped the newly announced cockpit-door market with a deal in March 2002 to supply 5,000 such protective devices. Rivals were forced to consider dropping out of the business.

But not all attackers have been terrorists; some are simply disturbed people.

The very nature of flying places great emphasis on safety, which includes passengers being strapped in with seatbelts for their own well-being in case of turbulence. Accidents in both the military and in civilian flying have been much reduced since the 1960s due to better training, examinations, and required updating of personnel, machines, and procedures, as well as technology. A certain number of military accidents are expected, due to the operational milieu, but many others have been preventable. The extraordinary safety record of the airlines—after all it is vital to the continuation of the business—has been due to both professional pride and to corporate and government supervision. Accidents have become so rare that each has become unique and newsworthy, as in the most unusual July 2002 mid-air collison over the German-Swiss border, at some 36,000 feet, of a Russian Tu-154 airliner and a Belgian Boeing 757 cargo plane.

"Hull losses" of aircraft for 1991–2001 showed that Africa was the least safe area of the world, with 9.8 per million departures versus .5 for the United States and Europe and 1.9 for China. And these figures, in turn, affected insurance premiums.

Much credit for flying safety is due the accident-investigation branches and the cooperation of manufacturers and other concerned parties worldwide.

GENERAL AVIATION

The third part of the manufacturing community—the general-aviation companies—has produced the largest number of units, but the smallest by weight. In the United States, the Beech and Piper aircraft corporations had by the 1980s moved from the leadership role of their founding dynasties to merge with or become other corporations, such as Beech-Raytheon; and Cessna Aircraft Company had changed management. These organizations had followed in the steps of what is now Learjet by introducing either turboprops or pure jets for business/executive use. Their products were also finding increasing acceptance on commuter airlines, which was a growing fraternity. However, in that field they faced competition especially from de Havilland of Canada (now Bombardier) whose turboprop DHC-6 Twin Otter (ER 4.2), DHC-7 Quiet STOL (QSTOL)(ER 18.6), and DHC-8 (ER 25.9) proved highly fuel efficient.

In the United States, where 65 percent of the free world's aircraft by number have long been produced, Cessna, a leader in general aviation, saw its sales go from 551 in 1951 to 3,116 in 1961, to 3,847 in 1971, peak at 8,400 in 1979, and then drop back to 187 in 1987. The umbrella General Aviation Manufacturers Association (GAMA) member sales for the same years were 2,302 (1951); 6,778 (1968); and 7,466 (1971), peaking in 1978 at 17,811, and dropping in 1986 to 1,495. The fifteen companies that had existed in 1947 had shrunk to nine by 1987, but they were producing bigger and more expensive business aircraft such as the Cessna Citation family.

The major U.S. general aviation manufacturers had gone into a nose-dive in the 1980s. Cessna and Beech had stopped production of their single-engine piston types, and although undoubtedly liability lawsuits were a contributing factor, so, too, were rising prices, FAA regulations, and stagnant designs versus exciting small cars and home video-recorder game simulations of flying, at pennies per flight. Innovation moved to experimental aircraft such as seen annually at the Experimental Aircraft Association (EAA) Fly-in at Oshkosh, Wisconsin, by a crowd of enthusiasts some 500,000 strong.

The General Aviation Revitalization Act of 1994 had also helped the U.S. general aviation industry recover with an eighteen-year statute of repose for lawsuits against manufacturers, from first delivery of an aircraft. However, Cessna single-engine machines did not go back into production until 1997. By 2000 the business had revived to the extent that there was a severe labor shortage in Wichita, Kansas, in a booming economy. In July 2001, Lycoming (now Textron Lycoming) had delivered its 300,000th opposed-piston engine, a 180 hp fuel-injected product, first manufactured in 1938 at 50 and 75 hp. But after September 11, 2001, a worldwide depression set in and caused manufacturers such as Boeing to cut back; Cessna had to lay off 250 of 1,000 workers due to the sales slump.

But yet another reason for the slow sales of the standard single-engine aircraft, such as the Cessna 172, has been the rise of home-builts like the Kitplane racer with a 575 hp Chevy engine capable of 405 mph (350 kn, 648 km).

During this time, Grumman replaced its Navy fighter contracts with the Gulfstream business jet series, and Hawker's smaller business jet was sold to Raytheon, which had also bought Beech. In Europe, Dassault continued to compete with its Fighting Falcon.

Then, too, the round-the-world unrefueled record was broken in nine days in December 1986 by Dick Rutan and Jeana Yeager in the unconventional piston-powered *Voyager* (ER 29). At the other end of the spectrum, a Boeing 747SP circled the world in thirty-six hours and fifty-four minutes with two refueling stops in 23,000 statute miles, only to be bested a few weeks later by a Grumman Gulfstream IV executive transport with thirty-six hours and eight minutes, with four stops. The difference would have been less if a pressure refueling system had not failed the 747 at

one stop, again emphasizing the importance of excellent ground support. The Gulfstream represented the best in modern corporate jets and proved that at the end of the twentieth century they could compete, with careful route planning, with both long- and short-haul airliners.

AIRPORTS

Growth of air travel worldwide can be understood simply by looking at the figures in the United States at the end of the twentieth century. In 1999, 1.5 million passengers flew every day. On Thanksgiving weekend that year, 20 million flew. In 2000, 225,000 passed through Chicago's O'Hare International Airport daily. In June and July 2000, some 97 million passengers boarded, but 125,000 of their flights were delayed for various reasons, one of which was a list of choke points—Boston, New York, Philadelphia, Washington, Chicago, Cincinnati, and Atlanta, all in the eastern United States. Newark, one of the New York Port Authority airports, could handle forty flights per hour in good weather, but sixty are scheduled by the airlines.

In 2000, some 682 million passengers boarded at U.S. airports, but at the same time clogged peak hours at places such as New York's LaGuardia Airport cost the airlines $6.5 billion and affected system-wide 119 million passengers. In 2000, unusual thunderstorms and heavy traffic volume contributed to a total of 309,482 delays, up 20 percent from 1999. These reports did not factor in flight cancellations.

To counter this, a slot lottery, peak-hour pricing, and new runways in the long-term were touted as solutions. But the question was whether or not a political will was present to release aviation trust funds in order to jump-start the building of new runways and bring capacity in line with consumer demand.

Another solution was seen in Turkey's rewriting of its aviation regulations to allow the entry of

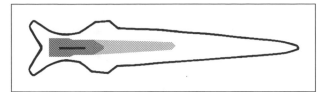

The 95 dB footprint of the 1958 Boeing 707 (white); the 80 dB footprint of the hush-kitted 1995 Boeing 727-200 (light gray); and the 95 dB footprint of the 1972 Airbus A-300B (dark gray). This clearly shows what technology can do when applied to a specific problem. The Gatwick Airport (London) runway (center black line) is 1.75 miles long. Extending far beyond the airport, the 707 footprint is 17 miles long; the A-300B's footprint is only 3.75 miles long.

new carriers. Conversely THY—*Turk Hava Yollari*—the national airline, has reduced capacity.

Because of noise curfews, major airports are only open eighteen out of twenty-four hours per day. In the fall of 2000 Zurich began to sharply increase its movements charges for noisy aircraft at the rate of double for every thirty minutes between 2200 and 0600 hours, or roughly a four-fold increase over the 2000 charges. Late in 2001, faced with urgent demands from freight operators for quieter engines for night operations (between 2300 and 0600 hours), Boeing, Rolls-Royce, and General Electric were developing the hushing that would meet Heathrow's quota count (QC2) noise-classification levels. These are important for Asian airlines, because due to journey and local times, they arrive in the very early morning and operate 80 percent with 747-400s.

Comparatively speaking, the decibel "footprint"—the graphic impression sound leaves—for a commercial jet airliner, in general, is said to be one-eighth that of certain military jet fighters. Much like Dallas-Fort Worth Airport, which covers 10,000 acres, the proposed conversion of the U.S. Marine air base at El Toro, California, has 4,700 acres, which will shield houses nearby from noise. The relative decibel footprints of the Boeing 707 and 727-200, and the Airbus A-300B, are

seen in the Gatwick db Footprint diagram. Moreover, the 85-decibel footprint of the commercial aircraft is but 12 percent of that of a U.S. Marine Corps fighter taking off.

A new problem for airports in our contemporary society has been a propensity for legal action. In 2001 a European court ruled that night-flying at Heathrow breached the human rights of those living close to an urban airport—their right to respect for family life and home. Mostly affected were the sixteen flights daily from Asia that arrive between 0500 and 0700 hours. The low number of flights did not enable the government to claim economic damage or infringement of the rights of a significant number of other people. In spite of double-glazing of house windows, the solution may ultimately be that of Los Angeles—clearing a dead zone around airports and perhaps filling it with warehouses.

Another problem, even with computer control, was gridlock at certain high-density airports. Of course it is not only on the air side of terminals that gridlock has occurred. Convenience and comfort facilities such as restrooms have simply been overburdened by the tidal flow of passengers when the newer and bigger airliners pull up to the gates.

The Higham-Bonwell version of Malthus' population laws specifies that traffic grows geometrically and facilities only arithmetically. In other words, passenger and freight loads grow on a 1, 2, 4, 8, 16, 32, etc., curve whereas facilities only expand on a stepped arithmetic basis. This is because airport expansions must be approved by a series of regulatory bodies and then be financed either by bond issues or trust funds, or a combination. A human oversight, especially with competition for funds, is to fail to project the consequences of growth as well as to neglect the lessons of history in both the special and comparable fields.

And now airports have had to seek ecologically and environmentally acceptable space clear of housing and connected to the city by highways and rail nets. One solution, considered for London then abandoned, was the creation of a man-made island such as at Japan's Kanái International Airport at Osaka. Another was the model of Germany's Munich II, and a third Hong Kong's 1998 Chop Lap Tek. In the search for a third London Airport (started in 1928), the development of more sophisticated air-traffic control of airways and landing and takeoff slots, together with ever larger aircraft, enabled Heathrow and Gatwick to sustain their traffic growth. But one of the regulatory stumbling blocks to the 2001 proposed British Airways-American Airlines alliance was the number of slots this union would have monopolized. As has been often the case, a barrier to growth has been planning permission—nine years for the still unbuilt fifth terminal at Heathrow.

Currently Heathrow handles 64 million passengers and 460,000 movements annually. With the completion of Terminal 5 in 2008, another 30 million can be accommodated. In the meantime, Europe's No. 3 Charles de Gaulle Airport will be able to handle 55 million and has direct rail service to European destinations. A third Parisian airport may be located seventy-eight miles north, at Chaulnes, and would open in 2015. But the French were beginning to rethink that after a change of ministries, just as in 1971 when the British had scrapped the plans for Maplin. Opposing factors are residential complaints around Orly and de Gaulle, promised aircraft movement limitations, and, conversely, the fact that 60 percent of the Paris traffic to the Mediterranean coast now goes on the TGV trains.

After a four-year public inquiry, Munich II will get a fourth runway in 2006, and its capacity will rise to 120 movements per hour. Amsterdam's Schipol Airport, with its new environmentally acceptable fifth runway, will by 2003 be handling 600,000 air transport movements annually. In South Korea, the new Inchon Airport opened in 2001, and a year later the government committed another $3.6 billion to ensure its expansion as a major Asian hub, with forty-three cities and a one billion population within three to five hours flying time—with further expansion already planned.

As in the past, the prospect of the arrival of a very large new aircraft raised questions as to what airports would need to do to be able to accept them—in this case, the Airbus A-380. Estimates to make fourteen U.S. airports compatible varied from the Airbus claim of $520 million to the U.S. General Accounting Office $2.1 billion.

The problems in Britain have arisen in part due to the recognition only in the 1970s that civil aviation was as vital to Britain's economic welfare as shipping used to be, and that London's airports were the gateway to Europe, especially for tourists. These travelers have become as important as business class, for the world's aging population has become affluent and can afford flying holidays. And as English has become the language of aviation, so it has also become that of tourism. In addition, with the arrival of the Euro in 2000 for credit-card and similar transactions, and in 2002 as a single currency within the European Community, so travel has become even easier, whether on group tours or not.

A parallel aviation business in Europe has been in charter airlines, whether owned by holiday companies ferrying people to warmer resorts or as affiliates of major airlines. These companies have been willing to use alternate airports, when available, where slots have not been a problem. However, their own viability was affected by the economic meltdown of 2001.

In the twenty-first century, the growth of population, traffic, and airports in Asia will make that the prime air transport area. Already in the decade ending in early 2001, ten new major airports or additional new facilities had opened: at Osaka (Kanái, 1994); at Hong Kong (1998); at Kuala Lumpur, Malaysia (1998); at Macau and at Shanghai (regionals, 1999); and, new terminals at Beijing, and at Taipei (Formosa), as well as terminals in process at Bangkok (Thailand), Chubu (central Japan), Guangzhou (China), and Singapore. Each of these new facilities will have a capacity of from 25–64 million passengers annually. Completed in 1998, Hong Kong's Chop Lap Tek airport could handle thirty movements per hour, but needed, and in 2002 received, China's approval for a second runway under the joint financing agreement.

Also new is the Athens 2001 Venizelos Airport at Spata, which has two parallel runways 0.94 miles (1.5 km) apart so that they can operate independently. It is open twenty-four hours a day and has no slot restrictions, but has 100 percent baggage screening. Most services are privatized, and the increase in costs to the airlines compared to the old Hellinikon Airport was a shock; but the charges are about the same as at Vienna and Amsterdam. The late 2001 activity was 600 movements per day by fifty-six airlines—or more than fifty per hour. Capacity is 16 million passengers annually, with the potential for 50 million.

The complexities of airport ownership hit Atlanta's Hartsfield International in 2002, which has 887,500 movements each year, the second busiest in the world after Chicago's O'Hare International. Hartsfield, established in 1925, is Georgia's largest employer and has revenues of $17 billion per year. But suburbanites want to wrest control of it from the city of Atlanta, which owns it, as Chicago does O'Hare. All other airports in the country are run by boards or authorities, except for the FAA-funded Hartsfield, an age-old quarrelsome point whenever the airport has received bad publicity from security breaches, a contract bidding scandal, or perhaps an ice storm.

What has happened to airports in the last forty years can be seen in the brief story of Chicago's O'Hare and Wichita's Mid-Continent airports. The former, with approximately 40,000 people employed in 1988, had 94,682 arrivals and departures in 1950 and handled 176,902 passengers. In 1987, the number of movements had risen to 792,897 carrying 57,543,865 passengers. Thus, the average of 1.86 passengers per movement of 1950 had become 72.6 just thirty-seven years later; but the number of movements had not increased proportionately because the size of aircraft had jumped instead from the 21-seat DC-3 to the 400-seat 747. At Wichita, by 1988 the city employed

101 people at the airport, while another 4,000 worked there, not one of whom was paid less than $20,000 a year. It had an operating budget of $10 million and, along with grants and the like, it spent $25 million a year. The revenues from the parking lot paid for the reliever airport. Cost accounting was used to determine landing fees.

Wichita Mid-Continent's direct economic impact on the community was in 1988 $192 million, and its multiplier effect was estimated at $482 million more. However, revenues were being hurt in the late 1980s by tax reform, by oil prices that affected the companies based in the area, and by the hasty reactions of the FAA to terrorism, which had caused Wichita-based general aviation aircraft to seek other, less-controlled airfields. The government paid the airport authority not to plant a good deal of the 3,500 acres of the field, and tenants rented 1,500 acres. Fire-fighting and snow removal were not nearly as costly as at Chicago's O'Hare, but were still a considerable part of the budget.

It is evident that major airports and airlines have become a significant part of their host city's economy, as well as the nation's as a whole. And hub-and-spoke airline systems are not only a critical dimension for passenger airlines, but also for freight and parcel services. United Parcel Service (UPS) began a standard parcel/shipping delivery business in 1953 and went to overnight delivery in 1982, when jets became available; by 1996, it had a fleet of almost 200 aircraft, using Louisville, Kentucky, for its domestic operations and Cologne/Bonn, West Germany, for its international. But hub-and-spoke systems had the disadvantages of ebb and flow of traffic, with consequent delays even in good weather. By 2000, bad weather could and did create catastrophe.

Fifth-ranked Northwest Airlines, with 300-odd planes in 1986, was an air force by current standards. Every day it dispatched 1,600 sorties, with 98 percent on-time departures, in contrast to a USAF F-15 Eagle squadron that still has only 75 percent of its aircraft available—the same percentage as of the RAF's Spitfires and Hurricanes in the 1940 Battle of Britain. (United Air Lines in 1994 had 545 aircraft with 79 on order, in contrast to the RAF's total of 1,271 machines, of which a fair proportion in 1995 were non-operational.) And the new 2002 Northwest Airlines terminal in Detroit featured a mile-long concourse.

This economic drive of the airlines' volume of movement helped allow the commuters to flow in as the trunk carriers pulled out of the regional airports in favor of settling into hubs, from which they sent out their spoke routes. In the United States, by 1988 most of the major commuters had been either taken over, become affiliated with, or at least operated under the wing of major companies, and had gates next to them in the terminals, joint fares, and access to their computers. The commuter lines, now in their affiliate's livery, were not as safe as the majors, but nevertheless remained far safer than automobile travel. And after 1996, in the United States they had to adhere to the same safety standards and training as the majors.

At the same time, the growth of air traffic with the new hub-and-spoke concept of airline operations caused an influx of passengers at the airports' physical facilities that were not necessarily capable of handling such massive numbers. The first new airport to be voted in by the public since Dallas-Fort Worth International was Denver International, the new $1.5 billion replacement for the mile-high Stapleton Airport. The new field had four north-south takeoff and two east-west landing runways, forty miles from downtown. With the new hushed jets, noise was not expected to be a factor, but convenience is, at this writing, until houses and motels encircle the new field, which had only opened in 1995 after persistent delays and after its baggage handling system was finally perfected.

The critical factor for airlines will remain efficient ground handling for minimum turnaround time in order to get eleven to twelve hours airborne daily from each aircraft. Even so, the bottleneck is still loading people into an aircraft at the gate. In 2002, Southwest's turnaround on the ground was thirty minutes per flight versus American Airlines' two and one-half hours—no wonder the majors lose money!

The future of major airports appears to be determined by the foresight of the planners, the reluctance of the voters, and the missteps by decision-makers, as well as by urban sprawl, noise, and water. Of equal importance has been the response of the airline and aircraft industry to noise restrictions, lack of expansion space, availability of landing slots, the growth of terminal facilities, and ground transport organization. Thus, London has sought that third airport since 1928 and will not complete its high-speed rail link to the city and the Continent, and its fifth terminal at Heathrow, until well into the twenty-first century.

By 2003, small airports worldwide that could be served by air taxis were very much under siege by a noise-conscious, voracious, land-hungry suburbia prepared to tax or legislate them out of existence.

The New Facilities

In general, the big jet is most economical on long-haul routes. But such large new aircraft of the period roughly 1948–70 demanded newer, longer, and stronger runways and reinforced taxiways, hardstands, and jetways. A spate of new airports and their associated developments have emerged, so that cities would not be by-passed by airlines. In Europe that peaked with Munich II Airport in the early 1990s. Not only did the Plateau Theory apply here, but the technological breakthroughs and investment in high-speed railways like the French TGV made surface intercity travel times and convenience highly competitive. The French, especially, recognized this with a rail terminal at Charles de Gaulle Airport, Paris, and the Swiss with theirs at Kloten, Zurich, where 45 percent of all non-transit passengers used the rail connection versus 31 percent at Amsterdam's Schipol Airport and 25 percent at Charles de Gaulle. The growth of high-speed intercity trains by mid-1999 had forced airlines to consider joining rail companies to provide seamless service for overseas and other passengers. At the same time they considered dropping such routes as London to Paris (240 miles) as not time-effective, city-center to city-center.

A further addition to service and facilities was a 2002 U.S. domestic code-share between Amtrak and Continental Airlines at Newark, which opened up connection possibilities to Philadelphia, Wilmington, Delaware, and Stamford and New Haven, Connecticut. But the question remained: Would Amtrak survive, even after a U.S. Department of transportation bail-out in July 2002?

In contrast in Britain, democracy and environmentalism delayed new airports, especially after the computer-generated Maplin (Foulness) planning fiasco of 1971. But land for new airports accessible to a city remains critical, and so in 1996 Tokyo was rethinking the idea of a floating airport offshore, as Osaka had done on its man made island.

AIRLINES

Major changes that affected airline development after 1945 included World War II, decolonialization, jet and turboprop engines, the introduction of tourist then economy and finally one-class service, cargo, and the inter-relationship of air transport and society at the airport, especially in the areas of noise, the environment, land use, crime, and mergers. In addition, a new aspect of airline business has been the success of the internet and the website. In 1998 the airlines in the United States sold $3 billion in tickets electronically, $8 billion in 1999, and $30 billion in 2000. What this will ultimately do to travel agents and the personal touch remains a question in the twenty-first century.

Not untypical of overall airline development was what happened in Britain. There the private airlines, Imperial Airways and British Airways

(1936) Ltd., had been forced into the state-owned BOAC in 1940. But at the end of the war, railway and shipping interests obtained the nationalized British European Airways (BEA) and British South American Airways (BSAA). The latter did not last due to accidents and too little capital, and was absorbed into BOAC in 1949. BEA began to poach in the 1960s in BOAC territory, when its new longer-ranged Comet 4 started flying to Beirut. Thus, in 1974 BOAC and BEA were merged into British Airways. In the meantime, a series of private companies had found the costs too great and in the 1960s wished BOAC to absorb their amalgamated British United. However, a 1969 government inquiry insisted on competition and gave the private sector and the African routes to the still independent British Caledonian, only to have that airline be forced to sell to either a foreign company or to British Airways, the latter winning in 1988.

Privatization, which began to affect the airlines in the 1980s, also reached the military in the twenty-first century with training, MRO, and aerial refueling being outsourced.

Outside of the Anglo-American world, economics affected airlines as well and, as example, pushed the creation in 1946 of Scandinavian Airline Systems, a joint partnership of Danish, Swedish, and Norwegian interests.

In the 1980s, although nationalism still prevailed, two new avenues of international linkages began to appear. First Delta and Swissair exchanged 15 percent of their stock, then KLM and Northwest cemented an alliance, to be followed by British Airways investing in U.S. Air. Then, United Airlines led off with advertising, code-sharing, and computer-reservation linkages. With dual designation, a passenger could hold British Airways tickets on a U.S. Air connection or Swissair bookings on a Delta trans-Atlantic flight, or vice versa.

In part, the future of the American manufacturers has been linked to that of the domestic airlines, and from 1978 to the 1990s the airlines had

Maintenance and overhaul must be done on schedule and in all kinds of weather, if not under climate-control. The size of the necessary facilities at Frankfurt can be judged from the 707 and DC-10 parked to the left. Note also the separate control tower to handle ground movements in these areas. (Frankfurt-am-Main)

The same place—Kansas City, Missouri—forty years later, with the cargo terminals to the left, three horseshoe-shaped passenger terminals in the center (a security nightmare, as every two gates must have screening facilities and staff), and the TWA overhaul base in the top-right rear. Free of noise protests, the airport has never been able to get approval of the required 51 percent of Missouri voters to protect itself with additional acreage. However, in the last quarter century, quieter engines have come to its aid with shorter takeoffs. (KCI)

The Gates Learjet (ER 25) that appeared in 1966 was almost a fighter with its quick performance—547 mph. It has since been further developed. (Learjet)

This 1950s view shows Mid-Continent Airport (MCI) at Kansas City, Missouri—now known as Kansas City International (KCI). The photo was taken shortly after the land was purchased and a runway laid down. (MCI)

The Grumman Gulfstream III of 1958 (ER 62, Gulfstream I; jet version of 1966, ER 313) has been a very successful turbo-prop business or executive aircraft. As access to major airports has become more difficult, as non-stop service across the Atlantic is possible from satellite urban airports, and as time-sharing aircraft have become available, executives are abandoning the airlines in favor of time-saving. (Grumman History Center)

Cessna entered the executive jet field in 1969 with the Citation (ER 14.5), and for a long time kept the straight wing that gave it excellent short field performance. By the end of the twentieth century, however, the new swept-wing Cessna 500 Citation (ER 23) had become available. In 1978 production of piston-engine aircraft for general aviation began a rapid decline in sales from more than 17,000 a year to about 1,000. One primary reason for this was a litigious society willing to enter into liability suits; a second reason was that much better profits could be made from million-dollar business airplanes. (Cessna)

The single piston-engine airplane rose in price from $12,000 of the 1960s to $36,000 of the 1990s, partly due to the natural increase in prices, especially after the 1968 inflation set in, but also because of liability suits, which could be brought even by the injured owner of an antique aircraft or by his or her survivors. Also affecting sales, however, was that many of the aircraft had remained unchanged since the early 1940s, and between entertaining video flying games and far less-expensive sports cars, buyers went elsewhere. Shown here is a Cessna 206 (ER 1.06), the first turbine conversion since 1984. (Cessna)

Crop dusting has become a big business around the world, operated by myriads of small entrepreneurs. It has to be done on still days, however, and thus it is often an early-morning task. The aircraft needs excellent slow-speed handling characteristics; safe, clean airflow over the cockpit; adequate hopper capacity; and an effective spraying system. Seen here is a Grumman Super Ag-Cat (ER n/a). (Grumman History Center)

The Beech Bonanza (ER 1.36, Model V35B) was first produced in 1947, with a V-tail. By 1977, 10,000 had been sold as a four-place machine capable of setting distance records. The Bonanza still has loyal owners; a 1976 or 1980 model today can sell for between $135,000 and $160,000, as compared to its 1947 base price of $8,945 or $11,355 fully equipped. (Beech)

The replica Vickers Vimy (ER 0.95) of the 1921 Smith Brothers standing by the 1976 Concorde (ER 4,262) well illustrates the tremendous advances of aviation—a 2,131-fold increase in efficiency in just over fifty years. (Vimy)

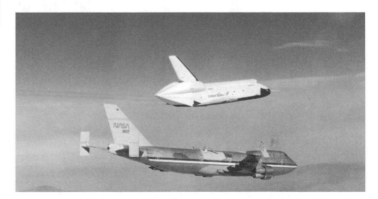

A space Shuttle, with aerodynamic fairing over its main engines, just after release from a NASA 747 that was carrying it piggyback—probably a test of the landing ability of the Shuttle *Enterprise* over Edwards AFB, California, in the late 1970s. The *Enterprise,* so named at the request of the fans of the television science fiction series, was a prototype that never flew in space. (NASA)

rough progress. Various factors affected the airlines' ability to make increased productivity pay:

- the decision to deregulate after years of control by the Civil Aeronautics Board (sunsetted in 1978);
- an expansion period following on the losses caused by the sudden surge in fuel prices due to the Arab oil embargo (from nine cents a gallon to ninety-nine cents in 1973);
- rising labor costs as a result of aging pilots and mechanics;
- non-discrimination against flight attendants and others;
- an overall sense of stability.

But deregulation brought chaos. Braniff and Eastern went bankrupt, Continental and TWA filed under Chapter 11 of the Bankruptcy Act, and Frontier became a holding company and then set up a non-union airline, Frontier Holdings, before folding into and along with People's Express, which also went bankrupt. By 2002, 178 airlines were gone, including in 2001 the venerable TWA. Part of the cause of all this turmoil was the entry into the field of a rash of new airlines not burdened with regulatory costs and requirements of serving unproductive markets or of providing social services, but free to operate only on lucrative routes from which they could skim enough cream using second-hand older aircraft. This seriously damaged established airlines, with their large financial commitments for new airliners and older mindsets. One of the most successful of these new entrants, however, has been the no-frills Southwest Airlines.

Just as the 1982 demise of the British Laker Airways brought in its wake international lawsuits, so the domestic pattern has been failure followed by lawsuits. All of this was later repeated with the establishment of the European Community in 1993. Ailing lines required either massive cash infusions or had to delay deliveries of new aircraft. And mergers, a rescue of sorts, ran the hazards of the U.S. Justice Department and the EC's Monopolies Commission.

The gradual consolidation of the U.S. airline industry resulted at the beginning of the twenty-first century in United and American airlines having 50 percent of the market, with Delta, Northwest, and Continental sharing 39 percent. And because everyone was flying the same types, it became increasingly possible to make cost-per-seat mile the standard competitive measure, as politicians noted. Passengers compared leg room, meals, and other services.

Entrepôt—market center—airlines such as KLM, Singapore, and in 2002 Qatar Airways, have used strategic position and financing to become players in the international air transport scene. Qatar carried 200,000 passengers in 1996 and 1.4 million in 2000. In November and December 2001, the United Arab Emirates ordered twenty-two Airbus 380s, three Airbus 330-200s, eight 340-600s, twenty-five Boeing 777-200ERs and -300s, with engine choices yet to be made in 2002 and deliveries through 2009. By 2002, Singapore Airlines had made a profit for thirty straight years, and had created a viable image of the "Singapore girls"—well-paid flight attendants who enjoyed their jobs—while providing full meals.

An offshoot of the creation of the EC has been the rapid rise of low-cost carriers, such as Easy Jet, with its twenty-six Boeing 737s, to be expanded to forty-eight by 2004. The British carrier expects to have Paris as its hub while serving sixteen European cities on thirty-five routes. Easy Jet is the ideal in that it operates only a single type and makes profits.

As an example of the difference between the majors and the low-cost airlines, British Airways posted a pre-tax loss for the fourth quarter 2001 of $229 million, a 19.9 percent drop. In contrast, low-cost Ryanair's revenue rose 18 percent, even as the company ordered one hundred Boeing 737-800s with options on fifty more to meet its target of forty million passengers per year by 2010.

The majors, such as British Airways, were slow

to react to the twin threats of industry slowdown and the challenge of low-cost rivals. Not until the mid-1990s did the airline begin to rethink its strategies. Old habits died hard, as British Airways, and other airlines, still tied revenues to high-end first class and business travelers, though they only accounted for 10 percent of the passengers carried. The result was that BA developed a high-priced reputation. It sold off GO (Go-Fly), its low-cost carrier, well managed by Barbara Cassani, and GO began 2002 with strong expansion plans, countering industry trends by moving to have a mix of aircraft. By 2006, it is to have a total of eighty jets as compared to twenty-two in 2002. Meanwhile, British Airways, in 2002, decided to cut capacity 20 percent, decrease staff, and seek to return to profitability in the changed times.

The smaller airlines, in many cases since 1978, moved up in size from twin-engine general aviation aircraft to commuter machines, and by the year 2000 to regional jets such as the Bae RJ 146-200. Indicative of this change has been both the consolidation of the commuters under a major's umbrella and the early 2000 order from Delta of 500 new regional jets from Bombardier of Canada in the 40- to 70-seat range. Such a fleet would give the Delta Connection great flexibility. To survive, Embraer and Fairchild also have to get into this market.

However, by 2003, sales of new regional jets were being endangered by scope clauses in union contracts, which limited the percentage of pilots in major airlines who could be employed on regional and commuter aircraft. In the cycles of mergers and disposals, the U.S. regionals faced the latter as 2003 approached.

WAR ON THE AIRWAYS SINCE 1945

The realities of the costliness of aviation started to appear in the early 1920s when airlines began to merge companies or to pool their services on the long thin routes. Natural growth was also enforced in the industry by government-prodded mergers or even by nationalization, as in France, Germany, and Britain. War, of course, put government at the helm, and both airlines and industry operated under directives, orders, and priorities.

After the 1939–45 war, the quantum leap made by aviation from biplanes to jets in less than a decade caused prices of new aircraft to rise nine times (DC-3 to Comet I). Airliners were able to fly non-stop westbound, London to New York, by the 1950s, and one million passengers were carried over the Atlantic alone in 1960. But the economic structure was constantly weakened by the political myth that competition was required to protect the public from price gouging. In fact, competition amounted to everyone flying the same machines with only different food service. What made for net profit was the ability to break even with ever-lower load factors, which dropped from the 117 percent for the Lancaster bomber conversion of 1946 to 41 percent for the 747-100 of 1969. Well-managed maintenance, labor, and fuel costs also played their parts.

Prominent in the airline management's war on waste, deficits, and costs was union busting, whether via negotiations for greater productivity, by mergers, or through bankruptcy proceedings. With companies in the early 1990s losing millions in any currency, savings had to be made. The French airline UTA *(Union de Transports Aeriens)* gave its pilots and cabin staff in 1988 the choice of productivity higher than flying thirty-four hours per month on Pacific routes, for instance, or lower pay. Ground crews have faced the same hard choices—break old habits, stop feather-bedding on new labor-saving, more maintenance-free machines, or retire. Or even more bluntly, grant concessions or lose the company and a job. In a few cases, such as United, the pilots have fought back and bought the company, only in 2002 to face a mechanics' strike. Others such as Frontier, People's Express, and British Caledonian have been merged and purged.

In the troubles of the 1990s, pilots, flight attendants, and mechanics gave wage concessions. By 2002 they wanted them back. One complication is that pilots are isolated from their employers having as their "office" the cockpit and rarely getting closer to the company than the briefing room. Interestingly, of aircrew, chief stewards are the best informed. Other workers, being ground-bound, are much more aware of corporate and their own concerns and futures. In 2002, pilots were finding that their attitudes of equal pay for equal work and the demand for their services were creating a global pay scale—not always to their liking

As we move farther into the twenty-first century, the airlines will still be subject to boom-and-bust cycles, and air forces will mostly be faced with out-of-theater peacekeeping operations with reduced forces.

Clausewitz said that war is the continuation of peace, or diplomacy by other means; so, too, peace is the continuation of conflict, by economic, political, and diplomatic grand strategies and methods. Grand strategy, however, has to be seamless. Nowhere in aviation has this been more true than in the airline business.

Ironically, man-powered flight first became a reality, and then began to follow the age-old patterns: successful flights; then across the English Channel; then, in 1988, from Crete to Santorini—74 miles.

Alliances

The story of the wars of the airways is also one of pooling and alliances, mergers and purges, all inevitably leading to larger corporate bodies less and less dominated by visible giants such as Juan Trippe of Pan Am, and more and more controlled by financiers such as Lord King of British Airways. The problems of creating alliances encompass not only both the personal compatibility of chief executives and the agreement of labor unions, who may themselves be stockholders, as in United, but also the availability of landing slots at airports and the

satisfaction of anti-trust and anti-monopoly laws and regulatory bodies.

By 1996 it was becoming increasingly obvious that outside the old Communist bloc, by the year 2000 probably only five airline systems would exist. These would be dominated by United Air Lines, American Airlines, British Airways, a Lufthansa-led European grouping, and one or two Pacific-rim consortia. *Airline Business* magazine (July 2001) surveyed alliances among the top 200 airlines by traffic ranking. At that time, Swissair had twenty-four arrangements, United had nineteen, and British Airways sixteen, with a number of duplicated partners. Global alliances by 2003 were so important that airlines had added an alliance manager—strategist, technologist, and politician—operating in uncharted territory. Such a person had to grasp marketing, operations, labor, technology, and regulatory-body knowledge, as well as cultural awareness, creativity, and innovative ideas.

Both the Star and One-World alliances were seeking new members for 2003 and beyond with their SabreNet integrated systems. One-World was moving to sharing codes, terminals, hangars, and other services.

Another change caused by the arrival of the European Community was that the twenty-three nation European Joint Aviation Authority (JAA) began to unify licensing regulations. The need to specify regarding civil aircraft maintenance and engineering arose because of the differing requisites in the EC: in Germany and Britain engineers held licenses for specific work granted by training, examination, and experience, and worked for an organization certified as competent by the U.K. Civil Aviation Authority; in France, maintenance engineers, technicians, and mechanics had academic qualifications and training, held no licenses, but worked for a licensed engineering organization. Although the old International Civil Aviation Organization treaty allowed both systems, the new JAA required both as of 1997.

In the United States, the FAA moved to har-

monize with the new JAA so that it could also license approved maintenance stations outside the
country. Thus, it became easier for engineers to
move and to be exempted from new examinations
elsewhere as a step along the road to globalization.
However, though English is the language of aviation, engineers may be required to have local
language competency. Moreover, in the legal description of skills, language and tradition played a
part in definitions and interpretations. Part of the
new studies course included human-factors awareness for pilots, but there was no need seen for
duty-hours regulations.

And gender and glass-ceiling issues have recently seen some breakthroughs. British Airways
had an American woman heading its charter business until it was sold, and China Airlines is chaired
by a woman, as is Qantas. Modern aviation is so
large and complex that few individuals of either
gender appear in the spotlight.

Yet, one of the problems of contemporary airline alliances and policy is the more the executives
have become detached from the aircraft and people,
the more passenger anger has arisen, with resentment at being treated like cattle. Part of this has
been caused by airline management of lines in the
private sector seeking to recover from the depression of the early 1990s when they lost millions
in every currency. This led to changes in leadership and restructuring, especially at Air France
and Sabena, among others, as well as to cramming
in more seats. British Airways successfully both
privatized and made money until 1999–2000.
Then, in 2001, Swissair, the fabled bellwether of
successful management, went bankrupt. However, in February 2002 it emerged from the bankruptcy, and the revived airline restarted services in
April to 125 destinations in 59 countries, with 128
aircraft and 10,000 employees.

And even though some U.S. airlines have lost
staggering sums, most are now run by financiers
and can tap large fiscal resources, including after
September 11, 2001, the U.S. government. In addition, the executives judge all purchases by their
contribution to productivity, whether buying aircraft or labor contracts, and by 1995 had begun to
get back into the black after years in the red (1989–
95). By 1998 revenues were booming, but airline
leaders were concerned by the coming of another
cyclical recession triggered by Asian and global
failures. And although they thought they had with-
stood it successfully, due to traffic growth, 2001
saw a free-fall of 20 percent, even before 9/11.

In the Far East, a Pacific consortium appeared
to be a voluntary solution, a natural evolution also
from pooling. In the USSR, of course, there was
no problem, as Aeroflot was the only airline until after 1991 when both Commonwealth of Independent States lines and private rivals appeared.
Nevertheless, the winds of Glasnost—the policy
of openness—swept it, too, in early 1988 with
massive reorganization and much more autonomy
to its divisions in order to create self-reliance and
economy in its massive fleet of 3,500 planes, from
crop dusters to jets. In 2003, the future was still
speculative.

Up until the late 1980s, China National Aviation Corporation (CNAC) was a holding company. It then spun off seven regional companies,
which provincial governments were allowed to
supplement with their own airlines. In China, the
multitude of new airlines came up against rivalry
in the economic crisis that swept Asia at the end
of the 1990s. The Civil Aviation Administration
of China (CAAC) had been commanded to consolidate the ramshackle industry with talk of a
compulsory merger of China Southern Airlines
(CSA) and Air China (AC). In June 1999, CSA
requested that trading of its shares in Hong Kong
and New York be suspended and then admitted
the rumor of merger was true.

In 1998, of the more than thirty airlines in
China, only four made profits in the wake of the
boom turned bust. Beijing ordered an end to fare
wars and a moratorium on new purchases.

The China Southern Airlines-Air China merger

was designed to allow Air China to float shares. Otherwise, as their headquarters are 2,000 miles apart, no economic benefits are to be seen. The State Council, in supporting the merger plan, was thought to want to use it to force alliances on the lesser companies, who resist because of provincial politics. Thus, China National Aviation Corporation was back on the scene as of 1995 as a holding company.

Undoubtedly the market is there, with 27.39 million enplanements in the first half of 1999. Tightened cost controls have brought benefits, offset by the cost of new aircraft. The CAAC has to weigh restructuring against the benefit of alliances with Delta and Northwest, the former being allied with Air France. Others have ties to American, Qantas, and Air Nippon. To be borne in mind is the projection that the largest boardings in the world will be in Asia and the Pacific.

Meanwhile, gaining momentum in 2002 was the idea that the TransAtlantic Common Aviation Area should come into being as a fully deregulated market.

CREW TRAINING

Pilot training and the size of the aircrew force needed by both airlines and the armed services has always been a "Barbed-wire Strand" proposition. Since at least World War II, assumptions as to forecast needs have proved to be wrong. First a war surplus affected projections, then, as that eroded, a more rapid growth in traffic than expected occurred, with both flight and duty-time limitations for aircrew at the end of the 1950s. The big jets followed and another rise in traffic that has continued with occasional recessions to the present. In addition, the trend, which actually started at the end of the 1920s with the autopilot, has led to reduced cockpit workloads and only two pilots for aircraft that once had three.

But by the mid-1980s the counter-trend came with the new very-long-range (VLR) machines

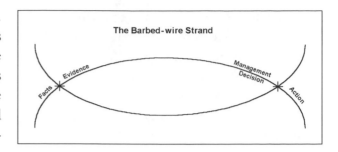

such as the 747-400 and the Airbus 330-340 series, whose fourteen- to sixteen-hour non-stop flights, longer than the allowed duty time, required two crews. And as after the end of the Cold War, when air forces shrank, so the major airlines had to worry once again about the source and cost of jet-trained pilots or raid the commuter and regional pools. Moreover, as Asian and other Pacific Rim companies such as Singapore Airlines have expanded, they have drawn qualified English-speaking pilots to their systems by rewards and promotions. By 1996, the push was on to train Asian pilots in places such as Australia and the United States, where good weather and space, as well as up-to-date facilities, were available.

Aircrew training and certification was basically of the hands-on in-the-air type until the 1960s. It was true that the primitive Link trainers had been used from early World War II for instrument-flying training, but after the war, simulators began to appear, which saved the airlines not only expensive flying hours but also were much safer. With three-axis motion and realistic "scenery," pilots and crew members could be brought up to proficiency level and then needed fewer hours in the air to be certificated, especially in glass cockpits.

However, one real safety problem that cannot fully be handled in a simulator because of lack of G forces are upset events, such as an uncontrolled roll to an inverted position. Loss of control in flight (LOCIF) resulted in the destruction of 577 aircraft in the United States during 1996–2000. This has been blamed upon the failure of the FAA over the last thirty years to insist upon the inclusion of spinning and other disorienting events during training.

Simulators are an expensive necessity. Airlines usually have their own if their fleets are large enough, or they and others send their pilots to specialist schools such as Flight Safety International. The business is steady and about eighty new simulators were by 2001 being created annually.

By the 1980s, companies could use simulators for much proficiency work, including in recent years attempts to fill the pilot shortage by retraining engineers. Alitalia, however, in 1983 found this not useful, for true compatibility between pilots, copilots, and cockpit management were not sorted out with the simulator. However, TWA, taking its flight engineers back into the right-hand seat, had more success when it treated them as *ab initio* students.

Lufthansa research at the end of the twentieth century revealed that not just crew resource management was needed, but also socialization. Five times as many flight-crew mistakes occurred as opposed to technical problems. The basic friction came from imbedded personality characteristics—poor communication, inadequate information management, deficient relationships, and diminished capabilities. In 1995, the FAA began to revise pilot flight- and duty-time regulations, but not even a draft had appeared by 2002.

Having drained their own pilot pools, the majors started on the 173 U.S. commuter lines. As a result, the latter were by mid-1988 experiencing up to a 70 percent annual turnover, even with the added resource of female cockpit crews. To deal with this new problem, Flight Safety International embarked upon a $100 million program to build simulators for commuter aircraft. These machines cost $4 to $5 million, much more than commuters can afford, but licensing requirements compelled them to send crews on a tuition-fee basis.

By the 1980s, the World War II group of pilots was gone. In 1980, U.S. pilots on the FAA rolls peaked at 827,071, but by 1986 had dropped to 709,168. Significantly, airline pilots showed a healthy increase, rising from 304,747 in 1973 to 410,079 in 1986. Non-pilot numbers during this time increased as well. By 1999, however, the airlines were threatened with a shortage again of qualified pilots for 2000 resulting from the sixty years-of-age grounding rule (insisted upon by the U.S. Federal Aviation Administration, but not by others), and because such careers were no longer considered quite as attractive. For the pilot, the irregular hours impinged on family life; and for the airlines, recruiting was sporadic and the quality of candidates low, and initial training costs were too great. In addition, information technology beckoned. The Barbed-wire Strand being at work, Boeing in 2002 predicted that the pilot shortage will last to 2008 and then get more serious. This is not expected to hit the majors as seriously as the regional carriers, whose pilot experience level upon hiring will probably drop from 1,500 to 500 hours, with a consequent rise in accidents.

But not only were aircrew in short supply periodically. Earlier, in the 1960s, BOAC had trouble hiring heavy-vehicle drivers for fuel bowsers and aircraft movers. In 2000, the airlines began to envisage a shortage of mechanics and, as in RAF Bomber Command in 1944, a severe shortage of avionics technicians. For the shortage in all of these specialties, the airlines were blamed for lack of foresight and unwillingness to create training centers now that the air forces no longer were a source of educated help. And as always, tuition at existing schools was above many willing entrants' abilities to pay.

Issues also arose in the airliner cabins. The lack of individual passenger responsibility led by the mid-1990s to the belief that cabin attendants were there to attend to "creature-comfort" needs rather than their ultimate safety. A public so well traveled and unconcerned about the likelihood of an emergency tended to ignore the routine safety announcements and requirements.

Another new commercial concern to airlines, which arose in 2001, was the likelihood of lawsuits from passengers who had experienced deep-vein thrombosis—blood clots in the legs caused by eight or more long hours in their seats. These

Civil Aviation

suits became a further detriment to air travel. By 2002 airlines were exploring the necessary proactive solutions. The issue pits scientific data versus anecdotal experience. By 2002, Boeing's latest 747-400ER boasted a medically correct interior for long-distance passengers.

LESSONS: SPARES, MAINTENANCE, AND SAFETY

A rough rule of thumb is that approximately 20 percent above the cost of an aircraft has to be allowed for initial spares that must be positioned within twenty-four hours at the required installation facility. Another is that the costs of fuel and maintenance will equal original capital cost in nine years.

In the period since 1945, a gradual evolution in aircraft maintenance had taken place, accelerated in the late 1950s by the arrival of the jet airliner. First came "lifing" of the airframe to 30,000 hours, rebuildable to 60,000 hours, and then this was expressed in either pressurization cycles or landings. Next components were also lifed so that progressive replacement of parts could coincide with annual overhauls or be scheduled for exchange during returns to the main base, working space on board being limited. And, finally, as the "C" (check) interval extended from the 2,000 hours of the mature 707 to the 4,500 hours of the 747 and of all the A-300 series, the system was changed in 1984 to be in accord with the Certificate of Airworthiness (C of A) category, so that the Airbus A-310 came on service with a "not to exceed one year" maintenance check, rather than an operational limitation. Concurrently, engines went from a time between overhaul of 1,200 to 1,800 hours for the pistons to the 14,000 hours of the Rolls-Royce Darts with their inspect-and-replace as needed philosophy, to the big jets that have now passed 30,000 hours in service or five years on the wing. Airframes and engines as well as other parts reflect the growing reliability of late twentieth-century aeronautical technology. In 2002, maintenance and repair organizations (MRO) were being affected by delayed inspections as well as delayed payments for work already done. The top thirty maintenance and repair organization companies in North America, Europe, and Asia supplied 75.1 million man-hours in 2001.

On the other hand, the demand to convert MD-11s to freighters was strong, but the systems of the 1960s DC-10s were too antiquated to be attractive without a complete rebuild, due to the recent electronics/computer revolution.

Safety has improved remarkably, as aviation is the most regulated and supervised of all industries. In the 1950s the worldwide accident rate was 30 per million departures; in 1997 it was only 1.4. Aviation personnel are safety conscious, but accidents do and will happen—yet rarely, percentage-wise, are they fatal. Air transport is far safer than the drive to the airport. In 1930, eighty-eight domestic scheduled air carrier accidents occurred in the United States, with a rate of 28.2 fatalities for every 100 million passenger miles flown. In 1950, thirty-nine accidents occurred per million miles, and the rate was 1.1. By 1970 the air accident rate was 0.8 versus 26.9 for motor vehicles. In 1985 the air accident rate was 0.5 and the motor vehicle rate was 19.2. In 1970, when total airline fatalities were less than 200, motor vehicle accidents had killed 54,633 people.

World airline accident rates declined significantly at the end of the century. Of the 778 people killed in 2001, 351 died in the four aircraft hijacked on September 11, and roughly another 3,000 on the ground on that day. The hijackings of the 1950s, including three airliners to Dawson's Field, Jordan, in 1970, did not generally involve human casualties. That changed in 1986. Hijackings always had been political, but from 1986 on the terrorists were state-sponsored.

And although the runway collision of two loaded 747s at Santa Cruz, Tenerife, occurred in 1977, killing 577, procedural rules have yet to be agreed to prevent such linguistic mix-ups. Bureaucracies move like treacle. Of much concern also was the declining safety record of the USSR, which started to slide in 1984 and did not begin to improve until 1992—which, of course, affected insurance premiums.

Then, too, in 2001 in the United Kingdom it was found that to cut costs pilots were being told to omit contingency fuel from their calculations on the grounds that it was to be used, not to be kept as a reserve against the unforeseen. In other circumstances, the 1996 TWA 800 accident and the Swissair 100 crash, and concern regarding the integrity of internal wiring, led to the development of NORA-based (National Office of Research Analysis) systems to check up to 5,000 wires and locate a fault to within one centimeter.

Safety consciousness on the part of all personnel is related to serviceability or availability. Remarkable strides have been made in the last three decades with the U.S. Navy, for example, reducing accidents from 3,348 pcr 100,000 flying hours in 1956 to 3.4 in 1987. And airlines have in the same period improved reliability by instrument—blind-landing—systems that allow aircraft actually to touch down in Category III conditions when the pilots' heads are literally still in the fog. This has been an economic necessity, with planes carrying up to 400 to 550 passengers, as on Air Nippon's domestic 747s, on tight schedules and with tons of cargo, and all the while depreciating at the bank by the minute.

The European Joint Aviation Authority was expected to have a single safety body in place by 2003, if nationalism could be overcome.

In the 1990s, concern was with the safety of twin-jet operations across the Atlantic, Pacific, and Indian oceans; in the twenty-first century, the focus was on long-range operations (LROPS) over environmentally hostile uninhabited areas of the world such as on trans-polar flights. It was debatable whether or not diversion in some of these regions was possible at all.

Thus far there has been no ditching of a large jet airliner, but on August 24, 2001, a Canadian A-330 ran out of fuel flying to Lisbon and glided to a safe landing in the Azores. The cause was a fuel leak and crew mismanagement of the subsequent emergency; if procedures had been followed, the aircraft could have made Lisbon safely.

The U.S. decision in 2002 to close in 2004 the mid-Pacific Johnston Atoll airfield posed new problems for trans-Pacific airlines operating twin-jet ETOPS aircraft, as did the imminent closure of Midway Island. No solution was in sight in mid-2002.

And birds continue to be an accident potential, especially if there is a failure to warn aircrew of their presence. The only USAF Boeing E-3B surveillance plane to crash was brought down just after takeoff in 1995 at Elmendorf Air Force Base, Alaska, by geese ingested into the port engines.

In Overview

The extraordinary growth of the airlines puts the Higham-Bonwell thesis into focus again—that while passenger and freight growth are geometric, facilities growth is arithmetic. The apparent solution to the gridlock in slots is larger and larger aircraft—thus the appeal of the Airbus A-380. According to Airbus in 1999, the world by 2018 will need 48 aircraft of 1,000 seats, 22 of 800 seats, 372 of 600 seats, 560 of 500 seats, and 302 80-ton freighters. Boeing by contrast sees the market as 360 aircraft of 500 seats and 570 of 400 to 499 seats. Airbus optimistically sees a market of 1,510 aircraft; Boeing sees a market of 930 including freighters.

The 2000 census in *Flight International* indicates that of the 14,341 Airbus and Boeing commercial airliners in service, 10,347 were from Seattle rather than from Toulouse, France.

The most numerous aircraft type was the 737, with 4,602 machines in service; the runner-up was the Airbus A-320, with 1,264. The third most prolific producer is Bombardier of Canada, with 401 CRJs and 513 Dash 8/Qs (formerly DHC-8).

Bombardier holds 45 percent of the total regional jet backlog of orders.

SEPTEMBER 11, 2001 — "9/11"

The media made much of the events of September 11, 2001, because of the spectacular nature of the coverage of the World Trade Center demise and the Pentagon crash. The casualties in the end were some 3,000, of an overwhelming possible 50,000. The shock to the United States was that the country was no longer immune to foreign attack. However, the security measures that subsequently were introduced and were claimed to change the world forever were only what Europe had put in place since the air hijackings of 1966. The media hype was reminiscent of the false furor about the coming of Y2K. Without diminishing the tragic loss of human life, the 1966 and the 2001 incidents, in fact, emphasize continuity and change, not dramatic alterations any more disruptive than a major winter storm. Risk management and common sense needed to be applied to the aftermath of 9/11. A somewhat similar phenomenon has long existed at sea—that of piracy. In 2001, 330 piracy incidents occurred worldwide, primarily against merchantmen. When losses have exceeded 10 percent of values, governments have acted.

On September 11, the United States went sky-silent, except for USAF and USN patrols. Canadian airports were full of diverted trans-Atlantic aircraft. But after the two days of enforced grounding, people should have wondered about results of the constant media coverage and the emotional impact on the American sense of freedom, as well as the ripple effects of the economic shock upon the already fragile aircraft industry. In the aftermath of 9/11 the USAF scrambled protective flights, but four months later reassessed the action in view of the wastage and consumption of airframe and engine hours and aircrew fatigue. Up to January 15, 2002, 13,651 such sorties had been flown with 200 aircraft on alert. Of these, 9,482 were by fighters, 3,427 by refueling aircraft, and the rest on support missions.

Immediately after 9/11, 5,692 U.S. airline pilots were furloughed—six percent of the 94,571 active airline pilots. But at the same time, Air National Guard units needed many pilots for twenty-four hour alerts and patrols.

The FAA in the United States after 9/11 lost its control of security screening. By 2002, questions were raised as to the competence of its training and the abilities of its inspectors who felt they were inadequately prepared (50 percent said they did not understand their checklist).

Britain was convinced by 9/11 that security of both aviation and information systems had to be globalized. But, in addition, airports have to be modernized, as does the U.K.'s transportation system.

The effects of 9/11 were worldwide. Wet-lease cargo carriers—those who contracted for the fuel and crew, along with the aircraft—were hard hit in a market already overcrowded. Australia's Qantas Airways, for example, had to cut capacity 11 percent as loads shrank 10–20 percent. Older 747s were retired and staff cut by 2,000, and large numbers were moved to domestic operations. And meanwhile, Qantas was trying to finish the acquisition of the bankrupt rival Ansett, which had shut down in September 2001, leaving thirty communities without service. The Qantas chairwoman was harshly critical of proposed powers to be granted to the Australian Consumer Competition Commission—the question being what was legitimate business-efficient practice versus anticompetitive behavior.

In November 2001 Sabena folded with $2 billion in debts; it is now part of SN Brussels Airlines. It had blamed Swissair, which also went under, while TAP, Aer Lingus, and Olympic were in precarious positions as no major had the finances to adopt them. And the low-cost carriers were cutting into mainland European business. Thus, the final collapse of the "chosen instruments"—the major airlines—of the 1950s was expected. The events of 2001 merely hastened the European airline crisis that had long been brewing. Analysts believed that only British Airways, Air France, and Lufthansa would survive into 2003. Mergers were thought less likely than alliances, due to the cloying effect of government regulations—a retarding nationalism as opposed to consolidation in other industries.

A two-year sales dip had occurred after the 1991 Persian Gulf War, and manufacturers forecast the same after 9/11. Following the decline, however, a return to an 8 to 10 percent annual growth rate was expected.

Distrust of the U.S. airlines was already evident in 2001 from their failure to tell the truth about delays for fear that passengers would transfer to other companies, and from computer projections set too optimistically.

In the aftermath of 9/11 and the severe traffic decline, suggestions were made to revive passenger interest: easier booking procedures, better parking at airports, shorter waits at ticket counters, on-time arrivals and departures, speedy and reliable recovery of checked bags, likelihood of non-stop flights, and fares that were equitable to all. These suggestions, of course, mirrored what had not been practice.

In Russia, the airline system had already collapsed, since 1999, when Aeroflot's passenger boardings fell from 90 million to 21 million. This hurt the maintenance and repair organizations accustomed to Soviet bounties. Moreover, as the factories stopped producing, they began to steal MRO work. And cash-short airlines practiced creative accounting, while the military had no funds at all for readiness.

The post 9/11 slump was being handled differently by Boeing, whose headquarters moved from Seattle to Chicago in 2001, and Airbus. Boeing downsized the company with layoffs; Airbus reduced with slowdowns and spreading the work to retain skills by reducing overtime, encouraging early retirements, not replacing departing workers, and cutting the trainees. Labor laws in Germany, France, and Spain make it difficult to lay off workers. The United Kingdom, however, is more flexible; workers will still receive the same wages, but will get compensatory time off. Generally a thirty-five hour week was in place in 2002, and the benefits should be added to by cost-cutting.

The fateful 9/11 affected airlines and airplane makers, and it began to ripple throughout the industry and its ancillary suppliers and manufacturers as Airbus and Boeing, Rolls-Royce, General Electric, Pratt & Whitney, and SNECMA laid off workers and slowed production.

Engine makers, now spread worldwide, after 9/11 saw their forecasts evaporate and their workforces slashed between 13 and 17 percent. Rolls-Royce cut 3,000 out of 28,000 workers, of whom 1,200 were released at Rolls-Royce Deutschland (BMW) in Germany and at its Allison Engine Company in the United States. On the other hand, China was not affected and at once began ordering.

In the aftermath of 9/11 and Boeing's cutback of production, Japanese manufacturers were expected to see a 20–30 percent decline in revenues in 2002 and beyond.

By early 2002, the combined effect of the U.S. and global downturn, of 9/11, and of the subsequent drop in traffic, was that stored aircraft rose from 5.2 percent of the world's airliners to over 12 percent. Where in 1990 482 were parked in the desert in the U.S. Southwest, this had risen by the end of 2001 to 2,076. By early 2002, United Air Lines had an idle fleet of 113. American had 39 stored and 67 idle; British Airways 24 and 33; and Iberia 11 and 43.

The "white-tail" fleet in the deserts changed in the latter quarter of the twentieth century. In the first thirty years, of the 1,400 aircraft stored, 1,200 had been scrapped due to age, excessive noise, and high fuel consumption. A few of these remain. Of the second group of 5,900 aircraft, twenty to thirty years old, 1,850 have been scrapped, 1,250 are parked, and 2,800 are active, currently in production; perhaps half of the parked will be scrapped. And the third group, of new and twenty-year-old transports, consists of 11,750, of which only 100 have been scrapped; 11,000 are active, and 650 are stored. Perhaps most significant is that the second group had a 30 percent lower fuel burn, whereas the third group has a 70 percent lower burn than the original 707s and DC-8s.

At the desert facilities, maintenance companies concentrate on aircraft likely to be recalled, and thus, retrofits, security upgrades, and reactivation have promised sound business for some years to come.

The white-tailing of airliners in the Arizona desert, together with used airliners being returned to manufacturers, had by 2003 become a boon to economy lines seeking low capital-cost planes, and to freight operators who saw the chance to buy cheap and convert eight- to ten-year-old rather than fifteen- to twenty-year-old airframes.

Foreign air forces were also finding gold in the desert, especially for such less competitive needs as anti-submarine warfare and maritime-patrol aircraft.

The fallout of 9/11, following on that of the Asian economic crisis, finally forced Asian carriers to contemplate consolidation and alliances, the loss of confidence in air travel, and the region's own economic difficulties, as well as the entry of the three newly consolidated Chinese airlines into the field—China Southern, Air China, and China Eastern. These three will be the only major Chinese carriers. The counter has to be alliances of the other Asian lines, such as possibly Garuda Indonesia, Malaysia Airlines, Cathay Pacific, Thai International, and Qantas—and perhaps Singapore.

A measure of the emergence of China from its old Red regime was that by the twenty-first century its air travel was growing at double-digit rates, and the country was the largest potential air transport market in Asia, with a population of 1.3 billion. By 2003, the Airbus A-340-500 could be billed as the longest-ranged airliner in the world at 10,000 miles, and three were being leased by Cathay Pacific for its non-stop Polar services to New York. Airbus argued that its operating costs were significantly below those of the rival 747-777 family.

The aviation industry ranks at the top of the world's industries with the airlines, and when combined with tourism has an enormous economic and pacific influence. The evolution and expansion of the industry is a fascinating study. The transition from the Wright Brothers to the stable airplane—the BE-2C scout plane—took seven years. The shift from operational biplanes in 1940—the Gloster Gladiator, the Fiat CR-42, and the Swiss Air Force Fokker DVII—to the jet Me-262 took less than four years. Conversely, extensive lags have occurred between the flight of the prototype and its last operational sortie, such as the Spitfire in 1936 and its final flight in the Royal Air Force in 1954, or the USAF B-52 Stratofortress, which first flew in 1954 and is not expected to be withdrawn until 2020—when it will be twice as old as its crews! Grand-strategic concept and political economy have been part of this equation, and inextricably part of the aviation industry.

CHAPTER 9

PATTERNS, PHILOSOPHIES, AND LESSONS

Up to the mid-twentieth century, advocates and supporters of air power tended to claim that it operated without precedents; their hatred of the older armed services had blinded them to realities of historical, technological, and corporate human experience. Politicians in various nationalistic ways shared these sentiments, and especially fears and myths of competition. And although the military forces have always been patriotic, an amicable international community of airmen has existed, even between former enemies.

The most important principles in military operations that have needed to be observed have been those of grand strategy, that seamless line of policy of which all else is the instrument, overtly or covertly.

Doctrine governs organization and structure, procurement, training, and tactics. It has to be related to strategy and, of course, grand strategy, as well as politics, diplomacy, economy, finance, and manpower because when war comes, it may either be limited, within a "business as usual" framework or, in a total conflict, it may be all-encompassing.

Doctrine has to provide basic guidance and purpose, but at the same time be resilient in the face of fresh technology, thought, situations, or combat lessons. Sound doctrine is based on a clearly established organizational base from which flexible operational action can be launched within the limits of national or inter-allied capabilities.

The early apostles of air power were full of idealism, but the attitudes of airmen have from the first contained a nineteenth-century thread of a quick, clean, mechanical, impersonal solution to problems with which others have struggled for years. Over time airmen have become more professional and more realistic.

Military use of air power has sometimes tended to prolong wars and threaten peace, yet the industrial apparatus needed to support air power in all its phases has been a stimulant to progress and employment. In the twentieth century, air power became a part of the political, economic, industrial, scientific, technological, medical, social, and ideological life of almost all peoples, and any interpretation of it must take into account the national characteristics and state of development of each nation and alliance studied. Much as electricity was a symbol of prestige in the second half of the nineteenth century, so air power became such a symbol in the twentieth, perhaps to be replaced by the total conquest of space in the twenty-first. The attack and defense ping-pong has been the same old sort of race as between guns and armor in the navies of the 1860–1945 days.

As airfields became vulnerable, by the late 1930s revetted dispersals to protect individual planes outdoors came into use, and anti-aircraft guns were developed and distributed. During mobile warfare from 1942, portable airfields were laid and airfield defense came into being, against enemy forces left behind on the ground, and to man anti-aircraft positions.

In the Cold War, Vietnam, and the Arab-Israeli Wars, and in Iraq and other vulnerable places, hardened shelters were constructed against which specially lethal "punch"—deep penetration—weapons were used. Other forms of hardened shelters were the U-boat pens of World War II and the underground hangars of the Swiss and Swedish air forces.

The desire for lethality also saw the development of mixed loads for aircraft and better explosives, such as the petrol/air bomb to provide stunning bursts over ground troops or the Exocet missile used at sea. Defenses also turned to anti-missile missiles to defeat the Exocet and, in 1991, to the Nike to down Iraqi V-2 type Scuds or very low-level, nap-of-the-earth sorties to destroy the immobile missile launchers.

Apart from the long-standing ground radar-based air-defense system of 1939–45 combining guns, aircraft, balloons, and sector control, by the late 1960s the airborne early warning (AEW) command and control aircraft had emerged and its evolution to an airborne command post using C^{4}I. At the end of the twentieth century, however, radar—unless of the look-down sort, beneath the line of flight—still had difficulty detecting enemy aircraft hugging the earth's surface.

In all of the above developments, computers since 1945 have played a significant role, from design calculations and drawings to the operation and direction of aircraft and their weapons systems.

To achieve lethality, airframes had to be developed or modified from the 1930 ability to carry 500-pound general-purpose bombs to packs of incendiaries, then to 22,000-pound armor and concrete-piercing special weapons; and the evolution, as well, in delivery techniques, has continued to the twenty-first century, yet sometimes with unpleasant postwar consequences.

Aviation has demanded a linking of resources, technology, and manpower, and as aircraft have become increasingly more mechanical to operate, and more technologically sophisticated, it has been natural to concentrate on the machine, while the importance of the human beings controlling it has appeared to shrink in proportion. Yet it must be remembered that almost all aircraft only obtain their impact from human control, whether it be by a national leader or by the pilot alone, all made possible by their ground organization. Aircraft are the visible symbols of air power, and it is not easy to think of that without envisaging warplanes or airliners as agents of destruction and construction. By the twenty-first century, the unmanned aerial vehicle—the UAV—carrying sensors, video cameras, and real-time transmission of data, is now changing the scene.

Theories concerning the use of air power in war evolved as the air service itself expanded. Ideally an air war calls for the quick seizure of air superiority, or control of the air, and consequent ability to attack any target within range and prevent the enemy from doing likewise. The victor can undertake grand-strategic bombing in such a way that he can break the enemy's will to fight before surface forces meet in a decisive engagement. At the least, the victor can hold air superiority over a limited area, so that his intelligence-gathering, strategic, and tactical forces can proceed unmolested and with air support as needed. His reconnaissance aircraft and his forward air controllers are free to come and go, and his movements are screened.

These ideals were set forth as early as 1915 by the Englishman F. W. Lanchester, a realist who knew that the implementation of many of these concepts was years in the future. Before the end of the First World War, P. R. C. Groves and Sir Frederick Sykes in Britain, and William "Billy" Mitchell in the United States, carried these theories to their logical extreme of expecting the next war to be won entirely by a preemptive air strike. In Italy, General Giulio Douhet and Count Caproni set out a more concrete, if bombastic, theory of war based upon Italian geographical considerations. The Soviets took a somewhat different, more Fullerite, approach in that they conceived of air power as unleashed on a front of perhaps 40 kilometers to hammer a hole through enemy lines in a supremely tactical air effort.

In post-1918 debates over the role of aviation, airmen tended to make exaggerated claims about what they could do, claims that would not become reality until the advent of the atomic bomb. The major problem with air-power theory was that it was out of touch with the actualities of political economy and of the length of time it took to mobilize an industrial war machine—which by 1935 was eight years.

In the meantime, the more practical theorists were those in the American and Japanese navies who developed the tactical carrier air forces, and in the German *Blitzkrieg* and Soviet deep-battle staffs who created air-supported mechanized armies.

Even after the Second World War, air-power leaders failed to learn that war cannot be won by theories that concentrate on only one aspect of human relations. History has long shown that capital cities are not the only sources of national power, and that frontal assaults, perhaps the most obvious way in which to attack, are less successful than more indirect approaches. For air power, too, guerrilla tactics, as in the grand-strategic air offensive of 1939–45, may be the more fruitful.

Moreover, in a war, where any form of missile or anti-aircraft are used in mountainous terrain and in poor weather conditions, even modern air power may become ineffective.

REALITIES

History makes clear that the realities of time, place, equipment, airfields, logistics, higher direction, money, and national character must be taken into account, together with the principles of war, in the application of air power. And these realities are often governed by the progression of the Wave Cycle, Plateau, Bamboo Basket, Pipeline Purdah, Barbed-wire Strand, and Cube theories earlier hypothesized.

The anticipated war may not be the one that eventually has to be fought. But this depends upon whether the cause is nation-, state-, or alliance-threatening, or a "colonial" contest, and whether or not the issue is seen as a matter of honor or retaliation. Intractable limitations may result in border skirmishes, which neither side wishes to escalate to total victory—as relations between India and Pakistan seem to demonstrate.

The First World War was the original large air war, but the official histories of its air aspects were delayed, or in some cases not provided for at all. As a result, of almost all those who wrote about it before the Second World War, none looked at the conflict impartially. If they had done so, they might have learned significant lessons. The Germans observed some of these teachings because they had been defeated; control of their air forces was thus largely kept in the hands of the army in its covert stage, and those who were to lead the air forces later were soundly indoctrinated with the basic rules of warfare.

One lesson from World War I for nations that had air services was that unless the enemy possessed the power to do irreparable harm at any time and place, air superiority was only worth fighting for when it was needed to defend the nation, to cover a particular operation on the ground or at sea, or to protect reconnaissance sorties.

Far more significant than the heroic fighter aces were the forward air observers who in the First World War directed artillery shoots, and much more attention needed to be paid to their equipment, morale, and protection. Fighting for air superiority merely for the sake of fighting used up men and machines and resulted in high casualties that led to deficiencies later when pressed by the enemy. Combat fatigue was not recognized in World War I and parachutes not always permitted. Training was as important as fighting. Unnecessary wastage meant that lesser theaters could not be supplied with air support from trained crews, yet it was in just such indirect approaches to victory that the greatest chance of success might lie.

The use of long-range grand-strategic bombing paid dividends where home defenses were not organized and populations unused to facing war, as in Britain during 1915–18. Relatively small forces could be used to effect in tying down enemy air power that might have been applied elsewhere. The mere threat acted as a deterrent and an inhibitor. But it was a violation of the principles of war to continue such attacks in the face of mounting opposition, for the defense eventually always got the better of the offense as long as the attacking forces pursued repetitive tactics.

With the Great War being regarded as an aberration, much as the Korean conflict would be many years later, few drew rules from it, especially airmen. Only in 1933 were the lessons of 1914–18 anti-aircraft experience released by the Air Ministry in London for their pilots' benefit, and with little impact.

The First World War also provided an example of the seesawing technical battle that could be expected in any air war and made clear the need for repair and salvage units. And, finally, the use of air power at sea had been worthwhile both offensively and defensively and might, in fact, have been more valid than continual fighting over a fixed battlefront.

The Ethiopian campaign of 1935–36 showed that air power could dominate but could not win a war in unsuitable territory, and that the use of bombs, and even gas, might produce significantly adverse reactions among neutrals.

In colonial operations, such as those of the Spanish, French, and British, reliability was perhaps more important for aircrews than their aircraft's effect upon the natives, for to fall into hostile hands could be excruciating.

But it was in Spain during 1936–39, and in China during 1931–45, that the lessons of war were again written clearly. The performance of fighters and bombers was tested and their weak-nesses observed. In China, attacks on enemy airfields that obeyed the rules of concentration and economy of force were apt to produce quicker results than grand-strategic raids against distant industrial targets. The war in China also showed that aircraft carriers could be used as mobile airfields that enjoyed relative immunity to land-based aviation, while naval air arms were particularly effective because of their training in long-range navigation and in striking pinpoint moving targets. The air-power revolutions of the 1930s have to include those at sea in both aircraft and in carriers and the doctrine to make the whole land-and-sea-based naval air arm effective.

Many of these same lessons were reinforced by experience in the Second World War, but with some new twists. The opening phases showed that air power was a gambler's weapon, and that coordinated air and ground forces used in a *Blitzkrieg* could punch their way to victory. In such dynamic campaigns, grand-strategic bombing by the victim was too slow to be of any use unless the attacker had to pass through blockaded bottlenecks. Events in Spain, China, Poland, and France demonstrated that even a technologically superior air force was no match for attacking air forces supported by ground forces that could overrun airfields and facilities—a tactic not possible beyond the English Channel.

The Battle of Britain reinforced the lesson that the defense could master the offense if enough time and money were devoted to the problem, while also making it apparent that an indirect approach might be the most effective even in air warfare. Because the air had no boundaries, strategists were sometimes misled by the ability to switch air power from one part of the war zone to another, sometimes finding themselves trapped by that very flexibility. The Germans were overconfident of flexibility and came to grief in the Soviet Union, because in spite of their by then limited transport force, they could not make *Blitzkrieg* work against a foe who could trade space for time and weather.

A grand-strategic bomber force was no substitute for dynamic tactical victory when actively engaged with the enemy in the field; but on the other hand, when the armies were not in action, grand-strategic bombing, such as attacks on British ports, was mistakenly neglected. Grand-strategic bombing campaigns, however, tied down enemy manpower in defenses and in repairs, and weakened the workforce by absenteeism, and ultimately eroded fighter defenses.

Both in the Soviet Union and in the Middle East, air forces with partly or wholly obsolescent equipment but professional morale and skills were able to stay in the field and harass the enemy because neither side had sufficient force with which to eliminate the other. Just as the U-boat at sea played a guerrilla game, so air power also followed the practice of war as seen by the Spanish guerrillas of 1809–14 and of Mao in China to 1949.

Air power could be used either grand strategically or strategically as a guerrilla force, thus posing the same problems for the defense as those faced by counter-guerrilla commanders, by attacking at the time and place of their own choosing and reaching their destination by devious routes—and by refusing battle under adverse conditions.

Gradually the tide of victory in any particular theater turned in favor of the side that could muster the largest air force and maintain it in excellent flying condition. Ultimately this meant a combination of industrial might, economic and military planning, training, maintenance and spares, repair and salvage, logistics, "manpower," and morale. The Germans could have won the Battle of Germany if they had concentrated on these aspects rather than dissipating the *Luftwaffe* over too many theaters; but they did not grasp the lessons of their own air campaign against Britain in the First World War. And they endured personality conflicts.

Additionally, the nations that won were those able to field highly trained forces, and that they were able to do so depended upon their recognition of the importance of instructors, fuel supplies, training facilities, and their ability to keep these beyond the range of the enemy. Both the Germans and the Japanese flew their trained units too hard, failed to recirculate personnel from them through the instructional system, and ended up with too few well-educated pilots at a time when their fighter forces faced both sophisticated new aircraft and seasoned enemy pilots.

The 1945 Burma campaign showed that air supply could free an army of traditional support, thus giving it a new speed of movement in difficult country, especially when there was no opposition in the air.

The war at sea from 1939 to 1945 emphasized the need for equipment designed for naval work, for viable carrier doctrine in both attack and defense, and for an understanding of maritime and mercantile strategy. Carrier doctrine could only succeed when supported by trained airmen and modern naval aircraft. The Japanese were lulled by their success over China and thus trained few replacements, only to see their pilots and mechanics devastated by the battles of the Coral Sea and Midway. The use of air power at sea in the Second World War established techniques that the Japanese had used to a lesser extent off China, as carriers were employed to provide cover for landing forces and even strategic attack against shore targets.

Since 1945, that technique has been refined and in fact over-used off Korea, Vietnam, the Persian Gulf, and perhaps in Afghanistan since 2001, in that expensive carriers were kept continually engaged in a land war. In the later Second World War campaigns, carrier forces were used successfully as *Judo Blitzkrieg* weapons to strike through the line of defensive atolls to the vital centers; but up to the latter part of 1942, the outcome of a battle in several cases hung in the balance and was decided as much by luck and fate as by admiralship or equipment. Toward the end of the war, American massed forces were skillfully employed, and the long periods between major actions enabled training to be undertaken. Replenishment at sea helped make the U.S. carrier task forces vitally effective, and the Allies benefitted from new equipment constantly updated.

The lessons from the post–Second World War period are largely a repetition of those that should have been learned by that time. The Arab-Israeli Wars showed the flexibility of centralized air power and its variable rapier use, as well as the importance yet again of training, logistics, and maintenance. In contrast, in Vietnam and Soviet Afghanistan, air power was employed clumsily and without the "Higher Direction" appreciating its assets and limitations. The Persian Gulf War was an aberration, like others before it, in that the air weapon had an unusual amount of time to build up in-theater. It was a disaster, as peace did not eventuate. And by 2000, the no-fly zone over Iraq was losing Coalition support. Conversely, in Afghanistan in 2001–02, offshore air power proved very effective under special circumstances.

Air power has a vast potential for peace as long as it is seen as a balanced system and its massive application is quick; it cannot be dribbled out, because it costs by the second, and its psychological strength dissipates after the first sudden impact. Thus, to escalate its use on a gradual basis is akin to subjecting a body to steadily increasing doses of poison at a rate not exceeding its tolerance to absorb the toxic agent. In anti-guerrilla warfare, air power's flexibility, supply, and propaganda functions are the most important.

Intercontinental bombers and ballistic missiles, if used only in a deterrent manner, can create a stand-off that will prevent the world's self-destruction. But once the deterrent, or the karate blow, has failed, then assuming the situation does not escalate into nuclear war, air power becomes tactical. As such it is an extension of surface forces and must be used to enable them to fulfill their roles on land and at sea. And this is likely to remain the job of a manned rather than a missile force for some time to come, UAVs notwithstanding—for the problem of accuracy still remains, no matter how lethality grows.

The successful use of the world's air space has come evermore to depend upon command, control, communications, computers, and intelligence (C⁴I,) whether for military or civilian purposes.

Flying control had enjoyed a hothouse growth in the latter part of World War II because it was recognized that aircrew were extremely valuable and that airfields were no longer the property of the local air force lord of the manor, just as in the First World War it had been realized that national cooperation had to override professional views.

In the postwar world of civil aviation, increasingly airline and airway efficiency depended upon a much extended air-traffic control, especially given the endurance of jets. By 2003, the range of airliners and of air-refueled military machines made the whole world one air space through which each craft had to be guided and directed from taxiing out to taxiing in at the end of the flight.

Whereas before 1941 the airlines were barely competing with surface transport, except on long-distance routes, especially the trans-oceanic, the 1939–45 war created viable transport machines and, within twenty years, the jets as well as airfields worldwide. From then on commercial aviation expanded, and the refinements led by the 1990s to the trans-oceanic executive/business jet as well. In our contemporary world, the leading companies in dollar terms have become aircraft manufacturers, aerospace companies, and airlines, as well as telecommunications firms.

That this was possible was due to revolutionary, yet evolutionary, developments in all areas of aviation and their acceptance by the public and politicians. These developments both suppressed materialism as costs became too great and created new alliances. One of these corsortia was the French firm Airbus; another was the growing consolidation of national and international airlines and their working partnerships with competitors, only held up from time to time by regulators until the climate and necessity allowed them. Perhaps in 2001 typifying these developments was the demise of TWA, America's second overseas airline after

Pan American. So, too, was the formal naming of the Airbus A-3XX the A-380 in 2001 and its commitment for production. This left the other major aerospace company, Boeing, to consider very seriously its future via the 747-400X or another airliner.

Both passengers and cargo by the end of the twentieth century had grown exponentially so that on Thanksgiving weekend 2000 more than 17 million flew on airlines within the United States alone. And air cargo and parcel service worldwide have shrunk the world, again in part because computers can handle the paperwork and track delivery. By 2003 aviation and the world were very different from that which the Wright Brothers had known.

AIRCRAFT MANUFACTURING

As often noted, the history of the airlines has been that of air forces inverted. Airlines have both been constantly "at war," and in friendly sporting rivalry. Ironically, competition and success have depended upon the human element even more than in the air army, due to the technologically level nature of the playing field—so often the aircraft are but minor variants of the basic machines. And the managers of the rival companies have generally kept in sight the necessity for cooperation in surveys, pooling, and other arrangements, such as handling each others' flights abroad, as much as has been permitted by law and project needs.

Industrial and transportational ideals are as important as military goals in the use of air power; certainly there are lessons to be found in these two civil facets of the subject that cannot be overlooked. The cycles of war and peace are observable in air transport activity as much as in military-industrial operations. In a sense, competition in air transport means that the cycles within the airline industry are shorter and sharper than in the military, where major wars are occasional disturbances of the norms of peace and peacekeeping. It must be noted, however, that the enormous and necessarily long-term expense of jet aircraft versus limited budgets has caused a lengthening of the cycles or distances between wave crests: twenty-and thirty-year life cycles for aircraft types are common and for individual aircraft are to be expected (for low-use bombers, an 80-year life is planned).

The aircraft used by the airlines have reflected military developments and have usually been governed by the same cycles of obsolescence, although the controlling criteria have been passenger demand or acceptance, financial practices, and carrier cost, rather than theoretical or actual conflict. The airlines have paralleled the military services, too, in their need for equipment and facilities that are economically viable and that best suit a particular route and traffic system. From 1945 to the 1990s, the American dominance of the air transport market tended to provide a uniformity of equipment; but the exact numbers required and the patterns in which they have been used have been determined by a mixture of domestic and international political and capital considerations, International Air Transport Association rules and fare structures, passenger and freight demands, schedule requirements, labor contracts and affirmative action, and maintenance schedules.

For both airlines and manufacturers, planned or informed guesses about the future ten to twenty years ahead have played a vital role in their selection of equipment and in the stimulation and development of air traffic to turn projects into viable realities. Success or failure has to be measured in long-term assessments of profits and losses rather than in any narrow conception of victory. An early write-off of major new pieces of equipment may result in paper losses that must be countered by adequate profits. In a continuous war there should not be any such thing as a final victory or a conclusive defeat, but bankruptcies will happen. And even if an airline is run as some form of a national social service, the airline president is still a manager—a general—who must keep the confidence of his backers or stockholders, and make sustaining profits.

AIRLINE PATTERNS

Airlines have developed in relation to both finances and technology. At first they were dependent upon fiscal support either in terms of direct subsidies or through mail contracts. Their survival also depended upon controlling competition and upon clearing-house arrangements, as well as upon labor-saving devices and accident investigation, and upon improved technology—i.e. aircraft. Many of these developments were slow to evolve and did so differently in the United States and Europe. Elsewhere, until about 1935, the airlines were closely related to general aviation.

The technological revolutions of the 1930s created both reliable aircraft and profit-making companies, which were in some cases protected by regulatory bodies. Then World War II saw the U.S. airlines boosted by their involvement in priority transport work, worldwide experience, the proving of new reliable airliners, and the free training of potential crews, ending with the cheap availability of surplus aircraft. The European airlines, except for Aeroflot, were handicapped or almost destroyed by the war and governmental ignorance as to their potential.

Postwar the hoped-for boom in general aviation took a long time to develop, in part because other than in the United States there was devastation and lowered incomes, and lack of open spaces, or small populations as in Canada and Australia.

For the airlines there was little choice of equipment—mostly used American or new designs, which did not always suit needs. But air travel was still first class until the mid-1950s, when lower fares began to generate tourism. By the time the big jets came on in the 1960s, people had the incomes to be air-minded and airlines continued to grow at 14 percent per annum, give or take a recession or two.

The regulations and the subsidies of the prewar period were either phased out economically or intensified technically, and privatization offered a whole new financial approach to nationalized airlines and to facilities as well. That, however, did not make them immune to economic downturns and even bankruptcy, which also affected leasing and manufacturers.

Aviation operations have constantly tested management to be efficient—a still unsettled story. Airlines are still growing and have new markets, notably in India, China, the Russian Commonwealth of Independent States, and ultimately in Africa, as well as Latin America.

The challenge will be to evolve an efficient transportation system under a minimum of regulation and in spite of the weather, and to do so at acceptable costs.

TECHNICAL CONSIDERATIONS

The weapons acquisitions process reflects national political, economic, social, and ideological characteristics and perception of the "enemy," as much as historical backgrounds and the necessities of geography and grand-strategic realities.

Before World War II the Germans concentrated on standardizing designs and production for a short war, but then in wartime tried too many innovations while believing the Fatherland was immune to air attack. Hitler's personal whims delayed designs by insisting that all be able to dive-bomb.

In France, national turmoil and the late formation of the French Air Force (1933) and its running battle with the army left it short of money for engineering, maintenance, and manufacturing until too late, though by 1938 the aircraft industry had at last switched from workshops to production lines.

In Russia, the five-year plans had helped the forward-looking Red Air Force produce viable types until the Spanish Civil War experience forced the development of new designs, which were produced by the just-displaced aircraft industry behind the Urals. The Soviets favored low-level machines that could aid and protect the army and swamp the enemy by numbers alone, as there were no viable strategic targets within range.

The Japanese, like the Germans, enjoyed early success and only too late realized they had to develop new designs and production facilities.

The British came to the 1939 war with a rapidly developing and merging industry, but with too many designs (fifty-nine), and, like the French, with an abhorrence of tactical air forces. The realities of war converted RAF fighters to fighter-bombers. But all through the war the prewar bomber-deterrent concept drained resources, finances, and manpower. After victory, the realities of defense costs pushed a second round of industry mergers following that in the 1930s, until with NATO and European unity the aviation industry was consolidated into British Aerospace and projects were shared, from Concorde (1962–76) with France and later Germany and others. The French were determined from 1945 to recreate their glory and prestige and succeeded with Mirages and Airbuses, until in the 1990s superseded by the German DASA organization, soon absorbed into the European Aeronautic Defence and Space Company (EADS), as Europeanization began to subvert nationalism.

But it was in the United States that production was combined with design to create a significant series of advances in both military and civilian manufacturing. Revolutions, continuity, and change together with the Cold War, as in the USSR, kept the process accelerating. But fear and distrust of competition and of wealth—along with national suspicions and ill-educated, yet ambitious congressmen—and the creation of multiple layers of bureaucratic checks and balances gradually assembled an unwieldy machinery with quadrennial management turnover. This added to the costs and lead times of new weapons systems, which had to battle not only operational desires and complex specifications but bureaucratic red-tape to such an extent that new systems proved to be late, costly, and unreliable.

Westernizing the Russian industries after 1990 saddled their excellent design-bureau system with the need to seek capital as well as to manage factories, heretofore separate production entities. Without anti-Communist glasses it is possible to see that the Soviet aircraft operation was in many ways a successful development, like the U.S. Navy's China Lake—even when the Soviet leaders were imprisoned—with design divorced from manufacturing. By 2003 a much stronger, streamlined sector was emerging, a rationalization, linking design and manufacturing.

In China, the evolution of the industry and the airlines has reflected doctrinaire politics, by 2003 rapidly changing to a modern organization and structure, including Western alliances.

Since 1945, jet-engine power has increased more than forty-fold from 3,000 pounds of thrust to 120,000; aircraft weights have gone up twenty-fold; and Efficiency Ratings (ER) have increased from 100 to 11,000. On the military side, the fighter has grown from an ER of 0.9 to 300–500, yet the heavy bomber is still at its 1960 level and is slowly fading away. Where the future lies will depend upon how many peacekeeping ventures will have to be made against well-armed enemies, perhaps by UCAVs.

Success has come not necessarily from newer and better or more lethal weapons or systems, but from more plentiful aircraft and weapons allowing for greater coverage and impact. Above all, however, it has come from thoroughly trained air and ground crews, experienced commanders and staffs, and strong support services.

Modern peacetime may be an asset to professionalizing military-naval-air personnel, but shrinking budgets may also be debilitating. In contrast, airlines have cycles not of war and peace, but of recession and growth, with expertise furloughed in the former and in shorter supply in the latter.

The functions of air power have been and will continue to be to intimidate, to help ground forces and allies, to reduce ground casualties, and to avoid war. The question will remain as to whether air power alone can win wars, and whether there can be war without it, for aviation and air power in the twentieth century have been a paradox of growth and power to achieve efficiency and diminish labor while miniaturizing.

Aviation has been on the cutting edge of technology for much of the twentieth century. As with communications, the irony is that the more efficient technology gets, fewer and fewer people are needed to do the job. Paradoxically, at the same time, the more complex the systems get, the more people are needed to build and maintain the infrastructure. And the result—until maturity was reached on the commercial side, as opposed to the military—was a constant workforce, though by 2003, the manufacturing force, both blue and white collar, was being shrunk in an effort to cut costs and to get greater productivity.

Aviation could still be faulted in 2002 for its failure to communicate—to mechanics, engineers, and others involved—the essential safety information learned from accidents. And while a faulty data system also played a part, the use of outsiders to criticize the FAA was unusual.

Yet, despite all, aviation has the ability to bring people together in commerce and tourism, to help alleviate poverty, and thus to quell unrest by peace.

2003 AND BEYOND

In the early 1990s, after the end of the Cold War and of the Persian Gulf War, aviation went through one of its cyclical crises that drove down airline traffic, pushed fuel prices up, and saw the hope of a "peace dividend." But maintaining an older aircraft fleet did not bring great savings.

In the twenty-first century, cancellations and delayed deliveries, moth-balled whitetails, and over-capacity were driving prices down. Mergers, which lowered assessed values and made the selling of new machines much more difficult, were being halted again by fear of anti-trust laws in North America, Europe, China, and Australia. Keeping up flight frequencies while lowering ca-

pacity to improve load factors was hampered by scope clauses in pilots' contracts, which limit the ratio of smaller to larger aircraft in the fleet.

Cost-cutting does not automatically reduce fuel consumption or fuel expense, as prices are linked to both the cost of crude and to volatile Middle Eastern and Central Asian politics. Realistic evaluation of the terrorist and world situation amidst the Afghanistan 2001–02 incursion no doubt concluded that an attack on Saddam Hussein's Iraq would raise oil prices and cause airline passenger boardings to drop, as would hostilities in Indonesia, the Philippines, Somalia, the Sudan, the Congo, and Yemen. Fortunately, the longer legs of modern jets enable them to by-pass such troubled areas.

Contrary to expectations, though true to Gresham's Law that bad drives out good, the low-cost carriers have grown, even as businesses have cut travel budgets and video-conferencing has become practical. Yet what was expected to affect the carriers was turnaround time, unless faster servicing processes could be developed.

The whole question of airline security is a matter of risk management, but bureaucracies and lawyers are affected by risks only after the fact because they do not have to pay for the costs of precautions, such as inspections of aircraft before every departure. Thus, there is no fiscal restraint on regulations.

In 2003 and beyond, another obstacle to be overcome between Europe and the United States was the fate of bilateral treaties, moving toward an open-skies policy that would see both the European Community and the Atlantic markets accessed by all. Linked here is the privatization of national airlines and the further consolidation of the nationalized flag carriers, once high debts, inflated staffs, and under-served domestic markets can be rationalized, and the barrier of no more than 49 percent foreign ownership removed.

Another area to be watched was the increasing move to outsource maintenance, distribution, and catering, as well as the leasing of engineers, and perhaps even a complete shift to ownership by another carrier. MROs around the world were making this possible.

Both airframe and engine manufacturers were expected not to recover their year 2000 output levels until 2004. And whether or not airframes delivered would drop from the 840 of 2000 to the 300 of 1993–94 remained to be seen. After 9/11, the world aviation crystal ball was too clouded to obtain predictions unless history was studied. Break-even load factors in October 2001 were at 88 percent, in spite of capacity cuts of 20 to 30 percent, though U.S. regionals had cut down only less than 3 percent.

What was to happen in Russian aviation was unclear, but President Putin's state financial aid was at least seeing indigenous airliners likely to become viable after a decade on hold in the hangars.

The defense sector in the European Community faced the struggle to sell the Eurofighter, especially since wartime wastage has been very light. And although a contract was signed at the end of 2001, assuming the first scheduled delivery to the RAF in 2008 was a challenge. Sales of thirty-three Dassault Mirage 2000–9 (ER 224.5, Mirage 2000) to the United Arab Emirates Air Force and possibly of the Saab JAS 39 Gripen (ER 78) to Austria, Czechoslovakia, and Hungary gave Sweden hope. The A-400M transport (ER n/a) was still enmeshed in the politics of budgeting and paying. In the meantime, the venerable Lockheed C-130 variants were being retained beyond their withdrawal dates and new orders added, or new Boeing C-17s substituted. In 2001 the USAF had placed a fully funded order for C-130s, which would flush spares through the system.

In general aviation, The Lancair Company and Cirrus had a substantial backlog of orders for their appealing light aircraft. Lancair is the manufacturer of the *New Spirit of St. Louis,* a Columbia 300 (ER n/a), which in 2002 successfully completed a non-stop flight across the Atlantic, retracing Charles Lindbergh's route, this time flown by his grandson Erik.

Yet other light aircraft manufacturers were having to search for funds. Numerous business aircraft, however, were on order as fractional ownership and leasing made them more attractive than airliner seats on a hub-and-spoke system with security delays.

Although the airlines tried to counter the trend toward company purchase of their own aircraft by offering business jets on lease, the sales and interest peak had passed. Like the American railroads, which did not take into account the potential growth of the automobile industry, the airlines have not faced the reality of automobile travel. However, airlines still have the advantage of speed and convenience at distances over 500 miles. But they must recognize that freight and non-business passengers—essentially tourists—have to be their income base.

As efficiency and miniaturization of electronic components continue to develop, trends of the last century will accelerate in the twenty-first. Business aircraft will make executive travel more convenient and more global, and will rejuvenate smaller more convenient airports while relieving the majors of some of their congestion. How soon video-conferencing will almost totally replace executive travel will be an on-going question related to the exchange of intelligence, the need for personal relationships in global businesses and trade, and to trust and honesty.

Looking beyond 2003, in the air the prime issues would be environmental concerns, including noise abatement, emissions, and effects on finite resources, as well as runway incursions and the need for ground-control radar to prevent collisions while taxiing—all issues of the twentieth century as well. The economic and political nuances of these concerns will continue to compel technical solutions, at a certain cost. The military services will find themselves also required to address and meet international standards while preparing for wars that may be deviations from the expected.

In 1936, one million tickets were sold on U.S. airlines. In June 2001, 49 million were sold, or roughly 588 million for that entire year, twice the U.S. population. And, thus, while the world's population increased 3.8-fold from 1903 to 2003, airline ticket sales went up "manifold."

This bodes well for the future, especially in Asia where airline usage has not yet developed to the same rate. Thus far expansion has taken place primarily in North America and Europe, but the greatest growth will come in Asia where three of the world's most populous regimes—China, the Indian sub-continent, and Indonesia—will become rich markets with global reach. China, moreover, is and will demand contract-sharing and licensing of the building of new aircraft because its skilled and lower-paid workforce and great market potential will make such agreements and the transfer of technology economically attractive. The same will apply to the dwindling military and naval aircraft sector.

Given distances and physical barriers, aviation still has an enormous potential.

With regard to international relations and air forces, the challenge will be to create an international peacekeeping force, especially for Africa, as enmities are ended. The patterns of history show that they eventually will be, as toleration, the emancipation of women, and the establishment of human rights is accomplished.

The heyday of everyone having offensive air forces passed with the twentieth century. Clearly the smaller air forces are either shrinking to inoperable levels or are being abandoned. What may remain will simply be national transport services with a maritime patrol and air-sea rescue capability. The market for new tactical aircraft will be consolidated as the European Community rationalizes and creates what would have been in the twentieth century an international air force, liable now to be used for out-of-theater peacekeeping operations. Moreover, as the cost in currency and wear-and-tear on equipment and manpower not only rises but is seen politically as unnecessary, a switch-over to the new immensely capable UAVs will be seen, and to their even newer armed combat versions. Their costs will decline rapidly with increased production of what will become widely utilized, miniaturized, urban surveillance machines.

One concern will be whether or not the aviation world can develop the means to flatten out the profit-and-loss cycle in a free-enterprise system of capitalism, or whether national and international bodies will be required to prevent cutthroat competition to ensure that both airlines and manufacturers can enjoy a reasonable profit and full employment in a stable economic environment adapted for unforeseeable events. This may also demand standards of management as well as an understanding of economic and technological patterns of concentration and controlled competition for the benefit of the traveling and shipping public.

In all of the above, managers and officers will at their peril overlook the human factor, whether it be in restroom facilities, passenger leg room, ease of travel in general, or in flight-duty times and combat fatigue.

Plato's pyramid now contains a few philosopher kings capable of master-minding the management of the world, a small coterie of military and civilian minions to run the systems, and a vast populace concerned mainly with their own lives and livelihoods unless something impinges upon that.

As democracy carries within it the seeds of its own destruction, or at least perversion, we must hope that the new globalism will seek a model from the history of aviation and air power in the twentieth century.

Looking back on the past one hundred years, 1903–2003, aviation and air power can be seen to have risen along a logarithmic curve, both technologically and in capability and capacity. While much of this can be credited to scientific, technological, medical, and other advances, aviation and air power remain instruments of human policy and pleasure, enormously stimulating, valuable, and a force for peace.

ACRONYMS AND ABBREVIATIONS

AC	Air China	ATC	air-traffic control: Air Training Command
ABDA	American, British, Dutch, Australian	ATO	air tasking order
ABM	anti-ballistic missile	ATFM	air-traffic-flow management
ACC	Air Combat Command	AVG	American Volunteer Group
ACM	Air Chief Marshal: air-combat maneuvering	AVIC	China Aviation Industry
		AWACS	airborne warning and control system
ADC	Air Defense Command		
ADGB	Air Defense of Great Britain Command	BA	British Airways
AEW	airborne early warning	BAC	British Aircraft Corporation
AFLC	Air Force Logistics Command		
AFM-1	Air Force Manual-1	Bae	British Aerospace
AGM	air-to-ground missile	BCR	bomber-combat-reconnaissance
AI	airborne interception (radar)		
ALARM	air-launched anti-radiation munitions	BE	Blériot Experimental
		BEA	British European Airways
ALL	all light level	BEF	British Expeditionary Force
ANC	African National Congress	BOAC	British Overseas Airways Corporation
ANZAC	Australian-New Zealand Army Corps		
		BSAA	British South American Airways
AOA	angle of attack		
AOC-in-C	Air Officer Commander-in-Chief	BVR	beyond visual range
AOP	air observation post	C	check (check interval)
ARVN	Army of the Republic of Vietnam	C^3	command, control, and communications
ASV	air-to-surface vessel	C^3I	command, control, communications, and intelligence
ASW	anti-submarine warfare		

C⁴	command, control, communications, and computers	CT	Communist terrorist
		CV	fleet carrier
C⁴I	command, control, communications, computers, and intelligence	CVE	a small, "baby flattop," escort carrier on merchant hull
		CVL	light carrier on cruiser hull
CAA	Civil Aeronautics Authority		
CAAC	Chinese Aviation Advisory Committee	DASA	Defence Analytical Services Agency (U.K.)
	Civil Aviation Administration of China		Deutsch Aerospace SA (German conglomerate)
CAD/CAM	computer-aided design/computer-aided manufacturing	DCA	Defense Communications Agency
			defense contra avions (anti-aircraft artillery)
CAF	Chinese Air Force		
CAP	combat air patrol	DEW	distant early warning
CAS	Chief of the Air Staff	DHC	de Havilland Canada
CAT	Civil Air Transport	DIA	Defense Intelligence Agency
CBW	chemical and biological warfare	DMZ	demilitarized zone
CCP	Communist Party of China		
CEO	Chief Executive Officer	EAA	Experimental Aircraft Association
CFD	computational fluid dynamics		
CFMU	central flow-management unit	EADS	European Aeronautic Defence and Space Company
CFT	conformal fuel tanks		
CIA	Central Intelligence Agency	EC	European Community
CINCPAC	Commander-in-Chief Pacific	ECM	electronic counter-measure
CINCPACAF	Commander-in-Chief Pacific Air Forces	EFTS	elementary flying training school
CINCSWPA	Commander-in-Chief Southwest Pacific Area	ER	Efficiency Rating
		ETOPS	extended-range twin-engine operations
CIS	Commonwealth of Independent States	EU	European Union
CNAC	China National Aviation Corporation	FAA	Federal Aviation Administration (U.S.)
CNAF	Chinese Nationalist Air Force		Fleet Air Arm (U.K.)
C of A	Certificate of Airworthiness		*Fuerza Aérea Argentina* (Argentina Air Force)
COBRA	coastal, battlefield, reconnaissance analysis		
COIN	counterinsurgency	FAB	*Force Aérienne Belgique* (Belgian Air Force)
COMOPSAIR	Command Operations Air		
CPDLC	controller-pilot data link communications	FAC	forward air controller
		FAN	*Fuerza Aérea de Nicaragua* (Nicaraguan Air Force)
CRFP	carbon fiber		
CRG	contingency response group	FAP	*Force Aérea Portuguesa* (Portuguese Air Force)
CSA	China Southern Airlines		

FAPA	*Force Aérea Populaire de Angola* (Angolan People's Air Force)	IRBM	intermediate range ballistic missile
FARM	*Force Aerienne Royale Marocaine* (Moroccan Air Force)	IT	information technology
FEAF	Far Eastern Air Force	JAA	Joint Aviation Authority
FL	flight level	JDAM	joint direct-attack munitions
FOAS	Future Offensive Air System	JPATS	joint primary aircraft training system
FLN/ALN	National Liberation Front/ National Liberation Army (Algeria)	JSF	joint-strike fighter
		JSTARS	joint surveillance target attack radar system
FRELIMO	*Frente nacional de Liberatacao de Mozambique* (Front for the Liberation of Mozambique)	KLM	Royal Dutch Airlines
		KMT	Kuomintang Party
FRETILIN	*Frente Revolutionária do Timor– Leste Independente* (East Timor)	LCA	light combat aircraft
		LANTIRN	low-altitude navigation and targeting infrared for night (system)
G	gravity		
GAMA	General Aviation Manufac- turers Association	LHR	London Heathrow Airport
		LMF	lack of moral fiber
GBU	guided-bomb unit	LOCIF	loss of control in flight
GCA	ground-controlled approach	LORAN	long-range navigation aid
GCI	ground-control intercept	LROPS	long-range operations
GEE	Grid ("G") radar navigation		
GO	Go-Fly (British Airways air- line)	MAAG	Military Assistance Advisory Group
GPS	global positioning system	MAC	merchant aircraft carriers
			merchant aircraft catapult ship
HARM	high-speed anti-radiation mis- sile		Miliary Airlift Command
		MACV	Military Assistance Command Vietnam
HCU	heavy conversion units		
HSA	Hawker-Siddeley Aviation	MAD	magnetic anomaly detection
HUD	heads-up display	MAN PADS	man-portable air defenses
		MASH	mobile army surgical hospital
IAF	Indian Air Force Israeli Air Force	MASINT	measurement and signature intelligence
IAI	Israel Aircraft Industries	MATS	Military Air Transport Service
ICAO	International Civil Aviation Organization	MEDEVAC	medical evacuation
		MIDAS	missile defense alarm system
ICBM	intercontinental ballistic missile	MIRV	multiple independently tar- geted re-entry vehicle/ warheads
IFF	identification, friend or foe		
IJN	Imperial Japanese Navy		
INS	inertial navigation system	MLU	mid-life upgrades

MPLA	*Moviemento Popular para la Liberación de Angola* (Popular Movement for the Liberation of Angola)	PLN	People's Liberation Navy
		PLO	Palestine Liberation Organization
MRO	maintenance and repair organizations	POL	petrol, oil, lubricants
		PRC	People's Republic of China
		PRU	photo-reconnaissance unit
		PSP	perforated steel plate runway
NACA	National Advisory Committee for Aeronautics		
		QC	quota count (noise-level classification)
NATO	North Atlantic Treaty Organization		
NATS	National Air Traffic Services (U.K.)	R&D	research and development
		R&R	rest and recuperation
NORA	National Office of Research Analysis	RAAF	Royal Australian Air Force
		RAF	Royal Air Force
NORAD	North American Air Defense Command	RAM	rapid area maintenance
		RBA	revolution in business affairs
NPA	New People's Army (Philippines)	RCAF	Royal Canadian Air Force
		REAF	Royal Egyptian Air Force
NORS	not operationally ready—supply	RED HORSE	rapid engineer deployable heavy operational repair squadron engineer. (RED HORSE units were elite engineering force units also trained in combat.)
NVA	North Vietnamese Army		
NVAF	North Vietnamese Air Force		
OAS	*Organization Armée Secréte* (Algeria)	RFC	Royal Flying Corps
ONUC	*Opération des Nations Unies au Congo* (United Nations Operation in the Congo)	RJ	regional jet
		RMA	revolution in military affairs
		RN	Royal Navy
OTU	operational training unit	RNAF	Royal Norwegian Air Force
		RNAS	Royal Naval Air Service
PACAF	Pacific Air Forces	RPV	remotely piloted vehicle
PAF	Pakistan Air Force	RRAF	Royal Rhodesian Air Force
PAIGC	African Party for the Independence of Guinea and Cape Verde	RRU	rapid reaction unit
		RSAF	Royal Swedish Air Force
		R/T	radio/telephone
PATCO	Professional Air Traffic Control Organization	RVNAF	Republic of Vietnam Armed Forces
PFF	Pathfinder Force	RVSM	reduced vertical separation minimum
PGB	precision-guided bombs		
PGM	precision-guided munitions		
PLA	People's Liberation Army	SAC	Strategic Air Command
PLAAF	People's Liberation Army Air Force	SADF	South African Defense Forces
		SAM	surface-to-air missile

SAR	search and rescue	TWA	Trans World Airlines
	synthetic aperture radar	UAV	unmanned aerial vehicle
SAS	Scandinavian Airline System	UCAV	unmanned combat aerial
	Special Air Service		vehicle
SBA	standard beam approach	UDF	unducted fan
SEAC	Southeast Asia Command	UDT	*União Democrática Timorense*
SEAD	suppression of enemy air de-		(Timor Democratic Union)
	fense	UNITA	*União Nacional para a Indepên-*
SEATO	Southeast Asia Treaty Organi-		*dencia Total de Angola* (Na-
	zation		tional Union for the Total
SHAA	*Service historique de l'Armée de*		Independence of Angola)
	l'Air (France)	UPS	United Parcel Service
SHAEF	Supreme Headquarters Allied	USAAC	U.S. Army Air Corps (1926–
	Expeditionary Force		41)
SHORAN	short-range navigation	USAAF	U.S. Army Air Forces (1941–
SIGINT	signals intelligence		47)
SNECMA	*Société Nationale d'Etude et de*	USAF	U.S. Air Force (1947–)
	Construction de Motears	USAFE	U.S. Air Force Europe
	d'Aviation (state-owned	USN	U.S. Navy
	French engine company)	USSR	Union of Soviet Socialist Re-
SS	submarine searching		publics
SST	supersonic transport	UTA	*Union de Transports Aeriens*
START	strategic arms reduction talks		(French airline)
STOL	short takeoff and landing	UTI	*Uchebno-Trenirovochny Istrebite*
SVNAF	South Vietnamese Air Force		(Russian trainer)
SWAPO	South West African People's		
	Organization	VC	Viet Cong
		VCR	videocassette recorder
TAAG	*Transportes Aéreos de Angola*	VDV	Russian air-assault forces
	(Angolan Airlines)	VLR	very long range
TAC	Tactical Air Command	VTOL	vertical takeoff and landing
TAF	tactical air force	VVS	*Voenno-vozdushnye sily* (Soviet
TAP	*Transportes Aéreos Portugeses*		Army Air Forces)
	(TAP Air Portugal)		
TBO	time between overhaul		
TBS	talk between ships	WASP	Women Airforce Service Pilot
TCAS	traffic alert and collision-	WPA	Works Progress (later Works
	avoidance system		Projects) Administration
TGV	*Train á Grande Vitesse* (high-	W/T	wireless telegraph
	speed French train)	WTO	World Trade Organization
THY	*Turk Hava Yollari* (Turkish Air-		
	lines)	Y2K	Year 2000

SELECTED EFFICIENCY RATINGS

Establishing dates for aircraft designs or types has not always been easy as these vary from specification to first flight, or occasionally from entry into service. In addition, data given varies from still-air range to combat radius and is not always clear. Combat range was multiplied by 2.5 to give still-air range that could be flown. Thus, the Efficiency Ratings herein should only be used to compare types roughly and to give a sense of progress.

In World War I, a type could be developed from sketch to operations in six months. In World War II, the rule was that four years were required to develop a fighter, and eight for a heavy bomber. Today, that might be twenty or more.

An additional problem in determining Efficiency Ratings has been caused by aircraft manufacturing companies changing their names through consolidation, or by companies ceasing business operations and selling their designs to successors (see page 12).

AIRCRAFT	YEAR	ER
Aerospatiale Alouette III Helicopter	1952	0.52
Aerospatiale Puma	1965	1.8
Aerospatiale Sud-Est Caravelle	1953	106
Aerospatiale Super Caravelle 12	1970	281.9
Aerospatiale/British Aerospace Concorde	1962	4,262
Aichi D3A1 Val	1940	3.5
Airbus A-300-B4	1969	1,178
Airbus A-300-600	1983	1,730
Airbus A-310-300	1978	2,248
Airbus A-320	1988	560
Airbus A-321 (320-100)	1988	560
Airbus A-321 (320-200)	1989	609
Airbus A-330/A-340 Series	1987	6,330
Airbus A-340-300	1987	6,330
Airbus A-380	2002	10,907
Airco DH-4	1916	0.096
Albatros D-1	1916	0.03
Alenia-Aerospatiale ATR-42	1985	26.5

AIRCRAFT	YEAR	ER
Alenia-Aerospatiale ATR-72	1995	26.5 (ATR-42)
Antonov 225 Mriya	1988	3,387
Antonov An-2	1947	2.1
Antonov An-12	1958	209
Antonov An-26	1957	16.8
Armstrong Whitworth Whitley	1934	21
Aviatik C	1916	n/a
Avro 146 (see also British Aerospace)	1973	115
Avro Anson	1936	2.38
Avro Lancaster I	1936	103
Avro Lincoln	1944	160
Avro Shackleton	1946	215
Avro Vulcan	1946	1,552 (1,483.5)
Avro Canada CF-18 Hornet	1980	124.4
Avro Canada CF-100 "Clunk"	1950	90
Avro Canada CF-105 Arrow	1953	223.2
Beardmore Inchinnan Airship *R-34*	1919	700
Beech 17 Staggerwing	1932	1.1
Beech 99/1900	1965	7.12
Beech Bonanza V 35B	1945	1.36
Beech Javelin	1928	0.48
Beech Racer	1929	0.48
Beech Travel Air	1928	0.48
Bell P-39 Airacobra	1935	4.25
Bell P-39D Airacobra	1941	3.15
Bell P-59 Airacomet and XP-59	1942	5.94
Bell P-63 King Cobra	1942	3.85
Blackburn Buccaneer	1955	184
Blackburn Roc	1938	2.9
Blackburn Skua	1934	2.9
Boeing 80A	1928	2.0
Boeing 247	1932	3.84
Boeing 314 Flying Boat	1935	109.7
Boeing 707	1954	1,733
Boeing 707-320	1959	1,733
Boeing 707-336	1959	2,407
Boeing 707-436	1959	2,407
Boeing 717 (McDonnell Douglas MD-90)	1989	374
Boeing 727	1960	641
Boeing 737	1965	232
Boeing 737-200	1967	363
Boeing 737-500	1990	354
Boeing 737-700	1998	n/a
Boeing 737-800	2000	n/a
Boeing 747-100	1966	5,989
Boeing 747SP	1970	5,628

Selected Efficiency Ratings

AIRCRAFT	YEAR	ER
Boeing 747–400	1988	8,760
Boeing 757	1978	663
Boeing 767	1978	1,088
Boeing 767–200	1990	1,104
Boeing 767–300ER	1983	3,044
Boeing 777	1986	3,845
Boeing B-17A/B/C	1934	25.8
Boeing B-17E	1941	101
Boeing B-17G	1942	75.98
Boeing B-29 Superfortress	1940	414
Boeing B-47 Stratojet	1944	992
Boeing B-50 Superfortress	1944	603
Boeing B-52 Stratofortress	1948	6,336
Boeing B-377 Stratocruiser	1947	423
Boeing C-17	1980	2,505
Boeing F-4B (USN) P-12 (USAAC)	1928	0.59
Boeing KC-97G Stratofreighter	1943	564
Boeing KC-135B Stratotanker	1954	1,769
Boeing P-26	1931	0.86
Boeing Sonic Cruiser	2001	n/a
Boeing Stearman PT-13	1933	0.32
Boeing Stearman PT-17	1938	0.33
Boeing V-22 Osprey	1995	164.5
Boeing XB-15	1935	145
Boeing YB-17	1934	24
Bombardier CRJ-70	1987	56.8 (Canadair 100)
Bombardier Global 5000	2000	n/a
Breda B-88 Lance	1936	9
Breguet Atlantique (Dassault Breguet)	1958	429
Brewster Buffalo	1939	4.42
Bristol Beaufighter X	1941	22.7
Bristol Beaufort	1936	19.6
Bristol Blenheim I	1934	7.28
Bristol Britannia 100	1952	517
Bristol Britannia 300	1956	710
Bristol Fighter F2B "Brisfit"	1917	0.083
British Aerospace Corporation BAC-111	1956	192
British Aerospace Avro 146	1973	115
British Aerospace Bae 146–200 RJ	1983	115
British Aerospace Bae EF 2000 Eurofighter Typhoon	1983	107.4
British Aerospace Bae Hawk TMK 1	1971	13.8
British Aerospace Bae Hawk 200	1971	14.27
British Aerospace Harrier GR1	1957	68
British Aerospace Sea Harrier	1969	75
British Aircraft Corporation/Aerospatiale Concorde	1962	4,262

AIRCRAFT	YEAR	ER
British Aircraft Corporation-Dassault-Breguet Sepecat Jaguar	1972	55
British Aircraft Corporation/Panavia Tornado	1969	72
British Aircraft Corporation BAC Canberra B-1	1955	275.2
British Aircraft Corporation BAC Lightning	1954	134
British Aircraft Corporation TSR-2	1957	1,197.5
Canadair CL-28 Argus	1952	574
Canadair CL-44 Yukon	1954	710.5
Canadair DC-4M Argonaut	1948	83
Canadair F-86 Sabre Jet	1949	31.4
Caproni Ca.30	1916	n/a
Caproni Ca.36	1917	0.84
Caproni Ca.42	1918	n/a
Caproni Ca.46	1918	1.05
Caudron G III/IV	1915	0.13
Cessna A-37 (T-37) Dragonfly	1954	14.56
Cessna 0-1A Bird Dog	1948	0.038
Cessna 206/207 Stationair 8	1962	1
Cessna Citation	1968	14.5
Cessna 500 Citation	1979	23
Cessna Crane / AT-17 Bobcat	1939	0.6
Chance Vought F4U Corsair	1938	13
Chase-Fairchild C-123 Provider	1943	44
Chengdu J-7 MF		n/a
Chengdu J-10		n/a
China State Aircraft Industry Factory Shenyang J-5 (MiG-17)	1952	26.6
China State Aircraft Industry Factory Shenyang J6/F6 (MiG-19)	1958	48
China State Aircraft Industry Factory Shenyang J-7 (MiG-21 derivative)	1953	40
China State Aircraft Industry Factory Shenyang J-8 (Mig-21)	1953	14.2
China State Aircraft Industry Factory Shenyang J-8II	1968	n/a
China State Aircraft Industry Factory Shenyang Q-5 (Nanchang A-5 derivative)		n/a
Consolidated B-24	1939	103
Consolidated (Convair) B-32 Dominator	1942	378
Consolidated B-36 Peacemaker	1941	2,042
Consolidated PBY Catalina	1933	16.6
Consolidated PB2Y Coronado	1942	43.56
Convair B-36J	1953	2,230
Convair B-58 Hustler	1952	2,508
Convair CV-990	1956	1,172
Convair F-102 Delta Dagger	1948	63

Selected Efficiency Ratings

AIRCRAFT	YEAR	ER
Convair F-106 Delta Dart	1954	212.5
Convair R3Y Tradewind	1948	504
Curtiss 75 Hawk	1934	1.67
Curtiss C-46 Commando	1940	36
Curtiss NC-4	1919	7.49
Curtiss P-36 Mohawk	1934	2.2
Curtiss P-36 Mohawk	1936	1.61
Curtiss P-40B Tomahawk	1937	2.5
Curtiss P-40F Warhawk/Kittyhawk	1942	7.3
Curtiss P-40N Kittyhawk	1944	6.46
Curtiss SB2C Helldiver	1938	10.36
Dassault Breguet Atlantic	1958	30
Dassault Falcon 900	1983	222
Dassault Mirage 2000	1975	224.5
Dassault Mirage 2000-9	1987	224.5
Dassault Mirage F-1	1965	54.7
Dassault Mirage III/50	1955	84.2
Dassault Mirage IV	1956	65
Dassault Mirage V	1964	65
Dassault Mystere IV	1955	16.4
Dassault Ourogan	1949	11.5
Dassault Rafale A	1985	336
Dassault Super Etendard IV	1956	32.4
DeHavilland Canada DHC-1 Chipmunk	1946	0.16
DeHavilland Canada DHC-3 Otter (U-1)	1951	2.1
DeHavilland Canada DHC-2 Beaver (U-6)	1946	4.2
DeHavilland Canada DHC-5 Buffalo	1964	51
DeHavilland Canada DHC-6 Twin Otter	1965	4.2
DeHavilland Canada DHC-7	1972	18.6
DeHavilland Canada DHC-8	1980	25.9
DeHavilland Comet I	1950	183.5
DeHavilland Comet 4	1958	520
DeHavilland DH-2	1914	0.064
DeHavilland DH-82 Moth	1931	0.12
DeHavilland DH-98 Mosquito FB Mk VI	1940	26.5
DeHavilland DH-103 Hornet	1943	59
DeHavilland Mosquito XI	1943	30
DeHavilland Mosquito PR45	1943	75.86
DeHavilland Vampire	1941	8
Dornier Do-17	1935	6.96
Dornier Do-19	1935	15.3
Dornier Do-22	1938	5
Dornier Do-26A	1937	98.3
Dornier Do-27	1949	0.76
Dornier Do-217	1938	30.2
Dornier Do-X	1929	28.5

AIRCRAFT	YEAR	ER
Douglas A-4 Skyhawk	1954	26
Douglas A-20 Havoc	1940	15.3
Douglas A-26/B-26 Invader	1944	25
Douglas AD-1/AE-1 Skyraider	1945	10.12
Douglas AD-2 Skyraider	1948	18.2 (AD-6, 1952)
Douglas AD-6 Skyraider	1952	18.2
Douglas Boston III (A-20)	1938	15.5
Douglas C-54A	1942	122
Douglas C-124 Globemaster	1947	420
Douglas D-558	1945	n/a
Douglas DC-2	1932	8
Douglas DC-3 (C-47) Dakota	1936	19.14
Douglas DC-4 (C-54)	1939	83
Douglas DC-6B Liftmaster	1946	278
Douglas DC-7 Seven Seas	1955	526
Douglas DC-8	1954	1,517
Douglas DC-8-30	1955	1,890
Douglas DC-9 (later McDonnell Douglas)	1963	49.5
Douglas DC-9-40	1969	53
Douglas DC-10	1966	2,967
Douglas F4D Skyray	1948	42
Douglas SBD Dauntless	1939	5.84
Douglas TBD Devastator	1933	3
Douglas World Cruiser	1924	3.07
Douglas XB-19	1938	n/a
Eindekker E-1	1913	0.029
Embraer EMB-120 Brasilia	1979	156
Embraer EMB-312 Tucano	1978	3.87
English Electric Canberra B-1	1947	147
English Electric Canberra PR-9	1955	305
English Electric Lightning (BAC Lightning)	1954	134
Eurofighter Typhoon 2000	1986	107.4
Fairchild C-119 Flying Boxcar	1941	67.5
Fairchild-Dornier 328 Jet	2000	n/a
Fairchild Republic A-10A Thunderbolt II	1972	26
Fairey Albacore	1938	3.17
Fairey Barracuda	1938	5.57
Fairey Battle	1935	5.46
Fairey Firefly	1941	11.5
Fairey Fox	1924	0.716
Fairey Fox II M (Belgian)	1933	0.84
Fairey Fulmar	1938	4.4
Fairey Swordfish	1933	1.4
Farman FE-2B	1914	0.095
Fiat CR-32	1933	0.87
Fiat CR-42	1938	1.36

Selected Efficiency Ratings

AIRCRAFT	YEAR	ER
Fiat G-50	1935	1.3
Fiat G-91	1959	25
Fiesler Fi 156 Storch	1936	0.15
Focke-Wulf Fw-172		6.96
Focke-Wulf Fw-190	1941	3.39
Focke-Wulf Fw-200 Condor	1936	46
Fokker 100	1986	182
Fokker DR-I Triplane	1917	0.03
Fokker D-VII	1918	0.83
Fokker F-18	1932	3.3
Fokker F-27	1950	16.69 (F-27-100)
Fokker F-50	1983	45.2
Fokker F-VII A	1925	3.3
Fokker / Fairchild F-27 100 Friendship	1952	16.69
Folland Gnat	1951	12.8
Ford Trimotor 5-AT-D	1925	3
Fouga Magister (Aerospatiale)	1952	n/a
General Dynamics F-16A Fighting Falcon	1971	113
General Dynamics F-16 C/D Fighting Falcon	1990	304
General Dynamics F-111 Aardvark	1962	1,189
German V-1 Flying Bomb	1943	?
Gloster Gladiator	1934	1.1
Gloster Javelin	1948	57.3
Gloster Meteor III	1940	15.3
Gloster Meteor IV	1945	22
Gloster NF11 Meteor	1948	27.3
Gotha LE-3 Taube	1915	0.006
Grigorovich M.24 Flying Boat	1922	n/a
Grumman A-6 Intruder	1957	84.5
Grumman E-2 Hawkeye	1957	61.2
Grumman EA-6B Prowler	1957	77.3
Grumman F-2A/F	1932	1.189
Grumman F3F	1934	1
Grumman F4F Wildcat (Martlet)	1936	3.9
Grumman F4F (FM-2) Wildcat (Martlet)	1944	4.94
Grumman F6F	1941	12.2
Grumman F7F Tigercat	1941	26.8
Grumman F 8F Bearcat	1943	12
Grumman F9F Cougar	1951	24
Grumman F9F Panther	1946	28
Grumman F-14 Tomcat	1969	129
Grumman F-14 Tomcat (of 1990s)	1991	463.6
Grumman Gulfstream I	1955	62
Grumman Gulfstream II	1965	31.3
Grumman Gulfstream III	1976	33.2
Grumman OV-1 Mohawk	1957	12.4

AIRCRAFT	YEAR	ER
Grumman S-2 Tracker	1950	15.6
Grumman SA-16A Albatross	1948	50
Grumman Super Ag-Cat		n/a
Grumman TBF Avenger	1940	10.5
Halberstadt D-11	1917	0.04
Handley Page 0/100	1914	0.52
Handley Page 0/400	1918	1.95
Handley Page Halifax I	1936	54
Handley Page Halifax III	1942	91
Handley Page Hampden	1932	17.56
Handley Page Victor	1946	527
Harbin Y-11 (An-2)	1990	n/a
Harbin Y-12II	1975	n/a
Hawker 192 Hart	1930	0.29
Hawker Fury I & II	1930	0.7
Hawker Hunter	1950	18.6
Hawker Hurricane I	1933	1.94
Hawker Nimrod	1926	0.66
Hawker Osprey	1930	0.73
Hawker Sea Fury	1942	11.95
Hawker-Siddeley (Blackburn) Buccaneer	1955	152
Hawker-Siddeley GR-7 Harrier	1957	27.7
Hawker-Siddeley Sea Harrier	1966	75
Hawker Tempest II	1943	19
Hawker Tempest V	1944	15
Heinkel He-111	1931	19.9
Heinkel He-177	1939	30
Henschel Hs 123	1933	1.10
Hunting (Percival) Jet Provost	1953	7.2
Ilyushin Il-2 Shturmovik	1938	3.7
Ilyushin Il-10	1943	4.3
Ilyushin Il-14 Transport	1952	16.5
Ilyushin Il-16	1952	1.29
Ilyushin Il-18	1955	322
Ilyushin Il-28	1948	37
Ilyushin Il-62	1963	1,614.7
Ilyushin Il-76	1971	898
Ilyushin Il-96-300	1986	2,045
Indonesia N.250	1980	n/a
Israel Aircraft Industries Kifir	1975	57.83
Israel Aircraft Industries Lavi	1986	2,940
Junkers CL-1	1918	0.092
Junkers Ju-52-3m	1929	6.7
Junkers Ju-86	1934	6.6
Junkers Ju-87	1938	2.22
Junkers Ju-88	1936	13.4

Selected Efficiency Ratings

AIRCRAFT	YEAR	ER
Junkers Ju-290	1937	18.6
Junkers W-13	1919	n/a
Kaman Ka-25 Helicopter	1950	n/a
Kawanishi N1K1-J Shiden (George)	1942	6.24
Lancair Columbia		n/a
Lavochkin La-5	1941	2.8
Learjet (Gates)	1958	25
Lockheed Electra	1954	232
Lockheed 10/12 Electra	1936	3.17
Lockheed 18 Hudson	1938	14
Lockheed C-5A Galaxy	1965	5,675
Lockheed C-56 Lodestar	1939	14
Lockheed C-69 Constellation	1943	114
Lockheed C-130 Hercules	1954	344 (C-130B)
Lockheed C-141 StarLifter	1960	1,470
Lockheed EC-121 Super Constellation	1949	422
Lockheed F-22 Rapier	1981	282
Lockheed F-80C Shooting Star	1944	27
Lockheed F-94 Starfire	1947	24.7
Lockheed F-104 Starfighter	1952	68
Lockheed L-049 Constellation	1946	113
Lockheed L-749 Constellation	1947	124
Lockheed L-1011 Tristar	1968	2,057
Lockheed L-1049G Constellation	1949	341.5
Lockheed L-1649 Starliner	1953	595.8
Lockheed P2V Neptune	1941	115
Lockheed P-3 Orion	1957	794.2
Lockheed P-38 Lightning	1937	8
Lockheed PV-1 Ventura	1942	23.2
Lockheed PV-2 Harpoon	1955	236
Lockheed S-3 Viking	1969	155.4
Lockheed SR-71 Blackbird	1964	2,040
Lockheed U-2 Gray Ghost	1955	45
Lockheed-Martin/Boeing F-22 Raptor	1981	282
Lockheed-Martin F-35 JSF	1990	n/a
LTV A-7 Corsair II (see Vought)	1964	101.4
LTV F-8 Crusader (see Vought)	1953	68
Macchi 200	1939	1.7
Macchi 200/MC 200 Saetta	1936	1.67
Macchi MC 202 Folgore	1941	2.25
Malmo J-3		n/a
Malmo MFI-9 "Minicon"	1958	0.19
Martin B-10	1932	4.19
Martin B-26B Marauder	1939	25
Martin Baltimore IV	1940	16.4

AIRCRAFT	YEAR	ER
Martin Maryland	1939	16.8
Martin Mauler	1944	31
Martin P6M Seamaster	1955	n/a
Martin RB-57 (formerly English Electric Canberra B-1)	1954	146.7
Martin RB-57 D/E	1953	185
McDonnell F2H Banshee	1945	34
McDonnell F3H Demon	1949	61
McDonnell F4 Phantom II	1954	370
McDonnell F-4 Phantom IIE	1979	236.4
McDonnell FH-1 Phantom	1942	33.5
McDonnell F-101 Voodoo	1946	252
McDonnell/Canadair CF-101 Voodoo	1954	252
McDonnell Douglas C-17	1980	2,505
McDonnell Douglas DC-10-30	1966	2,988
McDonnell Douglas DC-11 (MD-11)	1978	5,739
McDonnell Douglas F-15 Eagle	1969	187
McDonnell Douglas F/A-18E/F Hornet	1974	124.4
McDonnell Douglas MD-80	1977	402
McDonnell Douglas MD-80-90 Series	1989	435+
McDonnell Douglas MD-82/87	1985	439
McDonnell Douglas MD-90-30/MD-95	1989	374
Messerschmitt Me-109E (Bf-109)	1935	1.24
Messerschmitt Me-109G Gustav	1943	2.92
Messerschmitt Me-110	1936	6.0
Messerschmitt Me-163 Komet	1943	6.7
Messerschmitt Me-262	1938	9.92
Mikoyan-Gurevich MiG-15	1945	20
Mikoyan-Gurevich MiG-17F	1951	26.6
Mikoyan-Gurevich MiG-19	1953	48
Mikoyan-Gurevich MiG-21	1955	14.2
Mikoyan-Gurevich MiG-23/27	1966	274
Mikoyan-Gurevich MiG-25	1965	179
Mikoyan-Gurevich MiG-27	1966	274.7 (MiG-23MF)
Mikoyan-Gurevich MiG-29	1979	157
Mil Mi-6 Helicopter	1957	13
Mil Mi-8/M Helicopter	1960	2.56
Mil Mi-17 Helicopter	1980	2.87
Mil Mi-24	1965	3.2
Mil Mi-26	1975	21.32
Mitsubishi A5M (Type 96) Claude	1934	0.15
Mitsubishi G3M (Type 96) Nell	1934	34
Mitsubishi G4M (Type 1) Betty	1937	41
Mitsubishi J2M Raiden (Jack)	1942	6.96
Mitsubishi Zero A6M	1939	7.89
Morane-Saulnier MS-403	1934	1.6

Selected Efficiency Ratings

AIRCRAFT	YEAR	ER
Morane–Saulnier MS–406	1937	1.6
Morane–Saulnier MS D–3801	1941	1.78
Myasishchev M–52	1957	n/a
Nakajima B5N (Type 97) Kate	1935	5.24
Nanchang A–5 derivative	1958	n/a
Nanchang A–5 Fantan	1958	48
Nieuport 17	1917	0.037
Nieuport 28	1917	0.07
Noordyn AT–16 Norseman	1934	1.16
Nord NorAtlas 262	1949	29
North American AJ–1 Savage	1948	n/a
North American AT–6 Harvard (Texan)	1935	1.89
North American B–25 Mitchell	1939	23
North American F–86 Sabre Jet	1944	31.4
North American F–100 D Super Sabre	1949	90
North American OV–10 Bronco	1964	4.76
North American P–51A Mustang	1940	5.14
North American P–51D	1943	9.63
North American T–28 Trojan	1949	5.8
North American XB–70	1961	n/a
North American Rockwell B–1 Lancer	1969	6,279
Northrop A–17	1934	2.4
Northrop B–2 Spirit	1978	2,877.6
Northrop F–5 Freedom Fighter	1962	82
Northrop F–5E Tiger II	1955	128.2
Northrop F–20 Tiger II (Tigershark)	1970	88
Northrop F–89 Scorpion	1946	74
Northrop P–61 Black Widow	1941	83
Northrop T–38 Talon	1962	22.5
Northrop XB–35	1941	117.3
Northrop-Grumman Global Hawk UAV	2000	n/a
Panavia Tornado	1969	72
Petlykov PE–2	1941	11.71
Pfalz D–III	1917	0.1
Piaggio P180 Avanti	1983	19.51
Piasecki HUP–3 (UH–25C) Retriever	1948	0.4
Pilatus PC–7 Turbo-trainer	1978	4.83
Pilatus PC–9	1982	4.9
Polikarpov I–15	1931	0.39
Polikarpov I–16	1934	1.23
Polikarpov PO–2	1927	0.999
Porte F–2A Flying Boat	1917	1.189
Predator UAV		n/a
Republic F–105 Thunderchief	1959	26.3
Republic F–105 Thunderchief	1965	132
Republic F–84F Thunderjet	1950	78

AIRCRAFT	YEAR	ER
Republic P-47 Thunderbolt	1940	8.1
Royal Aircraft Factory BE-2C	1912	0.096
Royal Aircraft Factory FE-8	1915	0.3
Royal Aircraft Factory SE-5A	1917	0.18
Rutan (Scaled Composites) Voyager	1986	29
Ryan *Spirit of St. Louis*	1927	0.48
Saab 340	1980	19
Saab 2000	1988	61.7
Saab Gripen	1980	78
Saab J-29-F Tunnan	1948	24.6
Saab J-35 Draken	1949	35
Saab JA-37 Viggen	1967	162.7
Savoia-Marchetti SM-55	1924	15.7
Savoia Marchetti SM-79 Sparviero	1934	16.6
Savoia-Marchetti SM-82 Cangaru	1939	34
Scottish Aviation Prestwick Air Pioneer	1945	0.58
Sepecat Jaguar GR MK 1	1965	64.5
Seversky P-35	1935	3.9
Short S-23C Empire	1936	11.8
Short Belfast	1959	853
Short Stirling	1936	72
Short Sunderland	1936	63
Sikorsky S-3	1910	?
Sikorsky S-40	1931	n/a
Sikorsky S-42	1932	15.5
Sikorsky S-70 Helicopter	1974	4.14
Sikorsky Ilýa Mouromets	1913	0.52
Sopwith Camel	1917	0.96
Sopwith Pup	1916	0.934
Spad XIII	1917	0.135
Sukhoi Su-7 Fitter A	1958	82
Sukhoi Su-9 Fishpot	1960	14.26
Sukhoi Su-17/22 Fitter	1971	83.8
Sukhoi Su-27/30 Flanker	1971	173.6
Sukhoi Su-35	1992	173.6
Supermarine S-6B Schneider Trophy Racer	1929	0.496
Supermarine Seafire	1940	1.9
Supermarine Spitfire I	1934	1.9
Supermarine Spitfire VIII	1942	n/a
Supermarine Spitfire IX	1943	2.63
Supermarine Spitfire XIV	1944	3.5
Supermarine Swift	1946	15.2
Taylorcraft Auster	1938	0.13
Taylorcraft Auster XII	1942	0.09
Tupolev TB-3 (ANT-6)	1938	27
Tupolev Tu-4	1946	414

Selected Efficiency Ratings

AIRCRAFT	YEAR	ER
Tupolev Tu–16 Badger A	1952	2,594
Tupolev Tu–18 Blinder A	1959	2,594
Tupolev Tu–20B Blinder B	1960	2,652
Tupolev Tu–22 M Backfire (Tu–26)	1966	2,349
Tupolev Tu–28P Fiddler A	1961	629
Tupolev Tu–95 Bear	1952	2,121
Tupolev Tu–114	1956	1,977
Tupolev Tu–124D	1960	69
Tupolev Tu–144	1961	4,970
Tupolev Tu–154M	1971	393.8
Tupolev Tu–160 Blackjack	1980?	6,698
Tupolev Tu–204	1989	563
Tupolev Tu–214		n/a
Vickers 630 Viscount	1942	64
Vickers VC–10	1957	2,475
Vickers Super VC–10	1957	2,709
Vickers Valiant	1948	652
Vickers Vimy	1917	2
Vickers Vimy Commercial (Vimy IV)	1919	0.95
Vickers Viscount 810	1960	64
Vickers Wellesley	1933	5.57
Vickers Wellington I	1932	30
Vickers Wildebeeste IV	1928	1.7
Voisin 5	1914	0.007
Vought A–7 Corsair II (see LTV)	1964	101.4
Vought F–8 Crusader (see LTV)	1953	76
Vought-Sikorsky F4U Corsair (Chance Vought)	1938	13
Vultee BT–13 Valiant "Vibrator"	1938	0.75
Westland Lysander	1934	2.6
Westland Scout	1951	n/a
Westland Sea King Helicopter	1957	4.1
Witteman-Lewis Barling Bomber	1923	n/a
Xi'an F-7		n/a
Xi'an H-6		n/a
Xi'an Y-7 (50-passenger airliner)	1965?	n/a
Yakolev Yak-1	1938	2.36
Yakolev Yak-9	1941	4.14

BIBLIOGRAPHY

Bibliographic entries for aviation and air power in the twentieth century is a global topic to which a whole volume could be devoted. That is not possible here, thus limited suggestions have been presented in the following categories:

The selected works have been limited by publication space, the author's knowledge of languages, and his interests.

The criteria for selection was to include the latest coverage of the subject, or at least a volume that provides references to the wider and deeper literature. Entries include place of publication and publisher's name at time of issue. Many of the authors are prolific.

Because the years 1903–2003 were visual times, copious photographic resources are available, including movie and video footage. A short selection of videos is noted herein.

I. Reference Works

Aviation Year by Year. New York: Dorling Kindersley, 2001. A 900-page well-illustrated coffee-table account in annual installments.

Bishop, Edward. *The Daily Telegraph Books of Airmen's Obituaries.* London: Grub Street, 2002.

Bright, Charles D. *Encyclopedia of the USAF.* Westport, Conn.: Greenwood Press, 1992.

Cooksley, Peter G. *Air Warfare: The Encyclopedia of Twentieth Century Conflict.* London: Arms and Armour Press, 1997.

FAA Historical Fact Book: A Chronology, 1926–1971. Washington, D.C: Department of Transportation, Federal Aviation Administration, 1974.

Garrison, Paul. *The Illustrated Encyclopedia of General Aviation.* Blue Ridge Summit, Penn.: TAB Books, 1979.

Hallion, Richard P. *The Literature of Aeronautics,*

Astronautics, and Air Power. Washington, D.C.: Office of Air Force History, 1984.

Higham, Robin. *Official Histories.* Manhattan, Kans.: Sunflower University Press, 1970. Reprint, Westport, Conn.: Greenwood Press, 2000. A list of available official histories, with essays up to 1967.

Higham, Robin, and Donald J. Mrozek, eds. *A Guide to United States Military History.* Hamden, Conn.: Archon Books, 1975. Suppl. in 1981, 1985, 1991, and 1996. All include chapters on the U.S. Air Force and materials on U.S. Navy aviation.

Horton, John. *The Grub Street Dictionary of International Aircraft Nicknames, Variants and Colloquial Terms.* London: Grub Street, 1994.

Jefford, Wing Cdr. C. G. *RAF Squadrons: A Comprehensive Record of the Movement and Equipment of All RAF Squadrons and Their Antecedents since 1912.* Shrewsbury, U.K.: Airlife Publications, 1988.

Lopez, Donald S. *Aviation: A Smithsonian Guide.* New York: Macmillan Co., 1995.

Maurer, Maurer, ed. *Combat Squadrons of the Air Force, World War II.* Washington, D.C.: Office of Air Force History, 1982.

Noffsinger, J. P. *World War I Aviation Books in English: An Annotated Bibliography.* Metuchen, N.J.: Scarecrow Press, 1987.

Ravenstein, Charles A. *Air Force Combat Wings: Lineage and Honors Histories, 1945–1977.* Washington, D.C.: Office of Air Force History, 1984.

Smith, Myron J., Jr. *The Airline Bibliography: The Salem College Guide to Sources on Commercial Aviation.* Vol. 1, *The United States.* Vol. 2, *Airliners and Foreign Air Transports.* West Cornwall, Conn.: Locust Hill Press, 1986.

Sterling, Christopher H. *Commercial Air Transport Books: An Annotated Bibliography of Airlines, Airliners, and the Air Transport Industry.* McLean, Va.: Paladwr, 2001.

Taylor, Michael J. H., ed. *Jane's Encyclopedia of Aviation.* London: Studio Editions, 1980. Reprint, London: Jane's, 1991.

World War I in the Air: A Bibliography and Chronology. Metuchen, N.J.: Scarecrow Press, 1977. Provides access to older material not likely to be on the internet.

II. BACKGROUND

Arpee, Edward. *From Frigates to Flat-tops: The Story of the Life and Achievements of Rear Admiral William Adger Moffett, USN. "The Father of Naval Aviation," October 31, 1869–April 4, 1933.* U.S.: Published by the author, 1953.

Boyne, Walter J., and Donald S. Lopez. *The Age of the Helicopter: Vertical Flight.* Washington, D.C.: Smithsonian Institution Press, 1984.

Cadogan, Mary. *Women with Wings: Female Flyers in Fact or Fiction.* New York: Macmillan Co., 1992.

Chant, Christopher, and John Batchelor. *A Century of Triumph: The History of Aviation.* New York: Free Press, 2002.

Corn, Joseph J. *The Winged Gospel: America's Romance with Aviation, 1900–1950.* New York: Oxford University Press, 1983. A classic.

Crouch, Tom D. *A Dream of Wings: Americans and the Airplane, 1875–1905.* New York: W. W. Norton & Co., 1981.

Dassault, Marcel. *The Talisman: The Autobiography of Marcel Dassault, Creator of the Mirage Jet.* New Rochelle, N.Y.: Arlington House, 1971.

Dorman, Geofrey. *British Test Pilots.* London: Forbes-Robertson, 1950

Edgerton, David. *England and the Aeroplane: An Essay on a Militant and Technological Nation.* London: Macmillan Academic and Professional, 1991.

Friedman, Norman. *British Carrier Aviation: The Evolution of the Ships and Their Aircraft.* Annapolis, Md.: Naval Institute Press, 1988.

Fritzschke, Peter. *A Nation of Flyers: German Avi-*

ation and the Popular Imagination. Cambridge, Mass.: Harvard University Press, 1992.

Gibbs-Smith, Charles H. *The Invention of the Aeroplane, 1799–1909*. London: Faber & Faber, 1966.

Goss, Hilton Proctor. *Civilian Morale under Aerial Bombardment, 1914–1939*. Maxwell AFB, Ala.: Documentary Research Division, Air University Libraries, Air University, 1948.

Groehler, Olaf. *Geschichte des Luftkrieges, 1910–1970*. Berlin: Militärverlag der Deutschen Democratischen Republik, 1975. A solid East German view.

Gross, Charles J. *American Military Aviation in the Twentieth Century*. College Station: Texas A&M University Press, 2002.

Hallion, Richard P. *Strike from the Sky: The History of Battlefield Air Attack, 1911–1945*. Shrewsbury, U.K.: Airlife Publications, 1989.

Hart, Clive. *The Prehistory of Flight*. Berkeley: University of California Press, 1985. Chronologically the place to start.

Hone, Thomas C., Norman Friedman, and Mark D. Mandeles. *American and British Aircraft Carrier Development*. Annapolis, Md.: Naval Institute Press, 1999.

Iklé, C. *The Social Impact of Bomb Destruction*. Norman: University of Oklahoma Press, 1958. Suggests more studies of the impact of bombing.

Jane's. *All the World's Aircraft*. London: Janes, annually since 1909.

Jarrett, Philip, ed. *Biplane to Monoplane: Aircraft Development, 1919–1939*. London: Putnam, 1997.

Kennett, Lee. *A History of Strategic Bombing from the First Hot-Air Balloons to Hiroshima and Nagasaki*. New York: Scribner, 1983. In a class by itself. Comes from an author steeped in the French literature.

King, H. F., and J. W. R. Taylor, eds. *Kittyhawk to Concorde: Jane's 100 Significant Aircraft*. London: Jane's, 1970.

Kreis, John F. *Air Warfare and Air Base Defense, 1914–1973*. Washington, D.C.: Office of Air Force History, 1988.

Leary, William M., ed. *The Airline Industry: The Encyclopedia of American Business History*. New York: Facts on File, 1992.

Leary, William M., and William F. Trimble, eds. *From Airships to Airbus: The History of Civil and Commercial Aviation*. Proceedings of the International Conference on the History of Civil Aviation. Washington, D.C., Smithsonian Institution Press, 1995.

Lomax, J. *Sheila Scot*. London: Hutchinson, 1990.

———. *Women of the Air*. New York: Dodd Mead & Co., 1987.

McBean, John A., and Arthur S. Hogben. *Bombs Gone: The Development and Use of British Air-dropped Weapons from 1912 to the Present Day*. Wellingborough, U.K.: Patrick Stephens, 1990.

McKay, S. *The Tiger Moth: A Tribute*. Shrewsbury, U.K.: Airlife Publications, 1987.

Milberry, Larry. *Sixty Years: The RCAF and CF Air Command 1924–1984*. Toronto: CANAV Books, 1984.

Miller, Ronald, and David Sawers. *The Technical Development of Modern Aviation*. Westport, Conn.: Praeger Publishers, 1970.

Nalty, Bernard. *Winged Shield, Winged Sword*. 2 vols. Washington, D.C.: U.S. Government Printing Office (USGPO), 1997.

The 1998 National Aerospace Conference: The Meaning of Flight in the Twentieth Century. Dayton, Ohio: Wright State University, 1998. Contains an eclectic and wide-ranging set of essays from the beginnings to Concorde.

Paret, Peter, ed. *The Makers of Modern Strategy*. Princeton, N.J.: Princeton University Press, 1986. Revision of the 1943 edition by E. M. Earle.

Pelletier, A. J. *Beech Aircraft and Their Predecessors*. London: Putnam, 1995.

Potter, E. B., and Fleet Adm. Chester W. Nimitz. *Sea Power. A Naval History*. Annapolis, Md.:

Naval Institute Press, 1960. Best general history of naval affairs, and later editions.

Probert, Henry A. *Bomber Harris—His Life and Times: The Biography of Marshal of the Royal Air Force Sir Arthur Harris, Wartime Chief of Bomber Command.* London: Greenhill Books, 2001.

Robertson, Bruce. *Aviation Archaeology: A Collectors' Guide to Aeronautical Relics.* London: Patrick Stephens, 1977, 1983.

Robinson, Douglas H. *The Dangerous Sky: A History of Aviation Medicine.* Seattle: University of Washington Press, 1973. A fine starting point in that field.

Snow, C. P. *Science and Government.* Cambridge, MA: Harvard University Press, 1962. Later editions contain addenda.

Spencer, William. *Air Force Records for Family Historians.* London: Public Record Office (PRO), 2000.

Stanley, Col. Roy M. II. *World War II Photo Intelligence.* New York: Scribner, 1981. A careful, well-illustrated study of the aircraft, cameras, film, pictures, and clues revealed from this work.

Triggs, James M. *The Piper Cub Story.* Blue Ridge Summit, Penn.: TAB Books 1978.

Welch, Ann. *Happy to Fly: An Autobiography.* London: John Murray, 1983.

Wright, William C. *Rearwin: A Story of Men, Planes, and Aircraft Manufacturing During the Great Depression.* Manhattan, Kans.: Sunflower University Press, 2000.

Yeager, Jeanna, and Dick Rutan. *Voyager.* New York: Alfred A. Knopf, 1987.

III. Aviation and Air Power

Adkin, F. J. *Through the Hangar Doors: RAF Ground Crew since 1945.* Shrewsbury, U.K.: Airlife Publications, 1986.

Armitage, Air Marshal M. J., and Air Commodore R. A. Mason. *Air Power in the Nuclear Age, 1945–82: Theory and Practice.* London: Macmillan & Co., 1983.

Ball, D., ed. *Air Power: Global Developments and Australian Perspectives.* Sydney: Pergamon-Brassey's Defence Publishers, 1988.

Ball, S. J. *The Bomber in British Strategy, and Britain's World Role, 1945–1960.* Boulder, Colo.: Westview Press, 1995.

Bergerson, F. A. *The Army Gets an Air Force: Tactics of Insurgent Bureaucratic Politics.* Baltimore: Johns Hopkins University Press, 1980.

Beschloss, Michael R. *Mayday: Eisenhower, Krushchev and the U-2 Affair.* London: Faber & Faber; HarperCollins, 1986.

Blesse, Maj. Gen. F. C. *Check Six.* Tucson: Champlin Fighter Museum, 1987. Fighter memoirs.

Borman, Frank, and Robert J. Serling. *Countdown: An Autobiography.* New York: Silver Arrow Books/William Morrow & Co., 1988.

Brassey's Annuals. London: Brassey's, [1886–].

Brookes, Sq. Ldr. A. *V Force: The History of Britain's Airborne Deterrent.* London: Jane's, 1983.

Brown, M. E. *Flying Blind: The Politics of the U.S. Strategic Bomber Program.* Ithaca, N.Y.: Cornell University Press, 1992.

Buckley, John. *Air Power in the Age of Total War.* Bloomington: Indiana University Press, 1999.

Burrows, William E. *By Any Means Necessary: America's Secret Air War in the Cold War.* New York: Farrar, Straus & Giroux, 2001.

Cartier, Claude. *Marcel Dassault: la légende d'un siède.* Paris: Perrier, 1992.

Coffey, T. M. *Iron Eagle: The Turbulent Life of General Curtis LeMay.* New York: Crown Publishers, 1986.

Cohen, Col. E. *Israel's Best Defense: The First Full Story of the Israeli Air Force.* New York: Orion Books, 1993. Reprint, Shrewsbury, U.K.: Airlife Publications, 1994.

Constant, Edward W. *The Origins of the Turbojet Revolution*. Baltimore: Johns Hopkins University Press, 1980.

Cooling, Benjamin Franklin, ed. *Case Studies in the Achievement of Air Superiority*. Washington, D.C.: USAF Center for Air Force History, 1994.

Crosby, Ann Denholm. *Dilemmas in Defence Decision-Making: Constructing Canada's Role in NORAD, 1958–96*. New York: St. Martin's Press, 1998.

Daso, Dik Alan. *Hap Arnold and the Evolution of American Air Power*. Washington, D.C.: Smithsonian Institution Press, 2000.

Davis, M. *Winged Warfare: The Literature and Theory of Aerial Warfare in Britain, 1859–1917*. Manchester, U.K.: Manchester University Press, 1992.

Davis, Vincent. *The Admirals' Lobby*. Lexington: University of Kentucky Press, 1967.

The Development of Strategic Air Command. 1946–1986. Bellevue, Nebr.: Offutt AFB, 1986.

Douhet, Guilio. *The Command of the Air*. Italy, 1921. Reprint, New York: Coward-McCann, 1942. Reprint, Washington, D.C.: Office of Air Force History, 1983. A controversial classic.

Drewes, Robert W. *The Air Force and the Great Engine War*. Washington, D.C.: U.S. National Defense University Press, 1987.

Driscoll, Edward J. *Forming a Partnership for National Defense: Commercial Airlines and the Air Force. An Oral History*. Scott AFB, Ill.: U.S. TRANSCOM Research, 2001.

Futrell, Robert Frank. *Ideas, Concepts and Doctrine: A History of Basic Thinking in the United States Air Force, 1907–1964*. 2 vols. Maxwell AFB, Ala.: Aerospace Studies Institute, Air University, 1971.

Gardner, C. *The British Aircraft Corporation: A History*. London: Batsford, 1981.

Gililcrest, Rear Adm. P. T. *Vulture's Row: Thirty Years of Naval Aviation*. Atglen, Penn.: Schiffer Publishing, 1996.

Gooch, John. *Air Power: Theory and Practice*. London: Frank Cass & Co., 1995.

Goodison, Len. *Air Power at the Battlefront, 1943–1945*. London: Frank Cass & Co., 1998.

Gough, J. *Watching the Skies: A History of Ground Radar for the Air Defence of the United Kingdom by the Royal Air Force from 1946–1975*. London: Her Majesty's Stationery Office (HMSO), 1993.

Gunston, Bill. *Air Superiority*. London: Ian Allan, 1985.

———. *Grumman: Sixty Years of Excellence*. New York: Orion Books, 1988.

Hamer, David J. *Bombers versus Battleships: The Struggle Between Ships and Aircraft for the Control of the Surface of the Sea*. London: Conway Maritime Press; Annapolis, Md.: Naval Institute Press, 1999.

Hay, Doddy. *The Man in the Hot Seat*. London: Collins, 1969. The development of ejection seats is explained by one of the Martin-Baker "guinea pigs."

Heinemann, E. H., and Rosario Rausa. *Combat Aircraft Designer: The Ed Heinemann Story*. London: Jane's, 1980.

Jarrett, Philip, ed. *The Modern War Machine: Military Aviation since 1945*. London: Putnam, 2000.

Johnson, AVM J. E. *Full Circle: The Tactics of Air Fighting, 1914–1964*. London: Ballantine Books, 1964.

Jones, Neville. *The Origins of Strategic Bombing: A Study of the Development of British Air Strategic Thought and Practice up to 1918*. London: William Kimber, 1973. Provides the policy background.

Jordan, Robert S. *Norstad: Cold War NATO Supreme Commander—Airman, Strategist, Diplomat*. New York: St. Martin's Press, 2000.

Knight, ACM Sir M. *Strategic Offensive Air Operations*. Air Power: Aircraft, Weapons Systems and Technology Series, Vol. 8. London: Brassey's, 1989.

Komons, Nick A. *Science and the Air Force: A*

History of the Air Force Office of Scientific Research. Washington, D.C.: USGPO, 1966.

Kotz, Nick. *Wild Blue Yonder: Money, Politics, and the B-1 Bomber.* New York: Pantheon Books, 1988.

Laite, Gp. Capt. B.C. *Maritime Air Operations.* Air Power: Aircraft, Weapons Systems and Technology Series, Vol. 2. London: Brassey's, 1991.

Lanchester, F. W. *Aircraft in Warfare: The Dawn of the Fourth Arm.* Sunnyvale, Calif.: Lanchester Press, 1995.

Ledbetter, Col. M. N., and C. Bakse. *Airlift Tanker: A History of U.S. Airlift and Tanker Forces.* Paducah, Ky.: Turner Publishing, 1995.

Lee, Wing Cdr. Asher. *Air Power.* London: Gerald Duckworth, 1955. A useful book based on the author's observation of the Second World War as the RAF's expert on the German Air Force, and some work on the Soviets.

Lee, ACM Sir D. *Wings in the Sun: A History of the Royal Air Force in the Mediterranean, 1945–1946.* London: Ministry of Defence Air Historical Branch (RAF), HMSO, 1989.

Lovell, Mark. *Troubled Partnership: A History of Japan's Collaboration on the FSX Fighter.* New Brunswick, N.J.: Transaction Publishers, 1996.

Mason, AVM R. A. *To Inherit the Skies: From Spitfire to Tornado: Britain's Air Defence Today.* London: Brassey's, 1990.

Mason, AVM Tony. *Air Power: A Centennial Appraisal.* London: Brassey's, 1994.

Maydew, Randall C. *America's Lost H-Bomb! Palomares, Spain, 1966.* Manhattan, Kans.: Sunflower University Press, 1997.

McCarthy, Brig. Gen. J. R., Lt. Col. G. B. Allison, and Col. R. E. Rayfield. *Linebacker II: A View from the Rock.* USAF Southeast Asia Monograph Series, Vol 6, Mon. 8. Washington, D.C.: Office of Air Force History, 1985.

Meilenger, Phillip S. "The Historiography of Airpower: Theory and Doctrine." *Journal of Military History* 64 (April, 2000): 467–502.

———. *Hoyt S. Vandenberg: The Life of a General.* Bloomington: Indiana University Press, 1989.

Miller, Jerry. *Nuclear Weapons and the Aircraft Carrier: How the Bomb Saved Naval Aviation.* Washington, D.C.: Smithsonian Institution Press, 2001.

Mitchell, William. *Winged Defense: The Development and Possibilities of Modern Air Power Economic and Military.* 1925. Reprint, New York: Dover Publications, 1988. A classic.

Momeyer, Gen. William W. *Air Power in Three Wars.* Washington, D.C.: Office of Air Force History, 1978.

Nichols, John B., and Barrett Tillman. *On Yankee Station.* Annapolis, Md.: Naval Institute Press, 1987. The U.S. Navy off Vietnam.

Pach, C. J. *Arming the Free World: The Origins of the United States Military Assistance Program, 1945–1950.* Chapel Hill: North Carolina University Press, 1991.

Pape, Robert A. *Bombing to Win: Air Power and Coercion in War.* Ithaca, N.Y.: Cornell University Press, 1996.

Power, Gen. Thomas, with Albert A. Arnhym. *Design for Survival.* New York: Coward-McCann, 1964.

Puryear, E. F., Jr. *Stars in Flight: A Study in Air Force Character and Leadership.* Novato, Calif.: Presidio Press, 1980.

Rayner, H. *Scherger: A Biography of Air Chief Marshal Sir Frederick Scherger KBE, CB, DSO, DFC.* Canberra: Australian War Memorial, 1984.

Redmond, Kent C., and Thomas M. Smith. *From Whirlwind to MITRE: The R&D Story of the SAGE Air Defense Computer.* Cambridge, Mass.: MIT Press, 2000.

Reynolds, Clark G. *Admiral John H. Towers: The Struggle for Air Supremacy.* Annapolis, Md.: Naval Institute Press, 1991.

Royal Australian Air Force. *The Air Power Manual.* 2d ed. Canberra: RAAF Air Power Studies Centre, 1994.

Russell, Sir A. *A Span of Wings: Memoirs of Working Life in Aircraft Design Encompassing a Span from Biplanes to Concorde—Bristol Fashion.* Shrewsbury, U.K.: Airlife Publications, 1992.

Seversky, Alexandre de. *Victory through Air Power.* New York: Simon & Schuster, 1942.

Sherry, Michael S. *The Rise of American Air Power: The Creation of Armageddon.* New Haven, Conn.: Yale University Press, 1987.

Slessor, Sir John. *The Great Deterrent: A Collection of Lectures, Articles and Broadcasts on the Development of Strategic Policy in the Nuclear Age by Marshal of the Royal Air Force Sir John Slessor GCB, DSO, MC.* London: Cassell Publishers, 1957.

Sorrels, C. A. *U.S. Cruise Missile Programs: Development, Deployment and Implications for Arms Control.* London: Brassey's, 1983.

Spaight, J. M. *Air Power in the Next War.* London: G. Bles, 1938. A contemporary view.

Spick, Mike. *All-Weather Warriors: The Search for the Ultimate Fighter Aircraft.* London: A&AP, 1994.

Stephens, Alan, ed. *The War in the Air, 1914–1990.* Canberra: RAAF Air Power Studies Centre, 1994. Useful.

Stevenson, J. P. *The Pentagon Paradox: The Development of the F-18 Hornet.* Annapolis, Md.: Naval Institute Press, 1993.

Stewart, George. *Shutting Down the National Dream: A. V. Roe and the Tragedy of the Avro Arrow.* Scarborough, Ontario, Can.: McGraw-Hill Ryerson, 1988.

Tedder, Lord [Arthur]. *Air Power in War. The Lees-Knowles Lectures.* Cambridge, U.K.: Cambridge University Press, 1948.

Thomas, Andrew R., and Anonymous. *Air Rage: Crisis in the Skies.* New York: Prometheus Books, 2002.

Thompson, Maj. Gen. J. *The Lifeblood of War: Logistics in Armed Conflict.* London: Brassey's, 1991.

Till, Geoffrey. *Air Power and the Royal Navy, 1914–45: A Historical Survey.* London: Jane's, 1979.

Tusa, Ann, and John. *The Berlin Airlift.* Boston: Atheneum, 1988.

Twining, Gen. Nathan E. *Neither Liberty nor Safety: A Hard Look at U.S. Military Policy and Strategy.* New York: Holt, Rinehart and Winston, 1966.

United States Air Force, AFCHO (Chief, Office of Air Force History). *Air Interdiction in World War II, Korea and Vietnam.* Washington, D.C.: Office of Air Force History, 1986.

United States Air Force, School of Advanced Air Power Studies. *The Paths of Heaven: The Evolution of Air Power Theory.* Maxwell AFB, Ala.: Air University Press, 1997.

Vallance, Gp. Capt. A. G. B. *The Air Weapon: Doctrines of Air Power Strategy and Operational Art.* London: Macmillan & Co., 1996.

von Karman, Theodore, and L. Edson. *The Wind and Beyond: Theodore von Karman, Pioneer in Aviation and Pathfinder in Space.* Boston: Little, Brown & Co., 1967.

White, M. O. L. *The Foodbirds: Flying for Famine Relief. The Story of One of the Greatest Mercy Airlifts the World Has Known.* Oxford: Bookmarque Publishing, 1994.

Williams, G., F. Gregory, and J. Simpson. *Crisis in Procurement: A Case Study of the TSR-2.* London: Royal United Services Institution, 1969.

Winnefeld, J. A., and D. J. Johnson. *Joint Air Operations: Pursuit of Unity in Command and Control, 1942–1991.* Santa Monica, Calif.: RAND Corp./Naval Institute Press, 1993.

Wolk, Herman S. *Planning and Organizing the Postwar Air Force, 1943–1947.* Washington, D.C.: Office of Air Force History, 1984.

Wood, Derek. *Project Cancelled: A Searching Criticism of the Abandonment of Britain's Advanced Aircraft Projects.* London: Macdonald & Jane's, 1975.

Woolridge, Capt. E. T., ed. *Into the Jet Age: Conflict and Change in Naval Aviation, 1954–1975. An Oral History.* Annapolis, Md.: Naval Institute Press; Shrewsbury, U.K.: Airlife Publications, 1995.

Wrigley, H. N. Edited by Alan Stephens and Brendan O'Loghlin. *The Decisive Factor: Airpower Doctrine.* Canberra: Australian Government Publishing Service, 1990.

Wynn, Humphrey. *The RAF Strategic Nuclear Deterrent Forces: Their Origins, Roles and Deployment, 1946–1969. A Documentary History.* London: HMSO, 1997.

IV. Early Flight

Crouch, Tom D. *The Bishop's Boys: A Life of Wilbur and Orville Wright.* New York: W.W. Norton & Co., 1989.

Driver, Hugh. *The Birth of Military Aviation: Britain, 1903–1914.* Woodbridge, U.K.: Royal Historical Society/The Boydell Press, 1997.

Finne, K. N. *Igor Sikorsky: The Russian Years.* Washington, D.C.: Smithsonian Institution Press, 1987.

Jakab, Peter L. *Visions of a Flying Machine: The Wright Brothers and the Process of Invention.* Washington, D.C.: Smithsonian Institution Press, 1990.

Jarrett, Philip. *Another Icarus: Percy Pilcher and the Quest for Flight.* Washington, D.C.: Smithsonian Institution Press, 1987.

Lewis, Bruce. *A Few of the First: The True Stories of the Men Who Flew in and Before the First World War.* London: Leo Cooper, 1997.

Rickenbacker, Eddie. *Rickenbacker.* Englewood Cliffs, N.J.: Prentice-Hall, 1967. An autobiography by the man who went on to run Eastern Airlines.

Rolt, L. T. C. *The Aeronauts: A History of Ballooning, 1783–1903.* New York: Walker and Co., 1966.

V. Air Forces

The Air Force Communications Command, 1938–1986. Scott AFB, IL: 1987.

Air Ministry. *The Origins and Development of Operational Research in the Royal Air Force.* London: HMSO, 1963.

Arbon, Lee. *They also Flew: The Enlisted Pilot Legacy, 1912–1942.* Washington, D.C.: Smithsonian Institution Press, 1992. The U.S. Army experience.

Beaumont, Roger. *Right Backed by Might—The International Air Force Concept.* Westport, Conn.: Praeger Publishers, 2001.

Bell, Dana. *USAF Colors and Markings in the 1990s with Facsimile Color Paint Chips.* London: Greenhill Books, 1992.

Bentley, Geoffrey, and Maurice Conley. *Portrait of an Air Force: The Royal New Zealand Air Force 1937–1987.* Wellington, NZ: Grantham House, 1987.

Boog, Horst. *Die deutsche Luftwaffenfuhrung, 1935–1945.* Stuttgart: Deutsche Verlags-Anstalt, 1982.

Bowyer, Chaz. *RAF Operations 1918–1938.* London: William Kimber, 1988.

Boyne, Walter J. *Silver Wings: A History of the United States Air Force.* New York: Simon & Schuster, 1993.

Buckton, Henry. *Forewarned is Forearmed: An Official Tribute and History of The Royal Observer Corps.* Ashford, Kent, U.K.: Buchan & Enright, 1993.

Cain, Anthony Christopher. *The Forgotten Air Force: French Air Doctrine in the 1930s.* Washington, D.C.: Smithsonian Institution Press, 2002.

Christienne, Charles, and Pierre Lissarague. *A History of French Military Aviation.* Washington, D.C.: Smithsonian Institution Press, 1986.

Cooper, Matthew. *The German Air Force, 1933–1945: An Anatomy of Failure.* New York: Jane's, 1981.

Douglas, W. A. B. *The Creation of a National Air Force. The Official History of the Royal Canadian Air Force,* Vol. 2. Toronto: University of Toronto Press, 1986.

Finney, Robert T. *History of the Air Corps Tactical School, 1920–1940.* Washington, D.C.: USAF Center for Air Force History, 1992.

Greenhous, Brereton, and Hugh A. Halliday. *Canada's Air Forces, 1914–1999.* Montreal: Art Global and Department of National Defence, 1999.

Gupta, S. G. *History of the Indian Air Force, 1934–45.* New Delhi: Orient Longmans, 1961.

Hellenic Air Force General Staff. *Hellenic Wings.* Vol. 1, *An illustrated History of the HAF and Its Precursors, 1908–1944.* Edited and compiled by Flt. Lt. George J. Beldecos. Athens: Hellenic Air Force, 1999.

Hering, Sq. Ldr. P. G. *Customs and Traditions of the Royal Air Force.* Aldershot, U.K.: Gale & Polden, 1961.

Historia de la Aviacion Espanola. Madrid: Instituto de Historia y Cultura Aeronautica. 1988.

Homze, Edward L. *Arming the Luftwaffe: The Reich Air Ministry and the German Aircraft Industry, 1919–1939.* Lincoln: University of Nebraska Press, 1976.

Johnson, Brian. *Fly Navy: The History of Maritime Aviation.* Shrewsbury, U.K.: Airlife Publications, 1989.

Kendrick, L. *Music in the Air: The Story of Music in the Royal Air Force.* Baldock, Herts, U.K.: Egon Publishers, 1986.

Lee, ACM Sir David. *Wings in the Sun: A History of the Royal Air Force in the Mediterranean, 1945–1986.* London: Ministry of Defence, Air Historical Branch (RAF), 1989.

Mead, Brig. P. *The Eye in the Sky: A History of Air Observation and Reconnaissance for the Army, 1785–1945.* London: HMSO, 1983.

Mikesh, Robert C. *Flying Dragons: The South Vietnamese Air Force.* London: Osprey Publishing, 1988.

Milberry, Larry, ed. *Canada's Air Force at War and Peace.* Toronto: CANAV Books, 2000.

Murray, Williamson. *Strategy for Defeat: The Luftwaffe, 1933–1945.* Maxwell AFB, Ala.: Air University Press, 1983.

Odom, William A. *After the Trenches: The Transformation of U.S. Army Doctrine, 1918–1939.* College Station: Texas A&M University Press, 1999.

Omissi, David E. *Air Power and Colonial Control: The Royal Air Force, 1919–1939.* Manchester, U.K.: Manchester University Press, 1990.

Pearcy, Arthur. *A History of U.S. Coast Guard Aviation.* Shrewsbury, U.K.: Airlife Publications, 1989.

Peattie, Mark R. *Sunburst: The Rise of Japanese Naval Air Power, 1909–1941.* Annapolis, Md.: Naval Institute Press, 2001.

Potgieter, Herman, and W. Steenkamp. *Aircraft of the South African Air Force.* London: Jane's, 1981.

Rivista Aeronautica—1 primi cinquant' anni dell Aviazione italiana (Rome) 3 (March, 1959). This special issue of the journal covers the first fifty years of Italian aviation.

Smith, Malcolm. *British Air Strategy between the Wars.* Oxford: Oxford University Press, 1984.

The Story of the Pakistan Air Force, 1988–1998. Islamabad: Oxford University Press, 2000. The first volume, covering 1943–88 was published by OUP in 1988.

Strategic Air Command. *The Development of Strategic Air Command, 1946–1986.* Offutt AFB, Nebr.: Strategic Air Command, 1986.

Sturtivant, Ray. *British Naval Aviation: The Fleet Air Arm, 1917–1990.* Annapolis, Md.: Naval Institute Press, 1990.

Swanborough, F. G., and P. M. Bowers. *United*

States Navy Aircraft since 1911. New York: Putnam, 1983.

Terraine, John. *A Time for Courage: The Royal Air Force in the European War, 1939–1945.* New York: Macmillan Co., 1985. Published in the United Kingdom as *The Right of the Line: The Royal Air Force in the European War, 1939–1945.*

Turnbull, Archibald D., and Clifford L. Lord. *History of United States Naval Aviation.* New York: Arno Press, 1949. Carries the story into the interwar years.

Weeks, J. *Assault from the Sky: A History of Airborne Warfare.* New York: Putnam, 1978.

VI. World War I

Bailey, Frank W., and Christopher Corey. *The French Air Service War Chronology, 1914–1918.* London: Grub Street, 2002.

Bramson, A. *Pure Luck: The Authorized Biography of Sir Thomas Sopwith, 1888–1989.* Wellingborough, U.K.: PSL, 1990.

Cooke, James J. *The U.S. Air Service in the Great War, 1917–1918.* New York: Praeger Publishers, 1996.

Cooper, Malcolm. *The Birth of Independent Air Power: British Air Policy in the First World War.* London: Allen & Unwin, 1986.

Crowell, Benedict. *America's Munitions, 1917–1918.* Washington, D.C.: USGPO, 1919.

Cutlack, F. M. *The Australian Flying Corps in the Western and Eastern Theatres of War, 1914–1918.* Sydney: Angus and Robertson, 1923. Worth a look.

Davilla, James J., and Arthur M. Solan. *French Aircraft of the First World War.* Boulder, Colo.: Flying Machines Press, 2002.

Franks, Norman, and Hal Giblin. *Under the Guns of the German Aces: Immelmann, Voss, Goring, Lothar Von Richthofen. The Complete Record of Their Victories and Victims.* London: Grub Street, 1997.

Fredette, Raymond H. *The Sky on Fire: The First Battle of Britain.* New York: Holt, Rinehart and Winston, 1966.

Greenhous, Brereton. *The Making of Billy Bishop.* Toronto: Dundum Press, 2002.

Grinnell-Milne, Duncan. *Wind in the Wires.* New York: Mayflower-Dell, 1966. A classic World War I autobiography.

Haddow, G. W., and Peter M. Gross. *The German Giants.* London: Putnam & Co., 1962.

Higham, Robin. *The British Rigid Airship, 1908–1931. A Study in Weapons Policy.* London: G. T. Foulis, 1961.

Hudson, James L. *The Hostile Skies: A Combat History of the American Air Service in World War I.* Syracuse, N.Y.: Syracuse University Press, 1968.

Johnson, Herbert A. *Wingless Eagle: U.S. Army Aviation through World War I.* Chapel Hill: University of North Carolina Press, 2001.

Kilduff, P. *Germany's First Air Force, 1914–1918.* London: Arms & Armour Press, 1991.

Morris, Alan. *First of the Many.* London: Jarrolds, 1968.

Morrow, John. *The Great War in the Air.* Washington, D.C.: Smithsonian Institution Press, 1993. The place to start.

Murray, Williamson. *War in the Air, 1914–45.* London: Cassell Publishers, 1999.

Penrose, Harald. *British Aviation: The Great War and Armistice, 1915–1919.* London: Putnam & Co., 1969.

Powers, Barry D. *Strategy without Slide Rule: British Air Strategy, 1914–1919.* London: Croom Helm, 1976.

Priestley, R. E. *The Signal Service in the European War of 1914 to 1918 (France).* Chatham, U.K.: W & J Mackay, for the Institution of Royal Engineers and the Signal Association, 1921.

Robinson, Douglas H. *The Zeppelin in Combat.* London: G. T. Foulis, 1961. Rev. ed., 1967.

Winter, Denis. *The First of the Few: Fighter Pilots of the First World War.* Athens: University of Georgia Press, 1983.

VII. The Interwar Years, 1918–41

Baker, A., and Sir R. Ivelaw-Chapman. *Wings Over Kabul: The First Airlift.* London: William Kimber, 1975.

Balchen, Bernt. *Come North with Me: An Autobiography.* London: Hodder & Stoughton, 1959.

Bednarek, Janet R. Daly. *America's Airports: Airfield Development, 1918–1947.* College Station: Texas A&M University Press, 2001.

Bilstein, Roger E. *Flight Patterns: Trends of Aeronautical Development in the United States 1918–1929.* Athens: University of Georgia Press, 1983.

Brink, Randall. *Lost Star: The Search for Amelia Earhart.* New York: W. W. Norton & Co., 1994. An experienced airline pilot's explanation of the famous missing airwoman.

Brown, Jerald T. *Where Eagles Landed.* Westport, Conn.: Greenwood Press, 1990. USAAC airfield building.

Chadeau, Emmanuel. *Latécoère.* Paris: Olivier Orban, 1990.

Clark, Ronald W. *The Rise of the Boffins.* London: Phoenix, 1962.

Cobham, Sir Alan. *A Time to Fly: The Memoirs of Sir Alan Cobham.* London: Shepheard-Walwyn, 1928, 1986.

Cochrane, Dorothy, Von Hardesty, and Russell Lee. *The Aviation Career of Igor Sikorsky.* Seattle: University of Washington Press, 1989.

Cooke, James J. *Billy Mitchell.* Boulder, Colo.: Lynne Rienner Publishers, 2002.

Coupar, A. R. *The Smirnoff Story.* London: Jarrolds, 1960.

The Cutting Air Crash: A Case Study in Early Federal Aviation Policy. Washington, D.C.: Department of Transportation, Federal Aviation Administration, 1973.

Foxworth, Thomas G. *The Speed Seekers.* London: G. T. Foulis, 1989.

Gandt, Robert L. *China Clipper: The Age of the Great Flying Boats.* Annapolis, Md.: Naval Institute Press, 1991.

Glines, Carroll V. *Around the World in 175 Days: The First Around the World Flight.* Washington, D.C.: Smithsonian Institution Press, 2001.

Guangqiu Xu. *War Wings: The United States and Chinese Military Aviation, 1929–1999.* Westport, Conn.: Greenwood Press, 2001.

Gunston, Bill. *By Jupiter! The Life of Sir Roy Fedden.* London: The Royal Aeronautical Society, 1978.

Hegener, H. *Fokker: The Man and His Aircraft.* Letchworth, Herts, U.K.: Harleyford Publishers. 1961.

Higham, Robin. *Britain's Imperial Air Routes.* London: G. T. Foulis, 1960.

Hyde, H. Montgomery. *British Air Policy between the Wars, 1918–1939.* London: Heinemann, 1976.

James, John. *The Paladins: A Social History of the RAF up to the Outbreak of World War II.* London: Macdonald, 1990.

Kelsey, Benjamin S. *The Dragon's Teeth: The Creation of United States' Air Power for World War II.* Washington, D.C.: Smithsonian Institution Press, 1982.

Komons, Nick A. *Bonfires to Beacons: Federal Civil Aviation Policy under the Air Commerce Act, 1926–1938.* Washington, D.C.: Smithsonian Institution Press, 1989.

Lee, ACM Sir David. *Never Stop the Engine when It's Hot.* London: Thomas Harmsworth, 1983.

Lindbergh, Anne Morrow. *Listen! The Wind.* New York: Westvaco, 1990. The classic story of the 1933 Arctic air route exploration, by Charles A. Lindbergh's wife.

Lindbergh, Charles A. *The Spirit of St. Louis.* New York: Scribner, 1953.

Mackersey, Ian. *Smithy, The Life of Sir Charles Kingsford Smith.* Boston: Little, Brown & Co., 1998.

Macmillan, Norman. *Sir Sefton Brancker.*

London: William Heinemann, 1935. A fellow pilot's biography of the exuberant proponent of civil aviation.

Maurer, Maurer. *Aviation in the U.S. Army, 1919–1939.* Washington, D.C.: Office of Air Force History, 1987.

Migeo, M. *Saint-Exupéry: A Biography.* London: Macdonald, 1961.

Morrison, Wilbur H. *Donald W. Douglas: A Heart with Wings.* Ames: Iowa State University Press, 1991.

Nobile, Gen. Umberto. *My Polar Flights.* New York: Putnam, 1961.

O'Brien, P. J. *Will Rogers: Ambassador of Good Will.* London: Hutchinson, ca. 1935.

Overy, Richard. *Goering.* London: Phoenix, 2000.

Penrose, Harald. *British Aviation: Ominous Skies, 1935–1939.* London: HMSO, 1980.

Richardson, Gp. Capt. F. C. "Dickie." *Man is Not Lost: The Log of a Pioneer RAF Pilot/Navigator, 1933–1946.* Shrewsbury, U.K.: Airlife Publications, 1997.

Roskill, Capt. S. W. *Naval Policy between the Wars.* Vol. 1, *1919–1929.* Vol. 2, *1930–1939.* London: Collins, 1970, 1976. Regarding the Fleet Air Arm.

Shiner, John F. *Foulois and the U.S. Army Corps, 1931–1935.* Washington, D.C.: AFCHO, 1983.

Shute, Nevil. *Slide Rule: The Autobiography of an Engineer.* London: William Heinemann, 1954; William Morrow & Co., 1954.

Trimble, William F. *Admiral William A. Moffett: Architect of Naval Aviation.* Washington, D.C.: Smithsonian Institution Press, 1994.

Vander Meulen, Jacob. *The Politics of Aircraft: Building an American Military Industry.* Lawrence: University Press of Kansas, 1991.

Wells, K. B. Meekcom. *The British Air Commission and Lend-Lease: The Role, Organization of the BAC (and Its Antecedents) in the United States and Canada, 1938–1945.* Turnbridge, Kent, U.K.: Air Britain (Historic), 2000.

Wight, Monte Duane. *Most Probable Position: A History of Aerial Navigation to 1942.* Lawrence: University Press of Kansas, 1972.

Winterbotham, Gp. Capt. F. W. *Secret and Personal.* London: William Kimber, 1969.

Woolridge, E. T. *The Golden Age Remembered: U.S. Naval Aviation, 1919–1941.* Annapolis, Md.: Naval Institute Press, 1998.

VIII. WORLD WAR II IN EUROPE, 1939–45

Addison, Paul, and Jeremy A. Crang, eds. *The Burning Blue: A New History of the Battle of Britain.* London: Pimlico, 2000.

Allen, Wing Cdr. H. R. *Who Won the Battle of Britain?* London: Barker, 1974.

Babington-Smith, Constance. *Air Spy.* New York: Harper & Bros., 1957.

Beer, Siegfried, and Stefan Karner. *Der Krieg aus der Luft: Kärnten und Steiermark 1941–1945.* Graz, Austria: Weishaupt, 1992.

Beevor, Antony. *Crete: The Battle and the Resistance.* Boulder, Colo.: Westview Press, 1994.

Bekker, Cajus. *The Luftwaffe War Diaries.* Cambridge, Mass.: Da Capo Press, 1994.

Bender, Roger James. *Air Organizations of the Third Reich.* Palo Alto, Calif.: Aurora Press, 1967.

Bingham, V. F. *Bristol Beaufighter.* Shrewsbury, U.K.: Airlife Publications, 1994.

Bishop, Edward. *McIndoe's Army: The Story of the Guinea Pig Club and Its Indomitable Members.* London: Grub Street, 2002.

———. *The Wooden Wonder: The Story of the de Havilland Mosquito.* London: Max Parrish, 1959.

Blandford, E. L. *Target England: Flying with the Luftwaffe in World War II.* Shrewsbury, U.K.: Airlife Publications, 1997.

Boog, Horst, ed. *The Conduct of the Air War in the Second World War: An International Comparison.* New York: R. J. Berg & Co., 1992.

Bowman, M. W. *The Men Who Flew the Mosquito: Compelling Accounts of the Wooden Wonder's Triumphant World War II Career.* Wellingborough, U.K.: PSL, 1995.

———. *USAAF Handbook: 1939–1945.* Gloucester, U.K.: Sutton Publishing, 1997.

Braille, Robert V. *Angels Zero: P-47 Close Air Support in Europe.* Washington, D.C.: Smithsonian Institution Press, 2000.

Brew, Alec. *Boulton Paul Aircraft since 1915.* London: Putnam, 1993.

Brickhill, Paul. *The Dam Busters.* London: Evans Brothers, 1954.

Brown, Capt. Eric, RN. *Testing for Combat.* Shrewsbury, U.K.: Airlife Publications, 1994.

Brown, James Ambrose. *A Gathering of Eagles: Campaigns of the South African Air Force in Italian East Africa 1940–1941.* Cape Town: Purnell, 1970.

Brown, Louis. *A Radar History of World War II: Technical and Military Imperatives.* London and Philadelphia: Institute of Physics Publishing, 1999.

Bullmore, F. T. K. *The Dark Haven.* London: Jonathan Cape, 1956.

Bungay, Stephen. *The Most Dangerous Enemy: A History of the Battle of Britain.* London: Aurum Press, 2000.

Carl, Ann B. *A Wasp Among Eagles: A Woman Military Test Pilot in World War II.* Washington, D.C.: Smithsonian Institution Press, 1999.

Churchill, Jan. *On Wings to War: Teresa James Aviator.* Manhattan, KS: Sunflower University Press, 1992. A WASP's story.

Coffey, T. M. *Decision Over Schweinfurt: The U.S. 8th Air Force Battle for Daylight Bombing.* New York: David McKay, 1977.

Collier, Basil. *The Battle of the V Weapons, 1944–1945.* New York: Wiliiam Morrow & Co., 1964. An overall developmental picture.

———. *The Defence of the United Kingdom.* London: HMSO, 1957.

Coombs, L. F. E. *The Lion Has Wings: The Race to Prepare the RAF for World War II: 1935–1940.* Shrewsbury, U.K.: Airlife Publications, 1997.

Cowderoy, Dudley, and Roy C. Nesbit. *War in the Air: Rhodesian Air Force, 1935–1980.* Alberton, South Africa: Galago Publishing, 1987.

Craven, W. F., and Cate, James Lea, eds. *The Army Air Forces in World War II.* 7 vols. Chicago: University of Chicago Press, 1948–58.

d'Alzac-Epezy, Claude. *L'Armée de l'Air de Vichy, 1940–1944.* Chateau de Vincennes: Service historique de l'Armée de l'Air (SHAA), 1997.

Daniels, G., ed. *A Guide to the Reports of the United States Strategic Bombing Survey.* Vol. 1, Europe. London: Royal Historical Society, 1981.

Davis, Richard G. *Carl A. Spaatz and the Air War in Europe.* Washington, D.C.: Smithsonian Institution Press, 1993.

Dornberger, Gen. Walter. *V-2.* New York: Ballantine Books, 1954.

Dugan, James, and Carroll Stewart. *Ploesti, the Great Ground-Air Battle of 1 August 1943.* New York: Ballantine Books, 1962.

Durand, A. A. *Stalag Luft III: The Secret Story.* Wellingborough, U.K.: PSL, 1989.

Fisher, D. E. *A Race on the Edge of Time. Radar: The Decisive Weapon of World War II.* New York: McGraw-Hill, 1988.

Fletcher, E. *The Lucky Bastard Club: A B-17 Pilot in Training and in Combat, 1943–45. Mister Fletcher's Gang.* Seattle: University of Washington Press, 1993.

Fozard, J. W., ed. *Sydney Camm and the Hurricane: Perspectives on the Master Fighter Designer and His Finest Achievement.* Washington, D.C.: Smithsonian Institution Press. 1991.

Frankland, Noble. *The Bombing Offensive against Germany: Outlines and Perspectives.* London: Faber, 1965.

Freeman, Roger A. *U.K. Airfields of the Ninth: Then and Now.* Croydon, U.K.: After the Battle Publications, 1994.

———. *The Mighty Eighth: Units, Men and Machines.* London: Macdonald, 1969.

Fridenson, Patrick, and Jean Lecoir. *La France et la Grande-Bretagne face aux problems aériens (1935-mai 1940).* Vincennes: SHAA, 1970.

Furse, Anthony. *Wilfred Freeman: The Genius behind Allied Survival and Air Supremacy, 1939 to 1945.* Staplehurst, Kent, U.K.: Spellmount, 1999.

Galland, Gen. Adolf. *The First and the Last.* London: Methuen, 1955.

German Aviation Medicine in World War II. Washington, D.C.: USGPO, 1950.

Goodson, Lt. Col. James, and N. L. R. Franks. *Over-Paid, Over-Sexed, and Over Here: From RAF Eagles to 4th Fighter Group Hawks.* Canterbury, U.K.: Wingham Press, 1991.

Goulter, Christina J. M. *A Forgotten Offensive: Royal Air Force Coastal Command Anti-Shipping Campaigns, 1940–1945.* London: Frank Cass & Co., 1995.

Granger, Byrd Howell. *On Final Approach: The Women Air Force Service Pilots of World War II.* Scottsdale, Ariz.: Falconer Publishing Co., 1991.

Green, William. *Warplanes of the Third Reich.* New York: Doubleday, 1970.

Guerlac, Henry E. *Radar in World War II.* New York: American Institute of Physics, 1987.

Haarer, Sq. Ldr. A. E. *A Cold-Blooded Business.* London: Staple, 1958. Bomb disposal.

Haight, John McVickar. *American Aid to France, 1938–1940.* New York: Atheneum, 1970.

Hall, H. Duncan. *North American Supply.* 2 vols. London: HMSO, 1955.

Harclerode, Peter. *Arnhem: A Tragedy of Errors.* London: A&AP, 1994.

Harris, ACM Sir A. T. *Despatch on War Operations: 23rd February, 1942, to 8th May, 1945.* London: Frank Cass & Co., 1995. Note the preface and introduction by Sebastian Cox, and "Harris: a German View" by Horst Boog.

Harvey, Maurice. *Scandinavian Misadverture: The Campaign in Norway, 1940.* Turnbridge Wells, Kent, U.K.: Spellmount, 1990.

Hatch, F. J. *Aerodome of Democracy: Canada and the Commonwealth Air Training Plan, 1939–1945.* Ottawa: Directorate of History, Department of National Defence, 1983.

Hays, Gus, Jr. *The Alaska-Siberian Connection: The World War II Air Route.* College Station: Texas A&M University Press, 1996.

Higham, Robin. *Diary of a Disaster: British Aid to Greece, 1940–1941.* Lexington: University Press of Kentucky, 1986.

Hinsley, F. H., et al. *British Intelligence in the Second World War.* 6 vols. London: HMSO, 1979–88.

Holley, I. B. *Buying Aircraft.* Washington, D.C.: U.S. Army Center for Military History, 1964.

Holmes, Harry. *The U.S. 8th Air Force at Warton 1942–1945: The World's Greatest Air Depot.* Shrewsbury, U.K.: Airlife Publications, 1998.

Hooper, Bill, and Tim Hamilton. *The Life and Times of Pilot Officer Prune: Being the Official Story of TEE EMM.* London: HMSO, 1992.

Hughes, T. A. *Overlord: General Pete Quesada and the Triumph of Tactical Air Power in World War II.* New York: Free Press, 1995.

Huston, James A. *Out of the Blue: U.S. Army Airborne Operations in World War II.* New York: Stein and Day, 1979.

Irving, David. *The Destruction of Dresden.* Morley, Leeds, U.K.: Elmfield Press, 1974.

Jackson, A. S. *Pathfinder Bennett—Airman Extraordinary. Air Vice Marshal D.C. T. Bennet CB, CBE, DSO.* Lavenham, U.K.: Terrence Dalton, 1991.

James, T. G. G. *The Air Defences of Great Britain.* Vol. 1, *The Growth of Fighter Command, 1936–1940* (2001). Vol. 2, *The Battle of Britain* (2000). Vol. 3, *Night Defence during the Blitz, 1940–1941* (2002). London: Frank Cass & Co. The Air Ministry secret histories.

Jones, R. V. *The Wizard War: British Scientific Intelligence, 1939–1945*. New York: Coward, McCann, & Geoghegan, 1978.

Joubert, ACM Sir Philip. *The Forgotten Ones: The Story of the Ground Crews*. London: Hutchinson, 1961. Adds another dimension.

Kellett, J. P., and J. Davies. *A History of the RAF Servicing Commandos*. Shrewsbury, U.K.: Airlife Publications, 1989. The combat ground crew

Koch, Horst-Adalbert. *Flak, die Geschichte der deutsche Flakartillerie, 1935–1945*. N.p., 1954.

Leaf, E. *Above All Unseen: The Royal Air Force's Photographic Reconnaissance Units, 1939–1945*. Wellingborough, U.K.: PSL, 1997.

Lukas, R. C. *Eagles East: The Army Air Forces and the Soviet Union, 1941–1945*. Tallahassee: Florida State University Press, 1970.

Marshall, S. L. A. *Night Drop: The American Airborne Invasion of Normandy*. Boston: Little, Brown & Co., 1962.

Mason, Francis K. *Battle over Britain*. New York: Doubleday, 1969. Very detailed.

McGovern, James. *Crossbow and Overcast*. New York: William Morrow & Co., 1964. V-weapons.

Mets, D. R. *Master of Air Power: General Carl "Tooey" A. Spaatz*. Novato, Calif.: Presidio Press, 1988.

Middlebrook, Martin. *Arnhem 1944: The Airborne Battle, 17–26 September*. New York: Viking, 1994.

Ministry of Supply. *Periodical Review No. 1, Fires in Wellington Aircraft*. Issue 2 (Jan. 18, 1946). United Kingdom: R. D. T. (Fires) Directorate of Aircraft Research and Technical Development, Ministry of Supply, 1946. Part of a series.

Mitcham, Samuel W., Jr. *Eagles of the Third Reich: The Men Who Made the Luftwaffe*. Novato, Calif.: Presidio Press, 1997.

Morgan, Hugh, and Seibel, J. *Combat Kill: The Drama of Aerial Warfare in World War II and the Controversy Surrounding Victories*. Wellingborough, U.K.: Patrick Stevens, 1997.

Mortensen, Daniel R. *A Pattern for Joint Operations: World War II Close Air Support, North Africa*. Washington, D.C.: AFCHO, 1987.

Morzik, Gen. Maj. Fritz. *Die Deutschen Transportflieger im Zweiten Weltkrieg*. Frankfurt am Main: Bernard & Graefe, 1966.

Moulton, Maj. General J. L. *A Study of Warfare in Three Dimensions: The Norwegian Campaign*. Columbus: University of Ohio, 1967.

Moyes, P. *Bomber Squadrons of the RAF and Their Aircraft*. London: Macdonald & Jane's, 1974.

Neillards, Robin. *The Bomber War: Arthur Harris and the Allied Bomber Offensive, 1939–1945*. London: John Murray, 2001.

Nockolds, H. *Rescue from Disaster: The History of the RDF Radar Group*. Newton Abbot, U.K.: David & Charles, 1979.

Noltc, Col. Reginald G. *Thunder Monsters over Europe: A History of the 405th Fighter Group in World War II*. Manhattan, Kans.: Sunflower University Press, 1989. P-47 Tactical Air Force.

Orange, Vincent. *Coningham: A Biography of Air Marshal Sir Arthur Coningham KCB, KBE, DSO, MC, DFC, AFC*. London: Methuen, 1990.

Overy, R. J. *The Air War, 1939–1945*. New York: Stein and Day, 1980. A must-read treatment.

Parton, James. *"Air Force Spoken Here": General Ira Eaker and the Command of the Air*. Washington, D.C.: Adler & Adler, 1986.

Peake, Dame Felicity. *Pure Chance*. Shrewsbury, U.K.: Airlife Publications, 1993.

Pearcy, Arthur. *Lend-Lease Aircraft in World War II*. Shrewsbury, U.K.: Airlife Publications, 1996.

Perret, Geoffrey. *Winged Victory: The Army Air Forces in World War II*. New York: Random House, 1993.

Phelps, J. A. *Chappie: America's First Black Four-*

Star General. The Life and Times of Daniel
James, Jr. Novato, Calif.: Presidio Press, 1991.

Philpott, Bryan. In Enemy Hands: Revealing the
Stories Behind Wartime Allied Aircraft Losses.
Wellingborough, U.K.: Patrick Stephens,
1981.

Pile, Gen. Sir Frederick. Ack-Ack. London:
George C. Harrap & Co., 1949.

Pisano, D. A. To Fill the Skies with Pilots: The
Civilian Training Program, 1939–46. Urbana:
University of Illinois Press, 1993.

Plocher, Generalleutnant Hermann. The German Air Force versus Russia, 1941. USAF Historical Studies No. 153. Washington, D.C.:
AFCHO, 1965.

Postan, M. M., Denys Hay, and J. D. Scott. The
Design and Development of Weapons. London:
HMSO. 1964.

Pultney, Diane T, ed. ULTRA and the Army Air
Forces in World War II. Washington, D.C.:
USAF Warrior Studies, 1987.

Ramsey, Winston G., ed. The Battle of Britain,
Then and Now. London: After the Battle,
1982.

———. The Blitz, Then and Now. London:
Battle of Britain Prints, 1987. Several volumes.

Ray, John. The Battle of Britain: New Perspectives.
London: Arms & Armour Press, 1994.

Reitsch, Hannah. The Sky My Kingdom: Memoirs of a German Woman Test Pilot. Oxford.
The Bodley Head, 1955.

Rexford-Welch, Sq. Ldr. S. C. Royal Air Force
Medical Services. 1939–1945. 4 vols. London:
HMSO, 1954–58.

Ritchie, Sebastian. Industry and Air Power: The
Expansion of British Aircraft Production, 1935–
1941. London: Frank Cass & Co., 1997.

Robinson, Derek. Piece of Cake. New York:
Knopf, 1984. An excellent novel of a 1939–
40 RAF squadron.

Rosignoli, G. Air Force Badges and Insignia of
World War II. Dorset, U.K.: Blandford Press,
1976.

Rudel, Hans Ulrich. Stuka Pilot. New York:
Ballantine Books, 1958. Gives a unique look.

Rust, K. C. Fifteenth Air Force Story in World War
II. Terre Haute, Ind.: Sunshine House, 1993.

Saward, Dudley. The Bomber's Eye. London: Cassell Publishers, 1959. On radar bombsights in
World War II.

Schaffer, Ronald. Wings of Judgment: American
Bombing in World War II. New York: Oxford
University Press, 1985.

Schoenfeld, M. Stalking the U-Boat: USAAF
Offensive Antisubmarine Operations in World
War II. Washington, D.C.: Smithsonian Insti-
tution Press, 1995.

Sharp, C. M. DH: An Outline of de Havilland
History. London: Faber & Faber, 1960.
Reprint, Shrewsbury, U.K.: Airlife Publica-
tions, 1982.

Shores, Christopher. Aces High. 2 vols. London:
Neville Spearman, 1966.

Simons, Leslie E. German Research in World War
II. New York: John Wiley & Sons, 1948.

Sims, E. H. The Fighter Pilots: A Comparative
Study of the Royal Air Force, the Luftwaffe and
the United States Army Air Forces in Europe and
North Africa 1939–45. London: Cassell Publishers, 1967.

Smith, B. F. The Ultra-Magic Deals and the Most
Secret Special Relationship, 1940–1946. Shrewsbury, U.K.: Airlife Publications, 1993.

Smith, Perry McCoy. The Air Force Plans for
Peace, 1943–1945. Baltimore: Johns Hopkins
University Press, 1970.

Smithies, E., ed. War in the Air: The Men and
Women Who Built, Serviced, and Flew War
Planes Remember the Second World War. New
York: Viking, 1990.

Speer, Albert. Inside the Third Reich. New York:
Simon & Schuster, 1997.

Stanley, Col. R. M. To Fool a Glass Eye. Shrewsbury, U.K.: Airlife Publications, 1998. Air
photographs and camouflage.

Steadman, Kenneth A. A Comparative Look at
Air-Ground Support Doctrine and Practice in

World War II, with an Appendix on Current So-viet Close Air Support Doctrine. Fort Leavenworth, Kans.: Combat Studies Institute, U.S. Army Command and General Staff College, 1982.

Stouffer, Samuel A. *The American Soldier.* Vol. 1, *Adjustment During Army Life.* Vol. 2, *Combat and Its Aftermath.* Princeton, N.J.: Princeton University Press, 1949. Reprint, Manhattan, Kans.: Sunflower University Press, MA/AH Publishing, 1977.

Suchenwirth, Richard. *Historical Turning Points in the German Air Force War Effort.* USAF Historical Studies No. 189. Maxwell AFB, Ala.: Air University Research Studies Institute, 1959. Reprint, Manhattan, KS: Sunflower University Press, MA/AH Publishing, 1977.

Tedder, Lord [Arthur]. *With Prejudice.* London: Cassell Publishers, 1966.

United Kingdom. *The Strategic Air War Against Germany, 1939–1945. The Official Report of the British Bombing Survey Unit.* London: Frank Cass & Co., 1998.

United States Army Air Forces. *Pilots' Information File 1944: The Authentic World War II Guidebook for Pilots and Flight Engineers.* Atglen, Penn.: Schiffer Publishing, 1995.

Vaeth, J. G. *Blimps and U-Boats: U.S. Navy Airships in the Battle of the Atlantic.* Annapolis, Md.: Naval Institute Press, 1992.

Warren, John C. *Airborne Operations in World War II, European Theater.* USAF Historical Studies. No. 97. Maxwell AFB, Ala.: USAF Air War College, 1956. Reprint, Manhattan, Kans.: Sunflower University Press, MA/AH Publishing, 1977.

Webster, Sir Charles, and Noble Frankland. *The Strategic Air Offensive against Germany.* 4 vols. London: HMSO. 1961.

West, Kenneth S. *The Captive Luftwaffe.* London: Putnam, 1978.

Wheeler, Air Commodore Allen. *That Nothing Failed Them: Testing Aeroplanes in War.* London: G. T. Foulis, 1963.

White, G. *Allied Aircraft Piston Engines of World War II: History and Development of Frontline Aircraft Piston Engines Produced by Great Britain and the United States during World War II.* Shrewsbury, U.K.: Airlife Publications, 1995.

Wolff, Leon. *Low-Level Mission.* London: Longmans Green, 1958.

Wood, A. *A History of the World's Glider Forces.* Wellingborough, U.K.: PSL, 1990.

Wright, Robert. *The Man Who Won the Battle of Britain.* London: Macdonald, 1969. Published as *Dowding and the Battle of Britain* for British distribution.

Ziegler, Mano. *Rocket Fighter: The Story of the Me-163.* Garden City, N.J.: Doubleday, 1963.

IX. WORLD WAR II IN RUSSIA, AND THE USSR TO 1990

Antonov, V., et al. *OKB Sukhoi: A History of the Design Bureau and Its Aircraft.* Leicester, U.K.: Midland Counties, 1996.

Belyakov, R. A., and J. Marmian. *MiG: Fifty Years of Secret Aircraft Design.* Shrewsbury, U.K.: Airlife Publications, 1994.

Conversino, Mark J. *Fighting with the Soviets: The Failure of Operation Frantic, 1944–1945.* Lawrence: University Press of Kansas, 1997.

Duffy, P., and A. Kandalov. *Tupolev: The Man and His Aircraft.* London: Society of Automotive Engineers, 1996.

Hardesty, Von. *Red Phoenix: The Rise of Soviet Air Power, 1941–1945.* London: A&AP, 1982.

Higham, Robin, John T. Greenwood, and Von Hardesty. *Russian Aviation and Air Power in the Twentieth Century.* London: Frank Cass & Co., 1998.

Kerber, L. L. *Stalin's Aviation Gulag: A Memoir of Andrei Tupolev and the Purge Era.* Washington, D.C.: Smithsonian Institution Press, 1996.

Mikoyan, S. *Stepan Anastasovich Mikoyan: An Autobiography.* Translated by Aschen

Mikoyan. Shrewsbury, U.K.: Airlife Publications, 1999.

Pennington, Reina. *Wings, Women and War: Soviet Airwomen in World War II Combat.* Lawrence: University Press of Kansas, 2001.

Zamoyski, A. *The Forgotten Few: The Polish Air Force in the Second World War.* London: John Murray, 1995.

Ziemke, Earle F. *Stalingrad to Berlin.* Washington, D.C.: USGPO, 1968. The Soviet victory in the East is explained.

X. World War II in the Pacific

Banks, A. *Wings of the Dawning: The Battle for the Indian Ocean 1939–1945.* London: HMSO, 1996.

Bleakley, Jack. *The Eavesdroppers.* Canberra: Australian Government Publishing Service, 1991.

Byrd, Martha. *Chennault: Giving Wings to the Tiger.* University: University of Alabama Press, 1987.

Cornelius, W., and T. Short. *Ding Hao: America's Air War in China 1937–1945.* Gretna, La.: Pelican Publishing Co., 1980.

Craven, W. F., and Cate, James Lea, eds. *The Army Air Forces in World War II.* Vol. 4, *The Pacific: Guadalcanal to Saipan, August 1942 to July 1944.* Chicago: University of Chicago Press, 1950–66.

Daniels, G., ed. *A Guide to the Reports of the United States Strategic Bombing Survey.* Vol. 2, *Pacific.* London: Royal Historical Society, 1981.

Feifer, G. *The Battle of Okinawa and the Atomic Bomb.* Boston: Ticknor & Fields, 1992.

Francillon, René. *Japanese Aircraft of the Pacific War.* London: Putnam, 1970.

Franks, N. L. R. *The Air Battle of Imphal.* London: William Kimber, 1985.

Friedman, Norman. *U.S. Aircraft Carriers: An Illustrated Design History.* Annapolis, Md.: Naval Institute Press, 1984.

Gamble, B. *Black Sheep One: The Life of Gregory "Pappy" Boyington.* Novato, Calif.: Presidio Press, 2000.

Glines, Lt. Col. Carroll V. *Doolittle's Tokyo Raiders.* New York: D. Van Nostrand, 1964.

Goldstein, D. M., and K. V. Dillon, eds. *The Pearl Harbor Papers: Inside the Japanese Plans.* Washington, D.C.: Brassey's, 1995.

Green, William, Gordon Swanborough, and P. S. Chopra, eds. *The Indian Air Force and Its Aircraft.* London: Ducimus Books, 1982.

Hall, R. C., ed. *Lightning over Bougainville: The Yamamoto Mission Reconsidered.* Washington, D.C.: Smithsonian Institution Press, 1991.

Halsey, Adm. William F., and Lt. Col. J. Bryan, III. *Admiral Halsey's Story.* New York: McGraw-Hill, 1947.

Harper, S. *Miracle of Deliverance: The Case for the Bombing of Hiroshima and Nagasaki.* New York: Stein and Day, 1986.

Hata, Ikuhiko, and Yasuho Izawa. *Japanese Naval Aces and Fighter Units in World War II.* Shrewsbury, U.K.: Airlife Publications, 1990.

Hata, Ikuhiko, Yasuho Izawa, and Christopher Shores. *Japanese Army Air Force Fighter Units and Their Aces, 1931–1945.* London: Grub Street, 2002.

Horikoshi, J. *Eagles of Mitsubishi: The Story of the Zero Fighter.* Seattle: University of Washington Press, 1981, 1992.

Hoyt, Edwin P. *McCampbell's Heroes: The Story of the U.S. Navy's Most Celebrated Carrier Fighters of the Pacific War.* New York: Van Nostrand Reinhold, 1983.

Kenney, Gen. George C. *Dick Bong, Ace of Aces.* New York: Duell, Sloan & Pearce, 1960.

Kerr, E. B. *Flames over Tokyo: The U.S. Army Air Forces' Incendiary Campaign against Japan 1944–1945.* New York: Donald I. Fine Books, 1991.

Knebel, Fletcher, and Charles W. Bailey II. *No High Ground.* London: Weidenfeld & Nicolson, 1960.

Layton, Rear Adm. Edwin T. *"And I Was*

There": Pearl Harbor and Midway, Breaking the Secrets. New York: William Morrow & Co., 1985.

Lloyd, Alwyn T. Superfortress: The Story of the B-29 and American Airpower in World War II. New York: Detail & Scale, 1988.

Lundstrom, John B. The First Team: Pacific Naval Air Command from Pearl Harbor to Midway. Annapolis, Md.: Naval Institute Press, 1983.

Mikesh, Robert C. Broken Wings of the Samurai: The Destruction of the Japanese Air Force. Shrewsbury, U.K.: Airlife Publications, 1993.

Mikesh, Robert C., and S. Abe. Japanese Aircraft, 1910–1941. London: Putnam, 1990.

Morison, Samuel Eliot. United States Naval Operations in World War II. 15 vols. Boston: Little, Brown & Co., 1947–62.

Morrison, W. H. Point of No Return: The Story of the Twentieth Air Force. New York: Times Books, 1979.

Newton, W. P., and R. R. Rea., eds. Wing of Gold: An Account of Naval Aviation Training in World War II. The Correspondence of Aviation Cadet/Ensign Robert R. Rea. University: University of Alabama Press, 1987.

O'Brien, T. The Moonlight War: The Story of Clandestine Operations in South-East Asia, 1944–1945. London: Collins, 1987.

Phillips, Bob. KC8 Burma: CBI Air Warning Team, 1941–1942. Manhattan, Kans.: Sunflower University Press, 1992.

Prange, Gordon W., with D. M. Goldstein and K. V. Dillon. Miracle at Midway. New York: McGraw-Hill, 1982.

———. Pearl Harbor: The Verdict of History. New York: McGraw-Hill, 1986.

Reynolds, Clark G. The Fast Carriers: The Forging of an Air Navy. New York: McGraw-Hill, 1968.

Scott, Gen. Robert L., Jr. God Is My Co-Pilot. New York: Charles Scribner's Sons, 1943.

Sherrod, Robert. History of Marine Corps Aviation in World War II. Washington, D.C.: Combat Force's Press, 1952.

Shores, C., and Y. Izawa. Bloody Shambles. 2 vols. London: Grubb Street, 1992, 1996.

Smith, P. C. Impact! The Dive Bomber Pilots Speak. London: William Kimber, 1981.

———. Task Force 57: The British Pacific Fleet, 1944–1945. London: William Kimber, 1969.

Spector, Ronald. Eagle against the Sun. New York: Free Press, 1985.

Takaki, Ronald. Hiroshima: Why America Dropped the Atomic Bomb. Boston: Little, Brown & Co., 1996.

Tillman, B. The Dauntless Dive Bomber in World War Two. Shrewsbury, U.K.: Airlife Publications, 1993.

Tomlinson, M. The Most Dangerous Moment. London: William Kimber, 1976.

Treadwell, T. C. The Ironworks: A History of Grumman's Fighting Aeroplanes. Shrewsbury, U.K.: Airlife Publications, 1990.

Tunner, Gen. William H. Over the Hump. Washington, D.C.: Office of Air Force History, 1985.

Webber, Bert. Retaliation: Japanese Attacks and Allied Countermeasures on the Pacific Coast in World War II. Corvallis: Oregon State University Press, 1975.

Werrell, Kenneth P. Blankets of Fire: U.S. Bombers over Japan during World War II. Washington, D.C.: Smithsonian Institution Press, 1996.

Woodbury, D. O. Builders for Battle: How the Pacific Naval Air Bases Were Constructed. New York: E. P. Dutton, 1946.

Y'Blood, William T. Red Sun Setting: The Battle of the Philippine Sea. Annapolis, Md.: Naval Institute Press, 1981.

XI. The Red Air Force and China

Allen, K. W., G. Krumel, and J. D. Pollack. China's Air Force Enters the Twenty-first Century: Project Air Force. Santa Monica, Calif.: RAND Corp., 1995.

Braybrook, R. *Soviet Combat Aircraft: The Four Postwar Generations.* London: Osprey Publishing, 1991.

Bulowski, P., and J. Miller. *OKB MiG: A History of the Design Bureau and Its Aircraft.* Leicester, U.K.: Aerofax/Midland Counties, 1991.

Gunston, Bill. *Mikoyan MiG-21.* London: Osprey Publishing, 1987.

Gunston, Bill, and Yefim Gordon. *MiG Aircraft since 1937.* London: Putnam, 1998.

———. *Yakovlev Aircraft Since 1924.* Annapolis, Md.: Naval Institute Press, 1997.

Lake, Jon. *Jane's How to Fly and Fight in the Mikoyan MiG-29 Fulcrum.* New York: Harper-Collins, 1997.

Mason, R. A., and John W. R. Taylor. *Aircraft, Strategy and Operations of the Soviet Air Force.* London: Jane's, 1986.

Moon, H. *Soviet SST: The Technopolitics of the Tupolev-144.* New York: Orion Books, 1989.

Zaloga, Stephen J. *The Kremlin's Nuclear Sword: The Rise and Fall of Russia's Strategic Nuclear Forces, 1945–2000.* Washington, D.C.: Smithsonian Institution Press, 2001.

Zijun, Duan, ed. *China Today: Aviation Industry.* Beijing: China Aviation Industry Press, 1989. Translation published by the Chinese Social Science Press.

XII. Commercial Aviation

Bain, D. M. *Canadian Pacific Airlines: The History and Aircraft.* Calgary, Alberta, Can.: Kishom Publications, 1987.

Baker, Eugene E. *Contrails: A Boeing Salesman Reminisces.* Enumclaw, Wash.: TABA Publishing, 1996.

Bao, P. Lo. *An Illustrated History of British European Airways.* Feltham, Middlesex, U.K.: Browcom Group, 1989.

Bender, Marilyn, and Selig Altschul. *The Chosen Instrument: Juan Trippe and Pan Am, The Rise and Fall of an American Entrepreneur.* New York: Simon & Schuster, 1982.

Bernstein, A. *Grounded: Frank Lorenzo and Eastern Airlines.* New York: Simon & Schuster, 1990.

Blain, A. N. J. *Pilots and Management: Industrial Relations in the U. K. Airlines.* London: George Allen & Unwin, 1972.

Borins, Sanford D. *The Language of the Skies: The Bilingual Air Traffic Control Conflict in Canada.* Kingston and Montreal, Can.: McGill-Queen's University Press, 1983.

Bowers, P. M. *Boeing Aircraft since 1916.* London: Putnam, 1966.

Braden, B., and P. Hagan. *A Dream Takes Flight: Hartsfield Atlanta International Airport and Aviation in Atlanta.* Atlanta: The Atlanta Historical Society/University of Georgia Press, 1989.

Bray, Roger, and Ladimir Raitz. *Flight to the Sun: The Story of the Holiday Revolution.* New York: Continuum Books, 2002.

Burnham, Frank. *Cleared to Land: The FAA Story.* Washington, D.C.: USGPO, 1977.

Capelli, Peter, ed. *Airline Labor Relationships in the Global Era: The New Frontier.* Ithaca, N.Y.: Cornell University Press, 1995.

Cohen, Susan, and Daniel. *Pan Am 103: The Bombing, the Betrayals, and a Bereaved Family's Search for Justice.* New York: Signet, 2000.

Condit, John. *Wings over the West: Russ Baker and the Rise of Pacific Western Airlines.* Madeira Park, B.C., Can.: Harbour Publishing, 1984.

Corbett, David. *Politics and the Airlines.* London: Allen & Unwin, 1965.

Cowell, J. G. D. H. *Comet: The World's First Jet Airliner.* Shrewsbury, U.K.: Airlife Publications, 1976.

Culbert, Tom, and Andy Dawson. *Pan Africa: Across the Sahara in 1941 with Pan Am.* McLeon, Va.: Paladwr Press, 1998.

Cuthbert, G. *Flying to the Sun: Quarter Century of Britannia Airways, Europe's Leading Leisure Airline.* London: Hodder & Stoughton, 1987.

Dallin, Alexander. *Black Box: KAL 007 and the Superpowers.* Berkeley: University of California Press, 1985.

Davies, David P. *Handling the Big Jets: The Significant Differences in the Flying Qualities Between Jet Transport Aeroplanes and Piston-engined Aeroplanes.* London: Civil Aviation Authority, 1973.

Davies, R. E. G. *Aeroflot: An Illustrated History of the World's Largest Airline.* McLean, Va.: Paladwr Press, 1992.

————. *Airlines of Asia.* McLean, VA: Paladwr Press, 2000.

————. *Airlines of the United States since 1914.* Washington, D.C.: Smithsonian Institution Press, 1972. Rev. ed., 1988.

Davis, S. F. *Delta Air Lines: Debunking the Myth.* Atlanta, Ga.: Peachtree Publishers, 1988.

Dienel, Lans-Liudger, and Peter Lyth, eds. *Flying the Flag: European Commercial Air Transport since 1945.* New York: St. Martin's Press; London: Macmillan Press, 1998. Describes how "patriotic exclusivity" plagued profitability and efficiency.

Dobson, Alan P. *Peaceful Air Warfare: The United States, Britain and the Politics of International Aviation.* Oxford: Clarendon Press, 1991.

Donne, M. *Above Us the Skies: The Story of BAA.* London: British Airports Authority/Good Books, 1991.

Driscoll, Ian. *Airline: The Making of a National Carrier.* Auckland, N.Z.: Shorthand Publications, 1979.

Emerson S., and B. Duffy. *The Fall of Pan Am 103: Inside the Lockerbie Investigation.* New York: G. P. Putnam's Sons, 1990.

Endres, Gunther. *The Vital Guide to Major Airlines of the World.* Shrewsbury, U.K.: Airlife Publications, 2002.

Evans, Sir R., and C. Price. *Vertical Take-off: The Inside Story of British Aerospace's Comeback from Crisis to World Class.* London: Nicholas Brealey Publishing, 1999.

Freiberg, Kevin, and Jackie Freiberg. *Nuts! Southwest Airlines' Crazy Recipe for Business and Personal Success.* Austin, TX: Bard Press, 1996.

Gero, D. *Flights of Terror: Aerial Hijack and Sabotage since 1930.* Wellingborough, U.K.: PSL, 1997.

Gill, R. *Airborne: The Evolution and Birth of Malaysia Airlines.* Kuala Lumpur: Malaysia Airlines, 1992.

Green, William, and Gordon Swanborough. *The Illustrated Encyclopedia of the World's Commercial Aircraft.* London: Salamander Books; New York: Crescent Books, 1978.

Gunn, John. *Challenging Horizons: Qantas, 1939–1954.* St. Lucia, Aus.: University of Queensland Press, 1987.

————. *The Defeat of Distance: Qantas, 1919–1939.* St. Lucia, Aus.: University of Queensland Press, 1985.

Gunston, Bill. *Airbus: The European Triumph.* London: Osprey Publishing, 1988.

Handleman, Philip. *Chicago O'Hare: The World's Busiest Airport.* Osceola, Wisc.: Motorbooks International Publishers, 1998.

Hayward, Keith. *Government and British Civil Aerospace: A Case Study in Post-war Technology.* Manchester, U.K.: Manchester University Press, 1983.

Henderson S., and Walker, T. *Silent Swift Superb: The Story of the Vickers VC-10: Aircraft of Distinction.* Newcastle-upon-Tyne, U.K.: Scoval Publishing, 1998.

Hooker, Sir Stanley. *Not Much of an Engineer.* Shrewsbury, U.K.: Airlife Publications, 1984.

Hopkins, George E. *The Airline Pilots: A Study in Elite Unionization.* Cambridge, Mass.: Harvard University Press, 1971.

Horwitch, M. *Clipped Wing: The American SST Conflict.* Cambridge, Mass.: MIT Press, 1982.

Hubbard, David G. *The Skyjacker: His Flights of Fancy.* New York: Macmillan Co., 1971.

Hudson, Kenneth, and J. Pettifer. *Diamonds in the Sky: A Social History of Air Travel.* Oxford: The Bodley Head/BBC, 1979.

Irving, Clive. *Wide-Body: The Triumph of the 747.* New York: William Morrow & Co., 1993.

Johnson, R. W. *Shootdown: The Verdict on KAL 007.* London: Chatto & Windus, 1986.

Jones, Fred. *Air Crash: The Clues in the Wreckage.* London: Robert Hale, 1985.

Knight, Geoffrey. *Concorde: The Inside Story.* London: Weidenfeld & Nicolson, 1976.

Komons, Nick A. *The Third Man: A History of the Airline Crew Complement Controversy, 1947–1981.* Washington, D.C.: Department of Transportation/Federal Aviation Agency, 1987.

Kuter, Gen. Laurence S. *The Great Gamble: The Boeing 747.* Tuscaloosa: University of Alabama Press, 1973.

Lasserre, Jean, ed. *One Century of Aviation with Air France.* McLean, Va.: Paladwr Press, 2001.

Lewis, W. David. "Airline Executives and Federal Regulation: Case Studies in America Enterprise from the Airmail Era to the Dawn of the Jet Age," in *Historical Perspectives on Business Enterprise,* Mansel G. Blackford and K. Austin Kerr, eds. Columbus: Ohio State University Press, 2000.

McAllister, C. *Aircraft Alive: Aviation and Air Traffic Control.* London: B. T. Batsford, 1980.

McDaniel, William H. *Beechcraft: Fifty Years of Experience.* Wichita, Kans.: McCormick-Armstrong, 1982.

McGregor, Gordon, R. *The Adolescence of a Airline.* Toronto: Air Canada, 1980.

Middleton, D. *Civil Aviation: A Design History.* London: Ian Allen, 1986.

Milberry, Larry. *Air Transport in Canada.* Toronto: CANAV Books, 1997.

Moreira, J. G. *Lisbon Airport 1942–1992.* Lisbon: Edicoes Inapa, 1992.

Nance, John J. *Splash of Colors: The Self-Destruction of Braniff International.* New York: William Morrow & Co., 1984.

Ormes, I. *Leading Edge: The Pioneering Years of Aviation Insurance.* London: Hill Aviation, 1988.

Owen, Kenneth. *Concorde and the Americans: International Politics of the Supersonic Transport.* Shrewsbury, U.K.: Airlife Publications, 1997.

Penrose, Harald. *Wings Across the World: An Illustrated History of British Airways.* London: Cassell Publishers, 1990.

Petzinger, Thomas. *Hard Landing: The Epic Contest for Power and Profits That Plunged the Airlines into Chaos.* New York: Times Business/Random House, 1995.

Ramsden, John Michael. *The Safe Airline.* London: Macdonald & Jane's, 1976.

Reed, Dan. *The American Eagle: The Ascent of Bob Crandall and American Airlines.* New York: St. Martin's Press, 1993.

Robinson, Jack E. *Freefall: The Needless Destruction of Eastern Air Lines and the Valiant Struggle to Save It.* New York: Harper Business, 1992.

Rochlin, Gene I. *Trapped in the Net: The Unanticipated Consequences of Computerization.* Princeton, N.J.: Princeton University Press, 1997.

Sampson, Anthony. *Empires of the Sky: The Politics, Contests and Cartels of World Airlines.* London: Hodder & Stoughton; New York: Random House, 1984.

Scanlan, H. *Winged Shell: Oil Company Aviators 1927–87.* London: Alison Hodge, 1987.

Schiavo, Mary, and Saba Chartrand. *Flying Blind, Flying Safe.* New York: Avon Books, 1997.

Serling, Robert J. *Maverick: The Story of Robert Six and Continental Airlines.* New York: Doubleday, 1974.

———. *When the Airlines Went to War.* New York: Kensington Books, 1997.

Shore, Bernard. *The Flight of the Iolar: The Aer Lingus Experience, 1936–1986.* Dublin: Gill and Macmillan, 1986.

Skene, Wayne, and Don Weekes. *Turbulence: How Deregulation Destroyed Canada's Airline.* Toronto: Douglas & McIntyre, 1994.

Smith, Philip. *It Seems Like Only Yesterday: Air Canada, the First 50 Years.* Toronto: McClelland and Stewart, 1986.

Testrake, Capt. John, and David J. Wimbish. *Triumph over Terror on Flight 847*. New York: Fleming H. Revell Co., 1987.

Thompson, William D. *Cessna: Wings for the World, the Single-engine Development Story*. Bend, OR: Maverick Publications, 1991.

Thomson, Adam. *High Risk: The Autobiography of Adam Thomson. The Politics of the Air*. London: Sedgwick, 1990. British Caledonian Airlines.

Tiburzi, Bonnie. *Takeoff! The Story of America's First Woman Pilot for a Major Airline*. New York: Crown Publishers, 1984.

Transport Committee of the House of Commons, United Kingdom. *Airline Competition Computer Reservation Systems. Third Report*. London: Transport Committee of the House of Commons, HMSO, 1988.

Wallis, Rodney. *Lockerbie: The Story and the Lessons*. Westport, Conn.: Greenwood Press, 2001.

Woods, Eric. *From Flying Boats to Flying Jets: Flying in the Formative Years of BOAC, 1946–1972*. Shrewsbury, U.K.: Airlife Publications, 1997.

"X," Captain [Capt. B. Power-Waters, pseud.], and R. Dodson. *Unfriendly Skies: Revelations of a Deregulated Airline Pilot*. New York: Doubleday, 1989.

Young, G. *Beyond Lion Rock: The Story of Cathay Pacific Airways*. London: Hutchinson, 1988.

XIII. Wars since 1945

Air Ministry, United Kingdom. *The Malayan Emergency 1948–1960: Royal Air Force. AP3140. Restricted*. London: Ministry of Defence, June 1970. Declassified in 2000.

Aviation Week and Space Technology. *The Persian Gulf War: Assessing the Victory*. New York: AW&ST, 1991.Includes articles from 1990 and 1991.

Bailey, Robert. *Support, Save, Supply: Hercules Operations in the Gulf War*. Shrewsbury, U.K.: Airlife Publications, 1992.

Ball, S. J. *The Bomber in British Strategy: Doctrine, Strategy, and Britain's World Role, 1945–1960*. Boulder Colo.: Westview Press, 1995.

Beg, Aziz, ed. *Seventeen September Days*. Lahore, Pakistan: Babur and Amer Publications, 1966.

Berger, Carl, ed. *The United States Air Force in Southeast Asia: 1961–1973*. Washington, D.C.: Office of Air Force History, 1977.

Berguist, Maj. Ronald E. *The Role of Air Power in the Iran-Iraq War*. Maxwell AFB, Ala.: Air University Press, 1988.

Broughton, J. *Going Downtown: The War Against Hanoi and Washington*. New York: Orion Books, 1988.

Burden, R., et al. *Falklands: The Air War*. London: A&AP, 1986.

Cagle, Cdr. Malcolm, and Cdr. Frank A. Manson. *The Sea War in Korea*. Annapolis, Md.: Naval Institute Press, 1957.

Churchill, Jan. *Classified Secret: Controlling Air Strikes in the Clandestine War in Laos*. Manhattan, Kans.: Sunflower University Press, 2000.

Clancy, Tom, and Gen. Chuck Horner. *Every Man a Tiger: The Gulf War Air Campaign*. New York: Berkley Publishing Group, 2000.

Clark, Gen. Wesley K. *Waging Modern War: Bosnia, Kosovo, and the Future of Combat*. New York: Public Affairs, 2001.

Clodfelter, Mark. *The Limits of Air Power*. New York: Free Press, 1989.

Cordesman, A. *The Lessons and Non-Lessons of the Air and Missile Campaign in Kosovo*. Westport, Conn.: Greenwood Press, 2001.

Coulthard-Clark, Chris. *The RAAF in Vietnam: Australian Involvement in the Vietnam War, 1962–1975*. St. Leonards, NSW: Allen & Vrevin and The Australian War Memorial, 1995.

Crain, Conrad C. *American Air Power Strategy in Korea, 1950–1953*. Lawrence: University Press of Kansas, 2000. A solid new appraisal.

Cull, B., D. Nicolle, and S. Aloni. *Wings over Suez: The First Authoritative Account of Air Operations during the Sinai and Suez Wars of 1956.* London: Grub Street, 1996.

Flintham, Victor. *Air Wars and Aircraft: A Detailed Record of Air Combat, 1945 to the Present.* New York: Facts on File, 1990. A very useful work.

Francillon, R. J. *Vietnam Air Wars.* London: Temple Press/Aerospace, 1987.

Fricker, John. *Battle for Pakistan: The Air War of 1965.* London: Ian Allen, 1979.

Friedman, L., and E. Karch. *The Gulf Conflict, 1990–1991: Diplomacy and War in the New World Order.* Princeton, N.J.: Princeton University Press, 1993.

Futrell, Robert F. *The United States Air Force in Korea, 1950–1953.* New York: Duell, Sloan & Pearce, 1961. Rev. ed., Washington, D.C.: Office of Air Force History, 1983.

Futrell Robert F., and Martin Blumenson. *The Advisory Years to 1965: The United States Air Force in Southeast Asia.* Washington, D.C.: Office of Air Force History, 1981.

Godden, J. *Harrier: Ski-jump to Victory.* London: Brassey's, 1983.

Hallion, Richard P. *Air Interdiction in World War II, Korea and Vietnam.* Washington, D.C.: Office of Air Force History, 1985.

Hannah, C. *Striving for Air Superiority: The Tactical Air Command in Vietnam.* College Station: Texas A&M University Press, 2001.

Hiro, Dilip. *Desert Shield to Desert Storm: The Second Gulf War.* New York: Routledge, 1992.

Hoeffding, O. *Bombing North Vietnam: An Appraisal of Economic and Political Effects.* Santa Monica, Calif.: RAND Corp., 1968.

Israeli Defense Forces. *Commanders of the Six Day War and Their Battle Reports.* Tel Aviv: Ramdor, 1967.

Nathan, J. *Anatomy of the Cuban Missile Crisis.* Westport, Conn.: Greenwood Press, 2001.

Jackson, Robert. *The Berlin Airlift.* Wellingborough, U.K.: PSL, 1989.

———. *Suez: The Forgotten Invasion.* Shrewsbury, U.K.: Airlife Publications, 1996.

Joes, Anthony James. *The War for South Vietnam, 1954–1975.* Rev. ed., Westport, Conn.: Greenwood Press, 2001.

Kirkland, Richard C. *Tales of a Helicopter Pilot.* Washington, D.C.: Smithsonian Institution Press, 2002.

Levinson, J. L. *Alpha Strike Vietnam: The Navy's Air War, 1964–1973.* Novato, Calif.: Presidio Press, 1989.

Logan, D. *The 388th Tactical Fighter Wing at Korat Royal Thai Air Force Base, 1972.* Atglen, Penn.: Schiffer Publishing, 1995.

Matthews, J., and C. Holt. *So Many, So Much, So Far, So Rare: United States Transportation Command and Strategic Deployment for Operation Desert Shield /Desert Storm.* 95- 47485 CIP. Washington, D.C.: Office of the Joint Chiefs of Staff, Joint History Office, and United States Transportation Command Research Office, 1995.

Michel, M. *The Eleven Days of Christmas: America's Last Vietnam Battle.* San Francisco: Encounter Books, 2002.

Middlebrook, Martin. *The Fight for the "Malvinas": The Argentine Forces in the Falklands War.* New York: Viking, 1989.

Moriarty, J. M. *Ground Attack Vietnam: The Marines Who Controlled the Skies.* New York: Ivy Books, 1993.

Morse, S., ed. *Gulf Air War Debrief.* New York: Aerospace Publishing, 1991.

Mrozek, Donald J. *Air Power and the Ground War in Vietnam.* Washington, D.C.: Pergamon-Brassey's, 1989.

Odgers, George. *Mission Vietnam: Royal Australian Air Force Operations 1964–1972.* Canberra: Australian Government Publishing Service, 1974.

Peters, J., and N. Hanson. *Team Tornado: Life on a Front Line Squadron.* London: Michael Joseph, 1994. Persian Gulf War.

Ripley, T. *Air War Bosnia: UN and NATO Air-*

power. Shrewsbury, U.K.: Airlife Publications, 1996.

Robbins, C. *The Ravens: The Men Who Flew in America's Secret War in Laos.* New York: Crown, 1987.

Russian General Staff. *The Soviet-Afghan War: How a Superpower Fought and Lost.* Lawrence: University Press of Kansas, 2001.

Sharp, Adm. U.S. G. *Strategy for Defeat: Vietnam in Retrospect.* Novato, Calif.: Presidio Press, 1979.

Sharp, Adm. U.S. G., and Gen. William West-moreland. *Report on the War in Vietnam.* Washington, D.C.: USGPO, 1969.

Sherwood, J. D. *Officers in Flight Suits: The Story of the American Fighter Pilots in the Korean War.* New York: New York University Press, 1996.

Shore, Capt. Moyers S. II. *The Battle for Khe Sanh.* Washington, D.C: USGPO, 1969. The official U.S. Marine Corps account of 1968 action.

Sorivth, J. *George Bush's War.* New York: Henry Holt, 1992.

Sturkey, M. F. *Bonnie-Sue: A Marine Corps Helicopter Squadron in Vietnam.* Plum Beach, S.C.: Heritage Press International, 1999.

Thomas, Graham. *Flying Fury: The Story of the Men and Machines of the Fleet Air Arm, RAF, and Commonwealth Who Defended South Korea, 1950–1953.* London: Grub Street, 2002.

Thompson, W. *To Hanoi and Back: The U.S. Air Force and North Vietnam, 1966–1973.* Washington, D.C.: Smithsonian Institution Press, 2000.

Tilford, Earl H. *Crosswinds: The Air Force's Setup in Vietnam.* College Station: Texas A&M University Press, 1993.

———. *Search and Rescue in Southeast Asia, 1961–1975.* Washington, D.C.: USAF Center for Air Force History, 1992.

Venter, A. J., N. Ellis, and R. Wood. *The Chopper Boys: Helicopter Warfare in Africa.* London: Greenhill Books, 1994.

Warden, John. *The Air Campaign: Planning for Combat.* London: Pergamon-Brassey's, 1989.

Wilcox, R. K. *Scream of Eagles: The Creation of Top Gun, and the U.S. Air Victory in Vietnam.* New York: John Wiley & Sons, 1990.

XIV. TECHNICAL MATTERS

Adair, B. *The Mystery of Flight 427. Inside a Crash Investigation.* Washington, D.C.: Smithsonian Institution Press, 2002.

Adams, A. R. *Good Company: The Story of the Guided Weapons Division of the British Aircraft Corporation.* Warton, U.K.: BAC Guided Weapons Division, 1976.

Ballard, Jack S. *Development and Employment of Fixed-Wing Gunships, 1962–1972.* Washington, D.C.: Office of Air Force History, 1982.

Barlay, Stephen. *The Final Call: Why Airline Disasters Continue to Happen.* New York: Pantheon Books, 1990.

Beaty, D. *The Naked Pilot: The Human Factor in Aircraft Accidents.* London: Methuen, 1991.

Becker, John V. *The High Speed Frontier: Case Histories of Four NACA Programs, 1920–1950.* NASA SP-445. Washington, D.C.: National Air and Space Administration, 1980.

Bell, Dana. *At the Controls: Cockpits of the National Air and Space Museum.* Shrewsbury, U.K.: Airlife Publications, 2001.

———. *The Smithsonian National Air and Space Museum's Directory of Airplanes, Their Designers and Manufacturers.* Washington, D.C.: Smithsonian Institution Press, 2002.

Biddle, Wayne. *Barons of the Sky. From Early Flight to Strategic Warfare: The Story of the American Aerospace Industry.* New York: Henry Holt, 1991.

Black, Flt. Lt. K. *The Last of the Lightnings: A Nostalgic Farewell to the RAF's Favourite Fighter.* Wellingborough, U.K.: PSL, 1996.

Böhme, Klaus-Richard. *The Growth of the*

Swedish Aircraft Industry, 1918–1945. Manhattan, Kans.: Sunflower University Press, 1988.

Boot, R. *From Spitfire to Eurofighter: Forty-five Years of Combat Aircraft Design.* Shrewsbury, U.K.: Airlife Publications, 1990.

Bordoni, A. *Airlife's Register of Aircraft Accidents: Facts, Statistics and Analysis of Civil Accidents since 1951.* Shrewsbury, U.K.: Airlife Publications, 1997.

Boyne, Col. Walter J. *Beyond the Wild Blue: A History of the United States Air Force, 1947–1997.* New York: St. Martin's Press, 1997.

Bramson, A., and N. Birch. *The Tiger Moth Story.* Shrewsbury, U.K.: Airlife Publications, 1991.

Braybrook, R. *Supersonic Fighter Development.* London: G. T. Foulis, 1987.

Bruce, J. M. *British Aeroplanes, 1914–1918.* London: Putnam, 1956.

Calvert, Brian. *Flying Concorde: The Full Story.* Shrewsbury, U.K.: Airlife Publications, 2001.

Chadeau, Emmanuel. *L'industrie aéronautique en France, 1900–1950, de Blériot à Dassault.* Paris: Fayard, 1987.

Chant, Christopher. *Air Defence Systems and Weapons: World AAA and SAM Systems in the 1990s.* London: Brassey's Defence Publishers, 1989.

Chapman, Gp. Capt. R. *Military Air Transport Operations.* Air Power: Aircraft, Weapons Systems and Technology Series, Vol. 6. London: Brasscy's, 1989.

Clarke, Sq. Ldr. D. M. *What Were They like to Fly?* London: Ian Allen, 1964.

Congdon, Philip. *Behind the Hangar Doors.* Woodhall Spa, Lincolnshire, U.K.: Sonik Books, 1985.

Coombs, L. F. E. *Fighting Cockpits: 1914–2000. Design and Development of Military Aircraft Cockpits.* Shrewsbury, U.K.: Airlife Publications, 1999.

Cumming, C., ed. *Lost to Service: A Summary of Accidents to RAF Aircraft and Losses of Personnel, 1959–1996.* Halifax, N.S., Can.: Nimbus Publishing, [1997].

Daniel, R., and J. Cuny. *Les Avions Dewoitine: Collection Docavia,* Vol. 17. Paris: D'Editions Lariviere, 1982.

Davies, P. E. *Gray Ghosts: U.S. Navy and Marine Corps F-4 Phantoms.* Atglen, Penn.: Schiffer Publishing, 2000.

Davies, P. E., A. Thornborough, and T. Cassanova. *Boeing B-52 Stratofortress.* Marlborough: Crowood Press, 1998.

Dawson, Virginia F. *Engines and Innovation: Lewis Laboratory and American Propulsion Technology.* NASA SP-4306. Washington, D.C.: NASA, 1991.

Denham, T. *World Directory of Airliner Crashes: A Comprehensive Record of More than 10,000 Passenger Aircraft Accidents.* Wellingborough, U.K.: PSL, 1996.

Ellis, C., ed. *Smiths Industries at Cheltenham: The Story of Fifty Years at Bishop Cleeve, 1940–1990.* Privately published by Smiths Industries, 1990.

Elsam, Gp. Capt. M. B. *Air Defence.* Air Power: Aircraft, Weapons Systems and Technology Series, Vol. 7. London: Brassey's, 1989.

Endres, G. G. *British Aircraft Manufacturers since 1908.* London: Ian Allan, 1995.

Evans, H. *Vickers: Against the Odds, 1956–1977.* London: Hodder & Stroughton, 1978.

Everett-Heath, E. J., et al. *Military Helicopters.* Air Power: Aircraft, Weapons Systems and Technology Series, Vol. 6. London: Brassey's, 1990.

Faith, N. *Black Box: The Air-crash Detectives: Why Air Safety Is No Accident.* London: Boxtree/Channel 4, 1996.

Federal Civil Defense Administration. *Fire Effects of Bombing Attacks.* Washington, D.C.: Office of Civil Defense Mobilization, 1952.

Fishbein, Samuel B. *Flight Management Systems: The Evolution of Avionics and Navigation Technology.* Westport, Conn.: Praeger Publishers, 1995.

Flight International. *Fuel Economy in the Airlines.* London: Flight International, 1980. A Royal Aeronautical Society symposium.

Francillon, R. J. *Grumman Aircraft since 1929.* London: Putnam, 1989.

———. *McDonnell Douglas Aircraft since 1920,* Vol. 1. London: Putnam, 1995.

Gilles, J. A. *Flugmotoren, 1910–1918.* Frankfurt am Main: E. S. Mittler & Sohn, 1971.

Golley, John, and Frank Whittle. *Genesis of the Jet: Frank Whittle and the Invention of the Jet Engine.* Shrewsbury, U.K.: Airlife Publications, 1996.

Gorn, Michael. *Harnessing the Genie: Science and Technology Forecasting for the Air Force, 1944–66.* Washington, D.C.: Office of the Air Force History, 1988.

Gunston, Bill. *Faster than Sound: The Story of Supersonic Flight.* Wellingborough, U.K.: PSL, 1992.

Hardy, R. *Callback: NASA's Avation Safety Reporting System.* Shrewsbury, U.K.: Airlife Publications, 1990.

Hastings, S. *The Murder of TSR-2.* London: Macdonald, 1962. The story of Britain's last supersonic bomber.

Hearn, P. *Sky High Irvin: The Story of a Parachute Pioneer.* London: Robert Hale, 1983.

Higham, Robin, and Abigail T. Siddall, eds. *Flying Combat Aircraft of the USAAF-USAF,* Vol. 1. Ames: Iowa State University Press, 1975.

Higham, Robin, and Carol Williams, eds. *Flying Combat Aircraft of the USAAF-USAF,* Vol. 2. Ames: Iowa State University Press, 1978.

———. *Flying Combat Aircraft of the USAAF-USAF,* Vol. 3. Manhattan, Kans.: Sunflower University Press, 1981.

Hunt, Leslie. *Veteran and Vintage Aircraft.* 4th rev. ed. New York: Scribner, 1978. Locates and describes over 9,000 preserved aircraft around the world.

Hurst, R., and L. Hurst., eds. *Pilot Error: The Human Factors.* London: BCA and Granada TV, 1982.

Imrie, A. *The Fokker Triplane.* London: A&AP, 1994.

Jackson, R. *Flying Modern Jet Fighters.* Wellingborough, U.K.: PSL, 1986.

Jewell, John. *Engineering for Life: The Story of Martin-Baker.* Higher Denham, U.K.: Martin-Baker Aircraft Co., 1979. Ejection seats.

Johnson, Brian, and Terry Heffernan. *A Most Secret Place: Boscombe Down, 1939–45.* London: Jane's, 1982.

Kelly, O. *Hornet: The Inside Story of the F/A-18.* Shrewsbury, U.K.: Airlife Publications, 1990.

Kinsey, Gordon. *Martlesham Heath: The Story of the Royal Air Force Station, 1917–1973.* Lavenham, Suffolk, U.K.: Terence Dalton, 1975, 1983.

Landi, D. M. *Positioning Recoverable Spares in Military Airlift Networks.* Santa Monica, Calif.: RAND Corp., 1967.

Launius, Roger D. *Innovation and the Development of Flight.* College Station: Texas A&M University Press, 1999.

Lerche, Hans-Werner. *Luftwaffe Test Pilot: Flying Captured Allied Aircraft of World War II.* London: Jane's, 1977.

Lloyd, Ian. *Rolls-Royce: The Growth of a Firm.* London: Macmillan & Co., 1978.

———. *Rolls-Royce: The Years of Endeavour.* London: Macmillan & Co., 1978.

———. *Rolls-Royce: The Merlin at War.* London: Macmillan & Co., 1978.

Loomis, David. *Combat Zoning—Military Land-Use Planning in Nevada.* Reno: University of Nevada Press, 1993.

Lumsden, Allan. *British Piston Aero Engines and Their Aircraft.* Shrewsbury, U.K.: Airlife Publications, 1997.

Maguire, J. A. *Gear Up! Flight Clothing and Equipment of USAAF Airmen in World War II.* Atglen, Penn.: Schiffer Publishing, 1995.

McClement, F. *Anvil of the Gods: Modern Airplanes versus Violent Storms.* Philadelphia: J. B. Lippincott, 1964.

McKinnon, D. *Bullseye One Reactor.* Shrewsbury, U.K.: Airlife Publications, 1987. The Israeli Air Force attack on Iraq.

Ministry of Munitions. *History of the Ministry of Munitions.* London: Ministry of Munitions,

United Kingdom, 1922. Once secret twelve-volume history.

Mitchell, G. *R. J. Mitchell, World Famous Aircraft Designer: Schooldays to Spitfire.* London: Nelson & Saunders, 1986.

O'Leary, M., and E. Schulzinger. *Black Magic: America's Spyplanes, SR-71 and U-2.* Shrewsbury, U.K.: Airlife Publications, 1989.

Organ, Richard, et al. *Avro Arrow: The Story of the Avro Arrow from Its Evolution to Its Extinction.* Cheltenham, Ont., Can.: Boston Mills Press, 1980.

Owen, Kenneth. *Concorde: Story of a Supersonic Pioneer.* London: National Museum of Science and Industry, 1982.

Pedden, Murray. *Fall of an Arrow.* Toronto: Stoddart, 1978.

Pelletier, A. J. *Bell Aircraft since 1913.* London: Putnam, 1992.

Price, Alfred. *Panavia Tornado: Spearhead of NATO.* London: Ian Allen, 1988.

Ramsden, John Michael. *Caring for the Mature Jet: A First Principles Technical Report.* St. Albans, U.K.: John Michael Ramsden and *Flight,* 1981.

Ransom, S., and R. Fairclough. *English Electric Aircraft and Their Predecessors.* London: Putnam, 1987.

Report of the Presidential Commission on the Space Shuttle Challenger Accident. Washington, D.C.: USGPO, 1986.

Rich, B. R., and L. Janos. *Skunk Works: A Personal Memoir of My Years at Lockheed.* Boston: Little, Brown & Co., 1994.

Robertson, Bruce. *Aviation Archeology.* Cambridge, U.K.: Patrick Stephens, 1997. On the identification and recovery of wrecks and other pieces of the air branch of industrial archaeology.

Robineau, Francois. *Rafale: Wings for the Future.* Paris: Le Cherche Midi Éditeur, 1995.

Schlaifer, Robert, and S. D. Heron. *Development of Aircraft Engines; Development of Aviation Fuels.* Boston: Graduate School of Business Administration, Harvard University, 1950.

Sell, T. M. *Wings of Power: Boeing and the Politics of Growth in the Northwest.* Seattle: University of Washington Press, 2001.

Sherman, A. *Lightning in the Skies: The Story of Israel Aircraft Industries.* London: Stone 1973.

Smith, G. *What Were They Like to Fly.* Osceola, WI: Motorbooks International, 1990.

Smith, Herschel. *A History of Aircraft Piston Engines.* Manhattan, KS: Sunflower University Press, 1981. Provides an invaluable technical historical survey, of which we need a jet sequel.

Stait, Bruce. *Rotol: The History of an Airscrew Company, 1937–1960.* Stroud, Gloucester, U.K.: Alan Sutton, 1990.

Stevens, P. J. *Fatal Civil Aircraft Accidents: Their Medical and Pathological Investigations.* Bristol, U.K.: John Wright & Sons, 1970.

Stewart, Stanley. *Emergency! Crisis in the Cockpit.* Blue Ridge Summit, Penn.: TAB Books, 1991.

Sturtivant, Ray. *British Research and Development Aircraft: Seventy Years at the Leading Edge.* Yeovilton, U.K.: Haynes/Foulis, 1990.

Sullivan, K. H., and Milberry, Larry. *Power: The Pratt & Whitney (Canada) Story.* Toronto: CANAV Books, 1989.

Sweetman, Bill. *Stealth Bomber: Invisible Warplane, Black Budget.* Shrewsbury, U.K.: Airlife Publications, 1989.

Taylor, Douglas R. *Boxkite to Jet: The Remarkable Career of Frank B. Halford.* Derby, U.K.: Rolls-Royce Heritage Trust, 1999.

Tillman, Barrett. *MiG Master: The Story of the F-8 Crusader.* Shrewsbury, U.K.: Airlife Publications; Annapolis, Md.: Naval Institute Press, 1990.

Turnill, R., and A. Reed. *Farnborough: The Story of the RAE* [Royal Aircraft Establishment]. London: Robert Hale, 1980.

Vajda, Ferenc A., and Peter Dancey. *German Aircraft Industry and Production, 1933–1945.* Shrewsbury, U.K.: Airlife Publications, 1998.

Vincenti, Walter G. *What Engineers Know and*

How They Know It: Analytical Studies from Aeronautical History. Baltimore: Johns Hopkins University Press, 1990.

Walker, AVM J. R. *Air Superiority Operations.* Air Power: Aircraft, Weapons Systems and Technology Series, Vol. 5. London: Brassey's, 1989.

Weick, F. E., and J. R. Hansen. *From the Ground Up: The Autobiography of an Aeronautical Engineer.* Washington, D.C.: Smithsonian Institution Press, 1988.

Werrell, Kenneth P. *The Evolution of the Cruise Missile.* Maxwell AFB, Ala.: USAF Air War College, 1985.

Wesseling, Louis. *Fueling the War: Revealing an Oil Company's Role in Vietnam.* London: I. B. Taurus, 2000.

Westrem, Ron. *Sidewinder: Creative Missile Development at China Lake.* Annapolis, Md.: Naval Institute Press, 1999. An intriguing and informative story of innovation in its heyday.

Yeager, Chuck, et al. *The Quest for Mach One: A First-Person Account of Breaking the Sound Barrier.* New York: Penguin Studio, 1997.

XV. Miscellaneous Sources

Photos

Some countries are ultra-sensitive about taking photos of military installations or equipment. Obtain permission first.

Naval Institute Photo Service, 291 Wood Road, Annapolis, MD 21402-5034.

National Air and Space Museum, Washington, DC.

Archives

When writing or e-mailing any of these organizations, be sure to indicate your specific interest and secondary sources and records that you have already used; also provide your brief *vita.* Most archives cannot do research, but they can supply a list of competent persons who will, upon request. Ask for rates. Whether or not organizations can provide photocopies or photographs depends upon the circumstances and personalities at each facility. Photographs at one time were given out by public information and public relations departments. Increasingly, both corporations and air forces charge for illustrations, and impose a user fee. Ask before ordering.

Canada
Natinal Archives/Archives Canada. Ottawa, Ontario, Canada.

Australia
Australian War Memorial (AWM). Canberra, ACT, Australia. The AWM has the records of all three services.

Germany
Federal German Archives. Bonn, Germany. *Luftwaffe* records. Also available at the *Bundsarchiv* at Freiburg im Bresgau.

France
Service historique de l'Armée de l'Air. Chateau Vincennes.

Greece
Greek Air Force Institute of History. Hellenic Air Force, Athens.

Italy
Italian Air Force documents are held by the IAF, Rome.

United Kingdom
Ministry of Defence Information and Library Service. Whitehall Information and Library Center, 3–5 Great Scotland Yard, London SW 1 A 2HW, United Kingdom. The Ministry still prints its accumulation of articles and books, the *Modils Library Bulletin,* whose

ancestor was the *War Office Library Monthly Accession and Subject List.*

Royal Air Force Museum Library. Hendon, London.

Poland

Polish Air Force Archives. Warsaw.

Portugal

Portuguese Air Force Archives. PAF HQ, Lisbon.

Spain

Spanish Air Force Archives. HQ, SAF, Madrid.

Sweden

Military Archives. Stockholm. Swedish Air Force records.

United States

USAF Air Historical Division, Maxwell AFB, Ala. 36112.

National Archives and Records Administration (NARA). Washington, D.C., College Park, Md., and in presidential libraries.

U.S. Naval Historical Division and the U.S. Marine Corps Historical Division. Old Navy Yard, Washington, D.C.

Guides

Air Museums. Michael Blaugher, 124 East Foster Parkway, Fort Wayne, Ind. 46806-1020. E-mail:airmuseums@aol.com. Guide to over 900 aircraft museums. $12.

Guide to Federal Aviation Administration Publications. Washington, D.C.: Department of Transportation, Federal Aviation Administration. Various editions.

Official Guide to the Smithsonian National Air and Space Museum. Washington, D.C.: Smithsonian Institution Press, 2002. Information on this publication available at www.sipress.si.edu/books. $14.95.

Public Record Office. Kew, London. Holds most British official air records, for which finding aids are available. Mimeographed Pamphlet No. 16 covers operational records for the Royal Air Force.

Smith, D. J. *Britain's Aviation Memorials and Mementos.* Wellingsborough: PSL, 1992.

Spencer, William. *Air Force Records for Family Historians.* London: Public Record Office, 2000. Archives generally have finding aids similar to the U.S. National Archives and Records Administration aids for its Record Groups.

Museums

Most of the museums listed here have a variety of documentary holdings, usually extremely helpful on technical matters.

Aeronautica Militare Museum di Vigna di Valle (Rome), Italy.

American Airlines Museum. Dallas, Texas.

Australian War Memorial Museum. Canberra. With archives.

Belgian Air Museum. Brussels. Part of the Military Museum.

Canadian Aviation Historical Society. Willowdale, Ontario, Canada.

Canadian National Aviation Museum. Rockcliffe, Ottawa, Canada. Contains an excellent collection.

Experimental Aircraft Association Museum. Oshkosh, Wisconsin. American collection of experimental aircraft. Probably the most popular in the world, with some 500,000 attending the fly-in each summer.

Fleet Air Arm Museum. Yeovilton, United Kingdom. The Royal Navy's collection.

Fiat Museum. Turin, Italy.

Finnish Air Force Museum. Helsinki.

Imperial War Museum and the American Air Museum. Duxford, Cambridgeshire, England. Duxford was a famous World War II fighter station.

Italian Air Force Museum. Rome. Sources and

collections. Access through Historical Offices.

Military Aviation Museum. Soesterberg, The Netherlands.

Munich Museum. Munich, Germany. A part of the museum covers aviation.

Musée de l'Air (Air Museum) at Le Bourget, Paris, France. A fine display of French aircraft, as well as World War I German aircraft.

Museum of Flight. Seattle, Washington.

National Air and Space Museum. Washington, D.C., and Dulles, Virginia. The premier U.S. collection.

New England Air Museum. Bradley Field, Connecticut.

Portuguese Air Force Museum. Lisbon.

RAF Museum. Two locations: Hendon, in northwest London (primary location), and the Royal Air Force Museum, Cosford, Shifnal, Shropshire, England.

Romanian Air Force Museum. Bucharest.

Royal Thai Air Force Museum. At RTAF HQ, near the Don Maung International Airport, Bangkok.

Russian Air Force Museum. Moscow.

San Diego Air Museum. San Diego, California.

Shuttleworth Collection. Old Warden Aerodrome, Bedfordshire, United Kingdom.

South African Air Force Museum. Swartkop, South Africa.

Swedish Air Force Museum. Linköping.

Swiss Air Force Museum. Dübendorf. Zurich.

United States Air Force Museum. Dayton, Ohio. A very impressive collection.

United States Army Aviation Museum. Fort Rucker, Alabama.

United States Air Force Strategic Air Command Museum. Bellevue, Nebraska.

United States Marine Corps Aviation Museum. Quantico, Virginia.

United States Naval Aviation Museum. Pensacola, Florida.

USS *Lexington* Museum on the Bay. Corpus Christi, Texas.

USS *Yorktown*. Patriots Point Naval and Maritime Museum, Charleston, South Carolina.

Journals and Magazines

Aerofan. Italy. For the buffs. Sometimes has interviews with past personalities or solid technical historic articles. Summary in English.

Aeroplane Monthly. London. 1973–. Contains a wealth of "gen."

Aerospace. London. Formerly the *Journal of the Royal Aeronautical Society*.

Aerospace History (originally *Aerospace Historian* then *Air Power History*).

Air Britain. Sometimes has interviews with past personalities or solid technical historical articles.

Air Force Journal of Logistics. Washington, D.C.

Air Force Magazine. Washington, D.C.

Airline Business. 1987–. Sutton, Surrey, England.

The Airline Handbook. Air Transport Association, Washington, D.C.

Airline Pilot. 1931–. Washington, D.C.

Airpower Journal (formerly *Air University Review*). Superintendent of Documents, Pittsburgh, Pennsylvania.

Air Wars 1919–1939. 1985–. Poughkeepsie, New York.

Aviation Quarterly. Ottawa, Ontario, Canada. A full-color Canadian aviation magazine.

Aviation Week and Space Technology. New York. The standard U.S. weekly.

Boeing Air Liner. Seattle, Washington. A technical publication for airlines.

China Today: Aviation Industry. Beijing.

Cross & Cockade International Journal. West Yorkshire, England. World War I.

Dekko, magazine of the Burma Star Association, London.

Esso (Exxon) Air World. Contact your regional Exxon company. 1948–.

Flight International. Surrey, England. Started in 1911 and merged in 1967 with *The Aeroplane,* which was founded in London in 1909. *Flight International* and the *Air Force*

Magazine's annual Institution of Strategic Studies survey the world's air forces, airlines, maintenance organizations, helicopters, and accidents.

Flight Journal. Ridegfield, Connecticut.

Fly Past. 1986–. Britain's best-selling aviation history magazine.

Fokker Bulletin. Amsterdam, The Netherlands. Now discontinued. Many companies have had their own journals from time to time.

Hump Pilot's Association. Pine Bluff, Arkansas. Reviews of books rarely noted elsewhere.

ICAO [International Civil Aviation Organization] *Journal.* Montreal, Canada.

Icare. Paris, France. Magazine of the French Airline Pilots' Association. Very well illustrated, historically oriented publication.

Interavia. Switzerland. Covers a wide range of air affairs.

Japanese aviation magazines—various, in Japanese.

Journal of the American Aviation Historical Society. Santa Ana, California.

Journal of the Canadian Aviation Historical Society. Willowdale, Ontario, Canada.

Journal of the Royal Aeronautical Society. London. Superseded by *Aerospace.* Has a cumulative index, 1866–.

Journal of the Royal United Service Institution. London. Now the *RUSI Journal.*

Journal of Strategic Studies. London.

Le Fanatique de l'Aviation. France. French aviation periodical with much detailed information, for the buffs. Sometimes has interviews with past personalities or solid technical historical articles.

Military. Subtitled: *World War II, Korea, Viet-Nam, and Today.* Sacramento, California.

Naval Aviation News. U.S. Naval Historical Center, Washington, D.C.

The Navy Supply Corps Newsletter. Naval Supply Systems Command, Washington, D.C.

NumberLingual. Switzerland. Swiss Air Force HQ, Bern.

RAF Flying Review. United Kingdom. Tactical and professional articles.

Recrueil d'articles et etudes. Service historique de l'Armée de l'Air, Chateau Vincennes, France. The reprints and fresh studies cover a wide range of topics on French Air Force history.

Revue des Forces Armées. SHAA, Chateau Vincennes, France.

Royal Air Force Air Power Review. Joint Doctrine and Concerns Centre, Shrivenham, Swindon, Wiltshire, England.

Royal Air Force Historical Society Journal. United Kingdom.

Shell Aviation News. London.

Skyways, the Journal of the Airplane, 1920–1940. Poughkeepsie, New York.

Technology & Culture. Henry Ford Museum, Dearborn, Michigan. Scholarly.

Video Observer. Santa Monica, California.

War and History. United Kingdom.

War and Society. Australia.

Wings of Fame—the Journal of the Classic Combat Aircraft. London. Well-illustrated history.

World Air Power Journal. Aerospace Publishing, Greenwich, Connecticut.

WWI. Aero, the Journal of the Early Aeroplane. United Kingdom.

Additional Resources

Air Transport Association of America, 1301 Pennsylvania Avenue, Suite 100, Washington, D.C. 20004-1707.

Center for Aerospace Doctrine, Research, and Education (CADRE), USAF, Maxwell AFB, Ala. 36112-5532.

Pilots' Notes for Aircraft. [Air Ministry]. The Bookshop, RAF Museum, Hendon, London. How pilots were told to handle aircraft.

2002 Aerospace Source Book. New York: McGraw-Hill, 2002.

United States Air Force Historical Research Institute. Maxwell AFB, Alabama.

United States General Accounting Office.

Washington, D.C. GAO reports frequently contain detailed evaluation of U.S. aviation concerns.

United States Library of Congress. Washington, D.C.

United States *National Union Catalogue.* The armed services have their own publications, sometimes with varying titles, traced in the *National Union Catalogue.*

Aviation Videos

The "Top Ten" aviation videos, in the following categories, as listed in *Flight Journal,* 2002:

World War I
1. *The Blue Max* (1966)
2. *Dawn Patrol* (1938)
3. *Dive Bomber* (1941)
4. *Hell's Angels* (1930)
5. *Lilac Time* (1928)
6. *The Eagle and the Hawk* (1933)
7. *Wings* (1927)
8. *Aces High* (1977)
9. *Devil Dogs in the Air* (1935)
10. *Zeppelin* (1971)

World War II
1. *God is My Co-Pilot* (1945)
2. *Thirty Seconds Over Tokyo* (1944)
3. *Tora! Tora! Tora!* (1970)
4. *Twelve O'Clock High* (1949)
5. *The Dam Busters* (1954)
6. *The War Lover* (1962)
7. *Air Force* (1943)
8. *A Guy Named Joe* (1943)
9. *A Piece of Cake* (1989)
10. *Task Force* (1949)

Post-World War II
1. *The Bridges at Toko-ri* (1955)
2. *Strategic Air Command* (1955)
3. *A Gathering of Eagles* (1963)
4. *Bombers B-52* (1957)
5. *Top Gun* (1986)
6. *The Right Stuff* (1983)
7. *Flight of the Intruder* (1991)
8. *Fail-Safe* (1964)
9. *Dr. Strangelove* (1964)
10. *The Hunters* (1958)

Additional videos suggested by the author include:

Air America (1990)
Always (1989)
Breaking the Sound Barrier (1952)
Flight of the Phoenix (1966)
The Great Waldo Pepper (1975)
No Highway in the Sky (1955)
Only Angels Have Wings (1939)
The Spirit of St. Louis (1957)

INDEX

Crisis, September 1938, 86
Criteria for air power, Mahan's, 25, 175
Crop dusting, 345
Cultural changes, post–WWII, 196
Cultural Revolution, 229, 230, 231
Cunningham, Sir Andrew Browne, Admiral, 171
Curtiss, Glenn, 64
Curtiss aircraft, 60, 95, 143
Curzon, George N., Lord, 54
Cycles of war and peace, 363

d'Annunzio, Gabriel, 55
Dassault: Ouragan, 270; Mirage V, 300
Daylight raids, Axis air defense, 139
DC-2 *Uiver,* 76
de Gaulle, Charles, 204, 294
de Havilland: DHC, 270; DH-82 Moth, 83; Vampire, 238
de Havilland, Geofrey, 115, 230
de St. Exupery, Antoine, 92
de Saxe, Maurice, Marshal, 29–30
de Seversky, Alexander Procofieff, 28, 45, 70
Decibel "footprint", 339
Defense(s), 70, 358; Battle of Britain, 135; industry, 24; system, air, 63; system, V-weapons, WWII, 142
Defense, post–WWII, 200; Africa, 292; bases, Vietnam, 249; China, 234; nuclear age, 198; spending, Afghan War, 277
Defense industries, 198–99; Russian, 220
Defensive (policy), 28–29
Defoliants (herbicides), V, 249
Demobilization, post-1918, 24, 58
Denain, General, 59
Denfeld, Louis, Admiral, 203
Deng Xiaoping, 231, 232, 233
Denver International Airport, 342
Deregulation, 346
Deserts, "white-tail" fleet, 355–56
Design (designing, designers), 308, 326–27, 330; interwar years, 62; WWI, 37, 57; WWII, 168, 175
Deterrence (deterrent), 199–200, 362
Deterrent theory, post–WWII, 202–203
Development(s), 7, 10–12, 362–63
D-558 Skystreak, 238, 239
DH Canada DHC-I Chipmunk, 239
Diem, 250
Dien Bien Phu, 245
Diplomatic control (oversight), Afghan War, 279
Disarmament, 201
Disrupted production, WWII, 110–11
Doctrinal developments, 78
Doctrine(s), 6, 27, 30, 63, 357; Douhetism/Douhetian, 59, 62, 63, 70, 71, 74, 75, 147; of grand-strategic bombing, 71, 74, 147; tactical, 100, 164
Donald, David, 13
Doolittle, James H., Colonel, 72, 105, 155; raid on Tokyo, 183–84
Dornier: Do-17A, 83; Do-X, 67
Douglas (Aircraft Company), 61, 77, 82, 83, 91, 104, 115, 253, 254; AD Skyraiders, 207, 239; A-4 Skyhawk, 272; C-54 Skymaster, 310; DC-8, 311; DC-9, 325; DC-10, 324; F4D Skyray, 254; SBD Dauntless, 176, 178

Douglas, Donald W., 238
Douhet, Guilio, General (Douhetism), 6, 28, 39, 45, 55, 57, 257, 358–59; doctrine, grand-strategic bombing, 59, 62, 63, 70, 71, 74, 75, 147
Dowding, Sir Hugh, Air Chief Marshal, 63, 109, 155, 192; Battle of Britain, 135, 137
Dresden, WWII, 154
Dunkirk, WWII, 122
Dutch: East Indies/Indonesia, 295; Indonesia, 280; New Guinea, 295
Duval, Colonel, 44, 59
Duval Division, 44, 59

Eaker, Ira C., General, 113
Early-warning system, WWII, 123, 124
East Pakistan, 259
East Timor, 296
Eastern Front, WWII, 127, 129–35
Economic effect of bombing cities, 161
Economic intelligence, WWII, 106, 154–55
Education, air forces, 202
Efficiency Ratings (ER), 12–16
Egypt (Egyptian, Egyptians), 260, 261, 262, 293
Eisenhower, Dwight D., General/President, 153, 237, 245, 246, 258
El Salvador, 298
Electronics, 208, 331–32; Middle East warfare, 262; reconnaissance, Persian Gulf War, 266
Ellington Field, 104
Embraer: EMB 120, 334; Tucano, 303
Emissions, 331
Encyclopedia of Military and Civil Aviation, 13
Engines, 289, 324, 325, 329; failure, 87; after 9/11
England. *See* Britain
English Channel dash, 173
Enterprise, 180, 180–81, 184, 186, 187
Environmental concerns, 367
Equipment: orders, airline, 84; WWI, 33–40; WWII, at hand, 161
Eritrea, 281, 282
Escort carriers (CVE), 167
Ethiopia, 92–93, 282
Ethiopian campaign, 360
Eurocontrol, 336
Eurofighter, 209, 303, 315–16
Europe (European): aircraft industry, 309, 320, 321; airline crisis, 354–55; airports, 340; air traffic control, 336; air war campaigns in, 163; and America, civilian aviation, 312–13; interwar years, 80, 88; USAF, 244
Europe (European theater), WWII: air war at sea, 173; *Blitzkrieg,* 116–17; carriers, 168; June 1942, 126; naval aircraft, 164, 166
European Community, 346; airlines, 348; defense sector, 367
Executives, airlines, 349
Executive travel, 367
Exocet missiles, 263, 299
Expansions, airports, 339
Experimental work, 90
Expert teams, German, post–WWII, 205

Hump route to China, 134–35
Hungary, 2002, 215
Hunting (Percival) Jet Provost, 270
Hussein, Saddam, 265, 266, 267, 268–69, 366
Hydrogen bomb, 199

Identification, friend or foe (IFF), WWII, 114
Illustrious, 170
Ilya Mourometz, 21, 37
Ilyushin, 218; Il-96, 221; Il-16, 82; Il-62, 318; Il-2 Shturmovik, 127, 130–31
Ilyushin, Sergey V., 218
Immelmann, Max, 41
Imperial Airways, 84
Imperial Japanese Navy, 64, 65
Imperial Japanese Navy Air Force (IJNAF), 174; defeat of, 195
Imphal, 133
In-air failures, 331
Inaccuracy of bombing, British, WWII, 149–50
Incendiaries, 156
Independent Bombing Force, 55
India: and Pakistan, 258–60, 276; WWII, 132–35
Indian Air Force, 316
Indonesia, 295–96
Industrial and technological legacy, 30–32
Industrial development, Russia, WWII, 154
Industries, aircraft: defense, 198–99; interwar years, 59, 62, 79–90; PLAAF, 230, 231, 232; WWI, 56; WWII, 110–16. *See also* Aircraft industry
Industry associations, American, WWII, 111
Inertial-navigation systems (INS), 332
Information, lack of, bombers, 154
Information technology (IT), 333
Instant Thunder, 267
Intelligence, post–WWII, 211–12; Afghan War, 278; air, 237; Persian Gulf War, 269
Intelligence, WWII: economic, 106, 154–55; gathering and use of, 160
Intercontinental bombers, 362
International linkages, airlines, 343
International peacekeeping air force, 368
Internet, 333
Interwar years, 6. *See also under various countries*
Intruding (intruders), WWII, 142, 146
Invasion of Norway, 169
Iran–Iraq war, 236, 262–63
Iraq, war with Iran, 236, 262–63
Iraqi Air Force, 266, 268, 269
Irish, Congo, 283
Israel (Israeli), 31, 206, 207, 236, 260–62; military aircraft, 316, 317; Persian Gulf War, 265
Israeli Air Force (IAF), 6, 260, 261
Israeli–Arab wars, 260–62
Italian Air Force, 2001, 215
Italians, war in Libya, 22–23
Italy (Italian, Italians), interwar years, 59, 63; assessment, 1939, 99; doctrine of grand-strategic bombing, 71; Ethiopia, 92–93; long-range flight, 91; Spanish Civil War, 97–98

Italy (Italian, Italians), WWI, 19; 44–45; assessment, 56; strategic bombing, 55
Italy (Italian, Italians), WWII, 128; Atlantic–Mediterranean war, 168; attacks on shipping, 157, 158; navy, 164; Taranto, 170–71

Japan (Japanese), 30; aircraft carriers, 30
Japan (Japanese), interwar years, 63, 64, 65, 68; assessment, 1939, 99; rearmament, 86; Sino-Japanese incident, 70, 93, 96
Japan (Japanese), post–WWII, 294–95; aircraft industry, 312; and China, 221
Japan (Japanese), WWII, land-based air power, 144; air defense, 146; bombing of (and surrender), 155–56, 159–60; Burma campaign, 133–35; economic intelligence, 154–55; *Judo Blitzkrieg,* 117; naval air force, 107
Japan (Japanese), WWII, seaborne air power, 194–95, 361; and America, 179; Battle of Midway, 185–88; Battle of the Philippine Sea, 191–92; Coral Sea, 184–85; *Judo Blitzkrieg,* 178; Leyte Gulf, 192–94; Malaya, 182–84; mid-1942 to mid-1944 lull, 188–91; naval aircraft and carriers, 178, 179; Pacific theater, 174–79, 179–94; Pearl Harbor, 179–81; production, 174
Japanese Army Air Force, 174
Jastas, 42, 43
JB-I, 115
Jellicoe, Sir John, 36, 50, 64, 65; and WWII, 174–75, 181, 182
Jenny, 38
Jet engine, 197, 198, 215–17
Jets, 5, 242, 273, 308; Boeing, 307; corporate ownership, 315; military facilities, 291; Vietnam, 246, 252
Joffre, J. C. J., Generalissimo, 74
Johnson, Amy, 80, 92
Johnson, C. L. "Kelly", 89, 216, 254, 288
Johnson, Lyndon B. (LBJ), 250, 251, 252, 256, 258, 333
Joint Aviation Authority (JAA), 348, 349
Joint Operations Center, Korean War, 244
Joint Stand-off Weapon (AGM-154A) glide bomb, 275
Jomini, Henri de, 28
Journal of the Royal United Service Institution, 27
JSTARS (joint surveillance target attack radar system), 267
Ju-87/88, etc. *See* Junkers
Judo Blitzkrieg, 178, 190
Julius Caesar, 71
Jungles, 296, 297
Junkers, 67, 73; Ju-88, 102, 147; Ju-87 Stuka, 102

Kaga, 93, 186
Kahn, Herman, 205
Kaman Ka-25 helicopter, 225
Kansas City International (KCI) airport, 344
Katanga (Katangans), 282, 283
Kawanishi NIKI-J, 144
KC-97 Stratofreighter, 239
Kennedy, John F., 211, 243, 246, 258
Kenya, 281, 282
Kesselring, Field Marshal, 142
Khe Sanh, 256
Kiev, 223
Kingsford-Smith, Sir Charles, 60
Kingston-McCloughry, 28
Kinkaid, Thomas C., Admiral, 193, 194

KLM, 84

KMT (Kuomintang Party), Nationalists, 226, 227, 228

Konigsberg, 169

Korea (Korean War), 202, 203, 240–45, 275; helicopter, 210; PLAAF, 227; and production, 216; RCAF 212–13

Kosovo, 31, 274–75

Kruschev, Nikita, 225

Kurita, Takeo, Admiral, 193, 194

Kuwait, 265, 267, 293

L'Armee de l'Air, 120, 121

La Stampa Sportiva, 22

Lanchester, F. W., 6, 74, 358

Land-based airmen, 69

Langley, Samuel Pierpont, 21

Latin America, 321–22

Lawrence, Thomas E., 48

Lawsuits, airlines, 351–52

Leasing companies, 309

Lee, Asher, 28

Legacies, uses of air power in WWII, 161–62

Legal action, airports, 339

LeMay, Curtis E., General, 144, 257, 287; attack on Japan, 156; Far East, 146; Korean War, 241, 242; SAC, 204

Leopoldville, 283

Lessons (learned), 274, 352–53; Afghan War, 278, 279; Korean War, 243, 244, 244–45; Libyan War, 23; post–WWII, 362; psychological, bombing, WWI, 55; U.S. Navy, Midway, 187–88; Vietnam, 258; WWI, 359–60; WWII, 360–62

Lethality, 8, 358

Lettow-Vorbeck, Paul Emil von, 48

Lexington, 64, 65, 76, 180, 184, 185

Liberty 12-A engine, 21

Libya, 293–94; war in (Libyan War), 22–23

Licensing regulations, 348–49

Life, aircraft, 197

Limited wars, 29

Lin Biao, 231

Lindbergh, Anne Morrow, 92

Lindbergh, Charles A., 3, 5, 66, 87, 91–92

Linebacker operations I and II, 256; II, strategy, 257

Link, Edwin A., 81

Link trainer, 81

Lippisch, Alexander, 254

Liu Yalou, 227

Lloyd, Air Vice Marshal, 192

Lloyd, Hugh, Air Officer Commanding, 141

Locating the enemy, WWII, 101

Lockheed, 89; C-5A Galaxy, 300; C-141 Starlifter, 287; C-130 Hercules, 254; EC-121 Super Constellations, 239; F-94 Starfire, 273; F-104 Starfighters, 207, 289; L-049 Constellation, 310; L-1011 Tristar, 324; P-80 Shooting Star, 254; P-38 Lightning, 144; P2V, 272; Skunk Works, 287, 288; SR-71 Blackbird, 237, 288; S-3 Viking, 302; U-2 Gray Ghost, 287

Lockheed-Martin, 209, 315, 316, 317

Logistics: Korean War, 240–41; Vietnam, 251

London, 29; airports, 342; WWI, 53; WWII, 137, 147

Long-range flight, 91

Longest front, Soviets, WWII, 131–32

Loss of control in flight (LOCIF), 350

Losses, 247, 248; India and Pakistan, 258, 259; Persian Gulf War, 268. *See also* Casualties

LTV: Corsairs, 289; Vought F-8 Crusader, 224, 289

Ludendorff, Erich von, General, 43

Lufthansa, 84

Luftwaffe, 77; as NATO air force, 255; in Spanish Civil War, 97

Luftwaffe, WWII: Battle of Britain, 135–38; *Blitzkrieg,* 125; Dunkirk, 122; Eastern Front, 131, 131–32; grand-strategic bombing, 147; Poland, 117, 118; production, 111–12; replacements, 103; siege of Malta, 140, 142

MacArthur, Douglas, General, CINCSWPA, 181, 184, 188, 191, 193; post–WWII, 241, 244

MacArthur-Pratt Agreement, 78

Macchi 200, 104

Macedonia, 48

Machiavelli, Niccolo, 28, 199

Machine guns, airborne (on aircraft), 36, 41

Mahan, Alfred Thayer, Rear Admiral, 25, 29, 30, 175

Mahanian assessment: aviation countries in 1939, 98–99; power of aeronautical countries, WWI, 56–57

Mahan's criteria, 25, 175

Maintenance, 352

Malaya, post–WWII, 295, 296–97

Malayan Federation, 295

Malays, Muslim, 297

Malmo J-3 monoplane, 66

Malta, siege of, WWII, 140–42; use of land-based air power, 158

Malthus, Thomas Robert, 339

Malvinas, 236, 298–99

Management factor, 26

Manchurian Incident of 1931, 93

Manufacturers, aircraft, 84, 199, 309, 367

Manufacturing, 363; early air power, 22; WWI, 37, 40

Mao Tse-tung, 226, 228, 229, 233; Mao's wife, 231

March offensive, German, 1918, 44

Marines, 244

Maritime warfare and air power, 29

Markings, national, 40

Marshall Islands, 191

Martin: B-10, 73; B-26 Marauder, 104; Mauler, 189

Martin, James, 238, 302

Mason, R. A., 28

Mass-production, interwar years, 87

Mau Mau (emergency, insurrection), 282

McCain, John S., Admiral, 194

McDonnell: F-4 Phantom II, 272; F3H Demon, 254; F2II Banshee, 253

McDonnell, James, Sr., "Mr. Mac," 253

McDonnell Douglas, 223, 308, 313; DC-11, 324; F/A-18E/F Hornet, 209; F/A-18 Hornet, 302; F-15 Eagle, 301; F-101 Voodoo, 291

McNamara, Robert, 250, 258

Mecozzi, Amadeo, Colonel, 6, 59, 75

Mediterranean conflicts/area, WWII, 163–67

Me-163 Komet, 115

Messerschmit Me-109 (Bf-109) fighter, 97, 102, 107

Metallurgy, 15

Technological revolutions, 14, 79, 86, 193; of 1934–1945, 103; of 1930s, 364

Technology (technologies), 3–4, 27, 366; new, 69; rapid obsolescence of, 196–97; strides in, WWI and WWII, 101; technological battle, WWII, 154–55

Tedder, Sir Arthur, Air Chief Marshal, 126, 153

Teller, 198

Tempest II, 145

Templar, Sir Gerald, General, 296

Terrorism (terrorists), 276, 236–37, 336–37; Communist, Malaya, 297; Libya, 293; war on, 278

Testing, 20

Tet Offensive, 256

Thatcher, Margaret, 268, 298

Theories, war, 28, 100, 358–59

Theorists, British, 74

Thor IRBM, 290

Thunderbirds, 302

Tibbets, Paul W., Colonel, 145

Tondern, 51–52

Torpedo-bombers, 166

Torpedoes, 158, 164

Tours of duty, 109

Towers, J. H., Lieutenant, 64

Toyoda, Soemu, Admiral, 192–93

Tractor aircraft (machine), 36, 42

Trainers, 81, 287, 288

Training, 323, 350–52; early air power, 20–22; military, post–WWII, 208; Soviets, WWII, 131; Vietnam, 251; WWI, 33–40, 56

Training units, operational (OTU), WWII, 151

Transport, cargo, 319

Transport, post–WWII, 196, 197; China, 226; colonial conflicts, 280, 281; Malayan Emergency, 296–97; Soviets, 218

Transport service, WWII, 160–61

Travel agents, 322

Trenchard, Sir Hugh, 28, 36, 44, 55, 57, 257; interwar years, 60, 63, 64, 65, 68, 74, 75, 88

Trippe, Juan, 10

Truman, Harry S., 143, 196, 203

Tunner, William A., Lieutenant General, 239, 240

Tupolev, 224, 225; TB-3, 77, Tu-114, 311; Tu-154, 220–21; Tu-124D, 318; Tu-26 Backfire, 212, 225; Tu-204, 21

Tupolev, Andrei N., 218

Turboprops, 326–27

Turkish Dardanelles, Allied campaign, 48

Turks (Turkish), 23, 117; WWI, 48

U-boats, 49–50, 51. *See also* Submarines

U-boats, WWII, 158–59; Battle of the Atlantic, 156, 157. *See also* Submarines

Udet, Ernst, 64, 111, 160

U.K. National Air Traffic Services (NATS), 336

ULTRA, 123, 124

Underdeveloped areas (of the world), 200, 207

Uniformity, aircraft, 41–42

UNITA (National Union for the Total Independence of Angola), 285, 286

United Kingdom. *See* Britain

United Nations: colonial conflicts, 281; Congo, 283; Korean War, 243, 244; peacekeeping, RCAF, 214

United States: aircraft industry, 305–306, 312–13, 315, 365; airlines, 342, 343, 346; airlines, licensing regulations, 348–49; air-traffic control, 333, 336; contribution to WWI air war, 45; early air power, 20; general aviation, 337; Mahan's assets for success, 30; military aircraft since 1960s, 317; navy, 30; pre–WWI air operations, 23; September 11, 354–56; SSTs, 327, 330. *See also* America

United States, post–WWII: Afghan War, 276–79; Angola, 285; air services, 204; and China, 227, 228, 233; Cold War, 201; grand strategy, 275; Indonesia, 295; intelligence, 212; jet engine, 216; Libya, 293–94; NATO campaign in Bosnia, 274–75; nuclear age, 198; south of the border, 297–98

United States Air Force, 25. *See also* USAF, U.S. Army Air Corps; USAAF

Unmanned aerial vehicles (UAVs), 237

UPS (United Parcel Service), 341; DC-8, 319

USAAF: Eighth Air Force, 152; equipment, 107–108; grand-strategic bombing, 153; legacies of WWII, 162; Ninth Air Force, 128; post–WWII, 201, 226

USAF, 203; Afghan War, 276, 277; aircraft, 317, 320; Bosnia, 274, 275; Congo, 283; Europe, 244; Korean War, 202, 240, 241–45; nuclear weapons, 205; Persian Gulf War, 265–69; personnel, 323, 326; and RCAF, 213–14; SAC, 204; satellites, 211; September 11, 354; and U.S. Army, 241; Vietnam, 202, 246, 248–52, 256, 258

USAF Europe (USAFE), 275

U.S. Air Service, 18; Douglas World Cruisers, 91

USAF, Afghan War, 276, 277; aircraft, 317, 320; Bosnia,

U.S. Army: Persian Gulf War, 265–66; and USAF, 241; Vietnam, 248

U.S. Army Air Corps (USAAC), 74, 78, 96. *See also* U.S. Army Air Forces (USAAF)

U.S. Army Air Forces. *See* USAAF

U.S. Asiatic Fleet, 182

U.S. Marine Corps, 244

U.S. Navy (USN), interwar years, 63, 64, 65

U.S. Navy, post–WWII, 203, 217; Afghan War, 278, 279; Korean War, 242, 243; reduction, 215; and Russia, 210; and submarines, 270; Vietnam, 252, 258

U.S. Navy, WWII: equipment, 178–79; lessons of Midway, 187–88; loss rate, 179; Pacific war, 183–84; Pearl Harbor, 179–81; pilots, 189

USSR, Air Force, 25. *See also* Red Air Force; Soviet Air Force; Soviet Army Air Forces

USSR (Soviet Union, Soviet), interwar years, 69, 77; airports, 79; Sino–Japanese incident, 70

USSR, post–WWII: aircraft industry, 217–21, 223–25; air services, 204; Cold War, 201, 204, 212, 213; fall of, 218–19; intelligence, 212. *See also* Soviet Union, post–WWII

USSR (Soviet Union, Soviet), WWII, 30, 360, 361; aid to, 152, 153, 154; aircraft and tanks, 106–107; Eastern Front, WWII, 129–35; Russian aviation history, 100

USS *Wasp*, 141

U.S. Twentieth Air Force, attack on Japan, 156

Valleys, Afghanistan, 264

Vandenberg, Hoyt, 242

Vauban, Sebastien Le Prestre de, 175

ISBN 1-58544-241-0